TRUE STORIES OF

Great
Escapes

Reader's Digest

TRUE STORIES OF
Great Escapes

THE READER'S DIGEST ASSOCIATION, INC.
Pleasantville, New York/Montreal

True Stories of Great Escapes

Editor: Charles S. Verral
Art Director: Robert Grant
Research Editors: Monica Borrowman, Susan Brackett,
Rita Christopher
Copy Editors: Natalie Moreda, Susan Parker
Art Researcher: Erika Pozsonyi

The credits and acknowledgments that appear on pages 607–608 are hereby made a part of this copyright page.

Library of Congress Catalog Card Number: 77-84357
ISBN: 0-89577-041-5

Printed in the United States of America

CONTENTS

Many authors of fiction have written stories in which their characters make breathtaking escapes. Yet no matter how fertile a writer's imagination, a fictional escape rarely surpasses those that happen in real life.

History abounds with such thrilling episodes: the flight of Moses and the Israelites from the Egyptians; Napoleon's getaway from the prison island of Elba; Harriet Tubman gaining her liberty after years of slavery; General MacArthur slipping away from the Japanese during World War II. The list goes on and on.

When Reader's Digest decided to publish an anthology of escape stories, the editors began a search of past issues of the magazine, going back to its beginning year of 1922. They found many accounts of true escapes—some well known, others now almost forgotten. But all these stories contained one common ingredient: courage—the courage of men, women, and sometimes children who risked life itself to be free.

From these true stories, 40 were selected to appear in this volume. They range from the miraculous mass escape of almost an entire British army in World War II to the feat of one young man who crossed the Atlantic Ocean hidden in the wheel well of an airliner.

To these stories have been added two book-length condensations: "The Long Walk," the saga of a breakout of seven men from a Soviet labor camp in Siberia and their trek toward India, 4,000 miles away; and "The Colditz Story," an account of a prison in Germany that the Nazis believed escapeproof and of the Allied POW's who proved them wrong.   —THE EDITORS

*From the day the wall went up in Berlin, groups
of East Germans tried every means of escape. On January 24,
1962, a band of refugees crawled into West Berlin
through a tunnel they had laboriously dug. Here is the story of
that tunnel. It is a drama of breath-catching suspense,
eloquent proof of man's passion for freedom.*

The January Tunnel

By William A. H. Birnie

THE BECKER HOUSE was like hundreds of other homes throughout
East and West Germany. Its two-story stucco walls squatted
sturdily beneath a massive peaked roof covered with red tiles. With
its tiny vegetable and flower garden and five or six dwarf fruit trees,
the house bespoke reliability, frugality, and strong family ties. To be
sure, a startling conical dovecote towered above the roof, but what
really distinguished the Becker house was its location.

In the quiet East Berlin suburb of Glienicke, it stood directly on
the border that separates East from West, tyranny from freedom.
Only 30 yards from the rear of the house lay the suburb of Frohnau,
in the French sector of West Berlin.

In between lay the Berlin Wall—at that point composed of four
rows of barbed wire and a picket fence—which was constantly patrolled by details of heavily armed Volkspolizei ("People's Police"),
commonly called Vopos.

Late on Monday afternoon, December 18, 1961, two of the Becker
boys, Erwin and Guenther, arrived home from work together. The
instant they opened the front door, they heard a dull pounding coming from the cellar. Dashing down the steps to investigate—anything
out of the ordinary put nerves on edge in tense East Berlin—the boys
found their handsome, blond brother Bruno energetically chipping
away at the cellar wall with hammer and chisel. There was no need to
ask what he was doing.

Bruno looked up and wiped the stone dust from his damp forehead. "I know you think I'm crazy," he said. "But I've had it! That
damned wall gets longer and higher every day. Tunneling through
here is our only hope."

11

"Sure," said Guenther, his voice edged with sarcasm. "How long have you been working?"

"About three hours."

Guenther pointed to the wall. "And take a look at what you've accomplished!"

The surface of the stone-hard glazed bricks that lined the cellar wall had scarcely been scratched.

"Come on, Bruno," said Erwin. "There's some beer upstairs. Let's talk this over quietly."

So the three went upstairs to the kitchen, where Bruno continued to argue for his tunnel.

"You remember what happened when we planned to cut through the barbed wire," he said bitterly.

They remembered all right. It had been only a month since they had tried, vainly, to escape overland. That night at 9:30 they had turned off all the lights, so that the patrols would think they had gone to bed. Then they sat in the darkness, waiting. They didn't know that the patrols had been reinforced because a few people down the road had escaped several days before. All they knew was that the Vopos, with police dogs that growled at the slightest suspicious sound, came by with dismaying frequency. They were still waiting for the right moment when dawn broke.

After that failure Bruno had wanted to start digging a tunnel. But his brother Erwin disagreed, and now in the Becker kitchen he reviewed his reasons.

"Look at it this way, Bruno. If we cut our way through the wire, most of us will probably make it, even if one or two get caught or shot. But with a tunnel what chance have we got? The Vopos would be sure to hear us digging. Then we'd be sent to prison—or worse—with all our friends who knew about the tunnel and probably a lot of others who didn't."

Reluctantly, Bruno again agreed to his brother's suggestion that they make one more effort to cut their way through the wire. They would now time the attempted breakthrough for as soon as possible after the New Year.

The Beckers had never been politically minded. All they asked of politicians was to be left alone. But after the wall had gone up, imprisoning them, along with more than a million other East Berliners on August 13, 1961, their nerves were drawn to such a point of desperation that they preferred risking their lives to living under a suffocating Communist regime.

Frau Clara Becker, 53, slim and gracious, with a quiet smile, had been left a widow with six children when her husband died in a Russian prisoner-of-war camp in 1945. Released herself from a refugee camp in 1947, she and the youngsters had eventually settled down in suburban Glienicke.

Life was far from easy, but they managed to get by. An uncle who lived in the United States periodically sent money and food parcels until he died in 1955.

In 1950 the Becker family moved into the house on the border. The three younger sons completed their schooling and found jobs. (Arnold, the eldest, had gone to live with Frau Becker's brother in Dortmund, West Germany.) By 1961 Erwin, 27, was earning an above-average salary as chauffeur for the president of East Berlin's Art Academy. Bruno, 21, brought home fairly good pay each week from his job as an electrician, and his twin Guenther also did pretty well as a steamfitter.

The oldest daughter, Gerda, 22, crossed over into West Berlin every working day. There she had a job as a hairdresser and earned a good salary. Her sister, exuberant 18-year-old Christel, was training to become a salesgirl.

They were an industrious, optimistic family, and their home became a sort of informal community center for a number of the young people in the neighborhood.

"It certainly wasn't paradise," Frau Becker later recalled. "But it wasn't too bad either. We could go over to the bright lights of West Berlin any time we wished."

Then came the wall, and the Beckers' world closed in.

On Monday morning, August 14, 1961, Gerda started off for her job in West Berlin as usual. Half an hour later, much to her mother's astonishment, she was back home.

"The Vopos stopped me," Gerda reported. "They said I was no longer permitted to cross over."

"But what about your job?"

"They told me to forget about it, about *ever* going across again. They said we were now all standard-bearers in the People's Democracy. They said—"

Her voice broke, and her mother put an arm around her shoulders. "Now don't get upset, Gerda. In two or three days everything will be all right again."

But the next day the Vopos and "volunteers" from the factories came pounding along Oranienburger Chaussee, the border highway

13

that adjoins the Becker home, and with them came trucks carrying huge rolls of barbed wire.

The Vopos unreeled mile after mile of the ugly wire strands, continuing the prison wall from the Brandenburg Gate to quiet little Glienicke and far beyond.

Life behind the wall became a series of small crises. Gerda got a job as a hairdresser in an East Berlin establishment, but her new salary enabled her to buy less than half what she could with her West Berlin pay. In addition, the management, following the party line, encouraged her fellow workers to distrust her because she had been a *Grenzgänger* ("border crosser"). The Communists were spreading the word that anyone who had worked in West Berlin was probably infected with "capitalistic decadence."

The men in Bruno's electrical shop were told to volunteer for duty in the People's Army—which might be ordered any day to fire on fleeing fellow Germans. Bruno got out of it, thanks to a doctor's certificate attesting to deafness in one ear, but the threat still hung over him. Guenther was urged by a fellow worker, who identified himself as a member of the Security Police, to report anyone making subversive, antiregime remarks.

Every third or fourth evening a pair of Vopos would knock on the Beckers' front door and check the identification papers of all the inhabitants. Each time one of them would be sure to flick on the living-room radio—to see whether it had been left tuned to a West Berlin station. If it had, the Beckers were liable to prison terms as "ideological defectors."

FOOD SHORTAGES grew acute. Meat, potatoes, butter, milk, and vegetables were scarce everywhere. Actually, the Beckers were better off than most of their neighbors, because they had a well-tended garden and those few fruit trees. But, like most Germans, they were fond of liver and bacon, and it seemed there was no liver to be had anywhere in East Berlin.

"You know," Christel said, smiling, one night, "Herr Ulbricht, our dictator, has accomplished at least one miracle: he has raised a generation of animals without livers."

But the jokes grew fewer as the shadow of the wall grew longer. Petitions were circulated through the factories and the schools urging all workers and students to agree that neither they nor anybody in their families would accept any mail or food or clothing parcels sent in from the West.

Worse than the facts were the rumors. (East Berliners have learned through bitter experience that the worst rumors tend to come true.) Two in particular troubled the Beckers. First, a universal conscription law (later enacted) would make all able-bodied young men liable for service in the East German armed forces; that would likely take the Becker boys. Second, it was rumored that all border residents were to be resettled somewhere deep within East Germany far away from the West and all border houses destroyed; that would mean the destruction of the Becker home.

Having agreed to make one more try at escaping through the wire, the Becker brothers finally decided to stage the hazardous attempt on January 13, 1962. It was a Saturday night, and this time the Beckers were not to be alone.

First to show up that afternoon were the Schwartzes—Franz, 50, a sober-minded mechanic, and his wife, Ilse. (Fictitious names have been used except for members of the Becker family.) Recently the Schwartzes had thought of nothing else but crossing over from East Berlin. When the wall went up, Herr Schwartz had been cut off from his good West Berlin job. But, more important, two of the Schwartzes' four daughters were married and now living in West Berlin; and the two youngest, 16 and 18, had been crossing over each day to attend school there.

The wall abruptly separated the younger daughters from school and schoolmates. Then they found that they couldn't even gain admittance to an East German school. Invariably they were told, "As former border crossers you should *prove* your loyalty to the People's Democratic Republic by getting jobs in factories."

The two girls had no desire to wait for the inevitable: assignment to a factory of the regime's choice. They begged their parents to escape, but their father had been adamant. Like Frau Becker, he felt that the wall was only a passing horror.

"There's no need for anybody to risk his life," he repeated firmly. "Just be patient, that's all."

But 16 and 18 are no ages for patience. Knowing that they could not persuade their parents to change their minds, the girls made secret plans. After lunch on Saturday, September 16, 1961, they slipped across the border on their own. (This was scarcely a month after the wall had been erected, and there were still some loopholes in the security system.)

Three days later the Schwartzes received a letter: the girls were living with their married sisters in West Berlin. Thereafter, every few days all four girls stood on a hilltop in Frohnau and waved to their mother. Frau Schwartz watched them through binoculars, her eyes blurred with tears.

At first, Franz Schwartz was infuriated that the girls had tricked him and his wife. But as the days and weeks ticked off and life behind the wall turned increasingly sour, the Schwartzes, too, became determined to escape.

One afternoon Herr Schwartz went to the Becker house to ask Bruno if he could fix a television set. While they were talking, Franz kept looking through the windows facing Frohnau.

"You're *really* on the border, aren't you? Have you ever thought of cutting through?"

"Maybe," said Guenther. "Why?"

Schwartz told them what was on his mind. Frau Becker sensed the sincerity in his voice and instinctively trusted him.

"We're going to make a try for it Saturday night," she told him. "If you want to join us, you and your wife come over for dinner. Then after it gets dark . . ."

Shortly after dinner that Saturday evening another couple appeared—the Alfred Muellers. They were in their middle thirties, and with them was their blond, roly-poly, eight-year-old daughter, Gisela. Unlike the Schwartzes, the Muellers had decided to move to the West even before the wall. All through July 1961 they had smuggled shoes, clothing, and other essential articles across the border and stored them in the West Berlin office where Herr Mueller worked as a heating engineer.

After the wall trapped them, they determined to make the break as soon as possible. On the bus he took to work each day, Herr Mueller had struck up an acquaintance with Christel Becker. When he learned that her family's house was directly on the border in Glienicke, he dropped by one night. Within an hour Frau Becker and her sons had invited him and his family to come along on the Saturday night escape expedition.

That night the three families—Beckers, Schwartzes, and Muellers—drank coffee and talked about everything except what was on their minds until it was pitch-black outside. Then they concentrated on the tramp-tramp-tramp of the Vopos, who seemed to come by all too regularly. Occasionally the Vopos would flash their lights on the windows, instantly silencing all conversation inside the house until reassuring darkness returned.

At 11:45 Frau Becker's nerves were at the breaking point. "I

haven't heard the Vopos for a long time," she said, "Maybe now's the time. I'm going out to see."

"I'll come with you," said Herr Schwartz.

"I think it's too early," said Erwin. "Take a look if you want, but be very careful."

Frau Becker and Franz Schwartz walked out into the garden. All was quiet. Then, suddenly, from off to the left, came the sound of voices and the tread of boots. There wasn't time to dash back into the house, and they had no reasonable explanation for being out in the darkness right there on the border.

"Quick, lie down," whispered Schwartz.

They lay on the icy ground behind a pine tree and, as fortune would have it, the two Vopos stopped not 10 feet away. For half an hour at least—Frau Becker thinks it was two hours—the Vopos discussed the weather and when they would get off duty, and how much better life was back in Dresden.

(Most of the border police were brought in from other sections of East Germany so they wouldn't have personal ties with East Berliners and be tempted to assist would-be escapees.)

Scarcely breathing, Frau Becker and Herr Schwartz lay in the garden until the Vopos finally moved on. When they got back inside the house, Frau Becker was near hysteria.

"We'll *never* make it!" she cried.

It had been a frightening, frustrating night. It produced one positive result, however: The men were now convinced that they could never escape overland.

The Becker boys invited Herr Schwartz and Herr Mueller to come down into the cellar. There Erwin pointed to the dents that Bruno had made in the glazed-brick wall.

Instantly, Herr Schwartz said, "Of course—a tunnel! That's the only way to do it!"

Now the Becker boys were all enthusiasm, and Schwartz agreed to pitch in on the project immediately. Mueller, engineering-minded, was skeptical. For an hour they talked over possibilities, techniques, and the obvious dangers.

Finally, Mueller said quietly, "All right. I agree. Shall we start the first thing Monday morning?"

"Perfect," said Erwin. "We'll report sick at our jobs. Let's make it 7 o'clock Monday, then?"

"*Jawohl.*"

ON MONDAY MORNING Herr Mueller arrived at the Becker house before the sun was up, carrying an electric drill he had "borrowed" from the shop where he worked. Bruno's eyes sparkled when he saw it; he knew it could save hours of exhausting work. In the cellar he connected it, listened to it hum, and then shoved it against the spot on the brick wall where he had chiseled. Instantly, all hell broke loose. He cut the switch hastily.

"We can't use it!" he said. "A banging like that could bring the Vopos on the run."

So the drill was put aside, and for the rest of that day the men took turns with Bruno's hammer and chisel.

Herr Schwartz joined the group on Wednesday and worked during the mornings. (To avoid suspicion he did not yet want to report sick at his regular job, which required him to work only in the afternoon.) By then the others had equipped themselves with the necessary hammers, shovels, and pickaxes—smuggled into the Becker house under cover of their overcoats.

They soon discovered that the cellar wall, built in the late 19th century, was two feet thick and all glazed brick. Working in shifts of two at a time, their eyes and lungs filling with stone dust, they took three days to cut a hole four feet high and two feet wide. They wanted it large at the beginning because they suspected that, regardless of their ambitions, the tunnel would inevitably tend to grow smaller and smaller as freedom came closer.

By Wednesday, about 5 P.M., they had conquered the cellar wall and were up against the sand and clay outside. From then on the job progressed with exhilarating rapidity.

But now new difficulties had to be solved. First, there was the problem of dirt disposal. Guenther suggested an easy solution: dump the dirt down an abandoned well in the garden at the rear of the house. The others vetoed the idea; the Vopos might notice and, besides, they would have to spend most of their time and energy carrying the debris upstairs and outside. Instead, the men put up crude partitions like old-fashioned coal bins and piled the dirt right there in the cellar. (Eventually there was just a single churchlike aisle left leading to the tunnel opening.)

The second problem was the need for light. Already the tunnel was getting black inside, and the two who worked at the front could barely see. Electrician Bruno solved that by stringing an overhead extension cord into the tunnel and, as they dug on, lights were added every nine feet or so.

Their third difficulty was that the farther they dug, the more dirt they had to handle, and the harder it became to remove. Even at 10 feet out from the cellar, it was time-consuming and enervating to throw the dirt back by hand.

The twins, Guenther and Bruno, solved this problem. They found a wooden box two feet square and one foot deep. They cut holes on opposite sides and attached long ropes. The diggers in the tunnel would fill the box and then call softly, "Full up." Those waiting in the cellar then would haul the box back and dump the earth into the bins. Hour after hour the operation continued in virtual silence, broken only by the men's panting and the soft swish of the shovels digging into the sand.

By Friday, January 19, they were beyond the first barbed-wire fence and, more dangerous, directly under the highway that constitutes the border. Just three feet beneath the pavement, the diggers could hear the tread and even the voices of the Vopos as they tramped by directly overhead.

"If we can hear them," said Guenther, "why can't they hear us?"

"It's a risk we have to take," Mueller said grimly. "We'll just have to try to work quietly."

Bruno put down his beer. *"Nein,* we can do better than that. We'll use the lights in the tunnel as a signal. I'll connect a switch upstairs, and Gerda can stand by the window and keep watch. Every time she sees the Vopos coming, she can switch the lights off, and we can stop working until they're gone."

Thus began Gerda's vigil at the window. Henceforth, from dawn to dusk, she scanned the border, switching the lights off and on as the Vopos came and went. Usually the delays were only a minute or two in length, but once she had to leave the diggers in darkness a while longer when a pair of young Vopos stopped and called up to her, "Hey, what are you doing at that window?"

Gerda's heart pounded. "Thinking over my homework," she answered quickly.

One of the Vopos chuckled. "When I get off duty, I'll come up and do some homework with you." He nudged his companion. "My pal, too. How about it?"

"You do," said Gerda evenly, "and I'll just have to inform your commanding officer."

"Oh, that sort," said the first Vopo. The two men swaggered on down the border highway, and with a sigh of relief Gerda switched the lights back on.

Inside the tunnel it was hot, dirty, sweaty work. Thus far, fortunately, there had been no cave-ins. At the entrance they had shored up the tunnel with boards, but under the foundations of the highway they found it unnecessary. Even so, droplets of melting snow kept coming through, making them wonder uneasily if the tunnel would continue to stand firm.

Then, on Saturday, January 20, while Bruno was digging, an avalanche of sand suddenly deluged him and a stick of wood hit him on the head. The lights flashed frantically.

In a moment Gerda's voice reached Bruno from the cellar. "For God's sake, do something quick! One of the fence posts has slipped down, and the barbed wire is sagging. The Vopos will see it the second they come by."

Bruno thought quickly. "Go back upstairs and flash twice when the fence looks all right."

He grasped the post and pushed it up through the ground slowly, until two flashes came from Gerda.

Then he called to Guenther, "Here, make a brace for this post. We'll tunnel around it."

On Monday, January 22, the end of the job seemed imminent.

Herr Schwartz announced that he had also reported sick at his job and would now be able to work full time. That made five diggers, and the pace quickened. On the same day, the men estimated that they already had reached the West.

They decided to push up a rod from the end of the tunnel. From the window Gerda was to flash once if it came up in the West, twice if it was still in the East.

Bruno and Guenther shoved up the rod and watched the lights. For a moment, the lights stayed on. Then they flashed off and on, off and on. The boys pulled the rod down hastily and crawled back through the tunnel to confer with Gerda.

She was breathless. "You're still at least 10 feet inside the border," she said, "and two Vopos were coming. You got that rod down just in the nick of time."

Swiftly the men returned to attack the last 10 feet. When they quit work that night, they announced jubilantly that they were sure they would be able to break into the West the next day.

TO FRAU BECKER, that last Tuesday remains a kaleidoscope of nightmarish impressions. The mere thought that the tunnel was there, and the dread of what would happen to them all if it was discovered, chilled her. Then, to her astonishment, the house began to fill with unexpected guests.

First to arrive were a courtly white-haired gentleman, his 71-year-old wife, and another woman only a few years younger. Frau Becker had never laid eyes on any of them.

"Herr Mueller was kind enough to invite my wife and myself," the man explained, "and we took the liberty of bringing Frau Zeller here. You see, she is a widow; her two daughters married our two sons, and they live in West Berlin. We just couldn't go without her. I do hope you understand?"

"Of course," said Frau Becker, forcing calm into her voice. "Won't you please come in?"

In the next few hours Frau Becker found herself hostess to a bewildering succession of friends and strangers. Among them was Hilda, 19, a plump, quiet-spoken girl who had been in and out of the house for months. During the tunneling she had often helped brush off the men's clothes and given them a nod of approval before they left the house. Frau Becker regarded her as Bruno's sweetheart, but that night Bruno announced that she was his fiancee.

Even more surprising was the arrival of a tall, blue-eyed teenager whom Guenther introduced as his girl friend. (He had never before mentioned her to the family.)

Christel had left the house after lunch. Her brothers would have been furious if they had known she was inviting several of her friends to join in the night's adventure. But Christel's instinct proved to be correct; nobody informed on the Beckers—not even the few who declined to go along.

For Frau Becker the most agonizing moment came when the door-bell rang around 8 P.M.

Frau Schwartz answered, then reported, "There's a lady to see you—a very stout lady."

"Dear God," Frau Becker whispered to herself.

She knew who it was—Frau Krauss, a friend and close neighbor. Frau Becker had desperately wanted to invite her to come through the tunnel, but Frau Krauss was an unusually large woman, and her husband was asthmatic.

"He might have an attack," the diggers had insisted, "and she could never fit through at the far end."

So Frau Krauss had not been told about the tunnel, and now, with the house filled with strangers, Frau Becker knew she could not even ask her friend to come in.

She went slowly to the door. *"Liebe* Frau Krauss—"

"I was passing by and thought I'd drop in for a minute."

"How nice! But I'm so sorry, I—my head aches and I was just about to go to bed."

But Frau Becker couldn't leave it like that. "Please wait a second," she said. "I have something for you."

Frau Becker went back into the living room and picked up her mother's Bible. Then she returned to the door.

"I've been meaning to give this to you for some time," she said. "You mentioned once that your family Bible was lost when your home was bombed. . . ."

Afraid that she couldn't control her voice any longer, she leaned forward and kissed Frau Krauss on both cheeks. "Sleep well."

Frau Krauss thanked her and slipped off into the darkness. (Less than four months later Frau Krauss, her husband, and 10 others escaped through a tunnel dug from the cellar of the Krauss border home, only a few hundred feet from the Becker house.)

By 10:30 there were 28 people scattered through the rooms of the Becker house. All the lights had been turned off, and they waited in darkness, each one absorbed in thoughts of the past and future.

In the cellar all attention was focused on a new crisis. Tunneling upward to break out into the open, the diggers had run into a concrete conduit four feet in circumference. Mueller, the engineer, studied it from below and decided that it contained telephone lines. The problem was whether to tunnel farther under or to cut up beside it and risk coming out in the East Zone.

"How long will it take to tunnel under?" asked Erwin.

"Another 24 hours."

"I vote that we take our chances and dig straight up," said Erwin.

"Agreed," said Mueller.

Now, as Bruno and Guenther dug upward, they began to encounter roots of trees and bushes.

"Get me the shears," whispered Bruno.

Forty-five minutes later—just before 1 A.M. on Wednesday, January 24—Bruno broke through.

Bruno and Guenther scrambled back to the cellar. "Let's get going," Bruno said quietly.

Thoughtfully Herr Mueller said, "Wait a minute. When we come out, we should have some protection. The Vopos might hear us and start shooting. I suggest that somebody go through first and get the West Berlin police to stand guard by the opening."

"Good idea," Bruno said. "Who?"

Guenther pointed to Mueller. "You."

Mueller nodded and crawled into the entrance.

Bruno went upstairs and whispered the news to his mother.

"All right," she said, "tell the others, and ask Gerda and Christel to go through with me."

She went down into the cellar, her two daughters close beside her. The others followed silently. Bruno crawled in first.

"I'll show the way," he said.

Ten people lay silent in the tunnel, and 17 waited in the cellar—all the women in their Sunday best—while Herr Mueller clawed and fought his way up and out of the opening. He discovered with horror that they had come out directly under the picket fence. They were still three feet short of the small posts that mark the actual beginning of the West. Technically they were still within the East Zone, and technically the Vopos had the right to shoot.

Then from down the road came the tread of approaching Vopos.

"Quiet!" he whispered back to Bruno. "They're coming."

"Quiet," Bruno whispered back to his mother.

Scarcely breathing, Herr Mueller lay in the bushes as the two

Vopos passed. In the tunnel Frau Becker and the others lay listening to the ominous footsteps just three feet over their heads.

During those last, unbearable moments of tension, the thoughts of many of the refugees turned strangely to the everyday world. Christel thought of her pet tomcat, Peter. Unable to find him that night, she had left behind a note with some money, asking that someone take care of him. Now she wondered: "Who will get Peter?"

Erwin thought: "I'm glad the last thing I did was to go upstairs and hack down our rubber plant. Why should *they* get it?"

Frau Becker thought of Frau Krauss: "May God forgive me, and may Frau Krauss forgive me in the morning."

Then the Vopos were gone, and Herr Mueller whispered to Bruno, "All clear. I'm off."

They waited in stifling blackness while he clambered up the Frohnau hill, stumbled half a mile along the path, and knocked at the first house he came to. It was now 1:15 in the morning. A light came on, and an infuriated man opened the door. "What in the name—"

Herr Mueller blurted out his story. "Have you a telephone?"

"Yes, the only one within a mile. You're lucky. Come in."

A half hour later Mueller was back at the tunnel entrance with

three armed West Berlin policemen. Each of the policemen had a flashlight ready to turn on to reveal himself and his gun if any Vopos started trouble.

Up and out, the refugees emerged, dirty, gasping, trembling. First came Bruno, then Gerda.

"Mother's next," she whispered to Bruno.

Daughter and son reached down into the hole, took hold of their mother's arms, and pulled her out gently.

Disdaining help, Christel pulled herself up.

"This is nothing." she whispered.

But the wait in the tunnel had taken its toll of everybody's nerves, and a moment later she was lying beside her mother on the frozen grass, looking up at the stars and murmuring over and over, "Thank you, God. Thank you."

In the Beckers' cellar, those who were waiting crawled singly into the tunnel as it emptied from the other end. Frau Mueller strapped a doll around the waist of her eight-year-old daughter, Gisela.

"Courage, little one," she whispered.

Gisela was delighted that she could stand and walk at the beginning of the tunnel, but soon she, like all the others, had to crawl.

They came through quickly now, with military precision. Frau Schwartz caught sight of a uniform in the dim moonlight, thought the man was a Vopo, and ducked back into the tunnel. But her husband, with the confidence of desperation, reassured her, and the West Berlin policeman helped her out.

Last person into the cramped, 87-foot passage was the 71-year-old grandmother who insisted that her husband precede her: "You have always led, *Geliebter.*"

On the way through she lost a shoe, and as she tried to crawl out of the hole at the end, she fainted. Tenderly, her husband and one of the policemen pulled her out. A moment later she was lying on the ground beside Frau Becker.

"You know," she said, "I do believe that policeman thought I fainted. Isn't that ridiculous?"

The Becker tunnel, dug through desperation and hope, was empty at last. It had enabled 28 men, women, and children to crawl from tyranny to freedom.

The escapees spent the next few days at the Marienfelde Refugee Camp in West Berlin recovering from their ordeal before they left for their new homes in West Berlin, Dortmund, Hamburg, Munich, and other cities of free Germany.

A week to the day after they had crawled through, Gerda and Christel returned to the snow-covered Frohnau hillside across from their home. They descended the hill and looked at the tunnel opening, already caved in and surely blocked on the other side.

"It's so little," Christel said in a suddenly awestruck voice. "I don't see how we ever got through."

Just then the inevitable pair of Vopos came by, and the irrepressible teenager in Christel broke out. "Why don't you come over here?" she cried. "You know you'd like it much better."

Eyes straight ahead, the Vopos marched on, and the girls were left alone. Across the border and the barbed wire, their home stood empty and abandoned.

"Peter," Christel called to her tomcat. "Come, Peter. Come."

But Peter didn't come, and Gerda put her hand on Christel's shoulder and said, "Let's go, Christel. That life is over."

The girls then climbed back up the hill toward their new lives.

*For the captured Danish Resistance fighters
there seemed no hope of escape from the
tightly guarded Nazi prison—until the day the
planes came and the bombs fell.*

Breakout

By Christen Lyst Hansen

THE FIRST OF THAT day's series of improbable events occurred when a key grated in the lock of my tiny attic cell. The solid wooden door creaked open and there stood the chief of the Nazi prison guards, Trappart himself.

"Get your things together," he said. "You're leaving."

Leaving? I couldn't believe it. For four long months I had been a prisoner on the sixth floor of this sprawling, U-shaped building, once the Copenhagen offices of the Shell Petroleum Company but now Danish headquarters of the German Gestapo. I shared the prison with 35 other Danish Resistance leaders, and I had feared that I'd never leave the place alive.

"We are sending you to Froeslev concentration camp," Trappart said. "The car will be leaving in 15 minutes."

The door clicked shut and he was gone.

Incredulously, I glanced at my watch. It was 8:10 A.M. on March 21, 1945. For just a moment my future seemed immeasurably brighter. I knew Froeslev to be an easy camp; my chances of survival there would be much better than where I was.

Though I had once organized a Danish underground police force, the Gestapo had apparently come to consider me too unimportant to remain in Shell House attic, where they kept only those leaders suspected of being most dangerous to them. They were much more interested now in "interrogating" Danes who had masterminded the sabotage of German-run war factories and railways.

Naturally, I was glad to be getting out of that infamous building, but I felt a sharp pang of regret at leaving so many of my friends behind to die. From the interrogation room on the fifth floor just

27

below, I could hear the cries of fellow Danes undergoing "questioning." More and more of our group were being arrested every day, and many of them were being forced to talk. Consequently, the Gestapo's massive intelligence files, kept on the first three floors, were fast nearing completion.

Soon the Nazis would finish piecing together their complex jigsaw puzzle of information. Then most of my friends in the attic would be shot, or put to slower deaths. Worse, when the Gestapo's files were completed, scores of other Danish Resistance leaders would be arrested and executed. Our whole regional underground movement would be defeated.

8:30 A.M. The surly German guard named Wiesmer marched me across the corridor to the washroom for the last time. As we went in, Prof. Poul Brandt Rehberg came limping out, and I was shocked to see how badly crippled he was from Gestapo beatings. This eminent Danish physiologist, who had helped most of Denmark's 7,000 Jews to safety, was now paying a heartbreaking price for his valor.

On the way back to my cell, I caught a glimpse of young Poul Bruun, who had planned many acts of sabotage. We had all heard whispers of his impending fate.

"We've found out you have been lying to us," an SS officer had informed him the evening before. "Tomorrow you will tell us the whole story—if we have to tear it from you."

For the slightly built, gentle Bruun it was now "tomorrow."

Again conscience stabbed me. What right did *I* have to escape, when men who had done so much more for our cause and country would stay here and perish?

8:40 A.M. Back in my cell I listened to the rising moan of the wind. It would be gray and raw outside. No weather for flying. *They won't come today,* I thought—and was forced to smile grimly at the wild fantasies that desperation can bring to the mind. There was no sensible reason to believe "they" would ever come.

"As long as we've got you up here under the roof," our jailers had always reminded us, "your RAF friends will never attack. They know you'd be the first ones killed by their bombs. Besides, your Allied friends are too busy in Europe to be interested in a cause as trivial as yours. They've forgotten you."

Discouragingly logical arguments. Yet drowning men clutch at straws, and we prisoners in the attic had long clung to a last forlorn hope. If, we reasoned, our Resistance leaders outside should determine that Shell House must be destroyed at any cost, if they could prevail on the Royal Air Force to attempt the job, and if the pilots could single out our building in a crowded district where all the steep-tiled rooftops looked alike, then the damning records in Shell House *might* be destroyed and our underground movement saved. And the terrible ordeal might be quickly over for us "expendable" prisoners locked up in the attic.

8:55 A.M. The poker-faced Wiesmer and two other soldiers came to escort me out of the building. As we passed the second and first floors, I glimpsed the vast rows of filing cabinets filled with the incriminating records that threatened to doom my comrades. How I longed for a hand grenade!

We reached the door leading outside, but there Wiesmer stopped and swore furiously.

"The morning car has already gone. Now we'll have to wait until 1 o'clock for the next one."

So it was back to the attic—at 9:02.

I attached no significance to the delay, nor to the fact that I was now placed not in my old cell, Number 10, but in Number 6. What did a few more hours matter when, without even a word of farewell, I'd soon be leaving my friends forever? I kept glancing at the hands of my watch, slowly edging toward my departure time.

Ten o'clock came . . . 11:00 . . . 11:15 . . . little did I know that the long-hoped-for "impossible" air attack was almost upon us, that, using the bad weather as an element of surprise, 46 Allied planes—18 Mosquito bombers and 28 Mustang fighters—were streaking for their target—Shell House.

11:18 A.M. At the whine of diving planes, I jumped up. As the bombs hit Shell House, the attic floor heaved violently beneath my feet. Dust filled the air, making it difficult to see or breathe. The bed danced out across the floor, and everything loose in the cell whirled around me. This, I realized, was only the salvo from the first wave of bombers. Could they destroy the records just 30 feet below without destroying us, too?

I picked up my wooden stool and hurled it against the cell door. To my amazement, the panel shattered. Rushing into the corridor, I saw Wiesmer blocking my path. I grabbed him by the shoulders and shook him violently.

"The keys!" I roared at him. I was frantic. "Give me the keys to the cells! Hurry up!"

Wiesmer, however, was paralyzed with terror, and for a second we both stared in awe at the gaping hole that a bomb had torn in the roof.

Planes roared unbelievably overhead; machine guns stuttered and flicked red tongues. Bombs crashed all around us. I could hear the other prisoners beating away at their doors.

"The *keys!*" I screamed at Wiesmer again.

Slowly he began to pull a chain from his pocket. I snatched it from him and began unlocking the cell doors.

Here was my big chance—the one I'd thought would never come. But would there be time?

In seconds, I unlocked Cells 7, 8, and 9. Number 10, my old cell, was open and empty. As I rushed toward Number 11, the whole building reeled and shook with a new series of explosions, but I managed to reach and open 11 and 12, and, as a sheet of flame from the ruined west wing swept toward me, 13, 14, and 15.

Rushing out of their cells into the dust-choked corridor came leading figures of the Danish Resistance. Some, like Professor Brandt Rehberg, were limping so badly from "interrogations" that they could barely walk. But we were out—every one of us from the attic's south wing was free.

Some of us ran to help prisoners in the west wing, but found them impossible to reach; a bomb had ripped a gigantic hole in the floor, and we couldn't get across.

"Come on," I yelled. "Time to get out of here."

With the others behind me, I raced for the northeast stairs. A lucky choice: They proved to be one of the only two stairways in the building still left standing!

The few prisoners still alive in the blazing west wing were making even more spectacular exits. Poul Bruun, experiencing an even rougher day than had been promised him by the Gestapo, had fallen straight through to the fifth floor. His skull was fractured, but he was vaguely aware of fire surging toward him. It was either jump—from a fifth-story window—or burn to death. Bruun jumped. Spinning down, he landed in a tangle of barbed wire.

Meanwhile, our group raced down the stairs and burst into the open. There had been no time to think of the guards and guns that might await us there, but a glance revealed only corpses; the lucky guards had fled.

The gate of the barbed-wire fence was standing open. We ran through it, wildly, headlong.

By another freak of chance, the barbed-wire entanglement, our last obstruction, had been blown to bits, and a path was cleared for us precisely where—and when—we needed it.

The streets were mercifully deserted and filled with smoke. By now practically everyone else had dived into the air-raid shelters (among them, I learned later, my wife and 15-year-old son, who had watched the bombing from a shop not 700 yards away).

For a moment we seemed to have the entire city to ourselves. Only when the last ground-shaking explosions ended did we turn to look back. Shell House attic—about 90 seconds after we left it—had collapsed in a torrent of flames.

We quickly scattered in various directions, and in seven minutes I had reached a friend's house.

That evening I learned more about the air raid, one of the most daring and perilous of the war. Launched in cooperation with the Danish Resistance, the mission had been led by Britain's Air Vice-Marshal Sir Basil Embry himself. The bombing attack on Shell House had cost four RAF bombers, two fighter planes, and the lives of nine of the airmen.

But the assault had accomplished its mission. Though eight of the attic prisoners had died, the incriminating Gestapo records lay in ashes. Scores, perhaps even hundreds, of Copenhagen Resistance fighters had thus been placed beyond the reach of terror.

For us and for our families and friends it was a night for exuberant, if incredulous, celebration.

About a dozen survivors of Shell House are alive today. Every year they get together to talk about old times and to marvel that things turned out so well. The ordeal in Shell House taught them all a lesson—that no matter how bleak a situation may appear to be, it is never too late to hope for one last chance.

Christen Lyst Hansen, who died in 1974, was honored by King Frederik of Denmark with a decoration for his heroism during the bombing raid on Shell House.

*The weather-beaten Soviet trawler sailed across the
Black Sea under orders to proceed to a repair yard.
But its captain had a different plan—to defect to a Western
country with his ship and crew.*

Desperate Voyage

By George Feifer

E VENING WAS APPROACHING when distant thunder rumbled
through the air of Kerch, a Russian port on the northern shores
of the Black Sea. The weather would have seemed threatening to
most sailors, but to Pavel Ivanovich Dudnikov, captain of the elderly
Soviet fishing trawler *Vishera,* the prospect of a storm was pure balm.
From the wheelhouse he gave the order to cast off and rang down
"slow ahead." It was 7 P.M. on August 10, 1972. The *Vishera* had
begun her desperate voyage to freedom.

Nothing seemed unusual about the 160-ton trawler. Her gray and
white anonymity was enlivened only by the canary-colored hammer
and sickle painted on a red band around her narrow funnel. Her
orders were to proceed to a repair yard in Odessa, 485 miles to the
west. In fact, however, Captain Dudnikov and his first mate, Vladimir Dyusov, shared a daring plan: to strike south across the Black Sea
to the Bosporus, thence through the strait and on to Greece, the
nearest Western country where they considered it safe to ask for
political asylum. Though slow, the ship was newly refitted and fully
provisioned: 11 tons of fuel (enough for 10 days' sailing), plenty of
food and water for the crew of eight.

The notion of defecting with an entire ship was audacious indeed.
All craft movements throughout the Black Sea were closely watched
by Soviet patrols. Capture of a defector, with a likely charge of
"crimes against the state," could mean up to 10 years in a labor
camp—even, in rare cases, death.

Dudnikov and Dyusov could not tell the crew of their plan for fear
of risking denunciation to the Soviet police. At least one member of
every Soviet fishing crew is an informer. Fortunately, the identity of

33

the *Vishera's* informer was obvious: Engineer David Tskhadaya, 57, a dogmatic, slogan-spouting Communist Party member. Even knowing this, the captain could not always contain his feelings about Soviet rule. A few days earlier he and Tskhadaya had stood on deck, gazing at the hills above Kerch.

Tskhadaya had said: "If I were a local party secretary, I'd build a large statue of Lenin up there, dominating the city."

"This country has a million statues of Lenin," Dudnikov blurted

out. "I'd build a restaurant where people could go and *enjoy* themselves for a change!"

Aghast, Tskhadaya warned the crew of this "impertinence" and threatened: "When we get back, the KGB will look into this case."

Pavel Ivanovich Dudnikov had been born in 1929 of Russian peasant stock in a village bordering the Caucasus Mountains. In 1930 Communist Party officials forced farmers to give up their land and join collective farms. To acquire resources to start the collectives, the officials arrested some of the hardest-working farmers and their families as "exploiters," confiscated virtually everything they owned, and exiled them to the wilderness of the northern Ural Mountains. Among the victims was the Dudnikov family.

At 17, after an adolescence in near-famine conditions, Pavel became a seaman. Over the next decade he rose to the rank of mate, earning 150 rubles a month—enough to support a bachelor. But when he married and had to provide for a family, his pay did not suffice. He resorted to occasional smuggling and black-market transactions to make ends meet.

In 1962 the desperate Dudnikov bought some Western currency from an underground trader, intending to purchase and resell some

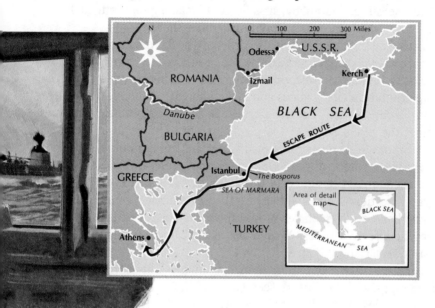

foreign clothing so that he could buy extra goods for his family. But he was caught and sentenced to eight years in a labor camp. In his first year there he learned that his wife had divorced him.

The harsh experience set his goal in life: to flee the Soviet Union. Shortly after his release from the labor camp in 1970, he met Vladimir Dyusov, whose ideas about the Soviet regime matched his own.

Three hours out of Kerch, a guard-ship signal light—"Identify yourself"—stabbed furiously at the *Vishera*. Dudnikov's first impulse was to ignore the challenge, even though the trawler was still on her assigned course. His slow response aroused suspicion, and the guard ship at once ordered the *Vishera* to come alongside.

Through a bullhorn, an officer asked, "Why didn't you answer? What are you trying to do?"

"Sorry," shouted Dudnikov.

He saw the officer pick up the radiotelephone to call the Command Point for Control of Ship Movements in Kerch. Five minutes seemed like hours. Then he was told he could proceed and was warned: "Watch yourself—or we'll watch you!"

Leaving the guard ship, the *Vishera* headed almost due south, instead of moving westward along the coast to Odessa. Luckily, Command Point had ordered all vessels to give a wide berth to the coast, where naval units would be engaging in night-firing exercises. This, of course, suited Dudnikov, since it would take him out into the Black Sea, away from the more heavily patrolled shore.

Five hours out of Kerch, he ordered the helmsman to come to starboard—to the freedom course, 232 degrees. To dispel the crew's curiosity, Dudnikov said this new course was necessary to take the ship around the firing zones and out of danger. Actually, the *Vishera* was heading directly for the Turkish Bosporus, 500 miles southwest across the Black Sea.

At midnight Dyusov relieved the captain. But Dudnikov could not sleep. He was too worried. On a recent 300-mile voyage the *Vishera* had encountered three patrol boats. These sea sentries knew the assigned location of every Soviet vessel and were ready to intercept any ships that were off course. Would these high seas and bad visibility provide effective cover? Would the electrical storms interfere with coastal radar surveillance?

August 11 dawned to more thundery squalls. The morning horizon was empty, and the *Vishera* seemed alone in the Black Sea's 170,000 square miles. Dudnikov was required to radio his ship's position twice daily, but he told his radio officer to contact no one. An industrious Lithuanian, the officer thought the order a curious one, but he did not question it.

However, the captain was soon suffering the disquieting presence of Tskhadaya, who climbed to the bridge to inspect the chart.

"Why are we so far from shore?" he asked.

"It's this rotten visibility," said Dudnikov. He gestured with his hand. "The coast is right over there."

In truth, they were more than 100 miles from land on a course slightly south of the major sea-lane.

Just after noon the next day a speck appeared ahead. Dudnikov and Dyusov were relieved when it turned out to be a Soviet freighter. Even so, merchant vessels had standing orders to report any Soviet ships considered off course. The two men watched the ship lumber past. No signal. Their luck was holding!

Several times in the tense hours that followed, the *Vishera* took evasive action to avoid Soviet merchantmen. These maneuvers did not go unnoticed by the crew. Some of them guessed correctly—but privately— what was afoot. Dudnikov and Dyusov became aware of a kind of tacit conspiracy as they saw some of the sailors exchange meaningful looks.

At 3 P.M. the magic moment arrived: the first view of Turkey to the south. Although five hours of steady steaming remained to reach the Bosporus, they would soon be in Turkish territorial waters. If a Soviet cutter appeared, Dudnikov could race for the shore, beach the ship if necessary or swim to land. Meanwhile, the crew had to be told what was up—everyone, that is, except Tskhadaya, who was down below in the engine room.

"I offer you my congratulations," Dudnikov said to each sailor in turn. "You are now in Turkish waters and a free man if you choose. I intend to sail to Greece. You can join me in requesting political asylum. If you want to return to the Soviet Union, you may do so when we reach Athens. The choice is yours."

The crew's reaction was not long in crystallizing. "Free!" they rejoiced. "We're going to be free!"

Tskhadaya obviously had to be told something. So he was informed that the ship had received radio orders to change course from Odessa to Izmail, a Soviet port located about 45 miles up the Danube delta from the Black Sea. Tskhadaya checked with the radio officer who, as instructed, confirmed the change.

There was still the serious business of getting safely through the Bosporus. At the rail Tskhadaya watched idly as the *Vishera* began negotiating "the Danube." The delicate passage took well over an hour. It was only at the south end of the Bosporus, opposite Istanbul itself, when the Sultan Ahmet Mosque, a famous Turkish landmark, came into view that Tskhadaya jerked back in disbelief.

"What does this mean?" he shouted. "This is Turkey!"

"Yes, I see," Dudnikov replied blandly. "Apparently I made a slight mistake."

"I will report to the Soviet Consulate in Istanbul immediately," spluttered Tskhadaya.

The captain proceeded through the Bosporus, then anchored and opened six bottles of Russian champagne to mark the occasion. Calmly he made Tskhadaya an offer: he would not lock him up if Tskhadaya stood watch until allowed to leave the vessel in Greece. Crestfallen, the informer agreed.

As it turned out, Tskhadaya never reached Greece. Shortly after, in the Sea of Marmara, a Turkish parol boat drew up to inspect the *Vishera*. As the vessels touched, Tskhadaya leaped onto the deck of the Turkish boat. Babbling in Russian and schoolboy German, both incomprehensible to the Turkish crew, he was whisked ashore with them. The Turks were convinced that he was seeking asylum from the Soviet vessel.

But this episode posed a new problem. The Soviet Navy kept an average of 50 ships in the Mediterranean. If Tskhadaya got word to Soviet officials before the *Vishera* could reach Greece, there was still danger of interception. Dudnikov ordered the trawler's identification markings painted out. (As it happened, Tskhadaya remained enmeshed in Turkish red tape too long to relay a timely warning to the Soviets.) In the early morning hours of August 14 the *Vishera* safely dropped anchor off Piraeus, the seaport of Athens.

When a Greek patrol boat came alongside, Captain Dudnikov told its skipper: "We want to ask for political asylum."

"You mean you yourself want asylum," the Greek corrected him.

"No, the whole crew!"

And so ended the voyage of the *Vishera*, the first Soviet craft to defect since World War II.

On January 8, 1973, Captain Dudnikov, First Mate Dyusov, and the rest of the Vishera's *crew boarded the Italian liner* Cristoforo Colombo *at Piraeus and sailed for the United States. Two eventually returned to the Soviet Union; the others are working in various parts of the United States. The fate of Engineer Tskhadaya remains unknown.*

*Green Beret officer James "Nick" Rowe was captured by the Viet-
cong in South Vietnam in 1963. Throughout his 62 months
of imprisonment, during which he suffered extreme physical and
mental torture, he managed to keep a diary. The following
amazing account of how one man endured a lonely, uneven struggle
against a totalitarian system is based on that diary.*

Five Years to Freedom

By Maj. James N. Rowe, U.S. Army

THE STOCKY VIETCONG soldier shoved me violently forward. My
arms were tied at the wrists and elbows, and this prevented me
from balancing as I slipped and struggled in the muddy rice paddy.
Another VC prodded me with his bayonet.

"Mau di!" he commanded ("Move fast!").

I stumbled into one of the deep irrigation trenches that bordered
the paddy. Underwater, panic seized me as I kicked, trying to get to
air. But the sides of the ditch were slick and offered no foothold.
Then I felt something solid and pushed myself upward, breaking the
surface and taking a deep breath before going under again. I heard a
harsh chuckle from one of the VC as the water closed over me.

A hand grasped the cloth binding my elbows and raised me. I
managed to roll onto dry land. Then I was pulled to my feet and once
more pushed along the path atop the canal bank where a short time
ago we had been shooting at one another.

I was exhausted, but through the whirling haze in front of my eyes,
I saw crumpled bodies strewn across the mud. Many of the bodies
were stripped, but on a few were the camouflage uniforms worn by
the South Vietnamese Special Forces. Each had a gaping hole in the
head, the face unrecognizable after the explosive exit of the bullet.
The VC were taking no wounded Vietnamese prisoners.

This was Vietnam in October 1963—before the arrival of United
States jets, artillery support, and combat units. I was an adviser, and
now, on patrol in Vietcong territory with three companies of South
Vietnamese, a fight had broken out and I had been captured.

I heard a commotion behind me, and Dan Pitzer, a medic, came
shuffling past, two VC trotting behind him.

"I'm sorry, Nick," he said as he passed.

A third American had also accompanied the patrol, Capt. Humbert "Rocky" Versace, an intelligence adviser. He had been hit in the knee, and I had just put a compress on the wound when the VC took me. I prayed that they hadn't killed him.

At a shouted command, my guards halted. I stood with my head hanging, trying hard to get my breath, dimly seeing a pair of sandaled feet in front of me.

"My khong?" came a rasping voice ("Is it an American?").

"Da Phai!" snapped a guard, and a fist came straight at me. My head snapped back; pain shot across my face, then blackness.

I came to with a guard kicking me in the back. I could feel the wetness of blood on my face, and I couldn't breathe through my nose. Yanked to my feet, I was led down the canal and put in a long, narrow boat. Shortly the boat pulled away, and I passed out.

I awoke blindfolded with one of the guards wiping my face, using a rag dipped in canal water. He swabbed my mouth and nose almost gently, for which I was grateful. Later, I was led ashore into what was apparently a small village and, in the company of Dan Pitzer and several Vietnamese prisoners, given some rice to eat. The blindfold had been removed.

I had no idea where we were. I recalled a chapter in the pamphlet

Escape and Evasion that said: "One should attempt to escape as soon after capture as possible, before the enemy can move you to a secure area." I wished that the author had included at least one paragraph on how to do it.

Night fell, and we came to a hut. To my relief we found Rocky Versace inside, lying on the floor. He was in obvious pain from his wound, but the bleeding had stopped. Most important, he was alive.

Again by water we moved on, blindfolded, accompanied now by Rocky. I lost all sense of direction. When we finally stopped and the blindfolds were removed, I could see low, thick-leaved trees, ferns, and reeds. I followed a guard through knee-deep water into a grove where we came to a cagelike structure with a low thatched roof and a floor. The walls were made of poles spaced about six inches apart vertically and horizontally.

We entered, and our arms were untied. We were given sleeping mats and mosquito nets. I asked for a drink of water. In a short time, a boy brought me a cup, and I drank greedily. Too late, I felt the slimy moss in my mouth. The water had been scooped up from the stagnant swamp outside our enclosure.

I was too tired to think any more about it. We climbed under the mosquito nets, and the guards departed, leaving one man outside the cage with a submachine gun.

The patrol on which we were captured had been directed against the village of Le Coeur, located in Vietcong-dominated territory some 140 miles southwest of Saigon. It was a countryside of rice paddies, banana and coconut groves, and scattered hamlets, located on the edge of the U Minh Forest. We had never ventured into this area before, and the close proximity of the legendary "Forest of Darkness," a Vietcong sanctuary, had made it a cinch for a fire fight. But instead of encountering the irregular guerrilla units we had expected, we had run into a main force battalion. Our retreat had been cut off with heavy losses. As a matter of fact, Dan, Rocky, and I were very lucky to be alive.

The sun was above the trees the next morning when I awoke. I gingerly felt the bridge of my nose and was rewarded with a sharp pain. I also had a graze wound on the thigh and several small punctures in my chest and legs from mortar fragments. Dan, who had caught fragments in his shoulder, cleaned our wounds.

Rocky Versace was a more serious problem. A trimly built, 26-year-old West Point graduate, he had volunteered for a six-month extension in Vietnam after a year as an adviser. His outthrust jaw and penetrating eyes were indications of his personality; his steel-gray hair looked as if it belonged on someone much older.

He was in severe pain, and his knee had begun to swell. Dan loosened the compresses, which had stuck to the dried blood, giving Rocky a little relief; but medical care was a necessity. Apparently this was not available, for we received only boiled water, some soap, and a mild antiseptic. We washed the wound as thoroughly as we could, and Dan rebandaged it.

The guards also gave us a breakfast of rice. I wondered how long I could go without some sort of real food. I was still thinking in terms of American rations. Before I finished my meal, I experienced wrenching stomach cramps. The guard responded to my frantic gestures by pointing toward a shaky walkway that led away from the cage into the brush. I barely made it to a small platform nailed above the water between two trees. The guard stood about 15 feet away as I went through the spasms of oncoming dysentery. Soon I was spending most of my time running to the latrine.

After a couple of days, Rocky was moved out of the cage, supposedly to be taken to a hospital. Later, we were assured that his wounds were being treated. Dan and I wondered what was in store for us. Before Rocky's departure, he had talked about another American who had been captured earlier and released after six months. We set that as the outside limit of our own detention.

On November 14 Dan and I were taken on a four-day trip to another prison camp among the mangrove swamps of the southern Camau Peninsula. This camp was more elaborate than the setup we had left. There was a log dock over the entry canal and long, narrow huts built on poles to raise them above water level.

Rocky Versace was already there in a thatched hut next to a small kitchen and mess hall. Dan and I were put in a separate hut with barred walls and were not allowed to communicate with him. It was becoming clear that the reason for his separation was not "hospitalization," which he had never received. Rocky, who spoke fluent Vietnamese, had assailed the Vietcong movement from his first encounter with the guards and had been marked as a "reactionary." Dan and I, who spoke little Vietnamese, were unknown quantities.

On the evening of our fourth day in the new camp, we heard excited shouts near Rocky's hut. The guards scrambled for their weapons and then disappeared into the trees, wading in mud up to their thighs, rifles held overhead. Shouting continued as they spread into a line, sweeping through the palms and fern thickets.

A camp official appeared before our cage carrying leg irons, and we were forced into them. We asked why. Visibly incensed, the man snapped, "Versace was very bad."

With a wounded leg and surrounded by deep mud and a camp full of guards, Rocky had tried to escape. He had more guts than brains to try it at this point, and he was caught pulling himself through the slime toward a canal. I learned later that he was attempting to reach the canal, where he could swim and possibly make it northward to a friendly outpost. The VC had assumed from Rocky's opinions that they had a hard case on their hands. Now they knew it.

The camp was run by a major who wore a khaki uniform. The VC also had a political representative there, Mr. Muoi. He wore black trousers and shirt, as did a third man. He was Mr. Ba, whom we called Plato because of his tendency to philosophize.

Plato spent part of each afternoon at the cage with Dan and me, gently probing our ideas about the U.S. involvement in Vietnam. He made no effort to contradict anything we said. His central theme was the generosity and leniency of the National Liberation Front toward prisoners. Then he began to push for a letter to our families stating that we were well and thanking the NLF for its lenient treatment. I refused, and eventually a compromise was worked out. We wrote to the International Red Cross, giving our names, ranks, and serial numbers, and stating that we were in reasonably good health.

One day Plato brought a piece of paper to be filled out. It was titled: "Red Cross Index Data Card." Beneath this heading were: Name, Rank, Serial Number, Date of Birth—all as prescribed by the Geneva Convention. But these questions were followed by a great many others of a military and personal nature.

"Mr. Ba," I said, "this form contains questions we cannot answer."

He looked surprised that I would refuse. "All the Front wishes to do is to notify your family that you are not killed."

"We wrote letters to the Red Cross," I reminded him. "They will notify our families that we are alive."

"No!" His answer was emphatic. "The Red Cross is a tool of the imperialist aggressors, and the Front does not recognize it. Consider your decision carefully. I will come back."

I was still attempting to determine several things. First, what was their purpose in taking us prisoners rather than killing us? Second, what requirements would be placed upon us that we could not fulfill? Finally, to what lengths would they go to ensure fulfillment?

My dysentery, which had grown worse, was now accompanied by

fever and nausea, but the probing of our thoughts went on. Ba and Muoi came in periodically, and on one visit Muoi asked, "Do you know that your President Kennedy was killed?"

I thought he was trying to shake us up. We had been told earlier that Ngo Dinh Diem had been overthrown and killed and that the government in Saigon was toppling. The possibility that these reports might contain some truth made me wonder what was happening on the outside. I dismissed them as false, but it was my first taste of an uncertainty that would grow to monstrous proportions.

Early in 1964 Dan, Rocky, and I were separated and moved to another camp, about two hours away by boat. Plato came to visit me soon after my arrival and pulled out the index data card again.

"You must complete the form," he said.

"What if I refuse?" I asked.

"Do not fear torture," he reassured me. "We are not barbarians who rely on torture to gain information." Then he explained a theory that I was to learn well in the days to come. "If you take an individual and control his body, you do not necessarily control the man. But if you can control his mind, you control the whole. Soon you will attend a school that will show you the truth about Vietnam."

I asked what happened if an individual refused to cooperate.

"He may rest here for a long time," Plato said calmly. "If we are unsuccessful in our instruction the first time, we must recommence."

On February 18 a guard marched me to the school hut. The inside had been decorated with slogans, painstakingly printed in English: "Welcome the lenient policy of the Front toward POW's," "Do not die for the profit of Capitalist-Imperialist." Two khaki-uniformed Vietnamese sat behind the desk. As I slid onto a bench, one began to lecture in a precise voice. Plato translated:

"The National Liberation Front has dispatched us to present to you the just cause of the revolution and the certainty of final victory. Your release will depend upon your good attitude and repentance of your past misdeeds."

My mind was fixed on the phrase "good attitude," and I barely heard Plato begin translating the first lesson: *Vietnam la mot* ("Vietnam is one country").

The next day it was Rocky's turn. I had learned that he was being held in both leg and arm irons, and I watched as he hobbled along to the school. From the angry expressions on his guards' faces, I could tell he was not going willingly.

His first words as he entered the school were: "I'm an officer in the

United States Army. You can force me to come here, you can make me sit and listen, but I don't believe a damn word you say!"

"Rocky," I thought, "bless you. You're a hard-core s.o.b.!"

The school continued through March 24 and covered a sketchy history of the war against the French, the Geneva Accords of 1954, Ngo Dinh Diem's accession to the presidency in South Vietnam, and the suffering that, they said, had occurred because of Diem and the intervention of the United States. Any facts that refuted their version of history were conveniently omitted from their recital of events.

On the evening of April 8, I heard Mr. Muoi's voice yelling in the direction of Rocky's cage. Rocky's voice was fainter, but clear, "All or just me?" They were moving Rocky out! In the commotion, I strained to see through the darkness, but the guards blocked my view.

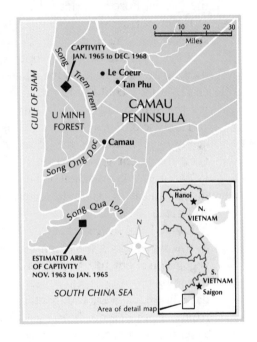

The next morning I was allowed for the first time to walk from my cage to the kitchen to get rice. Along the way a pile of bloody gray rags caught my eye. They were the pajamas given to Rocky, torn into shreds. I forced myself to look at Rocky's cage. Bars had been ripped from the side of the hut and either hung crazily from the tangle of poles or were strewn in the mud. The image of what had happened fixed itself slowly in my brain. Rocky must be dead.

Plato visited my cage later in the day, his mood unusually somber. He told me it was unfortunate that the Front had been forced to take drastic action, but they had no other choice. Rocky had shouted at him and questioned his instruction. Because Rocky had opposed the Front, he had paid. Plato said he hoped my attitude would improve.

I sat, trying to contain my boiling anger. My one thought was not to strike back until I could hurt them. It would have been useless to batter my head against a wall and only lose what slight freedom I had. My ultimate goal was clear: to gain my freedom without compromising my beliefs or harming my country.

Nearly six months had passed, and clearly our hope for an early release had been ill-founded. In fact, another year would pass in much the same way. It was a strenuous period of being moved from one camp to another, of deteriorating health, and of continual VC attempts to extract military information while instilling a proper attitude—acceptance of their version of the war.

I devised a cover story that allowed me to deny knowledge of the areas my questioners were interested in. I concealed the facts that I was a graduate of West Point and that I had trained in artillery and the Special Forces. Instead, I became an engineer with no knowledge of tactics. Bridges, roads, buildings I could discuss, but beyond these subjects I was useless.

I was trying to avoid any open opposition, since this would allow them to bring to bear on me whatever pressure they wished. I wasn't certain that I could hold out as Rocky had done, particularly when the pressure could be maintained for as long as they wanted.

The case of Rocky had a startling twist. One afternoon a guard was at my cage talking to me about the war and particularly about the good treatment given prisoners. I questioned this, saying that the POW's never knew when one of them might be executed. The guard, in defense of his statements, blurted out, *"Khong My chet!"* ("No American is dead!").

Later, I discovered that this was true. While bathing in a canal I overheard Rocky's voice coming from some huts in a clump of thick vegetation about 100 yards from ours. His "murder" had been staged; it was purely a deception meant to weaken our resistance. (Rocky's days, however, were numbered. In September 1965 we were to learn from a Radio Hanoi broadcast that he had been executed in retaliation for the execution of three VC terrorists in Danang.)

As the weeks passed, my health began to disintegrate. The diarrhea became so bad that the guards brought me a crock resembling a large flowerpot so that I wouldn't have to be released from the cage five or six times a night to go to the latrine. I also developed a fungus infection that began like ringworm, spreading rapidly until the raised red areas linked up in a patch extending from my knees to my arms. The constant itching became almost unbearable.

Curiously, after losing a lot of weight, I began to fill out again, although there had been no change in our diet: rice twice a day with *nuoc mam* (a kind of salty fish gruel) and an occasional piece of fish. I felt extremely tired, however, and noticed pains in my lower legs. Within a few months I had practically ceased to urinate, and the weight was an abnormal swelling in my legs and abdomen. I had beriberi and was bloated with stored fluid.

A VC medic, whom we called Ben Casey after the television doctor, treated me with injections of strychnine and vitamin B_1. Within three hours I was experiencing intense pain in my legs, and shortly after dark I began urinating, continuing through the night. The result was a thoroughly emaciated American. I stared at my skinny arms and legs in horror.

Dan was in bad shape, too. Once, for resisting being put in irons, he was strung up from trees outside his cage, spread-eagled, his wrists and ankles bound with wire that cut so deeply it left scars. Worse, however, was the slow starvation. He was little more than bone, and I was reminded of pictures I had seen of the Nazi concentration camp at Dachau. Any exertion left him exhausted.

In December our camp came under attack by American helicopters, and we had to flee into the jungle; then we were moved to a new camp. Dan passed out, going into a near coma for almost two weeks.

LATE IN JANUARY 1965 we moved back to the area where we had been captured, and in March our political indoctrination began again. Dan and I were taken to a hut and introduced to a man named Mr. Hai. He fixed us with a frigid stare.

"I can kill you. I can torture you," he said coldly. "But no, I choose to allow you to fulfill the requirements of the Front and display your knowledge on certain questions."

Back in my cage I was given paper, ball-point pen, and a questionnaire entitled "My Revelation," which asked for biographical and military data and essay-type answers dealing with religion, politics, and economics. I read and reread the form, fitting my cover story into the framework of the questionnaire. Then I began on the essay questions and merrily scribbled inane comments about home economics, mechanical drawing, and a number of other courses I had—and had not—taken in high school.

On April 9 I again met with Mr. Hai. Dan was already there, and I sat with him on the floor. Mr. Hai looked at me with a malefic stare. Suddenly he slammed the papers down hard on his desk. His eyes were flaming with rage.

"This is useless! You have not shown repentance! You continue to resist the Front!" His voice lashed out, carrying a physical impact with each word. "I can no longer allow you to live under the lenient policy. You will go where conditions will reflect your attitude."

I was sent to a separate camp, which I named the Salt Mines. It consisted of just four huts, one of them the familiar barred cage. Dan did not accompany me, but on May 15 another American was brought in, bedraggled but still defiant. This was Sgt. Dave Davila, who had first been captured in December 1964. (The names Dave Davila, Tim Barker, and Ben Wilkes have been fictionalized to protect the families of the actual prisoners.) Davila was a helicopter gunner from Hawaii. He had escaped from a nearby camp and had managed to evade capture for two days. His punishment was to be sent to the Salt Mines.

Two and a half months of utter hopelessness followed. The guards no longer talked about release. Our diet was reduced, and both Dave and I knew we were slowly starving. My fungus infection became much worse, threatening to cover my face and eyes. For days at a time there was no water to drink. I could feel the lining of my mouth drying and tightening as the weeks passed.

We both knew that we couldn't survive much longer. An attempt to escape, whatever the result, would be better than rotting away. I had been planning for months, and in our infrequent meetings Dave and I began to lay the groundwork for a getaway, sketching rough maps, hiding bits of dried fish.

By late August 1965 we were ready.

The night of the 28th was perfect. Rainstorms that rolled in at half-hour intervals would cover any noise we might make. The guards were all in their hut by the kitchen, leaving the path to the canal open. With my last bit of hoarded ink in an old piece of ball-point-pen filler, I drew out a false escape route. This I was going to drop near my cage as we left, hoping the guards would find it. It might keep them off our backs for a couple of extra hours.

About midnight Dave's voice came softly:

"Ready, Nicko?"

We checked our gear and slid into the dark. The paper with the false route was lying outside the cage as if I'd dropped it accidentally. Our guard was curled up, asleep.

The night was totally black. It took us about 10 minutes to cover the 60 feet to the reed-lined canal. Once there, we moved more rapidly, but found the canal less clearly defined the farther we got from camp. Dave suggested heading overland, going what we thought would be due east until we hit a larger north-south canal that we could follow. We decided to try it and found ourselves in a tangle of ferns and reeds. We sounded like a herd of elephants as we splashed through them. The mosquitoes were like a second skin, driving their stingers into every inch of our bodies.

We tried to move faster, but we were both tiring rapidly.

"Don't let me stop," Dave gasped.

Exhausted, we pushed on through high grass, reeds, and clumps of trees, driven by the thought of freedom. After two hours we came upon a canal, but we could no longer tell if it ran north to south or east to west. We moved on through the reeds, hoping frantically that we were heading east.

At last the sky lightened, and I decided to climb a tree, checking for the sunrise that should be ahead of us.

As I reached a vantage point, I almost wept. The sun was breaking through the clouds *behind* us. We had been traveling west. Worse, I saw the path that we had left in the tall grass. It marked our trail as if we had left road signs.

Desperately, I tramped out several false trails from our main path, terminating each in an area where the grass stopped and where we could conceivably have continued without making a distinct trail. We then backtracked for about 100 yards and headed due south, making certain to close the grass over our path as we moved away.

I cursed at our slow pace. I could picture the guards, like a bunch of bloodhounds, rapidly sweeping the area.

We had traveled another hour when we heard voices from a boat along a nearby canal. They had got near us too damn fast.

I couldn't think of anything that would aid us in evading them now, aside from a tremendous amount of luck. Dave and I camouflaged the narrow trail we had made into a dense clump of ferns, then lay down in the water, covered to our necks, with our heads pressed in close to the ferns. All we could do was wait.

I could hear my heart thumping as the voices came closer. I thought of the movies I'd seen as a young boy about the war in the Pacific, and how the hero had always miraculously escaped. What happened in real life?

A guard we called Cheeta suddenly broke into the patch of grass, his Russian burp gun carried in a ready position. Behind him came two other guards. We heard more voices from the south. Another group was sweeping in to link up with the others. I was suddenly very tired, very sick.

Cheeta shouted in alarm and jumped back. He had almost stepped on Dave. The others rushed over, training their guns on Dave as he unwillingly got to his feet.

"Where's Rowe?" Cheeta demanded. *"Toi khung hieu"* ("I don't understand"), Dave replied in a lifeless voice.

The guards fixed bayonets and began to tramp through the ferns, jabbing at the water.

I was only six feet away, sliding backward through the undergrowth as quietly as possible, when one of them tripped over me. Instantly there were bayonets all around my face, and I was ordered to get to my feet.

Dave sank to his knees utterly exhausted, only half conscious. A

guard named Leo shouted for him to stand, pointing his burp gun at him. I knelt beside him and lifted an eyelid. I saw nothing but white; he was passing out.

I told Cheeta I would have to help him. Instead, they bound my arms at the elbows. Dave started to slump.

I bent my knee, giving him something to hang onto. Deep strain twisted his mouth. His hand found the bend in my arm. He clung, pulled, and with his face contorted almost beyond recognition, stood upright, leaning heavily.

For six days after that I was held in leg and arm irons. My arms were pulled back and upward while my feet and legs were stretched painfully in the opposite direction. It was like being on a rack. I was released only to eat twice a day—rice with salt and almost no water. I was not allowed to go to the latrine. So for that period, still suffering from dysentery, I lay encrusted in my own filth.

If I were to repent of my crime, I was told, and to promise that I would never try to escape again, the Front would be lenient with me. I replied that I'd rather die trying to regain my freedom than starve in a prison camp. Then, late one night, the guard who had been on duty when we escaped came into my cage and kicked me viciously twice in the ribs. I decided then that enough was enough and agreed to their terms if both Dave and I would be allowed to resume our normal prisoners' life.

A guard handed me a piece of soap and a towel and told me to bathe. I felt a sudden catch in my throat and turned away, ashamed at the urge to cry. The relief was so beautiful!

I looked toward Dave's cage and saw him sitting by the door. He was a skeleton. The escape had pushed him to the limit. In his eyes was the reflection of the last months in the punishment camp, the slow death there, the near death in front of Leo's submachine gun, and now this. It was a tightening vise that left a man no place to turn, no hope for maintaining the shreds of individuality, self-esteem, or belief without sacrificing his life for that privilege.

On September 7, 1965, we were taken back to a camp we called the No K Corral and rejoined Dan Pitzer and another American prisoner, a black master sergeant named Edward "John" Johnson. John was in leg irons because he was thought to have been an accessory in Dave's earlier escape attempt.

On the morning of January 8 all of us heard a deep voice speaking English in the guard area. The man was talking extremely slowly, almost as if he were drugged. One of the guards called Dan over, and a few minutes later he reappeared at the edge of the compound. I caught my breath in shock. There, clinging to Dan's shoulder, was a hulk of human wreckage, a huge bone structure covered with tightly stretched, fungus-infected skin. What must have been a grin of joy at seeing other Americans looked like a leering death's-head. The deep voice echoed from the cavernous chest. "God! Americans!"

This was our introduction to Capt. Tim Barker, U.S. Army, captured a year before. One look at him and a strong feeling of kinship and responsibility swept through us. He must have lost at least 80 pounds, and his festering fungus sores were alarming. The first thing we did was to get him a bath and some clean clothing.

I spoke to the cadre about medication for Tim, and on January 13 we were given vitamins, a horse-liver extract, and several bottles of a fungicidal liquid. Our days now became a constant struggle to some-how keep Tim alive. But a year of imprisonment and starvation had destroyed his will to live.

On the morning of February 4, I went to Tim's net to help him get out and eat. He was crouching at the rear of the net, his eyes enormous, his pupils dilated.

"I don't want any rice!" he gasped. "I won't eat it!" Then he curled up in a tight ball and began to have spasms from the waist down, his legs twitching and jerking.

Dan slipped in beside me and called for John to get Intern, a VC medic. He arrived with a syringe of respiratory stimulant, injected it, and left. Tim's chest began to heave for a moment, then slowed and stopped. We rolled him onto his stomach, and I began artificial respiration. "Don't . . . die! Don't . . . die!" The rhythm went through my mind as I applied pressure, then released.

Intern came back and told us to carry Tim to the canal, where he would be put in a boat and taken to a "hospital." But as we placed him in the boat and shaded his head with a sleeping mat, I knew it would be the last time we would see Tim.

A few weeks later Dave Davila began to have a problem with rice. He would eat and vomit, try again and vomit again, until he finally got the rice to stay down. Soon he began to remain all day in his net, except when he had to go to the latrine. Then he refused to eat, just as Tim Barker had done. I went to see Major Bay, the camp commander, telling him another American would die unless he was given adequate food. His reply was an apologetic refusal.

I RETURNED DETERMINED not to let Dave die. We had been through the Salt Mines together, survived the escape attempt, and made it through the "correction" period. I knew he could lick the physical problem, but the psychological one was tougher—Tim Barker had shown Dave a new way to escape. I prayed for an idea that might help this Hawaiian boy get back to the islands he loved.

On the night of March 19 Dave's condition worsened and he became incoherent. It was agonizing to lie there in leg irons and listen to a man die, calling the names of old friends, his mind a thousand miles away. In the morning I tried to feed him, but it was impossible. He couldn't even get a cup of water down. Intern arrived and decided that Dave also had to be moved to the "hospital."

I gathered his belongings in a small bundle, and we carried him to the canal. As we lifted him into the boat, he clung to my forearm with a grip far beyond anything I imagined possible. I realized that it was the ancient warrior's arm clasp. Dave was bidding me farewell.

The impact of this second death drove our morale to abysmal depths. I felt bitterness and hatred building, feeding off the constant frustrations and anxiety. I knew that I could destroy myself if I allowed such negative emotions to dominate my thinking. So I turned to the one positive force our captors could never challenge: God.

I had never questioned religion, nor had I ever really accepted it. It was something I had lived with, because that's the way things were done. Now I was left with only the intangibles that form the core of our existence: faith, ethics, morals. I could only turn to the Power I believed to be so far greater than that which now imprisoned me. After Dave's death I really began to believe: "The Lord is my Shepherd; I shall not want."

The next months—indeed, the next year and a half—were a struggle as first one, then another of us succumbed to illness and sought desperately to find enough to eat to sustain the will to live.

Political indoctrination during 1966 and 1967 continued as before. The guards would bring the camp radio over for us to hear the English broadcast by Radio Hanoi. This was supposed to keep us abreast of the conflict so that we might evaluate the validity of the lessons taught us. For the first time we learned of the antiwar movement in the United States. Hanoi reported protests on campuses across the nation, which we took as normal exaggeration, but it stayed with us where the battle reports didn't.

Major Bay conducted several classes on "the just cause of the revolution and the injustice of the U.S. dirty war of aggression." He always claimed that no North Vietnamese troops were present in South Vietnam, and there were specific instructions to the cadre to deny any link with the Communist Party of Vietnam, headed by Ho Chi Minh. This link was the first thing an American prisoner looked for to justify his own beliefs. If the VC could convince him that a Communist-inspired insurgency didn't even exist, the rest of the POW's beliefs could be attacked.

Had I not understood some Vietnamese, I might have missed hearing the daily political classes attended by the guards in which the doctrine *Marx-it, Le-nin-it,* was taught to even the youngest. It was incongruous to hear the cadre teaching Marxist philosophy to the guards, yet denying any connection with communism when talking with Americans. The fact that the cadre felt the need to lie strengthened my conviction that I was right in my beliefs.

On September 14, 1967, the first indications of some big event began to unfold. A group of high-level interrogators and a VC journalist paid us a visit. Dan and John Johnson met with them together, and then, separately, so did I and Jim Jackson, a Special Forces medic who had joined us a month earlier. The journalist, who spoke English, informed me that these men were representatives of the Central Committee and had come to the camp to determine our condition and review our "progress." They asked me a few perfunctory questions and seemed to be bored by my answers. Then I was told that my attitude had been judged unsatisfactory.

Nonetheless, their visit sparked speculation about the possibility of release, and our hopes seemed justified, for soon our diet was improved. A second indicator came when John suddenly declared that he couldn't eat and began vomiting. This time medication came into the camp in amounts and types exceeding anything we had seen in all the other years combined.

On October 18 Mr. Hai reappeared to see if John was well enough to travel. That was the tip-off to what followed. Preparations were made by the guards for a trip, and the next day Dan, Jim, and John attended a special meeting with Mr. Hai and a cadre that had arrived with him. That afternoon my summons came, too.

I sat on a stool before the cadre, while Mr. Hai translated:

"You are POW Rowe, and you are here to learn the decision of the National Front for Liberation of South Vietnam. Your comrades are no longer prisoners. They are to be released under the lenient policy of the Front and allowed to return to their homes."

I knew what was coming, but it was still a shock. "You have shown a bad attitude," Mr. Hai continued. "You have foolishly tried to escape. You cannot recognize the just cause of the revolution. For these reasons you cannot be released."

He paused, then added, "Do not think that merely because the war ends you will go home. You can remain here after the war."

I felt like sliding through the floor poles. The thought of staying here alone until I died was terrifying.

That evening I ate my last meal with the other three. I gave Dan a message for my parents and wished them all a heartfelt Godspeed on their journey to freedom. Late that night they climbed into a boat and were gone. On November 3, I was told that they had reached Cambodia and would soon be home.

The loneliness after they left produced an overwhelming depression. At the same time, I was happy that they were free. I knew that none of them had bought the line that the cadre was throwing at us.

Christmas was approaching, and I planned to celebrate it no matter what the circumstances. The day before Christmas I spent the morning catching enough of the tiny *ca ro* fish for a substantial surplus. I was declaring the next day a holiday. I made a wreath out of tree branches and pieces of colored thread. Purple wild grapes took the place of holly berries.

As I prepared the evening meal, I sang Christmas carols, picturing the brightly lighted tree at my parents' home, the table spread with food, and, most important, the people. The fireplace in our living room was the window through which I saw Mom and Dad, seated on the couch, as the small dancing flames of my cooking fire became the roaring blaze on our hearth.

Mr. Hai had given me some cookies and tea to celebrate, "just like you do in America." I made the tea and offered a cup to my guard, Cheeta, with some cookies. He was surprised, but ate them with obvious enjoyment. Then he locked me in my leg irons for the night.

I now entered a terrible period of harassment and pressure to force a compromising statement from me. Adding to my torment, my fungus infection again developed into a serious problem. It covered most of my body except for my head.

The political lessons became almost more than I could take, as I had to sit and listen to the guards degrade my country and voice their confidence in our defeat. I was troubled by the increased use of American sources to substantiate the violence that seemed to be erupting across the United States. I began hearing more statements alleged to have been made by U.S. senators and congressmen, not only opposing our presence in Vietnam, but supporting the NLF.

DURING THE TET OFFENSIVE the news got worse. I heard that the NLF had hit major cities over the length of Vietnam (despite their own proposed seven-day cease-fire). City after city was being overrun, the South Vietnamese forces were disintegrating, and the American command was in turmoil.

Confused and anxious, unable to sleep, I developed a case of dysentery that soon became unbearable. I was denied medication unless I wrote an "appeal" to U.S. servicemen to go home. I resisted at first, but at last consented, signing the message just as my keepers wrote it, leaving in every grammatical error and inaccuracy. I felt lost when I gave them the paper.

News continued to pour in. The assassination of Robert Kennedy was carried on all broadcasts. I sat stupefied. First, President Kennedy, then Martin Luther King, now Bobby. My United States was being turned upside down. Escape was a remote dream, for I was told that the Tet offensive had broken Saigon's control of the countryside. Even if I did escape, there would be no place to go.

Finally, on August 18, Mr. Hai —who had once said, "I can kill you. I can torture you"—returned to camp, and I was called before him. I listened as he went through his main points: the hopeless struggle, the antiwar movement, President Johnson's decision not to run for reelection. I could feel the confusion building, the feeling of having to defend something that perhaps wasn't defensible.

"And now," Hai continued, "you must write for me your thoughts on the war and how it can be resolved. You must recognize the unjust cause of the U.S. imperialists, who sent you to die so that they might become enriched. You must believe that my recommendations are well received by the Central Committee and, if you show progress, you can be released."

The desire for release was strong, and writing what he wanted was the only way I could see to come out alive. The reasons I'd had for being willing to hang on, no matter what came, had been torn away from me. I couldn't condemn my country, yet I didn't want to die for supporting a lost cause. "Mr. Hai, I can't write those things." The words were out before I realized I'd said them. I panicked as I saw the coldness come into his eyes.

He retrieved his paper without speaking, then looked at me with a slight smile, confident in his control of the situation. "Go back to your house," he said. "We will talk again about this matter."

That night my clothes and mosquito net were taken from me. Mr. Hai, the s.o.b., had set this up. I cursed under my breath as the first group of mosquitoes bit into my exposed skin. I could actually feel the pulpy mass in my hand each time I slapped at a concentration of 50 or more. There was not a portion of my body that wasn't bitten. Blood and crushed mosquito bodies smeared my skin.

The hours wore on without relief. The rough metal of my irons made raw red stripes on my legs as I twisted and turned. My diarrhea broke loose, and I was unable to make the crock I used at night. The odor, the filth, the stings, the hopelessness made me want to cry out: "—you, Mr. Hai, and all your ancestors!" That was my final coherent thought before I was aroused by a guard.

My clothes were given back, and later I was ordered to Mr. Hai's hut. His countenance was a mask of innocence as he said, "I see your face is swollen. Why do you not use your mosquito net?" Then he launched into his spiel for several hours, ending by saying, "Now you can write for me what you have learned in our discussion."

"Mr. Hai, I'm tired," I said, "and can't really think straight."

His voice cut like a knife. "You must not try the patience of the Front! Consider carefully your path."

That night was a repeat of the previous one. My clothes and net were taken away again.

"Mr. Hai," I asked in the morning, "please tell me—am I being punished for something?"

"You are a criminal," he replied. "The U.S. aggressors have brought much suffering to our country, and they must pay their blood debts. If you do not repent your crimes, the Front can no longer allow you to enjoy the lenient policy."

No longer enjoy the *lenient* policy!

For a third night I suffered without my clothes or net. During periods of rationality, my one thought was: "I've got to stop this." I decided to make a trade, giving Mr. Hai something he wanted—in as ambiguous a form as possible—in exchange for relief and sleep.

The next morning I indicated my willingness to write for him, and the following day, after a satisfying rest, I listed the events of the war as Hai had related them. (A few days earlier, for example, he had told me: "In the dry-season counteroffensive launched by the imperialist aggressors in 1966 and 1967, 28 U.S. battalions were annihilated and 85,243 U.S. and satellite troops were wiped out.")

I had reached the point where the war in Vietnam was a mass of confusion in my mind. I had to buy time and try to get my physical condition under control. Mr. Hai left, and for two weeks I fed myself as well as I could and treated my ailments. He returned late in August with five lessons—"corrections" to my thoughts. The sessions ran through the days and into the nights. I knew I'd lie naked to the mosquitoes again unless he got what he wanted. There was too much to fight at one time. I wrote in my diary later: "Sessions a mental meat grinder—repeat, repeat, repeat, write. Enough truth to confuse the rest—certain points are unclear as compared with before—*have* to know *our* side!"

Mr. Hai left again, but returned a few days later and announced that I was to prepare for a "three-day excursion." The Central Committee had decided that I had progressed, but that my "writing" was still incomplete. So I was to be taken to my old post at Tan Phu, where the base had been overrun and the area "liberated," in order for me to see the "reality of the situation in South Vietnam."

We left on September 14 by boat. Hai explained the ground rules: no talking to civilians, keep my head lowered, look repentant in the presence of civilians, and rely on the cadre to protect me from the wrath of the people.

We spent the first night in a nearby village, then continued our journey. I didn't recognize the terrain until we came to a point where our canal intersected with a larger one and Hai pointed to a reed-covered bank. "There is Tan Phu post," he declared. I stared in disbelief. There wasn't anything there—no concrete bunkers, no watchtower, no people, only the reeds swaying in the hot breeze. Tan Phu had ceased to exist.

Hai took advantage of my surprise to emphasize the NLF's strength as proved by their ability to wipe out the post. I had no reply. It was obvious that nothing had been spared, and the confidence they had shown traveling through this zone seemed justified.

AT DUSK WE STOPPED at a village where the people were holding a meeting to discuss the revolution. This would be dangerous for me, Hai cautioned, since the villagers hated Americans. When he mentioned the name of the village, I was startled. We had run medical patrols to it in 1963, bringing food and clothing, and had developed quite some rapport with the people.

When we arrived, Hai spoke to the assembled crowd, pleading with them to realize that I was a prisoner and was learning of the crimes I had committed in order to repent and join the Vietnamese in their struggle for freedom. There was silence from the people as rows of curious eyes fastened on me. Then I felt a hand on my shoulder and flinched. *"Manh khong, Trung-Uy?"* ("Are you all right, Lieutenant?") a voice behind my ear asked. I managed to nod. The hand patted me and there was one word: *"Tot"* ("Good.").

Then I was roughly pushed out beside Hai by a guard and exhibited as a prize of war. A commotion broke out to my right, and a scrawny man leaped from the crowd with his fist upraised, screaming, "Down with the American imperialists!"

I tensed, awaiting the blow. But nothing happened. I glanced up, and the man was standing in front of me, his fist still clenched. This unusual tableau continued until suddenly a member of the cadre stepped belatedly forward and blurted out, "My compatriots, restrain your anger. Do not strike the prisoner."

It was like a grade-school play during which someone had missed his cue. When the speech was finished, the man in front of me was even more uncertain what to do next. Finally, he managed a sheepish grin and shuffled back into the crowd. Someone laughed.

Hai had just begun a closing speech when an old grandmother, chewing betel nut, walked up to me and poked a bony finger into my ribs. She squeezed my forearm until she touched bone. "Do you mistreat him?" she asked. "I remember this boy when he came to our hamlet. He was strong, and now he looks weak and sick."

A chuckle went through the crowd at the idea of this little old lady putting a powerful leader in a tight situation.

Hai slipped into his standard line. "You must remember that the Americans are criminals. But the Front is lenient. . . ."

The old woman interrupted him. "I know what it is to be hungry and sick, and there is no leniency in inflicting that on another."

Hai looked desperately at me. "Tell her you are well treated," he ordered. I lowered my head and looked repentant.

Two days later I was back in my forest cage, not knowing what to expect next, but feeling better equipped to deal with my confusion about the war. I had seen the vast difference between what the cadre wished me to believe and what actually existed. These people had known nothing but war for two decades, and out of its destruction they had always rebuilt. I had seen, if only in this area, the spark of resistance still burning. If they, in a Communist-controlled zone, were willing to resist, I was willing to help.

One morning, a few weeks after my trip to Tan Phu, I was called to a meeting in the guards' mess hall. Entering the hut, I saw not only Hai and his cadre but also an older man in his late 50's sitting at the head of the table. All the guards from the immediate area were gathered, too. I had been thinking constantly of release, but I felt only animosity from the assembled group.

The man at the head of the table spoke: "I am a representative of the Central Committee and have come to say a few words to you. It is fortunate that the peace- and justice-loving friends of the South Vietnam Front for National Liberation in America have provided us with information that leads us to believe you have lied to us."

My throat constricted, and my stomach wrenched. The guards' eyes all seemed to be boring into mine.

"According to what we know, you are not an engineer. You were not assigned to the many universities that you have listed for us. You have much military training that you deny. The location of your family is known. You were an officer of the American Special Forces.

59

Your father's name is Lee, and your mother's name is Florence."

The words became a blur. He was picking me to pieces. Desperately, I tried to remember the points he attacked, so I could build some sort of answer, but there was no way to cover all of them.

After five years of captivity, my whole miserable world had collapsed. Who would give them information about me? An American wouldn't do that to one of his own. I could understand opposition to war and a strong desire for peace. Dissent was a part of American life, but to support the enemy at the expense of another American was inconceivable. Yet there was no other place the VC could have got their information. I felt sick.

Shortly thereafter I discovered a frightening new development. During mealtime the guards spent at least 40 minutes in their mess hut, leaving me alone. Periodically, I went to their sleeping hut during this interval and leafed through the papers they kept in a .30-caliber ammunition box. In this way I was able to determine roughly what action of major importance was pending.

One day in December I was quickly checking the new papers in the box when one caught my eye. My name was on it! I read the heading and saw that it had come from the political office of the headquarters zone. I tried to decipher the sentences relating to me. *"Sang chuyen"* ("to transfer"). *"Ban dan dich van."* I was to be transferred to the Enemy and Civilian Proselyting Section at headquarters. Transfer meant the VC felt that the resources to deal with me at this level had been exhausted. I knew that at headquarters there was no pretense of "leniency and humanitarianism." I could expect to give them what they wanted or face execution.

THE MORNING OF DECEMBER 31, 1968, was dark and cold as my guard, nicknamed Porky, unlocked my leg irons. We were camped atop a low bank formed by the mud dug from a canal and now covered with the same cattail and bamboo reeds that filled the fields on both sides of us. A faint glimmer of a fire brushed the reeds with an orange glow. I could hear the other guards talking in low voices.

For 10 days our area had been under intensive attack by B-52's, F-100's, and helicopter gunships. We had been forced to leave our camp, keeping on the move during the day, bivouacking where we could at night. Rice was running short; we were limited to one meal a day. As the food supply dwindled, so did my value to the VC.

I was just cleaning my eating cup when I heard the sound of helicopters. They were heading straight for us. My throat went dry, even though the sound had been a common one during the past days.

The piercing foghornlike sound of a minigun, the electronic multi-barreled machine gun, caused all heads to snap in its direction. The aircraft had found something.

An HUI-A (Huey) command ship orbited in wide circles above us, observing the action. Below it four smaller choppers flew in pairs, sweeping back and forth across a huge field near us, almost touching the reeds. The first ship was blowing the reeds apart with the violent downdraft from its rotor blades, and as the reeds parted, the trailing ship would gun down anything that showed.

It was obvious that I, wearing Vietnamese pajamas, would look like one of the VC to a pilot, and my deeply tanned face, even with a beard, would be just another VC face. On the other hand, the guards had a standing order to kill an American prisoner if they couldn't guarantee his security. My chance for survival looked slim.

A Light Observation Helicopter made a pass directly over us. I was flat on the ground, anticipating the rain of steel that would follow. Reeds were battered down all around us by the prop wash, exposing our bodies to the trailing gunship. They began firing, but apparently at targets in the next field. Cold sweat covered my face. I heard one of the younger guards, his voice soft, sobbing, *Ma, ma.* How lost he sounded. How strange that he turned back to the source of love and comfort he had known before joining this revolution.

Porky, who was monitoring a radio, announced, "Troops are being sent into the area!" Mr. Sau, head of the military cadre, ordered us to move, crossing to the field of reeds behind us. The idea was to get as much distance between us and our campsite as possible.

It was a confused exodus, and I noticed that discipline was disintegrating. The helicopters continued their hunt, causing us to crouch frequently in the thigh-deep water. Sau still maintained a weak grip on the reins of authority, but the muttering behind me from Porky and another guard indicated their dissatisfaction with his leadership.

Sau called a halt and had a guard climb a low tree to observe. I turned and spoke quietly to Porky. "It is dangerous to put him where the helicopters will see him."

Porky's face was stoic. "Sau is not a wise soldier." he said. A break in confidence between cadre and guard! If only I could exploit it.

We set off again, and I could hear Porky muttering to himself as we slogged through the murky water. I frequently pointed out maneuvers that I had noticed the choppers using, assuring Porky that Sau was going to get us killed. Porky told me to be quiet, but after a while we began to fall farther and farther behind the main group. I murmured a quick prayer, asking the good Lord please to do what He would—I was going to try my best.

I stopped and turned to Porky, whose face was upturned, watching the gunships. "I'm afraid to follow Sau any farther, because the helicopters will spot him soon. If we go by ourselves, making a small trail, you will be able to fight later, while the others will be dead." I paused, studying his face for reaction.

"Di!", Porky commanded ("Go!"). He was pointing to the left, perpendicular to our line of travel and away from the main group! I followed, first taking my mosquito net out of my pack. It would be wise to wave something white at the helicopters.

Porky was breaking the reeds ahead of me, opening the minimum path that would allow us to pass. His attention was divided between the trail and the helicopters, and I found myself ignored. He had slung his burp gun across his back and was bent forward, enabling him to use both hands as he tunneled through the grass. The weapon was temptingly exposed, and from the position of the bolt I could see that there was no round in the chamber. All I had to do was get rid of his magazine! I reached forward and tripped the release at the rear of the magazine. Porky straightened up seconds later, and as he stepped forward, the magazine dropped unnoticed into the water. I stepped on it as I passed, grinding it into the mud.

Now the choppers appeared to be making wider circles, skirting the fringes of this field as if preparing to transfer their operation to another area or to depart entirely. I couldn't allow that. I searched the clumps of reeds for one of the numerous fragments of dead tree branches, selecting a short limb almost two inches in diameter. I stepped quickly behind Porky. The sharp blow caught him at the base of the skull. He sagged and dropped without making a sound. I chopped him twice with the edge of my hand, delivering the blows to the side of his neck below the jawbone. I didn't intend to kill him, but as I laid him across the reeds, I noticed blood running from his mouth and nostrils. It was too late to worry about it now.

I moved quickly across a narrow ditch and leveled an area of reeds, which allowed me to see the helicopters. Then I began to wave my white mosquito net wildly. One of the gunships passed overhead and banked sharply, circling me. It was joined by a second sleek craft, and now my heart was beating so hard I thought my whole body would vibrate. "They've seen me! I'm okay! They've seen me!" I was exuberant and waved even more frantically.

Up in the helicopters (I learned later) the radio crackled. "There's a VC down there in the open."

From the other ship came the reply, "Gun him!"

Then from the command ship came the voice of Maj. Dave Thompson, group flight commander. "Wait. I want a VC prisoner. Cover me. I'm going down."

The helicopters swept the surrounding terrain, laying a devastating hail of bullets on the hidden VC, who were firing at the descending ship. I watched as the Huey circled wide around me, then lined up for a low pass. The door gunners kept their fingers against the triggers of their machine guns as they waited to foil any trap. All of a sudden one of them, looking down, spotted my beard.

" Wait, sir!" The shout went over the microphone with a unique urgency. "That's an *American!*" The response was immediate.

I saw the helicopter swing into a tight, low turn, braving the fire directed against it, and settle at the edge of the water not more than 15 yards from me. I ran, stumbling, seeing nothing but the interior of the chopper. I dived onto the cool metal flooring and heard myself shouting, "Go! Go!"

The chopper lifted off. I watched as the trees and reeds began to drop away beneath the speeding craft. After five years I was out of the "Forest of Darkness." How many times I had looked up at airplanes, wishing that I could be in them above the mud, mosquitoes, and filth, flying free over the confines of my green prison. Now I could see the horizon—and the world seemed beautiful.

Twenty minutes later Lieutenant Rowe reached the U.S. base at Camau, where he learned that during his imprisonment he had been promoted to major. His first real meals, his first sight of friendly faces, his exuberance at having escaped were almost indescribable experiences. That night, bedded down on a soft, "capitalist-imperialist" mattress, he was unable to sleep and finally arranged his blankets on the floor.

Major Rowe was awarded the Silver Star and the Bronze Star for his actions as a POW. He left the army in 1974 and, after a try at politics, turned to writing. He is now married and the father of a daughter.

General Giraud had been captured by the
Germans once before and had escaped. Now he was
determined to gain his freedom again.

The Elusive
French General

By Frederick C. Painton

ON MAY 10, 1940, German infantry flowed out of the woods near
Le Catelet, France, and surrounded a French machine-gun
nest. After the emplacement had been pulverized by mortar fire, the
German officer called on the survivors to surrender. To his amazement, among them appeared a six-foot, gray-mustached man with the
five stars of a general on his kepi. For the second time in 25 years
Henri Honoré Giraud was a German prisoner of war.

It was a bitter humiliation for a man whose career had just reached
its peak. Giraud had been an outstanding officer since the turn of the
century. But ill luck followed him into battle. In the First World War
Giraud, then a captain, was wounded while leading a bayonet charge.
He was captured by the Germans and placed in a prison camp in
Belgium. But even before his wounds healed, he managed to escape
and, although permanently lamed by his wounds, finally rejoined his
regiment in France.

During the peace years he served with distinction in Africa and
commanded a military district at Metz. Then came the Second World
War, and he was made commander in chief of the Allied forces before Laon. When the Germans broke out of the Forest of Ardennes,
he rushed to the front to see how the tide might be stemmed, only to
be caught in a forward machine-gun nest.

Giraud had escaped before, yes. But now he was 61, and the rigors
of making an escape demanded youth. Nevertheless, he refused to
give his word not to make the attempt. He was taken to the fortress of
Königstein, perched on a sheer cliff 150 feet high, with all entrances
double guarded.

Immediately Giraud began to scheme for escape. He practiced his

German until he could speak it well. He obtained a map of the surrounding country and memorized every contour. With the twine from packages sent to him he patiently wove a rope that would support his 200 pounds. When it proved not strong enough, friends from France sent him 150 feet of copper wire in an adroitly prepared ham. He was allowed, of course, to write letters; his jailers did not know that an invalid prisoner, who had been repatriated, had conveyed a code to the general's wife. Using this, he sent out details of his plan bit by bit in the form of seemingly innocent letters.

He had only a French general's undress blue uniform to wear, but his raincoat could pass for a civilian garment. Presently, among the packages arriving for him was another luscious ham. If the Germans had looked inside it, they would have found a jaunty Tyrolean hat.

On the morning of April 17, 1942, Henri Giraud stood on the balcony, looking out over the sentry walk. Tied to his waist was a package containing chocolate, biscuits, the Tyrolean hat, and the raincoat. When the guard had passed, the general knotted his homemade rope to the balustrade and started his 150-foot descent. He wore gloves, but even so the skin was chafed from his hands. At last he reached the ground safely.

He limped to the cover of some trees, shaved off his mustache, and put on the Tyrolean hat and the raincoat. Two hours later he reached a bridge at Bad Schandau, five miles away. Calmly he leaned against the parapet and ate the lunch from his pack. There, at 1 o'clock, a lean young man carrying a suitcase and a hat in the same hand strolled toward Giraud. This was the prearranged signal. The young man had been sent by friends. Giraud and the young man went to the railroad station, boarded the first train that came along, and went into a lavatory. Giraud opened the suitcase and found his own Paris clothes. There were also identity papers bearing the name of an industrialist, a photograph that looked like him (without his mustache), and money. A few minutes later a grave, distinguished-looking businessman emerged from the lavatory.

Now Giraud put into operation part two of his escape plan. The alarm was out and the frontier guards would be extra alert. He could hope to avoid arrest only by traveling continuously on trains through Germany until the uproar died away.

Once, near Stuttgart, Gestapo agents began working through the train, verifying heights against the passengers' identity cards. Giraud's six feet could not be disguised. But he happened to be seated opposite a young *oberleutnant* of the Afrika Korps. He smiled at the lieutenant and remarked that he, too, had spent much time in Africa. The German dropped his magazine, delighted to find someone who knew the desert. They conversed animatedly.

By the time the Gestapo man arrived at his seat, Giraud was illustrating graphically with his hands his idea of how Rommel could beat the British. The German lieutenant watched, his eyes eager, his own hands poised.

The Gestapo man touched Giraud's shoulder. "Your papers,

please, gentlemen." The lieutenant, boiling to present his own point, looked up angrily. "Go away! How dare you interrupt us?" The man did as Giraud had guessed he would: apologized and backed off.

On another occasion, as the general was about to board a train, he saw Gestapo agents searching every passenger. He dallied outside until the train began to move. Then, with a supreme effort of the will, Giraud ran—without limping. His glasses jiggled. His cheeks puffed out. He had all the appearance of a flustered German businessman trying to make a train. His very boldness carried off the affair. One of the Gestapo agents actually helped the panting old gentleman aboard.

Finally he crossed the border into occupied France. He hoped to slip over the line into the unoccupied area, but found that German guards were stopping every man over 5 feet 11 inches tall. Back he went by train across southeastern Germany to the Swiss frontier. That, too, seemed tightly closed. But there were mountain trails that could not all be watched. One night he struck out over an unfrequented trail. Climbing and twisting among craggy peaks, he came suddenly upon three soldiers. Bayoneted rifles swung to cover him.

Then a soldier spoke—in a Swiss dialect. He was safe. The guards took Giraud into Basel, where he made his identity known. The Germans were furious, but the Swiss refused to surrender him.

Giraud finally made the dash for unoccupied France. He resorted to an old trick—that of changing cars several times on the lonely Swiss roads. The cars entered unoccupied France by different roads. The Gestapo stopped the wrong car.

In 1914, when he had first escaped from the Germans, Giraud had sent his wife a telegram when he reached Holland safely: "Business concluded excellent health affectionately Henri." Now he sent her another: "Business concluded excellent health affectionately Henri."

Yet Gen. Henri Giraud was not a free man. His escape had caught the imagination of a saddened French people, and he had become a public idol. The Germans had lost face. When Marshal Pétain refused the German demand to return Giraud under arrest, the Nazis tried to assassinate him. He was forced to go into hiding. Giraud found that he had merely escaped into a different kind of prison.

History, however, was to summon Henri Giraud from obscurity. On October 24, 1942, in an Arab farmhouse in Algeria, Lt. Gen. Mark W. Clark conferred secretly with pro-Ally French officers about the possible Allied occupation of French North Africa.

During the conference the French officers raised the point of choosing a leader around whom the many French factions could rally. General Mast said: "I can only suggest—General Giraud."

General Clark objected: "But that's impossible. He's practically a prisoner in France."

"He must be got out—by submarine."

Such a plan was put into effect a few nights later when a submarine reached the southern coast of France. The British secret service had informed Giraud, and he was ready. He arrived in North Africa in time to play an important part in the Anglo-American invasion.

Gen. Henri Honoré Giraud died in 1949 after being decorated with the Croix de Guerre and the Médaille Militaire. He was laid to rest at Les Invalides in Paris, where Napoleon and other great French military heroes are buried.

*The East German doctor had made careful
plans for his escape. But when he entered the
hostile waters of the Baltic Sea, he wondered if he could
endure the hours of struggle ahead.*

The Lone Swim

By Peter Döbler

I T WAS A WARM SUMMER afternoon in 1971. I was spooning down a
vanilla sundae and watching the throng of bathers at Kühlungsborn, one of East Germany's finest beaches on the Baltic Sea. From
time to time, armed patrols of border guards sauntered past. I was
wearing part of my scuba diver's wet suit, and my body glistened
with the kind of heavy grease used by Channel swimmers, but nobody seemed to be taking any special notice of me.

At about 5 o'clock I headed for the water, carrying a bundle with
the rest of my wet suit, together with diver's weights and a few
personal possessions. I paddled the bundle out to a sandbank and let
it sink, marking the spot mentally. Then I swam to and fro, to become part of the scene and also to watch the patrol activity. For,
unlike the other bathers, I was not there for recreation.

As the crowds began to leave for home about an hour or so later, I
dived for my gear and put on the rest of my suit in the water. The wet
suit and mask now covered my entire body, except for part of my
face. I had fins on my feet and homemade scoop-shaped swimming
aids fitted on my hands.

Tucked into the suit were a deflated plastic life belt for extra buoy-
ancy in an emergency and a roll of strong tape for mending defective
equipment. Next to them, wrapped in watertight plastic, I carried
two bars of chocolate, identification papers, and 50 East German
marks, plus a tube containing painkillers. On one wrist I wore a
compass, on the other a watch with a luminous dial. I was all set for a
28-mile swim—to freedom. If all went well, I reckoned I would be in
West Germany in another 26 hours.

It would not be my first trip to the West. A decade before, while

69

still at school, I had visited "capitalist" Hamburg, where I defended our peasants' and workers' state against skeptical West Germans. Yet I took back to my hometown of Rostock memories of the way West Germans spoke out freely, of their better-quality and less-expensive shoes, of the shiny new cars that even ordinary people drove.

I kept these impressions to myself while at school, learning to give the outward assurances of loyalty that our state required. In the summer of 1959 I confidently applied to study medicine at the University of Rostock, listing forestry as a second choice. But although I had always done well at school, the university administration informed me that there was no room in either department.

This rejection painfully reminded me of something I had found it convenient to forget. In a country where almost everything is state-owned and state-run, my father, an accountant, worked hard to keep his own small accounting firm private. This was enough to place our family outside the peasant and worker category, whose children were given preference in education.

That summer, however, my father died. When I subsequently reapplied to the university, this time as the son of a state employee (my mother worked in a state enterprise), I was promptly admitted to study medicine.

For a full year after I had completed my basic medical studies, I was unable to get a hospital post in Rostock. When they offered me a job as a doctor on a large fishing vessel I took it—with the consent of my wife, also a doctor, whom I had married that year. Since there were no apartments available in Rostock, we decided the shipboard job would be a practical solution until the housing authority found living quarters for us. Yet after three voyages to North Atlantic fishing grounds, there was still no apartment. My wife continued to live with her parents, and I went back to my mother.

Finally, there was a job for me in Rostock, at one of the most modern and best-equipped hospitals in East Germany. But the work was demanding and the pay poor. Because my wife and I worked different hours, we spent only an occasional Sunday together. Sadly but inevitably in our fourth year of marriage she and I agreed that life together had been a fiction, and we decided to get a divorce. In court I spoke out, blaming our breakup on the inability of the state to find us accommodations. Needless to say, this didn't make me any friends, but it did make me feel better.

Escaping to the West then became my main preoccupation. I proceeded to explore the Baltic coast so thoroughly that even to this day

I can draw a detailed map of it from memory. To check on conditions after dark, I took up night fishing at all the likeliest escape points. I familiarized myself with the movements of the mobile searchlight batteries that nightly scan the waters up to nine miles out and the patrol routines of the police boats and naval craft.

I also started on a program of physical conditioning. I took lengthy swims, the longest lasting about 20 hours. When I emerged after that, I was elated to discover that I still had energy left. At night I swam in rivers or lakes, avoiding the sea because it might arouse suspicion. To strengthen my arm muscles, I began rowing and lifting weights. I changed to a protein-rich diet, and to harden my body, I took regular winter dips in the Baltic.

For my starting point, I chose Kühlungsborn because it was not in a maximum-surveillance zone, not being especially close to either Denmark or West Germany. I plotted my course carefully on a sea chart and memorized it. For the first nine miles I would swim straight out; then, following an estimated 8½ hours of swimming, I would turn left toward the coast of Schleswig-Holstein. My next checkpoint would be Buoy Number One of Sea Lane Number Six, between Gedser in Denmark and Lübeck. From the buoy it would be another 14 hours' swim to shore.

On the evening of Friday, July 23, I dictated a tape stating my reasons for fleeing and stressing that I had informed no one of my plan. I put the tape in the desk of my room at the hospital. As I had the weekend off, I would be missed on Monday at the earliest; and if I had to call off my escape, there would be time to retrieve the tape.

At Kühlungsborn on Saturday morning the weather looked quite promising. The wind was strong enough to provide a gentle helping push and the surface chop I needed for concealment. Water temperature was ideal. Still, I delayed, afraid that something unforeseen might occur. But after finishing my vanilla sundae, I decided that it was now or never.

As I struck out from the sandbank, the lead weights held me low in the water. To make me even harder to spot, I swam the breaststroke, slower than the crawl but causing less splash. I had decided to stay with this stroke at least until darkness, then jettison my weights and switch to the crawl.

By nightfall I had passed the first buoy that marked the three-mile territorial-water limit. I stopped to check my compass and picked the star closest to my desired heading to guide me. Since I knew from long practice how fast I was swimming, I needed only to consult my watch to work out my progress and position. I glanced at my watch—and at first I didn't want to believe what I saw. It had stopped. One of my main navigating aids had failed. I would just have to rely on estimated time.

Meanwhile, searchlights from the coast were beginning to feel out the waters. One beam brushed directly over me, and I ducked until the darkness oozed back. I was past the three-mile limit—yet I knew very well that East German patrols pick you up, or shoot you, wherever they find you, except in another country's territorial waters.

For the rest of the night I concentrated mostly on my stroke. Occasionally, I rolled over on my back to relax, and once I munched a chocolate bar. In the misty half-light of predawn I calculated elapsed swimming time and made my left turn. Above the surface the only sound was my own rhythmic splashing; beneath the surface I was able to detect the continuous pulsations of faraway ships' propellers and the unsettling whoo-whoo-whoo of East German patrol boats.

About an hour after dawn I raised my head to look around. There, directly ahead, I saw a dark object in the mist. It seemed as high as a patrol boat, and I could make out a mast. Gingerly, I paddled ahead until the silhouette became sharper. Then I almost laughed out loud in relief. Before me lay Buoy Number One on Sea Lane Number Six. I had calculated correctly.

Now I could hear the thump of an approaching vessel. It was a large ferryboat bound for West Germany. I waved and shouted, but it slid past without stopping. More ships kept passing that day, but they were all too far away to spot me. Soon I gave up even attempting to hail them; it sapped too much strength.

Then I sensed that first warning twinge, and a cramp seared through my right calf. I went into the drill I had practiced many times. I wrenched off my hand fins, tucked them into my suit, bent the cramped leg, crammed the disabled toes behind the knee of the other leg, and gripped them between my good calf and thigh. I also swallowed a painkiller, washing it down with a gulp of seawater, and floated. Then I tested my leg; it seemed all right, and on I swam.

But now dark clouds loomed overhead, and a world of gray surrounded me—gray sea all around, gray sky above. Suddenly, in mid-afternoon, the skies opened, pouring forth sheets of rain. Lightning flashed, the wind whistled, and I found myself bobbing up over wave crests and down into troughs. I had been in the water more than 20 hours; my mouth felt crusted with salt, and I had to stop myself from swallowing water through my snorkel.

The thunderstorm lasted about an hour. When it finally lifted, there was land ahead. Before me lay the West German island of Fehmarn. Pleasure craft dotted the seascape, and one of them was coming in my

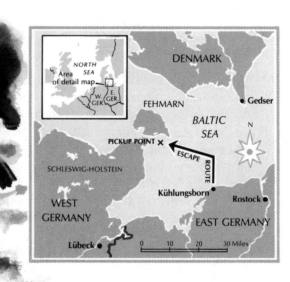

direction. "East Zone! East Zone!" I yelled. A man and two boys gaped down at me. Then they lowered a ladder, and I stumbled aboard. The next thing I knew, I'd downed a whole pot of steaming coffee. I was very cold now, my shoulders and legs ached, and the skin of my body was bluish-white and incredibly wrinkled. But I had made it!

Later on I was able to obtain work at a West German hospital and began to feel at home. People ask me if I would do it over again. If there were no other choice, I certainly would. As a doctor, I am accustomed to handling people's lives as a precious trust. But I also know that if a patient loses trust in his doctor, it's his privilege to switch to another. My new one is much better. His favorite remedy—freedom—is doing wonders for me.

The almost incredible story of a teenage boy
who escaped from his native Cuba by
flying the Atlantic Ocean stowed away in the
wheel well of a DC-8 airliner.

Stowaway

By Armando Socarras Ramírez
as told to Denis Fodor and
John Reddy

THE JET ENGINES of the Iberia Airlines DC-8 thundered in ear-splitting crescendo as the big plane taxied toward where we huddled in the tall grass just off the end of the runway at Havana's José Martí Airport. For months my friend Jorge Pérez Blanco and I had been planning to stow away in a wheel well on this flight, No. 904—Iberia's once-weekly nonstop run from Havana to Madrid. Now, in the late afternoon of June 3, 1969, our moment had come.

We realized that we were pretty young to be taking such a big gamble; I was 17, Jorge 16. But we were both determined to escape from Cuba, and our plans had been carefully made. We knew that departing airliners taxied to the end of the 11,500-foot runway, stopped momentarily after turning around, then roared at full-throttle down the runway to take off. We wore rubber-soled shoes to aid us in crawling up the wheels and carried ropes to secure ourselves inside the wheel well. We had also stuffed cotton in our ears as protection against the shriek of the four jet engines. Now we lay sweating with fear as the craft swung into its about-face, the jet blast flattening the grass all around us. "Let's run!" I shouted to Jorge.

We dashed onto the runway and sprinted toward the left-hand wheels of the momentarily stationary plane. As Jorge began to scramble up the 42-inch-high tires, I saw there was not room for us both in the single well. "I'll try the other side!" I shouted. Quickly I climbed onto the right wheels, grabbed a strut, and twisting and wriggling pulled myself into the semidark well. The plane began rolling immediately, and I grabbed some machinery to keep from falling out. The roar of the engines nearly deafened me.

As we became airborne, the huge double wheels, scorching hot

74

from takeoff, began folding into the compartment. I tried to flatten myself against the overhead as they came closer; then, in desperation, I pushed at them with my feet. But they pressed powerfully upward, squeezing me terrifyingly against the roof of the well. Just when I felt that I would be crushed, the wheels locked in place and the bay doors beneath them closed, plunging me into darkness. So there I was, my five-foot-four-inch, 140-pound frame wedged in a maze of conduits and machinery. I could not move enough to tie myself to anything, so I stuck my rope behind a pipe.

Then, before I had time to catch my breath, the bay doors suddenly dropped open again, and the wheels stretched out into their landing position. I held on for dear life, swinging over the abyss, wondering if I had been spotted, if even now the plane was turning back to hand me over to Castro's police.

By the time the wheels began retracting again, I had seen a bit of extra space among all the machinery where I could safely squeeze. Now I knew there *was* room for me, even though I could scarcely breathe. After a few minutes I touched one of the tires and found that it had cooled off. I swallowed some aspirin tablets against the head-splitting noise and began to wish that I had worn something warmer than my light sport shirt and green fatigues.

Up in the cockpit of Flight 904, Capt. Valentín Vara del Rey, 44, had settled into the routine of the overnight flight, which would last 8 hours and 20 minutes. Takeoff had been normal, with the aircraft and its 147 passengers, plus a crew of 10, lifting off at 170 miles per hour. But right after takeoff a red light on the instrument panel had remained lighted, indicating improper retraction of the landing gear.

"Are you having difficulty?" the control tower asked.

"Yes," replied Vara del Rey. "There is an indication that the right wheel hasn't closed properly. I'll repeat the procedure."

The captain relowered the landing gear, then raised it again. This time the red light blinked out.

Dismissing the incident as a minor malfunction, the captain turned his attention to climbing to assigned cruising altitude. On leveling out, he observed that the temperature outside was –41° F. Inside, the stewardesses began serving dinner to the passengers.

SHIVERING UNCONTROLLABLY from the bitter cold, I wondered if Jorge had made it into the other wheel well and began thinking about what had brought me to this desperate situation. I thought about my parents and my girl, María Esther, and wondered what they would think when they learned what I had done.

My father is a plumber, and I have four brothers and a sister. We are poor, like most Cubans. Our house in Havana has just one large room; 11 people live in it—or did. Food was scarce and strictly rationed. About the only fun I had was playing baseball and walking with María Esther along the seawall. When I turned 16, the government shipped me off to vocational school in Betancourt, a sugarcane village in Matanzas Province. There I was supposed to learn welding, but classes were often interrupted to send us off to plant cane.

Young as I was, I was tired of living in a state that controlled *everyone's* life. I dreamed of freedom. I wanted to become an artist and live in the United States, where I had an uncle. I knew that thousands of Cubans had got to America and had done well there. As the time approached when I would be drafted, I thought more and more of trying to get away. But how? I knew that two planeloads of people were allowed to leave Havana for Miami each day, but there was a waiting list of 800,000 for those flights. Also, if you signed up to leave, the government looked on you as a *gusano* ("worm") and life became even less bearable.

My hopes seemed futile. Then I met Jorge at a Havana baseball game. After the game we got to talking. I found out that Jorge, like myself, was disillusioned with Cuba. "The system takes away all your freedom—forever," Jorge complained.

Jorge told me about the weekly flight to Madrid. Twice we went to the airport to reconnoiter. Once a DC–8 took off and flew over us; the wheels were still down, and we could see into the well compartment. "There's enough room in there for me," I remember saying.

These were my thoughts as I lay in the freezing darkness more than five miles above the Atlantic Ocean. By now we had been in the air about an hour, and I was getting lightheaded from the lack of oxygen. Was it really only a few hours earlier that I had bicycled through the rain with Jorge and hidden in the grass? Was Jorge safe? My parents? María Esther? I drifted into unconsciousness.

The sun rose over the Atlantic like a great golden globe, its rays glinting off the silver-and-red fuselage of Iberia's DC–8 as it crossed the European coast high over Portugal. With the end of the 5,563-mile flight in sight, Captain Vara del Rey began his descent toward Madrid's Barajas Airport. Arrival would be at 8 A.M. local time, the captain told his passengers over the intercom, and the weather in Madrid was sunny and pleasant.

Shortly after passing over Toledo, Vara del Rey let down his landing gear. As always, the maneuver was accompanied by a buffeting as the wheels hit the slipstream and a 200-mile-per-hour turbulence swirled through the wheel wells. Now the plane went into its final approach; now a spurt of flame and smoke came from the tires as the DC–8 touched down at about 140 miles per hour.

It was a perfect landing—no bumps. After a brief postflight check Vara del Rey walked down the ramp steps and stood by the nose of the plane, waiting for a car to pick him up, along with his crew.

Nearby there was a sudden, soft plop as the nearly frozen body of Armando Socarras fell to the concrete apron beneath the plane. José Rocha Lorenzana, a security guard, was the first to reach the crumpled figure. "When I touched his clothes, they were frozen stiff as wood," Rocha said. "All he did was make a strange sound, a kind of moan."

"I couldn't believe it at first," Vara del Rey said when told of Armando. "He had ice over his nose and mouth. And his color—" As he watched the unconscious boy being bundled into a truck, the captain kept exclaiming to himself, "Impossible! Impossible!"

THE FIRST THING I remember after losing consciousness was hitting the ground at the Madrid airport. Then I blacked out again and woke up later at the Gran Hospital de la Beneficencia in downtown Madrid, more dead than alive. When they took my temperature, it was so low that it did not even register on the thermometer. "Am I in

Spain?" was my first question. And then, "Where's Jorge?" (Jorge is believed to have been knocked down by the jet blast while trying to climb into the other wheel well. He was arrested by Cuban police and served a short term in prison before being released.)

Doctors said later that my condition was comparable to that of a patient undergoing "deep freeze" surgery—a delicate process performed only under carefully controlled conditions. Dr. José María Pajares, who cared for me, called my survival a medical miracle.

A few days after my escape, I was up and around the hospital, playing cards with my police guard and reading stacks of letters from all over the world. I especially liked one from a girl in California. "You are a hero," she wrote, "but not very wise." My uncle, Elo Fernández, who lived in New Jersey, telephoned and invited me to come to the United States to live with him. The International Rescue Committee arranged my passage.

(Armando Socarras now lives in Florida. He is happily married and a college student.)

I want to be a good citizen and contribute something to this country, for I love it here. You can smell freedom in the air.

I often think of my friend Jorge. We both knew the risk we were taking and that we might be killed in our attempt to escape from Cuba. But it seemed worth the chance. Even knowing the risks, I would try to escape again if I had to.

AN EXECUTIVE OF THE Douglas Aircraft Co., makers of the DC–8, later said that there was "one chance in a million" that a man would not be crushed when the plane's huge double wheel retracts. "There is space for a man in there, but he would have to be a contortionist to fit himself in among the wheels, hydraulic pipes, and other apparatus."

Armando should also have died from both the lack of oxygen and the extreme cold. At the altitude of Flight 904 (29,000 feet), the oxygen content of the air was about half that at sea level, and the temperature was -41°F. An expert at Brooks Air Force Base School of Aerospace Medicine in San Antonio, Texas, said that at that altitude, in an unpressurized, unwarmed compartment, a man would normally retain consciousness for only two or three minutes and live only a short while longer.

Perhaps a Spanish doctor summed up Armando Socarras' experience most effectively: "He survived with luck, luck, luck."

Led by a brave girl and dedicated to a just cause,
the young heroes risked death at the hands of the Nazis
to win freedom for Allied servicemen.

The Lifeline Called Comet

By W. E. Armstrong

O N SUNDAY, OCTOBER 22, 1972, more than 200 men and women met in Brussels for a great reunion. Ambassadors and aristocrats, French, Dutch, and Belgian peasants, and a party of 35 wartime veterans of Britain's Royal Air Force—they gathered as they had every October for 27 years, to commemorate one of the war's strangest and most inspiring ventures. All had played a part in Comet, the escape line along which Allied airmen, shot down in northwestern Europe, were funneled back to Britain.

Many such lines were organized by courageous men and women in Holland, Belgium, and France. But whereas other chains were professional—under the guidance of trained agents and limited to getting escapees home—Comet was idealistic and passionate, dedicated to making a real contribution to victory by helping to keep the Allied air forces fully manned.

A conspiracy of youth, with few escorts or couriers older than 25, it was braver, more imaginative—and the most successful. Of 2,900 airmen returned to Britain by all escape lines between the outbreak of war in September 1939 and the Allied invasion of Normandy in June 1944, Comet was responsible for 770—nearly one in four.

The cost of this lifeline was grievous. Two hundred and sixteen of Comet's members, both French and Belgian, were shot or died in concentration camps. At least 700 were imprisoned for the duration of the war. Many were tortured and risked their lives—but the line's boost to aircrew morale was immense. RAF Sgt. George Duffee, whose Halifax bomber was shot down in Holland, recalls: "The knowledge that unknown friends were waiting below to pick you up was an enormous comfort on a raid, like having extra armament."

The Comet Line began as the compassionate impulse of an ardent young Belgian girl, Andrée de Jongh. At her home near Brussels, she and her sister were taught by their schoolmaster father, Frédéric de Jongh, to revere the memory of Edith Cavell, the heroic English nurse executed by the Germans in 1915 for helping Allied soldiers to escape. Andrée vowed that if ever war came again to Belgium, she would follow Edith Cavell's example.

In May 1940, when the Germans invaded her country, 24-year-old

Andrée promptly acted on her vow. For some seven months she nursed Belgian and British wounded in a Bruges hospital, under such strict German surveillance that any scheme for rescue was impossible. Then she returned to Brussels and took stock of the situation. With the Channel coast and all the Low Countries in enemy hands, hundreds of Allied servicemen hidden in Brussels and other big towns were trapped. As the German police got to work, more were captured and their hosts condemned for harboring them. Some way of escape to Britain was urgently needed.

The only route, Andrée decided, was via Gibraltar. It meant nearly 600 miles through Nazi-occupied France and almost another 600 through pro-Nazi Spain. It meant crossing three national frontiers and several military zones. It meant recruiting hundreds of underground workers willing to risk death for strangers in a cause that much of the world thought lost. It meant outwitting the most efficient and cruelly repressive secret police in Europe.

Even for a well-subsidized, experienced Resistance group, this was a daunting project.

Andrée de Jongh set to work alone, without funds, and with only a young fellow Belgian named Arnold Deppé, her father, and her own dauntless spirit to help her.

Escapees, they decided, would travel by train to the Belgian frontier at Quievrain; then would come a Somme crossing near Amiens, to bypass German checkpoints at the entrance to France's Occupied Zone; a train to Paris; a night train to Bayonne, some 20 miles from the western end of the Spanish frontier; a bicycle ride to Anglet, near Bayonne, for a day's rest in a "safe" house; a hike to a farm in the mountains around Urrugne, the frontier village; an all-night forced march over the Pyrénées to San Sebastián in northern Spain, and finally, with the help of the nearest British consulate in Bilbao, a car journey to Gibraltar via Madrid.

To secure the receiving end of the chain, Arnold Deppé went south to Anglet, where he established contact with Elvire de Greef, mother of a family of Belgian refugees. A woman in her thirties, with iron health and ruthless energy, she was to become second only to Andrée in the organization. Tactician and quartermaster, she found bicycles for escapees, bought their black-market food, and recruited Basque smugglers as guides for the march over the mountains.

With the line's southern end assured, Arnold Deppé moved north, working out passwords, train timings, contacts with French and Belgian Resistance workers, and, in Paris, setting up a halfway house where escapees could rest and change their clothes. Upstream from Amiens, he arranged to have a rowboat hidden on the Somme's reedy bank. Returning to Brussels, he reported that all was ready.

At Andrée's end, too, all was ready: the false papers and identity cards, the cover stories. To raise the necessary cash, Andrée sold her few jewels and Arnold Deppé took a salary advance from his firm. Everyone now had a code name. Andrée was "Dédée," her father was "Paul," Elvire de Greef was "Tante Go." The escapees were known as "parcels," or "children."

The first batch of "parcels," 11 Belgians including an elderly woman, left Brussels in early June 1941, with Andrée and Arnold Deppé as escorts. All went well until the party reached the Somme, where they were appalled to see a tent pitched near the rowboat. With campers so close by, the boat was unusable, but the river had to be crossed, and only four of the fugitives could swim.

With typical resourcefulness Andrée obtained a long coil of wire and an inflated inner tube from a nearby farm. She waited until after nightfall, stripped, swam the 40 yards to the far bank, tied the wire to a tree, and returned.

Supported by Andrée or Arnold Deppé and clinging to the tube, which was threaded to the wire on a running noose, all the fugitives reached the other side. The operation took two hours; Andrée swam the dark river 11 times.

"She made me brave," said one fugitive that night, "braver than I ever thought I could be."

The party reached Anglet without further incident at the end of June. Here they were handed over to Elvire de Greef for the march across the Pyrénées, while Andrée and Arnold Deppé, elated by this apparent success, returned to Brussels.

In August they escorted eight Belgians and a Scottish soldier. Only Andrée, with two Belgians and the Scotsman, got through; Arnold Deppé and the others were arrested by German police while changing trains at Lille. Deppé was tortured by the Gestapo but, knowing that the line's future depended on his courage, he refused to reveal the name of his leader.

In Anglet Andrée received more bad news: the Spanish government had repatriated all 11 Belgians in her first batch. Bitterly disappointed that people brought out so dangerously had been sent back to the Germans, she resolved in the future to help mainly British fugitives, who stood the best chance of reaching Gibraltar, and, further, to give priority to those who could resume the battle against the Nazis—at that stage of the war, aircrew.

Andrée now had to enlist the help of the British Consulate in Bilbao, 100 miles away. With her three "parcels," led by a smuggler-guide, she took the hazardous 14-hour night march across the Pyrénées. After a day's rest in San Sebastián, she reached Bilbao and confronted Vice-Consul Vyvyan Pedrick. Although by profession Pedrick had to be skeptical, he was deeply impressed by the candid girl with her eager face and remarkably youthful appearance.

"I was particularly struck by Andrée de Jongh's single-mindedness," he recalls, "and the passionate determination that showed clearly in her blue eyes."

Andrée soon convinced Pedrick of her good faith, but the consulate was required to carry out routine security checks. She was asked to return in a few weeks.

When she reappeared on October 17, this time with two Scottish soldiers, she got all she wanted from the British: money for the expenses of every fugitive brought from Brussels and for the Basque guides. About one condition she was adamant: her organization must be an entirely Belgian enterprise, completely independent of London. She would have no professional agents, no radio contact, no interference whatsoever.

With finances assured, results followed quickly. By Christmas 1941 Andrée had made her fifth crossing of the Pyrénées, escorting four airmen. She had found a new guide, a rugged Spanish Basque called Florentino, who became one of Comet's bravest and most faithful workers. Apparently as lighthearted and confident as ever, Andrée was now under great pressure, for the Gestapo in Brussels had been questioning Frédéric de Jongh about her movements. A wanted woman, she could not return to Belgium. Her father got a message through to her by courier: he would take over her role in Brussels while she continued to direct operations in France.

This was a solution typical of the line's impressive resilience—a resilience that may have inspired MI-9, the department of British Intelligence concerned with escape routes, to name the line Comet, because it is the nature of comets in general to vanish and reappear again.

Detailed vigilance became more and more necessary. Freedom could hang on the faulty tilt of a beret or an awkward gait in clogs. Since so few fugitives knew the French language, to speak was often fatal; sometimes, surprised airmen would find themselves locked in a sultry embrace with Andrée as police or customs men approached.

It was a grim, nervous game, but there were hilarious moments. Flight Sgt. Brin Weare, hidden in a German-infested area for months, was finally borne to safety in a coffin by grieving Resistance members, as punctilious Germans presented arms.

At Austerlitz station in Paris, when "informers" warned the Nazis that an airman was disguised in the garb of a priest, the escapee and his aghast but giggling escort watched in amusement while dozens of indignant ecclesiastics, bound on a pilgrimage to Lourdes, were unceremoniously frisked.

In February 1942 the Gestapo paid another visit to the De Jongh home near Brussels. Andrée and her father were both away, so the Gestapo took her elder sister for questioning and put a watch on the house. On his return to Brussels six weeks later, Frédéric de Jongh only just escaped arrest and fled to France. Within a few days three leaders of his organization were in prison.

To MI-9, which had been following reports of the line's activities with admiration and anxiety, the disruption of its northern section seemed to be the end of Comet. But a new leader, 36-year-old Belgian aristocrat Jean Greindl, materialized to tie the broken ends. He quartered Belgium into regions with reporting centers at Ghent, Namur, Liège, and Hasselt, where patriots brought airmen they had been hiding. The system paid off at once. Between June and October 1942, 54 aircrew, brought south in 13 teams, crossed the Pyrénées.

Safely back in Britain, the airmen told of the cheerful efficiency of their escorts; the long night journeys in crowded trains; the chilling police checks; the isolated farmhouse in Urrugne, where they rested before the last hard march into Spain—and, finally, of San Sebastián's lights, the heady lights of freedom. Above all, the airmen talked of Andrée. Some broke down when they remembered her, fearful that so gallant a spirit should be at risk.

Andrée was at greater risk than they knew. In November 1942 two German agents slipped through weak security in Brussels. As a result, from Brussels to Bayonne, more than 100 men and women were arrested and deported or sent to prison; none broke under torture.

Then, on the misty afternoon of January 15, 1943, Andrée was arrested with three pilots at Urrugne as she was about to start on her 37th passage through the Pyrénées. Since August 1941 she had personally escorted 118 servicemen to freedom.

Elvire de Greef, with her usual energy, organized two daring attempts to rescue Andrée from prison in Bayonne. They failed. Soon Andrée was moved to other prisons and eventually to Germany. In no less than 21 severe interrogations in various prisons, and in Ravensbrück and Mauthausen concentration camps, she gave only one piece of information. To protect her father from Gestapo suspicions, she admitted that she herself was the mastermind behind Comet.

To MI-9 and British observers in Spain, the line seemed destroyed beyond all mending. But, amazingly, a batch of airmen reached Bilbao a fortnight after the roundup at Urrugne. Once again Comet's vitality had triumphed. A new leader emerged in the south: a 23-year-old Belgian, Jean-François Nothomb, code-named "Franco," who had worked for months with Andrée. Meanwhile, time was running out for Comet's top men in the north. Jean Greindl was arrested, tortured, and condemned to death. He was killed—a bitter irony—when an Allied plane bombed the barracks in which he was held.

By spring 1943 Allied air strikes were drumming over northern Europe, and the escape lines had never been busier. Comet, handling 60 airmen a month, needed more escorts. In May, Frédéric de Jongh, who had his daughter's courage but not her cunning, recruited as guide a plausible Belgian youth called Jean Masson—a pathological traitor. Within a month De Jongh and his principal assistants were under arrest.

Still the line endured. Throughout that summer Comet kept up the flow of airmen into Spain. By now all its members were very tired, but the ardor of Andrée's undefeated spirit, coming from the misery of Mauthausen, upheld them.

"We felt we couldn't let her down," recalls Elvire de Greef. "Dedée was not simply the founder of Comet, she *was* Comet."

Meanwhile, the Nazis hardened their campaign against the escape lines. On October 20, eight of Jean Greindl's lieutenants, arrested with him, were shot on the military rifle range at Brussels, against the grass bank where, 28 years before, Edith Cavell had died for the same cause. In his last letter one of them wrote what could be a motto for the Comet line: "I die for the ideal we all shared."

In January 1944 "Franco," who had helped 215 men to freedom, was arrested in Paris. By February nearly all Comet's operators in the north were in Gestapo hands.

On March 28, 1944, Frédéric de Jongh was shot by the Germans near Paris. The line had begun with this gentle, scholarly man, for it was he who had inspired his daughter to create it. And, fittingly, the line ended shortly after his death, for the massive bombings that followed the Normandy invasion made the operation of escape lines virtually impossible. Instead, under a plan code-named "Sherwood," the airmen were gathered into forests on the Belgian frontier and in central France and supplied by parachute drops until the Allies liberated them in September.

Andrée was eventually freed from prison. Along with two other Comet members, she received the George Medal for her contribution to the Resistance. Later on she continued working for others by nursing lepers in Ethiopia. What force sustained her? As one airman she guided to freedom put it: "Andrée de Jongh was one of those rare beings who felt the misery of the world and would not let it rest."

*The young prisoner had all but given up hope of
breaking out of escapeproof Brandenburg
prison in East Germany. Then a solution came from
an unlikely source—his Communist guard.*

The Only Way

By Claus Gaedemann
and Robert Littell

THE FILE ON ALFRED LAUTERBACH, prisoner No. 1880 in Brandenburg Penitentiary, East Germany, was meager. It showed only that he had been sentenced to 25 years for the crime of conspiracy against the German Soviet State. The file did not tell how, in the last days of the war, this young German artist had watched his brother die by torture at the hands of Soviet soldiers. In retaliation, he had thrown himself into underground resistance, had been arrested, "tried" by a Russian military court, and summarily sentenced.

When our story begins, in May 1952, Lauterbach had been in prison three years. His hair was cropped; his restless, burning eyes were sunk deep in his drawn face; and he had lost 57 pounds.

Worst of all for artist Lauterbach was the knowledge that his skill of hand and eye was rusting away. All day he sat alone with his thoughts in a cell where he could hear children playing and laughing in the free world beyond the walls, yet never see them.

But one day Lauterbach was shown some Communist propaganda posters and asked to paint others like them. Though he hated the East German regime, he jumped at the chance to hold a paintbrush in his hand once more.

A young police officer escorted him to a long, narrow room with a high window on the top floor of the prison. On a trestle table lay paper, pencils, cloth streamers, and pots of paint. Then, given a dozen slips of paper with the text of slogans typed on them, he was locked in. Lauterbach shoved the table under the window, set the chair on the table, and climbed up for his first glimpse of freedom in three years. Then he went to work. There was such sheer joy in watching color spread under his brush that time flashed by; before he knew it, his guard was standing at the door to take him to his cell.

Noticing that the guard seemed unusually young for the master sergeant's stars he wore, Lauterbach looked at him more closely. Smart blue uniform, straw-blond hair showing under the jaunty cap, unblinking eyes set like marbles in an almost baby-pink poker face. Here was a perfect specimen of the new Communist-trained People's Police: green as a cucumber but hard as nails.

The guard, Horst Bock, was indeed young. Born in 1930, he had known only the Germany of Hitler, the war, and the Soviet regime. At 17, urged by a People's Policeman who was the father of one of his friends, he enlisted in the Volkspolizei—the Vopo. But Bock's politics went no further than the naïve belief that the Soviet regime was responsible for East Germany's postwar recovery.

Even the massive doses of Marx and Lenin that he got at police school didn't seem to affect him. If you were a good recruit, you stood dutifully in the rain, whether the downpour consisted of words or water. He learned to take it—and also to dish it out; he became fluent in Communist doctrine.

At the proper time he was told to join the Communist Party. He hesitated—until his friend's father pointed out to him that if he didn't join, he couldn't hope for promotion. "I saw no harm in it," Bock said later. "I just went along."

He emerged from his schooling a specialist. At Brandenburg he was assigned to the prison's three-man political division, where he censored East German newspapers before they were given to the inmates, looked after the library for the prison staff of 300, and lectured to them regularly on Communist history and ideology.

Life was good. Bock's young wife, also a Vopo, worked in the prison's teletype department. They had two small children, lived practically rent-free in one of the comfortable staff houses near the prison, and by East German standards were well paid.

If Bock was not a convinced Communist, he was at any rate an obedient, industrious, and appreciated servant of the state. He had no idea of "choosing freedom" or indeed anything but the path ahead of him—which clearly led upward.

From time to time during the weeks that followed, Bock would march his shaky, gray-faced prisoner to the studio workroom, to the task of painting posters or of blowing up to several times life-size the paunchy figures of puppet President Pieck or Premier Ulbricht. Words between them were few. But each was sizing up the other.

Lauterbach saw in Bock a tool of the power he feared and loathed.

But how ruthless or how pliable a tool, he did not know. So he kept his mouth shut and watched and waited.

Lauterbach, on the other hand, impressed Bock more and more by his talent, his concentration, and the passion he put into making a good job of dreary slogans. Bock could not feel, he said later, that Lauterbach was a criminal; rather, he thought of him as an opponent of the regime whom it was logical to lock up.

Imperceptibly, as time went on, the ice melted. The tone of Bock's commands softened. Occasionally he would offer a word of praise, now and then a mild joke. Curious about the prisoner, Bock looked up his record. It was starkly brief: There had been a two-minute trial, followed by a five-word explanation of a 25-year sentence. Bock wanted to know more.

One day in September when he went to take Lauterbach down from the workshop, Bock asked: "Just what are you in prison for?"

Impulsively, Lauterbach burst out: "I was branded as a criminal because I fought against crime!"

It was as if the cork had been pulled from a bottle; everything came pouring out. Lauterbach told the tale of heartless injustices so many people had suffered—decent people whose crime had been indignation and protest—and of sentences of a third of a lifetime for offenses they hadn't committed.

Bock's duty, according to regulations, was to interrupt the prisoner, accuse him of telling lies, and report him. Instead, he listened, fascinated. "He may be lying," Bock remembers saying to himself. "I must find out if it checks."

At one point in Lauterbach's tirade, Bock went to the door and opened it to see if anyone was listening. By this gesture, though neither of them realized it at the time, Bock had crossed the line: He and Lauterbach were on the same side of the fence.

Later, in his cell, Lauterbach was horrified at what he had done. Bock would report him. It meant weeks in the punishment cell deep underground—no light, no bed, and only dry bread to eat.

For a week he sat alone in dread, waiting for the ax to fall. And then one morning Bock came for him, escorted him upstairs, and set him a task as if nothing had happened.

But in Bock's mind and heart a great deal had happened. At that time the first steps toward an amnesty of political prisoners were being taken in Soviet Germany. Many of the inmates of Brandenburg were being questioned in the hope that some would confess and beg the government for mercy.

It was part of Bock's job to help with the preliminary questioning. Under this cover he talked to almost 100 prisoners and unearthed a sickening succession of cases of doctors, lawyers, teachers, and civil servants who had been sentenced to 10, 15, or 25 years for political "crimes" that were trivial, trumped-up, or grotesquely vague. Lauterbach had not been lying.

Bock said nothing, but Lauterbach sensed the change and began to push a little. He showed Bock selected newspaper clippings: "Ten Thousand Cheer Party Leaders," a Communist headline would boast—and Bock, who had been to the meeting himself, knew that only a few hundred had turned out.

One day Lauterbach launched into a savage attack on puppet Premier Ulbricht. Bock let the prisoner fire away. He was moved by Lauterbach's eloquence, his unanswerable facts. At the end he remarked: "Be glad you said all this to me and not to someone else."

Bock had committed himself.

And now, he began to try to help many of the prisoners. There were the smuggled notes between inmates, for example. When a note was intercepted by a guard and taken to Bock, he would secretly consult Lauterbach. If Lauterbach said the prisoner was OK, nothing more would happen to him. Even more dangerous was Bock's identifying, to Alfred Lauterbach, the stool pigeons among the prisoners. Lauterbach would then discreetly pass the word around that so-and-so was not to be trusted.

Then Bock fell ill. For four weeks he was at home with plenty of time to think things over. It became clear to him that he had in effect joined the underground. Sooner or later he would betray himself. There was only one solution. When he went back to the prison, he fastened his cool, steady eyes on Lauterbach and said: "The only way out of all this is—*out.*"

"That should not be difficult for you," replied Lauterbach.

"It's going to be extremely difficult," said Bock, "because when I go I shall take you with me!"

Lauterbach was speechless. A policeman and an inmate escaping together from Brandenburg—it was mad!

Brandenburg Penitentiary was what penologists call an "institution of maximum security." The buildings were enclosed within a 20-foot wall, at each corner of which stood a watchtower manned by guards with machine guns. At night searchlights glared pitilessly down upon a strip of bright-yellow sand just within the wall. Any prisoner who stepped onto this blinding beach was instantly shot. Everyone and everything that passed through the prison's double gates were scrutinized. At unpredictable times there were spot checks when men and goods were meticulously searched. No one had ever escaped from Brandenburg Penitentiary.

But Bock's determination was unshakable. Carefully he went over all the possibilities: fake papers, a guard's uniform, throwing the switch on the searchlights and scaling the wall in the dark, even the wild idea of arming enough prisoners to stage a gigantic delivery of all of them. And once he and Lauterbach were out, how would they cross the Havel River between Potsdam and West Berlin?

They were working hard on their plans when suddenly Bock was transferred to a post in Kottbus Prison. He left Brandenburg Penitentiary on a few hours' notice.

A stouter heart even than Lauterbach's would have despaired. He was seldom asked to paint now, or to letter posters. Time stretched out and out; nearly a year went by. Then Horst Bock was in Brandenburg again, transferred back at his own request. Lauterbach's hopes blazed when he realized that his guard was as keen as ever to attempt the double escape. Bock had been to Berlin and could easily have crossed over to freedom alone. Instead, he had come back for his friend Lauterbach.

Again for weeks they watched, planned, and eliminated one escape scheme after another. And then, when the whole thing seemed utterly hopeless, Bock had a flash of inspiration. A shortage of some 100 marks had turned up in the accounts of his political section. A small matter, but it caused a flurry among Bock's superiors. Why not make up the deficit by selling the old newspapers piled high in the top-floor storeroom? The authorities, relieved, told him to go ahead.

At 8 A.M. on Thursday, July 8, 1954, a covered truck backed up to the doors of the prison office building. It waited there while a squad of inmates, with M. Sgt. Horst Bock in charge, climbed back and forth to the storeroom, where Lauterbach handed each man a heavy bundle of newspapers.

The last bundle was taken down by Lauterbach. Inside it was hidden a suit of civilian clothes. Under the windows of the office staff, he carried the bundle of papers into the truck. Bock climbed in after him and quickly stacked the bundles around and over him.

It was raining as the truck pulled out. At the first gate two guards stepped out of their room. Turning up their collars against the rain, they peered into the truck. They saw Bock, who outranked them, sitting on top of a load of old newspapers. They waved the driver on.

The guards at the second gate were also satisfied. "Pass!" they said.

When Lauterbach heard the truck start up again, he peeled off his prison uniform and changed into the civilian clothes. As the truck slowed for a stop sign, he hopped off. A moment later Bock followed him. The two men walked into the city of Brandenburg 100 yards apart, like strangers.

It was now after 9 o'clock. At noon there would be a roll call of the inmates. As soon as Lauterbach was found missing, a crash alarm with roadblocks, radio cars, and police launches would triple-seal the border between Potsdam and West Berlin.

The two men had 30 miles and a risky swim before them. By taxi and bus the fugitives rode taut as watch springs into Potsdam. Then they walked, not too quickly, through the lawns and hedges of Babelsberg, where many Russian officers had their villas, and down to a deserted spot on the Havel River. They waded into the water and struck out for the far shore.

The rain made visibility bad, and the wind raised waves. Lauterbach, weakened from his prison fare, could not make good time. Halfway across they heard the sound they had dreaded most: the put-put of a motorboat. A police launch was bearing down on them.

Or was it? Unbelievably, the Soviet police, whom the men could see huddled in the cabin, did not spot them. The launch came abreast, a few dozen yards away, and then put-putted on.

They swam on, stumbled ashore, saw the friendly uniforms of the West Berlin police, and surrendered at last to freedom.

The rest, like all happy endings, is quickly told. After the usual screening, both men were granted political asylum and flown to West Germany. Bock's wife was placed under house arrest for some weeks but, being pregnant, was finally allowed to consult a doctor. Taking her two young children with her, she slipped into West Berlin, and from there to a small Bavarian town where the Bock family finally settled. Horst took up the study of photography.

Alfred Lauterbach directed his art talent to carving. He produced beautiful wood figures in the tradition of his native Saxony: a tiny goose teasing a little girl, dappled deer no larger than a watch charm, fairy-tale figurines sturdily but delicately alive.

For the Bocks and for Lauterbach, bound together by an act of patient, selfless courage, life hasn't been easy. But it's been free.

*The Cuban truck driver had a daring scheme so risky
that it defied belief. If it worked, it would bring
freedom to many. But if it failed, imprisonment or death
before a firing squad would swiftly follow.*

The Truck That Fled

By William Schulz

EUFEMIO DELGADO WAS a man obsessed with a single dream: getting out of Cuba. The wiry, 28-year-old father of four had vowed to himself that somehow, someday, he would take his wife and children to freedom. During the day, as he drove a huge tractor trailer for Fidel Castro's Transportes Nacionales, and lying awake at night, he searched for a solution. Finally, by the summer of 1968, he had a plan—a scheme so daring that it defied belief.

Strong-willed and outspoken, Delgado was just one of countless Cubans who felt themselves trapped and stifled in Castro's police state. On three different occasions he had blurted out anti-Castro sentiments within earshot of a government informer. And each time he had been arrested by G-2, the secret police, on "suspicion of counterrevolutionary activity."

"Is it a crime to say that the people don't have enough food?" he had stubbornly insisted. But he also knew that he could remain no longer in Guanajay, a town 30 miles southwest of Havana. The local G-2 chieftain had threatened to have him sent to a forced-labor camp. Reluctantly but realistically, Delgado moved as far away as he possibly could—615 miles away—to the little town of Contramaestre in Oriente, Cuba's easternmost province.

Even there life became unbearable. The terror of the regime had been stepped up. Neighbors simply disappeared, victims of G-2. The 8 hours that Delgado worked each day became 12 and sometimes 14 as he and hundreds of thousands of other Cubans "volunteered" to work overtime.

"We are told by the commissar that we are volunteering," he said to his dark-haired wife, Olga. "If you protest, you go to jail."

93

He received no pay for the extra work, but it made little difference. The pesos that he brought home each month were all but useless. Literally everything that money could buy was stringently rationed or simply unavailable. In a land where food was once plentiful, each of the Delgados was limited to a pound of beans, a half pound of meat, and a pound of lard per month.

"If you have ever heard a child cry from hunger, it is something you never want to hear again," Olga said when her husband returned from three weeks of hauling sugarcane.

"That does it!" he shouted. "We've *got* to get out of this place."

But how? The twice-daily Freedom Flights that carried refugees to Miami were available only to those with relatives in the United States. The Delgados had none. (The Freedom Flights, begun in September 1965, were discontinued in April 1973.) Escape by sea seemed impossible. The heavily patrolled waters between Cuba and the American mainland were known as Machine Gun Alley.

Delgado knew that he was by no means alone in his desperate desire to flee Cuba. Long-distance hauls took him to Havana, where he found almost everyone he knew bitter and disillusioned by the Castro revolution.

Joaquín Martínez (names have been disguised when necessary) was a victim of the 1968 "revolutionary offensive," during which Castro shut down 55,000 of Cuba's privately owned shops and restaurants. Jobless waiter Martínez found himself drafted into an agricultural brigade, in which he worked from 6 in the morning until 6 at night, seven days a week. And there was Lucila Cardona, who rose every morning at 4 to join the long lines at the nearest food outlet. Often, after hours of waiting, she would find the shelves bare, which meant that her children would subsist again on sugar dissolved in water. Or Gloria Morales, who was married to a dedicated Communist naval officer and lived a privileged life in Castro's Cuba. But the young couple had an 18-month-old daughter, a beautiful, curly-haired little girl who would be taken from home when she reached school age and sent to a revolutionary boarding school—the Círculos Infantiles. "She will not grow up a Communist," vowed Gloria.

Delgado had no idea how he could help his friends and relatives reach freedom. "But somehow we'll make it," he promised an older brother. "You have my word."

Then, in the summer of 1968, Eufemio was dispatched to Caimanera, a small town near the U.S. naval base at Guantánamo Bay, to pick up salt for delivery to Havana. There he learned of still others anxious to flee Cuba: blacks who had found the revolution a cruel hoax; fugitives from forced labor; students hungry for a taste of freedom. He established contact with the group's leader, a mechanic named Francisco Alonso, and in a series of clandestine meetings gained his confidence.

"Escape to the American base is possible," Alonso reported, "but risky. The Cuban side is heavily patrolled, and escapees are shot or captured and sent to concentration camps for 30-year terms. But if we could get a truck, we might be able to crash through."

"I'll supply the truck," Delgado said, referring to his 1958 American-built White, a large green van whose cab was now powered by a Soviet diesel engine. "We'll work together."

Alonso pulled from his shirt a soiled, much-studied map of eastern Oriente. For hours the two analyzed government defenses, discussed strategy, made plans. As Delgado headed back toward Havana, he felt relieved for the first time in many months. "I don't know whether we'll make it," he thought. "But at least we're trying."

Coordination between Delgado, who was now required to spend most of his time at Transportes Nacionales headquarters in Havana, and Alonso in Guantánamo was difficult. Both were reluctant to use the telephone for fear it was tapped by G-2. Finally, plans were completed: Eufemio would send 22 relatives and friends by train from Havana to Santiago, on the southeastern coast of Cuba some 50 miles from Guantánamo. They would wait there until picked up by him in his truck; then all would proceed to the city of Guantánamo, 15 miles from the U.S. base, for the rendezvous with Alonso's group and the break for freedom.

The escape was set for December 17. At first all went according to plan. With his wife and children already aboard the truck, Eufemio picked up his 22 passengers in Santiago on the morning of the 17th and headed for Guantánamo. But when he braked the truck to a stop at the final pickup site, he knew immediately that something was wrong. Only Alonso was there, and he was obviously distraught.

"G-2 is wise to us," he stammered. "They've got an ambush waiting at the base. You've got to turn back."

Delgado, stunned, climbed into the trailer and broke the news to the others. An auto mechanic slammed his fist into his palm in bitter frustration; several women wept silently.

"This is only a temporary setback," Delgado declared, trying to keep his voice steady. "We will return to our homes and move again when the time is right. There is nothing to worry about."

But Delgado knew this was untrue. As he drove back toward Havana, questions ran through his mind. How had G-2 learned of the escape? Could there be an informer in the group? Would G-2 be waiting when he returned to Transportes Nacionales headquarters? Fortunately, nothing untoward occurred.

On December 31 a courier whom Delgado knew only as Pedro arrived. An escaped political prisoner and comrade of Alonso's, Pedro brought welcome news: "Everything is set for January 6." That would be the Feast of the Three Wise Men, the day on which Latin Americans traditionally exchange Christmas presents. "It is some gift we will give ourselves and Fidel," thought Delgado.

He checked his work schedule and found that he was supposed to drive west that week from Havana to Pinar del Rio Province and then back to Camagüey, less than 250 miles from Guantánamo. A perfect cover. He next communicated with the friends and relatives who had made the first trip. No one backed out; indeed, others who had learned of the plan begged to come along. By January 3, when they left by train for Santiago, the Havana group had swelled to 36.

Delgado left Havana that same morning for a youth camp in Pinar del Rio. There he picked up 80 men who were to be transported to a sugar mill in Camagüey.

The trip took 22 hours. Bone-weary, Delgado delivered his workers, grabbed a few hours' rest, then headed for Contramaestre. He arrived home at 3 A.M. on January 5, parked the truck, and waited through the "longest day of my life."

At 1 A.M. on January 6, Delgado and his family walked out of their home for the last time, leaving behind everything they treasured. In less than two hours they reached Santiago, where the Havana contingent was waiting, disguised as agricultural volunteers on their way to the cane fields. Eufemio gave no hint of recognition as he herded them into the truck. "Hurry up! Get moving!" he barked. "There's cane to be cut."

Within minutes the van was heading toward Guantánamo, where Delgado would pick up Alonso and 20 more passengers. But, again, a surprise greeted him. When he arrived at the rendezvous, he was horrified to discover nearly 100 people—middle-aged women, teenage boys, babies in their mothers' arms—instead of the expected 20.

"There are too many. They make the escape too difficult," Delgado protested to Pedro.

"What can we do?" Pedro replied. "We cannot deny them."

Delgado agreed, then asked for Alonso. "He has pulled out," Pedro said. "He couldn't get any machine guns, and he says that without them we have no chance of holding off the guards."

Eufemio cursed bitterly—but he had come too far to turn back. "We've got the truck and two pistols," he said. "We will make it now—or die trying."

It was still dark when Delgado pulled out of Guantánamo with his 130-odd passengers shoehorned into the truck. Knowing that the crack Cuban guards stationed outside the U.S. base relaxed somewhat during daylight, he pulled off the road to mark time. Half an

hour later, with the first signs of dawn, he continued toward Caimanera along the three-lane road that would take him past the base. Four miles outside Caimanera, he saw the base, a mile off to the right. Driving parallel to it, he was passing guard posts every quarter of a mile, and he studied them intently, looking for the weakest point. He made his selection, then proceeded into Caimanera. There he asked a passerby for directions to a fictitious address. Informed that there was no such place, Delgado headed back the way he had come.

The sun was shining brightly as he approached the spot he'd chosen for the breakout. Slowing down as little as possible, he suddenly swerved off the road and headed for the Cuban-built barbed-wire barrier. In his rearview mirror Eufemio glimpsed eight soldiers sprinting from the nearest guardhouses. He pressed the accelerator to the floor. Machine-gun bullets whizzed past the truck; a tire blew. Delgado struggled desperately to keep his vehicle under control as it lurched across the bumpy terrain at 60 miles an hour. A quarter mile from the wire, his luck ran out. The truck careened into a ditch. He jumped out and opened the trailer doors. "Head for the fence!" he shouted. "Keep low! Keep low!"

Delgado and Jorge Pérez, an old friend from Havana, ducked behind the truck and fired at the rapidly closing guards. They dropped two, but their pistols were hardly a match for Czech-built automatic weapons. A half-dozen refugees fell as they neared the fence.

"Down!" Delgado screamed to the others. "Keep down!"

He and Pérez abandoned the truck to go to the help of the stumbling women and children.

Those who reached the barrier—four feet high and four feet across—ripped themselves badly as they clambered over. But still they fought, screaming and bleeding, across the wire.

Delgado got Olga and his own four children over, then heard Gloria Morales cry despairingly for help: "I can't make it. Take the baby. Get her to freedom!"

Eufemio took the child just as he saw his own brother and sister-in-law captured 50 yards away. The guards were moving in quickly now, taking prisoner after prisoner.

"Cross over! Cross over!" Olga screamed from the other side of the fence. Delgado tossed the baby across the barbed wire; then, with nothing left that he could do, he crawled over himself.

Less than 20 minutes had passed since he had turned off the road. When U.S. Marines arrived on the scene minutes later, they found 88 courageous men, women, and children who had made it to freedom. Sadly, more than 40 others had not.

It was 8 A.M., January 6, the Feast of the Three Wise Men. Eufemio Delgado had engineered the largest single escape in the 10 years of Fidel Castro's Communist regime. A frail little woman, her arms and legs streaked with blood, grabbed Delgado and sobbed her thanks. "You have given us the greatest gift of our lives," she cried. "We can never forget."

*The young lawyer had carefully prepared an elaborate
hoax to hoodwink the Communist authorities
in East Germany. On its successful conclusion rested
the liberty of five political prisoners.*

Operation Liberty

By Frederic Sondern, Jr.,
and Norbert Muhlen

THE WEST BERLIN RADIO interrupted its regular program one day in the summer of 1952 to make a startling announcement. Five prominent political prisoners of the Communists had escaped from the supposedly escape-proof East German prisons of Zwickau and Waldheim and had made their way to the safety of Berlin's Western sector. As details came in, it became clear that they had not broken out. They had been released by the Communist prison authorities, who had been hoaxed by forged release orders and telephone calls from a spurious state's attorney.

While West Germany laughed, the enraged State Security Service and People's Police dropped all other business to find the authors of the plot. Sixty officials were discharged. The Communist press and radio screamed that dastardly American agents had been at work.

Actually, the skulduggery had been devised by a young German ex-Communist named Hasso Lindemann and two of his friends.

Lindemann, a bookish, 23-year-old law student, had been rocketed to a position of Communist power by circumstances not unusual in East Germany. In 1949 the Communist authorities of Leipzig had discharged most of the experienced judges and prosecutors in the district as "politically unreliable." A milkman, an organ-grinder, and a 21-year-old girl became Leipzig's People's Prosecutors. They had power of life and death over their fellow citizens, but they needed someone to advise them about legal procedure. Lindemann, who had worked as a clerk in the Ministry of Justice, seemed "politically activistic" and obedient. He was made assistant to the state's attorney.

Comrade Lindemann was a shrewd investigator and wrote brilliant briefs in impeccable Communist legal style. His record was soon impressive. Several prominent industrialists whose cases he investigated had their properties expropriated and were sent to prison for long terms. A dozen young anti-Communist agitators went to jail after Lindemann had made the cases against them. Wisely modest and retiring, Lindemann let the People's Prosecutors take credit for these triumphs. As a result, he was very popular with his chiefs. He was well fed and housed, relatively well paid, and had a promising career ahead of him.

But Hasso Lindemann had a conscience. He had been a convinced and faithful Communist, but as the parade of Red injustice and cruelty—the trumped-up charges, faked evidence, and brutal sentences against innocent people—crossed his desk, he began to rebel.

"All the Communist philosophy in the world," he later said, "could not excuse for me the monstrous thing I was doing. Somehow I had to set these people free."

One afternoon, when most of the personnel of the state's attorney's staff were at their weekly Communist Party "indoctrination meeting," Lindemann took from his chief's desk a number of form letters used to order the release of prisoners, then fled to West Berlin.

"The forms, the clothes on my back, and a few marks were all I had," Lindemann recalls. "Everything else—job, future—I left behind. But I felt much, much better."

There were five cases that he was determined to rectify at once. Seventy-year-old Karl Mende had committed no crime, even under Communist law—the government had simply wanted his prosperous glass factories. He was convicted of "industrial sabotage" and sentenced to six years at hard labor; his factories were expropriated. Arthur Bergel, a prominent woolen manufacturer, was the victim of a similar conviction. His offense had been to pay his 1,700 workers a higher wage than the government allowed. Horst Schnabel, a high-school boy of 17, had been sentenced to two years in the penitentiary, to be followed by transportation to the uranium mines, for possessing a book banned by the Communists. Jürgen Poppitz and Ekkehard Schumann, 20-year-old students, had received four-year terms for firing rockets that showered Leipzig with anti-Communist leaflets.

The obstacles in Hasso Lindemann's way seemed insuperable. As a former Communist, he was suspect to the various refugee organizations in Berlin. Then, after he had finally convinced the principal anti-Communist committees that he was sincere, a new state's attorney, whose signature Lindemann did not know, was appointed for Leipzig. The new incumbent ruled that no release order was to be obeyed unless the prison director checked its validity by a personal phone call to the state's attorney or to his immediate subordinate.

It took Lindemann three months to obtain from a friend in Leipzig a document signed by Chief State's Attorney Adam, more time to practice a flawless forgery of the signature. Through a complicated system of couriers and deftly worded, seemingly innocent letters, he learned the exact technique and timing of the telephonic verification.

Finally, the months of preparation came to an end. One of Lindemann's aides, Hans Schmidt, was put in charge of the first operation. Lindemann had wanted to perform it himself, but his face was too well known to People's Police and State Security Service men.

With forged release orders for Mende and Bergel in his briefcase, Schmidt set out for Leipzig and for the particular postbox from which the state's attorney's communications were always mailed.

Twice Schmidt almost met disaster. Two police officers suddenly appeared in his train compartment and ordered him to open his briefcase for inspection. Such spot checks are routine in East Germany. Schmidt obeyed, his heart in his mouth. The policemen saw the envelopes stamped "Chief State's Attorney's Office."

"You are a courier of the Herr Oberstaatsanwalt? " one of them asked. "Of course," Schmidt replied.

"We are sorry to have disturbed you, sir."

Heels clicked, salutes were exchanged, and, without asking for his papers, the officers departed.

At the postbox in Leipzig, Schmidt had his other bad moment. Two People's Police were watching the box, on guard against the mailing of clandestine leaflets. But again the official envelope commanded immediate obeisance, and one of the Volkspolizei even politely held up the box flap as Schmidt dropped the letters in.

That night neither Schmidt in Leipzig nor Lindemann in Berlin slept a wink. The release orders should reach the warden of Zwickau Penitentiary in the morning. If the warden telephoned the state's attorney's office before the plotters could act, the game would be up.

At the earliest feasible moment, Hans Schmidt braced himself and telephoned Zwickau.

"This is Oberstaatsanwalt Adam," he bellowed into the machine. "Give me the director at once."

Since the German bureaucratic caste system under the Communists is as strict as it ever was, Schmidt calculated that the voice of an exalted chief state's attorney would not be too familiar to a warden. He was right. The director answered with great deference.

"Have you received the release orders for Mende and Bergel?" snapped Hans Schmidt.

"No, Herr Oberstaatsanwalt. But I will attend to them personally the moment they arrive."

"See that you do," Schmidt growled. "No return call to my office is necessary to verify these orders. Is that clear?"

"Of course, Herr Oberstaatsanwalt. I will not disturb you. I have been deeply honored by your personal call."

When Schmidt hung up, he was sweating. But the most dangerous part of the operation lay ahead. Mende and Bergel, thinking their release was legal, would doubtless go home, where they would soon be rearrested. They had to be warned to flee at once to West Berlin. Schmidt went to Zwickau to wait for them.

Watching Zwickau Penitentiary is a hazardous task. Anyone loitering nearby is immediately reported by the guards to the People's Police. But Schmidt found a café from which he could watch the institution's main gate. He sat and drank beer—and more beer. He explained at great length to the café keeper that he was trying to drown his domestic troubles. A People's Policeman examined his papers, fortunately rather carelessly.

Finally, Schmidt decided that the forgeries had been detected. Dejectedly he returned to Berlin.

Actually, the release orders had merely been slow in reaching the penitentiary. When they arrived, Mende and Bergel were brought before the warden and the prison's dreaded political commissar.

"The highest authorities in our state have decided to forgive your crimes," the commissar announced cordially, even offering them cigarettes to put them at ease. "We are releasing you."

Presently the two men, provided with civilian clothes, money, and a ration of food for the journey home, stumbled out through the prison gate in a daze.

Their freedom might not have lasted long except for Lindemann's thorough planning. Fearing that Schmidt might be picked up by the police, Lindemann had dispatched another friend—Kurt Braun—to guide Mende and Bergel to Berlin. Braun waited in the neighborhood of the prison for almost 48 hours—without sleep and with only three apples for food. He didn't dare go into a restaurant for fear there might be a police checkup.

Almost collapsing from fatigue and hunger, Braun also finally gave up and boarded a streetcar for the railroad station. As the trolley rumbled away, he took one more backward look at the prison. Two gaunt men whose clothes hung loosely from their shoulders were coming out the prison gate!

Risking his neck, he jumped from the car. For several blocks he walked behind the two men to make sure they were the right ones (prison changes people's appearances). Finally, he sidled up and pressed a slip of paper into Herr Mende's hand.

"Follow these directions," he said quietly. "Get to West Berlin. Your families are there."

Fear and suspicion were plain on the men's faces. They both knew

that this might very well be a cleverly arranged police trap.

"Please, *please,*" Braun urged desperately, "do as I say." With that, he vanished around the corner.

The next morning Herr Mende and Herr Bergel were safely in West Berlin. Still hardly able to believe their luck, they had found their families and had come to thank Lindemann.

"It was a strange interview—the former convicts and their former prosecutor," Lindemann reminisces happily. "But it was a very satisfactory one, particularly for me."

There were still three more prisoners to free—one in Zwickau, the others in Waldheim.

Schmidt was ready to start again for Leipzig when catastrophe struck. News of the two men's "escape" had leaked somehow, and a

West German radio station blared it out. Lindemann was beside himself with disappointment, when suddenly he realized that the trick might still work if they acted immediately. All Communist police and judicial chiefs habitually leave the city on Saturday for their country retreats and cannot be reached until their return around 11 o'clock on Monday morning. Lindemann was sure that his plan had more than an even chance of succeeding.

And he was proven right. The release orders arrived at Zwickau and Waldheim without delay. Schmidt repeated his first memorable telephone call to the two wardens. On Monday three bewildered boys found themselves on their way to West Berlin in the care of Hans Schmidt and Kurt Braun.

But it had been a close shave. Five minutes after the Zwickau gates had closed, a big car roared up to the prison. Herr Oberstaatsanwalt Adam himself, flanked by high-ranking police officers, stormed angrily into the institution.

The escape of Mende and Bergel had been discovered late Saturday by agents monitoring West German radio broadcasts. Gerhart Eisler, then propaganda minister, happened to be at his desk early Monday morning and was informed first. Roaring with rage, he tried to contact his colleagues. But no responsible police official could be reached until Monday noon. Then the entire State Security Service and People's Police was unleashed in an unprecedented manhunt. Trains were searched, automobiles stopped, innocent pedestrians dragged off to police stations for questioning throughout East Germany. They were too late.

In a comfortable restaurant in West Berlin Lindemann, his helpers, and his ex-victims were celebrating. The spare, usually shy young man raised his glass.

"We shall have to use other methods in the future," he said. "But I think we can do it again."

*As the airplane swooped low over the Communist cruise
ship, a man leaped from the stern into the
stormy, shark-infested waters of the Caribbean Sea.
It was all part of a daredevil escape plan.*

Rendezvous at Sea

*By Ken Agnew
as told to Kenneth Schaefer*

IT WAS NOW OR NEVER for Karl Bley. I put my single-engine airplane into a steep turn and raced directly at the East German ship.
My low pass was the signal for the 24-year-old machinist from behind the Iron Curtain to jump overboard.

Misgivings filled my mind. The Atlantic Ocean seven miles off the
Florida Keys is hostile water at best, and on this day-after-
Thanksgiving 1970, choppy swells were waiting to welcome his desperate leap to freedom. If he escaped the powerful suction of the
ship's propeller, he would have to take his chances with the sharks
until the rescue boat reached him.

For that matter, was Karl Bley even on board the ship? If he was,
would he jump, or would he lose his nerve at the sight of that 40-foot
drop into the churning wake?

Escape had been Karl Bley's dream since the night two years earlier, when, aboard the same East German cruise ship-freighter, the
M.S. *Völkerfreundschaft,* he had sailed past the glittering lights of
Miami. A thousand miles to the northwest in Villa Park, Illinois, lived
his older brother, Eric. Eric Bley had made it out of East Germany in
1955, followed a year later by his fiancée, Marlis. The two were now
U.S. citizens and were grateful to their adopted land. Eric had founded a successful machine-building firm in a suburb of Chicago.

For 15 years the brothers had corresponded regularly. (They had
worked out a code to get their messages past the ever-watchful East
German censors.) Immediately after his 1968 trip to Havana, Karl
wrote Eric that if he ever got that close to America again, "I'm going
to jump and swim for it." It was no idle boast. Eric knew the hunger
his brother felt. He had felt it himself.

He also knew that the chance was slim of swimming the seven miles from ship to shore. So there had been desperation on both sides of the Iron Curtain. It was at that point—two months before—that I had been pulled into the affair.

Eric had come to the Florida Keys, south of Miami, looking for help in the escape plan that he and his brother had plotted. On Duck Key he saw a sleek charter boat, the *Pequod*, belonging to my long-time friend, Capt. Bob Lowe. Fast, in prime condition, *Pequod* was the perfect boat to overtake the *Völkerfreundschaft* when she ran by the Florida coast at 18 knots. Eric found Bob Lowe, who listened in silence as he outlined his scheme.

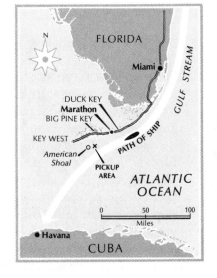

"You want to lay a rescue vessel alongside that Commie ship just when your brother is ready to jump?" Lowe demanded. "Is that the idea?"

Eric nodded. "That's right."

"It's going to need air-ground co-ordinating. And a definite signal to your brother that all's set before he makes the leap. It won't be easy."

Needing a pilot, Lowe brought Bley to see me. It was Lowe who sold me; I could tell that he liked what he saw in Eric Bley. Before he'd finished, I was as hooked as Bob by the desperate determination of a man fighting for his brother's life.

Eric had just about everything we needed to know about the cruise ship *Völkerfreundschaft,* thanks to an advertising brochure that Karl had mailed to him. Passengers would board at the Baltic seaport of Rostock, enjoy a trip to Havana, then return. The cover carried a picture of the ship; an inside page even gave the frequencies monitored by the ship's radio.

We worked out a plan. I'd fly the route most Communist ships take in making the Havana run: From the Bahamas they go straight toward Palm Beach, then follow the Florida coastline until they've nearly cleared the Keys. Once I'd spotted the ship, I would radio Bob and Eric, who would put out in the *Pequod.* As they closed in on the East German ship, I'd make a low pass in my light plane. That would be the signal for Karl to jump.

The second week of November Eric told us that Karl was aboard the ship. He would be off the Keys sometime on Thanksgiving Day. He would wear a bright jacket for quick spotting by his rescuers and would have a life preserver on under the jacket. But, the younger brother wrote, whether the rescue craft showed up or not, he was going to jump before the *Völkerfreundschaft* veered away from the last bit of America.

To provide day and night surveillance, we had enlisted George Butler, a retired engineer and enthusiastic pilot. For two days he and I had been flying our planes up to Palm Beach and across the 60 miles to the Bahamas, directly over the path the ship should take. We had also worked south along the Keys to American Shoal, an unmanned lighthouse 16 miles off Key West—the usual turnaway point of Soviet vessels bound for Cuba. We could report nothing but frayed nerves for our almost nonstop efforts.

At 5:30 on the morning after Thanksgiving a dejected Eric Bley was leaving his hotel on Duck Key for the airport and a reconnaissance flight with me. Suddenly, as he stared out at the blackness across the ocean to the east, he saw lights—*the ship!* He jumped into his car and roared off to the Marathon airport on Key Vaca. I was waiting for him, and the minute we lifted off the runway, we could see the ship, her whole stern lighted up like New York. I killed our wingtip lights and the brilliant strobe atop the fuselage so we wouldn't tip off our quarry. Flying high over the ship, we took out the brochure with its identifying picture. The sky and water were still dark, but with the deck lighting we had it—picture and ship matched exactly, even to the bright-red line along her hull.

In minutes we were back at Marathon, where a waiting Bob Lowe told us that there wasn't time to go north to Duck Key, get the *Pequod,* and still catch the cruise ship, now moving past the village of Marathon at a full 18 knots.

"It'll take a 40-knot boat to catch it," he said. "Come on, Eric! We'll get a boat even if we have to steal it!" Seconds later their car was speeding toward Big Pine Key, 19 miles to the south.

Butler had arrived by this time and was ready to fly the high watch at 2,000 feet while I took the low run. Just before we both took off, I asked Butler's wife to call the Coast Guard: "Tell them you got a garbled message that there's a man in the water off American Shoal and to get help out there right now!"

We had to have some kind of backup. I was afraid Bob and Eric wouldn't get a boat and that Karl had meant it when he said he'd jump even if there was no signal.

I flew down to Big Pine Key just as a 22-foot fiberglass outboard skiff came planing out of the Sea Center Marina, charging for the daylight beginning to show in the east. It was taking a brutal pounding as it hit the heavy chop of the open water. I didn't think Lowe could see the ship, and I skimmed over him to set him on an intercept course that would put him ahead of his target.

At that point the skiff went dead in the water! I watched Bob fiddle with the engine until it restarted. Another half mile and it quit again. "Bob's not going to make it!" I reported to Butler over the radio.

As I was debating whether to signal the jump anyway, I saw white froth behind the little boat as Lowe brought the engine alive once more. We were still in business!

I headed for my assigned point low and far ahead of the *Völker-freundschaft* to wait until Butler called that the skiff was closing in.

"Now!" came the word finally.

"Right. I'm going in!"

Soon I was hell-bent for the bow of the unsuspecting liner, barreling down her port side, whitecaps only a few feet below me. I caught sight of passengers at the rail—two dozen of the most stunned expressions I'd ever seen. At the fantail I made a tight turn to the left, so close that the flagpole at the stern almost caught my wingtip. If Bley was aboard, he had to have heard me! But for one awful second there was nothing—just people gawking from the rail as I roared up the starboard side of the ship.

"Nobody jumped!" I bellowed at the mike in my right hand.

Then it happened. A figure went over the rail and plummeted to the water. *"He jumped!"* I yelled.

There was an abrupt squawk from my radio, and Butler called from overhead: "There're two in the water!"

I gaped in disbelief at what was happening. From the side window I now saw not two, but *three*. No . . . *four!* Eric had previously warned us:

"If this boy jumps, look out—you're liable to get more." We had them.

Lord, I thought, what a gamble! None of the three knew of our plot. No one but Karl had a life jacket—only life rings they'd tossed to the turbulent sea just before jumping. I circled the floundering figures below, and as they struggled toward those orange-colored rings in the water, I knew I was looking at raw courage.

Lowe's pilotage of the rescue boat was magnificent. Almost before the last man hit the water, Bob was past the liner and Eric was pulling Karl into the skiff.

Then came the ship's response. We had known that the Reds were prepared for the possibility of a man overboard, and we'd talked at length about how long it would take the *Völkerfreundschaft* to make a 180-degree turn. We had guessed wrong.

Eric and Bob were still dragging the men from the water when the ship rolled into a tight turn at full speed. It was amazing to see a liner lean like that, and I had the fleeting suspicion that the captain wanted everybody overboard.

It was close! By the time the last man was picked from the sea, the ship was bearing down on the tiny rescue craft. Bob raced at top speed for shallow water close to shore, where the *Völkerfreundschaft* could not possibly follow. Finally, the East German ship broke off the chase, made a turn, and took the southerly heading for Havana. It was all over.

Afterward, I sat beside Karl in a room at the Key West Coast Guard station and looked at the earnest face of this slender, dark-haired youth from East Germany. His dream had come true out there in the ocean when he waved his arms in a sign of triumph and screamed at the man in the bow of the rescue boat, "Bruder! Bruder!"

The men who had leaped to freedom with him were Dr. Manfred Kupfer, a 37-year-old neuropathologist from Leipzig; his brother, Dr. Reinhold Kupfer, a 33-year-old pathologist from Zwickau; and Dr. Peter Rost, 37, a microbiologist, also from Zwickau. They had come on the cruise with unspoken hopes that just such a chance might be theirs. Karl's bold leap was the inspiration they'd hoped for so desperately.

Through Eric's interpreting, I learned that Karl had been on deck since early morning watching the lights along the Keys, studying the shoreline through binoculars for any sign of action. "I saw you when you took off from the airport," he told me. "I saw your bright light go out, and when I heard you in the dark high above the ship, I knew that Eric was coming."

Looking at this 24-year-old, who I knew now would have made that leap, signal or no, I suddenly realized what freedom means.

U.S. Marine Corps Pvt. Martin Kaylor's term of military service in the Korean War had come to an end—or so he fondly believed, until he found himself trapped deep behind enemy lines, a captive of the Chinese Communists.

The Long Way Home

By *John G. Hubbell*

K AYLOR," said the lieutenant, "tomorrow morning at 0600, when the regiment moves up, you are to report to S-1. Your dependency discharge has come through, and you're going back to Casual Company at Hamhung."

Bud Kaylor, marine machine gunner, was stunned, then elated. This was no foxhole rumor, this was for real. He was getting out of this frozen hell and going home. He'd be there in time for Christmas with his wife, Dorothy, and their family.

Early the next morning Kaylor said quick good-byes to his buddies. The 1st Marine Division and the army's 7th Infantry Division were moving north for an assault on the Chosin Reservoir. But for Bud Kaylor the war was over, or so he thought. This, however, was the morning of November 28, 1950, and no one knew that the stage was set for the attack by the Chinese Reds.

At S-1 the personnel officer told Kaylor he'd have to get back to Hamhung on his own. So he and Art Foley, a mail clerk, hitched a ride in the lead truck of a five-truck convoy. There were two other marine passengers in the back of their truck and another riding shotgun with the driver. Thus Bud Kaylor started the first leg of his journey out of Korea—and home.

The home he was headed for was near Hopkins, Minnesota, where Gladys and Charley Kaylor, Bud's parents, lived. It was there that the telegram was to arrive on January 5, 1951. It came from Marine Headquarters, with deep regrets: Pfc. Charles Martin Kaylor had been missing in action since November 28, 1950.

"The telegram said 'missing,' " Charley Kaylor related. "Bud is a little guy, but he's tough, cool, and a mighty quick thinker. He had always been an athlete. I figured he was still alive somewhere."

Neither could Bud's wife nor his mother nor his sisters give up. His daughter, Terry Jo, was only four, but she was sure her father would come back. Through the long months that followed, they all lived on the strength of interminable prayer and desperate hope.

Soon after Kaylor's convoy got under way that morning for the 70-mile trip, they came to a small village. The huts looked uninhabited, but in seconds a crowd of Koreans was streaming out. They shouted and pointed down the road.

"Poor gooks think the Commies are coming back," someone said.

The marines waved and laughed, and some threw candy and cigarettes. Soon they found out what the Koreans had been trying to tell them. Around a sharp bend they came upon a jeep in the middle of the road, with logs piled high on either side of it. The driver of the lead truck couldn't avoid hitting it. The jeep rolled off the road, and the driver bulled his way on.

Bud Kaylor looked over the edge of the truck. Chinese soldiers were six and seven deep in the ditches, and more were running down the hills on both sides of the road, shooting as they came. Kaylor grabbed his carbine and emptied it into one of the ditches. There wasn't time to aim, and the Reds were so thick it didn't make any difference anyway.

In a matter of seconds his ammunition was gone. He dropped flat on his back and saw two bullets sing past, within an inch of his nose. He *saw* them go by, because they had come right through the steel side of the truck, and it had slowed them down. Then one came through and got Art Foley, the mail clerk. Kaylor started to reach for Art's carbine, and he saw something yellow sail by. It was a grenade shaped like a potato masher. He leaped for it, but it wasn't there; so he thought it had bounced out of the truck. But when he lay down again, his head hit something hard; he reached back and grabbed the object. It was the grenade. He immediately threw it backward, clear of the truck, and heard it go off.

A minute later the driver was shot in the ear. The marine riding shotgun with him kept firing at the ditch on the driver's side of the road, trying to protect him. There were only two tires left, and the truck veered all over the road.

Kaylor grabbed Foley's carbine and sat up at the back of the truck. He was just in time to see a Chinese Red soldier lob one of those yellow grenades up from the ditch. It was a perfect throw, and Kaylor grabbed it by the handle and slammed it right back at him. It hit at

the Communist's feet and instantly exploded. The Red died with unbelieving surprise on his face.

Then the truck swerved off the road into the ditch. Kaylor went over the side and ran to some thin bushes. From there he could see the truck driver and his gunner running toward a frozen river about 500 yards away. The Reds shot at them from a hill, and Kaylor watched the bullets kick up the snow around their feet. Suddenly, the gunner dropped, but the driver kept right on going across the river, into the cover of thick woods.

A number of Reds showed up, and one threw a grenade that landed about five feet from Kaylor. It went off and knocked him down, and he was conscious of a burning sensation in his leg.

The Reds came up and stood all around him, looking at him and pointing their rifles. Then one moved in close and frisked him.

Kaylor saw the red stain come through his pant leg. The blood was running fast. His captors took him to a command post, where a Chinese officer called two orderlies over and gave them some instructions. Then he turned to Kaylor and made him take his parka off. The officer pretended that he was searching it, and he motioned to the orderlies to take Kaylor away. As Kaylor left, he saw the officer trying on his parka.

Bud was weak from loss of blood. He kept falling down, and the Reds kept pushing him along. Every step seemed colder than the last. It was -15°F, and all Kaylor wore now was his field cap, a shirt, pants, shoes, and long underwear. At a battalion aid station the Communist orderlies dressed his wounds.

Early the second morning, when they reached a Korean village, one of the Reds walked Kaylor to the door of a house and motioned him inside. Entering, Bud could see three Chinese officers at a table. A single candle illuminated the entire room. In a few seconds another officer came in. He was young and friendly, and his English was flawless. He put out his hand and smiled.

"I'm Lieutenant Fung," he said. "Won't you sit down?"

Fung asked his name, rank, and serial number. He translated swiftly to the three officers at the table. Then he asked Kaylor the names of marine officers in his outfit, how many tanks were there, and what kind of artillery. Kaylor started to say that he wasn't required to tell, when he felt a sharp kick at his leg. He looked around, and at the end of the bench he saw two Chinese overcoats piled over a body, with only the feet showing. Kaylor moved farther down the bench, away from the body, and told the lieutenant he couldn't answer him.

In a few minutes Fung left the room, and the body under the overcoats sat up and unveiled itself. It was the truck driver, 19-year-old Cpl. Fred Holcomb, from Hamden, New York, and he was more than a little indignant at having been captured, and all the Chinamen in Korea could go to hell.

"We don't tell them a thing," he said. "We don't have to."

Kaylor was sorry that Holcomb hadn't escaped, but glad he was finally in good marine company. They started talking about the ambush, and then Fung came back into the room. He talked to the two marines until dawn. He explained that the Chinese were not going to kill them, that they didn't even want them as prisoners.

"All we want to do with you guys," he said, "is get you out of Korea so you can't fight us anymore." He said they were going to take them to China, put them on a neutral ship, and send them back to the United States. Then he took their home addresses.

"I'd like to write you fellows after the war and see how things turn out for each of us," he said. He told them they would be moving out in the morning, shook hands, and said good-bye. And he left them with the memory of a warm and friendly person.

It was snowing heavily when they moved out with a Chinese column and started walking north. After four days they joined a group of 250 other prisoners, including 43 marines. They moved on north, Kaylor limping along on his wounded leg over the icy mountain trails. And finally, after they had walked for 11 days, and just when Bud thought he couldn't walk another mile, they stopped moving. They were in the village of Kanggye, near the Yalu River.

The Chinese divided them into two sections and billeted them in cold Korean houses, where most of them lay on the bare floor in a sleeping stupor for days. When they were strong enough to want to stop sleeping, the Chinese took their clothes and gave them Chinese uniforms. English-speaking Red officers began to interrogate them. It was kept mostly on a personal plane, and the officers kept it up until they got the answers they wanted. If Comrade Kaylor, for instance, said he earned $250 a month at his job in Minneapolis, he was obviously lying. This made the Chinese angry, and they would spend long hours explaining to him that he was among friends and there was no need for him to lie. Patiently, they would point out to him that his warmongering, capitalistic bosses on Wall Street had duped him into thinking he was well off.

When the prisoners realized what the Reds wanted to hear, they told them tales of wretched, hungry childhoods that had been lived in anticipation of joining the Marine Corps, where they could at least get some food and clothing. They told of aged parents who lived as best they could on the infrequent and niggardly charity of the Wall Street bosses. The Chinese seemed to like this.

The indoctrination began in a bleak, cold barn called the Big House. A Chinese "high commander" came out on a stage and made a welcoming speech. They were not, he explained, to think of themselves as prisoners. They were "newly liberated friends" and would be treated as such. The Chinese people were not angry with them for being in Korea, since they had been duped by their imperialistic bosses. They would be treated with kindness, but they must obey the rules set down for newly liberated friends. If they broke the rules, they would undergo severe punishment.

On Christmas night all the newly liberated friends were herded into the Big House. The Chinese had decorated the place with Christmas trees and candles, wreaths and red paper bells. There was a big sign saying, "Merry Christmas." Along the walls were signs reading, "If it were not for the Wall Street imperialists, you would be home with your wives and families this Christmas night." A high commander made a speech that repeated what the signs said, and he threw in a few unkind remarks about Truman, MacArthur, and Secretary of State John Foster Dulles.

By this time the POW's knew what the Chinese wanted of them, and word had spread that the "most promising" prisoners would be released before the war was over. So after the high commander finished speaking, a marine from Boston named McClean jumped up and shouted, "Down with the Wall Street bosses!" And another named Dickerson pulled his six feet seven inches from the floor and shouted in a Georgia drawl, "Down with the aggressive imperialists!" And a five-foot nine-inch marine named Kaylor limped over to a toothy interpreter named Lieutenant Pan, looked him squarely in the eye, and cried, "Down with the warmongers!" The newly liberated friends all over the Big House took up the cry, and the happy, smiling Chinese ran around the huge room, patting them on the back, shaking hands with them, and giving them presents. Each man received 10 pieces of candy, 6 cigarettes, and a Christmas card.

After Christmas each section was lectured every other day in the Big House. They listened to long orations by high commanders of varying rank. Sometimes the teachers spoke in Chinese, and this took the longest because an interpreter had to translate. Sometimes they would rattle along in a high-pitched, singsong English. First, they spoke on "Why Are We Treating You So Well?" Then, "Who Is the Aggressor in Korea?" Then, "Why Is the United States the Aggressor?" Then, "How You Can Fight for Peace."

After the lectures the section marched back to its house, where it would engage in a lengthy round-table discussion. An English-speaking Chinese officer would sit quietly by, listening and taking notes. Once in a while he would inject a comment, and the marines would all nod solemn approval.

The weeks stretched into months, and the pattern became routine.

And then dysentery hit. It hit everyone, and the ones it hit the worst died. Sometimes only one would die in a week, sometimes three, four, or five.

Worse than the dysentery was the malnutrition; they had nothing to eat but sorghum seed and millet. Malnutrition hit the legs with a screaming viciousness. When it hit Kaylor, he lay flat on his back for 28 days and cried and became delirious, while agonizing pains raced through his legs. When it would stop for a while, he would drift off to sleep and suddenly wake up screaming when the pains came back. Then, after days of this, exhaustion would claim him, and the pain would lie dormant while he slept. Finally, his legs felt better, and he was able to move around again.

IT WAS MARCH NOW, and the days got longer and warmer. And the rumors got thicker that some of the most "promising" friends were soon to be released. The combination kept the prisoners in anxious good spirits. But it was with some reluctance that every man in the camp signed the Stockholm Peace Petition. The Chinese thought it would be a good indication of their sincerity in their desire to fight for peace. The marines hoped that the names might somehow sift back and reach the United States.

And on March 21 the second telegram arrived at the house of Charley Kaylor in Hopkins, Minnesota. The message was from the army's provost marshal general, and it said that the name of Charles Martin Kaylor had been mentioned on an enemy propaganda broadcast out of Peking on March 16. That's all it said. But now the family's constant, desperate hope became a fire.

On Easter Sunday 60 prisoners were herded into the Big House. Inside, great care was taken to seat a certain 30 on one side of the room and the rest on the other side. Then a high commander delivered a lengthy singsong reiteration of all the lectures of the months before. He climaxed this oration with the news that one of these groups of 30 was to be released. It was felt, he said, that these men were "ready to carry on the fight for peace among their own people." The other 30 were being cited for "progress," but were being kept for a while to help instruct incoming newly liberated friends. Then he smiled and toyed with the 60 men.

"Which group is it?" he asked. "Who is going home? Is it the group on my right? Or is it the group on my left?" Bud Kaylor looked around at the faces in his group. Harrison, Estess, Dickerson, Holcomb, Maffioli—all were barracks bull-session artists, and all had given the Reds master snow jobs.

Finally, the high commander pointed to the group on his right. It was Kaylor's group. "This group," he said, "leaves tonight."

The 30 marines took the news with stone-faced joy, for they wanted the Reds to feel that they would just as soon stay there and be Communists as return home and be Communists. The other 30 also remained stone-faced, but they had trouble fighting back the tears.

The prisoners who were to be released moved out in trucks at dusk and rode for five nights. On the fifth night Lieutenant Pan, the interpreter in command, got them out of the trucks and told them they were in the Chunchon area.

"There has been an American offensive," he said. "It is too dangerous to let you go now. You might be killed."

The marines said they would take that chance, but Pan told them he was acting under orders. Then the trucks moved away, and the marines were marched to a prison camp.

They stayed in this camp six weeks. Then, on the night of May 15, the Chinese called out 19 of the 30 marines and marched them to a river. They gave them razors and soap and let them bathe and shave, then brought them chow. The food was pork and rice, and it was the first time in six months that any of them had seen anything but sorghum seed and millet. A lot of them ate too much too fast and got sick. Bud Kaylor was one of them. After they finished eating, Lieutenant Pan spoke to them.

"Word has come to release you men," he said.

Again they were loaded into trucks. On the third night they reached the Imjin River. Retreating Chinese troops were coming back across the river by the thousands. Pan turned his charges over to a field commander. The commander told them that another offensive had been started and they could not be released at this time. Then he left, saying he would be back about midnight and for them to be ready to move back up north.

T. Sgt. Charley Harrison, of Tulsa, Oklahoma, was fighting mad. He announced firmly that he was *not* going up north again. He was going home, and if anyone wanted to come with him they were welcome. U.N. artillery was whistling in close, and the guards were in foxholes. So all 19 marines sneaked off and waded across the shallow Imjin River. On the other side they ran for miles through the woods.

Just before dawn they stopped in a field where the wheat was high and went to sleep. They awoke to find four Chinese soldiers pointing guns at them and jabbering to each other. Then Harrison, who spoke Chinese, put on an act. He got up smiling. He explained that they were released prisoners of war and that the high command would be displeased if they were shot or taken back. The Chinese jabbered back at him, and then he talked some more. And then he started talking to the marines out of the side of his mouth.

"These birds aren't going to let us go," he said. "They're arguing whether they should shoot us now or take us in." Then he said something in Chinese. Then he spoke English again. "Estess and Dickerson, get the one on the left." More Chinese. "Kaylor and Hilburn, the one on the right; Nash and Holcomb, the one next to him." More Chinese. "Hawkins and Hayton, the other one." Then there was more Chinese, and finally Harrison gave the word: "Let's get 'em!"

The marines did their jobs as Harrison assigned them and completed them quickly when the others pitched in. This was a kill-or-be-killed situation. The marines overpowered the Reds and strangled them and smashed their heads with the gun butts. Then they ran.

In the next valley they came to a village. A bearded old Korean sent them up to a house on the top of a hill, where the mayor used to live, and promised to send them food and tobacco. They were to wait there until he could send a message to the American troops, who were only a few miles away.

Inside the house they lay and marveled that this was the only house any of them had seen in Korea with wallpaper. And then they heard the sound of an airplane. They looked outside and saw an L-5 artillery observer, an army plane, flying low. They quickly cut the wallpaper into strips and took it out to the rice paddy behind the house. They spelled out POW 19 RESCUE, and then they went back inside. Only Fred Holcomb stayed out in the rice paddy, waving his undershirt to attract the L-5's attention. Snipers fired at him from the hills occasionally, but they weren't coming close, and Holcomb was much too excited to care.

Soon Holcomb came running in. The L-5 had dropped a message: "Come out to the letters so you can be counted. We are sending tanks in to pick you up."

They went back to the letters, and in half an hour they saw the L-5 leading three tanks around a bend in the draw that stretched out beneath the rice paddies. Then Lt. Frank Cold, of Tampa, Florida, the only officer among the 19, lined them up in a column of twos.

"I know how we all feel about being rescued," he said. " But this is the army coming in to get us, and we're still marines. So let's be rescued like marines, in formation."

The tanks ground to a halt about 300 yards away to identify them. This was hard to do, since they were wearing Chinese uniforms. But finally they moved up close. The hatch of the lead tank opened and an army captain climbed out.

The 19 marines stood there, in columns of twos, in a soggy, worthless no-man's-land, somewhere in Korea, and tears as big as raindrops streamed down the face of every one of them. The army captain stood looking at them, and for a moment it seemed as though all Korea was silent. Then the captain said, "Come on, fellas, let's get the hell out of here!" So they climbed into the tanks and got the hell out of there, but they were rescued like marines.

IT WAS ON May 25 that the third telegram arrived at Charley Kaylor's house. It came from Marine Headquarters, and it said that Pfc. Charles Martin Kaylor would soon be home. The endless months of hoping and praying were over, and the miracle had happened. But the people in Charley Kaylor's house said one more prayer anyhow.

Almost suddenly, it was June 23, 1951, and Bud Kaylor was moving down the steps from the airplane while his eyes searched the faces at the end of the ramp. He saw them, right in front. He limped toward them. Then Dorothy was in his arms, the others clustered around him. Bud Kaylor had come the long way home.

*This is the amazing account of how two daring
young Canadians established an escape route through Nazi-held
France during World War II. More than 300 Allied airmen
and secret agents followed it to freedom.*

House of Alphonse

By John G. Hubbell

ONE NIGHT in January 1944 an announcer for the British Broad-
casting Corporation voiced a cheery greeting in French from
London: "Good evening to everyone in the House of Alphonse. I
repeat: Good evening to everyone in the House of Alphonse."

Across the Channel in German-occupied Brittany, in a small room
above a café in the village of Plouha, a young man named Raymond
LaBrosse, whose papers identified him as a salesman of electrical
medical equipment, switched off a radio and turned to the two other
people in the room.

"That's it," he said.

Stocky Lucien Dumais, known locally as a contractor, got to his
feet and nodded quickly to the third man, café owner François Le
Cornec. "Let's go!" he said.

The men slipped into the night.

A few minutes later the rear doors of half a dozen village houses
opened, and small groups of what seemed to be young French peasants edged silently out. They were not all peasants. Among them,
dressed in the same sort of clothes, were 13 American and 5 British
airmen who had been shot down in France. Silently, by twos and
threes, led by the French, the airmen moved through the woods behind the village. They carefully skirted the edges of open meadows to
avoid being seen by patrols of German troops.

After an interminable time they came to a stone farmhouse—the
"House of Alphonse," actually the home of Resistance worker Jean
Gicquel. Here, before a flickering candle, Dumais warned the airmen: "Many lives have been risked to bring you this far. There is just
a mile left, and it is the most dangerous you will ever travel. You will

121

maintain absolute silence and do exactly as you are told. There are enemy sentries and patrols in the area. If it becomes necessary to kill any of them, you are expected to help—use knives or your hands. Be quick, and above all be quiet; your lives and ours depend on it."

Then Dumais and the villagers led the airmen out again, through the darkness. Finally, they reached a cliff that dropped sharply 200 feet to the beach below. Clutching, sliding, tumbling, they scrambled down to a black cove.

From a hidden perch on the cliff, a French sailor had begun blinking the letter *B* in Morse code on a flashlight. The signal went out over the dark English Channel every two minutes.

For a long time there was no answer. Then, shortly before 2 A.M., four rowboats slid into the cove. The airmen hastily scrambled into the boats and were rowed out to a blacked-out British motor gunboat, No. 503, standing silently offshore.

The villagers returned to the House of Alphonse, where they waited for the clock to strike 6 A.M.—the hour the Germans lifted the curfew. Before going to bed in the house at Plouha, Lucien Dumais raised a wineglass to Le Cornec and LaBrosse.

"Eh bien. To our first success," he said. "It went off like clockwork. But we have a busy season ahead of us."

"Operation Bonaparte" was the key part of a larger escape network called Shelburne Escape and Evasion Line, which was to go on to become World War II's most successful escape route. For one of its two key men there was a prelude that began in London in August 1942, when Ray LaBrosse, a 22-year-old sergeant in the Canadian Army's 2nd Divisional Signals Regiment, was called in by a kilted British intelligence major to answer all sorts of seemingly nonsensical questions. Did he like sports? Adventure? As a boy, what games had he enjoyed most?

How did he feel about the war? About the Americans? The British? The French? As LaBrosse answered, the major sized him up. A native of Ottawa, LaBrosse was of French descent and spoke the language fluently. He was young but, according to his superiors, mature, enthusiastic, strong, imaginative.

Finally satisfied, the major put the proposition: He needed two good men to set up and run an escape organization for Allied airmen shot down in France. Capture, of course, would mean torture and a spy's death. Was LaBrosse interested? LaBrosse was.

He and a partner parachuted into France in 1943, and for six months they teamed up with the French Resistance in evacuating airmen. Then the apparatus was infiltrated by the Gestapo, and LaBrosse's partner was among those arrested. LaBrosse escaped via the Pyrenees to England. He was soon asked if he would return to help set up "Shelburne" to find, hide, clothe, feed, and evacuate escaping airmen. The role of "Bonaparte" was to get them out by sea from Brittany. He said he would.

The man selected to go with him this time was another bilingual Canadian, Sergeant Major Dumais, 38, of Montreal, a veteran of the August 1942 raid on Dieppe. (Captured there, he had escaped to England after living off the French countryside and making his way to Marseilles.) By the time the two men left England, both of them had had months of intensive training in jujitsu and the use of various types of weapons and explosives, as well as in the construction and operation of wireless sets. They were given fountain pens that fired a deadly gas, buttons that hid compasses, large amounts of francs, forged identity papers. For security reasons each had his own code, unknown to the other. Finally, on a night in November 1943, a light plane landed them in an isolated meadow 50 miles north of Paris.

The operation very nearly foundered before it got fairly started. Making their way to Paris, Dumais and LaBrosse succeeded in getting in touch with the Resistance. Soon afterward, LaBrosse went to keep a sidewalk rendezvous with one of its members, a woman. A flicker of her eye as he approached warned him just in time that two trench-coated figures idling nearby were Gestapo agents. Shaken, LaBrosse walked on past.

Soon thereafter, immutable rules for governing the escape organization were laid down. No one involved was to know anything except his own function. Cooperating Frenchmen were to be told only that if a "package" (airman) was found it was to be hidden and "rewrapped" (given peasant clothing), word passed secretly to a reliable friend, instructions awaited. No airman was to be given more than the barest essential information.

Soon escape procedures and routes were worked out, villagers screened and recruited, hideouts arranged. Dumais and LaBrosse rented separate quarters in Paris and met only when necessary. Dumais made no pretense at working as the mortician his Paris papers said he was; he traveled extensively and let the story grow in his neighborhood that he was a successful black-market operator. La-Brosse appeared to be every inch the dutiful salesman. He moved about picking houses known to be safe for his radio operations and exchanging coded messages with London.

As they had surmised, the season was busy. The air war over the Continent was reaching its peak of violence; ever-increasing numbers of crewmen from crippled bombers were parachuting down all over France. Typical was Lt. William Spinning, a bomber pilot from Birmingham, Michigan, who dropped into north-central France. Bewildered, alone, knowing that any second he might be spotted and shot, he spent days and nights hiding and walking, scavenging cabbages from farms. Once he was given a meal by a huge woodcutter who wept as he watched him eat, then wrapped him in his own worn jacket, and pointed him toward Spain. He experienced a torrential rain and a feverish illness, but at last he saw two men beckoning to him from a field. They gave him hot food and drink, hid him in a warm farmhouse, told him to wait. Though Lieutenant Spinning didn't know it, the Shelburne Line had picked him up.

ALL THE AIRMEN found were funneled first toward its organization in Paris, headed by Paul-François Campinchi. Undertaker Dumais was everywhere—watching, noting, instructing. Thus, in a wine warehouse 70 miles south of Paris, he watched while Resistance men taught four Allied airmen to act like ill-humored French laborers. They were not to look angry, just sullen, like the many French who refused to speak to the enemy. If stopped for questioning, they were to show their fake identity papers, say nothing, play dumb.

"The slightest mistake can betray you," they were told. "The way you smoke, for example. You people inhale great, greedy drags and often remove a cigarette from your mouth. The Frenchman savors a cigarette; he keeps it in the corner of his mouth and lets it build an ash. He rarely removes it, and he *never* offers cigarettes to others— cigarettes are too scarce in France these days."

Next day Dumais was outside a church near Compiègne, reading a newspaper, when a farmer drove up, presented a gift of eggs to the priest, explained he was Paris-bound with a truckload of hay, and wondered if Father had "packages" he wanted delivered. The priest nodded and told the man to drive his truck around back to the church cellar entrance. There the driver picked up two airmen who had been hiding in a stack of hay.

The Canadians were nearby one night in Paris waiting to hear if Resistance interrogators thought Lt. Manuel Rogoff, an American bombardier, was a Nazi agent. Rogoff was not to be trapped. He knew that the Pittsburgh Pirates of the National League had lost no games in 1942 to the Chicago Bears of the National League, because the Bears were a football team. He knew that Dizzy Dean had never pitched for the Detroit White Sox (and that it was the Detroit Tigers, not White Sox), but for the St. Louis Cardinals. He knew what movies had been playing in the theaters on his base in England prior to his last raid. He was well acquainted with the adventures of Tom Sawyer and Huckleberry Finn.

Every airman was interrogated, because German agents were always probing. One night a Free Norwegian airman was brought in. Dumais himself questioned him. The man had been flying with the RAF, he said, and was desperately anxious to return to England and rejoin the fight.

He had all the right answers about his squadron, base, even personnel. But he became oddly vague and impatient when quizzed on things Norwegian; he said he had not spent much time in Norway in recent years. Dumais' interrogation turned savage. The "Norwegian" panicked, confessed he was a Nazi agent, and pleaded for mercy. He offered to join the organization and promised invaluable help, but no chance could be taken. Shifted to a country house near Versailles, he was pumped for all the information he would give. Then he was shot.

There was the young man who identified himself as Robert K. Fruth, a U.S. airman from Defiance, Ohio, but could not answer the most routine questions. His squadron? His bomb group? The pilot of his plane? The names of others in his crew? The target his plane had last attacked? On all these questions he drew a blank. While the Resistance was considering whether to execute him, LaBrosse tapped out a short, coded message to London.

Two days later a BBC broadcast cleverly keyed to the coded query established that Fruth was genuine. Newly arrived in England from the States, he had been roused from bed in predawn darkness his very first night to replace a gunner fallen suddenly ill. That explained why he had had no time to acquire the most rudimentary information before he was shot down.

The transfer of airmen from Paris to the Brittany coast was tricky. Too many "packages" delivered to Plouha, the principal jumping-off point for Bonaparte escapes, might attract attention. Hence, the disguised airmen were first sent to a number of other small towns nearby. One of these was Guingamp, 15 miles from Plouha.

Before an airman boarded the train in Paris, he was well briefed. In his hand or stuffed in his left coat pocket he must carry a newspaper. As he crossed the Guingamp platform, a nondescript man would jostle him and give him a swift, discreet dig in the ribs. That was the sign of recognition.

Guingamp's Resistance leader was Mathurin Branchoux, a thrice-wounded World War I veteran Among his retinue was one François Kerambrun, who drove a small enclosed delivery truck for the Germans. To airmen he was carrying to a hideout near Plouha, Kerambrun would explain that the Germans allowed him to attend to his own private business in his off-hours. And this, he would grin, was his private business—doing what he could for France.

By the middle of March 1944 LaBrosse reported in his radio code to British intelligence that dozens of fliers and secret Allied agents were hidden around the Brittany countryside. Thus, on three March nights, there came again over the BBC the welcome message, "Good evening to everyone in the House of Alphonse. . . ." and, in separate groups, they were taken out.

Cautious and vigilant, the two Canadians nevertheless knew how to take risks. Soon after the Normandy invasion in June, they had to reach Brittany for an evacuation. Rail lines had been knocked out or commandeered entirely by German forces; so they started out on bicycles. In Rennes a German military policeman took Dumais' bicycle from him. Dumais signaled LaBrosse to keep moving and meant to flee himself on foot; then he thought better of it—boldness might arouse less suspicion than humility. He stormed into German military-police headquarters, shouting that he had been robbed.

"It is imperative that I be in St. Brieuc this evening," he roared at the commandant, "and you must get me there."

The commandant, fearing that he had a wealthy, influential French collaborator on his hands, provided a staff car. When LaBrosse pedaled wearily into St. Brieue the next day, a grinning Dumais was waiting for him.

German records later indicated that the Gestapo never came really close to untangling and destroying the undercover operation. But apart from that early near-disaster in Paris, there were many very close shaves. Once in Guingamp, with the town full of Germans, two Nazi officers hammered at the door of a house and said that it was being requisitioned for their troops. The housewife pleaded that she already was rooming several weary railroad men and had no more beds. She was given an hour to clear the rooms. The hour gave her just enough time to get rid of several Allied airmen. In François Kerambrun's truck, they were rushed somewhere else.

On another occasion German shore batteries spotted the British motor gunboat No. 503 as she approached for a pickup, and opened fire. She escaped but returned hours later in darkness and completed the rendezvous. Just as dawn lit the area, the 503 slipped over the horizon with more "packages" for London. (Eventually, the 503 came to a tragic end, though not on a Bonaparte assignment. Four days after Germany's surrender, she struck a mine in the North Sea and sank with all hands.)

Finally, the Germans themselves paid a hair-raising visit to the House of Alphonse. One night immediately after Dumais and café

owner Le Cornec had briefed a group of airmen and left the premises, a German patrol knocked on the door and instructed its inhabitants—Jean Gicquel and his family—to come out.

Instead of obeying, Gicquel slammed the door in their faces and hustled his ailing wife, his six-week-old daughter, and five airmen up to the attic. The Germans opened fire and in the confusion wounded one of their own men. They brought the injured man into the house to patch him up. Hiding in the attic, everyone lay motionless, ready for the fight to the death they were certain was coming. But the Germans, nervous and excited, unaccountably departed without searching upstairs. Gicquel and the pilots then slipped out of the house to a nearby wheat field, where they waited out the night. Next day Dumais and Le Cornec rounded them up and later got them out.

Eight times Bonaparte's men and women led Allied airmen and agents—Britons, Americans, Canadians, Free French, Belgians, Dutchmen, Poles—through that hazardous journey to the coast. When there were no more evacuations to be made by sea, the two Canadians fought in the Maquis around Plouha.

So tightly kept was the secret of Shelburne and Bonaparte that none of the *évadés,* as the escaped airmen came to call themselves, ever was able to learn that such a network existed. Most assumed they had just fallen in with a single escape operation. But years later one of them—Ralph Patton, a Buffalo, New York, businessman—tracked down the story while vacationing in France and learned that in seven months this network had rescued a total of 307 downed Allied airmen and secret agents. Bonaparte alone accounted for nearly half of the total. There had been eight trips by the British gunboat. Of all the escape networks on the European continent, Shelburne was the most successful in that it never lost a single "package." The only casualty was the House of Alphonse itself—the Germans, suspecting it to be a Resistance hideout, returned and burned it.

As a result of Ralph Patton's discovery, 50 of the American *évadés* gathered in Buffalo from all over the country one night in May 1964 to honor those who so willingly had risked death for them. On hand were Lucien Dumais, by then a Montreal businessman, and Maj. Raymond LaBrosse, a staff officer at the Collège Militaire Royal de St. Jean—Canada's bilingual military college. From Brittany, Guingamp's Resistance leader Mathurin Branchoux brought with him photographs of houses, people, and scenes the Americans and Canadians would readily recognize.

It was the only noisy rendezvous Operation Bonaparte ever had.

*His leg shattered, the East German youth lay
in the "death strip," where Western guards could
not go. Yet without help he would die.*

Incident at the Border

By Lawrence Elliott

O N THE evening of December 31, 1969, in the East German border town of Meiningen, a boy of 17 named Bernd Geis sat in a café trying to hide his loneliness behind a glass of beer. Around him strangers sang and noisily toasted the coming year, but Bernd had no one to celebrate with and nothing to celebrate. The one person he wanted to be with this New Year's Eve was his older sister, Irene, who lived across the forbidden frontier in West Germany. His mother and father had both died within the past 18 months. He had come to Meiningen to be with his married brother, but the brother had no room for Bernd in his small apartment. So every day the husky, brooding boy worked at his job as a carpenter's apprentice, and every night he came home to an empty room in a boardinghouse.

Now, at around 8:30, suddenly moved by the special melancholy that comes from being alone in the midst of great gaiety, Bernd paid up and went outside. And in the cold white night he turned, not toward his lonely little room, but down the snow-packed road that led

to the demarcation line between the two Germanys. With no fore-thought, without regard for the fact that the price of failure was prison and possibly death, Bernd had impulsively decided to flee to the West. He had no political quarrel with the regime; he had grown up under communism. He simply wanted to see his sister.

Since the Berlin Wall went up in August 1961, all sorts of people, a few even younger than Bernd, have attempted the dangerous flight to freedom. So strong is the human urge to be free that thousands upon thousands of East Germans have risked everything to cross the ugly, unnatural barrier. They have tunneled beneath it, crashed the walls with trucks, and dared the guards with false papers. But for every one who has succeeded, nine have been turned back. And on the first day of the new year, Bernd Geis, equipped with nothing but his resolve, would become the first of an estimated 10,000 who would try to reach the West before 1970 ended. Of all these, only 901 would make it.

Bernd spent that night and the daylight hours of January 1 hiding in a barn. When it was dark again, he struck out across the fields, through the deep snow, toward the place where he imagined the border to be. He knew vaguely about the border fortifications, that there were mines and high fences, yet he had no plan except that he was going to climb or burrow or run to get across.

At 8 P.M. the frightened youth came upon the barbed wire. It stood starkly revealed in the light of a cold moon, not 50 feet away. Beyond were two higher fences of wire mesh. He stood there shivering, listening, weighing his fear against his loneliness. Then he shuffled ahead through the snow and lay down on his back and in a few minutes had worked his way under the barbed wire.

It seemed so incredibly easy. Where were the guards? Was this all there was to it? He rested on his knees, brushing snow from his shoulders, measuring the next fence with his eyes. It was probably 10 feet high, but he was sure he could climb it. Suddenly he was sure of everything, that he would make it safely, that he would soon be with Irene. Up over the wire mesh he went, already gauging the last fence, and plunged toward it with joy and wild confidence.

Then Bernd's luck ran out. He was inside the 20-yard zone known as the death strip, a belt of barren land implanted with contact mines. And as he pitched through the waist-deep snow, a shattering explosion flung him forward. When he looked back, he saw that his right boot was dangling from his leg by a few shreds of flesh and that his spurting blood was staining the snow.

At that moment, about 200 yards away, on a small road that once led to Meiningen but now dead-ended at the demarcation line, a patrol of West German border guards listened intently.

"What was that?" asked recruit Wolfgang Schmitt uneasily.

"One of their mines," answered Sgt. Rudolf Romeis. "Probably set off by the weight of the snow."

But even as he spoke, an unmistakable cry for help sailed up to them and hung a moment in the cold night. Then it came again, faint, anguished. Romeis slipped his submachine gun off his shoulder and snapped at Schmitt, "You stay with the car." To the third man, Pvt. Alois Reis, he said, "Let's go!"

They struck out through a small wood that ran parallel to the demarcation line, marked on the Western side only by a series of intermittent stakes. The cries continued, drawing Romeis and Reis closer, until they came opposite the dark shape that lay crumpled in the death strip 150 feet away, just inside the wire fence.

"Hello!" Romeis called. "Who are you? What's the matter?"

And Bernd cried out, "Help! My foot is blown off. I'm bleeding very badly. I'm from Meiningen. My name's Bernd Geis. I'm trying to get away. Please help me!"

Sergeant Romeis swore aloud. At 22, he was a veteran of the federal border guards and was well aware that the pathetic souls on the far side of the fence were all too often pursued, shot at, and hauled back into East Germany. Now the life of one such human depended on him. Yet his orders were inflexible: Anyone who reached the Western side was to be protected and given every assistance; but none of his men was ever to set foot across the line of stakes that marked the actual boundary of East Germany. The Vopos—the East German guards—would need no further invitation to open fire. And as with every confrontation between East and West, this would have the potential to explode beyond a random exchange of shots.

"Listen," he called, "take your belt off and tie it around your thigh, tightly. That will stop the bleeding. Can you do that?"

"I've done that," came the reply. "But can't you help me?"

"We're going to try." He turned to Reis: "Stay here. Keep talking to him. I'm going to call headquarters."

He ran for the patrol car. It was equipped with a two-way radio, and soon, as Schmitt and a Bavarian border policeman, Paul Havlena, edged close to hear, he was detailing the situation to the duty officer at his post at Oerlenbach, 30 miles away.

"Any reaction from the Vopos?" asked the officer.

"No, sir. I think they must be celebrating New Year's. Can't we go in and get the fellow out? He won't last long in this cold."

"I can't make that decision," was the reply. "I'll contact the divisional commandant and call you back."

It would be a long time before he did. For the implications of such a confrontation were understood at every level of command, and the commandant knew that if he gave a go-ahead order, he would be held accountable. At 9 P.M. he put in an emergency call to the commanding general in Munich.

Meanwhile, Sergeant Romeis was shooting flares into the sky, turning it ghostly white. He had told Bernd that the Vopos would see them and either come to get him out or let the West Germans across the border tend to his foot. But Romeis was not as hopeful as he sounded: He had never known the Vopos to give anyone on the Western side permission to help an escapee, no matter how badly wounded. And it would take hours before the Vopos themselves could blast a safe path through the mine field. But he didn't know what else to do and kept firing flares while calling encouragement to the hurt boy. There was no response from the darkness beyond the death strip.

About 25 minutes had passed since Bernd had stepped on the mine. He lay so close to the wire fence that if he had had the strength to crawl another arm's length he could have touched it. It constituted the boundary of his world now, locking him inside with his mangled foot and the excruciating pain and the cold. He knew that without someone's help he would soon die. The pain was so bad that he began to think it would be better to close his eyes and let the cold take him.

"Please help me," he called, then put his head down on his arm.

Later, Sergeant Romeis would say: "I think that's what did it—he looked like he was giving up. Nothing we'd said to him about our orders meant a thing. All he understood was that he was dying and we were just standing there, 50 yards away."

Still there was no word from headquarters. "The hell with it!" Romeis suddenly said to Reis. "I'm going in. Are you with me?"

Without hesitation Reis replied, "Right."

Romeis ran back to the patrol car and got an ax. "We're going after him," he told Schmitt. "You cover us from here. If they start shooting, use the machine gun."

Schmitt took a deep breath: "Will they really shoot?"

"If they see us, you can count on it."

Romeis was aware that even if they got Bernd out they could all be disciplined for disobeying orders. But he didn't hesitate. Instructing Havlena, the civilian policeman, to stay where he was, Romeis stepped out beyond the line of stakes and crept across the no-man's-land to the wire fence. Reis waited at the demarcation line.

"Bernd," Romeis whispered, "we're going to get you out."

And Bernd, freezing and at the very limit of his resources, managed an exhausted, "Thank you."

Romeis tried first to pry up the wire mesh with the ax. When that didn't work, he hacked at it until, with ever more desperate swings, he broke the ax handle off. For an agonized moment he lay in the snow, breathing hard, unable to think of anything more to do. Then he bolted up and dashed back to where Reis stood: "The jack! Come on! Let's go back and get the jack!"

They ran for the patrol car, got the jack, then made their way back to where Bernd lay. They scooped snow out from under the fence and five minutes later implanted the metal extension tube of the auto jack under the mesh. Stroke by stroke, they pried the fence up. Romeis held up the mesh with his knee while Reis slithered under and began dragging Bernd through. Then they had him and hefted him up, Reis grabbing him under the armpits, Romeis by the legs. A couple of minutes later they were joined by Havlena who tried to hold the almost severed foot steady. Now, as they began slogging and staggering toward the woods, the 150 feet seemed interminable. But still there was no movement from the East, not a sound.

It was only when they reached the woods, just as they crossed over the demarcation line, that Schmitt came racing up: "It's okay, Sergeant! They just called in—the general says it's okay to get him out!"

Romeis smiled wanly. "Welcome to West Germany, Bernd," he said. "And happy New Year."

They took him directly to the hospital in Mellrichstadt, where the shattered foot was amputated at once. Two days later Irene was at his bedside. Although he was hospitalized for some time, by the summer he was settled in her house in Gelsenkirchen, learning to use an artificial foot. Later when he had a job in a chemical plant, Bernd said, "I would give the other foot, gladly, to be here."

As for the soldiers, Romeis, Reis, and Schmitt, far from being punished, they were all promoted and taken to Bonn for a special commendation by Interior Minister Hans-Dietrich Genscher for acting "as human beings in an emergency that was above the law."

But closed borders only rarely produce happy endings. Barely a year after Bernd's escape, and not far away, another young man stepped on a contact mine; although he managed to get across the border, he bled to death before help came.

This is a frank and brutal account of 15 years
spent among the living dead at the penal
colony in French Guiana—and of one prisoner's
final escape after many failures.

Dry Guillotine

By *René Belbenoit*
Foreword by *William LaVarre*
Fellow, The Royal Geographical Society

IN MAY 1935 while I was on the British island of Trinidad, a slender
waterlogged Indian canoe put in from the sea, carrying six starved
Frenchmen—fugitives from the penal colony of French Guiana. After
hearing their story, the officer of the port declared: "I am not going to
turn these poor men over to the French consul. French Guiana is a
plague on the face of civilization!"

Five of the six fugitives were big, powerful men—men of brute
strength, brute living, and brute mentality. The sixth, in contrast, was
astoundingly small, less than five feet, and weighed under 90 pounds.
He had only one possession, an oilcloth-covered package containing
30 pounds of closely written manuscript—the record of 15 years of
prison colony life, the most amazing document I had ever seen.

"Why don't you let me send your manuscript safely to the United
States to a publisher?" I asked. "It's impossible for you to actually gain
permanent freedom. You'll be lost at sea or arrested and sent back to
Guiana. You must understand that."

But he refused, and I thought that I would never see him again, that
his story would be lost. I was mistaken. René Belbenoit finally reached
the United States, with his book, *Dry Guillotine.*

IN 1920, WHEN I WAS 21 years old, I was sentenced to eight years at
hard labor in the penal colony in French Guiana, for theft.

The convict ship on which I sailed carried about 680 convicts,
herded into steel cages in the hold. Each cage contained between 80
and 90 convicts, with hardly one square yard for each pair of feet.

To prevent mass rebellion, the cage ceilings had openings through
which scalding live steam could be injected. Unruly convicts were
sent to the hot cells, sheet-iron cubicles next to the boilers, too small
for a man to straighten up in.

In the cages conversation turned naturally to Guiana and escapes.

137

Some prisoners had small maps of South America torn from atlases and spent their time studying these minutely, measuring distances and learning names of rivers and towns in the countries that surround Guiana, trying to pronounce words that a few months ago did not exist for them: Paramaribo, Venezuela, Orinoco, Oyapoc.

Cliques formed quickly. There was one distinct group, composed of the *forts-à-bras* ("strongarms"), the much-tattooed men who had lived many years in the military prisons in Africa and knew all the tricks. From the beginning they had tobacco and other comforts, and they quickly organized gambling games. Their lips turned suddenly into snarls, vomiting obscenities, and their bulging muscles made them the relentless bullies of the cage. During the night they stole anything they could and sold their loot to the sailors, who dropped a weighted line from the deck to the privy porthole. Each parcel of stolen goods brought five to six packages of tobacco.

One day two convicts who had long been enemies started fighting with knives made by sharpening spoon handles on the cement floor. They were out to kill each other.

We all lined ourselves up against the bars to hide the fight from the guards, and the *forts-à-bras* began singing to drown any cries of the struggling men. Suddenly, one of the fighters slipped, and the other was preparing to finish him off when the guards, becoming suspicious, entered the cage, revolvers in hand. The blood-soaked loser was taken to the infirmary, and his adversary was placed in a hot cell for the rest of the voyage.

As we reached the tropics, the heat and lack of air in the cage became terrible. Three-fourths of the men wore nothing but towels about their waists. The water became contaminated, and the sailors poured permanganate into it so it would be drinkable. Twice a day we were given a collective shower; the sailors came down into the hold with hoses and soused the steaming men with fresh salt water. It was a delicious relief.

One morning the shore appeared, and a few hours later we were being marched off the landing. A flock of blacks stood along the shore and lined our path. The black women laughed freely and gesticulated in our direction. But the many white men who were also there—*libérés* who had served their prison sentences but were still condemned to live in French Guiana—presented a miserable front. Mostly barefoot, all shabbily dressed, they seemed too wretched to be excited by our arrival.

We were taken to St.-Laurent Camp and locked into barracks in groups of 60. Presently, five men came up to the barred windows. "Tobacco?" they whispered. "Coffee! Bananas!"

"But how are we to pay?" I asked. "I have no money!"

"With your clothes," they answered, and then quoted prices. A pair of pants was worth 40 sous; a blouse, 30 sous; a blanket, 5 francs.

One new arrival sold a pair of trousers, another a blouse. And that night everybody had his cigarettes—and a few bananas.

On the second morning after our arrival, the commandant of the penitentiary assembled everybody in the compound and warned us against trying to escape.

"Here in Guiana you enjoy great liberty," he said, "and you can try to escape whenever you like. But we have two constantly watching guardians: the jungle and the sea. I know that in less than 15 days many of you will be off into the jungle; I know also that these will return soon, and I'll see them in the cells or in the hospital, except for those who are lying as skeletons picked clean by ants."

Then came the medical inspection. Nearly all, sick or well, were pronounced capable of any kind of work. But when I showed the doctor my title to a war pension, he classed me for light work. This saved me later from many a misery.

For I discovered that all convicts who are pronounced fit—whether young or old and regardless of their former occupations—are set to the same tasks. Consequently, in that damp, hostile climate, of some 700 that arrive annually, 400 die in the first year. Hence the total number of prisoners remains fairly constant. When a convoy comes, the total rises to 3,500; the hospital overflows, some disappear in the jungle, and in the 12 months before the next shipload arrives, the count has dropped again to 2,800. The policy of the administration is to kill, not to reclaim.

Within six months after they arrive, most of the convicts are reduced to a life little better than that of primitive beasts. They must go barefoot, for the wooden shoes issued—over the protests of many governors—are unsuitable for the environment. Underclothes and socks have been sold. The men do not even wash themselves in the morning, for the water in the barracks is never plentiful.

Each convict keeps his few francs and other valuables in a hollow cylinder about three inches long, made of aluminum or other noncorrosive metal, which is concealed by inserting it into the anus.

The prisoner must be equipped with a strong constitution to resist such conditions. I was small, physically weak, unused to hardship—how long, I wondered, would I be able to last?

Eight days after our arrival, I and a dozen other men were sent to Camp Nouveau, 14 miles inland. To our utter amazement, we were shown the path and left alone to walk unescorted through the jungle!

On the trail we encountered a group of half-naked men carrying axes. Seeing we were new, they stopped for a moment. They had finished their set task of felling lumber and told us they were going back to camp for their nets. Then they would go into the forest again and catch butterflies whose wings, sold to curio dealers in Cayenne, brought in a small amount of money.

AT CAMP NOUVEAU, a thatch-covered barracks set in a clearing, the bookkeeper registered our names and numbers and then indicated our bunks—which were hard, bare boards. At dawn I was assigned to the workshop where wide straw hats are made. With a pile of *awara* palm fiber I had to plait a braid 20 yards long each day. I usually started work before daylight and had my task finished by 10 o'clock. Then I went into the jungle where I could think things out.

At Camp Nouveau many convicts had vainly tried to escape through the Dutch colony across the Maroni River. I learned from them all the details of the route and promised myself that I too would escape, though all of them tried to convince me that it was sheer folly to attempt it.

Nevertheless, when presently I made friends with a young convict who was also anxious to escape, we agreed to pool the little money he had with my information and try together. Slipping out of camp, we boarded a raft we had secreted on the creek and let it drift down the current. We had half a dozen lumps of hard bread, some tins of sardines and condensed milk, and a bottle filled with matches, collected one at a time.

When night came, we were afraid to make a fire for fear of pursuit. Mosquitoes buzzed about us by the thousands, and our faces became swollen from the maddening bites.

After many hours of struggle with the treacherous currents of the Maroni, we succeeded in reaching the Dutch bank, a few hundred yards below Albina. Then, fumbling around for a trail through the jungle, we foolishly came out into a clearing where a group of Carib Indians were at work. They immediately started toward us, brandishing shotguns and machetes.

We gave them the little money we had, hoping to buy them off, but they held their guns on us and, intent on collecting the reward for escaped prisoners, took us to the Dutch authorities. The next day a launch transported us back to French territory, where we were both locked in the blockhouse.

There are four disciplinary blockhouses at St.-Laurent, usually containing about 250 convicts. Of the 40 men in my blockhouse the majority were in for *évasion* ("escape") and had been brought back from British or Dutch Guiana. They had sold all they possessed for tobacco, and not one of them had any clothes. A few had a piece of rag wrapped around their loins. The heat was stifling, for the only air entered through six heavily barred small openings about 12 feet above the floor. At night we slept with our heads to the wall and one ankle in an iron lock. The irons clanked and rattled incessantly.

The temper of these men is terrible. Without occupation, with no money for tobacco or extra food, and crazed by the unbearable stench and heat, their misery is abject. When a newcomer comes in and they discover he has money, if he is weak, he is soon plundered. If he complains, he is apt to be murdered.

The penalty for *évasion* is usually solitary confinement for periods ranging from six months to five years. However, since it was my first attempt, I was given only 60 days. After serving my time, I was sent back to Camp Nouveau, under guard, and put to work in the jungle clearings where they were trying to grow vegetables. The first day I was terribly bitten by huge black ants, and the next morning I was so swollen and feverish that I reported sick.

The doctor refused to send me to the infirmary, and I, for my part, refused to go out to work. For this insubordination I was sentenced to 65 days in the cells—where I was most certainly better off than at work in the clearings, even though I was kept in irons and put on dry bread for two days out of three.

When I was finally released from the cells, I was transferred to the infirmary at St.-Laurent as an attendant. Here, for the first time, I had an opportunity to acquire a *débrouille*—the chance to earn some money, which is coveted by all convicts. There was a chestnut tree near the infirmary, and I began a trade in chestnuts, which I roasted on a piece of tin and sold at two sous for 20.

Every prisoner who can arrange it has his *débrouille*, his graft. One sells coffee, at four sous, made from leftovers from the kitchen. A second nightly spreads a blanket for *la marseillaise*, a form of baccarat, and takes one-tenth of the winnings. A third has a box of candy on the blanket, and the players drop two sous into it and munch a piece while they sit absorbed in the gambling. The barracks-keeper economizes on the main lamp and sells the surplus oil to the convicts for their own lamps. The hospital attendant weakens the milk diet prescribed for the dying (made by mixing water and condensed milk) and sells the extra tins of condensed milk. It is his *débrouille*.

Little by little my capital increased, and when I had got together a sufficiency of clothes, I again planned to escape. For always existence in the prison colony holds but two alternatives: escape or die. This time, I told myself, I would not fail!

The night before Christmas, when the guards were already beginning to celebrate noisily, nine of us, sworn to the last man to gain liberty or die, slunk through the silent jungle to the creek where a canoe had been hidden. We quickly pushed off downstream.

The canoe was 30 feet long, with a sail fashioned from old trousers and hammocks. It was stocked with a supply of coffee, rice, tapioca, condensed milk, dried beef, and bananas. Our water tank was a privy barrel we had submerged in the creek for several days to remove its odor—after burning it out with fire and tar.

We reached the Maroni and three hours later had traveled the 13 miles down to the Atlantic. There we set the sail and were soon out upon the open sea. Suddenly, we heard a sound like thunder. We were approaching the breakers!

Marseillais shook Basque, who had claimed to be a navigator, and shouted excitedly: "We're in danger, Basque! I don't know a thing about a boat. Take the steersman's paddle!"

Basque sat up. He began moaning and begged us to forgive him. He knew nothing about sailing, he confessed; he'd posed as a navigator just to get us to take him with us. He had hardly ended his excuses when without warning a huge roller crashed in on us from both sides. As a second roller and then a third struck us, the mast snapped and the sail fell down on us as we bailed for our lives.

When, by a miracle, we were able to steer the canoe to shore, our water supply was ruined. We had lost practically all our food. And hardly nine hours had gone by since we had left the camp.

No sooner had he set foot on the sand than Marseillais said to Basque: "Get going before it's too late," and he took his long knife out of his waistband.

I think the rest of us would have pardoned Basque and allowed him to stay with us, but we hung dejectedly in a circle and said nothing. Basque looked hard at the threatening knife and then without a word walked slowly away with hanging head into the jungle.

Without comment, we turned to our own problems. Obviously, we could not now continue by sea. Practically all our supplies had been washed away. We agreed to rest until the next day and then set out for Paramaribo through the jungle.

Next morning Basque returned to our camp, crying: "Everything is flooded, I can't get through!"

In Marseillais' look I recognized Basque's death sentence. Then, with a curse, Marseillais leaped and struck. There was a piercing scream, and Basque sank to the ground. Marseillais dragged the body to the water, where the tide would claim it.

After three days of tramping through miles of mud and tangles of

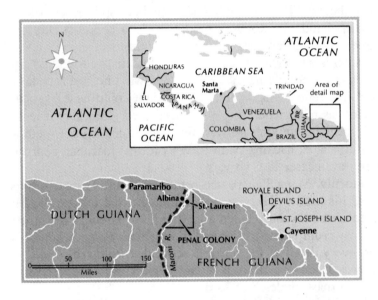

mangrove roots, we decided to get back to French Guiana as quickly as possible. Our food was almost exhausted, but we knew that our strength would last until we reached the Maroni River. There we planned to spend several months catching butterflies and thus get money for supplies for another escape. We had friends in the various camps, on whom we thought we might depend to help us hide out.

Progress became easier now, for we emerged into higher ground. Big Marcel and Marseillais were in the lead, slashing a trail with machetes. I followed with three others, and a short distance behind us were Gypsy and Robert.

Gypsy had a wooden leg, and this slowed him considerably; he fell often on the rocks and had difficulty bending low to avoid the vines. Robert and Gypsy had long been companions in the camp, and they walked in the rear and helped each other when the need arose.

At the end of the second day, famished and tired, we made camp. Soon Gypsy came out of the trail and joined us. He was alone.

"Where's Robert?" Marseillais asked him.

Gypsy said that Robert had lagged behind because he was sick. He'd be along presently.

An hour went by. Robert still did not come.

So Marseillais decided to go and look for him. He traced back almost a mile. As he was about to give up and turn back, he discovered Robert's still-warm body concealed under hastily cut branches beside the trail. The back of his skull had been split by a terrific blow. Close at hand lay Robert's food bag. It was empty. Gypsy had murdered his little friend for a few mouthfuls of tapioca and milk!

Marseillais returned to camp and told us he had found no trace of Robert. But secretly he told Big Marcel what he had found. Gypsy asked innocently what Marseillais thought could have happened.

"He was my friend!" Gypsy almost cried. "My *good* friend!"

Marseillais wouldn't answer him. He busied himself getting the camp in shape, hacking palm leaves with his machete, approaching nearer and nearer to Gypsy.

Suddenly, Marseillais passed behind him, and Gypsy, suspicious, turned his head to keep an eye on him. At that instant Big Marcel leaped on him—and planted a long knife squarely in his heart!

Gypsy crumpled to the ground. I remember even now, many years later, every detail of the horrible scene that followed.

It was Dédé, the brother of Big Marcel, who proposed it. "We ought to roast his leg," he said.

Marseillais agreed. "He was but a beast—and beasts can be eaten!" The others approved. Half an hour later Gypsy's liver, skewered on a stick, was grilling over the fire—which, ironically enough, had been kindled with Gypsy's wooden leg. And Marseillais chopped off Gypsy's good leg and placed it on the coals to broil.

Then they ate—and I ate too, since I dared not incur their dislike and become an outcast from the group.

That night there was no talk—not even the most cynical, I believe, could get away from the horrible events of the day. Three bodies lay now in the trail of our escape.

Two days later we reached an Indian village on the bank of the Maroni. Here we obtained food. But as we slept, after eating, the Indians reported us to the Dutch authorities. Soon four Dutch soldiers took us by surprise, pistols in hand.

Again I served time in the blockhouse, and then, classed as an incorrigible—or "inco"—was sent to Camp Charvein, where malaria and dysentery raged and where the other incos, toiling absolutely naked under clouds of mosquitoes, were little better than maddened animals. Fortunately, however, after 80 tormented days I was restored again to the normal life of the colony by a new director of the administration to whom I had sent a petition.

During subsequent years in French Guiana I attempted twice more, unsuccessfully, to escape. As punishment I was sent to Royale, one of three islands 10 miles off the mainland. (The other two are St. Joseph and Devil's Island—the latter, made famous by Alfred Dreyfus and other political prisoners, being usually confused by the general public with the entire prison colony.)

I served time in *La Case Rouge* on Royale, the Bloodstained Barrack, where the most vicious convicts in the entire prison colony were assigned. Each morning the guards take a look in the privy to make sure that a body is not sprawled there. It has happened hundreds of times—murder for vengeance or for robbery.

No outsiders are ever allowed on these islands, and very few people have visited them for other than official reasons. I suffered there beyond the power of telling. But I kept on living while all about me blood flowed and men died.

I spent time on the island of St. Joseph in solitary confinement, entombed in a dark cell. The convicts call it *la guillotine sèche* ("the dry guillotine"). At the bottom of a sunless pit the prisoner stays 23 hours out of each 24. He has no work, nothing to read, nothing to write on—nothing to occupy himself with. The only sounds he hears are those of the sea breaking on the rocks and the screams of the demented. Here sane men are deliberately reduced to raving idiots in order to discredit their reports to the press or to high French authorities of the abuses in French Guiana.

In November 1927, after I had been in the penal colony almost six years, I was transferred to Cayenne for the first time. I had now become an established convict, familiar with the ways of the prison colony. I had also come to understand the underhanded workings of the administration. I had seen convicts buy favored positions for 25 francs; I had seen unscrupulous officials sell the government clothes and blankets, so that the convicts had to wear rags for months; I had seen guards practice systematic and incredible rackets at the expense of the prisoners. And all this revolted me even more than did the vileness of the convicts, for it was a hideous advantage to take over helpless men who had no friends and no possible means of redress.

To see Cayenne is to see the depths of human degeneration. Although it is the main city of one of the oldest possessions under the French flag, it is the capital of a colony without colonists.

Back in the reign of Napoleon the Third, when the penal colony was planted, it was thought that if the convicts were made to stay on after completing their sentences, they would marry and have children, and the colony would thus become settled by hard, strong men. For this reason, the accessory penalty of *doublage* ("doubling") was resorted to. A freed convict had to serve as a *libéré* a period of exile equal to his original sentence.

But nobody wanted to have anything to do with the freed convicts. The black women would not marry them. The colony's bad name discouraged enterprising citizens in France. And so, since the days when the penal system was established, the possession has gradually dwindled into a place where lawlessness, degeneration, poverty, and misery surpass that of any other colony in the world.

French Guiana is the camping ground of futility. The only development is the penal system. And the adjacent prospering colonies of Dutch and British Guiana struggle to keep the wave of penniless convict would-be colonizers out of their boundaries.

France has long realized that the plan is a failure: Each new governor tries to develop something or other; one tries coffee, another cattle, another cocoa. But there is no element of population to sustain such efforts, and all fail completely.

The population of the capital is about 11,000, including 700 convicts and 300 *libérés*. An astonishing amount of freedom is permitted here, and convicts overrun the town by day, returning at night to be locked in the penitentiary.

WHILE I WAS ON THE ISLANDS, I had written an account of actual conditions there and secretly sent the manuscript to the new administrator of the penal colony, Governor Siadous. This interested the governor in me, and when I was transferred to Cayenne, he gave me the special task of placing the archives of the colony in order.

So for months I worked among stacks of papers, books, articles, reports on convicts, accounts of the administration, lists of food supplies, clothing materials. I took notes lavishly. Thus I got the knowledge and documentation, the facts and figures, that have enabled me since to expose irrefutably the corruptness of that hell.

I admired Governor Siadous very much. In his two years in office

146

he tried everything to better conditions. But he had no support from the corrupt penal administration. He was all that stood between me and the administration, and when he left the colony, I was sent back to Royale and spent the last three years of my stay in Guiana in solitary confinement. The many months of long-drawn-out loneliness closed in on me as I marked each day on the wall with my fingernail. And then, on November 3, 1934, nearly 15 years after I had been sent to Guiana, a key turned in the rusty lock, and a guard handed me a document—which I could scarcely read, my eyes were so dimmed by my dark cell. I was a *libéré*—a free convict!

A *free* convict! Free to live like a homeless mongrel dog. Free to live in the jungle but condemned to the colony for the rest of my life and barred from Cayenne for 10 years.

I adopted the only trade by which a *libéré* can keep in funds. Living in a jungle hut, I caught butterflies, I made odds and ends and toys out of rubber that I collected in the forest, and these I sold to the curio dealers of the town. I managed to have a parrot to roast for Christmas—shot with a bow and arrow. I celebrated New Year's Eve over a boiled armadillo, dug out of its hole with a broken pickax salvaged from an old dump. I had no teeth left, but that did not bother me, for I rarely had anything that needed chewing.

Money! Money was what I needed—to buy an escape from this living hell. A hundred francs would buy an Indian canoe. Fifty francs would buy food for two weeks at sea.

One day as I was thus brooding in St.-Laurent, a sun-helmeted tourist beckoned to me.

"Where can I find a prisoner who speaks English?" he asked in schoolboy French.

"I speak a little English," I said.

"I want to find a prisoner named Belbenoit," he said in English. "The man about whom Blair Niles wrote her book, *Condemned to Devil's Island.*" (I had at one time sold her several manuscripts, when she had visited French Guiana, on which she had based a novel.)

I laughed for the first time in years. "I am Belbenoit!"

He explained that he was an executive of an American motion-picture company. They planned a film story about Devil's Island—one that would feature a dramatic escape. He had flown down to study the colony at first hand. Would I give him information? If a prisoner tried to escape, how would he do it?

I spent the whole night answering his questions, making rough drawings of prison cells and punishment racks, describing my three attempts to escape through the jungle, answering every question while he took a bookful of notes. By dawn he had enough. The airplane in which he had arrived soon was but a speck in the Caribbean sky. But in my hands he had left $200! The money to escape!

"This time I'll make it!" I whispered.

I searched the penal colony like a hawk—for men whose plight was most terrible and whose physical aid would be greatest. At last I selected five convicts (one a sailor).

At 6 o'clock on the night of March 2, 1935, we met stealthily and noiselessly made our way to Serpent Creek, where a Chinaman had promised to hide a boat for us. It proved to be only half the size of the craft I had bargained for—a dugout canoe barely three feet wide. The provisions contained less than half of the things agreed upon before I had passed my cash to the Chinaman. I felt as though my escape had failed before it had begun.

But something told me not to turn back. I got into the canoe, urged the others to take their places, and soon we were paddling noiselessly down the river. At the mouth we hoisted our patchwork sail. Chifflot, our navigator, took the homemade tiller. The long slender canoe began to dance over the water.

Men in their right senses would never have gone out in such a craft—but we were driven by a quite insane desire to seek freedom at any price. The night passed all too slowly. Morning found us far out at sea, unpursued.

I lighted some charcoal in a kerosene tin, and strong tea soon revived us. I would have to stretch out the Chinaman's skimpy food supply very thin. But no one, during the first day, grumbled. We all talked with nervous gaiety.

The third night found us not such good friends. The sun and glare of the open sea and the soaking of the salt spray made us miserable. Cramped for 50 long hours against each other, we had talked ourselves out of hopefulness—and then everyone began to find fault. A turbulent sea arose, and we had all we could do to keep from being swamped. We did not even attempt to keep a course. A mighty wave washed the compass from my hands, and not a star was to be seen.

When at last dawn came, we were drenched, stiff, hungry, thirsty, and sick at heart. I dipped some water out of the keg—and discovered that salt water had got in. I mixed it with condensed milk, but my companions said it tasted terrible.

"We'd better try to reach the mainland!" Dadar said. "I'd rather take a chance on the jungle—there's at least plenty of water to drink!"

"We've only been gone three days!" I said. "I told you when we started that I would not turn back. If we reach Trinidad, we are safe. If we land anywhere on the mainland, we will be turned over to a French consul." Thus we quarreled all day long, and the following days and nights were nightmares.

"Blast it!" Bébert in the bow of the canoe snarled. "Change the course! I've had enough of this. I'm going to land on the coast and take my chance!"

"Stop!" I yelled at Dadar who had begun crawling toward the sail

sheet. I reached into my shirt and drew out a small pistol I had obtained for just such a desperate crisis. I am a very little man. I should have been no match for any of my companions in physical strength. But I had made up my mind to turn neither to right nor left. The five big men glowered at me.

"Rush me if you like," I said. "Here are six bullets—and I will kill each one of you if you insist."

"Put the sail over!" Bébert shouted to Chifflot. At the same instant Dadar sprang up and tried to snatch my gun. Before I could fire, Dadar had slipped and fallen against Chifflot, and both of them tumbled against the gunwale.

"Look over there!" Casquette yelled suddenly. "It's land!"

The others stood up and looked, but, thinking it was a trick to get me off guard, I didn't budge. They couldn't fool me that easily.

"It's Trinidad! Come, Belbenoit, and see for yourself!" Cautiously, I tried to get a clear view without risking a sudden onslaught. And as we crested a whitecap, I saw that they were not trying to outwit me. There, against the horizon, were high, green mountains.

The sight wiped out all animosity. We all shouted joyously.

A few hours later, after 14 days at sea, the canoe shot up on the glistening white beach. My companions tried to leap ashore, but they were so weak that they stumbled and sprawled on the sand.

In a thatched hut nearby we found a big kettle full of rice and salt fish. We dug our hands into it and ate like wolves, then rolled over and fell into an exhausted sleep.

When we awoke we made our way to a little hamlet. The authorities listened with sympathy to our story—the British hate French Guiana as a blot on civilization. They fed us well, allowed us to rest, and presented us with a new boat. A recent Trinidad law allows all fugitives from French Guiana 24 days on the island and a means of continuing their escape.

On June 10 a British Navy launch towed our boat, amply supplied with food, out to sea. Then we were cut loose and on our way. Ahead lay the other islands of the British West Indies—stepping-stones to freedom as we headed northward for Miami.

As one day followed another, we seemed to be making good headway, but saw no land at all. Six days finally passed before we admitted we were lost.

Sixteen days after leaving Trinidad, the sea threw us up on a long barren stretch of coast, shooting us with express-train speed through the rough surf. Before we could make any effort to save ourselves, we crashed on the beach, completely wrecking our boat. We rescued only our remaining food and personal effects.

We built a fire on the beach and prepared dinner. Before we had time to eat it, a group of Indians—naked, but armed with bows and arrows and spears—came up and began inspecting our rescued supplies. When we tried to stop them, they became menacing, and at last they took everything we had, even our clothing. One of them got hold of an oilcloth package containing my Devil's Island journals, written during 15 years of imprisonment. I grabbed the package and opened it hastily to show him that it contained only papers. He gave it back to me with a humorous grimace.

The Indians disappeared behind the dunes. They were, I found out later, the Cactus Eaters, savages of the coastal desert of Colombia.

So, all of us naked and armed with only a machete that we salvaged after the Indians left, we started over the hot sand.

For four days we saw no human being as we skirted the jungle shore. We caught some fish and frogs by spearing them with sharply pointed sticks. We made a fire by rubbing dried sticks for more than an hour and carried coals in a large seashell to start new ones. We were all covered with festering insect bites. Our feet were cut and very sore. But happily we had not, as I feared, started to quarrel. Naked, we kept together out of pure fright.

At sunset of the third day we came to a long grass hut, in front of which some very old nets were drying. The fishermen were away, but we saw a large sea turtle and cooked and ate chunks of the fat meat and then climbed up into the rafters eagerly hoping to find clothes. There was not a single pair of pants or a shirt—only seven old Mother Hubbards of cheap printed calico.

"Well, a dress is better than nothing!" Bébert said as he began to twist into one.

Soon we all wore petticoats. Clothed, we found that the insects bothered us less.

Next day, however, we were discovered by a squad of Colombian soldiers. With our bearded faces, we were an astounding sight.

"We must take them to show the general," the soldiers exclaimed. "Nothing so funny has happened in years."

In an hour we reached a little town—the Colombian coast town of Santa Marta—and were taken to the barracks. The general gave us clothes, food, and medicine, but he also notified the French consul.

The next day we were behind the bars of the high-walled military prison—waiting for a French boat to take us back to Guiana. Our desperate gamble had been lost!

Under this terrible disppointment my companions began bitterly to find fault with one another, and soon a bloody fight broke out. The noise of our combat brought guards. Mysteriously, I was picked out and locked up in a solitary cell. Then, and this is hard to believe unless you know the South Americans, the prison adjutant came to my cell with some paper and pencils and said: "Belbenoit, we are going to let you escape. Your friends are a different type of fugitive; they were convicted for far more serious crimes. We've checked up on you. Spend the day writing articles for *La Prensa*. The editor will pay you for them tomorrow afternoon. At night you will find your cell door open. Bon voyage!"

All day long I wrote about different phases of the French penal administration. In the late afternoon Don Paez Reyna, the editor, came into my cell. He read what I had written and handed me a roll of bills. Some hours later I went to the door and cautiously turned the knob—the door opened. And at the end of the building I found the outside gate ajar.

Later I learned that my companions were shipped back to the dry guillotine. Of all the men who escaped with me, I alone was free!

Mind often wins over matter. I know that only one thing brought me through the terrible days that followed. It was not my muscles, for I am very weak. It was not my knowledge of the jungle or of the sea, for I had none. It was not my experience in dealing with primitive natives, for the hostile tribes I met in the coastal wilds of Colombia were as strange to me as they would have been to you. The one thing that brought me through was just this: I kept repeating over and over, "I *will* reach the United States."

When my supplies were exhausted, I obtained food from the Indians by telling them that I would pay two pesos each for butterflies—and then sneaked out of their villages at midnight to steal a canoe in which to continue up the coast. I repeated this technique a dozen times and stole as many canoes. Food hardly mattered to me anymore. My days of struggle at sea hardly mattered. Nothing mattered en route, if only I was making progress toward the United States.

In the jungles of Panama I spent several months with a friendly tribe of Indians and snared a large collection of butterflies that I later sold to a curio shop in Panama City. With this stake, and always eluding passport and identification inspection, I worked my way up through Costa Rica, Nicaragua, Honduras, and into El Salvador.

There, at the little port of La Libertad, I found a freighter loading cargo. It was northward bound, I was told. I managed to go aboard unobserved and crawled through a trapdoor into a dark room packed with coils of hawsers and wire cables. There I lay until the ship's engines started turning.

I SPENT HOUR AFTER HOUR in the black hold until I thought at least two days must have passed. The little food I had with me was finished. I was very thirsty. I decided to go on deck, if it were night, and look for food and water. I climbed the ladder and raised the trapdoor. It *was* night. Only two yards in front of me was a big dish of food—left for a dog. Beside it was a tin pan of water. The dog was playing with a ball far down the deck. I crept out, drank the water, and took the food back to my hideout.

I did not know how many days went by, for I lived in complete darkness. Twice I was hungry enough to sneak up to the deck and steal the dog's food and water. Then I heard the ship's whistle blow. We were arriving somewhere. I pushed up the trapdoor and climbed out into broad daylight. We were alongside a dock, in what I thought must be some Mexican port. At the foot of the gangplank two men in uniform were stopping each sailor who left the ship. I noticed that they only frisked the sailors. They didn't ask for identification papers.

I decided to risk everything on one lone play. An officer was going ashore; I hurried along the deck and went down the ship's gangplank behind him. The uniformed men greeted the officer cordially—in English! I opened my only possession, the bundle of manuscript, as a signal for them to search me. One of them mechanically felt my pockets and motioned me to pass on. I walked ashore.

From some laborers I learned that I was in California and that it was Tuesday. I had been in the hawser room seven days and nights.

I walked on with a springing step. I was terribly emaciated. I had no teeth. I had one pair of cotton pants. One cotton shirt. One hand-made cotton coat. A pair of ragged shoes. That was all I possessed. But I was no longer afraid. For after 22 months of almost unbelievable trials, I had escaped from the hell of French Guiana to the safety of the United States.

I entered the outskirts of Los Angeles as happy as a lark.

René Belbenoit remained in the United States on a temporary visa until 1941, when he was deported to Central America as an illegal immigrant. Determined to live in the United States, Belbenoit headed north again, swam the Rio Grande, and then reentered the country near Brownsville, Texas. He was finally, after years of legal battles, granted U.S. citizenship in 1956.

Belbenoit married and had a son. He became the owner of a clothing store in Lucerne Valley, California. He died from a heart attack on February 26, 1959, at the age of 59.

Belbenoit was born in Paris, France, and from the age of 12 he lived without parental guidance, holding such jobs as errand boy, dishwasher, valet. Convicted of stealing pearls from an employer, he was sentenced to hard labor in the prisons of French Guiana.

Belbenoit's Dry Guillotine, *published in 1938, was a best-seller and was translated into many languages. It and a subsequent book,* Hell on Trial, *are credited with playing a major role in bringing about the abolition of the French penal colony.*

The getaway was from a deserted Cuban beach under cover of night. Seven humans crowded aboard a raft made from inflated tire tubes. Their destination was the United States, many ocean miles away.

Escape From Cuba

By Joseph P. Blank

THE STORM came to an end during the darkness of early morning. Antonio Vigo Cancio was afraid to guess how far the wild north wind might have blown them back toward Cuba. It was the sixth day of their attempted escape from the Castro regime, and their raft of six patched inner tubes, roped together, was looking flimsier than ever. Then, at dawn, came the appalling sight: In the distance the seven refugees detected the faint outline of the mountaintops of Cuba, perhaps 20 miles away.

Antonio tried his best to think. Nothing was left of their rations but a half-dozen portions of water and two small cans of condensed milk. Should they go back to Cuba, land at night, try to find water, and set out again? Should they chance being caught and clapped in prison? He decided against it. Veneranda, his wife, holding their baby, read the decision in Antonio's eyes.

"You men pick up those paddles," she said. "Let's get going."

Early in the Cuban revolution, Antonio had hoped that Castro

meant democracy. By 1960 he knew that Cuba had only exchanged one dictatorship for another. He became involved in a conspiracy to overthrow the government. Caught with explosives in his possession, he was sentenced to 30 years in prison. After two attempted escapes had cost him months in solitary confinement, he decided to become a model prisoner in the hope of earning a reduced sentence. In December 1969, after serving nine years, he was paroled.

On release, Antonio was ordered to a job as a truck driver with a federal agency that employed ex-prisoners and closely observed their behavior. After working 25 days, living in a barracks with other parolees, he was permitted to spend five days with his family.

"We can't live like this, always watched," he said to Veneranda. "We have no future here. We must leave." Veneranda agreed.

As a former political prisoner, Antonio wasn't eligible for the daily refugee airlift that went to Miami. The only alternative was an illegal trip across the Straits of Florida. Antonio began to consider the problem. He decided against attempting to steal or build a seagoing craft. That way he risked arrest before he even touched water. He had to find another way.

In April 1971, after parking his truck in his agency's garage one day, Antonio found himself staring at a big inner tube from a truck tire. *That* was it—a raft composed of inner tubes tied together and enclosed in a sheath stitched from burlap bags. A special advantage: The deflated tubes could be folded and hidden in a small space.

During the next few months Antonio stole six inner tubes from the garage. Two were in fair condition; the others had to be patched. Then he found four hardwood boards and shaped them into paddles with a machete. His wife collected food and burlap bags.

On August 17 Antonio and Veneranda assembled the raft while their two sons, 11-year-old Tony and 10-month-old Carlitos, looked on. Inflating the tubes by mouth took them an hour, and they felt as if their lungs were bursting. Antonio lashed the tubes into a six-by-nine-foot raft. After slipping the raft into the sheath of burlap sacks that Veneranda had stitched together, the couple bounced on the tubes to test the patches under pressure. Everything held.

A few days later Antonio began his monthly five-day leave. Checking the weather forecasts, he learned that no storms were expected along the northern coast of Cuba during the coming week. He estimated that it would take four to five days to reach the shipping lanes off Florida, where he hoped to be picked up by a passing cargo vessel or fishing boat.

He had his crew: Luis, his wife's brother; Silvio, her cousin; Julio, a friend of the family. He had a compass: a toylike giveaway that had come with a bottle of vermouth. Everything was ready.

On the afternoon of departure, young Tony asked his mother, who had been silent for hours, *"Mima,* are you thinking of the trip?" When she nodded, he said, "Well, only three things can happen. We'll get caught, which is the worst thing. Or we'll die, but we'll die as a family. Or we'll arrive safely, which will mean happiness."

She hugged him.

Shortly before 7 that evening a friend arrived in a truck. Antonio loaded it at a casual pace to avoid attracting attention, and the family climbed aboard. After picking up Luis, Silvio, and Julio, they drove to the launching site, a narrow, uninhabited stretch of sand called Hollywood Beach, about 25 miles east of Havana.

Silently, the men carried the equipment and supplies to the water's edge, then began blowing up the tubes. When, at last, the group climbed aboard, the raft sank lower in the water than Antonio had anticipated. As the men started paddling toward Key West, 90 miles to the north, everyone on the raft soon became wet to the waist.

Antonio had no charts, no open-sea experience. By day, he intended to navigate by compass; at night, by the North Star.

The four men, sitting cross-legged or with their legs dangling in the water, paddled rhythmically for six hours. Then Silvio and young Tony got violently seasick, and Julio's arms gave out. After 24 hours Antonio remained the only consistent paddler.

The refugees were now developing painful sores on their hips, thighs, and legs. The men suffered from continual friction with the burlap as they paddled, and Veneranda from her writhing, restless 28-pound baby. Her arms felt almost dead from trying to control and provide shade for the seemingly tireless infant.

At about noon on the third day a freighter hove into sight several miles away. "We're saved!" Silvio shouted.

"Wait!" Antonio ordered. "Get under the mosquito netting."

The raft's supplies included blue-tinted netting for camouflage, and now, as they floated haphazardly, Antonio stared hard at the freighter. When it plowed a few hundred yards closer, he spotted the red and white funnels that identified it as a Soviet vessel. For a long quarter hour the group cowered silently beneath the netting while the freighter slowly disappeared in the distance.

Later that night Antonio found that food and water were being consumed faster than expected, and he began rationing for all hands except the baby, Carlitos. He also discovered, to his dismay, that salt water had killed the flashlight batteries and ruinously corroded the mirror that he'd brought for flashing signals.

On the afternoon of the fifth day the sky darkened, and a brisk north wind began stirring up whitecaps. It was the kind of wind Antonio had secretly dreaded from the outset; the raft was now being inexorably blown back toward Cuba. The waves deepened, lightning flashed, and rain slashed down, ruining the remaining bread and sugar. Hour after hour the little group merely clung to the raft. And then, with the arrival of dawn, came the disheartening sight of the Cuban mountaintops.

Shortly after the decision against returning to the island for water was made, a good south wind sprang up to push the raft away from Cuba. The men paddled, rested, and paddled again. By the end of the day the rationed water for the adults was finished, though a little remained for the baby. Luis was shaking with fever.

With the next dawn came a cloudless blue sky, and soon the sun blazed down on them. They reached into the water for seaweed and chewed on the buds. Sometimes, in a tangled mass of seaweed, they found tiny, half-inch crustaceans, which they popped into their mouths, chewed once, and swallowed.

Antonio tried to conceal his anxiety about his wife. Her bloodshot eyes were sunken, her lips deeply cracked, her blouse virtually torn off her back by the baby's frenzied clawing as he screamed from thirst. The salt water had irritated the infant's skin, and he scratched himself until the blood ran.

Then, on the ninth day, there was a fearful change. Now the baby lay mercifully quiet—too quiet. Periodically, Veneranda shook him, or Antonio reached over to play with his hand. The infant would open his eyes, gaze vacantly for a moment, then return to sleep.

Except for Antonio, the crew was apathetic—thirst and weakness were destroying them. But Antonio firmly believed they were nearing their destination. Aircraft frequently passed across the sky six or eight miles to the east, and each time he pleadingly waved his paddle with a diaper tied to it.

Early on the 11th day Antonio was alerted by a change in the air. He smelled sweet water—somewhere to the east it was raining, and the wind was blowing rain clouds in their direction.

"It's going to rain!" he shouted exultantly. "Luis, you and Julio grab a plastic bag and catch water! When the rain starts, everybody turn your face up and catch water in your mouth."

Rain drenched them for about 10 minutes. No one spoke. Each was savoring the delicious luxury of fresh water. After the clouds passed, Veneranda filled an eight-ounce bottle for the baby and let him drink half of it. He screamed for more, but his mother set aside the remainder, knowing it should be reserved for the end of the day.

Although Antonio insisted that they had to be approaching the end of their terrible passage, the other men couldn't share his optimism. They had depended on his judgment for freedom. Now, in their shattered mental state, they blamed him for their despair.

During the night a rainless storm tossed the raft. Fearful of losing a passenger overboard, Antonio shouted, "Everybody awake! Use your paddle. Sit up straight." Then, around 4 A.M., the wind died, the waves grew shallow, and stars twinkled. Not too far away Antonio saw moving lights.

"That's a boat!" he cried. More lights peeped out of the night. "Boats! We're going to be saved! Everybody paddle!" The four men screamed for help, but their pleas went unheard.

"It doesn't matter," Antonio reassured them. "There are many boats out there. As soon as day comes, they'll see us."

The men somehow found strength and, as they paddled, suddenly out of the dark-gray dawn, about 200 yards away, loomed the gigantic shape of an oil tanker, the *Key Trader,* from Wilmington, Delaware. It moved slowly toward the refugees as Antonio shouted and waved a diaper. Then, with bells suddenly clanging and red lights flashing, the tanker came to a halt.

Antonio and Silvio paddled the raft to within 20 yards of the ship. A voice from the deck shouted in English, "Who are you?"

"We are Cubans," Antonio replied. "We have escaped. We've been at sea for 12 days."

A rope dropped from the tanker's deck. Antonio grabbed it and pulled alongside. On the raft the others were chattering hoarsely, for the most part incoherently, and trying to embrace one another. In a few minutes a flexible ladder was lowered from the deck. Veneranda touched her husband and said, "The baby."

He picked up Carlitos and, incredibly, climbed the ladder with the infant clutched in one arm. At the gunwale a sailor took the baby from him. Antonio was helped to the deck, where he collapsed.

Veneranda watched her husband and baby disappear into the safety of the ship. In her numb, near-unconscious condition, she wasn't capable of feeling joy or triumph. "We've gotten through," she murmured to herself. "We are there."

*The order of execution had been given. A grave large enough
to hold 18 bodies had been dug. It seemed that only a
miracle could save the Luxembourgers from sudden death—until the
Nazi corporal took matters into his own hands.*

The Doomed Prisoners

By Edwin Muller

FOR 15 YEARS CERTAIN people in the town of Differdange, Luxembourg, had been trying to find a certain German. They had a
score to settle with him.

They knew his name, Johann Punzel. They knew his serial number
in the German Army and the fact that he had been a member of the
Nazi Party. But until June 3, 1955, they had never caught up with him.

The thing that Punzel had done, the reason they were looking for
him, had happened in the spring of 1940. The war in Poland was
over, and the vast armies of Germany and the Western Allies faced
each other along the Maginot Line; Differdange lay between them.
But Luxembourg was neutral, and the townsmen of Differdange
hoped the German invasion would never take place.

Then at dawn on May 10, they were awakened by the roar of
planes. When they looked up, the sky was full of parachutes. The
Germans had come. Soon the French came too. Columns of their
cavalry rode out from the Maginot Line and occupied the town.

By the time the first shots were fired, the roads from Differdange
were jammed with fugitives. The HADIR steelworks, which employed 4,000 of the town's 15,000 inhabitants, closed down. But one
group of employees was called together: the 40-odd steelworkers who
doubled as a fire brigade. They were free to go, the plant manager
said, but shells might hit the plant and start fires. It was to the advantage of the company and the town that the property be preserved. He
called for volunteers to stay behind.

There was a moment of silence. Then Joseph Weiler, 50, a plant
foreman and chief of the brigade, stepped forward.

"I will stay," he said.

161

Fourteen others volunteered, among them Nicolas Wallers, an ambulance man of the company infirmary. Wallers' wife insisted on staying too. Someone, she said, would have to prepare food for the men. Later three more men joined the group, bringing the total number to 18 men, 1 woman.

They settled down in the air-raid shelter under the main office building. Through the thick walls they could hear the terrifying rattle of machine-gun fire and the crunch of exploding shells. The battle lasted two full days. Then, on the night of May 11, the French pulled out and the German paratroopers came pouring in, followed by tanks and artillery.

At first the Germans treated the firemen in a not-unfriendly way. There was work for them to do: cleaning up debris, burying dead animals, even putting out a few fires that broke out in houses where careless soldiers were billeted.

Then, after two weeks, there was a sudden change. On May 27 and 28, Differdange was bombarded heavily by the French from the Maginot Line. The fire was extraordinarily accurate. With uncanny precision the shells found the German ammunition dumps and the areas where tanks and other heavy equipment were camouflaged. A great amount of damage was done.

Late on the night of the 29th a detail of military police went to the air-raid shelter and kicked the sleeping firemen awake. They searched everybody in the room, including Mrs. Wallers. With detection equipment they checked all wires and electrical outlets in the room, and they tested the walls with hammers. At last they went away, but guards were posted around the plant. The firemen could no longer move about freely.

At intervals the bombardment continued. Three days later the military police came again to the steelworks and ordered the firemen to assemble in the street. In a column of twos they were marched past a place where soldiers were digging a big hole. The same horrible thought occurred to more than one of the firemen: The hole was big enough to hold 18 bodies.

Farther on they were halted at a cement wall next to a small garage and lined up. A lieutenant appeared, a hard-faced man with a dueling scar on one cheek. He walked slowly down the line of men, staring each one in the face. Then he spoke:

"We have established that one or more of you have sent signals to the enemy, enabling them to direct their fire. If the guilty person or persons do not confess, all of you will be shot."

The group was then locked in a small room at the rear of a garage. It had only one barred window to admit any light. The place was cold and the concrete floor damp.

Mrs. Wallers clung to her husband, sobbing uncontrollably. Some of the men also began to weep openly; others were on their knees, saying their prayers.

Weiler spoke up in a firm voice: "Has anyone anything to say about the charge that has been made?"

Nobody did. But some began hysterically accusing others. Weiler's voice cut through the discord: "Pull yourselves together. We can get out of this only if we stick together and face the Germans like men."

The hubbub subsided. Time dragged on. At last the door opened and the lieutenant appeared. "Are the guilty ready to confess?"

Silence.

"Very well. That means that the order of execution will be carried out in precisely one hour."

The lieutenant beckoned to a corporal, a blond, blue-eyed man of some 30 years of age.

"Corporal Punzel, you will take over the custody of these men until their execution. When the hour has passed, they are to be brought out two at a time. Their grave has been dug."

The corporal saluted, and the door was closed.

JOHANN PUNZEL WAS BORN in 1910 in the Bavarian town of Pressig, where his parents had a delicatessen. In World War I his older brother was killed.

Then came the 1920's, when wild inflation nearly destroyed the middle class of Germany. The Punzel family went steadily downhill. In that decade the worst off were the youth of Germany. Their lives were frustrated and despairing—no way to earn a living, nowhere to go. The suicide rate rose.

Johann alternated between occasional jobs and helping with the dying delicatessen. In those days Hitler seemed to offer a ray of hope to youths like Johann, who joined the Nazi Party when he was 17. He saw and heard Adolf Hitler and was carried away by the glamour of that evil genius.

Presently he got a full-time clerical job at party branch headquarters in Pressig. At the time war came Johann was married to a pretty, dark-haired girl, and they had two babies. He was called into the army and did well. When his regiment, the 330th Infantry, marched into Differdange, he was a corporal.

PUNZEL STOOD outside the garage door, somewhat confused. An order was an order and must be carried out. But those people in there—and the woman he could hear sobbing. He decided to pass the buck. Leaving guards posted, he hurried off to find Lieutenant Kelch, the regimental adjutant.

Kelch was too busy to be bothered.

"The matter belongs in the judge advocate's office," he said. "Go and see them about the sentence."

Punzel returned to the prisoners, who surrounded him, clamoring their innocence. Joseph Weiler quieted them and told Punzel that the charge was without foundation, that none of them had had an opportunity to signal the French.

"You have searched the air-raid shelter," Weiler said. "Cannot further search be made?"

Punzel was impressed. And then it occurred to him that the lieutenant had spoken of carrying out the sentence against "these men." He had said nothing about the woman. He pulled Mrs. Wallers to her feet, led her outside, and found a Wehrmacht truck bound for Luxembourg City. He put her into it, and the truck drove away.

At the judge advocate's office Punzel asked the lieutenant in charge if the sentence could not be deferred until further search for evidence could be made. To his surprise, the officer said he would look into the matter and told him to come back in three quarters of an hour.

When Punzel returned, the answer was: "No. The sentence is to be carried out unless the guilty confess. But it has been decided to reprieve the prisoners for 24 hours. However, if the French bombardment is resumed, the prisoners are to be shot at once."

Punzel became more and more confused. By now he was completely convinced that the men were innocent, but he could think of no way to do anything to save them.

However, he could do some little things for their comfort. He moved the prisoners from the garage to a storeroom across the street, where the floor was dry, and he had food and hot coffee taken to them from a regimental canteen.

That night Punzel slept badly. He kept listening for the French bombardment—which would mean the immediate death of the prisoners. But they would die anyway the next afternoon.

Next morning he went again to see the prisoners. They had nothing to say except to plead for mercy. Presently, Punzel went to the judge advocate's office, not to see the lieutenant but to make sure he was away at lunch. Then the corporal went back to the storeroom, noting that there were no soldiers nearby except the guards, his own men. He had some words with them. They looked at him curiously.

Punzel went into the room and asked one of the prisoners if he could get a truck at the steelworks. The man said that he could. Punzel sent two of the guards with him.

When the truck arrived, Punzel went into the room and spoke hurriedly: "You are free, all of you. Get into the truck quickly."

At first there was only stunned silence, then a bedlam of laughing and sobbing. The men crowded around him and tried to shake his hand and give him their watches and money. He shook them off.

"Be quiet. Get into the truck and go."

Nicolas Kremer, the youngest of the firemen, asked for his name. He gave it and his serial number, 105275A. Then the truck drove off toward Luxembourg City.

Back in his quarters Punzel shook all over as if with a chill. Now the thing he had done seemed incredible. He was sure to be found out. Perhaps his own men would turn him in—though several of them had congratulated him. In any case, the firing squad would soon come and he would be done for.

But Punzel was lucky. Within an hour a general order came through: the 330th Infantry was to move up to the Maginot Line. In the commotion that followed, nobody thought to inquire about the firemen of Differdange.

Nobody ever did.

Punzel never disobeyed another order, and he ended the war as a second lieutenant. He went back to Pressig, to the dreary business of trying to make a living for himself and his family in a beaten and despairing country. He had another go at the family delicatessen. It failed. He had other jobs, but they didn't last long.

Then in 1946 he was notified that he was under investigation by a Military Government court because of his former party membership. After some thought, he wrote to the Management of Mines in Differdange, telling who he was and what he had done in the matter of the firemen. He never received an answer. But later he was notified by the court that he had been cleared.

The years went by.

THE FLEEING FIREMEN found refuge with their families or friends and went into hiding. After the Franco-German armistice of 1940 it seemed safe to return to Differdange. Some of the men went back to their old jobs in the steelworks, now under German management.

There was much speculation as to who had sent the signals to the French, but the truth was never established.

Joseph Weiler died of a heart attack. So did Mrs. Wallers. Young Nicolas Kremer rose in the world, went into politics after the war, and was elected to the Luxembourg Parliament. He was the one who concerned himself with finding Johann Punzel. But in the disorganization of beaten Germany, it proved impossible to trace a soldier through only his name and serial number.

Then Kremer heard of the letter Punzel had written to the Management of Mines. Kremer wrote to the Military Government, stating the facts of the case, but got no reply—though his letter later proved to have been helpful in getting the charge against Punzel dropped. But when he tried to locate Punzel through the Military Government, he got nowhere.

After many unsuccessful attempts over a period of years, Kremer at last tried writing to the police departments of various German cities. In the spring of 1955 the Nuremberg police sent him Punzel's address in Pressig.

Kremer wrote Punzel, inviting him to visit Differdange for a reunion with his former prisoners. Punzel, touched and incredulous at this surprising turn of events, replied that he would come.

Punzel and his wife arrived at Differdange on June 3, 1955, the 15th anniversary of the prisoners' release. The surviving firemen had contributed to an entertainment fund, as had the management of the steelworks.

For three weeks the Punzels lived in a happy daze. At a big party, the first of many, a huge meal was prepared, toasts were drunk, and a gold watch inscribed *"Als Dank Für Hilfe 3.6.1940"* ("In Thanks for Your Help") was presented to Punzel amid thunderous applause. There were automobile trips, more gifts, and invitations everywhere for lunch and dinner.

Punzel was received by the Luxembourg Minister of Justice, who, in the name of the government, thanked him for what he had done. One Sunday there was a special service in the principal church of Differdange. The pastor—who had spent three years in a concentration camp—preached a sermon of gratitude to Punzel, and the choir sang a special hymn in his honor. Punzel broke down and wept.

Allied prisoners of war contrived many fantastic and
audacious methods of escape during World War II.
This exciting account of the infamous Nazi prison camp
Stalag Luft III is a classic escape story.

Tunnel to Freedom

By Flight Lieutenant Paul Brickhill
Royal Australian Air Force
as told to Allan A. Michie

STALAG LUFT III, at Sagan, Germany, halfway between Berlin and
Breslau, held some 10,000 captured airmen in the spring of 1943.
Nearly all were from the British and Commonwealth air forces, al-
though Americans were beginning to arrive in numbers.

In April the camp was enlarged by the addition of the North Compound, and 700 of us were moved into it. Already, prisoners in the
working parties that helped build the compound had studied its lay-
out and paced off its distances—with tunnels in mind. Escape was the
one hope that had kept us going through the months of captivity.

A few of the officers had dug tunnels at other camps, and around
them we built "X," our escape organization. Head of "X" was Squadron Leader Roger Bushell, a tall South African who had been a lawyer in London, then a fighter pilot until shot down over Dunkirk.
Bushell had already made two remarkable escapes and once had got
almost to Switzerland before he was caught.

North Compound was a square, each side 1,000 feet long, enclosed
by two tall barbed-wire fences, parallel and five feet apart, the space
between crammed with barbed-wire coils. Ten yards inside this barrier was the warning wire; step across it and the guards shot. Numerous sentry towers, 15 feet high, each with searchlight and machine
gun, were manned 24 hours a day. Twenty-five yards outside the
wire on all four sides were dense pine woods, which cut off any view
of the outside world—but which would also cover an escape.

As soon as we moved in, notices were posted asking for volunteers
to play cricket and softball. The notices were signed "Big X." Everybody knew what that meant, and 500 signed up for the tunnel work.
It was decided to start three long tunnels, "Tom," "Dick," and

Block 104

Trapdoor to tunnel shaft concealed under heating stove

30-foot-deep shaft

Air-pump room for air-conditioning Harry

Shop for preparing timbers to shore tunnel

"Harry," in the hope that one would get by undetected. We never used the word "tunnels"; too many guards understood English.

Tom was to be dug from Block 123 to the wire, 150 feet away, and then on to the shelter of the woods. Dick was to be dug from Block 122 toward Tom, so that it could either be joined with Tom's shaft or be dug all the way to the woods. Harry was to begin from Block 104 and drive to the woods on the north.

Of course, the tunnels would have to start from within our huts. Each hut was 100 feet long, with sleeping quarters, washroom, and small kitchen. The Germans had built these huts about a foot off the ground, so that the guards could look underneath to see if we were up to any funny business. There were usually several of these "ferrets" around, easily spotted by the blue overalls they wore. With torches

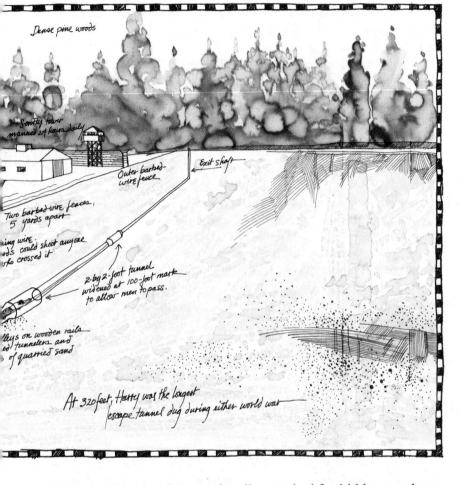

Dense pine woods

Sentry tower manned 24 hours daily

Outer barbed-wire fence

← Exit shaft

Two barbed-wire fences, 5 yards apart

...ing wire ...ts could shoot anyone who crossed it

2-by 2-foot tunnel widened at 100-foot mark to allow men to pass.

...lleys on wooden rails ...ed tunnelers and ...s of quarried sand

At 320 feet, Harry was the longest escape tunnel dug during either world war

and long steel probes they continually searched for hidden trapdoors and telltale sand from tunnels.

Three teams were organized, each under a veteran tunneler. Wally Floody, a Canadian mining engineer, was chief technician. Every volunteer was interviewed by the "X" chief of his block. Miners, carpenters, engineers were assigned to tunnel. Tailors were organized to turn out disguises. Artists set up a forgery shop to fake papers. Any man who spoke fluent German was assigned to make friends with a ferret, keep him always in sight, cultivate him, eventually try to bribe him to bring in items needed from the outside.

One day a new ferret, a particularly zealous one, appeared on duty and we labeled him "Keen Type." Within a month, however, a contact had so cultivated him that he lost his zest for antiescape vigilance.

He would come into the compound, walk straight to his contact's room, and say, "Keen Type here. Can I come in?" and then settle down for tea and a biscuit.

Prisoners without any special skills were assigned either as "penguins," to dispose of sand from the tunnels, or as "stooges," to keep watch on ferrets. For the next year we had 300 stooges working in shifts every day. They reported to "Big S," the head security officer, a tall, rangy American colonel.

Once the security system was working, we went ahead on the tunnels. The Germans had overlooked one detail. In each hut the washroom, the kitchen, and a small section where there was a stove had concrete floors and stood on brick and concrete foundations that had no openings through which the security guards could probe. These were the places from which we started work.

The first job was to build secret trapdoors. At any hour of the day or night the Germans would rush into a block shouting, *"Aus, Aus!"* ("Out, Out!") and then upset beds, pry into cupboards, and rip up floor and wall boards looking for tools, civilian clothing, buttons, nails, anything an escapee might use. Yet ingenuity, backed by three years of weary experience, built trapdoors they couldn't find.

By luck, we got hold of a little cement left over from building the camp. A Polish team cast a removable block to replace a slab about two feet square chipped from the floor of Block 123. When a little sand and dirt had been rubbed around the edges, nobody could spot it. This was Tom's entrance.

Dick's trapdoor in Block 122 was the most ingenious. In the washroom floor was an iron grating through which waste water ran into a concrete well three feet deep. The drainpipe that led from this sump was so placed that there was always some water in the well. While stooges kept watch outside, the Poles removed the iron grill, bailed out the well, and, with a cold chisel acquired by bribing a guard, freed the whole concrete slab that formed one side of the well so that it was removable. When the slab was in place and the cracks were sealed with soap, the waste water rapidly accumulated, making everything look most unsuspicious.

Harry's entrance was also tricky. The tall heating stove in Room 23 of Block 104 stood on tiles embedded in a concrete base about four feet square. The men moved the stove back, chipped the tiles free, and reset them in a concrete trapdoor that looked precisely like the original base. Five of the tiles cracked in the process. They were replaced by tiles stolen from a cookhouse in East Compound.

It had been risky business. Harry's floor was up for about 10 days in all, hidden from the ferrets only by a carelessly placed mattress, but we got away with it.

Now we were set for the more dangerous business of tunneling. The distances, directions, and angles of the three tunnels had been computed by rough trigonometry. We had learned that most German sound detectors could hear nothing below a depth of 25 feet, so we decided to sink shafts 30 feet straight down from the three trapdoors before heading for the woods.

The light, sandy soil was easy to dig, but it needed almost solid shoring. As a start, we made each man provide two bed slats. This first levy wasn't too bad, but by the time the fifth and sixth levies took more slats, it was hard to sleep.

Early in May 1943 the first sand was cut away. Teams worked from just after morning roll call right through to the evening roll call with only a short break for lunch.

The penguins had the troublesome job of disposing of the bright yellow sand, which showed up glaringly if dumped on the dun-colored soil above ground. Some of the sand could be stirred into the soil of our tiny gardens, but that didn't begin to solve the problem. So we took dozens of small towels and sewed them into sausage-shaped sacks. Then a penguin would hang one of these, filled with sand, in each trouser leg and wander casually out to the playing ground. There stooges would be staging boxing matches, volleyball games, or pretended brawls. Once in among the men, the penguin, with hands in pockets, would pull strings that freed pins at the bottom of the sausage sacks and let the sand trickle to the ground. There many scuffling feet would quickly discolor it and trample it into the surface. When we were

Heating stove pushed back to reveal trapdoor to shaft

going strong, we kept 150 penguins busy and disposed of tons of sand under the very noses of the ferrets.

The tunnels were scooped out with little coal shovels and iron scrapers made from our cookstoves. The bores were about two feet square and shored with box frames made of bed slats. We saved our few nails to build shaft ladders.

At the base of each shaft roomy chambers were dug for the use of carpenters and fitters and for the ventilating equipment. One day, when three diggers were thus enlarging the base of Dick's shaft, a frame began to leak sand. In a matter of seconds the leak became an avalanche. The ladder held and two diggers scrambled up. The third, Wally Floody, was almost smothered before the other two got him out. Dick's shaft filled almost to the top. It was a bitter setback, but the job was grimly done over again.

Veterans had learned that you could not tunnel far without fresh air and that holes poked up to the surface were not adequate. By luck, a copy of a modern-mechanics type of magazine came into camp, and it contained an article that described a homemade air pump. We promptly set to work to make one.

Our "tin bashers" collected Red Cross dried milk tins, cut off the ends, and fitted the cylinders together to build pipe. They wrapped the joints with German propaganda newspapers. The pipe was laid in a ditch along the tunnel floor and covered with sand. At the far end was a nozzle, which delivered fresh air. The air was forced through the pipe by shifts of pumpers who operated a bellows constructed from kit bags. This first outfit worked perfectly and we promptly built two more. Now we could close the trapdoors and work without fear of interruption from the ferrets.

Our electrical specialists rounded up odd bits of wiring left behind by the builders. Then they surreptitiously rearranged the camp wiring, gaining a few score feet in the process. They wired the three shafts and made hidden connections to the camp circuit. We stole bulbs from corridors and so had light to dig by. When the Germans neglected to switch on the power during the day, we used homemade lamps—tin cans with pajama-cord wicks burning in margarine.

The digging teams evolved a rigid system. Number one digger lay full length on his side and one elbow, hacking away at the tunnel face and pushing the sand back toward his feet. Number two lay facing the other way, his legs overlapping number one's. He collected the sand in special boxes that were placed on trolleys and hauled by homemade ropes back to the shaft.

These trolleys, strong enough to carry two sandboxes or one man, were first-class installations. They had carved flanged wooden wheels fitted with "tires" cut from tin cans. The hubs even had ball bearings, smuggled in by a tame ferret. The track rails were made from barrack moldings. When the tunnels became long, the diggers sprawled on the trolleys and pushed their way to the working face.

At times it was stifling hot in the hole. Men worked naked or in the hated long underpants issued to prisoners. Dirt stains on their outer clothes would have given the show away. Up above, we rigged rough showers where the diggers returning from the tunnel could quickly wash off all telltale sand before roll calls.

The diggers learned to take sand falls in their stride. Usually, the

One of the digging team loaded sand into boxes—to be hauled back to tunnel shaft

only warning would be a slight rustling sound, and then suddenly the number one digger would be buried under a pile of the suffocating sand, which smothered lamps and air line. Then the number two man would have to work at top speed to get him out before he smothered.

By the end of May, a month after digging commenced, each of the three tunnels was about 70 feet long. It was nearly summer, the best time for escaping, for we could sleep out and live off the land.

The X leaders decided to concentrate on Tom, which had the shortest distance to go. A week later they set up the first "halfway house" at the 100-foot mark. This was a little chamber built from the end frames of our wooden bunks. In it men could turn around without having to go back to the shaft. Calculations were that Tom's halfway house was just under the warning wire. That left 100 feet to go to get inside the woods.

Other X groups were busily preparing the equipment we'd need.

Our forgery department consisting of 50 men turned out phony passports and identity cards. We called it "Dean & Dawson," after the English travel agency.

Some of our guards could be tempted with a gift of coffee or chocolate, and once they had smuggled in one item, they couldn't refuse more, because we might give them away to the commandant. In this way we got colored inks, pens, brushes, special types of paper, magnets to make compasses, radio parts to build the illegal receiver on which we got daily news bulletins, a camera and equipment to make photos for our fake passports, hammers, saws, nails, and maps.

A few guards, smoothly cultivated by our linguists, were even persuaded to lend us their *Zahlbuch*, combined paybook and identity card, while our forgers made copies. The faking of documents was an incredibly finicky job. Whole sheets of simulated typewriting were drawn by hand, complete with strikeovers, imperfect letters, and bad shifts. Other documents called for lines of close print or countless whorls of "engraving." Forgers ripped fine paper from Bibles and linen covers from books to make identification books. One document needed in crossing frontiers was so complicated that it would take a skilled forger five hours a day for a month to make one. Letterheads were "embossed" with toothbrush handles. German eagle and swastika stamps were cut from rubber boot heels. Altogether, the escapees were outfitted with more than 400 forged documents.

An Australian pilot made compasses—the cases from melted phonograph records, the glasses from broken windows, the needles from sewing needles rubbed on a magnet.

In the tailor shop 60 men made civilian clothes out of RAF uniforms and turned out close copies of Luftwaffe uniforms. Escapees caught wearing exact copies would be shot as spies, but by the Geneva Convention we could use imitations.

Half a dozen mapmakers traced a variety of maps and ran copies off on a makeshift duplicator. They made the gelatin from fruit jello, the ink from the crushed lead of indelible pencils.

We learned that the Americans were to be moved in six weeks to a separate compound, and they had put in a lot of work on the tunnels. So evening shifts were added to hurry things up. We had to take even greater chances with sand. More of it was dug into our vegetable gardens, and some was scattered near the freshly upturned soil around a new camp theater.

One day a probing ferret turned over some bright yellow sand in a garden. This touched off a series of frantic but futile searches. The

Germans dug a trench between Block 123 and the wire, but it was not deep enough to reveal Tom.

By the end of June we calculated that Tom had reached just under the edge of the wood, and we prepared to dig a shaft straight up to the surface. Just then a horde of Germans suddenly appeared and began to cut away the trees! It was actually mere coincidence; they had decided to build a new compound there. They chopped the trees back for 50 yards; but time for the Americans was growing short, and it was decided to break Tom out anyway and let the escapees crawl the rest of the way to cover.

We had so much sand coming up that we were desperate. Someone suggested storing it temporarily in Dick. Every evening a stream of penguins carrying cardboard Red Cross boxes would stroll across to Dick's hut and there dump sand down the shaft. Even that was not enough. The X leaders decided to take a long chance: store sand in Red Cross boxes under our beds and hope that the Germans wouldn't find it until it could be properly disposed of.

Tom was now 260 feet long, with a few yards to go to its goal. Bushell decided to lie low for a few days to allay suspicion. Then ferrets found the boxes of sand in our huts! Heavy transport wagons were brought into camp and trundled all around the area in an effort to collapse any tunnels we might have. They only wrecked our vegetable gardens.

A day or so later, in a last suspicious search of Block 123, a ferret accidentally jabbed his probe into the edge of Tom's trapdoor.

That was the end of Tom.

The ferrets couldn't find how to open the trap, so they broke it in. They dynamited Tom and incidentally blew up part of the roof of Block 123. They were so relieved at discovering Tom that they took no reprisals or even precautions.

A mass meeting decided that work would go ahead on Dick and Harry. However, it was deemed wise to do no more until winter, when we assumed vigilance would slacken because it would be a bad season for escapes.

At the end of August 1943 the Americans were moved to their new compound, and we threw a great party for them on home-brewed raisin wine as a farewell.

While we were waiting for winter, it was decided to try some aboveground escapes. For one attempt the carpenters made imitation German rifles out of wood—they got the exact measurements by sneaking up behind guards with calipers and measuring the parts.

These they leaded with pencil to resemble metal and polished them until you couldn't tell them from the real thing.

Periodically, the German guards escorted small parties of prisoners through the gates for delousing our clothes, and the idea was to stage an unofficial delousing party of our own. Three prisoners, disguised as Luftwaffe *Unteroffiziers*, took 24 other prisoners in tow, passed the inspection at the gate, and made off into the woods. A few minutes later six senior officers, including the Battle of Britain fighter ace Bob Stanford Tuck, tried to get through but were detected.

We were all forced to stand on parade for nearly seven hours while the three missing men were identified. Later, all were rounded up. One man, a fluent Spanish speaker, who posed as a foreign worker, got to Czechoslovakia and then by train almost to the Swiss border, where he got out and walked right across a narrow strip of Swiss territory without knowing it and back again into Germany, where a frontier guard nabbed him. The other two got to a Luftwaffe airdrome, sneaked into an old Junkers trainer, and were just warming up the engine when a German pilot coincidentally came along to fly it and caught them.

We were ready to start tunneling again early in 1944. Dick was almost filled in with Tom's sand, and anyway the Germans had started to build a new compound where Dick was to have broken out. That left Harry. But snow lay deep on the ground and sand disposal stumped us. One of the tunnelers suggested we put it under the theater. He had noticed the Germans never looked there.

We had built the theater ourselves and had taken care to leave no openings for the ferrets to peek through. Underneath was a deep excavation, which could take tons and tons of sand. Our engineers adjusted one seat so that it swung back on hinges, and under it they cut a trapdoor. Into this the penguins dumped kit bags packed full of sand every night.

Three teams, 10 veteran diggers in each team, pushed Harry ahead up to 12 feet per day. By the end of January, the first "halfway house" was built 100 feet out. The planners had calculated that 300 feet of tunnel in all would bring us into the shelter of the trees.

It was a long dig, and conditions were getting worse. The ground was cold and damp. Every digger suffered continuously from colds. Most of them were spitting black from breathing the fumes of our fat lamps; we had run out of electric wire. Sand falls kept occurring nearly every day.

But by mid-February another 100 feet had been dug, and the second halfway house was put in. This was just about under the far boundary wire; there were 100 feet still to go.

Then we got a small break. German workmen hooking up loudspeakers laid down two large coils of electric wire, intending to use them in a few minutes. A prisoner calmly walked off with one coil. A mock fight broke out, and in the confusion we got the second coil. The German workmen were afraid to report the loss. (At the end, when the Gestapo found the wire in Harry, three of them were shot.)

That haul gave us 600 feet of wiring, enough for stringing lights clear up to the digging face.

The chief ferret again became suspicious. Wally Floody, our chief penguin, our security chief, and half a dozen of the key diggers were suddenly transferred to a compound several miles away. That was a blow. It was bad enough losing key men, but it was worse that the Germans obviously knew we were up to something.

By March 8, 1944, the final 100-foot section was dug and a chamber excavated at the end. In four days four of the best diggers carved straight upward, fitting ladders to the side as they progressed, until they struck pine-tree roots. They estimated that they were about two feet below the surface, just inside the woods. They boarded over the top of the shaft and left the remainder to be dug on the night of the break. By March 14 the tunnel was ready. The trapdoor was closed and its sides cemented up to wait for milder weather and a night suitable for our getaway.

The very next day the chief ferret sent his men to search Block 104. One of them even ran his probe around the cement that sealed Harry's trapdoor. It held.

About 500 men had worked on the tunnels, but we estimated that only 220 would be able to pass through it during the hours of darkness. Bushell was allowed to draw up a list of 60 workers, 20 more were nominated by secret ballot because of their work on the project, and 140 names were drawn out of a hat.

The lucky ones began their preparations. We had enough money to buy train tickets for 40 men; the rest were to walk across country. Bushell and other men who'd been loose in Germany conducted lectures, giving hints and advice. A Czech pilot described the border mountains of Czechoslovakia, 60 miles away, for which most of the foot travelers intended to head.

After roll call on the morning of Friday, March 24, Roger Bushell announced that the escape would take place that night. There was six inches of snow on the ground, which was not good, but there would be no moon. Our meteorologist thought there would be a wind to drown suspicious noises.

The forgery department boys filled in their documents and stamped them with the correct date, which of course couldn't have been done until then. Some escapees were to go as foreign workers, others as neutrals, others as German officials, soldiers, and civilians—and each man's papers had to fit his story.

A digger went out to Harry's end to see how far we had to go to break through. When he jabbed a stick upward three inches, he struck daylight, much to his surprise. At least, it seemed, there wouldn't be any difficulty in getting to the surface.

We laid blankets at the bottom of the shafts to deaden sounds and nailed planks on the trolleys so the escapees could lie on them and be pulled along. When darkness came, the escapees put on their disguises. Our improvised iron rations were issued, a revolting but nourishing combination of grated chocolate, oatmeal, crushed biscuits, vitamin pills, barley, dried milk, and other concentrated foods all boiled together.

By 8:30 P.M. it was announced that all was ready. Ten minutes later the first escapee went down the ladder, turned out in a civilian suit and carrying a homemade briefcase. The second, dressed as a workman, followed. Roger Bushell, carrying an attaché case and looking like a smart businessman in his gray herringbone lounge suit, black overcoat, and dark hat, went down among the first five.

There was a bad wait when the first man was unable to pry the roof boards loose. It was almost an hour, an agonizing time for the men lying along the tunnel, before the swollen boards came loose and the earth was removed. Up above twinkled a few stars, and down the shaft came the sweet fresh air of freedom.

But when the digger cautiously stuck his head out, he got a shock. Instead of being just inside the woods, the hole was 10 feet short of the trees, its gaping opening a bare 15 yards from a sentry tower.

We were stunned when he broke the news. Would the work of 500 men for more than a year end in complete failure? But the men were in no mood to be stopped. To go out now was risky. To wait a month for the next dark of the moon and in the meantime dig another 30 feet of tunnel was equally risky. Besides, the forged papers were all dated and would have to be redone. That decided it.

The first man up crawled to a brushwood fence, paying out a rope by which he could signal when it was safe for the next man to emerge. The sentry in the tower paid no attention to the woods but played his searchlight on the barbed-wire fence and compound. Two other sentries patrolled back and forth along the wire. When both were out of sight, the rope was tugged and the second man slipped across into the relative safety of the woods.

It took more than an hour for the first 20 to make it. They were all going by train, and they headed for the Sagan railway station a quarter of a mile away. From timetables smuggled in by guards we knew exactly when the trains were due.

Back in Block 104 the initial delay had been terrible. Obviously something had gone wrong, but what? Escapees sat around, a queer collection of well-dressed civilians, workmen, and a German corporal, hoping that ferrets would not appear. Just after 9:30 the men at the trapdoor felt a blast of cold air. It could only mean that we'd broken out. A muffled cheer went around the block.

There were other interruptions. Two bad sand falls held up the show for about an hour and a half in all. Sometimes the trolleys left their rails—more delays. Men going out with suitcases or blankets wrapped around them would find themselves jammed in a narrow tunnel, afraid to pull loose for fear of causing a fall. We were running far behind schedule.

At midnight the air-raid sirens sounded, and all lights, including our illegal ones in the tunnel, were switched off. It was obvious now that not more than 100 men would get away before daylight. Lamps had to be lighted and passed along the tunnel.

We up above heard the faraway sound of falling bombs, and the huts rattled as RAF blockbusters fell crashing on Berlin, 100 miles away. At any other time we would have cheered, but that night we cursed. It was about 2 A.M. before the lights came on again. In the meantime, one by one the escapees had been crawling silently from the tunnel mouth and away into the woods.

The worst moment came at about 4:30. The sentry in the tower shouted to a guard patrolling below. The guard went up the tower ladder, and the sentry descended and walked straight toward the hole. He could hardly miss seeing it. Steam from the heat of the tunnel poured out of it, and from it to the woods led a black trail across the snow where escapees had crawled. The sentry, apparently blinded by looking at his searchlight, came on until he was a bare four feet from the hole, turned around, and squatted down. For five minutes he remained there, while the men in the shaft hardly dared breathe. At last the sentry went back to his tower. More escapees slipped through the tunnel and away.

When it was almost 5, the RAF man in charge decided it was getting too light. "Get the next three men down," he said. "Then we finish. If all of them get away without detection, the Huns won't know a thing until morning roll call, and the boys will have an extra four hours before the hunt is on."

The last three men quickly descended. Just as the third man vanished up the tunnel on the trolley, we heard the crack of a rifle.

Two escaping men had reached the rendezvous tree in the woods, another man, crawling, was halfway to it, and a fourth man had just come out of the hole when the rope signaler saw a guard approaching. If he kept on coming, he was bound to step right into the hole. The men outside froze to the ground when they felt two sharp warning tugs on the rope. The German strode on. He was seven yards away and still hadn't seen the hole.

Left, right, he strode on, probably half asleep, and one foot came down only a bare 12 inches from the tunnel mouth. When he made his next step, he almost trod on the man lying alongside the opening. He took one more pace, and then he snapped out of his daze. He didn't even notice the man lying at his feet, but he must have seen the black track across the snow. Then he saw the man lying halfway to the wood and raised his rifle to shoot. At that moment one of the escapees waiting by the tree leaped into sight and waved his arms, shouting, *"Nicht schiessen, Posten! Nicht schiessen!"* ("Don't shoot, sentry! Don't shoot!")

The sentry, startled, shot wild. The two men at the edge of the woods and the man who had crawled halfway came slowly forward, hands raised. And then, right at his feet, the last escapee, still unseen,

Of the 76 escapees, only 3 reached safety, 50 were shot, 23 were recaptured

180

rose slowly. The guard jumped back a yard and looked downward. There in front of him was Harry's gaping mouth. He whipped out a torch and flashed it down the hole into the face of the 81st escapee, hanging precariously on the ladder.

The sentry blew his whistle. In a moment guards came running from all directions.

Harry's long life had ended.

In Block 104 there was a frantic scramble to burn our lists and papers, break up equipment, and get rid of civilian clothes. The men in the tunnel were inching back along the trolleys, expecting a shot from behind. When the last man came up, the trapdoor was sealed down and the stove replaced.

In a few minutes there came a scratching sound from below. A ferret had worked his way back along the tunnel and couldn't get out. We let him stay there.

By 6 A.M. the compound was swarming with guards, machine guns covered the doors and windows, and ferrets combed Block 104 calling, *"Aus! Aus! Efferbody aus!"* As each man came out of Block 104, a ferret grabbed him and forced him to strip in the snow, boots and all, while every article of clothing was inspected.

While the search was going on, an adjutant came running to implore us to open the trapdoor. The ferret was still down there, and they were afraid he would suffocate. The other ferrets couldn't find the trapdoor. We finally decided to open it for them. The ferret down below was not a bad type—he was the only one with nerve enough to go down the tunnel.

In a matter of hours the whole countryside was roused in one of the biggest manhunts of the war. The radio warned all civilians to be on the watch for the escapees. SS and Gestapo men, Luftwaffe men, and even naval men from Stettin and Danzig were mobilized by the thousands for the search.

Back in the compound we waited for reprisals. Harry had broken the world's record for the number of escapees who got away, and we expected the Germans to take it out on us. The Gestapo arrived to investigate, but its agents, never liked by the regular army, got no help from the ferrets and found nothing. We even managed to filch two of their flashlights. But they did uncover a black market—run by the commandant and his staff! The hapless commandant was promptly whisked off for a court-martial.

Most of the 76 men who got away were nabbed within a day or so, although some got as far as Danzig and Munich. All were taken to a

Gestapo prison in Gorlitz, 40 miles away. From Gorlitz, 15 men were brought back to Stalag Luft III. We could learn nothing more.

Then, a fortnight after the break, our senior officer was called to the commandant's office. Stiffly, the German read out the official report—of the 76 escaped officers, 41 had been shot!

Our senior officer called a meeting and announced the dreadful news. Under the Geneva Convention, drastic penalties must not be inflicted upon prisoners who attempt escape. The Germans had never before done such a thing. We thought most likely the announcement was a bluff to dissuade us from further escape attempts. We held a memorial service in the compound, however, and every man defiantly wore a black diamond of mourning on his sleeve.

When the Germans posted the list of the dead, it contained not 41 but 47 names, among them the leaders—Roger Bushell; Tim Walenn, who ran the forgery factory; Al Hake, the compass maker; Charlie Hall, the photographer.

For days the compound was shaken with grief and fury. Then three more names were added to the list of dead. The Germans never gave us any reason for the shootings or why they shot only 50 of 76. A couple of weeks later they brought in urns containing the cremated ashes of the dead, which we placed in a memorial vault.

In June a letter arrived, written in Spanish and signed with a fictitious name. That was the signal that one escapee, a Dutch pilot in the RAF, had succeeded in reaching England. A postcard from Sweden, signed with two false names, revealed that two Norwegians had also made it out. With 15 men sent back to Stalag Luft III and 50 reported shot, that left 8 unaccounted for.

Not till long afterward did we learn that they had been sent to the notorious Oranienburg concentration camp. Nobody had ever escaped from a concentration camp, the Gestapo boasted. However, within a few months the eight had tunneled out. They were eventually rounded up, but by then Germany was in the chaos of collapse and they were not shot.

If the Germans shot our 50 comrades to frighten us from building more tunnels, they made a psychological blunder. X was re-formed around two veteran tunnelers, and we immediately began work on "George," which started under the theater. George was on as grand a scale as Harry, and we were almost ready to break out when we were hurriedly evacuated. The Russians were only 30 miles away. We were forced to march for weeks half across Germany. We were at Lubeck on May 2, 1945, when the British 2nd Army set us free.

Since the Berlin Wall first went up, thousands
have managed to circumvent it in a variety
of ways. But no scheme was more audacious than the
one engineered by the Holzapfel family.

The Lion's Den

By C. Brian Kelly

A SUMMER NIGHT'S RAIN fell gently on the twin cities of Berlin, spattering the barrier that divides East from West. It soaked the four men crouched at the western base of the wall. They said nothing. They dared not even move.

High above them, on the eastern side of the wall, were the battlements of the House of Ministries, once Hermann Göring's Luftwaffe headquarters and now, in 1965, the central bureaucracy—the lion's den—of the Communist German Democratic Republic. Somewhere on the Ministries roof, beyond the brightly lit wall and the armed border guards of the National People's Army, a family of three— father, mother, young son—was crawling through the rain toward hoped-for freedom.

IT WAS HARDLY LIGHT when the alarm rang at 4:30 that morning, but Heinz and Jutta Holzapfel were already awake in their small Leipzig apartment. Their son, Günther, was still sleeping soundly.

"Günther, wake up!" his parents urged. "We have to catch the early train to Berlin."

Günther was nine years old and delighted about the trip. He would be visiting the great House of Ministries, where his father sometimes worked. He dressed quickly and stumbled after his mother and father into the cool morning air.

They took the 6:13 train to the capital. At 10:30 A.M. they stood in the vast entrance hall of the House of Ministries, surrounded by the crowd of visitors that gathered in the entrance every morning before obtaining passes and scattering in the hallways beyond. Heinz strode ahead toward the pass office, a small cubicle next to an armed

183

sentry. Jutta and Günther stayed a few paces behind. If Heinz were challenged, they could turn for home.

But no one paid attention to the slender man with the short hair and colorless features. And no one noticed that neither Heinz nor Jutta actually obtained new passes.

When Jutta stepped out of the pass office with Günther, Heinz was standing in the crowd before the sentry. Waving them through, the guard barely glanced at the outdated passes they showed (obtained on a previous visit and never returned). Inside, the three were soon lost among the throng of people.

THE HOLZAPFELS' STORY actually began in 1945, when the Russian armies captured Berlin. The son of a Leipzig cobbler, Heinz was a thin, pale boy of 14. He matured in the new schools the Communists established in the Soviet Zone and by 1953 was a member of the Free German Youth, the training ground for future comrades. He enjoyed the privilege of studying in a special economics school, where he applied himself diligently. It was there that he met a petite, brown-haired girl named Jutta, herself a Communist.

They fell in love, and in time they were married. In order to make enough money, Heinz went to work as a carpenter in a wood-veneer plant. On the side he studied Marxist economics at Leipzig University. Shortly after the Berlin Wall went up in 1961, he became an "expert planner" for 20 wood-veneer factories and a group leader for the Communist party committee in his office.

Because Heinz Holzapfel had relatives living in West Germany, he knew that he could rise only so far in the management ranks. Among his own group, however, he felt he was secure. And his wife, Jutta, was a great asset. She was first an editor of a factory newsletter and sometime later worked in the personnel department of the Leipzig trade and industrial fair. The Holzapfels were considered by most people to be "the perfect Communist couple."

Yet there were doubts, hesitant at first, then growing stronger. Neither dared mention them—until one winter evening in 1963 when it suddenly all came out in the open.

Heinz was late, held up by yet another of the interminable party meetings at the office. When he got home, he slammed the door behind him. Talk, talk, talk, he complained. Impossible production quotas. Facile exhortations to the workers. And all lies. He couldn't abide the hypocrisy any longer—the state's, the party's, his own. He wanted "to vanish from here."

Jutta was stunned. Never had she heard Heinz talk like that. What he was proposing was *escape*.

And what was she saying? Two words: "Me, too."

They stared at each other. There was nothing more to say.

In the next few weeks Heinz and Jutta discussed escape possibilities. But, as they soon learned, the borders between East and West really did form an Iron Curtain—too heavily fortified to crash openly, too heavily guarded to slip across unseen.

A year, then another six months, passed. Jutta remained at the trade fair. Heinz continued his work.

About twice a month, Heinz traveled to East Berlin on official business for his wood enterprise, which was a branch of the National Economics Council in the House of Ministries. And one day Heinz realized that the Ministries had become more than a place of business for him. At the rear of the building, only Niederkirchner Street—the "death strip"—separated it from the wall. Visiting his colleagues on the upper floors of the seven-story building, Heinz could look into West Berlin. He could see the traffic, a woman hanging wash, a boy like Günther on his way home from school.

At street level it would be easy enough to reach the border strip from the Ministries courtyard. Easy, but futile. There seemed to be no way that anyone could snip through the two barbed-wire fences, cross over the death strip, then scale the barrier itself without being stopped, or shot.

There had to be another way. Standing on the street one day, the huge structure looming above him, Heinz saw the solution in a flash. The roof! Of course. Who would expect an escape from the roof of the House of Ministries?

He also saw how it could be done. The lights that illuminated the forbidden strip of ground were the most obvious danger. But they pointed down. Anyone looking up from ground level would be blinded. The moment of real danger would come during the time of the descent. But the apparatus Heinz had in mind would reduce that exposure to only a few seconds.

That evening Heinz told Jutta his plan. It would work, he said. And Jutta agreed.

For help they turned to some of their old friends in West Germany. Routinely exercising their right to visit the Communist half of Germany, these friends met with the Holzapfels several times. They agreed to wait at the base of the wall, opposite the Ministries, on the night of the attempt.

Heinz, in the meantime, had begun a study of the Ministries roof. Fortunately, it was broken into layers, like the deck of a ship. It should be easy, Heinz figured, to drop from a seventh-story window to the sixth-floor roof, then to the fifth-floor level. From the fifth floor it was a sheer drop to the ground. How high was that level? Using floor-to-ceiling measurements made in a Ministries bathroom one day and a photograph of the building, Heinz calculated the distance at 75 feet. Next, he estimated the gap between the Ministries structure and the wall at 40 to 50 feet. All these figures were passed along to the West German helpers.

The three Holzapfels would need a hiding place—perhaps one of the sixth-floor offices Heinz visited on his official calls. But he had no key. Then, as he searched the top-floor hallways one day, Heinz passed a commonplace sign: *Herren.* Of course, the men's room!

Quickly, Heinz surveyed the building's lavatories. They were all on the wrong side, opening onto inner courts. All but one. In the most distant corridor from the wall, there was a single men's toilet overlooking the sixth floor, with only a short drop from the window to the ledge below.

Now everything fell neatly into place. At the appointed time they could retreat directly to this bathroom. It would be their hiding place *and* their escape hatch.

After they cleared pass control inside the front door that morning of July 28, 1965, the Holzapfels went their separate ways: Heinz to get a haircut; Jutta and Günther to the Ministries beauty salon. There Jutta relaxed for a bit. She had kept the briefcase containing their escape equipment. Both she and Heinz felt a woman would be less likely to be searched. As the hairdresser worked on her, Jutta had the bulging case at her feet.

When Jutta moved to the dryer and felt the hot cocoon come down over her head, her tension began to ease. Then a laugh startled her. The young woman who set Jutta's hair had the briefcase in her hand and was pretending to struggle with it. *"Mein Gott,* how heavy! What on earth is inside?"

Jutta had unaccountably left the case by the first chair.

She didn't dare answer. She felt her shaking voice would have betrayed her. So she took the case, and she and Günther left the beauty salon as quickly as possible.

Günther was too busy to wonder about anything but the fabulous building they were visiting. The gray Ministries was a small roofed city. The Holzapfels (Heinz had by this time rejoined them) visited the firefighting headquarters, the pharmacy, various shops, the huge cafeteria. After lunch, in the state bookstore, Heinz and Jutta held back a gasp as their son picked out a book on parachuting called *A Jump From the Clouds.*

By late afternoon they were back in the cafeteria. Heinz and Jutta, eyes on the clock, found little to say as they lingered over a snack and a hot drink. At 4:30, with the closing hour only 30 minutes away, Heinz said softly, "It's time to get going."

He and the boy traveled the elevator to the sixth floor and locked themselves into a men's room. Jutta rode a floor higher and vanished into a women's toilet she had found earlier in the day. It was closer to the rear of the building—and the wall—than the washroom Heinz had picked weeks before. Heinz and Günther joined her there at precisely 5:05 P.M. No one observed them.

Inside, Heinz immediately opened Jutta's bulging briefcase and pulled out the sign he had prepared—"Toilet closed. Please use the one at the end of the hall." He hung it outside the door. He then secured the bathroom door with two short, heavy crossbars. It would take several men to force an entrance.

Günther watched all this in astonishment. Now they told him the plan. If he followed instructions exactly, he would be given a bicycle once they were across the wall.

Silence fell. It would be a four-hour wait for darkness. While Günther slept, Heinz examined his signal lamp, a flashlight inside a candy bag with the tip of the bag cut out. It created a pinhead of light that could be seen only from the front and not from the side. He flicked it on and off several times.

ACROSS THE WALL, the Holzapfels' four confederates, carrying a 160-yard coil of blackened wire cable, headed for an abandoned junk truck. It was standing in a deserted lot close to the wall. The truck would make a firm anchor for their end of the Holzapfel railway. Dressed in dark clothing, the confederates faded into their shadowy hiding places next to the wall.

IN THE BATHROOM a block away, Heinz and Jutta waited impatiently. Nine o'clock had passed, and although there was no moon, it was still too light. Finally, at 9:30, they awoke Günther and pulled on their harnesses and "creeping socks," old ski socks Jutta had fitted with foam-rubber soles. Heinz opened the window. They climbed through and dropped to the sixth-floor roof. There they paused to darken their faces with soot. Heinz then motioned toward the rear of the building, toward the wall.

Heads down, bodies crouched, they flitted from one cover to another, shadows among the ventilation shafts and other projections that dotted the roof. They were on a ledge, framed on one side by the walls of the seventh floor and on the other by a 10-foot drop to the fifth-floor roof.

Soon they were more than halfway to the drop-off point to the fifth-floor level. But now a window threw a shaft of bright yellow light across their route. As Heinz studied it, recalling his explorations inside the Ministries months before, he realized it was the office of the *Stasi*—the State Security Service.

"Careful!" he whispered.

They nodded and followed him out to the very edge of the roof, away from the window. On hands and knees, all three Holzapfels began to pick their way carefully past the danger spot. Inside the room they saw, to their surprise, not armed police officers, but a group of men in their underwear. Seconds later the light in the room snapped off. The *Stasi* had gone to bed.

Straightening up, the Holzapfels quickly moved on.

The descent to the fifth-floor roof was easy enough, but now they were forced to crawl. There were few projections to hide behind on this final layer of roof, and a standing silhouette would be visible against the glow of West Berlin's lights.

Heinz went first, closely followed by Günther, then Jutta. Each adult had a heavy briefcase. Jutta's was full of equipment, Heinz's crammed with family papers and mementos. They both pushed their briefcases ahead, then pulled themselves forward, in a repeated push, crawl, push, crawl.

ON THE OTHER SIDE of the wall, meanwhile, a West German police patrol had stumbled on the Holzapfels' confederates and told them to leave. Early in the wall's history, West Berlin authorities had stood by to aid escape attempts. By 1965, however, the city government was anxious to avoid border incidents. And the police saw no reason to encourage this group who refused to explain their presence.

Finally, one of the confederates pointed at the gloom-shrouded House of Ministries.

"Look! There's a family up there on that roof," he told the officers. "They are planning to escape."

The police were incredulous. How could anyone escape from a

stronghold like the House of Ministries? It was quite impossible.

But the West German friends of the Holzapfels insisted, displaying the cable and explaining the operation in detail. The patrol leader heard them out, then radioed headquarters for instructions. Minutes later the conspirators returned to their posts—and 20 officers armed with submachine guns discreetly took up stations nearby.

IT WAS ALMOST 11 P.M. when the Holzapfels reached the far end of the roof of the fifth floor. Looking around for an "anchor," Heinz saw nothing close by. The only substantial thing in view was a tall flagpole at the opposite flank of the Ministries wing, at least 50 yards away. They started crawling again.

When they finally reached the flagpole, the Holzapfels were close to exhaustion. But there was no time to rest. Jutta quietly began unpacking homemade escape gear: wooden reels, a hammer, and a reel of tough nylon tennis gut. Heinz pulled out his bagged flashlight and signaled westward.

There was an answering blink.

Heinz reached for the hammer and tennis gut. He securely tied one end of the coiled gut to the flagpole, six yards from the roof's lip; the other end was attached to the hammer, which was wrapped in foam rubber to muffle the sound of its impact. Heinz stood up, swung the hammer tentatively, then hurled it with all his strength. He and Jutta heard the thin nylon feed out with a silken whisper. Then the line went taut, and they could see the brightly painted hammer on the ground, five stories down and some 50 feet away. It had landed just beyond the wall. So far, the plan was working.

After a short wait a blurred figure detached itself from the shadows near the wall and advanced toward where the hammer lay. Like a fish taking bait, it swallowed the object, then quickly retreated to merge again with the shadows.

Heinz waited—long enough, he felt sure, for his confederates to attach the cable to the gut. Yet, when he tugged at the line, it wouldn't give. Something was wrong.

On the western side of the wall, Heinz's confederates had fastened the gut to the wire cable. But the cable became snagged in underbrush, and the West Germans had to creep out to free it. Then they forgot to give Heinz any slack. His every pull continued to meet resistance. Both sides wondered what had happened. Had the others seen something they couldn't?

Finally, Heinz gave the nylon line a stiff jerk. The message was understood, for suddenly the thin line yielded. Minutes later, breathing quite heavily, Heinz and Jutta hauled the end of the wire cable over the edge of the roof. Smeared with black tar, it was barely visible. Down below, apparently unaware, the sentries remained quiet.

Moving very quickly now, Heinz looped the cable end around the flagpole, pulled the loop tight, and secured it with a snap hook. He then signaled the ground: "Ready here." They would need a few moments to draw the wire cable taut and anchor their end to the truck. Soon Heinz saw the pale green light winking.

Günther was to go off first. Even if the guards below spotted him, it seemed unlikely they could unsling their guns and aim before Günther cleared the wall. Tense and silent, the nine-year-old boy watched as his mother and father deftly attached his flimsy-looking escape vehicle to the cable. It was an eight-inch-wide wheel of hardwood with a deep groove on the cable-riding rim. Heinz had sawed hardwood pulley reels in half and installed ordinary metal bicycle hubs in the center holes. He then had glued and screwed the pulley reels

together. A pipe crossbar, inserted through the bicycle hub, was held securely in place by butterfly nuts. This provided a firm handle. Jutta, in the meantime, had made strong harness seats of extra-heavy-duty upholstery webbing, fitted to size for each family member.

Young Günther obediently crouched underneath the cable as they slipped his harness straps over the crossbar and secured them. They snapped a separate leather safety belt into place as well. Even if he lost his hold on the crossbar, Günther could not fall from the webbed seat.

But now it was quite apparent that the loop on the flagpole was too low, so low the cable pressed against the lip of the roof. If the passengers were to clear the edge, the escape track had to be lifted. Heinz quickly wedged himself under the wire cable, strained up with his shoulders—and Jutta then gave Günther a push.

The hunched figure of the nine-year-old went over the roof edge noiselessly. It was incredible how quickly he vanished into the blackness.

For young Günther, heart beating furiously, there was hardly time to realize what was happening. As the wind whipped past his face, he sensed rather than saw the lights flash past his feet. Then he struck a figure with strong, outstretched arms. In moments he was out of the harness, standing in an empty lot, the wall behind him. He had not uttered a sound during the trip.

On the roof Heinz and Jutta waited for the green blink that would tell them Günther was safe. When it came, they promptly signaled back, "Ready again."

Jutta floated down with a briefcase slung around her neck.

The police hurried Jutta and Günther to the safety of the nearest station house. The West German helpers stayed at their posts and waited for Heinz. But the cable was still. There were no warning vibrations from a third passenger.

On the Ministries roof, Heinz was desperate. He struggled to force the cable higher. It barely moved. Frantically, he tugged for more slack, but his cohorts on the ground did not understand. Finally, one of them rushed to the police station for Jutta's advice.

"He must need more slack," she said. "Loosen the cable!"

Minutes later Heinz had the added slack. Not all he wanted, but enough to raise the cable several inches. It would have to do.

Heinz hooked his harness onto the crossbar of the last reel. He eyed the cable, quivering just above the roofline. There still was no room to ride over the edge. Grabbing the cable below the reel with both hands, he jammed himself, on his back, between the cable and the lip of the roof. He forced himself to ease his legs, and finally his entire body, over the edge. Then he fell through space.

He was in his harness, however, and the wheel fell into place on the cable. Suddenly, he was rolling, faster and faster, down and away. He cleared the wall and struck the group of West Germans at the end of the cable like a cannonball.

Hours later, when dawn came, Heinz and Jutta were still up with their friends, their hotel room full of smoke and talk. Günther, soon to be the proud owner of a bicycle, was sound asleep. And back at the wall, as the cable took shape in the growing daylight, a lonely helmeted border guard was sent to haul it in.

*The dramatic account of an incident in
the South Pacific during World
War II involving the escape of a future
president of the U.S.A.*

Survival

By John Hersey

ONE DAY IN AUGUST 1943 an officer of a PT squadron in the Solomon Islands wrote home these distressing words: "Last night George Ross lost his life for a cause he believed in stronger than any of us, because he was an idealist of the purest sense. Jack Kennedy, ex-ambassador's son, was on the same boat and also lost his life. The man that said the cream of a nation is lost in war can never be accused of making an overstatement of a very cruel fact."

A couple of days later a mass was said in the squadron area for the souls of Kennedy, Ross, and the other 11 men of PT 109.

But sorrow at the PT base was premature. This is the account of what really happened. It shows that among all the horrible things in the Pacific war, there was one wonderful thing: the will of men to live.

SKIPPERED BY Lt. John F. Kennedy, PT 109 was out one starless night patrolling Blackett Strait in the mid-Solomons. At about 2:30 A.M. Kennedy, at the wheel, saw George "Barney" Ross, up on the bow with binoculars, turn and point into the darkness. The man in the forward machine-gun turret shouted, "Ship at 2 o'clock!"

Kennedy saw a shape and spun the wheel to turn for an attack, but the motor torpedo boat, running on only one of her three engines so as to make a minimum wake and avoid detection from the air, answered too sluggishly. The shape became a Japanese destroyer, cutting through the night at 40 knots and heading straight for the 109. All hands froze to their battle stations as the destroyer crashed into the PT and cut her in two. Kennedy thought "This is how it feels to be killed." In a moment he found himself on his back on the deck, looking up at the destroyer as it passed through his boat.

Only McMahon, an engineer, was below decks. He was thrown painfully against a bulkhead. A tremendous burst of flame came at him from the gas tanks. He put his hands over his face, drew his legs up, and waited to die. But he felt water hit him after the fire, and he was sucked down as his half of the PT sank. He began to struggle upward through the water. Over his head he saw a yellow glow— gasoline burning. He broke the surface and was right in the fire..He splashed hard to keep a little island of water around him.

Johnston, another engineer, had been asleep on deck. The collision dropped him overboard. The destroyer's turbulent wake took him down, turned him over and over, shook him, and drubbed on his ribs. The next day his body was black-and-blue.

The undamaged watertight compartments forward kept Kennedy's half of the PT afloat. The destroyer rushed off into the dark. There was an awful quiet: only the sound of gasoline burning.

Kennedy shouted, "Who's aboard?"

Feeble answers came from three enlisted men, McGuire, Mauer, and Albert, and one officer, Thom.

The survivors in the water answered Kennedy's hails: Ross, the third officer, and Harris, McMahon, Johnston, Zinsser, Starkey, enlisted men. Two did not answer: Kirksey and Marney, enlisted men.

Harris shouted from the darkness, "Mr. Kennedy! Mr. Kennedy! McMahon is badly hurt."

Kennedy, who had been on the Harvard swimming team five years before, dove into the water and swam to McMahon and Harris, 100 yards away, then took McMahon in tow and headed for the PT. A gentle breeze kept blowing the boat away from the swimmers. It took 45 minutes to make what had been an easy 100 yards. On the way Harris, who had hurt his leg, said, "I can't go any farther."

Kennedy, of the Boston Kennedys, said to Harris, of the same hometown, "For a guy from Boston you're certainly putting up a great exhibition out here, Harris."

Harris complained no more, and he made it to the hull. Then Kennedy swam from man to man, to see how they were doing. All were wearing life preservers. Those who couldn't swim had to be towed back to the wreck by those who could. It took nearly three hours to get everyone aboard.

The men stretched out on the tilted deck. Some collapsed into sleep. The others talked about how wonderful it was to be alive.

When it got light, the men saw, three miles to the northeast, the monumental cone of Kolombangara Island; there, they knew, 10,000

Japanese swarmed. To the west, five miles away, they saw Vella Lavella—more Japs. To the south, only a mile or so away, they actually could see a Japanese camp on Gizo. Kennedy ordered his men to keep low so that no moving silhouettes would show against the sky. The listing hulk was gurgling and gradually settling.

McMahon, horribly burned, and Johnston, who coughed continually from gasoline fumes that had gotten into his lungs, had to have room to lie down. Kennedy ordered the other men into the water and went in himself. All morning they clung to the hulk. They cursed war in general and PT's in particular. At about 10 o'clock the hulk heaved a moist sigh and turned turtle. McMahon and Johnston had to hang on as best they could.

It became clear with each passing moment that the remains of the 109 would soon sink. Kennedy said: "We will swim to that small island," pointing to one of a group three miles to the southeast. "We have less chance of making it than some of these other islands here, but there'll be less chance of Japs, too."

Those who could not swim well grouped themselves around a long timber that had been knocked loose by the collision. They tied several pairs of shoes to it, as well as the ship's lantern wrapped in a life jacket to keep it afloat.

Kennedy took one end of a long strap on McMahon's Mae West in his teeth and swam breaststroke, towing the helpless man. The salt water lapped into his mouth, and he swallowed a lot.

It took five hours to reach the island. It was only 100 yards in diameter. Kennedy lay down, exhausted. He had been in the sea, except for short intervals on the hulk, for $15\frac{1}{2}$ hours. His stomach was heavy with the salt water he had swallowed. But he kept thinking. Every night for several nights the PT's had cut through Ferguson Passage on their way to action. Ferguson Passage was just beyond the next little island. Maybe . . .

He stood up. He put a rubber life belt around his waist, and hung a .38 around his neck on a lanyard. He picked up the ship's lantern, a heavy battery affair, still wrapped in the kapok jacket. He said: "If I find a boat, I'll flash the lantern twice. The password will be 'Roger,' and the answer will be 'Wilco.' "

It took Kennedy half an hour to swim to the reef around the next island. Now it was dark. He blundered along the uneven reef in water up to his waist, making his way like a slow-motion drunk, hugging the lantern. He cut his shins and ankles on sharp coral. At about 9 o'clock he came to the end of the reef, alongside Ferguson Passage.

He took his shoes off and tied them to the life jacket, then struck out into open water. He swam about an hour, until he felt he was far enough out to intercept the PT's. Treading water, getting chilled, waiting, holding the lamp, he listened for the muffled roar of motors.

He looked west and saw flares that indicated an action beyond Gizo, 10 miles away. Kennedy realized that the PT boats had chosen, for the first night in many, to go around Gizo instead of through Ferguson Passage. There was no hope.

Kennedy started back, but this swim was different. He was very tired, and the current was carrying him off to the right. He saw that he would never reach the island; so he flashed the light on once and shouted, "Roger! Roger!"—to identify himself.

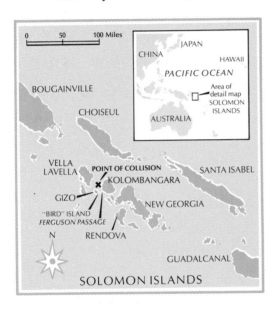

The men saw the light and heard the shouts. They thought that Kennedy had found a PT. They walked out onto the reef and waited. They waited a long time, but they saw nothing and heard nothing. They went back, very discouraged. One said despairingly, "We're going to die."

Johnston said, "Aw, shut up. *You* can't die. Don't you know that only the good die young?"

Kennedy had drifted right by the little island. He thought he had never known such deep trouble, but something he did shows that subconsciously he had not given up hope. He dropped his shoes, but he held onto the heavy lantern, his symbol of contact with his fellows. He stopped trying to swim. He seemed to stop caring. His body drifted through the wet hours, and he was very cold. Darkness and time took the place of a mind in his skull. For a long time he slept, or was crazy, or floated in a chill trance.

The tide shoves and sucks through the Solomon Islands and makes the currents curl in queer patterns. Jack Kennedy drifted in a huge circle—west past Gizo, then north and east past Kolombangara, then south. When light came at about 6, he saw that he was in Ferguson

Passage, exactly where he had been the night before when he saw the flares beyond Gizo.

For a second time he started back. He thought for a while that he had lost his mind and that he only imagined that he was repeating his attempt to reach the island. But the chill of the water was real enough, and his progress was measurable.

This time he made the island and crawled up on the beach. He was vomiting when his men came up to him. He said, "Ross, you try it tonight." Then he passed out.

In the afternoon Ross waded into the water and swam across to Island B. He took a pistol to signal with and spent the night watching Ferguson Passage. Nothing came through.

The next morning everyone felt wretched. Some prayed.

Johnston said: "You guys make me real sore. You didn't spend 10 cents in church in 10 years, then all of a sudden you're in trouble and you see the light."

When Ross came back, Kennedy decided that the group should move to a larger island to the southeast, where there seemed to be more coconut trees and where the party would be nearer Ferguson Passage. Again he towed McMahon, with the strap in his teeth, and the nine others grouped themselves around the timber as before. The swim took three hours.

The men were suffering most from thirst. When they found some coconuts lying on the ground under the trees, they broke them open and avidly drank the milk. Kennedy and McMahon, the first to drink, were sickened, and the others were careful to drink sparingly. During the night it rained, and someone suggested moving into the underbrush and licking water off the leaves. In the morning they saw that all the leaves were covered with bird droppings. Bitterly, they named the place Bird Island.

On the fourth day of their ordeal the men were low. Even Johnston was low. McGuire had a rosary and Johnston said, "McGuire, give that necklace a working over, will you?"

McGuire said quietly, "Yes, I'll take care of all you fellows."

Kennedy was still unwilling to admit that things were hopeless. He asked Ross to swim with him to an island called Nauru, to the southeast. They were both very weak, but after an hour's swim they finally made it and staggered up on the beach.

They walked painfully across Nauru to the Ferguson Passage side. There they found a box of Japanese candy and hardtack, a keg of water, and a one-man canoe. The two had a wary feast. When night fell, Kennedy took the canoe and a can of water from the keg out into Ferguson Passage. But no PT's came; so he paddled to Bird Island and gave out small rations of hardtack and water.

Before dawn Kennedy started out in the canoe to rejoin Ross, but a wind arose and the canoe was swamped. Some natives appeared from nowhere in a canoe, rescued Kennedy, and took him to Nauru. They showed him where a two-man canoe was cached. Kennedy picked up a coconut with a smooth shell and scratched a message on it with a jackknife: "ELEVEN ALIVE NATIVE KNOWS POSIT AND REEFS NAURU IS-LAND KENNEDY." Then he said to the natives, "Rendova, Rendova"— the island where the PT base was located.

The natives seemed to understand just what he meant. Taking the coconut, they paddled off.

Ross and Kennedy lay in a sickly daze all day. When it got dark, conscience took hold of Kennedy, and he persuaded Ross to go out into the Ferguson Passage with him in the two-man canoe. Ross argued against it. Kennedy insisted. The two started out. As they got into the passage, the wind rose. The waves grew until they were five or six feet high, and eventually they swamped the dugout. The two men clung to it, Kennedy at the bow, Ross at the stern. The tide carried them toward the open sea; so they kicked and tugged the canoe, aiming for the island. They struggled that way for two hours.

The weather got worse; rain poured down and they couldn't see more than 10 feet. Kennedy shouted: "Sorry I got you out here, Barney!" Ross shouted back: "This would be a great time to say I told you so, but I won't!"

They saw a white line ahead and heard a frightening roar—waves crashing on a reef. It was too late to do anything except hang on for dear life and wait.

A wave broke Kennedy's hold, ripped him away from the canoe, and turned him head over heels. His ears roared and his eyes pin-wheeled, and for the third time since the collision he thought he was dying. Somehow he was not thrown against the coral but floated into a kind of eddy. Suddenly, he felt the reef under his feet. He shouted, "Barney!" There was no reply.

Kennedy thought of how he had insisted on going out in the canoe, and he again called, "Barney! Barney!" This time Ross answered. He, too, had been thrown on the reef. His right arm and shoulder had been cruelly lacerated, and his feet, already infected from earlier wounds, were cut some more.

They struggled to the beach, fell down, and slept. In the morning

they were awakened by a noise. They looked up and saw four husky natives. One said in an excellent English accent: "I have a letter for you, sir." Kennedy tore the note open. It said:

> On His Majesty's Service. To the senior officer, Nauru Island. I have just learned of your presence on Nauru Is. I am in command of a New Zealand infantry patrol operating on New Georgia. I strongly advise that you come with these natives to me. Meanwhile, I shall be in radio communication with your authorities at Rendova, and we can finalize plans to collect balance of your party. Lt. Wincote.

Everyone shook hands, and the four natives took Ross and Kennedy in their war canoe across to Bird Island to tell the others the good news. There the natives built a lean-to for McMahon, whose burns had begun to rot and stink, and for Ross, whose arm had swelled to the size of a thigh. Then they put Kennedy in the bottom of their canoe, covered him with sacking and palm fronds in case Japanese planes should buzz them, and made the long trip to New Georgia.

Lieutenant Wincote came to the water's edge and said formally, "How do you do. Lieutenant Wincote."

Kennedy said, "Hello. I'm Kennedy."

Wincote said, "Come up to my tent and have a cup of tea."

That night Kennedy sat in the war canoe waiting at a rendezvous arranged by radio with the PT base. The moon went down at 11:20. Shortly afterward, Kennedy heard the signal—four shots. He fired four answering shots.

A voice shouted, "Hey, Jack!"

Kennedy answered, "Where the hell you been?"

In a few minutes a PT came alongside. Kennedy jumped onto it and hugged the men aboard.

The PT picked up the men on Bird Island and roared back toward base. The squadron medic had sent some brandy along to revive the weakened men. Johnston felt the need of a little revival. In fact, he felt he needed quite a bit of revival. After taking care of that, he retired topside and sat with his arms around a couple of roly-poly, mission-trained natives. And in the fresh breeze on the way home, they sang together a hymn all three happened to know:

> Jesus loves me, this I know,
> For the Bible tells me so;
> Little ones to Him belong,
> They are weak, but He is strong.
> Yes, Jesus loves me; yes, Jesus loves me.

Antis was a war dog. Born on a World War II battleground,
he became a decorated hero. Yet, to his master, Antis was
simply a friend, loyal and steadfast.

The Dog
From No Man's Land

By Anthony Richardson

T HE DEAFENING crash was followed almost at once by a long,
grinding roar. The noise was terrifying, and the German shepherd puppy, reacting frantically, struggled to get on his feet. He fell
over helplessly, uttering a tremulous cry. He was too weak from
starvation to stand up.

The farmhouse that was his home lay in no man's land between the
Maginot and Siegfried Lines. A few days earlier—it was now February 12, 1940—great thunderblasts of artillery had toppled the farmhouse walls, killed his mother and litter mates, and sent the farm
family scurrying. The puppy had lain alone in the ruined kitchen ever
since, cowering whenever the shelling recurred.

But that last blast had not been gunfire. It was the crash of a low-
flying reconnaissance plane, followed by an explosion of gasoline and
the roar of flames. A few minutes later two airmen from the French
1st Bomber-Reconnaissance Group, both lucky to be alive, spotted
the ruins of the farmhouse. The pilot, Pierre Duval, had taken a
bullet through his calf; so it was Jan Bozdech, observer-gunner, who
strode forward to investigate.

As he stepped inside past the sagging kitchen door, automatic pistol in hand, Jan heard the sound of quick, excited breathing.

"Put up your hands and come out," he ordered, covering a suspicious-looking pile of rubble.

There was no reply. With pounding heart, the airman carefully
moved forward and peered over the debris.

"Well, I'll be damned," he said. Then he began to laugh.

Pierre hobbled in, trailing blood. "What is it?" he asked.

"Look! I've captured a German," Jan replied. Reaching down, he brought up the tawny German shepherd puppy. Although the animal was quivering with fright, it bared its milk teeth, snarled defiantly, and even nipped at his hand.

"Here now," Jan said, stroking the base of the dog's ears, "you've just been saved from execution. I almost shot you, you know." Under this reassuring touch, the puppy relaxed in Jan's arms.

A ground fog had thus far protected the two downed airmen from German eyes. But this might lift at any time, and it would not be safe to try for the French lines until dark. They settled down to wait.

The wounded Pierre rested in a chair and closed his eyes. Jan dug out his chocolate ration and offered a lump to the dog. It sniffed the morsel, but did not eat until Jan lit a match and melted a piece. He rubbed the softened chocolate on his fingers. Once started, the puppy happily licked the airman's fingers clean again and again. Then it snuggled into his arms and slept contentedly.

Using one hand, Jan spread out a map on the floor and studied it. It showed a wood about a mile away. If they could make this, they should be in French territory. At 6 o'clock Jan shook Pierre awake.

"It's dark," he said. "We'd better be getting on."

For a moment they studied the puppy, sleeping on the floor. They couldn't take it along, for if it whimpered it might betray them. They left some of their rations beside a pan of water. Jan pulled the sagging door off its hinges and propped it sideways across the entrance so the puppy could not follow. Then they stole away.

As they set off for the wood, an exchange of gunfire broke out. They inched forward on hands and knees. Before they had moved 30 yards, a magnesium flare sputtered almost overhead, brilliantly lighting the terrain, and the two men flattened themselves instinctively. As the flare died away, Jan heard the noise he had been dreading— the frantic yelping of a puppy who knew he was being abandoned.

The animal would have to be silenced. Jan felt for his knife and, motioning Pierre to lie still, crept back. As he neared the farmhouse, he heard the puppy hurling itself against the barrier he had braced across the entry. Two forelegs momentarily hung over the edge while the hind legs scrabbled desperately. Then the dog slipped back down.

Jan peered over the barricade, straight into the puppy's imploring eyes. He turned away. It was unthinkable to kill a dog with a knife. He searched the ground for a heavy stick with which to stun the animal, but there was none. Thinking of Pierre lying injured in the darkness, he began to panic; he must hurry. Then he heard an anguished whimper from the other side of the door.

"Oh, hell," he muttered, and the last shreds of his firm resolution snapped. Reaching down into the dark, he lifted the puppy up and slipped it inside his flying jacket.

It took the two men almost seven torturous hours to reach the fringe of the protective wood. Pierre, weakened by his wound, was at the limit of his endurance, and even Jan collapsed, utterly spent.

During all this ordeal the puppy hadn't made a sound. But now he began to whine uncontrollably.

The noise roused Jan from near-sleep. "Be quiet," he muttered.

"Listen," Pierre said. "He hears something that we can't."

Then, like a pistol shot in the dark silence, a twig snapped and half a dozen figures emerged from the trees. Jan sprang to his feet, holding the dog with one hand and reaching for his automatic with the other one. But in the shifting moonlight he saw the uniforms of the French infantry. They'd made it to safety!

Using their rifles and a greatcoat to improvise a stretcher, two of the soldiers carried Pierre to the nearest blockhouse. Next day he was sent to the hospital. And Jan, gently clutching the puppy, was driven back to his squadron base at St. Dizier.

Here he belonged to a particularly close band of seven Czech exiles. All seven had been members of the Czech Air Force before Hitler invaded their country. They then had escaped through Poland, joined the French Foreign Legion in Africa, and later had been attached to the French Air Force. All had the same fighting spirit, the same determination to strike back against the Germans at all costs.

Perhaps it was their very homelessness that made them so susceptible to Jan's puppy. They loved him at once, immediately adopted him as a mascot, and after some discussion named him "Antis" after the A.N.T. bombers they'd flown back in Czechoslovakia. As Joshka, a slight, curly-haired youth from Moravia, commented, "The name should be unique, short, and typically personal for our dog."

"*My* dog," Jan corrected. But he assented to the name.

Every night Antis slept in the blockhouse at Jan's feet. As the weeks passed, he flourished and grew and, being intelligent and lovingly instructed, he learned to shake hands with each of his friends.

France tasted defeat that spring when Hitler's panzer divisions drove south with demoralizing speed. The squadron fled from one threatened airdrome to another until the day Paris fell. Then it was assembled for the last time.

"Gentlemen," the adjutant announced solemnly, "the unit is disbanded. Now it is every man for himself. May God be with you!"

The seven Czechs held a council. "We came here to fight, not to run away," said Vlasta, the senior member of the group. "I suggest we stick together, try to get to England, and carry on from there."

There was no dissent. Within 15 minutes the seven had piled all their possessions on an ancient cart and, perching Antis atop the load, joined the stream of refugees fleeing southward. And, because they were both determined and lucky, some two weeks later they found themselves in the small Mediterranean seaport of Sète. From there they made their way to the British naval base at Gibraltar.

Once the British had satisfied themselves about the Czech fliers' credentials, they assigned all seven to the Royal Air Force and ordered them to proceed on the trawler *Northman,* bound for Liverpool. They were finally going to England!

There was, however, one small problem: No dogs were allowed on board. British regulations absolutely forbade it. A flying wedge of Czechs smuggled Antis up the gangplank in a raincoat and spirited him into the stokehold. Jan loyally remained with the dog, spreading a blanket on the grimy coal.

On the second day out the *Northman's* engines broke down, and all passengers were ordered to transfer to another vessel. Hurriedly the Czechs divided Jan's baggage among themselves so that there would be room to conceal Antis in his duffel bag. All went well until they reached the deck of the new ship, where Jan paused momentarily to shift the weight of the bag.

"Move along, please," the ship's interpreter remarked curtly, and at the sound of the strange voice the duffel bag wriggled perceptibly. As it did, Jan lost his grip on the cord enclosing its neck. Immediately Antis thrust his head through the opening and looked out—directly into the astonished eyes of the British officer of the watch. The seven Czechs all stood as if paralyzed.

"Hullo," said the officer with a grin, "a stowaway! Well, let the poor beggar out before he suffocates." He released the cord and Antis dropped to the deck, shaking a cloud of coal dust around him.

"Now get him below and give him a bath before the captain sees what a mess you've made of his deck," the officer said, turning away to check off another group of transferees. Jan was pushed along in a daze, with Antis trotting at his heels.

The rest of the trip was made in luxury—real bunks, clean laundry, washbowls in the cabins. Antis, given his freedom, regained his vitality and glossy coat.

But as they approached Liverpool, the fliers received devastating news. All animals had to be quarantined in port for six months; animals whose owners could not pay the kennel fees would be destroyed. All the money the fliers had among them would not ransom Antis for more than three weeks.

But resourceful men have coped with greater problems. And by then the Czechs were seasoned conspirators.

When the ship docked at Liverpool the next evening, Jan and Vlasta wangled the assignment of overseeing the unloading of the detachment's baggage. After the last of it had been stacked in the cargo net, they then carefully placed a large, oddly shaped duffel bag stenciled "Jan Bozdech" on top of the pile.

Within the hour the bags were stacked neatly on the platform at Liverpool Central Station, Jan's still on top of the heap. Three minutes before their train steamed in, a platoon of soldiers marched up, halted, and ordered arms. A rifle butt struck the bag labeled Bozdech, and a loud yelp of protest arose.

Immediately the military police converged on the pile. The Czech detachment, always eager to help, joined in the search, heaving the baggage about and passing Jan's bag from hand to hand under cover of the general confusion until it was well clear of the suspected area. Surreptitious yelps with an imperceptible Czechoslovakian accent also misled the pursuers.

When the airmen's train arrived, the police gave up in disgust.

A quarter of an hour later the eight comrades were on their way to their first camp in the United Kingdom. It was July 12, 1940.

For men who had been on active combat duty, going back to flying school was irksome. At Cosford, and then at the Duxford RAF station, the Czechs also spent many exasperating hours poring over a book called *Fundamentals of English*. They almost welcomed the sporadic German air attacks that disrupted their study routine.

Jan devoted his spare time to training Antis. He was no expert handler and treated the animal simply as though he were a fellow human being. Antis responded with the most devoted and intelligent obedience. He quickly mastered all the standard commands, learned to close doors when ordered, and unfailingly fetched Jan's gloves when his companion dressed to go out.

While Jan was in class, Antis stayed with the armorers. He developed an unusual ability to detect enemy aircraft and was always minutes ahead of the base's high-frequency direction finders. The warning system worked only when the planes were flying high. When the Germans came in at treetop level, it was of little use. But Antis, the armorers claimed, invariably alerted them in time to take cover.

JAN WAS SKEPTICAL, for he had always been in class at the start of the raids. But one night, when he was studying in his bunk, Antis suddenly woke up and trotted to the window, ears cocked. There was no sound except the hiss of rain, but the dog began to growl.

"Go and lie down," Jan said. "There's nothing out in this weather."

Antis whined persistently. Then, seeing that Jan had no intention of moving from the bunk, Antis flattened his ears reproachfully and lay down. Half an hour later Joshka looked in as he came off duty from the Operations Room.

"Thick out," he said. "I wouldn't have been up there tonight for anything. I'll bet the German who came over was lost."

"Tonight?" Jan asked. "I didn't hear a thing."

"About half an hour ago," Joshka said. "Very high. We were plotting him just over 15 miles away when he turned back."

"Well, I'll be damned," Jan said, and by way of apology reached down and rubbed Antis' ears. The canny dog had been right.

That fall, when the Czechs were transferred to Speke airfield, five miles from Liverpool, Antis' peculiar ability became very important. Liverpool was a major target, subject to heavy bombardment. The dog's warnings were uncannily accurate, and the men came to depend on him to alert them whenever the immediate area was threatened.

One night when Jan and Vlasta were returning from liberty in town, the dog began to whine just as they neared a massive archway beneath the Speke viaduct. Over Liverpool the air was ribbed with searchlights and the horizon blinked with exploding bombs, but as yet there had been no warning siren.

"They *must* be headed this way," Jan said as the animal's whine grew more insistent. "Come on, let's hole up under the archway."

Almost immediately they heard the approaching engines. The first bomb burst just as they flung themselves under the viaduct.

Now explosion followed explosion; a girder fell, splitting the granite pavement; masonry toppled at either end of the arch. Where there had been a neat row of houses beside the viaduct there was only rubble. A long silence ensued, then someone began to scream.

"Come on," Vlasta yelled. "We've got to get them out."

They ran into the street. A man with blood spurting from a mangled arm blundered into them.

"Save her!" he shouted. "She's under there. We were having a cup of tea . . ." His voice trailed off.

A rescue worker thrust a pick into Jan's hands. Antis, standing by the shattered remains of a kitchen cupboard, his forepaws deep in broken china, began to bark. Jan looked closely and saw five fingers moving in the rubble. Digging quickly, he uncovered a dazed and blood-streaked woman.

"Good dog," the rescue worker said. "Bring him over here, will you? There's bound to be others. Lord, what a shambles!"

Jan followed the man to a pile of smoking plaster and shattered furniture. "Seek!" he ordered.

Halfway up the heap Antis stopped short, sniffing. An RAF officer started to dig where Antis stood, and within a few minutes he had a man out who had been totally buried and was still unconscious.

They continued working until 2 in the morning. When the rescue-squad leader passed the word that the job was done, the dog's coat was matted, his paws cut and bleeding from scrambling over the wreckage.

"There's no more we can do here," Vlasta said. "Let's go back and have Antis tended to."

But Antis was straining at his leash again, dragging Jan toward a sagging brick wall.

"No more, boy," Jan said. "We've had enough—"

A crash cut him short as the wall collapsed. Horrified, he felt the leash jerk out of his hand.

"Antis!" he shouted in the din. "Antis!" Vlasta flashed his light to where the wall had been. There was now only a head-high pile of brick and timbers. Instantly Jan was on his knees, pulling up chunks of plaster and flinging them in every direction. Again he shouted almost hysterically, "Antis!"

From somewhere behind the rubble came an answering bark. The men quickly broke through to a little room knee-deep in debris. A woman, sprawled on her back under a mass of plaster, was dead. But in the far corner Antis stood by a crib; the child in it was still alive.

The rescue-squad director was visibly moved. "You know, boy," he told Antis, "we just couldn't have done the job without you."

By early January 1941 Jan, Stetka, and Josef had completed their flying-school and flight training and, with Squadron No. 311 (Czech Squadron of Bomber Command), were posted to East Wretham for combat duty. The move reunited them with the other Czechs who had been training elsewhere and gave them at long last a chance to get at the hated enemy. But it meant that Antis, for the first time, had to accustom himself to separations from Jan. For the night bombing missions, which the squadron was soon flying, ofter lasted from late evening until dawn.

For weeks Antis was moody and dispirited. Then he established rapport with the maintenance crew assigned to *Cecilia*, his master's plane, and seemed to adjust himself to the absences. The dog would accompany Jan to dispersal, see him get aboard the big Wellington bomber, then retire to the maintenance tent, which stood at the edge of the field. Once there, he would settle down for the night and not budge as long as the planes were out.

But sometimes before dawn he would suddenly rise and cock his ears, and the maintenance crew knew then that the squadron was returning. As soon as Antis discerned the particular pitch of *Cecilia's* propellers, he commenced to bound and prance excitedly—his "war dance," the mechanics called it—and then he would trot out to watch the planes come in and to greet Jan. The ritual never varied.

But one night in June, after Jan had flown more than 10 missions, the mechanics noted a sharp departure from routine. Shortly after midnight Antis became unusually restive. "What's the matter with him?" one asked. "Are we expecting visitors?"

"No," replied Adamek, the crew chief, "no Jerries about tonight." He spoke directly to the dog. "Antis, calm down."

But the dog ignored him and went to the tent flap. Suddenly he lifted his muzzle and let out a long howl. Then he lay down outside,

not resting, but with his head up as if preparing for a long vigil.

At half past one the first returning Wellington blinked her identification lights and rumbled down the runway. She was followed at regular intervals by other planes until all but *Cecilia* were accounted for. Two hours passed; there was still no sign of Jan's aircraft.

"No point hanging on here," one of the mechanics finally said. "She'd have run out of gas by now."

"We'll give it 15 minutes more," Adamek said. When the time was up and the plane had not appeared, the crew reluctantly decided to disperse for breakfast.

"Come along, Antis," said Adamek. The dog would not move.

Just then the squadron's popular wing commander, Josef Ocelka, drove up to the tent. A longtime admirer of Antis, he had promised he would look after the dog if Jan ever failed to return from a mission.

"Any news of *Cecilia*, sir?" one of the mechanics asked, while Adamek struggled with Antis.

"Not yet. Give him a shove, Corporal," Ocelka suggested.

"It's no good, sir." Adamek replied. "He won't move until Jan shows up. I know him."

"So do I, dammit," Ocelka said. "Let's go. Perhaps he'll change his mind when he gets hungry."

After breakfast Adamek went back to the tent with a plate of liver. Antis ignored it, as he ignored the driving rain that had begun to fall. When Adamek saw that no amount of coaxing would move the dog, he spread a tarpaulin over him and left.

Late that afternoon Operations Room was informed that *Cecilia* had been hit by flak over the Dutch coast but had managed to limp back to Coltishall airfield with only one casualty. Air gunner Jan Bozdech was in Norwich Hospital undergoing treatment for a superficial head wound. The Czechs were elated at the good news. But no one could convey it to the dog.

All that night Antis stayed at his post. Next morning, at the time when the squadron customarily returned from raids, he stood up and paced about. An hour after dawn, when no plane had appeared, he began to howl disconsolately.

"He'll starve," Ocelka said, "and drive us crazy while he does. We've got to think of something."

It was the station chaplain, Padre Poucnly, who provided the solution. He went straight to the heart of the matter by telephoning the medical authorities at Norwich. Sergeant Bozdech was not seriously hurt. Would it be possible to run him out for a short trip in an ambulance and then board the dog at the hospital for a few days? (A medical consultation followed.) Yes? It would? Thank you so much.

And that was that. The ambulance arrived that afternoon, and the two inseparables rode back together to Norwich Hospital. There both of them were outrageously spoiled by the nurses until Jan recovered.

By the time Antis had waited out 30 of *Cecilia's* missions, all the crew felt that they knew his habits thoroughly. But one night shortly after the aircrew roll call the dog disappeared. Although there was no trace of him anywhere, and it was unlike him to alter a long-established routine, no one was particularly concerned. Antis had long ago proved that he could take care of himself.

When the plane leveled off at 8,000 feet, Jan gave a last worried look at the Wretham airfield, now indistinguishable in the darkened English countryside. Then he put the dog out of his mind and concentrated on checking his guns.

"Navigator to wireless operator," the intercom crackled suddenly. "Can you hear me?"

Engrossed in his own duties, Jan only half listened to the reply. But the navigator's next words jarred him to full attention.

"Am I going round the bend, or do you see what I see?" he asked.

There was a flurry of incredulous profanity. Then, "He must have got into the emergency bed by the flare-chute. Someone forgot to check it. Jan, open your turret door—we have a stowaway."

Jan knew at once what had happened. He opened the hatch and, as nonchalantly as if it were an everyday occurrence, Antis crawled into the turret and settled down between his feet.

"You villain!" Jan exclaimed. "We ought to drop you out with the bombs." But nothing could be done about it. The Wellington droned on, and Antis drifted off to sleep.

As they went over the target, a dense curtain of flak rocked the aircraft, but the dog stayed calm as long as Jan appeared unmoved. In response Jan found himself forcing signs of encouragement despite the intensity of the barrage, and thus each drew strength from the other. Then in a few moments the danger had passed, and they were on their way home unscathed.

They had just disembarked when Ocelka drove up. Since it was against Air Ministry regulations to take an animal on missions, the men braced themselves for a tongue-lashing. Like many easygoing officers, Ocelka could be vitriolic when the occasion demanded.

"How did you all make out?" he asked coolly, casting a sidelong glance at Antis. The pilot, Jo Capka, briefly described the run and the heavy fire they had encountered. The crew shuffled nervously as the recital came to a conclusion.

"Heavy fire, eh? What do you think of that?" Ocelka asked, looking Antis squarely in the eye. "Don't you think these poor boys need someone to hold their hands?"

Jan could stand it no longer. "I can explain, sir," he began, but Ocelka cut him off.

"What the eye doesn't see the heart doesn't grieve," he said curtly. "I've enough trouble on my hands with two-legged beasts without looking for any from four-legged ones. Now let's get back to Operations and make out the reports."

From then on Antis was accepted as a regular member of *Cecilia's* complement. His unruffled behavior under fire was all the more welcome because the men were nearing the end of their standard tour of combat duty. This was always a time of increased tension for any aircrew, for they all knew that more than one plane had gone down on its last trip. Unaware of their anxieties, Antis raced for the plane as if each mission were a pleasure trip, and inevitably something of his élan communicated itself to the crew.

He began to amass quite a respectable combat record and eventually sustained two wounds in the line of duty. The first occurred over Kiel, when a fragment of shrapnel lacerated his left ear, which acquired a permanent droop. The second ended his flying career.

DURING AN ATTACK on Hanover, as *Cecilia* was turning homeward after releasing her bombs, a shell exploded directly beneath the plane. The engines were not damaged, and no one reported being wounded; but when they reached East Wretham, the undercarriage jammed and they had to belly in for a landing. Only then did Jan discover that Antis had a three-inch shrapnel wound in his chest.

Jan rushed the dog to Station Sick Quarters, where he was stitched up. Thereafter Antis was grounded and barred from the field. Much as the dog resented the restrictions, they were somewhat easier to bear because he did not know Jan was still flying. While *Cecilia* was being repaired, the crew was assigned another plane, and since its propeller pitch was unfamiliar, Antis simply ignored it.

A short time later Jan completed his tour of 41 missions (of which Antis had shared 7) and was relieved of further combat duty. He spent the remaining two years of the war first as an instructor, then in flying antisubmarine patrol.

The first years of peace were blissfully happy ones for Jan. When he returned to his triumphantly liberated country, he was given a captaincy in the Czech Air Force and eventually was assigned to the Ministry of National Defense in Prague. Both he and Antis became well known to the public, for Jan wrote three books about service in the RAF. Almost every newspaper in Czechoslovakia carried tales of his war experiences with the dog.

When Jan married a golden-haired girl named Tatiana, Antis distinguished himself at the wedding by becoming entangled in the bridal veil. (He later made up for it by his steady devotion to Tatiana.) And when a son, Robert, was born to his idols in 1947, the baby became the dog's personal charge. At night he slept near the crib, instantly alert if the child awoke or cried. The dog would then rise, steal to the side of the big bed, and thrust his cold nose against the mother's bare shoulder. And if this failed to waken her, he would drag the covers away.

It was a wonderful time for all of them, but it was not to last.

On March 7, 1948, Jan Masaryk, Minister of Foreign Affairs and godfather to little Robert, telephoned from the Cernicky Palace.

"Please come round and see me, Jan," Masaryk said. "I have a present for your little boy."

As he put down the telephone, Jan knew that this summons might bring his life crashing about his ears. He had seen Masaryk only the previous day, so why should this good friend ask to see him again at this moment? There could be but one reason, and Jan approached the Cernicky Palace with dread.

"You are high on the Communist blacklist, Jan," Masaryk told him. "The blow can fall any time now. You must keep this completely to yourself. Even Tatiana must not know. You've got to get out of Czechoslovakia as soon as possible."

This then was the "present" for little Robert. But even that ruse had been necessary, since every telephone was tapped.

Acting through the Czech Communist Party, Soviet Russia was implacably taking over all the country. As the cold war intensified, everyone who had had associations in the West became suspect, and for months Jan had been aware that his apartment had been under surveillance. His friends knew it and no longer dared visit him. The Defense Ministry was now being packed with Communist informers, many of whom spoke Russian. Recently, two strange officers had been installed in his own department—ostensibly learners, but unquestionably spies.

Three days after Masaryk's warning was issued, it was grimly underscored by the fact that Masaryk himself was dead. According to the Communists, he had jumped from a Foreign Office window.

Jan faced an agonizing dilemma. He could not leave his wife and son while there was any possibility of a life for them together. But if he were imprisoned, they would be in a far worse position than if he fled. It was hard to know what to do, and for weeks he vacillated. Then one morning General Prachoska of the Czech intelligence service summoned him, and the decision was taken out of his hands.

"Sit down, Bozdech," the general greeted him. "Major Marek, my aide, would like to ask you a few questions."

"You are the author of these?" Marek began curtly, handing Jan three books and a folder of press clippings.

Jan nodded.

"And there have been broadcasts, radio plays, all glorifying the British?" Marek continued.

"I served in the RAF," Jan explained. "My writing is only a record of my experiences, without political significance—"

"On the contrary," Marek interrupted. "This work is treasonable. If you continue writing, your attention will be directed to the Red Air Force only. That is an order." He paused. "And there is one other matter. You are a member of the Air Force Club?"

"Yes, sir," said Jan. The fliers' organization was often referred to as the "English Club" because of the high percentage of members who were ex-RAF officers.

"We know that all sorts of opinions are expressed in this establishment, and we are interested in them. To put it bluntly, Captain, we want you to listen to, and if necessary encourage, criticism of the present regime. You will then report to this department the names of members whose remarks indicate that they are enemies of the state."

Jan was aghast. But as he began to protest, Marek brandished a blue document that had been lying on his desk. "I have here a police warrant for your arrest, dated Friday. You have three days to make up your mind. Is that clear?"

Jan did not return home until late that night. Long after dark he walked the streets alone, desperately seeking some way out of the trap set for him. He would never spy on his friends; that much was sure. If he remained in his post and defied the Communists, imprisonment and death were almost certain. His course was plain. No option remained but to flee the country.

To his great surprise, he woke the following morning with his mind refreshed and his nerves calm. Now that the long-dreaded blow had fallen and his intentions were resolved, his problems seemed almost preternaturally clarified.

He set off for his office at the usual time.

Some 50 yards from the Ministry of National Defense, a passerby awkwardly blundered into him.

"Excuse me, Brazda," Jan said in embarrassment, recognizing the man as a casual acquaintance, one of the instructors at the sokol physical-training college.

"If you are in trouble," Brazda said in rapid undertones, "listen to me. Tonight at 8. The Café Pavlova Kavarna at Strahove. The password is, 'May I offer you a vodka?'"

Then begging Jan's pardon for his clumsiness, Brazda left. The machinery of the underground movement had begun to turn.

AT 8 THAT NIGHT, when Jan appeared at the Café Pavlova Kavarna, the machinery caught him up smoothly. A dapper little man led him to a small upstairs room where he was confronted by two other members of the underground, a student and an elderly man who had obviously once been a soldier. The former military man, who was the leader of the group, wasted no time on formalities.

"Captain Bozdech," he said, "the deadline for your arrest is Friday. That gives us only one day to get you out of the country. It is not much time. You must make your decision quickly.

"You understand the risks, of course. If you are caught attempting to cross the frontier, they shoot first and ask questions later. So you must go alone, and perhaps we can arrange for your family to follow later by a less dangerous route. Agreed?"

Jan's heart sank, but he nodded.

"Very well," the spokesman said. "Now here are your instructions. Listen carefully." And for the next five minutes the three anonymous agents outlined down to the smallest detail what Jan would have to do the following day. Then with a warm bon voyage they dismissed him.

Tatiana was asleep when Jan returned home that night. Looking at her face, sweet in repose, he recalled Masaryk's warning, "Even Tatiana must not know." Of course Masaryk was right, Jan mused as he turned out the light. Both for her safety and little Robert's, it was best that he slip off this way. But next morning when he said good-bye to her, he found it almost impossible to keep his voice steady, and the closing of the door behind him was like a blow above the heart.

When he reached the office, he summoned his civilian clerk, Vesely. He had decided during the night that, risky as it might be, he would have to make one change in the underground's careful plans. Antis would have to come with him. Otherwise, as Jan knew from long experience, the dog would stubbornly refuse to eat; and Jan simply could not condemn him to certain starvation.

"Vesely," Jan said, "I've an appointment for Antis at the vet's at 11 o'clock. Would you go round to my flat later and collect him? I'll give you my gloves so he'll follow you."

"Very good, sir," Vesely replied.

Two hours later, when his unwitting accomplice returned with the dog, Jan knew that the time had come. The escape was now to begin. As he went out the door, he stopped for a moment casually. "I'll be back after lunch if anyone wants me," he said.

One of the Stalinist spies looked up from his paperwork. "We'll hold the fort," he said sarcastically. "Take your time."

"Thanks," said Jan. "I will."

Following the underground's instructions, he took a tram to the Vaclavska Namesti and went into the busy public lavatory there. When he asked a prearranged question, the attendant at once handed him a parcel containing a change of clothing. He was to travel as a peasant with a knapsack full of butter to sell.

The attendant kept Antis while Jan changed in one of the booths. Everything was complete, the sizes right—from the rough felt hat to the heavy boots. There were also a dozen packages of butter.

"You look a treat," the attendant muttered as Jan emerged from the booth and handed him a 500-crown note along with the parcel (which now contained Jan's smart air force uniform). "I hope you get a good price for your butter."

It was 150 yards to the Wilsonova Station. But no one took the least notice of him as he clumped through the tumult of traffic in his strange new boots, entered the station, and bought a ticket. The train came in, and he and Antis climbed aboard. Six minutes later, still following instructions, he alighted at Smichov.

This was but the beginning of a long and circuitous course that eventually brought Jan to a certain farmstead where he spent the night. Next morning a taciturn driver concealed him, along with Antis, in the back of a two-ton van. After a long ride they stopped at a remote cottage in a heavily wooded area.

"This is Anton's," the driver said. "I leave you here."

"Who is Anton?"

"A forester. He will guide you over the border."

As the van drove away, a tall, tanned man stepped from the cottage.

"What can I do for you?" he asked evenly, his eyes on the dog.

As he had been told to do, Jan offered him a package of a certain brand of cigarettes. The man turned it over in his hand ruminatively. Finally he said, "Why have you brought the dog?"

"Wherever I go, he goes too," Jan said.

Anton's face darkened. "Wherever you go, he goes," he repeated. "My God! Do you think this is a picnic outing? One bark from him and we're dead. You'll have to leave him behind."

"Then I'd better start back," Jan said.

"You'll have a warm welcome. The alarm will be out by now."

Jan realized this was true, for it was now Friday. But about Antis his mind remained stubbornly set.

"So you really want to risk your neck for the dog, eh?" Anton said. "Well, we'll see what Stefan says. He'll be coming with us."

He called into the cottage and in a moment a bearded, erect man emerged. Anton explained the situation to him, but the man said nothing, staring at Jan and Antis as if trying to recall something.

"Antis is trained," Jan said quickly. "He won't make a sound, and he may be able to help us."

"Antis," Stefan said. "That's it. I've read about you two and seen your picture in the papers. He can come, as far as I'm concerned."

Anton shrugged, then smiled at Jan. "You'd have found it a long walk back to Prague," he said. "But I like your spirit. You'll do. Now wait here, both of you."

He went into the house and returned immediately with two revolvers. "I hope we don't have to use them," Anton said, "but the positions of the observation posts are always changing. You never know."

Squatting, he began to trace a map on the ground with a stick. "Here," he said, pointing, "is our first obstacle, a forest about two miles deep. It's infested with patrols. We come out of the forest here," he indicated the spot, "then cross a small valley, which is also constantly patrolled. Then here is the West German frontier, and half a mile past it the village of Kesselholst. Once we're there, we're safe.

"We'll leave immediately. I want to reach the far side of the forest in daylight. Then we'll hole up and make the last dash across the valley after dark."

A car carried Jan, Anton, Stefan, and Antis 15 miles to the edge of the forest, and early that afternoon they plunged into the matted underbrush. Unavoidably they made a lot of noise, and as a precaution against being surprised by roving border patrols, Jan sent Antis ahead with instructions to "seek." Twice the dog stopped, growling a low warning when no other sound was audible, and seconds later the three men heard the faint, far-off sound of snapping twigs and hailing voices. They lay in the underbrush without stirring until the patrols passed, then moved cautiously on. It was almost sunset when they finally reached the far side of the wood.

From its border they carefully scanned the open valley that lay between them and Kesselholst. To their left was a narrow road and, paralleling it, a turbulent river. No patrols or strongholds were visible. As the evening light waned and the lights in the village began to go on, Anton murmured, "All right, let's go."

They had covered only a short distance when they heard Antis growl. Jan dropped to the ground, as did his companions. A moment later four dim figures stole past them down the slope.

Without warning, two searchlights suddenly split the night, sweeping across the valley. Rocks, bushes, and boulders seemed to leap out of the darkness as the light beams passed, converging, separating, then pouncing simultaneously on their prey. Four men, scarcely 50 yards from Jan, were caught scrambling frantically for the trees. They were obviously other escapees. Before they could reach the cover of the trees, machine guns opened fire, and all four fell.

As Jan, Anton, and Stefan watched, two trucks then sped up the road. Men alighted, picked up the bodies, and drove off.

"We're lucky to be alive," Anton whispered. "The way I intended to take is blocked by a new post, and if those four hadn't passed us, we'd have walked right into it. We'll have to double back and take another route across the river."

They crept silently back to the wood and then spent a hellish hour struggling blindly through the close-set firs to the riverbank. As soon as Jan stepped into the water, holding Antis by the collar, the current began to undermine his footing.

"Link hands," Anton said.

Jan clamped Antis' jaws onto the tail of his coat, and the four of them, clinging tightly to one another, edged their way toward the center of the swift-flowing river. As the current swirled about their waists, Jan slipped on a loose stone, staggered, and lost his grip on his companions' wrists. Immediately he was swept downstream, dragging Antis with him, until he struck a boulder and managed to grasp it. Recovering his balance, he saw that he had been carried into shallower water and he waded the few yards to the far shore.

Antis was with him, but there was no sign of Anton and Stefan. He dared not shout. Kneeling beside the dog, he ordered, "Seek!"

For several minutes after Antis had gone, there was no sound but the roar of the river. Jan wondered if he had been a fool to send the dog on such a hopeless errand—the current could carry a man 50 yards in a few moments. Then suddenly he felt a blow on the shoulder, and as he reached for his gun, a voice beside him began to curse. It was Anton and behind him was Antis.

"Sorry," Anton said. "I was crawling and bumped you with my head. Thank God for the dog. We'd never have got back together without him. Do you think he can find Stefan?"

At an order from Jan, the dog again disappeared. It was some time before he returned, leading his bedraggled and exhausted quarry.

"I was swept a long way downstream into a pool," Stefan explained. "But Antis found me. I think he saved my life."

After a moment's rest they pressed on, climbing toward a ridge that lay within a few hundred yards of the frontier. A dense fog shrouded the forest near its crest, and it became impossible to see a foot ahead. Antis ran from man to man, as a sheep dog handles his flock, guiding them. But at the top of the rise Anton decided that it was useless to continue the journey while the mist obscured all landmarks, and the four settled down to await the dawn.

At FIRST LIGHT they moved behind a giant boulder to plan their final dash across the border. Jan posted Antis atop the rock as lookout.

Since Anton had no idea what new posts they might encounter, they decided to cross the valley one at a time, and Anton broke a twig in lengths for lots to see who would go first. As he extended his hand, Antis growled and leaped from the top of the boulder. There was a clatter of stones, a stifled cry, and savage snarling.

Gun in hand, Jan ran around the rock. Antis was straddling a soldier who lay sprawled on his back, his rifle useless beneath him. Anton sprang at the guard, his knife upraised.

"No!" Jan cried. Anton hesitated.

"Jan is right," Stefan said. "It would be murder."

"The swine deserves to die," Anton said, but he grudgingly got off the man's chest. Quickly they gagged him and lashed him to a tree, then ran down toward the valley.

At the edge of the wood they stopped abruptly. In the meadow ahead a single guard post, with telephone wires running from its roof, blocked their way. Helpless, they crouched in the brush for almost an hour, watching the hut. There was no sign of movement.

"Try the dog," Anton whispered, and Jan sent Antis to seek.

Antis trotted out and stood sniffing beside the closed door. Then he barked. There was no response.

"I think there was only one guard in there," Stefan said, "and now he's tied to a tree."

Jan was on his feet, shaking with excitement. "Let's go," he cried, and they sprang into the open field. Far off down the valley someone shouted, but the three men and the dog raced on, down the slope and across the stream at its base. From far behind them they heard a telephone jangling in the hut in the meadow, and the sound of a distant whistle reached them.

"On! On!" Anton cried.

Another open field lay before them and, beyond, a wood. They ran for the sanctuary of the trees, and at last they knew that their feet were on German soil.

As soon as he had delivered his charges safely to the West German authorities, Anton bade Jan and Stefan farewell. He would return to Czechoslovakia and risk his life again to keep the escape route open for other proscribed men.

"Pray God we meet again in happier times," he said in parting. "I certainly was wrong about the dog. He was our salvation."

Within a week after his arrival in West Germany Jan received some heartening news from his homeland. A Czech refugee who had known him in Prague brought word that Tatiana and Robert had suffered no reprisals and were living quietly with her parents. After he received this report, he was convinced that his decision to flee Czechoslovakia had been the right one. He applied for reenlistment in the RAF and was accepted.

On this trip to England, however, there was no squad of loyal Czechs to smuggle Antis past the inspectors, and Jan had no choice but to surrender him for the legal six-month quarantine. Now a familiar difficulty arose. Upon reenlistment Jan had reverted to the lowest rank in the service, and his entire salary would not cover the cost of the kennel fees. Thus in desperation he applied for help to the People's Dispensary for Sick Animals in London, submitting a full report on the dog's history.

The clinic's response went far beyond Jan's expectations. Not only were the fees paid, but Antis' story was widely publicized. As a result, in March 1949 he was awarded an unprecedented tribute. He became the first non-British dog to receive the Dickin Medal, the Victoria Cross of the animal world. In a moving presentation speech Field Marshal Archibald Wavell, one of England's greatest soldiers, cited

Antis' "outstanding courage, devotion to duty and lifesaving on several occasions while serving with the Royal Air Force."

"I am sure," the field marshal concluded, "that everyone will join with me in congratulating you on your award, Antis, and we wish you many years in which to wear it."

Actually there were to be few more years for Antis, but during that time he and Jan were closer than ever. Jan heard no more from his wife, son, or parents, so Antis became his only family. As Antis' sight dimmed and his muzzle whitened with age, he could not bear even the slighest separation from his beloved master.

Each year, wherever they were posted, Jan performed an unvarying ritual on Christmas Eve. Beside a miniature Christmas tree, glittering with tinsel and artificial frost, he propped up photographs of Tatiana, Robert, and his parents, thus preserving at least one tangible link with home. On Christmas Eve of 1952 Jan finished his small arrangement and went to bed early. Sometime that night he awoke, conscious of a strange weight on his chest. Reaching out, he found that it was Antis, resting his head there.

This was most unusual. Once the dog had retired for the night, he could be depended upon to stay on his blanket until morning.

"What's wrong, Antis?" Jan asked. "Go back to bed, old-timer."

Jan heard a tremulous sigh, followed by the scrabbling sound of the dog's paws on the floor, then the sound of a falling body.

Instantly Jan switched on the light. Antis was lying on his side, unable to rise. Jan carried him to his bed and began to massage his legs, continuing the treatment at intervals all that night. By noon of the next day Antis managed to stand, but he was too weak to follow his master outside, and Jan stayed with him during the base's Christmas festivities. From his window he could see the lights in his mess and hear the sound of laughter and singing, and twice friends looked in to suggest that Antis might be left for a while. Jan thanked them, but he stuck to his vigil.

He sat by the table with the Christmas tree on it and took up Tatiana's photograph. She looked radiant in her wedding dress, and he remembered how Antis had become entangled in her veil when they left the church. Now across at the mess they were playing "Silent Night," and Jan remembered Christmases at other posts. The room was full of ghosts: Adamek and Joshka, Ocelka and Vlasta; scores of them trooped in. And soon Antis would be with them.

It seemed to Jan that 100 years had passed since the day—12 years before—when he had found that small puppy in no man's land.

*Determined to escape from a Soviet
slave-labor camp near the Arctic Circle, a small band
of desperate men set out on foot on an
incredible journey of more than 4,000 miles. Only the
hardiest of the band survived the awesome
trek to reach their final goal—India.*

The Long Walk

*By Slavomir Rawicz
as told to Ronald Downing*

SLAVOMIR RAWICZ was a 24-year-old lieutenant in the Polish Army when he was arrested in 1939 by the Soviet secret police and charged with spying. Vigorously maintaining his innocence, he was subjected to a year of physical and psychological torture before he was declared guilty of espionage and plotting against the people of the U.S.S.R.

Rawicz was sentenced to 25 years of forced labor and sent to Siberia. The journey from Moscow to the prison camp was a brutal one, first by cattle car, then on foot through subzero temperatures. Rawicz has recounted the story of his ordeal and ultimate escape in a book, *The Long Walk*. Parts of that extraordinary document are reproduced here, beginning with Slavomir Rawicz's arrival in northern Siberia at Camp 303 close to the Arctic Circle.

LIFE IN CAMP 303

A FAINT EARLY-MORNING HAZE dissipated, and in the cold, clear light of day I looked around at the place to which I had been consigned to spend 25 years of my life. Camp 303, lying between 300 and 400 miles south of the Arctic Circle, was a rectangular enclosure about a half-mile long and about 400 yards broad, at each corner of which stood a guard tower raised high on solid timber stilts, manned by machine-gun crews. The main gate, around which were built the troops' quarters, the kitchens, storehouses, and administrative huts, faced west in one of the shorter sides of the oblong. Roughly in the center of the enclosure was an open stretch of ground that served as the security no man's land between the soldiers and the prisoners.

Between us and the surrounding forest were the typical defenses of a prison camp. Looking from the inside, the first barrier to freedom was an unbroken ring of coiled barbed wire, behind which was a dry moat six feet deep, its inner side cut downward at an angle of about 30 degrees and its outer wall rising sheer and perpendicular to the foot of the first of two 12-foot-high log palisades presenting a smooth surface inward but strongly buttressed on the far side. Both outer sides of the two wooden walls were protected by rolled barbed wire. The space between the two provided a well-beaten track giving access from the main gate guardroom to all four control towers. It was patrolled by armed sentries accompanied at night by police dogs, who shared kennels near the west gate with a pack of sled dogs.

Mingling diffidently with us that first morning were about a thousand men, a large proportion of them Finns, who were already installed when our bedraggled crowd of some 4,500 arrived. They came from four big huts at the eastern end of the compound.

These log-built prisoner barracks were about 80 yards long by 10 yards wide, conforming in situation with the general plan of the camp itself. The doors faced west in the narrow end and were protected from the direct blast of wind and snow by a small covered porch with a southerly opening. It was obvious that there were no accommodations for us newcomers.

Speculation was cut short by orders from the troops to line ourselves up for food. We shuffled along in line to the open window of the kitchen, one of the buildings to the left of the main gate. There was the usual issue of ersatz coffee and bread. Each man drank up as quickly as he could and returned his tin mug through another window. There was plenty of hot liquid but a shortage of utensils.

Soldiers carried a portable wooden platform out into the middle of the parade ground. Around it, under orders from junior officers and NCO's, they formed a ring. We prisoners were then hustled to form ourselves into a big circle around the troops, facing inward toward the platform. Accompanied by a small armed guard, two Russian colonels walked through the ranks to the foot of the platform. One of them stepped up.

From my place in the front row I eyed him closely. He was tall, slim, and distinguished looking, his hair graying at the temples, a typical example of a professional soldier in any army. His small gray mustache was carefully trimmed, and his lean face showed two deep lines etched from a firm mouth into a strong chin. He was facing a hostile audience, a mob of ill-treated humans whose bitter hate of all things Russian was almost a tangible thing, but he gave no sign. He stood perfectly relaxed with no movement of hands, feet, or body.

He spoke clearly and crisply in Russian. "I am Colonel Ushakov," he said. "I am commandant of this camp. You have come here to work, and I expect from all of you hard work and discipline. I will not talk to you of punishment since you all probably know what to expect if you do not behave.

"Our first job is to provide shelter for you. Your first task, therefore, will be to build barracks for yourselves. How quickly you get inside out of the weather depends on your own efforts.

"If you have any complaints, I will always listen to them, and I will do what is in my power to help you. There are no doctors here, but there are trained soldiers who can administer first aid. Those of you who are now too sick after your journey to work will be housed in the existing barracks while the rest of you get on with the new buildings. That is all I have to say."

He stepped down. Immediately the other colonel took his place. He did not step up so much as leap forward in eagerness. There was nothing relaxed about this man. If there was a sense of restrained authority about Ushakov, this fellow wore his power like a flaunting banner. He was better dressed than the commandant. He wore a sheepskin jacket, and his well-made high boots were of soft leather, brightly polished. He was young enough to have been Ushakov's son.

If I ever knew his name, I do not remember it. He was the political officer, and we never called him anything but the Politruk, the short title by which all such officials were known.

He stood for fully a minute just looking at us, smiling faintly, eminently sure of himself, a picture of well-being and arrogance. The men stirred uneasily and stayed quiet.

He spoke strongly, harshly, and insultingly. "Look at you," he said, hunching his shoulders and placing his gloved hands on his hips. "You look like a bunch of animals. You are supposed to be the highly civilized people who fancy they can run the world. Can't you now appreciate what stupid nonsense you have been taught?"

Fortified by his anonymity in the restless crowd, one brave man had the temerity to answer back. His voice shocked the silence of the pause that the Politruk had allowed himself for dramatic emphasis after his opening onslaught. "How can we look any different? You won't let us shave; there's no soap and no clean clothes."

The Politruk turned in the direction of the voice. "I'll get your food ration stopped if I am interrupted again."

He was not interrupted again.

"After a time here," he went on, "and under the guidance of Comrade Stalin, we shall make useful citizens of you. Those who don't work don't eat. It is my job to help you to improve yourselves. You can attend classes to correct your way of thinking. We have an excellent library, which you can use after working hours."

There was some more in the same vein. Then, briskly, "Any questions?" A prisoner asked, "When does spring come here?" Replied the Politruk, "Don't ask stupid questions." The meeting ended.

The first few days of building the new prisoners' barracks were chaotic. All were willing enough to work, but it was most difficult to direct the men with the best qualifications to the work for which they were suited. The positions sorted themselves out smoothly enough after about three days. There were teams of architects and surveyors to plan out the ground and mark with stakes the plots for each hut. There were teams of young laborers hacking away at the frozen earth to make deep postholes for the main structural timbers. There were builders, men skilled in the use of axes to rough-shape the virgin wood from the forest. The main labor force issued forth from the camp gate every morning at 8, in the charge of armed soldiers.

I joined the forest workers. The camp was awakened by a bugle at 5 A.M., and there was an early morning procession of half-asleep men to the latrine trenches inside the wire behind the building site. The lineup for breakfast would follow. Tools were issued from the store on the left side of the gate, carefully checked out, and as scrupulously checked in again at the end of the day. As we marched out of the gate, a tallyman ticked off our names against his lists.

The forest was mainly of pine, but there was also an abundance of birch and larch. I worked in a felling team, handling one end of a heavy, crosscut, two-man saw. Occasionally I was able to get some variation by lopping with an ax the branches of the trees. Since the days of my boyhood at Pinsk I had always been handy with an ax, and I enjoyed the work. I found my strength coming back daily. I became absorbed in the bustle and activity. There was a glow of pride and satisfaction in being able to use my hands again. At 1 P.M. we went back to the camp, manhandling for delivery to the builders the timber we had cut. We received a midday issue of soup and returned to the forest to work until the light faded. Each day the line of huts increased in length.

Two weeks after our arrival the huts were finished. They lay in two lines with a wide "street" between each line of 10 huts. I was allocated a bunk in one of the last half dozen to be completed, and I well remember the wonderful feeling of shelter and warmth, protection and comfort I felt the first time I came in out of the chilling night into my new home. The air smelt deliciously of fresh-cut pine. Down each long side wall of heavy timbers were 50 three-tier bunks, simply made of planks laid out within a strong, four-post framework. Three square, sheet-iron stoves equally spaced out down the length of the room blazed red into the gloom, fueled by short pieces of sawn log, of which a supply was brought in daily by the forest working parties. Following the example of those already installed in their huts, we had brought in as much moss as we could carry in our kapok-padded jackets, called *fufaikas,* to spread on the hard boards of our beds. There were no chimneys for the stoves; the smoke issued from a short stovepipe and curled away through vents in the roof.

We had to spend many hours in our huts. After 6 P.M. all prisoners had to be back in their own quarters. A certain amount of movement in and around the huts was allowed as long as there was no standing about in large groups. Both lines of barracks were under close supervision from the towers at the eastern end of the compound, but as long as prisoners obeyed the strict order to keep away from the wire, the guards took no action. There was nothing much to do in the huts. There was nothing to read and no light to read by. The only activity permitted after the 6 P.M. deadline was a visit either to the Wednesday night lecture by the Politruk or to the library, the other Politruk-controlled enterprise.

It was a lively, cynical, and entertaining Czech occupying a bunk near me who persuaded me to go with him to one of the Politruk's Wednesday night talks, compulsory for all off-duty troops. The Politruk made no secret of his pleasure at seeing us and addressed a few special remarks to us before proceeding to deal with his military class. He spoke of the might of Russia, of her dominating place in the world (with asides to us on the decadence of the evil capitalist system). Soldiers asked questions, and the Politruk answered with the dogma of Marx and quotations from the speeches and writings of Lenin and Stalin. He was smiling as we left. He would not have been smiling a few minutes later had he watched the Czech put on a magnificent show for the benefit of the prisoners in our hut of the Politruk's education of the Red Army. I joined in the uproarious laughter. The Czech was a born actor and mimic.

BY THE END OF the first month the camp had settled into a disciplined rhythm of life, and there was a general feeling that, harsh though existence was in this remote, winter-bound spot, conditions could have been much worse. All working prisoners were given 400 grams (some 14 ounces) of bread a day. The bread was issued with the early morning coffee; part was eaten then, another portion went down with the midday soup, and the rest was taken with the hot drink handed out at the end of the day's work.

There was an occasional treat on Sunday when we were given dried fish, but bread remained our staple diet and the most important single factor in our lives. Tobacco, too, was important. There was a fairly generous issue once a week of the coarse *korizhki*, with a sheet of very old newspaper to act as cigarette paper. Bread and tobacco were the only commodities of value in the camp. They were the currency of the camp, the only means of payment for services.

The mortality rate continued high in that first month. Many of the men who survived the death march wrecked in body and mind never did any work. They were given bunks in the existing huts when we arrived and, worn-out beyond endurance, just lay there day after day until they lost their feeble grip on life. Volunteer burial parties from among their friends carried their bodies under armed escort to a clearing about a quarter of a mile from the camp, labored to hack graves out of the frozen earth, and committed them at last to rest.

Twice I went out with burial parties and in so doing discovered that the commandant was provided with an airplane. Our way took us past what seemed to me to be an inadequate runway cut out of the forest at its highest point. The plane, protected by tarpaulins, stood under the shelter of some trees. It was a small Tiger Moth trainer type. One of the guards said Ushakov piloted it himself to attend conferences at area army headquarters at Yakutsk.

The Russians interfered very little with our lives outside working hours. Inspection of our quarters was infrequent and perfunctory. Prisoners working in felling teams in the forest found new friends and at first sought permission to change from one hut to another to bunk near their teammates. The authorities offered no objection and let it be known that such moves could be made as a mutual arrangement between prisoners. Most men could be persuaded to switch places from one hut to another by a bribe of tobacco, and there was therefore a constant movement in those early weeks as men sorted out themselves and their friends.

I knew none of my companions particularly well, although I still occasionally saw Grechinen, who had been my companion on the march to Siberia. Apart from him there was only the Czech, whose wit and gaiety I admired but who was never a close friend.

I used to lie on my bunk in the long evenings looking up to the smoke vent 20 feet above me and think about it all. The insistent, hammering thought always was, "25 years in this place." Many of the men I now knew would die as the years passed. There would be fresh entries. And I would get older and older. Twenty-five years. As long to go as I had already lived. But how to get out? And having beaten the wire, the moat, and the formidable wooden fences, where would one escape to? Did anyone ever get out of Siberia? No man could hope to fight his way out alone against the crushing hazards of this country with its immense distances. Where, having planned an escape, could one find resolute men to make the attempt? These and other questions I put to myself. And I had no answers.

I fell in with Grechinen on the way to the latrines one evening. "Grechinen," I said, "if I could one day think up a plan of escape, would you come with me?" A frown creased his forehead. "Are you serious?" I nodded. Grechinen ran his fingers slowly through his beard. "Rawicz," he answered finally, "I will think about it tonight and tell you tomorrow."

Cautious Grechinen. I saw him the next day in the wide space between the two rows of huts.

"No," he said. "I would come with you if there was a chance, but the snow and the cold would kill us before we could get anywhere, even if the Russians didn't catch us." I shrugged my shoulders. "I still don't want to die young," added Grechinen.

I put the same question to the Czech. He thought at first that I was joking. Then he sat down on the edge of his bunk and motioned me down beside him. He put his hand on my shoulder. Quietly, in a voice just above a whisper, he said, "Yes, I would come with you, but you want strong and healthy men. My stomach plagues me, and I think it will eventually kill me. If I came with you I would die that much sooner out there, and you would suffer for having me with you." We sat there in silence for a few minutes after that. Then the Czech spoke again. "If you get the chance, clear out, my boy. Keep your eyes peeled, pick your men. I shall wish you luck, anyway."

We worked hard for six days and had an easy day on the seventh. Sunday was the day when the commandant addressed the prisoners. He would talk of the work target for the following week, draw attention to any infringements of camp rules, and make any necessary announcements affecting the life of prisoners.

We had been there a month when the commandant called for volunteers for a new job. He wanted men who had experience in making skis. There was no response at first. Said the commandant, "Volunteers will receive an immediate increase of their daily bread ration, and there will be more if the skis turned out are of good quality."

Sixty men volunteered, and I was one of them. I had once made a pair of skis. I could not claim to be an expert, but for an extra three or four ounces of bread a day I was willing to try my hand.

The ski shop was the other half of the building occupied by the library. Half a dozen of the volunteers were real experts at the job, and by common consent they divided the rest of us into a team of handymen for the actual process of manufacture and an outdoor crew for felling the birch trees, sawing the wood into the right lengths, and keeping up a steady supply of the right timber to the shop. My achievement in having once made a pair of skis earned me a job inside the hut on the last stage of steaming and shaping.

Working in the warmth of the ski shop, with the big stove roaring all day for the steaming of the wood, I felt I was getting back toward my full strength again. It should have made me resigned to my sentence, but instead it turned my thoughts more and more to escape. I began to wonder how I could preserve and hide some of my extra bread. I still had no workable plan, and I could not know then that I was soon to get help from a most unexpected quarter.

THE WIFE OF THE COMMANDANT

I HAD VOLUNTEERED ONCE and struck it lucky. I volunteered again one cold blustery Sunday morning in mid-March as flurries of snow swept about the hunched-up prisoners at the weekly parade.

"In my quarters," said Ushakov, "I have a radio set. It is called a Telefunken. Is there any one of you who knows this make of set well enough to do a repair job?"

I knew the Telefunken, because we had one at home—a German make. Men turned their heads to see who might step forward. There was a full minute of silence, and nobody made a move. I knew the set, but could I repair it? If I could, there was the exciting prospect of hearing some news from the outside world. I had a sudden panic that somebody else would get the job. I stuck up my hand and called out. An NCO stepped up and took my name and my place of work. "I will send for you when I want you," said the commandant.

It was to be a fateful decision, launching me into the last and most extraordinary phase of my stay at Camp 303. In this isolated community of between 5,000 and 6,000 men under sentence and a battalion strength of officers and men, there was but one woman. The defective Telefunken was to be the means of my meeting her, and, so far as I knew, I was the only prisoner who ever talked to her.

The following afternoon, as I worked in the ski shop, the commandant's messenger, a moon-faced private named Igor, called for me. "The commandant wants you," he said. "Come with me." As we left, the other men in the shop called out, "Find out how the war's going," and "Get us some news from Poland," and so on. I waved my hand. I confess I felt nervous as I walked away from the ski shop, across in front of the big gate, past the officers' mess to the commandant's house standing on the other side of the camp at the northwest corner of the parade ground. It was, like all the other buildings, built of logs with the typical porch opening south to keep the wind and snow away from the front door. As I stepped inside, I saw it only differed from the style of the prisoners' barracks in that it had an inner skin of smooth plank walls, a wooden ceiling and floor, and a stovepipe that went all the way up through the roof.

Igor ushered me in. Ushakov stepped forward toward the door, dismissed Igor, and motioned me in. "I have come to look at the set, *Gospodin Polkovnik,*" I said in Russian, using the old Russian style of respectful address to a colonel.

"Yes, of course. I will show it to you." He stepped past me.

The woman sat in front of the stove, which had been placed so that it protruded through the partition that divided the house into two rooms, thus heating both halves. The colonel murmured a conventional introduction to his wife. I bowed and said something formal, and she smiled with a small inclination of her head. I found myself staring at her. She was the first woman I had met since I left my mother in Pinsk. I felt awkward and ill at ease, painfully aware of my ugly clothes, my beard, and my long hair that curled over the neck of my jacket. I could not take my eyes off her.

She stood up, and I saw she was tall for a woman. She wore a long thick skirt and a dark woolen cardigan over a white, flower-embroidered cotton blouse. Her brown hair, tightly plaited and wound in the Russian style like a halo around the head, had a live, well-brushed sheen, and I was struck by the clearness of her skin. I was never much good at guessing women's ages, but I think she would have been nearing 40. She was not beautiful, but she had that quality of essential womanliness, a way of holding herself, an ease of moving, a way of looking at one, that would command attention anywhere. I came out of my fleeting trance to find her blue eyes regarding me with frank pity and sympathy. I turned my head away and saw Ushakov standing in the doorway between the two rooms looking at me in that preoccupied and detached manner of his.

"Let me show you the radio," he said.

The inner room was their bedroom and his office combined. Along one wall nearest to the stove was a heavy wooden bunk, at the head of which was a cupboard in which I could see his uniforms hanging. Near it, against the wall farthest from the door, was a solid wooden chest. The bed was to my left as I walked in through the partition door, the chest immediately in front of me. The part of the room to my right was Ushakov's office. Hanging on the wall was a big contour map of eastern Siberia. There was also a plan of the camp and a colored portrait of Joseph Stalin. On a bench under the all-seeing eye of Stalin was the radio, a brand-new, battery-operated Telefunken.

Ushakov gave me a Pushki cigarette, fetched over a kerosene lamp, and set it down on a bench near me. I took the back off the set and began running my fingers along the leads, suspecting a loose connection somewhere. Ushakov asked me questions about the set—where it was made, what it cost, how it worked.

Hesitantly, I inquired where he had got it.

"I happened unfortunately," Ushakov answered, "to be in charge of troops in Poland in 1939, and I acquired it there."

My mind seized on the use of the word "unfortunately." It tied in with the theory that the prisoners expressed that even to be commandant of a camp in Siberia was in the nature of a punishment. I had the impression then—and it was later to be strengthened—that Colonel Ushakov owed his appointment to Siberia to some indiscretion on his part during the Polish campaign.

He went back to the fire and sat down on the polished bench with his wife. I worked on, unhurriedly checking the circuit. After about half an hour I was aware that she was busying herself in the next room, and then he called me to the fire, while she poured out two mugs of tea, saccharine sweetened. The colonel drank first and then gave his mug to me. I went back to the radio, and as I worked, I surprised myself with the thought that I was not going to rush this job, that this was my most pleasant experience since my arrest, and that I must make it last. When Igor came to take me back, I explained that checking all the leads and valves was a slow business.

"Very well," said Ushakov, "you must come again. I will send for you." He gave me another cigarette, and I went off with my escort.

"What's the news?" the men called out to me when I got back.

"I haven't got the set going yet," I said, "but I'll tell you what's happening as soon as I do."

Igor fetched me again the next day. As I fiddled with the set, the colonel and his wife both talked to me. She was impressed by the fluency of my Russian. I told her my mother was Russian.

"What did you do to get sent here?" the colonel asked.

"Nothing," I said.

"You have 25 years, haven't you?"

"Yes."

There was a short pause, and then she spoke again. "Twenty-five years is a long time. How old are you?" I told her that I was 25.

The three-way conversation was interspersed with some odd silences. They sat close together on the bench; I was on my haunches looking over the top of the Telefunken. Surprisingly, Ushakov asked me if I thought Russia would be involved in another war. The last war for Russia, as far as he was concerned, was that of 1914. I mentioned Finland and Poland. "Ah," he replied, "that wasn't war; it was liberation." I wondered if he really believed it. I popped my head over the top of the radio and looked at him. He was gazing up at the ceiling, and his face was expressionless. He returned to the question of Russia being involved in war.

"In Poland," I said, "it was common knowledge that Goering came to us to get us to give the Germans a corridor through which they could attack Russia. Germany is ready, and the attack is inevitable." I gabbled it out fast. I expected to be told I was talking too much. But neither Ushakov nor his wife made any comment.

It occurred to me that they did not seem anxious to hurry the repair of the radio. I had found what I believed to be the fault, a loose battery lead. But I just did not want to put the back on the set, connect the radio, and switch it on. I thought my visits must then end.

Slavomir
Rawicz

She asked me about prewar Poland. What were the women's fashions? They were often elegant, I said, straight from Paris. And high-heeled shoes? Yes, I said. They, too, were very attractive.

Two days went by before I was summoned again.

On this third visit I started straightaway to get the Telefunken working. Ushakov was busy at his desk, and the woman did all the talking. She asked me about the films I used to see and was surprised to hear that Russian films were banned in Poland. As she talked, I switched the radio on. It hummed into life, and I began to turn the dials. Ushakov left his work and came over beside me. We heard a concert from Moscow. I went from station to station, picking up fragments of news, and finally we heard the voice of Hitler, ranting in his own unmistakable fashion, at a youth rally in the Ruhr.

Ushakov gave me a whole packet of korizhki tobacco and a sheet of old newspaper. As Igor stood in the doorway waiting to escort me away, Ushakov said, "If the set needs any attention, I will send for you again. I am afraid we do not understand how it works." I went back and told the men all I had learned from the wireless. Their greatest interest was in Germany and the speech by Adolf Hitler.

It was now nearing the end of March. I worked uninterruptedly for several days in the ski shop and began regretfully to think that the Telefunken episode was over. Just about that time I came to know a remarkable man named Anastazi Kolemenos. I had seen him come in occasionally to warm himself at the big fire. He was one of the finest physical specimens I have ever seen, over six feet tall, blond-haired and blond-bearded, with curious gray-green eyes. In spite of the privations he had endured, he must have weighed close to 200 pounds. He was a kind and helpful giant of a man, whose job it was to carry the birch logs and split them for use in the ski shop.

I was standing outside the ski shop door watching him one day. I walked across to where he had piled some logs and went to lift one to take it over to him. The end came up easily enough. I tried to get a grip around the middle to hoist it up. It defied my efforts. Then, suddenly, Kolemenos was beside me.

"That's all right, friend," he said, "I'll do it."

He bent down and swung the log onto his shoulder in one powerful movement. I did not regard myself as a weakling, but this man's strength was phenomenal. I spoke to him, spontaneously telling him who I was. Kolemenos told me his name and volunteered the information that he had been a landowner in Latvia and was now 27 years of age. The old escape idea came surging into my mind, but this was no place to talk of it. "We will have to talk some time," I said.

"I shall be glad to," answered the giant.

Over the clatter of workshop activity they called out to me, "Your friend has called for you again."

Igor stood stolidly inside the door and beckoned. I put down a ski I was testing, dusted myself off, and walked out with him.

Ushakov was there and so was she. He told me that the set was not working too well. I tested it, and it seemed to function, although the signal strength was down a little. I told him he would be advised to get spare batteries, and he said he would arrange that. He put on his greatcoat, murmured something to her about having to attend an officers' meeting, and went out. There was great understanding between these two, and they were completely devoted to each other.

"I will make some tea for you," she smiled. "You can find me a station with some good music."

She talked on for a while about the music she liked, praised Chopin, but declared that her favorite composer was Tchaikovsky. She told me that she played the piano and that having to leave her piano behind was one of her greatest hardships here in Siberia.

I found her the kind of music she wanted, and, with a symphony orchestra as the background, she talked about herself. She talked to draw me out, to get me to tell her about myself. It was as though she were saying, "This is me; this is my life. You can trust me."

I didn't quite know why this was happening to me. I said to myself that in spite of his exalted position here, these are really exiles and outcasts. She, especially, is almost as much a prisoner as I am. She is here only because he is here, and probably the real ruler of Camp 303 is the Politruk.

We sipped hot tea, and she kept her voice low. This was the story she told me. Her family had been army officers for generations before the revolution. Her father had been a colonel in the czar's personal guard and had been shot by the Bolsheviks. Her young cadet brother died of wounds received in the defense of the Smolny Institute. Her mother had fled with her from their home near Nijni Novgorod, and when, later, the mother died, she had adapted herself to the new order of life, got herself a work card, and found a job. She did well and earned herself a state holiday with other favored workers at Yalta. And there she met Ushakov. I gathered that from then on he was the only man in her life.

She was very loyal to Ushakov. She did not tell me why he had suddenly been posted from Poland. He went first to Vladivostock, and she had no word from him for six months. She knew some party people with the right influence. They told her that he was going to be put in charge of a camp in Siberia, and she strove unceasingly until her friends got her a travel permit to join him.

All the time I was telling myself: She talks to me because I am a prisoner and she is sorry for me and because she cannot talk about these things to her own people. Yet, amid lingering doubts, there was the conviction that this was an intelligent, sensitive, and most compassionate woman, and this camp, which surrounded her with the evidence of cruelly wasted lives, had shocked her. It was no place for a woman. She was a Russian, and she believed passionately in the great destiny of Russia. But she was also a woman, and I don't think she liked what she now had to see, day after day, month after month.

Those clear blue eyes held mine. "Do you ever think of escape?" The question panicked me. There was awful danger in it. I had my mouth open but could not speak. I put the cup down with a clumsy thump. And her eyes, wide open and blue and candid, still held me and watched my flutterings of fear.

The quiet voice was going on. "You do not answer, Rawicz. You do not trust me. I thought you might want to talk about it. There is no danger in talking to me about it. . . ."

Escape. It was as though she had looked into my mind and plucked out that one word of danger and longing and hope. Yes, I wanted to tell her about my perilous dreams. But she had shocked me into silence. The words would not come.

Then came Igor, and I turned to go, disconcerted and miserable, like a man who has turned his head from the extended hand of a friend. She spoke coolly and formally. "You will come again if the set needs adjusting?" My words came in a rush. "Yes, yes, of course I will. I shall be glad to."

I felt a slow burn of excitement as I waited through the next few days to see if I would get another call. I met a man named Sigmund Makowski, a 37-year-old captain in the Polish frontier forces. A precise, clear-thinking fellow, he was fit, active, and bore the stamp of the regular army officer. I marked him down, as I had marked Kolemenos, but I said nothing of my plans at this stage. I do not know what I expected of the colonel's wife, but at least I thought she would be in a position to advise.

Call for me she did. She was alone, and when I had tuned in the radio, dallying round the dial to pick up some news items for my friends, she started to talk of the approaching short Siberian summer.

I took the plunge. "I am sorry about the last time," I said. "Of course, I do think of those things, but the distances are so great, the country so difficult, and I have no equipment to face such a journey."

"You are only 25," she answered. "You need not have been afraid to admit that you do not look forward to the next 25 years in these surroundings. I am quite well looked after here. We have comfortable quarters, better food than yours, and as many cigarettes as we need. But I couldn't spend 25 years here. So escape must be an idea close to your heart, and it may do you good to tell me what you think."

So we talked of it as an abstract thing, as though it were being contemplated by some third person. We posed the question: Supposing a man could get out of the camp, where could he head for? The only possibility for such a man, in my opinion, would be to make a dash due east the short 600 miles to Kamchatka and from there find his way ultimately to Japan.

The attempt would be a failure, in her opinion. The Kamchatka coast was a number one security commitment and would be heavily guarded. Could he smuggle himself onto a westbound train, maybe find himself a job in the Ural mines, and possibly make his way out of Russia later? There would be difficulties of travel and work permits and other vital papers, she said.

That was all the exploring we did that day, and it was not until I lay on my bunk that night thinking things over that I realized the one escape route she appeared deliberately to have ignored—south, past Lake Baikal. Whence from there? Afghanistan was the name that popped into my mind. It sounded sufficiently neutral and obscure.

It was the colonel himself who next sent for me. He genuinely could not work that simple radio set, a fact that greatly surprised me, for he was an intelligent man. He seemed to be a little in awe of it and liked to have me find the stations for him. He wanted news, and as I got it for him in various speeches and bulletins, he said he now felt certain that Russia would soon be involved in war. I don't think he wanted war, but in war obviously lay his chance to get out of Siberia and back to the real job of soldiering for which he was trained.

There was no fanciful talk of escape when the commandant was there. I imagine he would have been horrified to know that his wife had ever broached such a topic with a prisoner.

When the time came for me to go, he stayed near the radio and she walked behind me to the door.

"Don't worry," she said. "You will be all right."

That night I spoke to Makowski. I walked him over to the latrines. "What would you think of an escape?"

"Don't be crazy, man. We have nothing to escape with, even if we got outside the camp."

"I might get a little help."

"If you can, I'm with you. To hell with this place."

The colonel's wife appeared to be actively enjoying her role as conspirator in chief. I have been unable to decide whether she ever believed I would really attempt an escape. It might be that all this was an intriguing exercise for the sharp wits of a woman bored by depressing camp life.

The business had emerged from the abstract. She was planning away as the radio gave us one of her favorite Tchaikovsky symphonies. "You will want a small number of the fittest and most enterprising men. You, from your extra rations, will save a quarter of a kilo of bread each day, dry it at the back of your ski shop stove, and then you will hide it. I will find some sacking to make into bags. Skins you will need for extra clothing and footwear. The soldiers trap sables, and the officers shoot them. They hang them on the outer wire. The men working outside must grab one a day. No one will miss them. Plan your own way out and then head south. Wait for a night when it is snowing heavily, so that your tracks are covered."

And then, almost as an afterthought, "Colonel Ushakov will be leaving for a senior officers' course at Yakutsk shortly. I would not want anything to happen while he was in command."

A very loyal wife, this one.

I sought out Makowski immediately. "We are getting out," I said. "There will be a little help for us."

"How many men will you want?"

"About half a dozen," I said.

"Good. We'll find them. I know one I can recommend."

I thought of Kolemenos. "I know one, too. We'll start rounding them up tomorrow."

PLANS FOR ESCAPE

T HERE HE IS NOW." Makowski, standing beside me at the midday break the next day, indicated a prisoner standing a little apart from the rest. "Let us wait here a couple of minutes so that you can look him over." The man's shoulders were squared, and the shapeless clothes could not disguise that ramrod back.

"You are a cavalry man," said Makowski at length. "You should recognize the type."

"Who is he?"

"He's a Pole. Sergeant of Cavalry Anton Paluchowicz. He's 41, but strong and fit, well-trained, experienced. I'd go anywhere with him. Shall we talk to him?"

We went over and talked. I liked the look of Paluchowicz. He accepted the proposition like a good soldier undertaking a mission of war. He was glad to know I was a lieutenant of the Polish cavalry.

"We shall do it," he said. "It won't be easy, but we shall do it."

That evening I came up behind Kolemenos. I tapped him on the shoulder, and he turned. He smiled. "Oh, it's you again."

"Kolemenos, I am getting out of here with some others. Would you like to join us?"

He put one big hand on my shoulder. "You mean it? Seriously?"
I nodded. "Yes, seriously. Perhaps very soon."

The big man smiled happily through his blond beard. "I shall come." He laughed and brought the weight of his hand down twice on my shoulder. "I could carry you on my shoulders if necessary."

Now there were four of us. We began to plan with a sense of urgency. It was the end of March, and I felt we had not a great deal of time. We began to watch things closely. We noted, for instance, that the starting of the dog patrol around the perimeter at night was always signaled by the yelping and whining of the sled dogs showing their annoyance at being left behind. That signal came only once every two hours. We discovered the patrol always went around counterclockwise, covering the long south side first. We decided the escape must be through the southerly defenses and that therefore we must get ourselves established in the end hut on that side. We began to bribe and cajole ourselves bunks in that hut.

Paluchowicz brought Zaro into the scheme. Eugene Zaro came from the Balkans, a Yugoslav I think. He was 30 and, before the Russians had caught up with him, had been a clerk. "If you want some fun on the way," said our sergeant, "Zaro is the man."

Like an inspection committee, Makowski and Paluchowicz and I watched him in the food queue. He was a well-built man, below average in height, and his almost black eyes had a constant gleam of laughter and mischief. The men around him roared in joyous gusts, and Zaro stood there, his eyes twinkling in a mock-serious face.

"All right," I pronounced, "we'll have him."

"I've always wanted to travel, and this sounds good," was Zaro's answer to my approach.

"It's going to be the worst trip you ever had," I told him.

"I know," he replied, "but I'm coming with you anyway." There was a pause. "The Russians have no sense of humor. It will do me good to get away from them."

So Eugene Zaro came in, and we were five.

I went on with my daily chore of drying a quarter of a kilo of my bread behind the big stove to add to the growing store hidden beneath the pile of rejected skis in the far corner of the shop.

Escapee number six was brought in by big Kolememos. He was a 28-year-old Lithuanian architect named Zacharius Marchinkovas, tall and spare-framed, with alert brown eyes. I was impressed by the manner in which he had already weighed the odds against us and decided that the slightest hope of success was worth the attempt.

When Sergeant Paluchowicz brought into our hushed deliberations the name Schmidt, I thought this must be one of the Russo-German colony who had joined our prison train at Ufa in the Urals. These Russians with German names were descendants of German craftsmen imported by Peter the Great.

"Is he German?" I asked the sergeant.

"His name is Schmidt, but I do not know," was the answer. "He speaks Russian very well and easily. He stands apart from the others. He does a great deal of thinking by himself, and he gives me excellent advice on everything. I recommend him to you."

Makowski and I announced our intention of meeting Mr. Schmidt the next day. "I will point him out to you, then," said the sergeant with a smile.

Schmidt was coming up to the window of the kitchen for his coffee when Paluchowicz indicated him with a jerk of the head. Makowski and I strolled over.

My first impression was that he might be too old for the rigors of the adventure we were planning. I judged him to be about 50. He was well built, wide-shouldered, and slim-waisted. His thick hair and beard were tinged with gray. He had seen us coming and, probably because the sergeant had warned him of the meeting, showed no surprise when I spoke. "We would like to talk to you."

I spoke in Russian. He answered in Russian, "Walk toward the huts, and I will join you." He moved on and we walked away.

Holding his mug of coffee, he fell in with us and, clear of the crowd, we stopped. He faced us and smiled. "Gentlemen, my name is Smith. I understand you have a proposition."

Makowski and I stood there, mouths agape. *"Smith?"* We repeated the name together.

"I am Smith, Mr. Smith. I am an American." He grinned happily at our astonishment. "You are surprised, gentlemen."

We just could not believe our ears. His Russian was impeccable. I could detect no trace of an accent.

"It is hard to believe," I said. "How did you get here?"

He had an easy, patient, almost professorial manner of speech. "Let me repeat, I am an American. By profession I am an engineer and was one of a number cordially invited by the Soviet government to help build the Moscow Metro. There were about 50 of us. That was 9 or 10 years ago. They arrested me in 1936, convinced themselves I was a professional foreign spy, and gave me 20 years." He drank his coffee. We were still looking at him like a pair of fools.

"Now I'll take my mug back and we shall walk together to the huts."

The three of us walked slowly to the huts. By now, the beginning of April, Makowski and I had got ourselves bunks near the door of the end hut. Kolemenos had also managed the switch, and the others hoped to join us within a few days.

We invited Mr. Smith into our hut. Sitting on Makowski's bottom bunk, I cautiously outlined our plans. I told him I had sound reasons for believing that only the long road south held any chance of success, although some of the others were still reluctant to drop the idea of the short route east to Kamchatka.

He did not rush to answer. He asked a few shrewd questions. We sat silent as he thought things over. And then, "Gentlemen, it will be a privilege to join you. I agree that the south route is the best. You can count on me."

We sat long with Smith. All our histories, our Russian dossiers, followed a similar pattern. Smith was different. He was the odd man out, and he intrigued us. He told us much, but neither then nor ever did he tell us his Christian name. Later, when we six Europeans addressed one another by our first names, the American was always, as he first introduced himself, Mr. Smith, the "Mister" somehow being accepted as a substitute for the name we were never told.

He had a ridged scar curving lividly from right to left from the crown of his head to the nape of his neck, some eight or nine inches long. He received it, he explained, when some scaffolding fell on him during the Metro building.

"Apart from the accident that give me this scar," he told us, "I had a good time in Moscow for a few years. The work was interesting, I was highly paid, and I found the Russians easy to work with. They had skilled engineers themselves, but key positions went to foreigners like myself. The reason, I think, was that this Metro scheme was a great prestige prospect, and if anything went wrong, national pride would be saved by having a foreigner as a scapegoat. I was quite happy. I had wanted to see Russia, and I was being financially well rewarded for the experience."

In a Moscow obsessed between the wars with its five-year plans, Smith and his friends, installed in well-appointed apartments and with money to spare to buy luxuries in shops where the entry permit was either a party membership card or a foreign passport, must have been conspicuous. Smith had a car and traveled around freely—a circumstance that must have earned him an underlined report in secret police records. He had a Russian girl friend; the police would not have liked that. But they let him go on, working hard and playing hard.

"I never saw the blow coming," he went on. "After a year's work, the Russians, without any move from me, doubled my salary, which had been fixed by contract, to show their appreciation of the steady progress that was being made with the work. From then on I thought I was well in with them."

Smith was in his flat with the girl after midnight one evening in 1936 when the NKVD called in force. They were quiet, determined, and most efficient. Smith and the girl were both arrested. He never saw her again. Other occupants of the flats probably never saw or heard a thing. When dawn came, Smith was occupying a cell in the Lubyanka—it was to be his home for the next six months. They refused his demands to see someone from the United States Embassy.

"What a transition," mused Mr. Smith. "One day a successful engineer, the next a professional foreign spy. It seems that apart from keeping a general watchful eye on my activities they had been opening my mail home. The main charge was that I had been sending out information about Russia in my letters to my folks in America.

"The trial was secret and farcical. I got 20 years, as I told you. They confiscated my car and all my possessions, so perhaps they got back most of the extra salary they had so generously awarded me."

He questioned us closely about our plans. He wanted as clear and detailed a picture as we could give at this stage. He asked us very shrewdly about the distances involved. Had we realized it would be 1,000 miles of foot slogging to the borders of Mongolia alone? We talked, almost in whispers, for a long time, as other occupants of Hut Number One came in past us, stamping snow off their boots, calling out to friends, standing in groups around the three red-hot stoves. I told him we would help him make the move from his hut in the middle of the line to this one. I urged that time was short.

He stood up, nodded thoughtfully. "Good-bye for now," I said. "Good-bye, gentlemen," he answered and walked out. The others readily accepted the seventh and last recruit to the party.

BY THE END OF the first week in April we were all in the same hut—a triumph of preliminary organization. We were gathering an impressive store of skins, most of them pulled off the wires by Kolemenos on his frequent trips to pick up the birch logs for the ski shop. On the grindstone in the ski shop I flattened and sharpened a six-inch nail into an instrument that could be used to cut and pierce holes in the tough pelts. Our final collection included sable, ermine, Siberian fox, and, a real prize, the skin of a deer that one of the officers had shot for the pot. We cut long thongs of hide for lacing up the simple moccasins we fashioned in the nightly gloom of the hut. We plaited thongs together and used them as belts. Each man made and wore under his fufaika a warm vest with the fur turned inward toward the body. To protect the legs, we made fur gaiters.

Our acute fear at this time was that we might be betrayed. Our feverish efforts were bound to attract some attention. Had a word been dropped to the Russians, the informant would have been well paid in extra bread and tobacco. But there was no Judas.

I told the colonel's wife that I had found six friends. She did not ask me who they were, and I do not think she wanted to know. She gave me a gift that was to be of inestimable value—an ax head.

"That will be on my conscience all my life," she said. "It is the first thing I have ever stolen."

I made a handle for it, and Kolemenos wore it for safekeeping inside the back waistband of his trousers.

One other priceless article I made in the ski shop was a fine three-inch-wide and foot-long knife. It was originally a section of broken saw blade, which I heated in the workshop stove, hammered into shape, and ground on the grindstone. The handle was two pieces of wood tightly thonged together by long strips of deerskin. As Kolemenos became the keeper of the ax, so I took over the custody of the knife. These were perilous possessions inside the camp. The discovery of either would have wrecked the whole scheme.

The problem of making fire was one we already had the answer to. Here, where matches were counted a luxury, there existed an effective, if primitive, method that made use of a thick fungoid forest growth that the Russians called *gubka* (literally "sponge"). It could be tugged off the trees in sheets. It was then boiled and dried. The fire-making equipment was completed with a bent nail and a piece of flintstone. The dry gubka, a supply of which we all carried stuffed into our jacket pockets, readily took the spark from the flint and could be blown into a red smolder.

The word reached us that in a week's time it would be Easter Sunday. It fell in 1941 on April 13, as I have discovered since then. The Sunday before, April 6, marked the end of our preparations. Our escape wardrobe was then complete with the making of seven balaclava caps of fur with extension flaps down the back that could be tucked into the necks of our jackets. We were all tense and ready to go, worried about our valuable new possessions—the skins, the ax, the knife, the store of dehydrated bread—and fearful that at this point some of them might be stolen.

And on that day the colonel's wife sent for me and said, "My husband has gone to Yakutsk. That is why he did not attend the parade today. I have made seven bags out of provision sacks. You will have to take them out one at a time." She was perfectly calm. My heart was hammering with anxiety. When she handed me the first of these bags, I saw that she had provisioned it, too, and I wondered how we could possibly hide it. I tucked the bag under my arm inside my jacket, stuck my hands in the deep pockets, and walked back to the prisoners' lines hunched up and bending over like a man in deep thought. Six times more in the next few days I made that hazardous trip, knowing each time that if any Russian guard discovered what I was carrying, disaster would be sudden and complete. We made pillows of the bags, covering them with bits of animal skin and moss. Every hour we were away from the hut we sweated in apprehension.

We acquired in those last few days a discarded and well-worn soldier's sheepskin jacket. I told the others of an old poacher's trick in which a sheepskin was dragged along behind to put the gamekeeper's dogs off the human scent. We could try the trick ourselves, I suggested. The others agreed.

We watched the weather, so essential a part of our escape plan. We wanted snow, big-flaked, heavy-falling snow, to obscure our movements. Monday was cold and very clear. On Tuesday there was wind-driven, icy sleet. Midmorning on Wednesday a lead-gray and lowering sky gave us the boon we sought. The snow thickened as the day went on. It began to pile up in the untrodden no man's land between us and the wire. At the midday break the seven of us met briefly. The word went around: "This is the day."

At 4 P.M. I left the ski shop for the last time with my fufaika bulging with my hoard of bread and the knife blade cold against my leg in my right boot. We drank our evening mug of coffee, ate some of the day's bread issue, and walked to the hut in ones and twos.

There were frequent walks to the latrines as we tensely talked over the final plans. It was Smith who advised that we must not start our break too early. The camp must be allowed to settle down for the night before we moved. Midnight, he thought, would be a reasonable time to run for it. Meanwhile, we must try to keep calm. And the blessed snow kept falling in big, obliterating cottonlike flakes, covering everything.

It was Zaro who had the preposterous idea of attending the Politruk's Wednesday evening indoctrination. We laughed at first, and then Makowski said, "Why not?" So we went, all seven of us, leaving our precious, moss-camouflaged bags on our bunks and telling ourselves that now, on this last night, nothing could go wrong. We sat ourselves at the back, and the Politruk beamed a faintly surprised welcome at us. We smiled right back at him and tried not to fidget.

It was the most exciting political meeting I have ever attended, although the element of excitement owed little to the speaker. The Politruk, now the camp's senior officer in the absence of Ushakov, was in good form. We heard again about the miracle of the Soviet state, about the value of toil, of self-discipline within the framework of state discipline, of the glorious international ideal of communism.

There was about an hour and a half of it before we stood up to go.

"Good night, colonel," we chorused.

"Good night," he answered.

Back in Hut Number One the men were beginning to settle for the night. Smith and Zaro, in the bunks nearest the door, were to give us the starting signal. We all broke up and climbed onto our bunks and lay there. Six of us lay wide awake and waiting, but big Kolemenos in the bunk below me was gently snoring.

I lay thinking and listening to the thumping of my heart. I remembered I had not said good-bye to the colonel's wife. I decided she would not have wanted me to.

The hours dragged by. Gradually the hut grew quiet. There was a loud snoring from someone. A man babbled in his sleep.

Smith tapped my shoulder. "Now," he whispered.

Gently I shook Kolemenos. "Now," I repeated.

THE GETAWAY

WE SWUNG OUR BAGS off the bunks by the rawhide straps that we had fitted for slinging them across our backs. We piled the moss coverings back in pillow form at the heads of our beds. "Everybody ready?" I whispered. From all around me came the hissed answer, "Yes." "Anybody changed his mind?" There was no reply.

"Let's go," said Makowski.

I dropped my bag near the door and stepped outside. The camp was silent. It was snowing as heavily as ever. I could not see the nearest wire. In the southeast guard tower, our nearest danger, they could not have had 20 yards visibility. We could be thankful that in this place of no piped water supply and no electricity, there were no searchlights to menace us.

The inner wire was 100 yards from the hut door. The success of the first part of the operation depended on the observation that the frost-stiffened wire coils did not faithfully follow the contours of the ground. There was a dip in the ground straight ahead of us, which we reckoned would provide a couple of feet of clearance if we burrowed through the snow and under the wire.

We went out one by one with about a minute's interval between each. Zaro went first, and I prayed he found the right spot at the first attempt. Then the Lithuanian. Then Mr. Smith. Then Makowski and Paluchowicz. Kolemenos turned and whispered to me, "I only hope they've made a great big hole for me to get through."

I watched him run off into the night like the others, carrying his bag in front of him, ready, according to plan, to shove it through the gap ahead of him. Then it was my turn, and the palms of my hands were moist with sweat. I took a last swift look around. The men in the hut were sleeping on. I turned and bolted.

When I reached the wire, Smith was under it and slowly wriggling forward. Two were through. The rest of us crouched down and waited. Agonizing minutes passed by as first the sergeant and then Makowski squirmed and grunted, bellies pressed flat against the earth, under the wire. The big bulk of Kolemenos went head first into the gap, and I held my breath. He was halfway through when the barbs took hold on the back of his jacket between the shoulder blades. He shook himself gently, and little pieces of ice tinkled musically down the coils of the wire.

"Lie still, Anastazi," I whispered. "Don't move at all."

Someone on the other side had pulled his bag through and was reaching through over his neck to try to release him. The minutes ticked by. I was aware that my jaws were clamped tight, and I was trying to count the passing seconds on my fingers. Kolemenos lay very still as the hand worked between his shoulders. Someone spoke on the other side, and the big man went forward again. I let out my breath in a long sigh and followed through. The first obstacle was behind us. It had taken a full 20 minutes.

We knelt down along the edge of the dry moat and looked across to the first tall wooden fence as Kolemenos slithered in and braced himself against the steep-sloping near side. We used him as a human stepping-stone, and as we clambered over him, he took our feet in his

linked and cupped hands and heaved us one by one onto the ledge at the base of the 12-foot palisade. More vital minutes were lost in pulling Kolemenos out of the ditch. By standing on his shoulders and reaching out at full stretch, we hauled ourselves over the top. Then perched on the lateral securing timber on the other side, we were able to lean over and help up the later arrivals.

Anchorman Kolemenos again posed us a problem. Straddling the top of the fence, our legs held firm, Makowski and I leaned heads downward and arms outstretched to haul at him, one arm each. Three times we got his fingers to within inches of the top, and three times we had to lower him down again. We paused, trembling with exertion and near despair, and tried again. His fingers scrabbled for a hold on the top, gripped. To our straining he began to add his own tremendous strength. He came up, up, and over.

To clear the coiled wire at the foot of the fence, we threw ourselves outward, landing in a heap in the deep snow. One or two failed to leap quite clear enough and were scratched as they pulled themselves away. We were in the patrol alley between the two fences. Time was running out. If I had heard the sound of the sled dogs announcing the start of a patrol, I think I might have been physically sick.

We ran the few yards to the outer fence and this time shoved Kolemenos up first. We were probably making little noise, but it seemed to me the commotion was deafening. This time I was last up, and it was Kolemenos who swung me up and over. In a final mad scramble we leapt and tumbled over the last lot of barbed wire at the foot of the outer fence, picked ourselves up, breathlessly inquired if everyone was all right, and, with one accord, started to run. Round my waist was tied the old sheepskin jacket. I tugged it free, dropped it, and heard it slithering along behind me attached to the thong looped on my wrist.

We gasped and choked and wheezed, but we ran and kept running into the great forest among the looming, white-clothed trees. We ran south, with the camp at our backs. One and then another stumbled, fell, and were helped to their feet. The first headlong rush slowed to a steady, racking lope. We jogged along for hours, into the dawn and beyond it to another snow-filled day, our packs bumping and pounding our backs as we went. When we stopped to draw air into laboring lungs, I made them start again. And I made them struggle on until about 11 A.M., when hardly one of us could have moved another step. I picked up the old sheepskin and held it under my arm. We looked around at one another. Paluchowicz was bent over double with his hands on his knees, his shoulders heaving, fighting to get his breath. Two of the others were squatting on their haunches in the snow. All of us were open-mouthed, panting like spent animals.

This place was a shallow, bowl-like depression where the trees grew more widely spaced. We had stumbled down into it and could not, without a rest, have attempted the slight climb out of it. We stood there for about 10 minutes, too breathless to speak and in a lather of sweat in spite of the subzero temperature.

The snow still came down, thinning a little now, and there was a moaning wind through the trees that made the gaunt branches shake and creak miserably. Like hunted animals, we were all straining our ears for sounds of the chase from behind us. In all our minds was the thought of the dogs. But there was only the wind, the falling snow, and the stirring trees.

Up the slope to our left the trees grew more closely together. "We will get up there," I said, finally. "There is more shelter, and we shall be better hidden." There were groans of protest. Smith joined in, "Rawicz is right."

So we labored our way out of the hollow and picked the broad base of a great tree as the location for our shelter. We scooped the snow away down to the tree roots and cleared a space a couple of yards square. Then we built up the snow around into a solid low wall. Kolemenos cut branches with his ax, and we laid them on top in a close mesh, piling on more snow to complete the roof. It was a lesson we had learned the hard way in Siberia: Get out of the wind, because the wind is the killer. Just wrap snow around you, and you'll sleep warm as though you were in a feather bed.

Here it was that we had our first real look at the contents of our packs. Each man had a flat baked loaf, a little flour, about five pounds of pearl barley, some salt, four or five ounces of korizhki tobacco, and some old newspaper. All this in addition to the dried ration bread I had managed to save. On the top of each pack were the spare moccasins we had made and the leftover pieces of skin. We crawled into the little snow house, all jammed closely together, and talked in low voices. There was a discussion as to whether we should smoke. We decided the additional risk was quite slight and the benefit to jangling nerves great. So we smoked and lay close together in the warm blue haze of burning tobacco.

There was, this relatively short distance from the camp, no question of lighting a fire, so we wolfed some of our bread. And in so doing we made a discovery about Sergeant of Cavalry Paluchowicz.

He had not a tooth in his head. Eating this hard bread was agony for him. The only way he could cope with it was by soaking it—in this case, where there was no water, by kneading it with snow.

"I had a nice set of dentures when they took me prisoner," he explained. " Then those bastard NKVD fellows knocked them out of my mouth, and they smashed on the floor. They laughed at that trick, but it was no joke to me, trying to get my gums around that prison bread, I can tell you. First thing I do when we get to where we are going will be to treat myself to another set of teeth."

"And have them gold-plated. You'll deserve them." This from Zaro. We laughed, and Paluchowicz joined in, too.

We slept through the remaining few hours of daylight, only one man remaining awake at a time to keep a listening guard near the small opening. Kolemenos went off to sleep like a tired child and snored gently and musically. No one had the heart to stir him for guard duty. Marchinkovas roused us as the light outside began to fade. We ate some more bread, smoked one cigarette each, and then crawled out. The snowfall had diminished to light flurries, and the wind was getting up. It was very cold, and we were stiff and sore.

All seven of us knew it was imperative that we should get clear of the camp area as soon as possible. All through that second night we alternately ran and walked. It never seemed to be completely dark, but the going was nevertheless difficult through two and three feet of crisp snow, the undulations of the ground masked by close-growing trees. Near morning we crossed a frozen stream, steeply banked on the other side, and when we scrambled up and got away from it into the continuing forest, we made our camp.

For the first four or five days we stuck to this night movement and daylight holing up. There was no sign of pursuit. Hopefully, we decided that, our tracks having been well covered by the first night's snow, the hunt had probably been organized eastward as being the shortest and most feasible escape route. Cautiously we congratulated ourselves on the choice of the flight to the south. We started to travel by day, advancing roughly abreast in a spread-out formation and making up to 30 miles a day. Watching the occasional watery sun, reading the sign of the moss growing on the sheltered side of the trees, we held to an approximate course south. Several more ice-bound streams were negotiated, and I judged they were all flowing southward to drain into the great Lena River. It was a time of hardship, of a constant battle against cold and fatigue, but our spirits were high. Most of all at this time we wanted to be able to light a fire, and we spurred ourselves on with the promise that we should have one as soon as we sighted the Lena.

After about a week of travel we began to sort ourselves out. The two regular soldiers, Makowski and Paluchowicz, kept close together. Marchinkovas, reserved and serious but with an occasional unexpected dry wit, was befriended by Kolemenos. Smith, now completely accepted as a kind of elder counselor of the party, was my own particular companion. The buoyant, fun-loving Zaro was impartially friendly with everyone and moved happily from group to group. A rare fellow, this Zaro. I saw him, at the end of a grueling day when we had to flog our aching muscles for the energy to build the night's hideout, mocking at his own and our weariness by squatting down in the snow, hands on hips, and giving us a lively version of a Russian dance until Kolemenos was bellowing with laughter, tears running down into his beard. Nothing could ever daunt Zaro. Of all the gallant jokers I had met, Zaro was undoubtedly the greatest. He taught us all that the grimmest twists of life were not entirely humorless.

ON THE EIGHTH or ninth day the going was unmistakably easier. The ground was falling away in a long, gradual slope southward. The bare earth between the trees began to show tufts of the typical tough, rustling Siberian grass; there was more moss on the tree trunks. In the early afternoon the forest suddenly thinned out, and we saw the Lena River, ice-sheathed and well over half a mile wide, at this point already a mighty waterway with still some 1,500 miles to run to its many-mouthed outlet into the Arctic Ocean. We stood, partially under cover in an extended line, listening and watching. The day was clear, and sounds would have carried well, but all was silent.

The American walked quietly over to me. "We'd better stay on this side tonight," he suggested, "and cross over at first light tomorrow."

I agreed. We built a shelter, and as darkness came on, we lit our first fire, setting it off with gubka moss and dry twigs that we had carried for days inside our jackets against our fur vests.

Quietly, as the wood smoke curled up into the upper branches of the trees and disappeared into the night, we celebrated with a hot dinner—a steaming *kasha,* or gruel, made of water, pearl barley, and flour, flavored with salt. Our only cooking pot was an aluminum mug of about one-pint capacity. We had a couple of crudely made wooden spoons, and the mug was passed around the circle, each man taking a couple of spoonfuls at a time. When the first lot disappeared—and it went very quickly—we melted some more snow and made a fresh mugful. The sergeant was allowed to soak his bread in the gruel, and we all congratulated ourselves on a fine meal. All night long we kept the fire going, the man on watch acting as stoker.

In the faint light of the day's beginning we silently crossed the Lena, mightiest river in this country of many great rivers, and came to the steep bank on the far side. There for some minutes we stood, looking back across the ice. Some of the tension of the past weeks was already falling away from us. In all our minds had been the idea we might never reach the Lena, but here we were, safe and unmolested. We could face the next stage with fresh confidence.

Inconsequentially, someone started to talk about fish. It set me on a train of thought and memory. I told the others that in winter back home in Poland it was possible to catch fish by hammering a hole through the ice.

"And having made the hole," interjected Zaro, "what do we do next—whistle them up?"

No, I explained, the fish, stunned by the hammering, will be forced out through the change of the air pressure when the ice is broken through. The others laughed and bantered, congratulating me on my ability as a teller of tall tales.

"All right then," I said, "let's try it."

Kolemenos went off and returned with a solid piece of timber, and we walked out about 20 yards onto the river ice. Kolemenos wrapped his arms around the timber, Zaro and I took hold near the bottom to direct the business end, and we started thumping away with pile-driver blows. Eventually we broke through. The water gushed up like a geyser, swirling icily around our feet. And yes! There were fish— four of them, about the size of herrings. We swooped on them and picked them up. We were all as excited as schoolboys. The others crowded around me, slapping me on the back, and Zaro made a little speech of apology for having doubted my word. Then Smith, looking anxiously around, said we had better not play our luck too hard and should get moving under cover again. We had a drink of the cold, clean Lena water and moved off.

We turned south again, climbed the riverbank to the higher ground beyond, and headed on the next leg of our journey with Lake Baikal as the immediate objective.

That first night across the river we spent in a copse of trees on a low hillock and lightly grilled our fish spitted through the gills on a skewer-pointed twig, ate sumptuously of our first fresh food, and finished up with more gruel.

By now the issue of rubber boots had been discarded as worn out. Our feet were still wrapped in the long strips of thick linen that had been handed out in the camp. All of us were now wearing moccasins with skin gaiters wound round with straps of hide. Movement south was at the steady rate of about 30 miles a day, and we kept going for a full 10 hours daily.

A FUGITIVE GIRL

OUR WAY LAY THROUGH TREES for some days. On about the third day we were enveloped in an early-morning ground mist as we started out. We abandoned for once our practice of advance in extended line and pushed on through the mist in a bunch. Somebody hissed urgently for silence. We stopped dead and listened.

Ahead of us and quite near came a violent thumping on the ground and a succession of crashing noises as though some heavy body were hurling itself toward us through the undergrowth. We stood as still as a collection of statues. Then I reached down for the knife, and Kolemenos heaved his ax up to his shoulder.

The furious commotion stopped. We waited a full minute, straining our ears. Faintly came the sound of choked, labored breathing. Another minute went by. The uproar exploded again, and we felt the vibrations as the earth was pounded. Kolemenos came up beside me.

"What is it?" he whispered.

"Must be an animal," I said.

"Well, it's not coming any nearer," said the big man. "Let's go and look." We spread out and went forward.

Through the mist a few yards away I saw an animal thrashing convulsively from side to side, its head down and hidden from me. I made the remaining short distance at a crouched run. The others came up fast behind me. There, kicking, snorting, and struggling, its muzzle flecked with spume and its breath pumping out steamily to join the morning's white mist, was a full-grown male deer. It was trapped and could not run. The fine spread of antlers was locked fast in the tangled roots of a fallen tree.

From the chaos around, from the beaten ground and the fact that the animal was almost spent with its efforts to break free, it seemed that it must have ensnared itself hours earlier. We looked at Kolemenos, and Kolemenos looked at the stricken beast.

He stepped up onto the trunk of the fallen tree and swung the shining ax blade down with a vicious swish. The edge struck home where the back joined the neck and the deer slumped, quite dead. We all ran forward and unitedly tried to get the head of the animal free. Kolemenos got his shoulders under the roots and heaved upward, but even he could not release the antlers, and eventually he brought his ax out again and hacked the head from the body. We hauled the carcass into a clear space, and I cut it open and carefully skinned it.

The thing had happened very quickly, and in the flurry of killing and cutting up the animal, we had not spoken much, until Makowski, speaking to us in a general way, but with his eyes on Mr. Smith, said, "What are we going to do with this lot?"

"We had better have a conference," said the American.

Mr. Smith opened the meeting with the statement that we could not carry all this meat, and we could not afford to leave any behind.

Marchinkovas propounded the obvious solution: "We must stay here for 24 hours and eat as much meat as we can hold. What's left we ought to be able to carry."

Zaro, licking his lips, said he was quite sure he could help to greatly lighten the load.

"All agreed, gentlemen?" asked Mr. Smith. There was an instant chorus of approval.

Paluchowicz busied himself gathering wood, laying and lighting a fire, while the rest of us built a shelter and completed the butchering. Within an hour we had choice cuts of venison grilling on a wooden spit over the flame, and the melted ice and barley gruel was steaming fragrantly with the addition of tidbits of liver and tender meat. We could not wait for the joints to cook through; I kept hacking slices off and handing them around. It took a bit of chewing, but it was excellent meat. Paluchowicz borrowed my knife and cut his share into small pieces because of his lack of teeth, and we let him later have the first go at the mug of gruel. We ate and ate, the fat of the meat running down into our beards, and we belched loudly and laughed, congratulating ourselves on our miraculous good fortune. All of us smoked and dozed in the shelter for an hour or two afterward and then decided we must get to work on the skin.

The preparation of the skin took some time. We armed ourselves with some pieces of wood and painstakingly scraped off the adhering lumps of fat. We made moccasins, 14 pairs of them. We each put one pair on over those we were wearing and packed the spare pair in our sacks. And there was still a piece of skin left for each of us. I carried mine rolled on the top of my sack. We broke off from our shoemaking to cook and eat another great meal, and again at night we fed off venison until our bellies were blown out with food. Not quite so heartily, but still willingly, we ate meat again just before dawn and distributed the best of what was left among our packs.

We continued on our southern course for Lake Baikal. And as the weeks slipped by into the middle of May, we noted gratefully the first signs of the short Siberian spring. The wind was milder, and there were a few buds on the trees. The streams we crossed were still frozen hard, and the carpet of snow lay undisturbed, but conditions generally were much easier.

The last thing we wanted was to meet other men, and in this our luck held. We crossed occasional roads only after thorough reconnaissance. There were nights when we saw afar the lights of a village. There were days when we saw the faraway outlines of buildings and tall chimneys plumed with white smoke. In these areas we proceeded with extra caution.

Then we began to meet real roads, probably of secondary importance but far better than anything we had encountered since we broke from camp. Borne on the wind from the direction of the lake came the sound of a distant factory hooter.

We came to a high point from which we could look down at the beginning of Lake Baikal. Miles away to the west groups of factory buildings caught the eye. Far below, between us and the water, there wound a road alongside which were telephone poles with their big white insulators carrying a weight of wires that indicated the presence of a fairly important highway. Our difficulty was to discover at what point we had struck the lake. We talked it over and finally made up our minds that we had swung too far west and were now somewhere near the northeast corner. This meant that we should have to follow the north shore westward until it turned down to point our route through southern Siberia.

For upward of an hour the seven of us squatted there, absorbed in the widespread scene below. We were in good humor at the thought of having attained another objective on our long trek south, but we faced the fact that our food supplies were down to a few scraps, including some small pieces of high-smelling venison.

Smith finally broke up the session. "Let's go down and take a look around," he suggested.

It took longer than we expected to reach the road. A weather-beaten signboard showed the direction and distance of a town, or village, named Chichevka, which must have been the place with the factories we had seen from the heights. We bolted across the road and into the undergrowth on the other side. Between us and the lakeside was a mile of flattish country in which junipers grew in profusion amid oak, ash, birch, lime, and willow. We broke through a fringe of small trees to find ourselves on the edge of a river.

We had to decide whether or not to cross. It was only about 150 yards wide, but the ice had broken up in the middle channel, and the brown water swirled on a swift current. Here we found that all of us could swim. The general opinion was that as we should have to negotiate many rivers from now on, there was no point in delaying our first test. I volunteered to go first.

We unwound our yards of rawhide strap from about our waists to make a safety line. Each man had up to seven turns of the stuff around him; the joined line was impressively long. The others kept watch as I trod carefully out on to the ice edge. It gave way suddenly with a crack, and I was in the water and gasping to get my breath. I struck out the short distance to the ice across the channel, reached it, and tried to climb up. The ice broke away and I tried again. It seemed a long time before I was able to haul myself out. Chilled and wet, I signaled the others to follow.

It was not so difficult for the rest but no less uncomfortable. They came across with the line to guide them, one by one, and Smith, the last to cross, was hauled over with the other end of the line around his waist. The next time I went over one of these half-frozen rivers, I took the ax with me and chopped away at the ice until the blade bit in, using it to help me out of the water.

We ran under cover as quickly as we could and then took off our three garments—the padded trousers and jackets and the fur vests— one by one and wrung out as much water as we could. We put them on again to dry on our bodies and went off briskly toward the lake to bring back circulation to our limbs.

LATE IN THE afternoon we huddled together to make plans for the next immediate stage of the journey. Common sense dictated that to hug the lakeshore too closely was to invite discovery by inhabitants of fishing villages that were well spaced here in the north but clustered thicker together on the southern side toward the sizable cities within reach of the Trans-Siberian Railway. The proposal we all approved, therefore, was to bear away north and make our way clear of roads and towns on a course parallel with but safely distant from the lake.

We accordingly set off obliquely northeast, aiming to cross the road again farther along. Our clothes were still damp, and we moved at a fast pace to dry ourselves off. We had covered about five miles when we saw ahead of us a line of trees marking the bank of another river.

Over to my right Zaro gave the halt and alert signal with upraised arm. I repeated the signal, and the advancing line straggled to a stop. Zaro pointed urgently in the direction of the river. I saw something moving between the trees. It could have been an animal, or it could have been a man—at this distance of several hundred yards in the fading light it was impossible to tell—but we had to investigate. I went over to Zaro and asked him what he thought he had seen.

Zaro said, "It might be a man. Whatever it is, it acts as though it has seen us and is trying to hide."

The others crept up to us. "If it's a man," said Makowski, "we shall have to hit him on the head and throw him in the river. We can't risk anyone giving us away."

We spread out again, Smith and Zaro on my left, Paluchowicz, Makowski, Marchinkovas, and Kolemenos on my right. Crouching low we moved forward from bush to bush until we were able to see that the line of trees was about 50 yards from the river, its waters now clearly visible. About 10 yards from the first of the belt of trees I stopped and listened. The others pulled up, too, and everyone peered ahead. Suddenly, a figure that had been motionless behind a tree trunk threw itself forward and downward into a clump of bushes. In that flash of movement I saw trousers and heavy boots. I broke cover and ran forward, the others at my heels.

The boots were rubber soled, felt topped, and knee length. They stuck ludicrously out from the bush as I threw myself on them and hauled outward to bring the owner into view. The next instant I was asprawl with the boots held in my hands. Kolemenos was breathing heavily down my neck, peering down at a ridiculously small pair of linen-swathed feet and slim ankles. And from beneath the bush came terrified, heartbroken sobbing. We looked at one another, still panting from our run, in sudden embarrassment. Someone whispered in awed tones, "It must be a woman."

Kolemenos bent down, shouldered aside the bush, and gently lifted. We all crowded around. It was a girl—a slip of a girl, round-eyed with fright, her tears making clean rivulets through the grime of her face. Moments ago we had been a bunch of desperate men who could have contemplated killing to prevent discovery. Now we stood around, clumsily contrite, like a crowd of romping boys caught in mischief and seeking the words to repair some act of over-rough horseplay. Through her tears she stole a look at my face and cowered back.

"Don't be afraid of us," I said in Russian.

She looked at me again, and her eyes went from me to the other six solemn and anxious bearded faces. She went on crying, and I cannot blame her; we must have looked like the worst gang of desperadoes she had ever had the ill luck to meet.

"Please don't cry, little girl," said Sergeant Paluchowicz.

She was still very frightened. She was fighting hard to stop her sobbing. "We won't hurt you," I tried to console her. "We all have sisters and sweethearts of our own."

Everything she wore seemed too big and bulky for her. Her thin shoulders were hunched in a long, wide, padded winter jacket, and her slim ankles emerged incongruously from a pair of heavy padded trousers. Like our own, both garments were of some somber black heavy material. Beneath the jacket showed the upper half of a well-worn and dirty purple velvet dress, the skirt of which was tucked into the trousers. From two sleeves of a green woolen sweater she had made herself a scarf, which was wrapped about her neck. Her tear-brimming eyes were very blue. Wisps of chestnut hair strayed out from under a moth-eaten fur hood. She looked like a schoolgirl masquerading in the clothes of a grown man.

She lifted her hands to draw the jacket sleeves across her face, and I saw she was holding a little crucifix. She dropped her hands, looked down at her feet, and turned her eyes on me. She was standing all but barefoot in the snow—and I was still holding her boots. I bent down and helped her slip her feet back into them.

She spoke then, in a quaint mixture of Polish and halting Russian. "I have lost my way to the kolkhoz where I work. I am Polish, and I was deported here to work." The look she gave us was apprehensive.

Paluchowicz and Makowski both pushed forward. I talked and they talked in a rush at the same time. In the gabble of explanation she finally understood we were telling her that we were Poles, too, that we were escaping prisoners, and that she had nothing to fear. Impulsively, she flung herself into my arms and cried her relief and sudden happiness. Over and over again she repeated, "God is good to me." The other two Poles awkwardly patted her head and shoulders.

Smith had moved apart and had been keeping an anxious watch. In Russian he called out: "Break it up. Are you forgetting where we are? For God's sake, let's get under cover."

The group quickly broke up. We moved off to find a hiding place.

H ER NAME WAS KRISTINA POLANSKA. She was just 17. She had not
eaten for two days, and she was very, very hungry. We rum-
maged in our bags and handed her our scraps of food. She ate like a
half-starved wild animal, with absorbed concentration, every now
and again sniffling and rubbing her padded sleeve across her nose.
She fascinated us. We squatted on our haunches and never took our
eyes off her. Only Mr. Smith sat back a little, watching her, too, but
with a more detached air of appraisal.

"I am not lost from the kolkhoz," she volunteered. "I ran away. I
have been running for many days." She paused. "And you are the
first gentlemen I have met since I left my home." She put a lot of
emphasis into the word gentlemen.

"Where was your home, Kristina?" I asked.

"My father had a farm near Luck, in the Polish Ukraine," she said.
"I last saw it in 1939. I have no home now."

Quietly, the American interposed with a question about our immediate plans. It was getting dark, he pointed out, and he thought we
should make some distance along the riverbank northward to a point
that looked favorable for a crossing early the next day. He suggested
that it would be senseless to give ourselves another soaking that night.
At least we could sleep dry.

There was no argument. We walked for four or five miles along
the tree-fringed river. I saw the girl several times looking at Smith.
She did not speak to him. I think she sensed that in this calm and
thoughtful man was the only likely opposition to her presence among
us. We Poles talked to her, but Smith said nothing.

It was quite dark when we found a place to rest. We built a shelter
against a fallen log. We laid down our food sacks for her, and she
curled up among us, completely trustful, and slept. Ours was a more
fitful rest. Throughout the dark hours we took sentry duty in turns,
according to our practice. She slept on like a tired child, oblivious of
the chill of the night. She still had not awakened when, in the first
hint of day, Mr. Smith touched me on the shoulder and beckoned me
away from the group.

He came to the point at once. "What are we going to do with this
young woman, Slav?"

I had known it was coming, and I did not know what to say. It might be a good thing, I said, to find out from her what her plans were. It was evading the question, and I was well aware of it. Out of the corner of my eye I saw Makowski talking to Paluchowicz. They strolled over to us. On their heels came Kolemenos. A minute later the other two joined us.

"Very well," said the American, "we'll make it a full conference."

We talked, but we did not come to the point. Were we going to take the girl with us? That was the only question. We decided that we would talk to Kristina first, then reach some decision afterward.

We woke her gently. She yawned and stretched. She sat up and looked at us all. She smiled in real happiness to see us. We grinned back through our beards and basked in that rare smile. Busily we fussed around to scare up some food, and we all quietly breakfasted together as day began to break. Paluchowicz, clearing his throat embarrassedly, asked Kristina how she came to be where we found her and where she was heading.

Kristina
Polanska

"I was trying to get to Irkutsk," she said, "because a man who gave me a lift on a farm truck and was sorry for me told me that if I got to the big railway junction there I might steal a ride on a train going west. He dropped me on the road a few miles away, and I was trying to find a way around the town."

Her glance rested on the American. He returned the look gravely. Her fingers fluttered to the strands of hair straying outside her cap and tucked them away in a gesture pathetically and engagingly feminine. "I think I should tell you about myself," she said. We nodded.

It was a variation of a story we all knew. After the First World War Kristina Polanska's father had been rewarded for his war services by a grant of land in the Ukraine under the reorganization of central European territory. He had fought against the Bolsheviks, and General Pilsudski was thus able to give a practical expression of Polish gratitude. The girl was an only child. They were a hardworking couple, her parents, and they intended that Kristina should have every advantage their industry could provide. In 1939 she was attending high school in Luck, and the Polanskas were pleased with her progress.

Then came September 1939. The Russians started moving in. The news of their coming reached the Ukrainian farm workers ahead of the Red Army "liberators." The well-organized Communist underground was ready. It needed only a few inflammatory speeches on the theme of the overthrow of foreign landowners and restoration of the land to the workers, and the Ukrainian peasants were transformed into killer mobs. The Polanskas knew their position was desperate. They knew the mob would come for them. They hid Kristina in a loft and waited. "Whatever happens, stay there until we come back for you," said her mother.

She heard the arrival of the mob, the shouts of men, the sounds of destruction as hammers and axes were swung. Kristina thought she recognized the voices of men from the nearest village. Outside in the yard her father called by name to some of the men he knew. The appeal came through clearly to the terrified child in the loft. "Take away what you want, but don't destroy our home and land." Silence for a minute or two after this. A growling murmur followed, then someone began to harangue the men loudly. The phrases were violent and venomous. Kristina heard her father's voice raised once more; however, it was immediately drowned out by a sudden uproar. Her mother screamed again, piercingly, and then Kristina pressed her hands over her ears to shut out the sound.

Kristina stayed in the loft for what seemed like hours, but she thought perhaps it was not really very long. The men had gone. The house was very still. All the personal servants had fled the day before. Kristina crept down through the silent house and into the yard. Her father and mother lay dead in the yard, near the side of the house. She crept to them and looked upon them for the last time. They had been beaten and then strangled with pieces of barbed wire.

I watched Kristina's white face closely as she told of the horror of that bright September morning. She spoke flatly, with little or no change of expression, as a person does who is still under the influence of profound shock.

"I went back into the house then," she said, "and I picked up some food and wrapped it in a cloth. I ran very hard for a long time."

She did not remember the next few days in detail. Some compassionate people in villages she passed through gave her a night's shelter and some food. She was obsessed with the idea of having to keep ahead of the Russians and out of their hands. Ironically, they caught her in the act of crossing the border when she did not even know she was near it. The Red Army handed her over to a civilian court, which swiftly sentenced her to be deported to Russia as a kolkhoz worker in the Yenisei River area of western Siberia.

Vividly she described her life on the Soviet farm. Most of the workers were strapping, big-bosomed, tough Russian women, and Kristina was the only Pole among them. On the second day after her arrival she was set to threshing and moving huge sacks of corn. The other women taunted her for her refinement and her weakness. They laughed at her failure to do the heavy work they managed themselves with ease. Aching from head to foot, she would cry herself to sleep at night. Food was poor, and the main item was one kilo of bread a day—for her as for the other workers.

But it was not the women who eventually caused Kristina to run. The farm was controlled by a foreman, whose attentions the other women were always inviting. Kristina was frightened of him and tried to keep out of his way. He was a big fellow, she said, swarthy and powerful. He would occasionally seek out the girl and try out some heavy pleasantries, telling her how different she was from the Russian women and that she needed someone to look after her.

There came the day when she was told she would not accompany the other workers in the horse-drawn farm cart but would report to the foreman's house "for interrogation." His intentions were obvious from the start. He promised there would be no more heavy work for her if she were kind to him.

Kristina panicked and appealed to him to let her go after the others and join them. What followed was a plain attempt at rape. Kristina screamed, clawed at his face, and frenziedly kicked out with her heavy boots. Surprised at the fury of her resistance, he relaxed his hold just long enough for her to break away and bolt blindly out and back to the women's quarters. He called vile names after her and threatened that he had means to make her change her mind.

She waited until the light began to fade in the afternoon, expecting all the time that he would come for her, but he did not show up. When she felt that the return of the other women must be imminent, she slipped out, keeping the kolkhoz buildings between her and the foreman's house, and ran. She slept that night in reeds by a river, and after following the river along for many miles the next day, finally reached a road and was given the first of two long lifts eastward by drivers of big farm trucks.

"All Russians are not bad," said Kristina. "These two were sorry for me and gave me some of their bread to eat. The second one told me to try to get to Irkutsk, but he could not take me any farther."

She looked around at us all, and her eyes finally rested on Mr. Smith. "So that is how I came to be here," she added.

The American dug his hands into his fufaika pockets. He spoke levelly. "We are not going near Irkutsk; we are heading south around the other side of the lake. What are you going to do now?"

Kristina looked surprised and taken aback. She turned an appealing gaze on the other six of us. We, said nothing. We knew what we wanted but were content to let Mr. Smith handle this his own way. Her lips trembled slightly. Then she jutted out her little chin. "I am coming with you. You can't leave me on my own."

The American looked over her head for some moments at the river beyond. "Can you swim?"

"I swim very well," she said, and there was no mistaking the note of pride. "In school I was a very good swimmer."

Through Mr. Smith's gray-streaked beard came the glimpse of a smile. We relaxed as we heard him tell her: "Forgive me, child, if my questions have seemed to be abrupt. We just thought you might have plans of your own. All we can offer you is a lot of hardship. Our food has run very low, and we have a great distance to travel. You must consider, too, that if you are caught with us you will not get off as lightly as you would if you remained on your own. If you want to join us, however, we accept you completely."

"Thank you," replied Kristina simply. "The only thing I wanted was to be with you."

THE GIRL WENT AWAY from us then into a screen of bushes, and in her absence I called for a check on food. All seven sacks were opened up, the rolled-up skins set on one side, and the food brought out. We were, as we feared, badly off. There remained perhaps a couple of pounds of barley among the lot of us, a little flour, some salt, and a few pounds of almost black deer meat. We decided on strict rationing to one small meal a day until we could replenish our stocks. The only item still in plentiful supply was the gubka moss for fire lighting.

Probably each one of us had, in addition to the communal food openly displayed, at least one piece of hard, dried bread, stuffed deep down in his long jacket pocket. I know I had one, and there was evidence later that the others also had this tiny personal cache. There was nothing dishonest or antisocial about it. To hide away bread was a prisoner reflex, a symptom of captivity. A prisoner holding one crust of bread felt that he still had a hold on life, as a man in civilized surroundings will carry around with him a lucky coin to insure that he will never be penniless. It was a measure of the great affection we developed for this waif Polish girl that later on one and another of us would dig out this last piece of bread to allay her hunger.

We ate hurriedly there that morning and decided to make an immediate river crossing. This first hour of daylight gave promise of a fine spring day, and we had a common desire to make distance fast and to return as soon as possible to a straight course to the south.

For the girl this first river was a new ordeal. We persuaded her to take off her warm jacket, trousers, and boots. I had a moment of great pity for her as she stood with us in the shelter of the trees in her faded purple dress. I went carefully out to the edge of the ice with the line paying out behind me, the ax stuck firmly in the back waistband of my trousers, and I made it fairly quickly across the open channel to the other side. Kolemenos crossed, holding her rolled-up clothes, with some difficulty, above water. Paluchowicz and Makowski came over together, the girl behind them with the bight of a length of spare line about her, the ends held by the two Poles. The other three followed, one of them bringing the girl's boots. We ran for cover, winding in the line as we went.

Kristina was blue with cold, and she could not stop her teeth from chattering. Kolemenos handed her her clothes.

"Don't stand still, child," the American told her. "Run off from us now and take that dress off. Wring it out quickly, wipe off as much water as you can, and jump into your dry trousers and jacket."

She nodded and ran.

We stripped, danced around, wringing out our garments as we did so. The operation did not take long, and in our wet rags we waited a few minutes for the girl to rejoin us. She came running, with her dress and underwear under her arm in a soggy bundle.

"Did you see? I *can* swim, can't I?"

Mr. Smith grinned. "Yes. I saw." And, aside to me, "The little lady is not going to be much trouble, after all."

We walked hard all through the day, halting for only the briefest rests, and Kristina kept up with us uncomplainingly. The midday May sun was pleasantly warm, helping, with the heat of our exertions, to dry out our clothes. We must have covered 30 miles northeast away from Lake Baikal by nightfall, and we all slept easier for being back among tall timber.

On the third day after leaving the lakeside, I judged we were in a position for turning south on a route that would take us down to the border, with Baikal lying some 50 miles to our right. It was guess-

work, but I don't think the estimate was far off, although it would have been impossible to maintain a truly parallel course. The country was hilly and well wooded, and our progress was a series of stiffish climbs, with scrambles down into steep-sided valleys carrying small rivers and streams. These valleys ran almost uniformly southwest. Many of the streams were fordable, although the current, swollen by the breakup of the ice, was strong. Kolemenos led the way across these, prodding ahead of him with a long sounding pole.

I marveled at the way the girl stood it all. I fear we all still had misgivings about her frailty, and I am sure she was aware of them. In these early days she never once held us up. She was even lively and happy when we were soured and foot-weary after a particularly trying march. She treated us like a crowd of big brothers—all except Mr. Smith. Between those two there grew almost a father-daughter relationship. Often in the night shelter she would get him to tell her about America, and on more than one occasion I heard him suggest that when this was all over, she should come to the states with him. He would gently tease her about her big Russian boots and then say, "Never mind, Kristina, in America I will buy you some beautiful dresses and elegant high-heeled shoes." And Kristina would laugh with the wonder and promise of it.

She grew on us until there was not one of the bunch who would not cheerfully have died to protect her. She would wake in the morning, look at the unhandsome collection around her, and say, "It is wonderful to see you all. You make me feel so safe." On the march she loved to get Zaro up to his funny business. Even Zaro sometimes was glum, but Kristina never failed to chaff him back to his normal sparkling humor. Zaro, spurred on by her interest, would effervesce with fun. Sometimes as I watched them together, I found it hard to realize we were on a desperate mission, half starved and with the worst of the journey yet to come. Most reserved of the party was Marchinkovas, the Lithuanian. He talked little and generally only gave his advice when he was asked for it. Kristina would walk alongside him for miles, talking softly and seriously, and then there would be the phenomenon of Marchinkovas smiling, even laughing out loud.

Now, too, the party had a nurse. Kolemenos began limping with sore toes. Kristina bathed his feet for him, tore strips off her petticoat, and bound up the raw places between his toes. When my leg wound opened up, she dressed that. A cut or an abrasion was her immediate concern.

When the bandages were finished with, Kristina washed them in stream water, dried them, and then put them away for further use.

Approaching what was probably the Bargusin River, about half-way down the lake, Kristina was herself a casualty. She began to drop behind, and I saw she was hobbling. I stopped the others and went back to her. "My boots are hurting me a little," she said.

I took them off. The soles and backs of the heels were raw where blisters had formed and burst. She must have had hours of agony. The boots had been much too heavy and too big for her. All seven men fussed about Kristina while she insisted that she was quite well enough to continue. I bandaged her feet with some of her own linen and then finally persuaded her to let us throw the boots away and make her some moccasins.

So I made Kristina a pair of moccasins. I lavished on them all the care and artistry of which I was capable with the materials at hand. The others watched every cut of the knife and every stitch of the leather thonging. I doubled the soles so that they would be stiff and long-wearing, and I lined them with sable. Everybody congratulated me on my handiwork, and Kristina planted an impulsive kiss right in the center of my forehead.

We began to feel that the girl was good luck for us. We suffered no real slowdown until, only five days after turning south at the lake tip, we reached, at night, the Bargusin River.

THE TRANS-SIBERIAN RAILWAY

THE BARGUSIN CROSSING took place at the end of May and was the last of the major water hazards. On the south bank the Siberian summer seemed to be waiting for us. The sun beat down, all was green, there were flowers, and the birds were back from their distant migrations. In six weeks we had walked out of the bitter tail end of central Siberian winter into the warm embrace of the southern summer, where village orchards in the distance were gay and beautiful with blossoming cherry and apricot trees. Sleeping out became less of an ordeal, even when it was considered prudent not to risk lighting a fire. During the day we were forced to discard our fur vests, but we put them on again after sunset to protect us against the night's chill.

For a full two days after crossing the Bargusin we ate nothing, and the thought of food obsessed all minds. Then it was that we saw the horse through the trees betraying its presence with restless movement in the shafts of a crude sledge. It had scented our approach and obviously did not like what it smelt. Zaro and I went forward for a close look. The horse turned the whites of its eyes over its shoulder toward us. It had every reason to suspect our intentions. We were all quite ready to eat horsemeat.

Zaro and I saw it at the same time—an old single-barreled 12-bore shotgun, stock and barrel held together by windings of copper wire. It lay across the sledge alongside a little leather pouch, which we guessed to be for the ammunition. The thought struck me hard: We must get that gun before the owner can reach it. I ran forward with Zaro and whipped it quickly under my arm, barrel pointing down. I waved the others forward. Kristina, with Mr. Smith's arm protectively about her shoulder, stood well back as the rest of the party came up to Zaro and me. Kolemenos went toward the horse to talk to it and to try to quiet its restiveness, but the animal shied from him.

The man must have been quite near, near enough to hear the nervous movements of his horse. We faced him in a tense bunch. He was about 60, a solid, broad-shouldered woodcutter, his big ax held on his right shoulder. He was heavily bearded, but both his beard and long hair were neatly trimmed. His approach impressed me. He saw us, but his slow, deliberate walk did not falter. His eyes looked steadily ahead and took in the fact that I held his gun under my arm. He gave no sign of fear or alarm. He went to the horse's head, ran his hand through the mane, turned aside, and swung the blade of his ax into the bole of a tree, where he left it.

He looked at me and beyond me to where the girl stood with the American. "Who are you?"

Smith answered, moving forward as he did so. "We are prisoners escaping. We shall not harm you. We only want food."

"Times have changed," said the man. "At one time you would have found food waiting for you and no questions asked."

There was a simple dignity about the man. He looked us all over with easy frankness. He turned his head toward Kristina again, and I thought he was going to ask us about her. But he said nothing. Instead, he walked around the horse's head and reached down to the sledge for a long, slim sack, which he picked up. His fingers busied themselves with the leather thong around the neck.

"You don't have to worry about me," he said. "I live alone, and I am the only man for miles around here."

From the sack came treasure. A loaf of dark brown bread. Four smallish dried fish. A thick, mouth-watering hunk of salted fat pork.

From his belt he took a long hunter's knife. These were the provisions of a man who was intending to be away from his home for a whole day, and it was evident he had not yet eaten. We watched his performance with concentrated attention. Carefully, he cut off one slice of bread and one slice of salt pork, which he replaced in the sack. He motioned to Kolemenos, positioned nearest to him. Kolemenos took a couple of paces forward, and the woodcutter put into his big hands the loaf of bread, the lump of pork, and the dried fish.

Kolemenos stood for so long looking down at the food in his hands that eventually I said to him, "Put it in your bag, Anastazi, and we'll portion it out later."

The sound of my voice caused the Russian to turn toward me—and to the gun I was holding. There was an unspoken question in his eyes. I walked over to Smith, and we talked about the gun. We agreed the thing would be useless to us. We could not hunt with it because the noise of it would attract attention to us, especially in the well-populated southern areas we were now approaching. Nevertheless, security demanded we should not leave it with the woodcutter. Paluchowicz and Makowski added their opinions, and the final decision was that we could not afford to take the slightest risk of the gun being used against us or as a signal to summon assistance.

I faced the Russian. "We are sorry, old man, but we have to take your gun with us."

For the first time he appeared perturbed. He lifted his hands as though to appeal to us, dropped them again. "It will not be safe for you to use it," he said. "I understand the way you feel. Hang the gun on a tree somewhere, and perhaps one day I shall find it."

We turned to go. Once more he looked at Kristina. "Good luck to you all," he called after us. "May you find what you seek."

We moved on for about an hour without much talk, all of us feeling a nagging sense of guilt at having taken that shotgun, a thing of inestimable value to a man like the woodcutter.

About five miles from the scene of the encounter I hung the gun on the low branch of a tree overhanging a faint track, having first bound a piece of deerskin around the breech. It was the best I could do.

The food remained untouched until that day's march ended at nightfall. Kolemenos divided it into eight portions. So small was each lot that I could have bolted down mine in a couple of minutes and still remained hungry. But the well-developed instinct of hoarding food against the possibility of even worse trouble prevailed with all of us. We decided to use what we had as an iron ration spread over three days—a little for this night and the two following nights. Kristina listened to our talk and ate as we did, one-third of her small store. She looked very white and tired that night, I remember.

In spite of the natural preoccupation with food, our progress remained good as we pressed south over a succession of low ranges. The farther we went, the more the signs of human settlement increased. Our method was to approach the top of each hill warily and scout from there the country ahead. Frequently we saw people moving about in the distance. We swung off course to avoid roads along which went telephone poles—always the mark of an important route—and which carried a fair amount of truck traffic. On other occasions we heard men calling to one another and the clatter of tractors. There was often the sound of a not-far-distant factory hooter.

DAYLIGHT TRAVELING WAS getting hazardous. One day after the last of the woodcutter's food was gone, we sat down to review our situation. This was a day, I recall, when Kristina had been unable to keep up. Several times she had slipped away and held us up. There had been good-natured grousing. She was away from us now as we discussed plans for covering the dangerous terrain between us and the border.

"What is the matter with the little girl?" asked Paluchowicz.

I turned rather sharply on him. "There is nothing the matter with her that a day's rest won't cure. Don't forget she is a woman. All women become unwell. Have you forgotten?"

Paluchowicz' face was a study of consternation. "I hadn't thought of that," he said slowly. Nor had the others, apparently. "The poor child," murmured Makowski.

Mr. Smith spoke up. "We shall have to revert to night marches very soon. We might as well start the new scheme now, and Kristina can have her rest. Slav, you are the youngest of us. You have a quiet word with her and tell her we won't start until she feels fit to go."

I met her as she came out from among the trees. "Kristina, we are all going to rest for a day and then start traveling at night."

"Is it because of me?" There was a bright pink spot in each cheek.

"No, no. It will be safer at night."

"I have been holding you back today. I am very sorry. But I could not help it, Slav. I am very tired today."

"I understand. Please don't worry."

She turned away. "You are very kind, Slav. You are all very kind. Thank you." And I led her back to the others. And everybody was immediately talkative in an elaborately casual way. Then Kristina sat down beside Mr. Smith and said, "Tell me some more about what the women wear in America." He smiled and talked. She listened without saying a word, her chin on her knees.

The new arrangement was a pleasant one. We slept during the heat of the day and had the light of the moon to guide us through the pleasant cool of the night.

It was in bright moonlight that hunger forced us for the first and only time to raid a village. The scattered lights of houses about a mile and a half away stopped us on the crest of a rise. A single, thin squeal of a pig came to us clearly.

Zaro made a sucking noise through his lips. "My mother used to make beautiful pea soup with a pig's tail in it."

Kolemenos touched my shoulder. "Let's go and find that pig."

We weighed the risks. We had to eat. Smith offered the strongest opposition, then gave in. The pig-hunting party was selected—Kolemenos, with the ax, I with the knife, and the Lithuanian Marchinkovas as a third member.

The big Latvian and I set off, Marchinkovas following us a few yards behind. We made a beeline in the direction from which we thought the squeal had come and came to an orchard of young trees on the fringe of the village. Grass grew thickly among the trees.

At the edge of the orchard we left Marchinkovas on sentry duty and started a hands-and-knees crawl toward a small, barnlike wooden building at the other end. We looked up to the roof of the building to make sure it was not after all a human dwelling place. We were reassured. There was no chimney.

I crept forward and flattened myself against the side of the building with my ear pressed against the wood. I could hear the pig moving around in rustling straw. He had scented me, too, and was snuffling at me inches away on the other side. Kolemenos joined me. We felt along for a door. There was none. "It must be around the other side," I whispered to him. The other side faced the village and its few lighted windows.

I found the door on the far side. It opened by a simple latch and creaked and groaned for lack of oil as I sweated to inch it open. Kolemenos squeezed in after me into the blackness. I moved over to the far side where from outside I had heard the pig moving about. By feel I discovered a small gate that lead to a penned-off corner. I jumped as the pig grunted a foot away from me and brought its snout against my leg. Kolemenos came from behind me, slipped his powerful arms gently around the animal, and gave a tentative heave to test the weight. "It's surely much too heavy for us to carry," he said.

There was only one alternative. We had to persuade the pig to come with us. "Make friends with it," I whispered. "Tickle its belly. Then get behind it and be ready to give it an occasional push." Kolemenos and I got to work. The pig grunted with pleasure. I took it by the ear and started toward the door. Kolemenos encouraged it from behind. There were a few breathtaking seconds of indecision before it moved. We went out, shutting the door after us, got into and through the orchard, crouching low and murmuring endearments to keep the animal in the right frame of mind to stay willingly with us.

A white-faced Marchinkovas met us at the top of the orchard and fell in behind us to cover our retreat.

With the luck of desperate men we made it. About a hundred yards from the rendezvous with the others, Kolemenos dispatched the pig with one swift ax blow. It died soundlessly. I felt a sharp pang of regret. It had been a very trustful pig. We worked fast, gutting the carcass in the moonlight and crudely cutting it up into pieces that could be carried by the seven men.

The killing had taken place only about three-quarters of a mile from the village, and the signs could easily be found in the morning. There was an extreme urgency about putting as much distance as possible behind us before daylight. We were jogging along most of the hours before the sun began vaguely to show in the east. We climbed a rock-strewn hill and, when we had almost despaired of finding a hideout, stumbled finally on a dank cave with a narrow opening well screened by dwarf trees.

As the sun came up, we had a clear view across a plain to a long ridge a couple of miles away in the direction from which we had come. There were no signs of life, but we took great care not to expose ourselves. The meat-heavy sacks were dropped well inside the cave. Anxiously we deliberated what to do with the pork. In this June warmth it would not long remain edible, and we knew it must be cooked quickly. The solution again must be to gorge as much meat as we could while it was fresh-cooked. There was no alternative to the risk of lighting a fire.

The fire was set going with the driest wood we could find well back inside the cave. Kristina turned the stake on which the joints of pork were spitted. The fire spluttered and hissed as the sizzling fat dropped on the burning wood. A delicious smell of roast pork and wood smoke filled the cave.

Throughout that day we cooked and ate and slept, maintaining one man on sentry duty in approximately two-hour shifts. By midafternoon I was in the throes of the most racking stomachache. Smith, Paluchowicz, and Makowski were also rocking in sheer agony, holding their clasped hands across their stomachs. All of us suffered from the effects of loading our digestions, idle for days, on the rich fattiness of half-cooked pig meat. Toward evening the cramping pains eased, and we drove ourselves to eat more.

Someone made the suggestion that we should try to smoke the meat we were to carry with us so as to preserve it. Dusk was falling as we piled green juniper boughs on the flames. The smoke billowed up, causing an epidemic of coughing and streaming eyes. For a couple of hours we smoked the lumps of meat until they were dark brown. Then we packed them in our sacks and set off on the night march.

At this stage of the journey I knew we must be within a week's travel of the border. The knowledge made us edgy, silent, and exaggeratedly watchful. I had the feeling that we were moving among hostile people and that the odds were that we must at some time run into some of them. I feared the imminent crossing of the Trans-Siberian Railway even more than I did the frontier. Already we were near enough to have heard in the far distance the passing of trains. Mr. Smith shared my fears.

"The railway will be heavily patrolled," he said anxiously.

"We will cross at night," I replied.

It was difficult to sleep during the day. There was no need to post sentries. Everybody was alert. Only Kristina seemed to enjoy peace of mind. Her trust in us was absolute.

From high ground we saw through the clear air of a June morning the Trans-Siberian Railway five miles distant from us. Near the track and separated by four or five miles were two small villages; on the outskirts of each, hard against the side of the tracks, was a signalman's or maintenance man's stone house. On our side of the railway, the northern side, was a protective belt of trees, beyond which could be seen some kind of fence, both having the purpose of preventing snow from drifting and piling up on the line. All day we watched. Several long trains passed in both directions.

The advance toward the railway was made immediately after dark. The fence offered no difficulties. At the foot of the embankment there was a ditch. We climbed into and out of it. We crawled slowly up onto the tracks and lay there listening. I put my ear to the nearest metal rail. There was no sound.

"Come on," I jerked my arm, jumped to my feet, and leapt for-

Mr. Smith

Anastazi Kolemenos

Sigmund
Makowski

ward, taking Kristina with me by the elbow. There was an agitated scramble down the embankment on the far side, and then we were all running like crazy fools. We had covered about a hundred yards when someone shouted, his voice sharp with panic, "Down! Down! Get down!"

I glanced over my shoulder and saw the lights of an oncoming passenger train. I dropped, pulling the girl with me. The train rushed past, in a whirlwind of sound.

It had been a near thing. If anyone on the train had seen us, we would have been ruthlessly hunted down. And there was still the chance that someone had caught a glimpse of us. We had to move on quickly.

The morning found us, after hours of hard travel, basking in sunshine on the secluded bank of a clear-water river. Smith said he thought it would be better if we got over to the other side as soon as possible. Unlike the rivers of the Baikal Range, these waters moved slowly and were warm. The swim across was pleasantly refreshing. The country on the south side of the river was fairly flat and gave us good cover. We made good time.

We were very near the border when we ran into two Buryat Mongols. There was no avoiding the meeting. We saw one another at the same moment at a distance of not more than 50 yards, and there was nothing to do but continue toward the pair.

One was middle-aged, as best as I was able to determine, and the other one was definitely a young man. They could have well been father and son. They stopped and waited for us to come up to them and grinned widely and nodded their heads. They bowed together as we came to a halt.

The conversation was embroidered and

276

ornamented with politenesses, and I took
the pattern from them. They spoke slowly
in Russian. They inquired solicitously
whether our feet carried us well in our travels. I assured them that our feet had carried
us well and returned the inquiry. The older
man was naively curious to know about us.

"Where do you come from?"

"From the north—Yakutsk."

"And where are you going?"

"We are traveling very far south."

The old man looked shrewdly at me from
beneath his wrinkled lids. "You go perhaps
to Lhasa to pray."

I thought that was an excellent idea.
"Yes," I replied.

But the old man hadn't finished. He
looked us over carefully. "Why do you have
the woman with you?"

A bit of quick thinking was required.

"She has relatives who live on the way," I
said. "We promised to deliver her there."

The two Mongols exchanged smiling
glances as though approving of our protect-
ing the girl on her journey. Then they both
dug their hands deep in their pockets and
withdrew them clutching fistfuls of peanuts, which they cheerfully handed around.

Each in turn wished us that our feet
would carry us well and safely to our destination. They turned away together and
walked from us. We waited to see them out
of sight. They had gone only a few yards
when the old man turned back alone.

He walked straight up to Kristina,
bowed, and gave her a big handful of peanuts for herself. He repeated his good wishes to her and to us all and left us beaming
goodwill.

We set off at a fast pace. We were too
near the frontier to take chances now.

Eugene Zaro

Zacharius
Marchinkovas

Anton Paluchowicz

277

PHASE ONE OF THE ESCAPE ended with the crossing of the Russo-Mongolian border at the end of the second week in June. It was notable for two circumstances: the ease of the crossing and the fact that we stepped out of the Buryat-Mongol Autonomous Soviet Socialist Republic with about 100 pounds of small early potatoes pulled out of a field only a few hours from the frontier. The timing of the potato-field raid—at dawn on the day in which later we were to make our exit from Siberia—was particularly gratifying to me. I felt that, having gone into captivity with nothing, we were leaving with a valuable parting gift, even though the donors were not conscious of their generosity.

We reached the crossing point in late afternoon. There was nothing to challenge our progress. The dividing line was marked by a nine-foot-tall red post surmounted by a round metal sign carrying the Soviet wheatsheaf, star, hammer, and sickle emblems over a strip of Cyrillic initials. To east and west one more post was clearly visible in each direction. They were so spaced in accordance with the contours of the country that an observer standing at any one post could always see two others.

I stepped around the post to see what might be inscribed on the other side of the plaque, but the reverse was blank.

There was the sound of sudden laughter as Zaro called out, "What's it like in Mongolia, Slav?"

Zaro cavorted across to me with a hop, skip, and a jump. The others followed with a rush. We pranced and danced, slapped one another on the back, pulled beards, and shook hands. Kristina ran around, kissed each one of us in turn, and cried with happiness and excitement. Mr. Smith put a stop to the noisy rejoicings by pointedly swinging his potato-filled food sack onto his back and moving off. We ran after him, still laughing.

"Let's get away from this place," Mr. Smith said, "as fast as we can go. We can't be sure how far below this border Russian influence extends. We don't know where we are or where we are going."

We walked fast after that, our sacks bumping against our backs. Behind us the frontier markers were swallowed into the distance and the darkness. The American had started a train of serious thought. I estimated that we had covered about 1,200 miles in not much more than 60 days. It was a feat of speed as well as endurance.

Paluchowicz broke in on my thoughts. "How far do we have to travel now?"

I thought about it. "About twice as far as we've traveled already," I guessed. Paluchowicz grunted his dismay.

Here it was that we first discussed seriously where we were going. Up to now we had thought ahead no farther than the escape from Siberia. Back in the camp I had talked, without any great conviction, of making for Afghanistan. It sounded like a safe, out-of-the-way small country where we might be received without too many questions asked. Now we turned our thoughts toward India. And the key to this, I think, lay in the talk we had had a day earlier with the two Mongols. Lhasa. It was a word we could use in a country where few knew our language, a sound that could be understood and that would always evoke the response of a flung-out hand to indicate direction. We talked mainly of Tibet in that first hour. India then seemed too far to contemplate.

The American spoke truly when he said we did not know where we were. We had no maps, and there was no one to tell us.

We were climbing steadily into the mountains two hours after leaving the border. Sweat oozed from us. The thunder spoke out nearer and nearer, and a warm, sighing wind blew up from nowhere, rapidly increasing in strength as we plodded on.

Around midnight the gathering storm exploded. The first overhead thunderclap boomed like a near-at-hand battery of long-range artillery firing a simultaneous salvo. It was an assault on the ears. Lightning streaked and blazed across the black heavens while the thunder rolled, crashed, and reverberated about us. A few large raindrops urged us to look for cover, but the lightning revealed only a wilderness of rocky slopes. The torrent was upon us as we groped in the tumult. The rain dropped down by sheer weight, its vertical fall unaffected by the whining wind.

My clothes were soaked in a matter of minutes. Streams of water trickled down the back of my neck inside my jacket. It was the worst electrical storm I have ever experienced.

We lasted that night out, the eight of us, in a shallow crevice between two smooth rocks. Only the innermost couple enjoyed any degree of comfort. The girl, in the most favored position, huddled shivering in her wet clothes throughout the unending dark hours, bewildered at the unabating fury of the storm.

It was a relief to get moving at first light. The rain sheeted down all through the day as though it would never stop. It went on teeming throughout the next night and until evening of the second day. Then the downpour ceased as spectacularly as though someone had turned a tap off in the heavens. In the morning a hot sun transformed our dreary world, and steam rose in clouds from the rocks. We dried our clothes and again began to take an interest in our position.

The continuing ascent was tiring but not difficult. The 15 to 20 pounds of potatoes each of us carried did not make the effort any easier, but no one grumbled on that account. From the heights on the fourth day there was a clear view of the range running roughly east and west and splaying out to the south like a series of great probing fingers. Our accidentally chosen route crossed the middle of three ill-defined peaks, its summit a broad, uneven-surfaced plateau.

The negotiation of the mountains took about eight days. The last stages of the descent were notable because we were able to find wood to light a fire and cooked the last of our stinking pig meat. We laid a flat stone across one corner of the fire and roasted potatoes, which made a memorable meal.

COMING DOWN ONTO THE PLAIN from the cool heights was like stepping into an oven. Off came the bulky fufaikas, and we sweltered bare-armed in our camp-made fur vests. Kolemenos carried Kristina's padded jacket, and she walked along with her faded purple dress opened at the neck. The ground was hard as cement and coated with a powdery reddish dust. The mountains outcropped in an odd succession of low, oval mounds. Our exposed arms turned bright red, blistered, peeled, and finally took on a deep tan. The 20 to 30 miles a day we imposed on ourselves were infinitely tiring, and the nights brought with them a severe chill.

The treatment of sore feet became a preoccupation. Deep cracks developed between the toes, and there were raw patches where the fine dust chafed inside our moccasins. We had occasion to bless the foresight of Paluchowicz, a chronic foot-sufferer, who had collected the fat drippings from the cooking pork back in the cave in Siberia and carried it in a roughly hollowed wooden cup shaped like half a coconut shell. This fat we applied to the cracks and sore patches.

The country, we discovered, was crisscrossed with rivers, but we marched a couple of days before we struck the first one. At noon on a sun-scorched day through a shimmering heat haze, the promise of its cool waters sent our dragging feet lifting over the dry ground. It was a beautiful sight, about 100 yards wide, its banks green-clothed with grass, its verges supporting flourishing growths of the long-stemmed, bamboo-jointed water plants we had met all through Siberia. We lay on our bellies and drank, then we sat in bliss soaking our aching feet. We washed ourselves, using fine sand as a scourer, and soaked the dust out of our clothes. We baked and ate some of our potatoes and lay down in the grass with a sense of relaxed well-being.

Along the river an hour after our arrival came a small sampan-type boat, high-built at bow and stern, broad-bottomed, and with a flimsy canopy amidships. Athwartships, just forward of the canopy, ran a long stout pole extending beyond the boat a few feet on each side to the ends of which were lashed two thick bundles of sticks riding an inch or two above water. At first I thought they were fenders, but afterward I concluded they were stabilizers, which, dipping into the water as the craft slewed, would keep it on an even keel. The boatman was Chinese. He was barefoot and wore a coolie sun hat, linen trousers ending below the knees, and a loose flapping shirt with ragged sleeves torn off at the elbows.

The sampan was poled along with a length of strong bamboo. The spectacle was new to all of us, and we waved as the sampan glided by. The boatman grinned and waved back. Three or four more craft moved past while we rested there. Propulsion was the same for all—a long bamboo pole—although one had a stumpy mast that could have been used for a sail.

There were many other boats on many other rivers in Outer Mongolia, but the men who plied their trade in them were always Chinese. On the roads I never once met a Chinese. Road travelers always seemed to be Mongols.

Our face-to-face meeting with the natives of the country occurred after we had crossed the river and moved a few miles to the south. We were following no track but planning our progress according to the lay of the land—avoiding small hills, seizing on a landmark ahead, and then walking steadily toward it. Our path was cut eventually by a road lying east and west.

Coming slowly from the west was a group of travelers, and it was obvious that if both they and we maintained our pace, we must meet. We were less than 50 yards from the road when the Mongols drew abreast. They stopped and waited for us. They were talking busily among themselves as we came within earshot but became silent as we halted before them. They smiled and bowed, keeping their eyes on us all the while.

There were a dozen or more men, one camel, two mules, and two donkeys. The animals were lightly laden and were also saddled for riding. Only the camel was being ridden now. Perched comfortably on it was an old man with a wispy gray beard. The men might have been a family party, of which the old man was the patriarch. All wore the typical Mongolian conical caps with their long earflaps turned back alongside the crown, in material that ranged from leather to quilted homespun cloth. All wore calf-length boots of excellent soft leather, and the old man's boots, in green leather simply embroidered on the outside of the leg in colored silk or woolen threads, were of especially fine quality.

When the bowing on both sides had been completed in silence, the graybeard got down from his camel. We bowed again, and he returned the greeting. He spoke in his own language, and we shook our heads. Mr. Smith whispered to me, "Try him in Russian, Slav." The old man heard and turned his attention to me.

"May your feet carry you well on the rest of your journey," I addressed him in Russian.

A long pause followed.

In Russian, haltingly and with an obvious searching for words in an unfamiliar tongue, came the answer: "Talk more, please. I understand you well, but I speak little Russian. Once I spoke this language, but not for many years."

I talked slowly, and he listened intently. I said we were going south, that we had crossed a river some hours before. I didn't know what else to say. There was such a long silence when I finished that I thought the parley was over. But the old gentleman wanted to satisfy his curiosity and, as it turned out, was grappling with his rusty Russian in order to phrase his questions. The conversation, in the fullness of time, proceeded thus:

You have no camels?—We are too poor to have camels.

You have no mules?—We have no mules either.

You have no donkeys?—No donkeys.

Having established us on the lowest stratum of society, he went on to question me about our journey. The word Lhasa came up. He pointed to the south.

"It is a very long way," he said. "and the sun will come around many times before you reach this place."

The question he had been itching to ask came at last. He looked at Kristina. Her hair, bleached several shades lighter by the sun, was in sharp contrast to the dark tan of her face, from which the blue eyes

frankly returned the old man's gaze. He asked how old she was, if she were related to any of us, and where we were taking her. I answered as I had done that other old man to the north.

This leisurely catechism had taken over half an hour and the patriarch had appeared to enjoy it immensely. I suspect he was proud of the opportunity of showing his younger kinsmen how he could converse in a foreign tongue.

He turned from us and spoke in his own language to the others. They smiled among themselves and bustled about the packs on the animals. From the packs they brought him food, and smilingly he distributed it among us. He handed around nuts, dried fish, some partly cooked swollen barley grains, and scone-sized oaten cakes.

We all bowed, and I, as the spokesman, thanked him in the finest phrases I could lay tongue to.

We parted with many expressions of felicitation for our respective journeys and many kind wishes for the continuing health of our feet. It was perhaps our most interesting encounter in Mongolia, but we were to find that all these people, whatever their station in life, had those typical qualities of courtesy, complete trust, generosity, and hospitality. The help we received was according to the means of the giver, but that help was always cheerfully given.

By the end of our first two weeks in Mongolia our methods of advance had been modified from those employed in Siberia. No longer was it necessary to post night sentries. The urge to keep on the move persisted; it had become a habit of our existence. But we were not now bedeviled by fears of imminent recapture; we could make contact with the people of the country. We did long day marches from the cool hour before dawn until the late evening setting of the sun, but we had adopted the hot-country custom of resting in shelter for the two hours of fiercest heat at midday.

To relate time and distance has been the greatest of my difficulties in recording the story of this bid for freedom. Particularly is this so concerning the passage through Mongolia, where we had no common speech with the inhabitants and where, even if we were given the names of rivers, villages, or other landmarks, there was no means of setting the sounds down to help the memory in later years. But I believe our progress through inhabited Outer Mongolia to the wastes of Inner Mongolia occupied us from six to eight weeks.

This much I remember: The entry into the Gobi Desert was not an abrupt transition. Twice we thought we were in it as we traversed long sandy stretches, but on each occasion a range of fairly tall hills intervened, and at the foot of the second range there was the boon of a shallow, sandy rivulet, beside which we camped for the night. That was our last drink of fresh water for a long, long time.

Toward nightfall of the next day we encountered a caravan trail at right angles to our course, alongside which were seated four Mongolians watching over a steaming iron cauldron suspended from a metal tripod over a fire. They all appeared to be aged between 30 and 40.

The usual courtesies were exchanged, but this time none of our hosts knew Russian. They motioned us to sit on one side of the fire while they faced us across the flames.

These were poorer travelers than those we had first met. I noticed that their jackets had been neatly patched in places. They had one mule among them, on which the bare necessities for their journey were carried. More water was added to the pot while we grinned and gestured futilely to show our pleasure at the unexpected meeting. In deference to Smith's gray-streaked beard, the oldest-looking Mongol directed his attention to the American, whom he obviously regarded as the senior member of our party and therefore its leader.

Eventually, Mr. Smith used the magic word Lhasa, and the Mongol, after a minute of deliberation, pointed the direction we should take. Then from inside his coat he withdrew a contraption that I can best describe as a metal cylinder on a long rod. From this cylinder he drew out a length of silk ribbon in the manner that a Westerner will produce a tape measure of the mechanically retracting kind. The silk was covered with symbols in a series of frames like the separate pictures on a movie film. He spent some time tranquilly contemplating the ribbon and finally, with a spinning motion of the hand, returned the roll within its case. This performance we took to mean a prayer for the happy completion of our pilgrimage. Mr. Smith bowed his acknowledgment.

The man in charge of the cauldron produced a brick of compressed tea, black in color, broke off a piece, and fed it into the water. For several minutes he stirred the brew with a large long-handled wooden spoon, and the fragrance from the boiling pot assailed our noses most agreeably. Next was produced a wooden jar from which the lid was removed to reveal a substance that looked to me like honey but which later turned out to be butter. Spoonfuls of the stuff were added to the brew, and the stirring and simmering went on for some time.

Two mugs were produced. The procedure for passing around the tea was rather amusing, since it involved guessing our ages in order that the more senior on both sides should be served first. About Mr.

Smith they had no difficulty. The first two cups dipped into the brew went to him and the oldest Mongol. When we turned over our own mug to the cook, he filled it and passed it without hesitation to Paluchowicz. I saw the sergeant make a face of great distaste at his first gulp, look at the American, and then smack his lips as Smith was doing to show appreciation of what he was drinking. Mr. Smith had sipped away with great composure.

Kristina and I were the last to be served. While we awaited our turns, I teased her about the custom of a country that ruled "Ladies last." She replied that placing her last might mean only that they recognized her as the youngest of us. The Mongols watched the laughing exchanges between us, and I am sure they would have loved to know what we talked about. When our turns did come, I could sense the others looking at us surreptitiously. The tea was comfortingly hot, but it tasted foul. We kept our faces straight and avoided each other's eyes.

The savor of the fragrant leaves was overborne by the sickening tang of rancid butter, which floated in glistening globules of fat on the surface. But we got through it, and I had to exercise great self-control to stop from laughing out loud as Kristina gave out a couple of decorous lip-smackings.

The Mongols' hospitality was rounded off with the gift of a little tobacco and a few nuts. We all stood and made our farewells. We walked away, and when I looked back from 50 yards away, they were squatting down again, their backs toward us. In that short distance we had passed out of their lives and they out of ours.

I was to remember later that they thought our trail to Lhasa merited a special prayer. We were striding into the burning wastes of the Gobi, waterless and with little food. None of us then knew the hell we were to meet.

HUNGER, DROUGHT, AND DEATH

TWO DAYS WITHOUT WATER in the hillocky, sand-covered, August furnace of the Gobi and I felt the first flutterings of fear. The early rays of the sun rising over the rim of the world dispersed the sharp chill of the desert night. The light hit the tops of the billowing dunes and threw sharp shadows across the deep-sanded floors of the intervening little valleys. Fear came with small fast-beating wings and was suppressed as we sucked pebbles and dragged our feet on to make maximum distance before the blinding heat of noon. From time to time one or another of us would climb one of the endless knolls and look south to see the same deadly landscape stretching to the horizon. Toward midday we stuck our long clubs in the sand and draped our jackets over them to make a shelter. Alarm about our position must have been general, but no one voiced it. My own feeling was that we must not frighten the girl, and I am sure the others kept silent for the same reason.

The heat enveloped us, sucking the moisture from our bodies, putting ankle irons of lethargy about our legs. Each one of us walked with his and her own thoughts, and none spoke, dully concentrating on placing one foot ahead of the other interminably. Most often I led the way, Kolemenos and the girl nearest to me, and the other ones bunched together a few yards behind. I was driving them now, making them get to their feet in the mornings, forcing them to cut short the noon rest.

As we still walked in the rays of the setting sun, the fear hit me again. It was, of course, the fundamental, most oppressive fear of all—that we would die here in the burning wilderness. I struggled against a panicky impulse to urge a return the way we had come, back to water and green things and life. I fought it down.

We flopped out against a tall dune, and the cold stars came out to look at us. Our bone-weariness should have ensured the sleep of exhaustion, but, tortured with thirst, one after another twisted restlessly, rose, wandered around, and came back. Sometime after midnight I suggested we start off again to take advantage of the cool conditions. Everybody seemed to be awake. We hauled ourselves upright and began again the trudge south. It was much easier going. We rested a couple of hours after dawn—and still the southerly prospect remained unaltered.

After this one trial there were no more night marches. Makowski put a stop to it.

"Can you plot your course by the stars?" he asked me. The others turned haggard faces toward me.

I paused a long moment before answering. "Not with complete certainty," I confessed.

"Can any of us?" he persisted. No one spoke.

"Then we could have been walking in circles all through the night," he said heavily.

I sensed the awful dismay his words had caused. I protested that I was sure we had not veered off course, that the rising sun had proved us still to be facing south. But in my own mind, even as I argued, I had to admit the possiblity that Makowski was right.

In any case, the seed of doubt had been sown, and we just could not afford to add anything to the already heavy burden of apprehension we were under.

So we went on through the shimmering stillness. Not even a faint zephyr of air came up to disperse the fine dust hanging almost unseen above the desert, the dust that coated our faces and beards, entered into our cracked lips, and reddened the rims of eyes already sorely tried by the stark brightness of the sun.

The severely rationed food gave out on about the fifth day, and still we faced a lifeless horizon. In all this arid world only eight struggling human specks and an occasional snake were alive. We could have ceased to move quite easily and lain there and died. The temptation to extend the noonday halt, to go on dozing through the hot afternoon until the sun dropped out of sight, invited our dry, aching bodies. Our feet were in a pitiable state as the burning sand struck through the thin soles of our worn moccasins.

I found myself croaking at the others to get up and keep going. There is nothing here, I would say. There is nothing for days behind us. Ahead there must be something. There must be *something*. Kristina would stand up and join me, and Kolemenos. Then the others in a bunch. Like automatons we would be under way again, heads bent down, silent, thinking God knows what, but moving one foot in front of the other hour after desperate hour.

On the sixth day the girl stumbled and, on her knees, looked up at me. "That was foolish of me, Slav. I tripped myself up." She did not wait for my assistance. She rose slowly from the sand and stepped out beside me. That afternoon I found to my faint surprise and irritation that I was on my knees. I had not been conscious of the act of falling. One moment I was walking, the next I had stopped. On my knees, I thought . . . like a man at prayer.

I got up. No one had slackened pace for me. They probably hardly noticed my stumble. It seemed to take me a very long time to regain my position at the head again. Others were falling, too, I noticed from time to time. The knees gave, and they knelt there a few unbelieving seconds until realization came that they had ceased to be mobile. They came on again.

There was no dropping out. These were the signs of growing, strength-sapping weakness, but it would have been fatal to have ac-

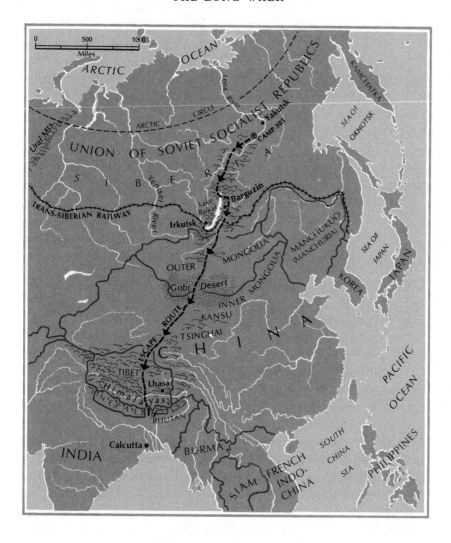

knowledged them for what they were. They were the probing fingers of death, and we were not ready to die yet.

The sun rose on the seventh day in a symphony of suffused pinks and gold. Without much hope we watched Kolemenos climb laboriously to the top of a high mound. One of us did this every morning as soon as the light was sufficient to give clear visibility southward to the horizon. He stood there for quite a minute with his hand over his eyes, and we kept walking, expecting the usual hopeless shrug of the shoulders. But Kolemenos made no move to come down. He flung out his right arm and pointed. My sight blurred over. For some seconds I could not focus. I rubbed my eyes and looked again. There was *something*, a dark patch against the light sand. It might have been five miles distant from us. Through the early morning haze it was shapeless and defied recognition. Excitement grew as we looked.

"Could it be an animal?" asked Paluchowicz.

"Whatever it is, it certainly is not sand," Mr. Smith replied. "Let's go and investigate."

It took us a good two hours to cover the intervening distance. There were *trees* all right—real, live, growing, healthy trees, in a clump, outlined against the sand like a blob of ink on a fresh-laundered tablecloth.

"Where there are trees, there is water," said the American.

"An oasis," somebody shouted, and the word fluttered from mouth to mouth. "An oasis!"

Kristina whispered, "It is a miracle. God has saved us."

If we could have run, we would have done so. We toiled that last half mile as fast we could flog our legs along. I went sprawling a few times. My tongue was dry and felt swollen in my mouth. The trees loomed larger, and I saw they were palms. In their shade was a sunken hollow, roughly oval shaped, and I knew this must be water. A few hundred yard from the oasis we crossed a clearly defined east-west caravan track. On the fringe of the trees we passed an incongruous pile of what looked like rusting biscuit tins, like some fantastic mid-desert junkyard.

The trees, a dozen or more of them, were arranged in a crescent on the south side of the pool and threw their shadows over it for most of the day. The wonderful cool water lay still and inviting in an elliptical depression hemmed with big, rough-worked stones. The whole green, life-giving spot could have been contained inside half an acre.

Zaro had the mug, but we could not wait for him to fill it and hand it around. We lay over the water lapping at it and sucking it in like animals. We allowed it to caress our fevered faces. We dabbed it around our necks. We drank until someone uttered the warning about filling our empty bellies with too much liquid. Then we soaked our food sacks and, sitting on the big stones, gently washed our cracked and lacerated feet. The very feel and presence of water was an ecstasy. Our spirits zoomed. We had walked out of an abyss of fear into life and new hope. We chatted and laughed as though the liquid we had drunk was heady champagne.

The full extent of our good fortune had not yet been discovered. Some 20 yards east of the pool, on the opposite side from which we had approached, were the remains of a still-warm fire and the fresh tracks of camels and many hoofprints, telling of the recent halt of a big caravan. It had probably departed at sunrise. These men, whoever they were, had cooked and eaten meat, and the bones, as yet quite fresh and untainted, were scattered around the wood ashes. They were the bones of one large and one small animal, and the meat had been sliced from them with knives, leaving small, succulent pieces still adhering. We portioned out the bones and tore at them with our teeth, lauding our luck. Poor toothless Paluchowicz borrowed the knife from me and did as well as anybody. When there was no more meat, we cracked each bone with the ax and sucked out the marrow.

For two or three hours during the heat of the afternoon we lay stretched out near the water under the blessed shade of the palms. The sun's rays began to slant, and I came out of a sleep haunted by blazing light and never-ending desert. I picked up the mug, climbed over the stones, scooped up water, and drank again. The American stood up, stretched, and joined me. Soon we were all up and about.

"I'm going to have a look at that pile of tins," Zaro said.

THE PUZZLE OF THAT DUMP of civilized junk in the heart of the south Gobi must remain unsolved. There were about a hundred of the boxlike metal containers, and they had been there so long that, even in the dry air of that place, they had rusted beyond use. From beneath the pile, half buried in the sand, Zaro pulled out a complete coil of rust-covered quarter-inch wire held together by circlets of thinner wire that broke away at a touch. I held a handful of sand in a fold of my sack and rubbed away at the heavy wire until I cleared the rust. The coating was thin; the wire was strong and sound. No one had any clear notion what to do with it, but we just could not bring ourselves to leave treasure behind. Since we had to take it with us, the discussion finally boiled down to shaping it into an easily portable form.

That was how we came to spend hours that day cutting off about four-foot lengths, turning the ends into hooks, and making loops that could be slung around the neck. The metal was tough, and bending it required hard work with the back of the ax head while the wire ends were jammed and firmly held in interstices between the close-set stones. When each of us had been supplied with a loop, Zaro and a couple of others made a few metal spikes about two feet long, one end beaten out to a point and the other looped to hang on the belt. Plenty of wire still remained when we had finished, but we thought we had all we could carry. The operation gave us a sense of achievement.

Inevitably came the question of when to depart. Two of our problems were insoluble. The oasis had water but no food. We had nothing in which to carry water. Makowski argued that if we waited here a few days, we stood a chance of meeting a caravan and securing ourselves a stock of food for the next stage. But I wanted to go. I said that, as we had just missed one caravan, there might not be another for weeks. We would wait on for days until we were too weak from lack of food to move at all, and the next travelers might find us dead from starvation. We were in desperate straits, and we had to decide immediately one way or the other. The thing was decided late that evening. We would set out before dawn.

We were on our way when the sun came up, and for half a day we could look back and see the trees of the oasis. I was glad when I could no longer see their shapes against the skyline.

For the first three days I thought we moved surprisingly well. On the fourth day the inescapable, strength-draining heat began quite suddenly to take its toll. This was the pre-oasis journey all over again. Stumbles and falls became increasingly frequent, the pace slowed, speech dried up into short grunted phrases. I remember Makowski saying, "Hell can't be hotter than this bloody desert."

On the fifth day Kristina fell to her knees. I turned slowly around to look at her, expecting her to get to her feet as she had done before. She remained kneeling, her fair head bowed down on her chest. She was very still. I moved toward her, and Kolemenos stepped back at the same time. Before we could reach her, she swayed from the hips and slumped forward, her face in the sand. We reached her at the same time and turned her on her back. She was unconscious. I opened the neck of her dress and started talking to her, gently shaking her, while Mr. Smith set to work with a stick and fufaikas to provide some shade for her.

She came to quickly. She looked at our anxious ring of faces, sat up, smiled through split lips, and said, "I feel better now. I must have fallen over—I don't know how it happened."

"Don't worry," I consoled her. "We'll rest here awhile and then you'll be all right again."

She leaned forward and lightly patted the back of my hand. "I won't fall down again."

We sat there awhile. Kristina reached down to scratch her ankle, and my eyes idly followed her hand. I saw that the ankle was swollen so that the skin pressed outward against the narrow-fitting ends of her padded trousers.

"Has anything bitten you, Kristina?"

"No, Slav. Why?"

"Your leg looks swollen."

She pulled up the trouser leg and looked, turning her foot about as she did so. "I hadn't noticed it before," she said.

We struggled on for a few more hours. She seemed to be refreshed. Then she fell again, and this time her knees buckled and her face hit the sand in almost one movement without even the action of putting her arms out to break the fall.

We turned her over again and wiped away the sand that had been forced into her nose and mouth. We put up the shelter. She lay with eyes closed, breathing in harsh gasps through her mouth. I looked at her ankles, and they were a pitiful sight. Both were badly discolored and so swollen that it seemed they would burst the restricting bottoms of the trousers. I took out my knife and slit the cloth upward. The skin appeared to be distended by water right up to the knees. I touched the swelling, and the mark of my fingers remained plainly visible for some seconds.

Kristina was unconscious for about an hour while we tried to stifle our gnawing anxiety with banalities such as, "It must be just a touch of sunstroke." I had a feeling like lead in the pit of my stomach. I was very frightened.

She was quite cheerful when she came around. "I am becoming a nuisance," she said. "What can be the matter with me? My legs are getting quite thick."

"Do they hurt you, Kristina?"

"No, not at all," she quickly replied. "They must be swelling because I have walked so far."

The time was afternoon on the fifth day. She walked on for hours without more than an occasional small stumble and was still keeping up with Kolemenos and me when the sun had gone and we stopped for the night. Sitting there among us she stole frequent looks at her legs. She said nothing, and we pretended not to notice.

It was a disturbed night. Everyone except Kolemenos seemed too weary and worried for sleep, Kristina lay very still, but I sensed she remained wide-awake.

During the first two hours of the sixth day the air was cool, and walking was as pleasant as ever it can be in the desert. But soon the sun began to blaze at us from a sky empty of clouds.

I took Kristina's elbow. "Can you keep going in this?"

"Yes, I think so."

Five minutes later she had folded up and was out, face down in the sand. Again we ministered to her and waited for her to open her eyes. She appeared to be breathing quite normally, like a tired child.

I stood a few steps away from her, and the others came over to me. "She is very swollen," I said, my voice lowered. "Do any of you know what that means?"

Nobody knew the symptoms. We went back to her and waited. I flapped my cap over her face to make some air.

She smiled at us. "I am being a bother again." We shook our heads. "I am afraid you had better leave me this time."

We all broke into protest at once. Kolemenos dropped down on his knees beside her. "Don't say that. Don't be a silly little girl. We shall never leave you." She lay there for another half hour, and when she tried to force herself up on her elbows, she fell back again.

I spoke to Kolemenos. "We must give her a hand." We lifted her to her feet. "I can walk if you stay near me," she said.

Amazingly, she walked, Kolemenos and I lightly holding her elbows. After a quarter of a mile we felt her start to fall forward. We steadied her, and she went on again. She pulled herself erect, and there was not a sound of distress, not a whimper. The next time she slumped forward we could not hold her. She had played herself utterly out; even the gallant will in that frail body could not produce another torturing effort. We were all in a bunch around her as the sun climbed up over our heads. Kolemenos and I each put an arm about her and, half-carrying, half-dragging her, set off again. A mile or so of that and I had no reserve of strength to give her. We stopped, and I bent over double fighting for breath.

We made a shelter there and remained for perhaps three hours through the worst heat of the day. She lay still—I do not think she could move. The ugly swelling had advanced past the knees and was heavy with water.

The sun began to decline. Kolemenos bent down and swung her into his arms and trudged off. I stayed with him, and the rest were all about us. He covered fully a quarter of a mile before he put her down that first time. He picked her up again and walked, her head pillowed on his great shoulder. I can never in my life see anything so magnificent as the blond-bearded giant Kolemenos carrying Kristina, hour after hour, toward darkness of that awful sixth day. His ordeal lasted some four hours. Then she touched his cheek.

"Put me down on the ground, Anastazi. Just lay me down on the ground. Please, Anastazi."

I took her weight from him, and together we eased her down. We gathered around her. A wisp of a smile hovered about the corners of her mouth. She looked very steadily at each one of us in turn, and I thought she was going to speak. Her eyes were clear and very blue. There was a great tranquility about her. She closed her eyes.

"She must be very tired," said Sergeant Paluchowicz. "The poor, tired little girl."

We stood around for several minutes, dispirited and at a loss to know what to do next. The shoulders of Kolemenos were sagging with exhaustion. We exchanged glances but could think of nothing to say. I looked down at Kristina. I looked at the open neck of her dress, and in a second I was down at her side with my ear over her heart. There was no beat. I did not believe it. I turned my head and applied the other ear. I lifted my head and picked up her thin wrist. There was no pulse. They were all looking at me intently. I dropped her hand, and it thumped softly into the sand.

The American spoke, hardly above a whisper. I tried to answer but the words would not come. Instead the tears came, the bitter salt tears. And the sobs were torn from me. In that godforsaken place seven men cried openly because the thing most precious to us in all the world had been taken from us. Kristina was dead.

I think we were half crazy there beside her body in the desert. We accused ourselves of having brought her here to her death.

The American intervened, his voice cold and flat. "Gentlemen, it is no use blaming ourselves. I think she was happy with us." The talk ceased. He went on, "Let us now give her a decent burial."

We scraped a hole in the sand at the base of a dune. Little pieces of stone that we sifted from the grains as we dug deeper we laid apart. I slit open a food sack and laid the double end gently under her chin. We lowered the body. On her breast lay her little crucifix. We stood around with our caps in our hands. There was no service, but each man spoke a prayer in his own language. Mr. Smith spoke in English, the first time I had heard him use it. As I opened out the sacking and lifted it over her face, I could not see for tears. We covered her with sand, and we dotted the mound around with the little stones.

And Kolemenos took her tall stick and chopped a piece off it with a stroke of his ax. Then he bound the one piece to the other, using a leather thong to make a cross.

So we said good-bye to her and went our empty way.

The awful thing was that there was so little but the girl to think about. Walking was sheer painful habit—it required no thought to perform. The sun beating down hour after hour would addle my brains and check the orderly sequence of thinking. I found I could imagine she was still there, just behind my shoulders, and I'd scuff along for mile after mile, seeing her. But there always came a time when the idea of her presence was so strong that I must turn my head, and bitter grief would knife at me all over again. I awoke slowly from a troubled, thirst-ridden sleep that night, and I was sure once more that she remained with us. And each fresh realization of her death renewed the agony.

It took another bitter tragedy to dull the sharp edges of our memory of Kristina.

On the eighth day out from the oasis, Sigmund Makowski pitched over into the sand. His arms were still at his sides when his face thumped down, and he had made no effort to use his stick to prevent the fall. He lay there a minute or two and was barely conscious. We looked down at him and saw the telltale sign. Over the tops of his moccasins the flesh was soft and puffy. We exchanged glances and said nothing. We turned him over and flapped our sacks in his face, and he recovered quickly. He got to his feet, shook his head from side to side, grabbed his stick, and plunged off. He keeled over again and again, but he kept going. And all the time the sickening flabby swelling grew upward and weighed upon his legs.

Makowski lasted longer after the first onset than Kristina had. On the ninth day he must have slumped down half a dozen times in a couple of hours.

That night he seemed to sleep peacefully, and in the morning of the 10th day he was not only still alive but appeared to have regained some strength. He set off with the rest of us, dragging his feet but unaided. He moved for half an hour before his first fall, but thereafter he pitched over repeatedly until Kolemenos and I again went to his rescue. When the time came to make our noonday halt, he was draped about our shoulders like a sack, and his legs had all but ceased to move. Mr. Smith and Paluchowicz eased his weight away from us and gently laid him down on his back. Then we put up the shelter and squatted down around him. Makowski lay quite still—only his eyes seemed to be alive.

After a while he closed his eyes, and I thought he had gone, but he was still breathing quietly. He opened his eyes again. The lids came down, and this time he was dead. There was no spasm, no tremor, no outward sign to show that life had departed the body. Like Kristina, he had no words for us at the end.

The dossier for Sigmund Makowski, aged 37, ex-captain of the Polish Frontier Forces, was closed. Somewhere in Poland he had a wife. I would like her some day to know he was a brave man. We buried him there in the Gobi. Kolemenos made another small wooden cross; we said our prayers and left him.

I tried hard to keep count of the days. I tried, too, to remember if I had ever read how long a man can keep alive without food and water. My head ached with the heat. Often the blackest pall of despair settled on me, and I felt we were six doomed men toiling inevitably to destruction. With each hopeless dawn the thought recurred: Who will be next? We were six dried-out travesties of men shuffling, shuffling. The sand seemed to get deeper, more and more reluctant to let our ill-used feet go. When a man stumbled, he made a show of getting quickly on his legs again. Quite openly now we examined our ankles for the first sign of swelling, for the warning of death.

In the shadow of death we grew closer together than ever before. No man would admit to despair. No man spoke of fear. The only thought spoken out again and again was that there must be water soon. All our hope was in this. Over every arid ridge of hot sand I imagined a tiny stream, and after each waterless vista there was always another ridge to keep the hope alive.

The only life we saw in the desert about us were snakes. They lay still, heads showing, with the lengths of their bodies hidden in deep holes in the sand. I wondered how they lived. They showed no fear of us, and we had no desire to molest them.

THE LAST OF THE GOBI

Two days after Makowski's death, Slav Rawicz and his five companions were reaching the end of their endurance, yet they staggered on across the blistering sands of the Gobi Desert. Each man knew that if a miracle did not happen soon, they could never expect to survive. Then a chance discovery revealed an almost dried-up creek. It gave them enough muddy water to stave off immediate death. But still there was nothing to eat.

"I think snakes are our only chance," the American, Smith, said. "It's not unknown for men to eat snakes. The poison is in a sac in the head. When you cut off the head, you remove the poison."

Unquestionably, it was the snakes of the Gobi that saved them, Slav Rawicz later wrote. Two were soon caught, skinned, cooked, and eaten. They were just the first of many the men ate, as the dreadful southward trek across the flat, never-ending desert went on and on.

Then one morning they awoke to make an exciting discovery. The land far ahead was beginning to slope upward to a series of foothills, and beyond, perhaps 50 miles away, was a mountain range.

So UNINFORMED WERE WE of central Asian geography that we speculated on the possibility that the tall eastern barrier could be the Himalayas, that somehow we had bypassed them to the west, that we might now even be on the threshold of India. We were to learn that the whole considerable north-to-south expanse of Tibet, ruggedly harsh and mountainous, lay between us and the Himalayas.

We plodded on for two more exhausting, heartbreaking days before we reached firm ground, a waste of lightly sanded rocks. Lifeless and naked, the rocky ridge sloped easily into the distance above us. In my mind was the one thought that over the hump there might be water. We rested a couple of hours before we tackled the drag upward. We took off our moccasins and emptied them of sand. Then we went up and out of the Gobi.

Over the ridge there was more desolation. By nightfall we had dropped down into a stone-strewn valley. In the morning we climbed again. We did not reach the next summit for several hours. From the top there was the view again of the great range to the east, looking even more formidable than at our first sight of it. Below us the floor of the valley appeared to be covered with sand, and we decided to get down before dark to search for snakes.

It was the merest accident that we did not miss the water on our way down. We had all passed it when Zaro turned around and yelled the one wonderful word. It was no more than a trickle from a crack in a rock, but it glinted like silver. It crept down over the curve of a big round boulder and spread thinly over a flat rock below. We turned quickly and scrambled back. We found that the source of the little spring was a crack just wide enough to take the fingers of one hand. The water was sparkling, clean, and ice-cold. We channeled the tiny stream to a point where we could lead it into our battered and much traveled metal mug. The mug was passed around, and each man took a gulp. No nectar of the gods could have tasted so wonderful. Again and again we filled the mug and drank.

The time was around the middle of the day. We agreed readily that we should stay close to the spring for another 24 hours.

The next morning we were on our way again. We traveled down the long slope, across the hot valley, and up the hillside facing us—a total of at least 15 miles. From the top of the ridge we took fresh bearings. Directly ahead were some formidable heights, so we set our course over easier ground about 10 degrees east of the line due south. Toward evening we were all heartened by the discovery of the first vegetation we had seen since the oasis. It was a rough, spiky grass clinging hardily to dry rootholds in fissures between the rocks.

The wearing trek went on day after day. Our diet was still confined to an occasional snake—we lived on them altogether for upward of three weeks from the time of our first sampling back in the desert. The specter of thirst receded as we found clear-running rivulets. It was rare now that we had to go waterless for longer than a day.

There came a morning when we breasted the top of a long rise and looked down unbelievingly into a wide-spreading valley, which showed, far below, the lush green of grazing grass. Still more exciting, there was a flock of about a hundred sheep, crawling like specks five miles or more distant from and below us. We made the descent fast, slipping and sliding in our eagerness to get down. We had about a quarter of a mile to go to reach the flock when we saw the two dogs, long-coated liver-and-white collie types. They came racing around the flock to take up a station between us and their charges.

Zaro called out, "Don't worry, we won't hurt them. Where's your master?" The dogs eyed him warily.

Kolemenos growled, "I only need to get near enough to a sheep for one swing of my old ax. . . ."

"Don't get impatient, Anastazi," I told him. "It is fairly obvious the shepherd has sent his dogs over here to intercept us. Let us swing away from the flock and see if they will lead us to their master."

We turned pointedly away. The dogs watched us closely for a couple of minutes. Then, apparently satisfied that they had headed us away from the sheep, they ran off at great speed together toward the opposite slope of the valley. My eyes followed the line of their run ahead of them, and then I shouted and pointed. A mile or more away rose a thin wisp of smoke.

"A fire at midday can mean only one thing—cooking," said Marchinkovas hopefully.

The fire was burning in the lee of a rocky outcrop, against which had been built a one-man shelter of stones laid one above the other as in an old cairn. Seated there was an old man, his two dogs, tongues lolling, beside him. He spoke to his dogs as we neared him, and they got up and raced off back across the valley to the flock. Steaming over the fire was a black iron cauldron. The American went to the front and approached bowing. The old man rose smiling and returned the bow and then went on to bow to each of us in turn.

He was white-bearded. The high cheekbones in his broad, square face revealed a skin that had been weathered to the color of old rosewood. He wore a warm goatskin cap with earflaps turned up over the crown in the fashion of the Mongols we had met in the north. His felt boots were well made and had stout leather soles. His unfastened three-quarter-length sheepskin coat was held to the body by a woven wool girdle, and his trousers were bulkily padded, probably with lamb's wool. He leaned his weight on a five-foot-tall wooden staff. There was no doubt of his friendliness and his pleasure at the arrival of unexpected visitors.

He talked eagerly, and it was a minute or two before he realized we did not understand a word. I spoke in Russian, and he regarded me blankly. It was a great pity because he must have been looking forward to conversation and the exchange of news. I think he was trying to tell us that he had seen us a long way off and had prepared food for our arrival. He motioned us to sit near the fire and resumed the stirring of the pot that our coming had interrupted. I looked into the stone shelter and saw there was just room for one man to sleep. On the floor was a sleeping mat.

As he wielded his big wooden spoon, he made another attempt at conversation. He spoke slowly. It was no use. Mr. Smith cleared his throat. He gestured with his arm around the group of us. "We," he said slowly in Russian, "go to Lhasa."

The shepherd's eyes grew intelligent. "Lhasa, Lhasa," Smith repeated, and pointed south. From inside his jacket the old shepherd pulled out a prayer wheel that appeared as if it had been with him for many years. The religious signs were painted on parchment, the edges of which were worn with use. He pointed to the sun and made circles, many of them, with his outstretched arm.

"He is trying to tell us how many days it will take us to reach Lhasa," I said.

"His arm's going around like a windmill," observed Zaro. "It must be a hell of a long way from here."

We bowed our acknowledgment of the information. From out of his pocket he produced a bag of salt and invited us to look into the cauldron as he sprinkled some in. We crowded around and saw a bubbling, grayish, thick gruel. He stirred again, brought out a spoonful, blew on it, smacked his lips, tasted, and finally thrust out his tongue and ran it slowly around his lips.

He chuckled at us like a delighted schoolboy, and his good humor was so infectious that we found ourselves laughing aloud in real enjoyment for the first time in months.

The next move by the old man had almost a ritualistic air. From his shack he produced an object wrapped in a linen bag. He looked at us, eyes twinkling, and I could not help thinking of a conjuror building up suspense for the trick that was to astound his audience. I think we all looked suitably impressed as he opened the bag and reached into it. Into the sunlight emerged a wooden bowl about five inches in diameter and three inches deep, beautifully turned, shining with care and use, of a rich walnut brown color.

Into the bowl he ladled a quantity of gruel and laid it on the skin rug. He disappeared into the shack and came out holding an unglazed earthenware jar, dark brown and long necked. It held about a gallon of ewe's milk, a little of which he added to the gruel in the bowl. He handed the bowl and spoon to Zaro, who was seated nearest to him.

Zaro ate a spoonful, smacked his lips, and made to pass the bowl around, but the shepherd indicated he was to finish the portion.

Zaro made short but evidently highly enjoyable work of it. "By God, that tastes wonderful," he exclaimed.

IT WAS MY TURN NEXT. The main ingredient seemed to be barley, but some kind of fat had been added. The sweet, fresh milk had cooled the mixture a little, and I fairly wolfed it down. I belched loudly, smacked my lips, and handed back the bowl.

The shepherd saw to the needs of each of us in turn before he ate himself. To what was left in the cauldron he added several pints of milk and started stirring again, making enough extra to give us each another bowlful.

He took the cauldron off the fire to cool off, moving it with some difficulty because it had no handle, although I noticed there were the usual two holes in the rim. To our unspeakable joy he then produced tobacco from a skin pouch and handed us each enough for two or three cigarettes. Out came the pieces of hoarded newspaper. We lit up with glowing brands from the fire.

We were happy in that moment and brimming over with gratitude toward a supremely generous host. And he, bless him, sat there crosslegged and basked in our smiles.

Away he went after about half an hour, refusing offers of help, to wash the cauldron and the precious bowl at a nearby spring. He came back, stoked the fire, and made us tea, Tibetan style, and this time we

even faintly approved the taste of the rancid butter floating in globules on the surface.

I felt I wanted to do something for the old man. I said to Kolemenos, "Let's make him a handle for his cauldron out of one of the
spare wire loops." Everybody thought it an excellent idea. It took us
only about 30 minutes to break off a suitable length, shape it, and
fasten it. Our host was delighted.

We tried to think of some other service we could render. Someone
suggested we forage for wood for the fire. We were away about an
hour and came back with a pile of stuff, including a complete small
tree which Kolemenos had hacked down with his ax.

The shepherd had been waiting for our return. As we came in, he
was finishing sharpening his knife on a smooth piece of stone. He had
his two dogs with him again. He made us sit down and, with his dogs
at his heels, strode off.

He returned shortly, dragging by the wool between its horns a
young ram, the dogs circling him in quiet excitement as he came. In
something like five minutes the ram was dead, butchered with practiced skill. He wanted no help from us on this job. He skinned and
gutted the carcass with a speed that made my own abilities in this
direction seem clumsy. The carcass finally was quartered. Salt was
rubbed in one fore and one hind quarter, which were hung inside the
stone hut. He threw the head and some other oddments to the dogs.

Half the sheep was roasted on wooden spits over the blazing fire
that night, and we ate again to repletion. We made signs that we
would like to stay overnight, and he seemed altogether willing that
we should. The six of us slept warm around the fire, while the shepherd lay the night inside his hut.

From somewhere he produced the next morning a batch of rough
barley cakes—three each was our share. There was more tea and, to
our astonishment, because we thought the limit of hospitality must
already have been reached, the rest of the ram was roasted and portioned out, and a little more tobacco distributed.

We left him in the early afternoon, after restocking his fuel store.
We did not know how to thank him for his inestimable kindness.
Gently we patted his back and smiled at him. I think we managed to
convey to him that he had made six most grateful friends.

At last we stood off a few feet from him and bowed low, keeping
our eyes, according to custom, on his face. Gravely he returned the
salute. We turned and walked away. When I looked back, he was
sitting with his back to us, his dogs beside him.

I THINK IT PROBABLE that at the time we encountered the old man and his sheep we had not even entered Tibet but had come out from the desert into the highlands in the narrow neck of the Chinese province of Kansu lying along the northeastern border of Tibet. The time then was about the beginning of October 1941, and it was to take us over three months to cover about 1,500 miles of difficult country to the Himalayas. We tried always to do at least 20 miles a day. Often we did more. There were occasional days, too, when we did no traveling, glad of the rest and refreshment provided by friendly Tibetan villagers. The tradition of hospitality to travelers was an innate and wonderful part of the life of these people; their generosity was open-handed and without thought of reward. Without their help we could not have kept going.

We came across our first village some five days after leaving the shepherd. We had been on the move for about an hour after dawn when I saw, over to the left of our course and about 10 miles distant, a smear of smoke. We were hungry, stiff, and not very warm. We decided to investigate. We came down a hill that was scrub-covered on its upper reaches, giving way to grass of good sheep-grazing quality. As we got nearer, we saw the smoke came from several fires and knew we were approaching some kind of settlement, hidden from us by the rounded shoulder of the opposite hill.

It was well past noon when we reached the village. The hill threw out a green-clothed buttress like a long arm, and 10 boxlike houses nestled there like a child in the crook of its mother's arm. Each house was about 20 feet by 12 feet, flat-roofed with overlapping wide boards weighted down with stones. The roofs sloped slightly forward in the direction of the overlap. A few of the dwellings were backed by a fenced-in enclosure containing a small outhouse a couple of yards square. The slopes around were dotted with dozens of long-haired sheep. We came in slowly on an almost due west-east track, frequently pausing to look around so that the villagers would have ample warning of our visit. We did not know then what reception to expect.

A closer view of the village revealed the presence of a number of children, some chickens, goats, and the first yaks any of us had ever seen outside a zoo. At a leisurely shuffle, strung out in couples, we came near to the first house and stopped, interested in the novel spectacle of a man harnessing a yak to a high two-wheeled cart. He had seen us but had his hands too full with the task in hand to do anything about it. Half a dozen shy but frankly inquisitive children, the eldest about 10 years old, positioned themselves about the cart and eyed us. The yak, its long silken hair riffling in the breeze blowing through the valley, was being difficult and was doing its best not be attached to the cart. Possibly it had got wind of us and did not care for the evidence of its nose. (I couldn't have blamed it for any adverse opinion based on the smell of us!)

The villager decided suddenly to give up the struggle. He dropped the harness and let the beast go free. We stood our distance as he turned toward us. We bowed, our eyes on his young, flat, glistening face. Meticulously he returned the salutation. The children watched silently. Kolemenos and I stepped forward a few paces, smiling. The children broke out into a chatter at the impressive stature of Kolemenos, surprised by his long blond beard and hair. We stood in front of the man and bowed again. He talked, and I talked, but all the pair of us learned was that we could not understand each other. The small children grouped themselves behind the man and listened to the exchange. All the time they kept darting glances at the blond giant. The villager turned around and motioned us to follow. The children ran ahead through the village to spread the news of our coming.

At about the middle of the uneven row of buildings the guide stopped. This dwelling followed the same unassuming pattern as the others, but it was distinguished from them by being slightly larger and having a porch formed of two sturdy timbers at its door.

"This looks interesting," Mr. Smith whispered to me as the man disappeared through the door.

"I think he's gone inside to fetch the mayor," said Zaro.

There was not much time for further speculation for, almost as though he had been waiting behind the door, a new figure emerged through the porch. I judged him to be about 50; he wore the normal dress of the country topped with a loose sheepskin jacket. We exchanged the usual greetings before he spoke in the language of the country. I shook my head and replied in slow, precise Russian. His face lit up, and he beamed at me.

"Welcome," he said in Russian. "Now we shall be able to talk."

We were rather taken aback. He spoke Russian easily and without hesitation. I had to remind myself that there could be no danger in a chance encounter with a Russian so far south of the Soviet Union.

He waited a moment for me to reply, and when I did not, he went on eagerly, "I am a Circassian, and it is a long time since I met anyone who could speak Russian."

"A Circassian?" I repeated. "That is most interesting." I could not think of anything less banal to say. I knew little of the region in the Caucasus where he was from.

His questions tumbled over themselves. "Are you pilgrims?" he asked. "There are not many Russians who are Buddhists. You came through the Gobi on foot?"

"Yes, on foot."

"It must have been a terrible experience for you. Once I myself nearly died on that journey."

He was going to ask more questions but suddenly stopped, remembering his duty as a host. He apologized and invited us into his home. We trooped inside. A stone partition divided the one big room. I caught a glimpse of a woman I took to be his wife hustling three or four children out of the front half of the room, presumably to the kitchen at the rear.

Within half an hour of our arrival we were being regaled with tea and oaten cakes. Nobody spoke much until the food was gone. We were too busy filling our empty stomachs. Then our host produced a pipe and bowl of tobacco and handed the bowl around. Soon the place was a haze of blue smoke, which drifted out through the open door.

"So you are going to Lhasa," he said between puffs of his pipe. He said it politely, more as a conversational gambit. I do not think he necessarily believed it.

"Don't forget," he warned us, "that the nights are fiercely cold, especially on the heights. You must never be tempted to seek sleep without adequate shelter. You must never be too tired to build yourselves a fire. If you go to sleep unprotected on the mountains, you will be dead in the morning.

"You are going in the right direction for Lhasa. There is a track from here for the next stage of your journey that you will find easy to follow. Tonight you must all stay here, and in the morning I will show you how to go.

"If you come across any village toward nightfall, stay there until the morning. You will always have a roof over your heads and be given a meal. No one will ask you for payment."

"Our trouble," Mr. Smith broke in, "is that not one of us knows the language."

Our host smiled. "That is not such a handicap. If you bow to a

Tibetan and he bows back, no other introduction is needed. You are accepted as a friend."

In the early evening we were treated to a meal of roasted mutton, which one of the Circassian's elder sons had killed soon after our arrival. While we ate, the father cut off strips of meat for the younger children, and they ran out through the door with the meat in their hands. Salt was produced in a bowl to help our eating, and I fear I ate a lot more of it than a thoughtful guest should have. It was a delight to savor its sharp piquancy again.

After the evening meal half a dozen men neighbors joined our party. The hardworking Tibetan wife produced more tea. Each of the neighbors proudly produced a fine wooden bowl of the kind that the lone shepherd had shown us five days before. Here again it was quite evident that these were very precious possessions.

The men drank tea from their bowls, and when they had finished, the bowls were taken away and washed. Although they all looked alike to me, each man knew his own bowl, and they were affectionately stowed away in linen bags before the pipes were brought out and the tobacco handed around. Smoke was puffed out in great clouds. The Circassian was kept busy translating the busy talk between us and his neighbors. In this community he was obviously of great eminence, much respected for his gift of tongues and knowledge of matters of the big world outside the valley. He was human enough to enjoy his role, but he carried it off with dignity and modesty.

THE NEIGHBORS BADE US good night and went their way. They went like men who have had a rare and enjoyable evening. I could imagine that we had provided them with material for many a reminiscent talk to brighten their uneventful lives.

We slept in bunks—our first night under a roof since our escape. I felt able to relax. I had a glorious feeling of complete safety. I slept a deep, refreshing sleep and only half woke at the urging of the rising sun. They let us lie on until the day was a few hours old. The household had long been astir, and two of the younger children were peering in at us as we sat up in our beds. They ran out, and I heard them chattering to their father.

Our benefactor came in with some squares of thick homespun linen over his arm. "Perhaps you gentlemen would like to wash?" he inquired with a smile.

"This is real hotel service," Zaro joked. He bowed to the Circassian. "Just lead us to the bathroom."

The Circassian joined in the laugh. "It is at the end of the village—nice, clean, flowing water."

The six of us went down to the stream. The morning air was sharp, but we stripped to the waist, immersed our heads in the cold water, gasped, splashed, and rubbed vigorously. We were tempted to wash our jackets and fur vests but decided that we should have to wait too long for them to dry.

We were given more meat, more oaten cakes, more tea. Then it was time to go.

"When you come back this way," said the Circassian earnestly, "do not forget this house. It will always be a home to you."

The American answered, "Thank you. You have been very kind and generous to us."

I said, "Will you please thank your wife for all she has done for us. We are grateful."

He turned to me. "I won't do that." he said quietly. "She would not understand your thanks. But I will think of something to say to her that will please her."

He spoke to her, and her face broke into a great smile. She went away and returned with a wooden platter piled with flat oaten cakes, handed them to her husband, and said something to him.

"She wants you to take them with you," he told us. We portioned them out gratefully.

There was one other parting present—a fine fleece from the man, handed over with the wish that it might be used to make new footwear or repair our worn moccasins. We never did use it for that purpose, but later it made us half a dozen pairs of excellent mittens to shield our hands from the mountain cold.

He walked with us out of the village and pointed out our way. For the only time in our travels we received specific and detailed instructions of our route.

"Some of the tracks you will follow will not be easy to find," he warned. "Don't look for them at your feet; look ahead into the distance—they show up quite clearly then."

He described landmarks we were to seek. The first was to be a crown-shaped mountain about four days distant, and we were to take a path that would lead us over the saddle between the two north-facing points of the "crown." From the heights we were to set course for a peak shaped like a sugarloaf, which we would find to be deceptively far way. It might take us two weeks to reach it, he thought.

More than that he could not from here tell us accurately, but eventually we should reach a road that at some point forked east to the city of Lhasa and southwest to the villages of the Himalayan foothills. We left him there, a little knot of children at his heels. When we turned around, he made a most un-Mongolian gesture—he waved his arm in farewell to us.

Marchinkovas spoke for us all when he said, "These people make me feel very humble. They do a lot to wipe out bitter memories of other people who have lost their respect for humanity."

We disciplined ourselves not to touch our oatcakes until the third day—we had three each—and then we spread out the eating of them as an iron ration. Our track was clearly marked, and the way was not too hard. At the end of the fourth day we camped at the foot of the crown-shaped mountain our host had described and started our climb at first light the next day. The ascent was long but not difficult, and the crossing took us two days.

It had been fully a week since our last real meal when we came across a mixed herd of sheep and goats and found the two houses of the Tibetans who owned them. The day was warm and brightly sunny after the freezing temperatures of the heights. There were scattered bushes of a species of wild rose, attracting the eye with gay blooms of yellow and red and white.

The house into which we were taken by the Tibetan herdsman was in the same style as that of the Circassian but smaller and not so well equipped. But the courtesy and the hospitality were of the same impeccable standard. We were given milk to drink on arrival and later two massive meals of goat meat. By signs we were urged to spend the night and willingly accepted the offer. The whole family turned out to bow their farewells in the morning.

The explicit directions of the Circassian led us to the looming bulk of the sugarloaf mountain and over it. On the other side we found a stretch of country that presented comparatively easy traveling.

ON TO THE HIMALAYAS

THE WEEKS DRAGGED ON, October made way for November, the days were cool, and the nights were freezing. Over long stretches of country too barren to support even sheep and goats, we sometimes went for four and five days without food. There were bleak, mist-enveloped mornings when I felt leadenly dispirited, drained of energy, and reluctant to flog my weary body into movement. The meals we were so generously given from time to time in the villages we came to were massive, but we lacked fresh greenstuff. The result was that we continued to be ravaged by scurvy. But we counted ourselves fortunate that no member of the party suffered a major breakdown in health, and the march went on. We swam turbulent rivers when we had to. We negotiated formidable-looking peaks that turned out on closer acquaintance to offer surprisingly little difficulty; we struggled over innocent-looking hills that perversely offered precipitous resistance to our advance.

It was about this time that we discovered a use for the strong wire loops we had brought with us out of the desert. One day we found our way blocked where the track over a hill had been broken away by a fall of rock. To get around it we had to face the climber's hazard of an overhang surmounted by a sharp spur. We made a 10-foot length of plaited thongs, tied it firmly to Kolemenos' loop, and had him from his superior height try to lasso the tip of the rock spur. It took a dozen throws before the wire settled over. Then, gradually, Kolemenos put the strain of his still considerable weight on the rope. It held firm. Zaro, as one of the lighter members, volunteered to go up first. He climbed with great care, not trusting absolutely to the rope but making use of what slight handholds and footholds there were. With Zaro tending the anchored end, we all made it quite easily, Kolemenos climbing last.

There was a well-spaced-out succession of unremarkable villages and hamlets, alike in their simple architecture and in the full measure of hospitality they accorded us. They presented no feature by which I can remember them individually.

In the fullness of time we came to a fork in the rough trail that we confidently accepted as that mentioned to us by the Circassian—the eastward branch leading to Lhasa and the other southwest to India. A few hours later we saw far off in the distance a big caravan of possibly 50 men and animals creeping slowly away from us in the direction we imagined to be Lhasa. It was the only large traveling group we ever saw in the country.

We found this to be a country not only of rugged ranges but also of great lakes. Near the end of November our way led us to a vast sheet of water like an inland sea. We bathed in the fresh cold water and camped the night around a fire that did not throw out quite enough heat to keep out the damp night air from the lake.

Then followed a period of comparatively easy progress. The lakeshore was our guide for many miles. A couple of days later we were in broken country again. There was a cluster of a few houses where we stayed for only one meal, and upon our refusal to stay overnight, we were given food to carry with us. We were moving well and our morale was excellent.

Three or four days after leaving the great lake, we camped in a valley strewn with stark rocks. We settled down in a shallow cave to eat what still remained of our flat cakes made from coarse-milled flour. We sat together for warmth. There was nothing then to warn us that this was a setting for tragedy.

As ALWAYS WE SLEPT, with the exception of Kolemenos, fitfully. One and another would awake mumbling from half-remembered dreams to get up and tend the fire. It was Zaro who rose and went out as another day began palely to light the still desolation of the valley. I lay propped on one elbow as he came back.

"There's some mist about, and it's cold," he said to me, "Let's get moving." He stepped over the others, rousing them one by one. Paluchowicz lay next to me, and Marchinkovas was huddled between Smith and Kolemenos. I stood up and stretched, rubbed my stiff legs, flapped my arms about. There was a general stirring. Kolemenos pushed me with elephantine playfulness as I limbered up.

Zaro's voice cut in on us. "Come on, Zacharius. Get up!" He was bending over Marchinkovas, gently shaking his shoulder. I heard the note of panic as he shouted again, "Wake up, wake up!"

Zaro looked up at us, his face tight with alarm. "I think he must be ill. I can't wake him."

I dropped on my knees beside Marchinkovas. He lay in an attitude of complete relaxation, one arm thrown up above his head. I took the outstretched arm and shook it. He lay unmoving, eyes closed. I felt for the pulse, laid my ear to his chest, and lifted the eyelids. I went through all the tests again, fearful of believing their shocking message. The body was still warm.

I straightened up. I was surprised at how small and calm my voice was. "Marchinkovas is dead," I said. The statement sounded odd and flat to me, so I said it again. "Marchinkovas is dead."

Somebody burst out, "But he can't be. There was nothing wrong with him. Nothing! I talked to him only a few hours ago. He was well. He had no complaint. . . ."

"He is dead," I said.

Mr. Smith got down beside the body. He was there only a minute or two. Then he crossed the hands of Marchinkovas on his chest, stood up, and said, "Yes, gentlemen, Slav is right."

Paluchowicz took off his old fur cap and crossed himself.

Zacharius Marchinkovas, aged 28 or 29, who might have been a successful architect in his native Lithuania if the Russians had not come and taken him away, had given up the stuggle. We were all stunned; we could not understand it, and we did not know how death had come to him. Perhaps he was more exhausted than we knew and his willing heart could take the strain no more. I don't know. None of us knew. Marchinkovas, the silent one with the occasional shaft of cynical wit, Marchinkovas, who lived much with his own thoughts, the man with a load of bitterness whom Kristina had befriended and made to laugh—Marchinkovas was gone.

In the rocky ground we could find no place to dig a grave for him. His resting place was a deep cleft between rocks, and we filled up the space above him with pebbles and small stones. Kolemenos carried out his duty of making a small cross, which he wedged into the rubble. We said our farewells, each in his own fashion. Silently, I commended his soul to God. The five of us went heavy-footed on our way.

The country changed again, challenging our spirit and endurance with the uncompromising steepness of craggy hills. We learned to use our wire loops as climbing aids on difficult patches. We tried always to find a village to spend the night under cover, but all too often the end of the day overtook us with no human settlement in sight.

Once from the heights we saw, many miles off, the flashing reflection of the sun from the shining roofs of a distant, high-sited city, and it pleased us to believe that at least we had seen the holy city of Lhasa.

The days were cold now, the nights colder. Snow-charged clouds hung menacingly over the distant, gaunt foothills of the Himalayas. We stayed one night in a poor hamlet of four stone-built shacks and the next morning spent several hours making warm mittens from the Circassian's gift fleece.

There came one clear day when we saw the snowcapped, cloud-topped soaring hump of the Himalayas, deceptively near. We were, in fact, a long way off and were to find the intervening distance fraught with trial and hazard.

Winter had overtaken us, and the night temperatures fell well below zero. There were occasional heavy snowfalls, sleety rain, winds that whipped down off the hilltops with the chill of the heights in them. Bitter though the conditions were, they had not the severity of the Siberian winter. But they were grim enough for us, underfed and weakened as we were by nine long months of continuous foot travel.

In February we encountered our last village, just eight or nine houses snuggled in a hollow a couple of hundred feet above a narrow valley. Behind the village reared the forbidding rampart of tall hills over which we had struggled for two days. Across the valley, hazy in the light of a wintry afternoon sun, another range heaved itself up toward the clouds. The houses had, for Tibet, a rare distinction. They were the only two-story buildings we had seen in the whole country, or, indeed, since we had left Siberia. We had descended to a point west of and below the little settlement and had to climb up to it along a rough track. We were profoundly tired, miserable, and very hungry. Paluchowicz was limping on his right foot, the arch of which had been bruised when he had stepped on a sharp stone.

The Tibetans, when they understood by our signs whence we had come and where we intended to go, showed amazement at our hardihood, or our foolhardiness. We were gently ushered into one of the houses, made to sit down on low benches polished with years of use, fussed over, given steaming hot tea, and fed with mutton and the usual filling oaten cakes. Paluchowicz was given some grease to rub into his sore foot. From all the houses men and children came to look at us. There was much smiling and bowing and slow nodding of heads. Undoubtedly, our arrival was an extraordinary event and it would long be a topic for wondering talk.

When we left the little mountain hamlet, we were loaded down with food, which included a complete side of a roasted sheep. Up to now we had kept whatever food we had been given in one sack, which was carried in turns. We decided at this stage to share the meat and flat cakes equally among us because of the danger of losing the lot if the precious single sack disappeared with its owner on one of the increasingly difficult climbs we were now encountering.

That night, around a small fire, we sat talking for hours trying to assess our position and how much farther we had to go. When the conversation flagged, the extraordinary stillness and silence of the brooding mountains engulfed us. I had a feeling of great pity for myself and for us all. I wrestled with a desperate fear that now, with thousands of heartbreaking miles behind us, the odds might be too much for us. Often at night I had these bouts of despair and doubt. The others, too, I am sure, fought the same battles, but we never voiced our waverings. With the coming of morning the outlook was always more hopeful. Fear remained, a lurking thing, but movement and action and the exercise of the mind on the daily problems of

existence pushed it into the background. We were now, more strongly than ever, in the grip of the compulsive urge to keep moving. It
had become an obsession, a form of mania. Like automatons we set
out each morning, triggered off by a quiet "Let's go" from one or
another of us. No one ever pleaded for half an hour's respite. We just
went, walking the stiffness out of our joints and the chill of the dark
hours from our bodies.

We rationed the food out thinly, and it lasted, one meal a day, for
over two weeks. It was insufficient for the heavy climbing and the
perilous descents in which we were now involved, but at least we had
the comfort of knowing we could not starve while it lasted. Several
times we were caught out on the heights and had to resort to the
lessons of our Siberian experience in making a snow dugout and
holing up sleepless until the dawn of another day.

Of the art of mountaineering we learned much as the weeks crept
by. I had done some climbing in Poland before the war, but it bore
little resemblance to this grim Himalayan business. Then I had stout
spiked boots and all the civilized paraphernalia, plus the services of
an expert guide. And we had climbed in summer, for sport.

Here we would claw our way upward for hours, sacks lashed on
our backs, only to find our way blocked by a sheer, smooth, outward-
thrusting rock face. We would cling to our holds and rest our toes,
cramped and sore with their prehensile curling inside the soft moccasins for footholds. Then we would turn about and go down and down
until we found a place from which to attempt a different approach to
the summit.

Under these circumstances the going was very slow. Our total
mountaineering equipment consisted of one strong rawhide rope
limited in use by its short length, the ax—by far the greatest single
asset—the broad-bladed knife, and the loops and spikes we had made
back in the heat of the Gobi.

We climbed as individuals, but in set order. Zaro, the lightest man,
led the way upward, testing the holds with the ax, breaking through
the ice crust on the snow, blazing a trail for the rest of us. I came next,
sometimes changing over leadership with Zaro to give him a rest,
then Kolemenos, Mr. Smith, and Paluchowicz. We tried to make
things as easy as possible for the two older men, but they always
insisted on taking the lead on the descents.

We still carried our trusty sticks, and on gentler slopes we used
them for probing through the snow to detect hidden crevices. At
other times we carried them stuck through our belts at our backs.

Zaro would have made a skilled and intrepid climber in any company. A clumsy device we thought up and made for getting us past bulging overhangs of rock was a weighty piece of smooth, hard, black stone, waisted in the middle like a figure 8, to which we tied our rope. This we would throw up and over, again and again and again, until eventually, unseen somewhere above, it would jam itself and take hold. Kolemenos would haul gently at first at the rope until it took his full weight. Then Zaro heroically would start to climb while we watched from below with our hearts in our throats, knowing that the penalty for a slip was death. When on a few occasions I saw by what flimsy chance the stone had taken hold on the original throw, my stomach turned over.

Occasional bright days brought the additional trial of sun glare off the white snow. We were distressed, too, by a new experience of intense physical discomfort: The cold struck at our foreheads until they seemed to be held in frigid bands of ice. This trouble we overcame by making sheepskin masks with slits for the eyes, the upper parts held under the rims of our caps and the lower parts hanging loosely at nose level.

The masks were effective for the purpose for which they were designed. They also seemed to help with the trouble of snow glare, but we found that moisture gathered beneath them, trickled, and froze around the nose and mouth. There were times when I had to stop and thaw out the gathering ice by holding the lower part of my face in my mittened hands. We kept our hands covered as much as possible, but when climbing demanded the use of the fingers, our mittens hung from our wrists by thongs.

With the masks around our heads and tied at the back of the head, and the earflaps of our Russian-style caps in position, we found it difficult to hear one another. Irritation piled on irritation. We were deadly tired, morose, always hungry. My nerves were strung as tight as piano wires.

THE ABOMINABLE SNOWMEN

TOWARD THE END OF MARCH 1942 we were convinced that at last we were very near the sanctuary of India. Barring our way ahead reared the tallest and most forbidding peaks we had yet seen. We told one another that one final effort must bring us to the country where we were sure ultimate freedom, civilization, rest, and ease of mind awaited us. Individually we needed all the assurances and encouragement we could get. I was tortured with the fear that the exertion of one more great climb would finish me. I feared the onset of the insidious sleep on the heights from which there was no awakening. All my fears were sharpened by that shared conviction that after 4,000 miles we were near success. I could not now banish the specter of bitter failure.

We sat around a fire made from the last of our hoarded scraps of fuel and ate the last crumbs of our rations. We got out the rawhide rope, the ax, the knife, the wire loops, the slim spikes, and examined them and tested them. We gave ourselves a couple of hours before dark for repairing footwear. When we had finished, we were as well prepared for the last assault as we could be. The fire burned down and became ashes before midnight, and we spent a restless night until the first glimmer of dawn. Zaro wound the rope about him, took the ax from Kolemenos, and started off. I was relieved to be on the move.

We were blessed with fair weather. The wind was cold, but the sun shone strongly enough to attack the top layer of snow so that it melted sufficiently to re-form in the freezing night temperatures into a skin of crisp, treacherous ice. We climbed more surely, more cautiously, than ever before. Zaro double tested every foothold and each handhold as he led the way upward, chipping away with the ax, steam issuing in little clouds from his nose and mouth beneath the mask.

At the beginning of the third day we were over the top, only to find ourselves confronted with another peak. It was the stuff of which nightmares are made. Always it seemed there was another mountain to block our way. Two days were spent scrambling down the south face from our exposed high perch, and I found it more wearing on the nerves than the ascent. Down in the valley we made ourselves a snow shelter out of the whip of the wind and managed to get ourselves an uncomfortable few hours sleep in preparation for the next ordeal.

This next mountain was the worst in all our experience. From valley to valley its crossing took us six days and taxed our endurance to such a degree that for the first time we talked openly of the prospect that we might all perish. I am certain that one blizzard of a few hours duration would have wiped us out.

Two days up, the top still hidden by swirling white clouds, I dug my knife into a crevice to give myself extra purchase in hauling myself up from a narrow ledge. With my body pressed close against the rock, I loosened each hand and foot in turn so that I could flex my cramped fingers and wriggle my stiff toes. Then I reached for the knife handle above me and began to haul on it with my right arm. Suddenly the knife sprang like a live thing, leaped from my hand, and flew over my head with the steel singing. I took fresh hold and, digging in with fingers and toes, dragged myself to safety. The knife was gone. There was no sign of it. I felt as though I had lost a personal friend.

Near the summit on the third day the climbing became easier, but we began to doubt seriously whether we could make it. The cold was terrible, eddying mist dropped down about us and lifted, dropped and lifted again. The effects of high altitude were draining from us what slight reserves of stamina we still had. Every step was a fight against torturing lassitude, making one want to sit down and cry with weakness and frustration. I could not get enough air into my bursting lungs, and my heart thumped audibly, hammering against my chest. Willpower became a flaccid thing. Any one of us, alone, could have given up thankfully, lay down happily, closed his eyes, and drifted into death. But somebody was always crawling on, so we all kept moving. A final refinement of misery was nosebleed. I tried to stop mine by plugging the nostrils with bits of sacking, but the discomfort of breathing only through the mouth was too much and I removed the plug. The blood poured down into my beard, freezing and congealing there.

We knew we would have to spend the night in this rarefied atmosphere, and the knowledge did our spirits no good.

"We must keep going while there's light," Zaro said. "We must try to get over the top before dark."

So we went on and on, painfully. We made long traverses to right and left to avoid the impossible extra exertion of a frontal assault. I do not remember going over the summit. I remember only the point at which I noticed with vague surprise that Zaro, leading, was slightly below me. We climbed again a little, and then we knew with certainty that the descent had begun.

That night was the crisis of the whole enterprise. On a broad, flat ledge where the snow had drifted and piled, we axed through the hard crust of the surface and dug laboriously through a few feet of snow to make ourselves a barely adequate refuge against the rigors of the night. We had no fire. We were all so bone-weary we literally could have slept standing up, but we knew it would be courting death even to attempt to doze.

It was the longest night of my life. We huddled there standing, with our arms about one another. Sleep lay on our lids like a solid weight, and I found myself holding my eyes open with fingertips pressed against the eyeballs under my mask. Three times Kolemenos, the arch-sleeper, let his chin sag on his chest and began to snore, and each time we punched and shook him back to consciousness. Each man was his brother's keeper, watching for drooping eyelids and the nodding head. At intervals we would stamp slowly around in a close ring. Even during this grotesque dance I began to swim down into beautiful, velvet sleep, but the American dragged me back by gently cuffing me, pulling my beard, and shaking me hard. There came that awful predawn period when fatigue and cold together combined to set me shivering in an uncontrollable ague from head to foot.

"Let's get going," said someone. "Let's get down to someplace where we can breath again."

Paluchowicz spoke: "I could not last another night like that."

It was barely daylight, but we broke out and started on our way, Paluchowicz leading and Zaro and I in the rear. Even now I could not convince myself we would make it. Once, around noon, we were marooned for fully an hour when the track of our descent ended abruptly on a foot-wide shelf over a terrible drop. We inched our way back, climbed upward in our old tracks, and tried again in another direction. This time we succeeded, but not without great danger and frequent use of the rope and ax.

In about 10 hours of grueling toil we must have come down about 5,000 feet before nightfall. Breathing became easier, morale improved, hopes rose a little again. We dragged on through another depressing, wakeful night and continued the descent the next day until we were able to see the valley below quite clearly.

IN THE AFTERNOON we found a cave. It was untenanted, but there was a stack of brushwood near the entrance. If we had needed a sign that Providence was still on our side, this was it.

Hanging from a peg in the roof was something wrapped in soft lambskin. Someone lifted it down and unwrapped it. Inside was a leg of goat meat, partly smoked and nearly black. We were too hungry to be fastidious. We decided to get the fire going and cook it.

What a fire that was. We stoked it until the dancing flames lit up the far corners of the cave. Watching the meat cooking, we thawed out for the first time in weeks. Without the knife we had to do some crude carving with the ax, leaving half the joint to be eaten in the morning and tearing up the rest in strips. Toothless Paluchowicz took longer than the rest of us to eat his portion, but we all managed to take the edge off our hunger.

We slept the night through. When we awoke, the day was already a couple of hours old, and the fire had long since died out. Hurriedly we ate the rest of the goat meat cold and left.

It was profitless to speculate any further on how near we might be to our journey's end. Not even now were we out of the mountains. The lesser peak we set ourselves to surmount two days after the cave episode was, had we known it, the last outpost of the Himalayas, beyond which the foothills led down into northern India. I do not remember any of the details of this last climb, but I know we pulled ourselves up the northern face for two days without attaining the height that brought on altitude sickness. When we started down the other side, the sun was shining brightly and the air was startlingly clear. Southward the country fell away dramatically. I knew I was looking, at last, at India.

In all our wanderings through the Himalayan region we had encountered no other creatures than men, dogs, sheep, goats, and yaks. It was with quickening interest, therefore, that in the early stages of our descent of this last mountain Kolemenos drew our attention to two moving black specks against the snow about a quarter of a mile below us. We thought of animals and immediately of food, but as we set off down to investigate, we had no great hopes that they would await our arrival. The contours of the mountain temporarily hid them from view as we approached nearer, but when we halted on the edge of a bluff, we found they were still there, 12 feet or so below us and about 100 yards away.

Two points struck me immediately. They were enormous, and they walked on their hind legs. The picture is clear in my mind, fixed there indelibly by a solid two hours of observation. We just could not believe what we saw at first, so we stayed to watch. Somebody talked about dropping down to their level to get a close-up view.

Zaro said, "They look strong enough to eat us." We stayed where we were. We weren't too sure of unknown creatures that refused to run away at the approach of men.

I set myself to estimating their height on the basis of my military training for artillery observation. They could not have been much less than eight feet tall. One was a few inches taller than the other, in the relation of the average man to the average woman. They were shuffling quietly around on a flattish shelf that formed part of the obvious route for us to continue our descent. We thought that if we waited long enough, they would go away and leave the way clear for us. It was obvious they had seen us, and it was equally apparent that they had no fear of us.

The American said that eventually he was sure we would see them drop on all fours like bears. But they never did.

Their faces I could not see in detail, but the heads were squarish, and the ears must have lain close to the skull because there were no projections from the silhouettes against the snow. Their shoulders sloped sharply down to powerful chests. The arms were long, and the wrists reached the level of the knees. Seen in profile, the back of the head was a straight line from the crown into the shoulders—"like a damned Prussian," as Paluchowicz put it.

We decided unanimously that we were examining a type of creature of which we had no previous experience in the wild, in zoos, or in literature. It would have been easy, had we merely seen them waddle off at a distance, to dismiss them as either bears or big apes of the orangutan species. From close range they defied facile description. There was something of both the bear and the ape about their general shape, but they could not be mistaken for either. The color was a rusty kind of brown. They appeared to be covered by two distinct kinds of hair—the reddish hair that gave them their characteristic color forming a tight, close fur against the body. This mingled with long, loose, straight hairs, hanging downward, which had a slight grayish tinge as the light caught them.

Dangling our feet over the edge of the rock, we kept them closely under observation for about an hour. They were doing nothing but moving around slowly together, occasionally stopping to look around them like people admiring a view. Their heads turned toward us now and again, but their interest in us seemed to be of the slightest.

Then Zaro stood up. "We can't wait all day for them to make up their minds to move. I am going to shift them."

He went off into a pantomime of arm waving, Indian war dancing, bawling, and shrieking. The things did not even turn. Zaro scratched around and came up with half a dozen pieces of ice about a quarter-inch thick. One after another he pitched them down toward the pair, but they skimmed erratically and lost direction. One missile kicked up a little powder of snow about 20 yards from them, but if they saw it, they gave no sign. Zaro sat down again, panting.

We gave them another hour, but they seemed content to stay where they were. I got the uncomfortable feeling that they were challenging us to continue our descent across their ground.

"I think they are laughing at us," said Zaro.

Mr. Smith stood up. "It occurs to me they might take it into their heads to come up and investigate *us*. It is obvious they are not afraid of us. I think we had better go while we are safe."

We pushed off around the rock and directly away from them. I looked back and the pair were standing still, arms swinging slightly, as though listening intently. What were they? For years they remained a mystery to me, but since then I have read of scientific expeditions to discover the Abominable Snowman of the Himalayas and have studied descriptions of the creature given by native hillmen. I believe that the five of us that day may have met two of the animals. If so, I think recent estimates of their height as about five feet are wrong. The creatures we saw must have been at least seven feet.

I think that, in causing a deviation of route, they brought our final disaster upon us.

It was about midday when we set off to continue our descent. Everything went well, and we made good time. Our spirits were up in spite of our empty bellies. We found an almost ideal cavity among the rocks to spend the night and were greeted by another clear, fine April morning breaking through a thin, quickly dissipated mist.

Two hours later it happened. Zaro and I had the rope's end belayed around our two stout sticks at the crest of a slope. I was laughing at something Zaro had said about the two strange creatures of the day before. The slope was short and hardly steep enough to warrant the use of the rope, which lay loosely thrown out as a safety line in case Paluchowicz, crawling down backward on all fours, should slip into an unseen crevice. Behind him were Smith and Kolemenos, well spaced out. All three were astride the limp rope without holding it.

I saw Paluchowicz reach the end of the slope. I turned to Zaro and in that instant saw the rope jerk about the sticks and become slack again. Simultaneously there was a brief, sharp cry, such as a man will make when he is suddenly surprised. Zaro and I swung together. It was a second or two before the awful truth struck me. Smith was there. Kolemenos was there. But Paluchowicz had vanished.

Like fools, the two of us stood there calling out his name. No one answered. The other two, with their backs to Paluchowicz, did not know what had happened. They had stopped at our first shout and were looking up at us.

"Come back!" I called out to them. "Come back! Something has happened to Anton."

They clambered back. I hauled in the rope and tied the loose end

about my waist. "I am going down to see if I can find him," I said.

I reached the point where, from above, the slope appeared to fall gently away. Zaro took in the slack of the rope and I turned around as I had seen Paluchowicz do. The sight made me catch my breath. The mountain yawned open as though it had been split clean apart with a giant ax blow. I was looking across a 20-yard gap, the narrowest part of the chasm that dropped sickeningly below me. I could not see the bottom. I felt the cold sweat beading out on my forehead. Futilely I yelled, "Anton, Anton!"

I turned and went back to join the others, so shaken that I held tightly to the rope all the way.

They all talked at once. Had I seen him? Why was I shouting? Where was he?

I told them what it was like down there, that there was no sign of Paluchowicz.

"We will have to find him," said Kolemenos.

"We will never find him," I told them. "He is gone."

Nobody wanted to believe it. I did not want to believe it myself. With difficulty we broke a way to a new point from which we could look down into the abyss. Then they understood. We heaved a stone down and listened for it to strike. We heard nothing. We tried a bigger stone and dropped that down. We listened, straining our ears, but there was still no echo of the strike.

We hung around there a long time, not knowing what to do. The disaster was so sudden, so complete. One minute Paluchowicz was with us, then he was gone, plucked away from us. I never thought he would have to die. He seemed indestructible. Tough, toothless, devout old Sergeant Paluchowicz.

"All this way," said the American. "All this way, to die so stupidly at the last." I think he felt it more than any of us. As the two older men, they had been close together.

Kolemenos took his sack from his back and very deliberately tore it down the seams. We all stood silent. He put a stone in the corner and threw it out into space. The stone fell out and the sack floated away, a symbolic shroud for Paluchowicz. He took his stick and with the blunted ax chopped an end off and made a cross and stuck it there, on the edge of the abyss.

We climbed on down, trying to keep in sight the spot from which Paluchowicz had disappeared, vaguely hoping we might discover his body. But we never found the bottom of the great cleft, and we never found Paluchowicz.

There were some quite warm days after this. We could look back and see the majesty of the mountains we had crossed. We were in terrible need of food, and now that the supreme effort was over, we could barely keep ourselves moving. One day we saw a couple of long-haired wild goats, which bounded off like the wind. They need not have been afraid. We hardly had the strength to kill anything bigger than a beetle. The country was still hilly, but there were rivers and streams and birds in trees.

We had been about eight days without food when we saw far off to the east on a sunny morning a flock of sheep with men and dogs in charge. They were too far off to be of any help to us and were moving away from us, but our hopes rose at the sight of them. Soon we must certainly be picked up.

Exhausted walking skeletons of men that we were, we knew now for the first time peace of mind. It was now that we lost, at last, the fear of recapture.

They came from the west, a little knot of marching men, and as they came closer, I saw there were six native soldiers with an NCO in charge. I wanted to wave my hands and shout, but I just stood there with the other three watching them come. They were very smart, very clean, very fit, very military. My eyes began to fill, and the tears brimmed over.

Smith stepped forward and stuck out his hand.

"We are very glad to see you," he said.

INDIA

I T WAS HARD TO COMPREHEND that this was the end of it all. I leaned my weight on my stick and tried to blink my eyes clear. I felt weak and lightheaded like a man in a fever. My knees trembled with weakness, and it required real effort to prevent myself from slumping down to the ground. Zaro, too, was hunched over his stick, and one of Kolemenos' great arms was drooped lightly about his shoulders. The rough, scrubby country danced in the haze of a warm noon sun. The soldiers, halted but five yards from us, were a compact knot of men in tropical shorts and shirts swimming in and out of my vision.

I dropped my head forward on my chest and heard the voice of Mr. Smith. He talked in English, which I did not understand, but there was no mistaking the urgency in the tone. His speech went on for several minutes. I had to flex my knees to stop their trembling.

The American came over to us, his face smiling. "Gentlemen, we are safe." And because we remained unmoving and silent, he said again in Russian, very slowly, "Gentlemen, we are safe."

Zaro shouted, and the sound startled me. He threw down his stick and yelled, his arms above his head and the fingers of his hands extended. He threw his arms about the American, and Smith had to hold him tight to prevent his running over to the patrol and kissing each man individually.

"Come away, Eugene," he shouted. "Come away from them. I have told them we are filthy with lice."

Zaro started to laugh and jig inside the restraining arms. Then he had the American going around with him in a crazy, hopping polka, and they were both laughing and crying at the same time. I do not remember starting to dance; but there we were, the four of us, stamping, kicking up the dust, hugging one another, laughing hysterically, until all of us collapsed one by one on the ground.

Kolemenos lay sprawled out repeating softly to himself the American's words: "We are safe . . . we are safe. . . ."

The American said, "We shall be able to live again."

I thought a little about that. It sounded a wonderful thing to say. All that misery, all that sorrow, the hardship of a whole year afoot, so that we might live again.

We learned from Mr. Smith that this was a British patrol on exercise. They would take us, if we were not too weak to march, a few miles to the nearest rough road where they had a rendezvous with a military truck from their main unit. He had told them that we had come so far a few more miles would not kill us. With the main unit there would be real food.

The patrol produced groundsheets from their packs and rigged up a shelter to protect us from the sun. We lay beneath it resting for about an hour. My head throbbed, and I felt a little sick. We were handed a packet of cigarettes and some matches. Even more than food just then I wanted to smoke. To handle so ordinary a civilized commodity as a box of matches gave me a warm thrill. The smoke itself was bliss. From somewhere came a big can of peaches, ready opened, and we dug our fingers in, stuffed the peaches in our mouths, and crushed the exquisite juice and pulp from them. We drank water from army water bottles and were ready to go.

It seemed to me that none of us could have recalled details of that cross-country trek. The patrol adjusted its pace to our weary shamble, and it must have taken about five hours to cover 10 miles. Zaro marched with me, and we buoyed ourselves up with the pretense that we were getting along at a swinging military pace.

"The heroes' return," Zaro said with a grin. "All we need now is a band to lead us."

The altogether delightful quality of everything that happened to us at the end of the march was that it required no resolution or decision from us. There was a bumping ride by truck at that breakneck speed that is the hallmark of army driving anywhere in the world. We were as thrilled as schoolboys with the trip. We were in the process of being gathered up, looked after, told what to do, tended, and later even pampered. The British took over completely.

I never found out exactly where we were. At that time I did not care. Any guess I might make from perusal of maps could be hundreds of miles off. Smith must have found out, but if he ever told me, the information did not register. I hugged to myself only the great revelation that this was India.

The young British lieutenant who watched us ease ourselves down over the truck tailgate was amazingly clean, spruce, and well shaven. I observed him as the American told him our story. His expression as he stood listening in the shade of the trees at the small roadside encampment was incredulous. His eyes kept wandering from Smith to us. He was trying to understand. He asked several questions, nodding his head slowly at each answer. I thought how young he looked. Yet he was about my own age.

The American told us, "He believes me now. He says he will make arrangements for us to be deloused and cleaned up here because he can't take us back to their base in this condition. He says he will have to isolate us from his troops until this is done but that we will be well fed and cared for. He says we need not worry."

That night we were given a hot meal that ended with stewed fruit and steamed pudding. I had my first experience of hot, very strong canned-milk army tea, lavishly sweetened. We were given cigarettes and first-aid treatment for our torn and bruised feet. And that night we slept secure, wrapped in army blankets, in a tent.

The novelty, the bustle, and the excitement of it all kept me going. There was no time for me to stand still and discover how near to collapse I was. Breakfast the next day absorbed my attention—more tea, corned beef, Australian cheese, butter from cans, and, unbelievably, white bread, canned bacon rashers, and marmalade.

The delousing was a very thorough affair. We stripped off all our clothes—the sheepskin surcoats, fufaikas, fur vests, caps, masks, padded trousers, sacks, and skin gaiters—and piled them in the open. The blankets we had slept in were thrown on top of the heap. Head and body hair was shorn off, bundled, and thrust among the clothes. Over the lot they poured gasoline, and suddenly it erupted into a roaring bonfire, billowing black smoke into the sunny, clear air. Everything went, consumed in flame.

Kolemenos said, "I hope those bloody lice die hard. They have had a good time at my expense."

I turned to him and he to me. Then we were all exchanging looks, and the laughter was bubbling out of us. We had realized we were seeing one another for the first time—really seeing for the very first time the lines, the set of the mouth, the angle of the chin, and the character of the faces of men who for 12 months and 4,000 miles had shared the wretched struggle for survival.

It seemed the most comical thing that had ever happened to us. I had never thought of what might lie beneath the matted hair, and neither, I suppose, had they. It was like the midnight revelation from some fantastically prolonged masked ball.

"Why, Zaro," I said, "you are a good-looking man."

"You look all right yourself," Zaro answered.

And Mr. Smith was not as old as I had thought him to be, now that he was shorn of his graying hair. And Kolemenos, in spite of the ravages that marked us all, was as handsome as a big, fine-bodied man could be. The four of us sat there laughing and joking in our nakedness while the fire roared.

Scrubbed clean, our cuts, sores, and scratchings anointed, we were made ready for our reentry into a civilized community. We received white, crisp new underwear, bush shirts, stockings, canvas shoes, and, to top the lot, dashing Australian-type light felt hats. Smith dressed in a leisurely, careful way, but the other three of us hurried through the operation in an enthusiastic race to be ready first. We looked one another over and liked what we saw. We joked about the stark whiteness of our knees.

They drove us away westward. I had a curiously detached feeling about it, like an exhausted swimmer allowing himself to be carried along in a tide race. We came to a military garrison, but I had no chance to look at it. We were immediately lodged in sick quarters.

The army doctor had been waiting for us. He examined us gravely, eyes narrowed behind thin tortoiseshell spectacles. He nodded his head, thinning on top, in acknowledgment of Smith's answers to terse questions. He was aged about 40, quick-moving, sympathetic behind his professional facade of impersonal efficiency. We needed a lot of care, he told Smith. We needed to take things easy. Recovery might take quite a long time.

For a few days they kept us there. The doctor dosed us with medicines and pills. We lounged and lay about, chatting and dozing. We ate most magnificently and were plied with fresh fruit. Kolemenos amused the small staff with his huge appetite. We were allowed to smoke as often as we pleased.

Here it was that we temporarily parted from Smith. He said he was being taken away to see the American authorities. "You three will be taken to Calcutta. Whatever happens I shall see you there."

We shook him by the hand. There didn't seem to be anything any of us could say.

"Just keep your spirits up," Mr. Smith said. "The doctor tells me that we are all going to be very sick before we recover from our trip. But he says that with the proper attention we shall get in a big hospital, we should pull through all right."

I thought we were not as ill as that and said so. I did not appreciate then that I was feeling a quite spurious sense of well-being, that I was a little drunk with the excitement of these wonderful last few days, that the reckoning was yet to come.

He went away from us like a figure slipping out of a dream. Zaro said, "We shall be seeing him in Calcutta," as though India were a small place and Calcutta were just around the corner. It was the way we felt. Everything was taken care of. We were spent forces, content to be carried along. All the hammering urgency and the iron-hard resolution of the last bitter year had drained from us. We were more sick than we knew.

I HAVE SMALL RECOLLECTION of the journey to Calcutta, except that it was long and tiresome and I was shrouded in black depression. We smoked incessantly.

It was a symptom of our condition, I suppose, that when we were driven in a bus through the teeming Calcutta streets, we were all bright as crickets, pointing out the sights one to the other, almost hysterically good-humored. I could have persuaded myself then that recovery had already begun. I was being fooled again by the fever of a new excitement.

The bus drove between the tall main gates of a hospital, and an orderly took Zaro, Kolemenos, and me away for a preliminary medical examination. At first we were bogged down in language difficulties. After some time it was understood that between us we spoke Russian, Polish, French, and German—but no English. Eventually we were interviewed by an orderly who spoke French. They wanted medical histories from childhood, so Zaro told the orderly about our measles and our whooping cough and our operations. It all went down on a set of stiff cards. We were examined by doctors, weighed, measured, given a bath, decked out in pajamas, and tucked in bed in a long ward, Zaro and Kolemenos in adjoining positions on one side with me directly opposite.

I remember my awakening the next morning quite clearly, a spotless vision of a nursing sister standing beside my bed laying her strong brown arm against my white one and joking with me until I smiled up at her. Then came the breakfast of fresh eggs with wafer-thin white bread and butter.

I went back to sleep that morning and dropped into a bottomless pit that stole all mind and recollection from me for nearly a month. I learned all about it later, and it was Mr. Smith who gathered the story and told it to me.

They gave me sedatives and kept a day and night watch over me. Meanwhile, Zaro and then Kolemenos went under. At night I screamed and raved in madness. I ran from the Russians all over again; I crossed my deserts and my mountains. And each day I ate half my bread and slyly tucked the remainder under the mattress or in the pillowcase. Each day they gently took away my precious little hoard. They talked to me and brought in great white loaves from the kitchens and told me that I would never have to worry again. There would always be bread. The assurances meant nothing. I kept collecting bread for the next stage of my escape.

The climax came after about 10 days, I was told. After that I was quieter, very weak, exhausted, and on the danger list. Kolemenos and Zaro, too, were in a bad way.

But, said the hospital staff, neither of the others matched the performance I put on during the second night of my stay in the ward. I got out my saved-up bread from where I'd hidden it; rolled up my mattress, bedclothes, and pillows; and, to their astonishment because they had not believed I had that much strength left, set off staggering under the load for the door. By the time I had rolled up my bedding, the night sister had the doctor there.

He had said, "Leave him; let us see what he does."

At the door the doctor, the sister, and two male orderlies blocked my way. The doctor talked quietly as he would have done to a sleep-walker. I went on. The orderlies held me, and I dropped my burden and fought with savage fury. It took all four of them to get me back to bed. I have no memory of the incident.

Four weeks after my admission to the hospital, I awoke one morning feeling refreshed, as though I had slept the night through dreamlessly and restfully. I could not believe it when I was told that my night had been a month long.

Mr. Smith came to see us. He looked lean and spruce in a lightweight civilian suit. For a week, he said, he had been close to death. He had been to see me a couple of days earlier, but I had shown no signs of recognizing him. He had talked to the doctors about us, told them in detail what we had been through.

"You are going to be all right now, Slav," he said. He gestured over to where Zaro and Kolemenos were sitting up in bed and beaming across at us. "And so are they."

One of the soldier patients in the ward wanted to know our names. The American told him, but the soldier had difficulty in getting his tongue around the unfamiliar syllables. A compromise was reached. We became Zaro, Slav, and "Big Boy."

Our story got around. From other parts of the hospital, staff members came along to take a peep at us. The British soldiers in our ward showered us with kindnesses. One of them went around with his hat collecting cigarettes, money, chocolate, and little personal gifts and shared the offerings among us.

The American came to see us again later. He gave me a silver cigarette case and some money.

"What are you intending to do when you are better, Slav?"

I told him there was only one course open to me. As a Polish officer I must rejoin the Polish Army.

"Are you sure that is what you want to do?"

"It is the only thing I can do."

"We shall meet again after the war, of course," the American said. "Where shall it be, Slav?"

"In Warsaw," I replied. And I wrote down for him the address of my family's house in Warsaw.

"I should like that," he said. "We will meet in Warsaw."

A British officer and a Polish interpreter came to see me. It was a long talk, but the characteristics of security interrogation were not overstressed. A long catechism about Poland, its people, and its politics tested my bona fides. Then I was called upon to repeat once again the stories about the Russians, the prison camp, and the journey.

The interpreter returned alone the next day, bringing me a gift of half a dozen white handkerchiefs and an Indian ivory cigarette holder. He told me that transport was being arranged through the British for me to join up with Polish forces fighting with the Allies in the Middle East.

The night before I left, Kolemenos, Zaro, and I had a farewell celebration in the hospital canteen.

Mr. Smith came to the hospital to see me off on that last day, bringing me a small fiber case in which to pack my few belongings. I had resolved to make the parting from Zaro and Kolemenos as painless as possible. We said good-bye in the ward, and the soldiers called out "Good luck" and "All the best, Slav," and things like that.

I walked toward the door, Smith ahead of me. Zaro and Kolemenos followed behind. I wanted them to stay where they were, but they kept on walking. I turned at the door, and big Kolemenos ran forward and hugged me, and then came Zaro. And the tears came so that I had to drag myself away. The American walked with me, blowing his nose in his handkerchief.

He rode on the bus with me into Calcutta, where they dropped him off. "Look after yourself, Slav," he said. "And God bless you."

The bus pulled away toward the transit camp where I was to await a troopship that would take me to the Middle East. I looked back at him once, and he waved.

I felt suddenly bereft of friends, bereft of everything, as desolate and lonely as a man could be.

Slavomir Rawicz served with the Polish armed forces in the Middle East during World War II, then was sent to England. He was in training with the Royal Air Force when the war ended. Rawicz remained in England, settling in the Midlands. He married an English girl, and they have two sons, three daughters, and four grandchildren. Rawicz's escape story came to the notice of a newspaperman, Ronald Downing, and together they produced this chronicle. No contacts have ever been established with the other three survivors of The Long Walk.

*The only chance of escape for the shell-torn
frigate and her crew was to make a suicidal dash
down the Yangtze River to the sea.*

The Epic
of the *Amethyst*

By George Kent

THE THIRD OF AUGUST is no holiday in Hong Kong, but on that
day in 1949 the city was a riot of flags; firecrackers exploded,
bands played, and on the decks of British and American men-of-war
crews in dress uniform stood at attention. The object of all this celebration was a low-slung, battered frigate with shell holes in her hull
and haggard men at the rails. The 1,430-ton *Amethyst* had come into
port after a heroic exploit—the latest in the long exploit-starred history of the British Navy.

The story begins on April 20, 1949. The *Amethyst,* one of several
warships assigned to furnish sanctuary and protection to British citizens caught in the war between Nationalist and Communist Chinese,
was making her way up the Yangtze River. Large Union Jacks were
painted on her sides, proof of her neutrality.

As she approached Rose Island, Communist guns, hidden behind
tall reeds, let go without warning at point-blank range. Shells blasted
the *Amethyst*'s bridge and wheelhouse and entered her hull above and
below the waterline, killing 17 men, wounding 30 others. The skipper
fell by the binnacle. The doctor dropped in the shattered sick bay.
The second and third officers were both badly wounded. The helmsman slumped lifeless over the wheel, slewing the vessel aground in
the Yangtze mud.

The destroyer *Consort* dashed up, guns blazing. She in turn was
fired on, losing 10 dead, 21 wounded. The following day the cruiser
London and the frigate *Black Swan* attempted a rescue and together
lost 13 dead, 22 wounded. All three vessels finally retired under the
relentless fire.

Below decks on the *Amethyst* a petty officer with a piece of shrapnel in his neck emptied fuel and ballast tanks to lighten the ship and get her off the mudbank. Another with a crippled shoulder unraveled the tangled electrical system. And communication with the outside world was maintained by Jack French, the frigate's only radio operator, who stayed on duty for five days and nights, taking only occasional catnaps.

Finally the *Amethyst* shuddered free of the mud and moved into a creek, which seemed safe. A volley from the Red batteries reminded her that such was not the case. Here most of her wounded were taken ashore and put aboard a Sunderland aircraft that landed with a doctor. Both plane and wounded were fired on.

The next day the ship moved to a position off Ta Sha Island, where she remained, under the muzzles of Communist guns, until the dramatic night of July 30.

On April 22 Lt. Comdr. John Simon Kerans, Royal Navy, entered the scene. A tall, thin man of 33 with a brilliant war record, he was ordered from his post as assistant naval attaché in Nanking to take command of the *Amethyst*. A comfortless situation confronted him. Seventeen dead men, roughly sewed in canvas, awaited disposition. Below were the wounded who had been unwilling or unable to move. The deck was a litter of blood and torn metal. Hundreds of rats had come aboard through shell holes.

Kerans found that most of the crew were youngsters fresh out of England with no battle experience.

"I gave them plenty to do," he later reported, "because I wanted them tired, too tired to think." He also ordered the best meals the ship's stores could provide.

He had the remaining wounded ferried over to the Nationalist side of the river, whence they were helped overland to Shanghai. Then he read the prayer over the dead and consigned them to the yellow waters of the Yangtze.

He used up his slim store of disinfectant to remove the gore from the decks. He had the shell holes stuffed with tightly rolled hammocks and kit bags and destroyed the damaged radar lest it fall into the hands of the enemy.

The Communist artillery was now emplaced on a commanding high knoll nearby, and trigger-happy sentries patrolled the shoreline. Ships were halted for inspection of papers by bursts of machine-gun fire aimed across their bows, with bullets frequently spattering the *Amethyst's* deck.

Early in May, Kerans had the first of 11 talks with the Communists concerning a safe-conduct. Col. Kang Mao-chao, the officer in charge, made it clear that the slightest move downriver would mean the annihilation of the *Amethyst*. Kerans soon realized that nothing would come of these talks. Methodically he began to plan a getaway.

To escape, he needed an adequate supply of oil; and to conserve it, he began shutting off power for 24-hour, then 59-hour, periods.

"Living in a ship with nothing running," said Kerans later, "was a

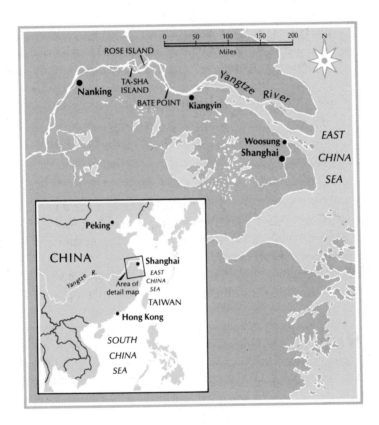

most unpleasant experience. It was like living in a grave."

Fans, too, had to be turned off, and the temperature below decks rose to 110° F, but sleeping on deck was frequently impossible because of the rains. Rats were everywhere. They ate the books—valuable morale-builders—raided the stores, and ran over the sleeping men. Mosquitoes were also bad, but a daily dose of paludrine kept all hands free of malaria. Prickly heat was the universal curse.

By the beginning of July, Kerans suspected that the enemy was going to try to starve him into submission. He cut rations in half. Meanwhile, he pored for hours each day over the shrapnel-shredded, blood-stiffened chart, learning it by heart. The piece showing the river immediately ahead was gone.

The Yangtze is a twisting stream, with mudbanks, hairpin curves, and a narrow, constantly shifting channel. It is one of the rivers on which the Admiralty permits its vessels to use pilots. In daylight pilots will not travel faster than five knots; at night they are reluctant to travel at all.

Part of Kerans's scheme was to mislead the Reds. In letters to his commanding officer, Adm. Sir Patrick Brind at Hong Kong—letters he knew the Communists read—he complained bitterly of his lack of fuel and kept asking for charts and a pilot. He also made it a point to give the vessel's top speed as 16 knots. Actually, helped by the current, the ship could do $22\frac{1}{2}$ knots. Moreover, Kerans knew he had fuel enough to cover the 140 miles from his anchorage to the sea with a little left over.

On July 24 Kerans had his 11th futile talk with Colonel Kang. The next day he made up his mind. He could not consult in code with Admiral Brind, because the code books had been burned in the shelling. So he communicated in double-talk, demanding instructions on how to behave should a typhoon arise. It was a question no British officer would ask; he is supposed to know.

Sir Patrick got the point. His reply was: "The golden rule of making an offing and taking plenty of sea room still applies." It was clearly permission to go.

On Friday, July 29, Kerans ordered the crew to pack the anchor chain with burlap and to place canvas, covered heavily with oil, beneath it, so that the chain could be slipped into the water noiselessly. By thus leaving chain and anchor behind, they could get under way in a matter of minutes. This was the only hint to the men that something was brewing.

At 8 o'clock the next night he explained to the crew that the breakout was to start in two hours. "If we don't get away now, we may never have another chance," he said.

On instructions from Kerans, the crew placed crates and boxes on the superstructure; over them and over the guns went yards of black canvas, altering the ship's silhouette to resemble an LST's, many of which, converted to commercial use, plied the river regularly. Buckets of black paint were splashed over the gleaming bridge and forward sections.

The *Amethyst* was beginning to get up steam, but the smoke would mean nothing to the Communists. Smoke had been pouring through the funnel all day from the stoves in the galley.

At 10 o'clock a brightly lighted steamer flying the Communist flag came chugging slowly downriver. Here was a break. The moment it was past, Kerans ordered his men to let go the anchor. The chain slipped silently into the water.

In a matter of seconds the ship was under way, and Kerans murmured the old Admiralty prayer: "Lord, Thou knowest how busy I shall be this day. If I forget Thee, do not Thou forget me."

The *Amethyst* trailed the steamer—the *Kiang Ling Liberation*—by about 200 yards. Kerans hoped that the glare from its lighted portholes would blind the Communists ashore and that in the flurry of inspection his ship might slip through unnoticed. Just as the *Kiang* came abreast of the shore batteries, flares illuminated the water brilliantly. A moment later the *Amethyst* inched past. Flares challenged her. Kerans's only reply was to increase speed.

With that, all hell broke loose. Machine-gun bullets ricocheted from the *Amethyst's* bridge, even from Kerans's tin hat, which fell off. As he stooped to pick it up, another burst cut the aerial wires close behind him. Then came the roar of the heavy stuff. Meanwhile, through the voice pipe, he could hear the man at the echo sounder chanting his minute-by-minute report of the river's depth: "Seven fathom, seven fathom, six fathom . . ."

A Communist gunboat anchored below the batteries began firing hysterically, mostly at the Red batteries ashore. The *Amethyst*, capable of using only one four-incher because of her shortage of men, let fly a single shell, then blazed away with her antiaircraft batteries. From her funnel poured a black smoke screen.

A 75-millimeter shell slammed into the *Amethyst* forward of the bridge, above the waterline. "Full speed ahead," the bridge telegraph clanged. But the vessel had acquired a sharp list to starboard and did not pick up speed. "Under heavy fire and am hit," said its radio. The helmsman was having trouble with the wheel; where ordinarily a touch did the trick, now he had to spin it hard over. Kerans swore. Here was disaster before he had gotten well under way. But he was able to note with satisfaction that his shots had started a great blaze ashore. In the water were two other fires: the *Kiang Ling Liberation* and the gunboat, both burning briskly after having been hit by the Red batteries.

The *Amethyst* continued to move like a man with a pain in his side,

and Kerans scanned the shore, looking for a place where he could beach her. He had planned for this emergency also. Twenty-four detonators were cached in the stern. Should it become necessary, he would blow her up.

Suddenly—Kerans still doesn't know how it happened—the ship returned to an even keel. At 10:15 she passed Rose Island, where the original shelling had taken place. At 12:24 Sunday morning, July 31, she went by Bate Point at a fast clip. At both places there were guns, but the speed of the *Amethyst* caught them unprepared. In the engine room, with sea doors shut and fans off, the stifling heat passed 150° F.

One-third of the run having been completed, the chart was now usable. To appreciate Kerans's feat, it must be remembered that the always unstable Yangtze was in flood; markers and landmarks had been covered or washed away. The flood helped the ship over the shallow places, but there was always danger that she would miss the course and run aground. It was a tar-black night, and the *Amethyst* was doing better than 22 knots.

Shortly after midnight a junk loomed suddenly under the bow. Before the *Amethyst* could swerve, she had sliced the craft in two. But there was no time to pause.

At 12:57 the *Amethyst* reached the forts at Kiangyin. Her speed again caught the Reds napping, and she was abeam before the guns began to fire. Once more the funnel vomited black smoke and the shells buried themselves in vapor. "Under heavy fire at Kiangyin," said the radio.

Twelve minutes later the radio spoke again: "Still under heavy fire, nearing boom."

The boom, a river block, consisted of a row of sunken merchant vessels, with only a narrow passage marked in normal times by two lights. On this night there were no lights. Kerans inched up to the boom, finally spotted the narrow lane, and drove through.

Machine guns on the boom let go a rattle of bullets, but Kerans rushed on. There was no heavy artillery to overtake him.

Now only 40 miles remained, and there was only one major obstacle, perhaps the most serious one yet encountered—Shanghai's heavily gunned forts at Woosung, which guarded the confluence of the Whangpoo and the Yangtze. But Kerans knew that the cruiser *Concord* was awaiting him at the mouth of the river, prepared to open fire on Woosung should it become necessary.

At 5:03 A.M., with the sky graying, Kerans saw Woosung's powerful searchlights sweeping the river. Somehow they missed the *Ame-*

thyst. Perhaps the tricky light of early dawn explains their failure to focus on the ship.

A half hour later Kerans was in the open sea alongside the *Concord* and radioing: "Have rejoined the fleet. No damages or casualties. God save the King."

Then in return Admiral Brind promptly sent a radio message: "Welcome back to the fleet. Your passage today will be epic in the history of the Navy."

King George sent this message: "The courage, skill, and determination shown by all have my highest commendation. Splice the main brace." In the British Navy the main brace is spliced by a formal gathering of all hands around a barrel of rum to drink His Majesty's health. This was done immediately.

Another message announced the award to Kerans of the Distinguished Service Order, one of Britain's highest decorations. From his old schoolteacher Kerans received this telegram: "Well played. Your mathematics must have improved."

One award that caught the public's fancy was the Dickin Medal given to the ship's cat, Simon, for valiant service in keeping down the rat population. The crew's version of the citation read: "Though recovering from wounds, Simon did single-handedly and unarmed stalk and destroy Mao Tse-tung, a rat guilty of raiding food supplies."

At Hong Kong, Malta, Gibraltar—wherever the ship paused on her trip home—there were festive celebrations. Finally, on November 1, the *Amethyst* docked at Plymouth. Shortly thereafter the ship's company paraded for the people of London and was received personally by King George.

What Kerans and his crew had done was summed up admirably in *The Illustrated London News:* "The affair of the *Amethyst,* measured by worldly reckoning, is a very small affair—a remote river incident. But measured in terms of the human spirit it matters a great deal, more perhaps than the brave men who manned her at the time realized."

*Slipping elusively from the role of theologian to that
of secret agent, the Irish-born monsignor engineered
the escape of thousands of Allied servicemen in wartime Italy
from under the very noses of the Nazis.*

Vatican Pimpernel

*By Lt. Col. Sam Derry
with David MacDonald*

IN ROME, LONG AFTER the end of the Second World War, my wife
and I crossed the vast expanse of St. Peter's Square to the top
steps of the basilica.

"Right here," I said, "he used to wait for us."

So often, during the German occupation of 1943-44, I saw Msgr.
Hugh O'Flaherty standing there large as life. Over six feet in height,
with a rugged Irish face bent over a breviary, glasses glinting on his
big nose, he'd look over the square for a familiar figure—one of our
agents—while murmuring Latin in a Kerry brogue. To sightseeing
Wehrmacht soldiers, he was just another priest at prayer. Nothing
about him suggested that this was the "Vatican Pimpernel," up to his
clerical collar in wartime intrigue.

As a theologian for the Holy See, Monsignor O'Flaherty officially
dealt in Catholic dogma. *Ex officio,* he led the underground British
Organization in Rome, which saved almost 4,000 runaway Allied
prisoners of war from the Germans. The key to its amazing success
lay in Monsignor O'Flaherty's makeup. Besides awesome courage,
sharp wits, and the impish ways of an oversized leprechaun, he had
more compassion than anyone I've ever known.

We met when I was 29. A British Army major, captured by Rommel's Afrika Korps and held in Italy for 15 months, I jumped off a
POW train in October 1943 and landed with a partisan farmer less
than 15 miles from Rome. Since several Allied envoys were still
inside the neutral Vatican, a village priest agreed to take a note there
for "anybody English." Back came money—and a summons to Rome
from someone he called "my superior."

Dressed as a laborer and smuggled into Rome under a cartload of cabbages, I was eventually led to the Vatican by a courier named Aldo. A burly man in black gazed down from the basilica's left-hand steps. Muttering "Follow me," he bustled through the Bernini colonnades, up an alley, into a building marked Collegio Teutonico—the German College—outside the Vatican but still on neutral ground. Escorting me into a small bedroom-study, he said with a twinkle: "Make yourself at home! Me name's O'Flaherty and I live here."

But why was I here? The 45-year-old priest grinned mischievously. "Ye'll soon find out," he said. "Meanwhile, how would you like a nice warm bath?" I must say I wasted no time in accepting.

At dusk, both clad in cassocks, we bluffed our way past the Swiss Guards and jackbooted Germans to the Vatican's nearby Ospizio di Santa Maria, the home of the refugee British legation. Our minister there, Sir D'Arcy Osborne, told me about Hugh O'Flaherty.

As a young seminarian from Ireland, he'd been posted to Rome in 1922, the year Mussolini's dictatorship began. A Vatican monsignor by 1934, he was deeply devoted to golf and assorted good works. In the early war years he used to tour Italian POW camps, seeking out new prisoners still "missing in action" and reassuring their families whenever possible via Vatican Radio as to their physical condition.

After the Allied forces' landings and Italy's capitulation in September 1943, thousands of POW's—mostly Britons—were let loose, and many reached Rome, just as German troops seized it. Recalling O'Flaherty, the ex-prisoners turned to him for help and advice. He hid hundreds with Roman friends or with rural partisans, meanwhile scrounging money to support them. But now, Sir D'Arcy related, an officer was needed to lend a hand.

"*That* is why we sent for you," Sir D'Arcy told me. "Are you prepared to take the command?"

Fascinated by O'Flaherty, I readily agreed. He decided we'd share his room at the Collegio. To the monsignor's mind—now devious, now direct, always unpredictable—a British conspirator should be safest in a place filled with German clergy. So he let me sleep on his sofa, obtained a civilian suit for me, and produced identity cards converting me from Sam to "Patrick" Derry and from an Anglican to a Dublin-born Catholic employed by Holy Mother Church.

Tramping around Rome with him, I marveled at how his organization had so far concealed more than 1,000 ex-POW's—in convents, in crowded apartments, on outlying farms. His favorite such billet was an apartment directly behind SS headquarters.

"Faith," he chortled, "they'll not look under their noses."

Given the tacit blessing of Pope Pius XII, the monsignor secured aid from an odd collection of monks, nuns, Communists, nobles, a Swiss count, two Free French secret agents, and a cockney butler, John May, at our U.K. legation. As John put it: "Our Irish friend knows everyone, and they all adore him."

A notable exception was SS Col. Herbert Kappler. Chief of SS forces in Rome, he'd learned of an escape line run by a mysterious priest and, unknown to us, had Gestapo men scheming to catch him.

The colonel almost succeeded. Once when the monsignor called on Prince Filippo Doria Pamphili, a prominent anti-Fascist who backed the network with money, Kappler raided the Palazzo Doria. As rifle butts banged on the front door, O'Flaherty fled to the cellar, where sacks of coal were just then tumbling through a trapdoor. He quickly stripped to trousers and T-shirt, stuffing his cassock and clerical hat into one bag. Smeared with soot, he crept out behind the delivery truck, shuffled past a score of SS officers, and vanished before they could realize that the "coalman" carried a full sack *away*.

As chief of staff to this artful dodger, I ordered all our escapees to stay under cover lest they compromise the Italian *padroni* ("patrons") who courted death by harboring them. Yet the gravest security problems were posed by the monsignor himself. He delighted in deliberately flirting with danger.

After we'd long kept a British general cooped up in a secret room, O'Flaherty took that star boarder, garbed in Donegal tweeds, to a papal reception and introduced him as an Irish doctor—to the German ambassador! I was furious.

"Ah, now," he said, winking, " 'twas a nice break for him."

As POW's turned up, the monsignor usually guided them to their secret billets or "cells"—often in clerical robes—because he couldn't bear asking anyone else to run the risk. But early in 1944, with the Allied armies pinned down below Monte Cassino about 100 miles away, O'Flaherty himself was compelled to take cover.

First, an escapee in one of our rural billets was recaptured. Threatened with torture, he turned in 12 other POW's and their *padroni*. O'Flaherty's reaction was typical, a gentle "God forgive him."

I couldn't. A further betrayal led the SS to 16 more POW's in two Rome hideouts where the monsignor and I were known. Some were shot. The German ambassador then informed O'Flaherty that he'd been denounced to Colonel Kappler as the escape line's leader. "If you ever step outside the Vatican, you will be arrested." he warned.

Under pressure from German authorities, his church superiors also ordered him to stay put and to get his "guest" out of his rooms. So I covertly moved into the British legation, carrying on our clandestine business as before. Undeterred, the monsignor met our agents openly on St. Peter's steps.

One day a former helper named Grossi brought word of an injured POW in a village 30 miles from Rome. Without telling me, the monsignor promised to go there the next Sunday. A last-minute message from another agent saved his life: Grossi has sold out to Colonel Kappler, who'd baited a diabolical trap for O'Flaherty by playing on his known Samaritan sympathies.

The Allies finally broke through at Monte Cassino on May 18 and swept toward Rome. When the city awoke on June 4, the gray hordes were gone, retreating north as Allied troops rolled into the Eternal City to a tumultuous welcome.

While some 250,000 people massed in St. Peter's Square for the pope's benediction, I went looking for Monsignor O'Flaherty. He was in the German College, giving thanks to God.

In nine months Monsignor O'Flaherty's makeshift organization had taken care of 3,925 escapees, including 1,695 Britons. (In all, 122 men were recaptured and half a dozen shot.)

Yet O'Flaherty *couldn't* stop there. Overnight, his boundless compassion embraced our foes as well. When U.S. Gen. Mark Clark came to pay his respects, O'Flaherty quizzed him sharply to make sure that German prisoners were well treated. In a plane lent by the Allied commander in chief, Gen. Sir Harold Alexander, the monsignor flew to see thousands of Italian POW's in South Africa and then visited Jewish refugees in Jerusalem.

He was awarded a CBE (Commander of the British Empire), the U.S. Medal of Freedom with silver palm, and other decorations from Canada and Australia. But when Italy's first postwar government awarded him a lifetime pension, he never accepted one lira of it. He wanted nothing for himself.

While I stayed in Rome, arranging repayments to all those who supported O'Flaherty's network or otherwise aided the Allies, many Fascist collaborators came to trial. Among them were two double agents, a doctor who'd rented one of our hideouts and the courier Aldo who'd first taken me to the Vatican. Incapable of spite, the monsignor testified on their behalf.

"They did wrong," he admitted. "But there's good in every man."

He sincerely believed it. After SS Colonel Kappler was jailed for life as a war criminal, O'Flaherty often went to visit him. "To me," Kappler once wrote, "he became a fatherly friend." And when Colonel Kappler later entered the Catholic Church, he was baptized by Monsignor O'Flaherty.

Although seldom together following the war, the monsignor and I kept in close touch. Made Notary of the Holy Office, he remained at the Vatican until 1960, when he suffered a stroke and retired to his sister's home in County Kerry.

Three years later I was maneuvered into a London television studio, the unwitting subject of *This Is Your Life*. Before an audience of former POW's, colleagues from the British Organization in Rome came forth to share old memories. A white-haired Monsignor O'Flaherty appeared on film, sending greetings from Ireland in a halting, quavery voice, because, it was explained, his doctors had warned him not to travel. But suddenly the monsignor appeared and walked slowly out on stage. Blinking in the limelight, he grinned and threw his arms around me. We both wept for joy.

That was our last time together. Within months, he died peacefully at 65, after a good life that another priest summed up in these few, true words: "Hugh O'Flaherty was above all a generous honest-to-God Irishman. His big heart was open to any and every distress."

*One of the most exciting adventures in Winston
Churchill's colorful life occurred when, as
a young man, he made a dramatic escape from a
Boer prisoner-of-war camp.*

My Escape

By Winston Churchill

IN 1899 A WAR BROKE out in South Africa between Great Britain and
the Boer republics of the Transvaal and the Orange Free State. As a
young journalist in England, Winston Churchill was appointed War
Correspondent for the *Morning Post*, a London newspaper, and dispatched to South Africa to cover the hostilities. Churchill later wrote
of his experiences in a book, *A Roving Commission*. An excerpt from
that publication telling of his capture by the Boers and his daring
escape is presented here. The account begins with the author's arrival
at the Natal port of Durban in the fall of 1899.

IT HAD BEEN MY INTENTION to go from Durban to Ladysmith, but I
could get no further than Estcourt, a tiny mining township of a
few hundred inhabitants, beyond which trains no longer ran. The
Boers had occupied the stations beyond. There was nothing to do but
to wait at Estcourt with such troops as could be collected to protect
the southern part of Natal from the impending Boer invasion. A
single battalion of Dublin Fusiliers, two or three guns and a few
squadrons of Natal Carabineers, two companies of Durban Light
Infantry and an armored train were the only forces which remained
for the defense of the territory. All the rest of the Natal Army was
blockaded in Ladysmith.

The days passed slowly and anxiously. The position of our small
force was most precarious. At any moment some 12,000 mounted
Boers might sweep forward to attack us or cut off our retreat. Every
morning cavalry reconnaissances were sent out to give us timely notice should the enemy advance; and in an unlucky moment it occurred to the General in command to send his armored train along
the 16 miles of intact railway line to supplement the cavalry.

Nothing looks more formidable than an armored train; but nothing is in fact more vulnerable. It was only necessary to blow up a bridge or culvert to leave the monster stranded far from home and help, at the mercy of the enemy.

This did not seem to have occurred to our commander, who decided to put two companies of infantry into the train and send it out to reconnoiter. Captain Haldane was selected to command this operation, and although he did not conceal from me his misgivings, he invited me to come along for the adventure and I accepted.

The armored train proceeded about 14 miles towards the enemy without a sign of opposition. We stopped for a few moments at a station to telegraph our arrival to the General. No sooner was this done than we saw, on a hill between us and home, a number of small figures hurrying forward. Certainly they were Boers. There was not an instant to lose. We started immediately on our return journey.

As we approached the hill, I saw a cluster of Boers on the crest. Suddenly three wheeled things appeared among them, and instantly bright flashes of light opened and shut several times. A huge white ball of smoke sprang into being and tore out into a cone, only a few feet, it seemed, above my head. It was shrapnel—the first I had ever seen in war, and very nearly the last! The steel sides of the truck tanged with a patter of bullets. There was a crash from the front of the train, and a series of sharp explosions.

The railway curved round the base of the hill on a steep down gradient, and our pace increased enormously. The Boer artillery, three guns, had only time for one more discharge before we were round the corner out of their sight. It crossed my mind that there must be a trap farther on. I was about to mention this to Haldane when there was a tremendous shock; he and I and all the soldiers in the truck were pitched head over heels to the floor. The front of the train had been thrown off the rails.

In our truck no one was seriously hurt. From the enemy's hill, 1200 yards behind, now came heavy rifle fire. Bullets whistled overhead and rang and splattered on the steel plates like hail. Haldane and I debated what to do. It was agreed that he and his Dublin Fusiliers should hold the rear, and that I should go forward to find out the extent of the damage.

I nipped out of the truck and ran to the head of the train. One truck had turned completely over, killing and terribly injuring some of the men; two others were derailed, blocking our homeward path. The rails, however, appeared to be intact. The enemy's rifle fire was continuous, and soon there mingled with the rifles the bang of the field guns and the near explosion of shells.

The train had been made up with the engine in the middle, three trucks being pushed before it and three drawn behind. The engine and three rear trucks were undamaged, but the three forward trucks now lay across the rails, blocking the rest of the train. I conceived the idea of detaching the engine and using it as a ram to push the wreckage off the track and clear the way. With a small detachment of men, I now set about this task.

I was very lucky in the hour that followed not to be hit, as I was working almost continuously in the open, directing the engine-driver. The work absorbed me completely, though I remember thinking that it was like working in front of an iron target at a rifle range. We struggled for 70 minutes among those clanging, rending iron boxes, amid repeated explosions of shells and a ceaseless hammering of bullets. The engine tugged and butted, pushed and pulled, until only some six inches of twisted ironwork stood in the way.

At last I decided to run a great risk—to hurl the engine full tilt at this one remaining obstruction. It might mean derailing the engine and sealing our doom, but with the artillery fire steadily increasing, we had to take the chance. The engine backed away, then charged towards the blockade. There was a harsh, crunching tear. The engine reeled on the rails, and, as the obstructing truck reared upwards, ground its way past and gained the homeward side—free. But after the engine had passed, the obstruction fell back on the rails, isolating the three trucks which carried the Fusiliers. Under the constant bombardment we dared not start the lengthy operation all over again. By a margin of six inches, we had failed. It was one of the bitterest disappointments of my life.

I WENT BACK TO Captain Haldane. We agreed that the engine should go slowly homeward with the wounded, and that the others should retreat on foot, sheltering themselves behind the slow-moving engine. Upwards of 40 men, most of them streaming blood, were crowded in the engine and its tender, and we began to move. I was in the cab, directing the engine-driver. The shells burst all around, some striking the engine.

The pace increased, the infantry outside began to lag and soon were 300 yards behind. I forced the engine-driver to stop. Close at hand was the bridge across the Blue Krantz River, a considerable span. I told the engine-driver to cross the bridge and wait on the other side while I went back to find Captain Haldane and his Fusiliers.

But while these events had been taking place everything else had been in movement. I had not retraced my steps 200 yards when, instead of Haldane and his company, two figures in plain clothes appeared upon the line. "Boers!"

My mind retains its impression of these tall figures, clad in dark, flapping clothes, with slouch, storm-driven hats, poising on their leveled rifles hardly 100 yards away. I turned and ran back towards the engine, the two Boers firing as I ran between the metals. Their bullets, sucking to right and left, seemed to miss only by inches.

We were in a small cutting with banks about six feet high on either side. I flung myself against one bank. It gave no cover. Another glance at the two figures; one was now kneeling to aim. Movement seemed the only chance. Again I darted forward: again two soft kisses sucked in the air; but nothing struck me.

This could not endure. I must get out of the cutting—that damnable corridor! I jigged to the left, and scrambled up the bank.

At the top was a wire fence, which I got through unhurt. Outside the cutting was a tiny depression. I crouched in this, struggling to get my breath again.

About 200 yards away the rocky gorge of the Blue Krantz River offered plenty of cover. I determined to make a dash for it. Suddenly on the other side of the railway, separated from me by the rails and two wire fences, I saw a horseman galloping furiously, a tall, dark figure, holding his rifle in his right hand.

He pulled up his horse almost in its own length and shaking the rifle at me shouted a loud command. We were 40 yards apart. I put my hand to my belt, but the pistol was not there. When engaged in clearing the line I had taken it off.

Meanwhile the Boer had covered me with his rifle. His horse stood stock still, so did he, and so did I. I looked towards the river. The Boer continued to look along his sights. There was no chance of escape; if he fired he would surely hit me, so I held up my hands and surrendered, a prisoner of war.

My captor lowered his rifle and beckoned to me to come across to him. At his side, I tramped back to where I had left Captain Haldane and his company. They were already prisoners. We found ourselves in the midst of hundreds of mounted Boers.

Such is the episode of the armored train and the story of my capture on November 15, 1899.

It was not until three years later, when the Boer Generals visited

England to ask for a loan on behalf of their devastated country, that I was introduced at a private luncheon to their leader, General Botha. We talked of the war and I briefly told the story of my capture. Botha listened in silence; then he said, "Don't you recognize me? It was I who took you prisoner. I, myself," and his bright eyes twinkled. At the time of our adventure he had not yet been made an officer.

Few men that I have known have interested me more than Louis Botha. An acquaintance formed in strange circumstances and upon an almost unbelievable introduction ripened into a friendship which I greatly valued. I saw in this grand, rugged figure the Father of his country, the wise and profound Statesman, the farmer-warrior, the deep, sure man of solitude.

But let me return to my story.

IT HAD BEGUN TO RAIN. As I sat drenched and miserable on the ground with the prisoners and some mortally wounded men, I cursed not only my luck, but my own decision. I could quite decently have gone off on the engine; I had not helped anybody by attempting to return to the company; I had only cut myself out of the possibilities of further adventure and advancement. I meditated blankly upon the sour rewards of virtue. Yet this misfortune was to lay the foundations of my later life. I was not to be done out of the campaign. I was not to languish as a prisoner. I was to escape, and by escaping was to gain a reputation or notoriety which made me well known among my countrymen, and acceptable as a political candidate in a great many constituencies.

But these events and possibilities were hidden from me. My gloomy reflections took a darker turn when I found myself picked out from the captive officers and ordered to stand apart. I had enough military law to know that a civilian in a half uniform who has taken an active part in a fight, even if he has not fired a shot himself, is liable to be shot at once by drumhead court martial. None of the armies in the Great War would have wasted ten minutes upon the business. I therefore occupied myself in thinking what answers I should make to the short, sharp questions which might soon be addressed to me, and what sort of appearance I could keep up if I were suddenly told that my hour had come.

After about a quarter of an hour I was much relieved when I was curtly told to rejoin the others. Indeed I felt quite joyful when a Boer field cornet told me: "We are not going to let you go, old chappie, although you are a correspondent. We don't catch the son of a lord every day."

I need never have been alarmed. To the Boer mind the destruction of a white man's life, even in war, was lamentable and shocking. They were the most good hearted enemy I have ever fought against in the four continents where I have seen active service. So it was settled that we were all to be sent to Pretoria as prisoners of war.

Prisoner of War! It is a melancholy state. You are in the power of your enemy. You owe your life to his humanity, your daily bread to his compassion. You must obey his orders, await his pleasure, possess your soul in patience. The days are very long. Hours crawl like paralytic centipedes.

Moreover, the whole atmosphere of prison, even the most easy and best regulated prison, is odious. Companions quarrel about trifles and get the least possible pleasure from each other's society. You feel a constant humiliation in being fenced in by railings and wire, watched by armed men, and webbed about with a tangle of regulations and restrictions.

DURING THE FIRST THREE WEEKS I was engaged in arguing with the Boer authorities that they should release me as a Press Correspondent. They replied that, even though technically I had been taken unarmed, I had forfeited my noncombatant status by the part I had taken in the fight. As soon as I learned of this decision I began to weigh the chances of escape. I shall transcribe what I wrote immediately after the event:

"The State Model Schools, where we were held, were surrounded on two sides by an iron grille, and on the other two by a corrugated iron fence about ten feet high. In themselves, these were not serious obstacles, but the armed sentries at 50-yard intervals made them well-nigh insuperable.

"After continual watching, it was discovered that at some points on their beats the sentries were unable to see a few yards of the wall near a small lavatory on the eastern side. The electric lights in the middle of the quadrangle brilliantly lighted the whole place, but this wall was in shadow. To pass the two sentries near the lavatory it was necessary to hit off the exact moment when both their backs were turned. After the wall was scaled one would be in the garden of the villa next door. There the planning came to an end.

"I was determined that nothing should stop my taking the plunge. One evening, after careful preparation, I strolled across the quadrangle and secreted myself in the lavatory. From there I watched the sentries. For some time they remained stolid and obstructive. Then one walked up to his comrade. They began to talk. Their backs were turned. Now or never!

"I stood on a ledge and drew myself up to the top of the wall. My waistcoat got entangled with the ornamental metalwork on the top, and I had to pause to extricate myself. In this posture I had one parting glimpse of the sentries, still talking. One was lighting his cigarette; I remember the glow on the inside of his hands. Then I lowered myself lightly into the adjoining garden and crouched among the shrubs. I was free! The first step had been taken, and it was irrevocable.

"The gate which led into the road was only a few yards from

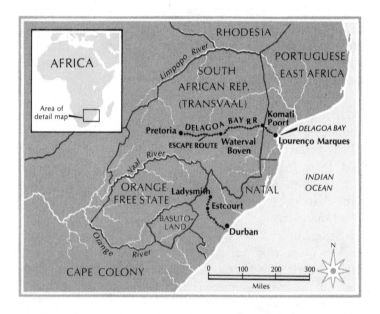

another sentry. I said to myself, *'Toujours de l'audace,'* put my hat on my head, strode into the middle of the garden, walked past the windows of the house without any attempt at concealment, and so went through the gate and turned to the left. I passed the sentry at less than five yards. Most of them knew me by sight. Whether he looked at me or not I do not know, for I never turned my head. I restrained with difficulty an impulse to run. But after walking 100 yards and hearing no challenge, I knew that the second obstacle had been surmounted. I was at large in Pretoria.

"I walked on leisurely through the night, humming a tune and choosing the middle of the road. The streets were full of burghers, but they paid no attention to me. Gradually I reached the suburbs, and sat down on a little bridge to consider.

"I was in the heart of the enemy's country. I knew no one to whom I could apply for succor. Nearly 300 miles stretched between me and neutral Portuguese territory at Delagoa Bay. My escape must become known at dawn. Pursuit would be immediate. Yet all exits were barred. The town was picketed, the country was patrolled, the trains were searched, the line was guarded. I wore a civilian brown flannel suit. I had £75 in my pocket and four slabs of chocolate, but neither compass nor map. Worst of all, I could not speak a word of Dutch or Kaffir. How was I to get food or direction?

"But when hope had departed, fear had gone as well. I formed a plan. I would find the Delagoa Bay Railway. After walking south for half a mile I struck a railroad. Was this the line to Delagoa Bay and freedom? I could not be sure, but resolved, nonetheless, to follow it. The night was delicious. A wild feeling of exhilaration took hold of me. I was free, if only for an hour.

"The fascination of the adventure grew. Unless the stars in their courses fought for me, I could not escape. Where, then, was the need of caution? I marched briskly along the line. Here and there the lights of a picket fire gleamed. Every bridge had its watchers, but I passed them all. Aside from making short detours at the dangerous places, I took scarcely any precautions. Perhaps that was why I succeeded.

"After walking for two hours I perceived the signal lights of a station. I left the line, and waited for the train in a ditch about 200 yards beyond the platform. An hour passed. I began to grow impatient. Then great yellow headlights flashed into view, and the train pulled up. In five minutes it started again.

"As it passed, gathering speed, I hurled myself at it, grasped some sort of handhold, was swung off my feet, my toes bumping on the line, and with a struggle seated myself on the couplings of the fifth truck from the front. It was a goods train, and the trucks were full of soft sacks, covered with coal dust. I crawled on top and burrowed in among them. They were warm and comfortable. Where was the train going? Would it be searched? What should I do in the morning? Ah, never mind that. Sufficient for the night was the luck thereof. I resolved to sleep.

"I woke before daybreak, conscious that I must leave the train, drink at a pool and find some hiding-place while it was still dark. I could not risk being unloaded with the coal bags. The train was running at a fair speed. I took hold of the iron handle at the back of the truck, and sprang. My feet struck the ground in two gigantic strides, and the next instant I was sprawling in the ditch, shaken but unhurt.

"It was still dark. I was in the middle of a wide valley, surrounded by low hills and carpeted with high grass. I searched for water and soon found a clear pool. Long after I had quenched my thirst I continued to drink, that I might have sufficient for the whole day.

"Presently the dawn began to break; I saw with relief that the railway ran steadily towards the sunrise. I had taken the right line, after all. Having drunk my fill, I set out to find some hiding-place in the hills. As it became broad daylight I entered a grove of trees on the side of a deep ravine. Here I resolved to wait till dusk."

I wrote these lines many years ago while the impression of the adventure was strong upon me. Then I could tell no more without compromising the liberty and perhaps the lives of those who helped me. For many years these reasons have disappeared. I can now relate the events which changed my nearly hopeless position.

DURING THE DAY I had seen two or three trains pass each way. Assuming that the same number would pass at night, I waited through four hours of darkness. But when midnight had passed with no sign of a train, I lost patience and started out on foot. I made little progress. Every bridge was guarded; there were many villages along the line; the veld was bathed in the bright rays of the full moon. To avoid these dangerous places I had to make wide circuits. I fell into bogs and swamps, brushed through high grass dripping with dew, and waded across the streams over which the bridges carried the railway. I had been able to take very little exercise during my month in prison, and tired quickly.

There was nothing for it but to plod on—but in an increasingly hopeless manner. I felt very miserable when I saw the lights of houses and thought of the warmth and comfort within them, but knew that they meant only danger to me. In the darkness to my left gleamed two or three fires; they must be, I thought, the fires of a Kaffir kraal. I had heard that Kaffirs hated the Boers and were friendly to the British. They might give me food and a dry corner to sleep in; I set out towards the fires.

I must have walked a mile in this resolve before a realization of its imprudence overtook me. I retraced my steps, perhaps half the distance. Then I stopped and sat down, completely baffled, destitute of any idea what to do or where to turn. Suddenly, without the slightest reason, all my doubts disappeared. It was certainly by no process of logic that they were dispelled. I just felt quite clear that I would go to the fires. I had sometimes in former years held a "planchette" pencil and written while others had touched my hand. I acted in the same subconscious manner now.

I walked on rapidly, and after some time perceived that the fires were not from a Kaffir kraal, but from the furnaces which ran the machinery of a coal mine. There was a group of houses about the mouth of the mine. I approached the most prominent—a substantial two-story dwelling.

The odds were heavy against me, and it was with reluctant steps that I advanced towards the silent house and knocked at the door.

There was a pause. I knocked again and an upper window opened.

"*Wer ist da?*" cried a man's voice.

I felt the shock of disappointment and consternation to my fingers.

"I want help; I have had an accident," I replied.

Some muttering followed. Then I heard steps descending the stairs. The bolt of the door was drawn, and it was opened abruptly. In the darkness of the passage stood a tall man, hastily attired, with a pale face and dark mustache.

"What do you want?" he said, this time in English.

"I am a burgher," I answered. "I have had an accident. I was going to join my commando at Komati Poort. I have fallen off the train. We were skylarking. I have been unconscious for hours. I think I have dislocated my shoulder."

It is astonishing how one thinks of these things. All this leapt out as if I had learned it by heart. Yet I had not the slightest idea what I was going to say next.

The stranger regarded me intently, and after some hesitation said, "Well, come in." He pointed into a dark room. I walked past him and entered, wondering if it was to be my prison. He lit a lamp. I was in a small room, evidently a dining room and office in one. My host laid on the table a revolver, which had been in his hand.

"I'd like to know more about this railway accident of yours," he said, after a considerable pause.

"I think," I replied, "I had better tell you the truth."

"I think you had," he said.

So I took the plunge and threw all I had upon the board: "I am Winston Churchill, War Correspondent of the *Morning Post*. I escaped last night from Pretoria. I am making my way to the frontier. Will you help me?"

There was another long pause. My companion rose from the table slowly and locked the door. Then he advanced upon me and suddenly held out his hand. "Thank God you have come here! It is the only house for 20 miles where you would not have been handed over. We are British, and will see you through."

It is easier to recall across the gulf of years the spasm of relief which swept over me than it is to describe it. I felt like a drowning man pulled out of the water and informed he has won the Derby!

My host introduced himself as John Howard, manager of the Transvaal Collieries. He had become a naturalized burgher of the Transvaal some years before the war. But out of consideration for his British race he had not been called up to fight the British. He remained on the mine to keep it in order until coal-cutting could be resumed. He had with him four British subjects; all would be guilty of treason in harboring me, and liable to be shot if caught.

I said that I did not wish to compromise him. Let him give me food, a pistol, a guide, and if possible a pony, and I would make my own way to the sea.

He would not hear of it. He would fix up something. But he enjoined the utmost caution. Spies were everywhere. He had two Dutch servant-maids in the house, and there were many Kaffirs employed about the mine. He became very thoughtful.

Then: "But you are famishing."

I did not contradict him. In a moment he had bustled off into the kitchen and returned with the best part of a leg of mutton and various other delicacies; leaving me to these, he let himself out of the house by a back door.

Nearly an hour later, he returned.

"It's all right," he said. "I have seen the men, and they are all for it. We must put you down the pit tonight, and there you will have to stay till we see how to get you out of the country. One difficulty will be the food. The Dutch girl sees every mouthful I eat. The cook will want to know what has happened to her leg of mutton. I shall have to think it all out during the night. You must get down the pit at once. We'll make you comfortable enough."

Before dawn I followed my host to the shaft. We entered the cage and shot down into the bowels of the earth. Two Scottish miners were waiting at the bottom with lanterns, a mattress and blankets. We walked through a pitchy labyrinth, and finally stopped in a chamber where the air was cool and fresh. Here my friends left me.

"Don't move from here, whatever happens," was their injunction.

Viewed from the velvety darkness of the pit, life seemed bathed in rosy light. I counted upon freedom as certain, and soon slept the sleep of the weary.

Mr. Howard told me that the Boer Government had been making a tremendous fuss about my escape. But on my second day underground, he announced that the hue and cry seemed to be dying away. The Boer officials now believed I must be hiding with some British sympathizer in Pretoria; they did not believe I could have escaped the town. In these circumstances he thought I might shift to quarters above ground. Thereafter I had a fine stroll in the glorious fresh air and moonlight each night, and took up daytime quarters behind packing cases in the office.

On the 16th, the fifth day of my escape, Mr. Howard told me of his plan to get me out of the country. A Dutchman named Burgener was shipping a consignment of wool to Delagoa Bay on the 19th. This gentleman was well disposed to the British. He had been made a party to our secret, and was willing to assist. The bales of wool could be so packed as to leave a small place in the center, where I could be concealed. A tarpaulin would be fastened over each truck after it had been loaded; and it was unlikely that it would be removed when the train crossed the frontier. Did I agree to take this chance?

I was more worried about this than almost anything that had happened to me so far. The idea of being perfectly helpless, at the caprice of a searching party at the frontier, was profoundly harassing. I should have been still more anxious if I could have read some of the notices which were circulating, offering a reward for my return, "dead or alive." In the end I accepted the proposal of my rescuer.

At two o'clock on the morning of the 19th my host appeared. He beckoned. Without a word, he led the way through the front office to the railroad siding where three freight cars stood. Three figures, evidently the English miners, were strolling about in the moonlight. A gang of Kaffirs were lifting an enormous bale into the rearmost car. Howard strolled along to the first car, and pointed. I nipped on to the buffers and saw before me a hole between the wool bales, just wide enough to squeeze into. From this there led a narrow tunnel through the wool. In the center was a space wide enough to lie in, high enough to sit up in.

I took stock of my new abode and its resources. There was a revolver. There were two roast chickens, some slices of meat, a loaf of bread, a melon, and three bottles of cold tea. The journey to the sea was not expected to take more than 16 hours, but no one could tell what delay might occur to commercial traffic in time of war.

All day long we traveled east through the Transvaal, and at night we were laid up at a station which, according to my reckoning, was Waterval Boven. I had accomplished nearly half the journey. During all the dragging hours of the day I had been haunted by anxieties about the search at the frontier, an ordeal inevitable and constantly approaching. Now another apprehension laid hold upon me. I wanted to go to sleep. Indeed, I did not think I could possibly keep awake. But if I slept I might snore! And if I snored while the train was in the siding, I might be heard. I decided in principle that it was only prudent to abstain from sleep—and shortly afterwards fell into a blissful slumber from which I was awakened the next morning by the jerking of the train as the engine was again coupled to it.

ALL THIS DAY, TOO, we rattled through the enemy's country, and late in the afternoon reached the dreaded Komati Poort. Peeping through a chink, I could see this was a considerable place. There were many voices and much shouting and whistling. I retreated into the center of my fastness, and covering myself up with a piece of sacking, lay flat on the floor to await developments.

Three or four hours passed; I did not know whether we had been searched or not. Meanwhile darkness had come on, and I had to resign myself to an indefinite continuance of my uncertainties. It was tantalizing to be held so long in jeopardy after all these hundreds of miles had been accomplished, and I was now within a few hundred yards of the frontier. Again I wondered about the dangers of snoring. But in the end I slept without mishap.

We were still stationary when I awoke. Perhaps the delay was because they were searching the train thoroughly! But at last we were coupled up, and almost immediately started. If I had been right in thinking that the station in which we had passed the night was Komati Poort, I was already in Portuguese territory. At the next station I peered through my chink and saw the uniform caps of the Portuguese officials on the platform. I restrained all expression of my joy until we moved on again. Then, as we rumbled and banged along, I pushed my head out of the tarpaulin and sang and shouted and crowed at the top of my voice. Indeed, I was so carried away by thankfulness and delight that I fired my revolver two or three times in the air as a *feu de joie*. None of these follies led to any evil results.

It was late in the afternoon when we reached Lourenço Marques. My train ran into a yard, and a crowd of Kaffirs advanced to unload it. I thought the moment had now come for me to quit my hiding-place, in which I had passed nearly three anxious and uncomfortable days. I had already thrown out every vestige of food and had removed all traces of my occupation.

I now slipped out and, mingling unnoticed with the Kaffirs and loafers in the yard—which my unkempt appearance well fitted me to do—I strolled through the gates and into the streets.

Burgener was waiting outside the gates. We exchanged glances. He turned and walked off, and I followed some 20 yards behind. We walked through several streets; presently he stopped and gazed at the roof of the opposite house, I looked in the same direction, and there—blest vision!—I saw floating the gay colors of the Union Jack. It was the British Consulate.

The secretary of the British Consul evidently did not expect my arrival. "Be off," he said. "The Consul cannot see you today. Come to his office at nine tomorrow, if you want anything."

At this I became so angry, and repeated so loudly that I insisted on seeing the Consul personally at once, that that gentleman himself looked out of the window and finally came down to the door and asked my name.

From that moment every resource of hospitality and welcome was at my disposal. A hot bath, clean clothing, an excellent dinner, means of telegraphing—all I could want. Happily the weekly steamer was leaving for Durban that very evening; on this steamer I embarked.

I REACHED DURBAN to find myself a popular hero. The harbor was decorated with flags. Bands and crowds thronged the quays. The Admiral, the General, the Mayor pressed on board to grasp my hand. I was carried on the shoulders of the crowd to the steps of the town hall, where nothing would content them but a speech. Sheaves of telegrams from all parts of the world poured in upon me, and I started that night for the Army in a blaze of triumph. Here, too, I was received with the greatest good will.

Churchill's escape made him an overnight hero in Britain and set the stage for his long and successful political career. After lecturing in England and the United States on his South African adventures, Churchill was elected to Parliament in 1900. By the time of the outbreak of World War I in 1914, he had become a member of the Cabinet, serving as First Lord of the Admiralty. His greatest fame came during World War II when, as Prime Minister, he led his beleaguered country in the victorious fight against Nazi aggression. In 1953 not only was Churchill knighted, but he was awarded the Nobel Prize in Literature. By an act of Congress in 1963 he was made an honorary citizen of the United States, the first person in history to be so honored. One of the great statesmen of the 20th century, Sir Winston Churchill died in 1965 at the age of 90.

An interesting postscript to Winston Churchill's escape is this letter that he wrote to Mr. de Souza, secretary to the commandant-general of the Transvaal Government, just prior to his breakout from the Pretoria prison camp:

STATE SCHOOLS PRISON, PRETORIA.

DEAR MR. DE SOUZA—I do not consider that your Government was justified in holding me, a press correspondent and a non-combatant, as a prisoner, and I have consequently resolved to escape. The arrangements I have succeeded in making with my friends outside are such as to give me every confidence. But I wish, in leaving you thus hastily and unceremoniously, to once more place on record my appreciation of the kindness which has been shown me and the other prisoners by you, by the commandant, and by Dr. Gunning, and my admiration of the chivalrous and humane character of the Republican forces. My views on the general question of the war remain unchanged, but I shall always retain a feeling of high respect for the several classes of the Burghers I have met, and on reaching the British lines I will set forth a truthful and impartial account of my experiences in Pretoria. In conclusion, I desire to express my obligations to you, and to hope that when this most grievous and unhappy war shall have come to an end, a state of affairs may be created which shall preserve the national pride of the Boers and the security of the British, and put a final stop to the rivalry and enmity of both races. Regretting that circumstances have not permitted me to bid you a personal farewell, believe me, yours very sincerely,

WINSTON CHURCHILL.

December 11, 1899.

---

*It was just a chess game played between two
strangers; yet one of the players knew that he was
using his own life as a pawn.*

"It's Your Move,
Hungarian!"

By Ferenc Laszlo

I WAS TRYING HARD to suppress my anxiety that September morning in 1946 as I stood in the dismal Keleti railroad station in
Budapest, Hungary. Panic, I knew, could wreck my hopes. I was
waiting prayerfully for the name of Oscar Zinner to be called—even
though I knew that it might mean my doom.

Until 10 days before I had never heard of Oscar Zinner. Then an
old friend of mine, who had information about the evacuation of
Austrians living in Budapest, had come to see me in secret.

"One man on the list for resettlement," he said, "has not replied to
letters informing him about the last train taking Austrian refugees
home to Vienna. He may even be dead. This man is a portrait painter
named Oscar Zinner. Would you care to risk attempting the trip to
freedom under his name?"

Would I! It was imperative that I flee my country as soon as possible. During the Nazi occupation, and later on as an unwilling subject
of Hungary's Communist regime, I had been an Allied intelligence
agent in Budapest. But recently the Soviet trap had snapped shut on
several of my close colleagues, and I had gone into hiding.

In changing my identity from Ferenc Laszlo to Oscar Zinner no
passports would be involved, because the Russians had looted and
burned all documents in virtually every Budapest home. My friend
spread typewritten pages of Zinner's biographical data before me.

"You are now the painter Oscar Zinner," he said. "Sit down and
learn. You must become Zinner in every action, in every thought."

He tapped the papers. "The Communist frontier guards will have a
copy of this. I need not tell you how closely they check. Another copy
will be held by the supervisor of your group. He is not acquainted

with Zinner. But when the name is called out at the station, *wait* before replying."

"Wait?" I asked.

"There's a chance that Zinner might show up at the last minute," he explained. "If two of you should answer, it would be embarrassing to the one who isn't Zinner."

For the next few days I studied Oscar Zinner's life story. I could describe the house where he was born in Graz, Austria. I knew his educational background, his habits, his likes and dislikes, even his style of painting. I could recall what critics had said of his pictures, the prices the paintings had brought, and who had purchased them.

Finally, late the night before my scheduled departure, I crossed the Franz Josef Bridge and let the incriminating biographical notes, torn into tiny shreds, flutter into the Danube.

A sudden sharp crackle from the loudspeaker in the railroad station snapped me back to the present. A rasping voice began to call out a list of names, alphabetically.

My stomach was knotted. Why did my new name have to begin with the last letter of the alphabet?

Finally, "Zinner—Oscar Zinner!" the voice barked.

I wanted to shout. But instead I waited, my heart pounding, my ears straining, my mind praying that there would be no answer.

"Zinner!" the voice called again, this time with annoyance.

I stepped forward. "Here!" I said timidly.

There was no challenge from the real Zinner. We were separated into groups of 10 and herded into compartments on the train.

Over and over I unrolled the story in my head. "I am a portrait painter. I was born in Graz. My father was an architect. . . ."

A shrill whistle from the station platform signaled the train to start. It didn't move. Suddenly, loud Russian-speaking voices could be heard at the end of our car. Four Soviet officers marched past our compartment door. They stopped at the next compartment, and I heard them order the occupants out into the corridor. Then they took over the space and soon were laughing amid much clinking of glasses. The whistle blew again, and the train jerked into movement.

As we picked up speed, I wondered when I would see my country again. But I realized suddenly that sadness was out of place. I was now Oscar Zinner, going home to Vienna.

The train groaned to a halt at Kelenföld. This was checkpoint number one. We did not have to wait long for the Soviet inspecting officer and his interpreter. In the corridor, accompanying Russian soldiers, heavily armed, stood stolidly watching the proceedings.

The Soviet officer, a rock-faced little man, started with the woman across the way. Shuffling the flimsy biographical sheets, he barked questions in Russian, which the interpreter translated into German. He came to the man sitting by the window on my side of the compartment. I began rehearsing once again what I would say: "I am a painter. I was born in Graz, Austria. My name is . . . My name is . . ."

Sweat broke out on my forehead, and my heart slid into my throat. A strange mental block, caused doubtless by my nervous tension and suppressed panic, let me remember everything about the man I was pretending to be except his name!

From a misty distance I heard the sharp voices of the examiner and the interpreter as they moved to the woman beside me.

"Please, God," I prayed, "what is my name? I am a portrait painter. My name is . . ." It was no use. The name would not come.

Just then I heard the door of the next compartment slide open. There was a brief flurry of conversation in the passageway, and then a Red Army colonel poked his head into our compartment.

"*Wer spielt Schach?*" he asked ("Who plays chess?").

Our examining officer turned and glared at the interruption, then stepped back respectfully under the gaze of his superior. As I was closest to the door, the colonel's next question seemed directed at me.

"*Spielen Sie Schach?*" he asked.

I hadn't played chess in 10 years, but it didn't matter. This was the breathing spell I needed. No one else in the compartment spoke.

"*Ja. Ich spiele Schach,*" I said.

The colonel gestured for me to follow him.

In the Russians' compartment were two other colonels and one much-bemedaled general, a fattening but still-powerful giant in his early fifties. Evidently it was he who wanted the chess game, for he gestured me to a seat opposite him.

Beside me were dozens of sandwiches and a box of candy. On the small table under the window were glasses, vodka, Hungarian brandy, and wine. The general gave me an appraising look, then pointed to the food and vodka. "*Davai,*" he growled in Russian ("Go on").

I ate in tortured suspense. At any moment one of the Russians might ask my name, or worse, the examiner might intrude.

As the train started, the general produced a chessboard and began arranging the figures.

"God help me," I thought. "This is the game of my life. I must make it good, and yet I can't afford to win." I had never known a

Russian who didn't hate to lose or a chess player who liked to play for long unless his opponent could make it interesting.

As we played, some of the tricks of the game slowly returned to me. The other officers watched the game in silence, apparently believing the general was a wizard at it. As a matter of fact he was quite a good player, but I was able to make him work for every advantage.

Time flew, as it does on every tense battlefield of chess, and with a start I realized that the train was slowing down at Györ, our checkpoint number two. My mind began to race. Now the door of the compartment slid open, and the supervisor of the Austrian group stepped in: "This man has not yet been questioned," he said firmly.

I need not have worried. The general rose, spread his huge bear's paw of a hand against the man's chest, and expelled him into the corridor. Then he slammed the door and pointed to the chessboard.

"*Davai, Magyar!*" he roared ("It's your move, Hungarian!").

Hungarian! I *was* coming from Hungary, of course, but his slip of the tongue, if it was that, set my scalp tingling.

When we finished the first game, from which the general emerged the victor, he said something to the officer who spoke German. "The general enjoys your style," the latter interpreted. "He will play you another game."

Before we began again, however, the general insisted that we drink. Reckless with the warm flood of confidence that came from the vodka, I lost myself in this game and suddenly found myself on the brink of winning. We were in the last crucial moves as the train slowed for Hegyeshalom, our final checkpoint. Here I would win or lose—not merely a game but everything I lived for.

This time dozens of Red soldiers, rifles slung over their shoulders, grenades hanging from their belts, led the procession of interpreters and security guards. They merely glanced into our compartment and went on to the next. There the angry little group leader must have told them of the "Austrian" who was sitting with the officers, for one guard came back to investigate. He stepped smartly in the door, saluted, and spoke rapidly in Russian, at the same time pointing to me.

Once again my brain froze in fear. Surely the general would let them question me, if only to forestall any further interruptions. "I am a portrait painter and my name is . . . ," I began saying to myself desperately. But I could not remember.

As the guard spoke, the general's face slowly purpled. I had no idea what the guard was telling him, but it made him as angry as any man I'd ever seen. He looked at me, his eyes blazing. Then he carefully placed the chessboard on the table under the window and stood up.

"This is the end for me," I thought. "To come so close—"

The general crossed his arm in front of his body, as a man would do to draw a sword. When he brought it up in a sweeping arc, the back of his hand smashed across the guard's mouth. The man reeled backward and struck the corridor wall.

The general slammed the door so hard it shook our window, then returned to his seat, muttering something under his breath. He picked up the chessboard and studied the pieces. *"Davai, Magyar!"* he said. My heart was bursting with

relief. No one would dare come in again—of that I was sure. As the train gathered speed, release from the awful tension flooded over me, so that, for the first time, I smiled. The general looked up from the board and smiled in return. He spoke to the young officer, who said to me: "The general wonders if you would enjoy playing him sometime in Vienna. Where can he reach you?"

Automatically I mentioned a well-known Vienna hotel. "And your name?" prodded the young officer.

Now, without the awful, clutching terror, I hesitated, but only for a brief moment. How could I ever have forgotten those two simple words, I wondered.

Aloud I said, "My name is Oscar Zinner."

*Aiding the fugitive to escape from the
dreaded Gestapo was an impul-
sive gesture of mercy that was to have its own
lifesaving repercussions.*

Turnabout

By Roman Turski

I WAS BORN in Poland, where before the last war religious intoler-
ance was not uncommon. In spite of my father's objection to my
participation in anti-Semitic demonstrations in Warsaw, I very often
heaved stones at windows of stores owned by Jews. I had no qualms
about my actions, and later it took months of hardship and persecu-
tion—and a Jew—to show me how to abide by the Biblical injunction
"Love thy neighbor as thyself."

Here's the story.

When Hitler annexed Austria and war seemed imminent, I quit my
job as instructor of a flying club in Lyons, France, and started for
home in my plane. The engine developed magneto trouble, and I had
to land at Vienna and stay there overnight to have it repaired.

The following morning, just as I stepped out of my hotel to buy a
few souvenirs before checking out, a man who came running past the
door bumped into me and sent me reeling. Outraged, I grabbed him
and was about to give him a piece of my mind when I saw that his
face was white with fear. Panting heavily, he tried to wrench himself
from my grip and said, "Gestapo—Gestapo!" I knew only a little
German but quickly understood that he was running away from the
dreaded German secret police.

I rushed him into the lobby and upstairs to my room, pointed to
the foot of my bed, and motioned to him to lie down. I covered his
slender, jackknifed body with artfully draped blankets so that the
tousled bed looked empty. Then I pulled off my jacket, tie, and collar
so that I could pretend I'd just gotten up if the Gestapo men came. In
a few minutes they did.

They examined my passport, returned it, and shouted questions, to which I replied, *"Ich verstehe es nicht"* ("I don't understand it"), a phrase I knew by heart. They left without searching the room.

As soon as they had gone, I locked the door and lifted the blankets. The poor man let out a stream of rapid German. It was not necessary to understand a word to comprehend his gratitude.

I got out my flight chart and, by gesturing and drawing pictures on the margin of the map, explained that I had a plane and could take him out of Austria. He pointed to Warsaw, and his expressive hands asked, "Would you take me there?"

I shook my head and made him understand that I had to land for fuel in Cracow. I drew pictures of police and prison bars to illustrate that he would be arrested upon arrival at any airport and made it clear that we would land in some meadow just over the Polish border and he could get off. He nodded with satisfaction, and his narrow face and dark brown eyes again conveyed deep thanks.

The customs and immigration men at the airport waved us through when I told them my friend wanted to see me off. My plane was warmed up and ready for flight. We quickly climbed into it and were soon in the air.

We crossed Czechoslovakia and soon saw the thin ribbon of the Vistula River and the city of Cracow. Landing in a large field by a wood near a country railroad station, I showed my companion where we were on the map, gave him most of my money, and wished him luck. He took my hand and looked at me wordlessly, then walked rapidly into the woods.

When I arrived at the Cracow airport, there was a detachment of police waiting beside the immigration inspector. One of the police said, "We have a warrant to search your plane—you have helped a man escape from Vienna."

"Go ahead and search it. Incidentally, I'd like to know what the man was wanted for?"

"He was a Jew!"

They searched my plane very thoroughly and, of course, had to let me go for lack of evidence.

The war came, and after Poland's short and bloody struggle against the Germans, in which I served as a fighter pilot in the Polish Air Force, I joined the thousands of my countrymen who wanted to carry on the fight for freedom. We crossed the border into Romania and were promptly caught and sent to concentration camps.

I finally managed to escape and joined the French Air Force. After the collapse of France, I went to England and fought in the Battle of

Britain. The following June I was wounded while on a fighter sweep across the English Channel when the Luftwaffe hit us over Boulogne. On those early offensive missions we were always outnumbered and outperformed by the Luftwaffe, and our only superiority was our morale.

As we started for home, I rammed an Me-109 and was hit by a piece of its sheared-off tail. I was half-blinded with blood. My squadron covered my withdrawal across the Channel, but I was unconscious when my Spitfire crash-landed in England. (I learned later that my skull had been fractured and that I was so near death the head surgeon of the hospital to which I was taken believed it would be almost useless to operate on me.)

When I returned to consciousness and opened my eyes, I realized that a narrow face with large brown eyes was looking down at me.

"Remember me?" their owner said. "You saved my life in Vienna." He spoke with only a trace of a German accent.

His words ended my confusion. I recalled this sensitive face and managed to say, "How did you find me?" Then I noticed his white smock. "Do you work here?"

"It's a long story," he replied. "After you dropped me off, I made my way to Warsaw, where an old friend aided me. Just before the war I escaped and reached safety in Scotland. When one of your Polish squadrons distinguished itself in the Battle of Britain, I thought you might be in it; so I wrote to the Air Ministry and found you were."

"How did you know my name?"

"It was written on the margin of your map. I remembered it."

His long fingers felt cool on my wrist. "Yesterday I read the story in the newspapers about a Polish hero shooting down five enemy planes in one day and then crash-landing near this hospital. It said that your condition was considered hopeless. I immediately asked the Royal Air Force at Edinburgh to fly me to this hospital."

"Why?"

"I thought that at last I could do something to show my gratitude. You see, I am a brain surgeon—I operated on you this morning."

The plan was to capture the Cuban naval vessel and make a run for freedom. No one thought that double the number of escapees would turn up.

The Incredible Mission

By Joseph P. Blank

IT WAS AN IMPOSSIBLE scheme. If Rafael Rodriguez had counted the seemingly limitless chances for failure through betrayal, mistakes, and bad luck, he would have recognized the utter folly of his plan to escape from Cuba. Failure meant death—certainly for his wife and himself, and possibly for his eight children as well as dozens of other men, women, and children.

But Rafael, a quietly authoritative man of 48 with a weathered face, graying, curly hair, and deep wrinkles at the corners of his mouth when he smiled, was so driven by the compulsion to escape from his homeland that he didn't permit himself to linger very long over "bad" thoughts.

Rafael had grown up in the little town of Guanabo, about 14 miles from Havana. Before finishing elementary school he went to sea. Over the years he saved his money, married, and eventually invested in a vessel to carry cargo between Cuba and Central America.

Rafael's interest in politics was purely personal. He wanted to live without fear, to carry on his business, and to improve the welfare of his family. Under Castro, these things were denied him.

"We had been promised a government controlled *by* the people," he said later. "We got a government committed to absolute control *of* the people. I had to get out. This was not easy. It meant leaving the country you love, the country where you were raised."

In July 1961 Rafael was arrested on suspicion of attempting to leave Cuba illegally. He was imprisoned for seven months, and the government confiscated his vessel.

"After my release," he says, "I was more determined than ever to leave. The main reason now was the children. They were all under steady indoctrination. My cell mate in prison had been denounced by his 14-year-old son. If this can happen, the father is no longer a father. He simply breeds for the state."

The only way to escape was by sea; yet the coast, especially to the north, was continuously patrolled by fighter planes and gunboats.

Rafael bought a fishing boat, available only because the hull leaked and the engine could not be repaired because of the lack of parts. He moored it on the southern coast, across the island from Havana, and began patching the hull and tinkering with the engine. Soon a pair of men came and questioned him. He told them he intended to use the boat for fishing.

He knew they knew what was in his mind, but he decided to continue work and to keep their surveillance focused on the boat. His real hope now, however, was to steal a second boat. To reduce the chances of being stopped and inspected, the getaway vessel would have to be a normal and familiar part of coastal activities.

For several months Rafael bided his time. He noticed that a sturdy 75-foot government lighthouse tender journeyed regularly up and down the southern coast. If he could somehow hijack this boat, designated the *H-11*, an escape could be effected under the guise of an ordinary service run. If . . . !

At a port bar a few days later, Rafael sat down next to the tender's captain, Reinaldo Armas, a slim man of 30, neatly dressed in duty khakis and the peaked cap of the Cuban Navy. They chatted about ships and the sea, and soon Rafael was buying his new companion drinks and dinner.

In the course of subsequent meetings, Armas complained about raising a family on his small navy salary and confided that he was fed up with the political coordinator who boarded his vessel each time it reached port. In fact, he eventually admitted, he was sick of the whole political business.

"A lot of people feel the same as you," Rafael assured him. "But you're in a more fortunate position. You have a good boat."

By the early summer of 1963 these cat-and-mouse conversations had reached the stage where both men knew, without expressing it in words, what lay ahead.

Rafael's plan had begun to grow. He invited a trusted friend, Dr. Jose Garcia (a fictitious name), to join him.

"I want to give the regime a message," he said. "I want to take people from every part of Cuban life—maybe 40 in all."

Rafael invited several couples who wanted to escape with their children. Dr. Garcia told others, and so also did Captain Armas.

"I worried," Rafael recalls. "I worried about word leaking. I worried about Armas' allegiance."

At Rafael's request, the Cuban underground sent Armas a letter, informing him that he would be killed if he betrayed the plan.

Despite the possibility that he was committed to destruction, Rafael continued to implement the plan. He gave Armas money for extra fuel. He then selected a second-in-command, Carlos Perez, and worked over the full plan with him. Using forged orders identifying themselves as "naval headquarters officers," Perez and two other men would board the *H-11* prior to the escape and make certain that the crew raised no alarm and that the vessel followed a certain schedule of movement. Perez would pass sleeping powders to Armas to slip into the crew's coffee on the night of the departure.

The escape route would lead the refugees through an uninhabited, insect-infested swamp to a barren point on the southern coast where the *H-11* would take them aboard. Posing as a fisherman, Rafael went over the route numerous times, calculating the time required to pass through the swamp. Because the swamp channel was too deep for children to cross on foot, he memorized the location of two large flatboats to be used for transportation. Fearful that his high-strung wife, Hilda, might collapse if she knew the actual plan, he told her that he intended to take the whole family soon to the Isle of Pines for a vacation.

On September 2 Armas received orders to sail up the coast to Cape San Antonio on September 4. After giving the crew 24 hours' liberty, he and Rafael rowed to the *H-11* to check over the vessel and review plans. The two men agreed on a system of signals and a rendezvous time of 4 A.M., September 4.

That night Rafael told his wife and children that they would leave "for vacation" the next day. In dozens of other homes information was received that the escape would take place the following night and that certain cars would pick up individuals and families and carry them to the staging area at an isolated farm.

At 7 the following evening Rafael shepherded his family into his car. "This was the worst moment of all," he recalls. "I now was committing the lives of my children."

When Rafael drove into the remote farm and Hilda saw clusters of people standing in silence, she turned to her husband, her eyes wide in question. He nodded, and she began crying.

He held her for a moment, then said, "Now I have work to do. Do

you want to go, or do you want to stay and have your children grow up in this kind of life?"

"I want to go," she said between sobs.

Rafael expected 40 refugees, but, by 9:30, 85 had gathered behind the farm's barn. Unwittingly, he was leading the biggest mass escape ever from Castro's Cuba.

"I don't know some of you," he told the silent throng. "We have a six-hour journey to the sea. You will break up into small groups and follow the guide. I will be the last man. Nobody can quit now. I warn you that I will shoot any person who tries it. This is the only way to protect all of us."

The refugees filed into the woods. Rafael carried his three-year-old son Jose on his back and his eight-month-old son Nelson in his arms. After an hour's march they reached the flatboats and loaded on women, children, luggage, and rations.

The night was moonless, and the men, pulling and pushing the flatboats, slipped and stumbled through the muck, sometimes sinking up to their hips. They hacked with machetes at the undergrowth and tore apart stiff, razor-edged stalks of vegetation with their hands. Branches jabbed them. Vines ensnarled their feet. Great swarms of hungry mosquitoes rose from the humid swamp. No one spoke. The only sounds were heavy breathing, groans, and the sucking of mud. Once a helicopter drifted overhead at about 1,500 feet. Everyone froze into immobility. Exhaustion overtook the elderly. One man sprawled on the channel bank and told Rafael, "I can't make it. Go on." Rafael ordered two older girls, one of them his daughter Milady, out of a boat and lifted the man in.

At 4 A.M. they reached the coastal edge of the swamp and halted in two feet of water. Rafael tied a flashlight around his neck and waded a quarter mile to the rendezvous point. He stood in four feet of water, straining his eyes and ears. He heard engines but could see nothing.

Things had not gone well aboard the *H-11*. Perez and his two fellow "inspectors" had rowed to the ship. Perez passed the sleeping powders to Armas. After ordering coffee for all hands, the captain slipped the powders into the drink but forgot to include additional sugar to disguise the bitter taste of the drug. Two crewmen grimaced at the first taste, and Armas, realizing what had happened, yelled at the cook, "How did my medicine get into the coffee!" He quickly emptied the pot into the galley sink and ordered fresh coffee.

The vessel got under way around 2 A.M., and Armas told the five men in the crew to catch some sleep while he took the wheel during the first leg. Perez decided to have Armas tell the crew that Rafael's signal was probably a call of distress. Then he, as an official from naval headquarters, would announce his suspicion that the fishermen were really escaping traitors who must be captured.

As the *H-11* neared the rendezvous point, Rafael finally saw its lights. He signaled—short, long, short. Armas answered, slowed his engines, and brought the *H-11*, with its 5½-foot draft, into eight feet of water. As his crew awakened, he said to them, "There was a signal for help. Must be trouble."

Rafael waded back to the group. He estimated that about a half mile separated them from the *H-11*, so he instructed Juan Cortes and Jose Garcia, Jr., two 18-year-olds, to swim to the tender and tell Armas to bring the vessel in closer.

When young Garcia breathlessly pulled himself aboard the *H-11* and opened his mouth to speak, Perez gave him no chance. "Shut up, you capitalist dog!" he snarled. To the crew he said, "There must be others. We'll wait for them."

Rafael heard no sounds from the tender. Darkness was running out, and he could wait no longer. He directed the loading of the first flatboat with women, children, and rations, and he and seven other men pushed the loaded boat into the sea, swimming with one hand and pushing with the other.

Nearing the *H-11*, the refugees suddenly recognized a Cuban naval vessel and assumed that they had been caught. The men cried, "No! No!" and the women wailed and clutched their children.

Rafael shouted, "It's all right! Get aboard!" He pulled himself over the side of the tender, and Perez snapped to attention, saluted, and said, "Good work, Major. Are there more traitors?"

Rafael stared at his accomplice, caught on, and replied, "Yes. Send a lifeboat for them immediately." Scrambling aboard the tender, the women unbalanced the flatboat and dumped all their rations and baggage into the sea.

Dawn was breaking by the time Rafael got the second boatload of "traitors" aboard. He ordered Armas to put the vessel on its normal course down the coast. A crewman tapped Perez' arm and said, "It sure was a great catch, wasn't it?"

"A great catch, yes," Perez agreed. "But you're the fish."

Both the crew and the refugees now began to grasp the truth. The crew, heavily outnumbered, did not make trouble. As Rafael circulated among his charges, he felt himself choking up with gratitude. No one appeared harmed by the ordeal. And so much could have happened—injury in the swamp, drowning at sea, discovery by the militia. Rafael felt that surely there must have been some divine intervention on their behalf.

All morning long the *H-11* gently plowed through the sea at its maximum speed of six knots. Rafael kept the refugees jammed into the hold, which soon grew stiflingly hot. Women fainted. Small children bawled incessantly. It was cruelty, but Rafael had no choice: the boat had to appear to be on a routine mission.

At 3 P.M. the vessel approached the Cuban naval base of La Coloma, the most dangerous point on the coast. Only Rafael, Armas, and Perez were on deck. The tender's crew was ordered below—at knifepoint. Suddenly three fighter planes flashed overhead. A torpe-

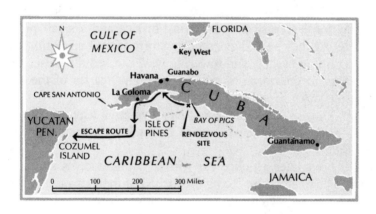

do boat put out from the base and crossed the *H-11*'s bow. Rafael waited. It went on. The harbor slowly receded into the distance. Rafael held to the coast till 10 P.M., then turned sharply south and made for the open sea.

At 6 the next morning the *H-11* underwent an alteration. The cargo boom and hatch cover were removed. The red star and "H-11" on the bow were painted out and replaced with "Nelson I," in honor of Rafael's youngest son. Across the stern appeared a new registry: ".7979 Miami, Fla." The passengers assembled on deck. In silence they watched Rafael lower the flag of Cuba and raise a U.S. flag that had been secretly and laboriously sewn together weeks before from pieces of clothing and curtains. Some refugees broke into tears; a few boys sang snatches of "The Marines' Hymn," thinking it was the U.S. national anthem.

At 11 A.M. Rafael caught a Cuban flag in his binoculars. It was a gunboat. Slowing down within a half mile of the *Nelson I*, it circled curiously. Rafael decided that if the gunboat ordered him to heave to, he would obey, then ram the vessel when it drew close. But the circling gunboat lost interest, picked up speed, and disappeared.

In the early afternoon Rafael put the *H-11* on a due-west course. The vessel was about 100 miles south of Cuba, 200 miles east of Mexico's Yucatan Peninsula, and 580 miles from Florida. He knew that the original plan to reach Florida could not be fulfilled. The loss of food from the flatboat made it impossible. They would have to head straight for the closest land: the island of Cozumel, off Yucatan, two days away.

Those two days were a nightmare. The burning sun made even the deck insufferable; it had to be doused continually with seawater. Adults were limited to a small cup of water every two hours, and the one daily meal consisted of a serving of rice and a small piece of chocolate. As they neared Cozumel, a storm kicked up. Rain poured down, lightning flashed, and towering waves tossed the vessel about. Rafael kept to the open sea during the night, fearful of the rocky, treacherous coast.

At 10 A.M. on September 8, four days after leaving Cuba, the *Nelson I* slipped into the harbor of Cozumel. Rafael and Dr. Garcia rowed ashore.

A half hour later a police car with a public-address system was cruising the streets, announcing the arrival of the Cubans and asking the people of the town to contribute clothing. Crowds gathered at the docks to cheer the refugees. The children were taken to the local hospital, where they were examined, bathed, and given a hot meal. Clothing stores donated dresses and shirts. Restaurants invited refugees to be their guests. Housing was found. People stopped them on the street to shake their hands. As 62-year-old Manuel Blanco said later, "This was the great moment. To have made it. To be free."

As for Rafael, now that it is all over, he is certain that their escape was made possible by Providence.

"After all," he said, "the good Lord must smile whenever any of His people escape from bondage."

The Nelson I *was impounded by Mexican authorities and returned to Cuba together with two members of the crew; three other crew members elected not to go back.*

*Acting was his life, and on the stage he played
many roles. But his finest performance came the day he
faced the mob of would-be murderers.*

Shatouni
The Magnificent

By Rouben Mamoulian

T HE HERO OF THIS STORY is Vahan Shatouni. When I first knew
him, I was a young boy in Tiflis, in the Caucasus Mountains
near the Russo-Turkish border, and he was a promising young actor
on the Armenian stage. He stood over six feet, with wide shoulders,
no hips, and a walk that combined the grace of a tiger with the high
spirits of a stallion. Strikingly handsome, he had huge dark eyes, full
of smoldering fire, the curved proud nose of an eagle, and bold black
eyebrows that met at a dashing angle. He was the doom of every
young girl and every woman—and the envy of every man.

In those days Shatouni's loftly ambition was to play two parts: one
was the melancholy Dane in Hamlet; the other, the lead in a popular
drama called *Ouriel Akosta*. This latter part he finally did play, under
most peculiar circumstances. Whether he ever played Hamlet I don't
know, but at the time I knew him he was assigned the lesser role of
Laertes in the Shakespearean drama—and he made the most of it.

To Shatouni, even more than to the average actor, entrances and
exits were of utmost importance. Needless to say, with his figure and
legs he looked sensational in tights. So his entrance in the fourth
act—where Laertes appears, sword in hand, to challenge the king—
was not unlike an earthquake in its effect. Shatouni would stop for a
moment in the open doorway and then leap over the threshold onto
the stage. There was always a satisfying gasp from the audience.

But at one performance disaster occurred. The dashing figure appeared, posed for a second—a black silhouette in the doorway—and
then, instead of that famous leap, his foot caught on the threshold and
he fell flat on his face! Six feet two inches of superb manhood hitting
the floor. There is nothing funnier than a glamorous entrance that

goes sour, and in a second the audience would have burst into loud guffaws. But in that first split second Shatouni was up, in one high bound, like a rubber ball, facing the king with such fury in his flaming eyes that no one dared laugh. He played the scene with such ferocity, in fact, that the king and queen went pale with fear under their makeup. He was actor enough to turn disaster into triumph.

An incurable romantic, Shatouni had a great gift for telling exciting stories. They were all about himself: his adventures, his acting triumphs, his escapades with women. No one believed a word, but everybody listened anyway, fascinated.

When World War I started, Shatouni enlisted at once in the cavalry. It was an undeniable fact that he looked tremendous in uniform. The sight of Shatouni striding down the street, his spurs clanking, his top boots shining like two black suns, his silver filigree Caucasian sword cutting a dashing curve at his side, was pure theater. Then he left Tiflis—for the front, he said. Others, who knew, said he left for the city of Yerevan, assigned to a staff job. In any case, after a few months Shatouni decided that it was time for the second-act climax.

He received two weeks' leave and came back to Tiflis. Just before alighting from the train, he put his left arm into a black silk sling— and thus made his appearance. To anxious questions he replied that he had been wounded in battle and told how hundreds of Turks had paid dearly for that wound. No two people heard the same story; yet all agreed that if anyone ever looked the brave hero Shatouni did.

Then came the Revolution of 1917—and eventually Shatouni's great third act, which proved to be a performance of actual unmitigated heroism. With the Revolution all the officials of the old regime were booted out of their mighty offices, some into the streets and some into kingdom come. The commandant of the city of Yerevan was one of them, and Shatouni was elected to take his place.

The people of the city adored him. Several times a day, and many times at night, he drove through the streets of the town just to show the people that he was keeping an eye on their welfare. He used a smart open touring car. (He never sat in it but stood up, the better to observe his domain, and also the better to be observed.) In front of his car six cavalry soldiers in Caucasian dress rode their spirited horses at full gallop, and six more followed. As he went by, in a blaze of sound and glory, people on the streets instinctively shouted, "Hurrah!"

Partly because official business bored Shatouni, and partly because he thought it romantic, he decided to have a "heart condition." He never *said* he had it, but implied it through mysterious references to the brevity of life and the immortality of the soul, and at times by an eloquent clutching at his chest with his hand, bending double, and asking in a soft, gentle voice for a glass of water. He would take a few sips, then, half closing his long curved lashes, say quietly and firmly, "It is nothing, nothing at all!" It gave him an added aura of somberly romantic grandeur. When overly bored by an interview, he would have such an "attack," then leave the office.

While Shatouni was perfecting his role as commandant, events were preparing a climax for his career. Shortly after the 1917 Revolution the Russian Army, with sagging war spirit, began to leave the fighting fronts almost en masse. Long trainloads of armed soldiers were soon passing through Yerevan on their way from the Russo-Turkish front back to Russia proper. These soldiers had suffered much during the czar's regime, and they nursed a bitter hatred for their officers. Now they had accounts to settle.

One morning a train pulled into Yerevan from the front. It was a train of freight cars and one passenger car with 65 officers aboard. Shortly after it, another train arrived, this one filled with hundreds of soldiers. Within seconds the first train was completely surrounded by a solid mass of armed and angry men who insisted that the officers come out and submit themselves to an immediate tribunal. This request meant only one thing: the officers would all be shot!

With the possibility of a massacre hanging thickly in the air, the stationmaster telephoned the local military headquarters. An old lieutenant general arrived, accompanied by his aide-de-camp. The brave general faced a wall of shiny rifles and hostile eyes. He cleared his throat and began to speak: "I order you . . . I *ask* you to disperse . . . go into your coaches." A soldier's voice interrupted harshly, "Shut your mouth, old man!" Another cried, "We'll try you with the rest of them!" In one more moment they would have torn the old warrior to pieces, but he knew when to retreat.

In the meantime, the stationmaster had been telephoning everybody for help. In vain. Then he had an inspiration: "The commandant! Shatouni the Magnificent!" A quick telephone call; an explanation. Then, just as the old general left, the soldiers heard what sounded like distant thunder—hoofs, horses' hoofs. And, while they watched, the glorious cortege came into view. Twelve horsemen were in front this time, 12 in the rear; in the middle was an open touring car, wherein stood the commandant.

With one eagle's glance, Shatouni took in the whole situation. Before the car had come to a full stop, he was out of it, striding swiftly along the platform, proud, handsome, and alone. The soldiers watched openmouthed as he strode past them, his silver spurs tinkling sharply. In three tigerish bounds the commandant reached the top of a pile of packing cases and stood there, the setting sun behind him. Then, stretching out both arms toward the crowd of uniforms, he shouted, "Soldiers, come to me!" They hesitated, then came on again until they had reached the packing cases—a sea of shining bayonets and puzzled faces staring up at the young Zeus.

Shatouni looked around, meeting each pair of eyes squarely with his own. Then, when the pause was ripe: "Brothers in arms, lend me your ears! I am the Commandant of the City of Yerevan, elected by the Revolutionary Will of the People! I am Shatouni!"

He stopped. There was a great silence. The name meant utterly nothing to any of them.

And now Shatouni did the unexpected. Moved by some inspiration that must have come to him directly from heaven, as it had no connection with sense or reason, he tore his uniform open with both hands, baring his chest, golden buttons scattering on the cement platform, and embarked on the soliloquy from *Ouriel Akosta,* the drama he had always longed to play. It starts: "Throw stones into my chest! Unleash your fury!" and goes on for three fiery pages. It had not the remotest bearing on the situation at hand, but how Shatouni read it! And how he acted it! The few townspeople who witnessed the scene said later that it was the greatest performance they had ever seen.

The soldiers stood breathless, so engrossed they were oblivious to the fact that the train containing the 65 officers was slowly pulling out of the station. Not so Shatouni. Out of the corners of his dark eyes he watched its progress. And when he finished the last sentence of the soliloquy, the train was a mere puff of smoke on the horizon.

The whole crowd broke into a thunder of applause. And now . . .

Now, suddenly, the commandant clutched at his heart and bent double. A dead silence fell at once. A soft voice said, "A glass of water, please!" Several soldiers dashed away and came back with many glasses of water. Others supported the commandant with their strong arms. Shatouni took a few sips, then said gently, "It is nothing, nothing at all." He was helped into his car; this time he sat, leaning back on the cushions. In a few seconds his cortege was out of sight, the sound of many hoofs dying away like distant thunder.

When the soldiers recovered their emotional balance, they turned back to the problem at hand. But, instead of the train containing the 65 officers, they saw only empty tracks glistening in the sunset.

*The plan to kidnap the German general was smoothly
executed. But then the two British officers faced the problem
of how to escape with him from occupied Crete.*

The Fantastic
Adventure

By Greg Keeton

O NE NIGHT IN 1944 two young British officers, both under 25, sat
in a café in Cairo. On leave after a long spell of fighting, they
were trying to think up a piece of devilment that would hurt the Nazis.
Suddenly, they had an idea: Why not kidnap a German general?

On the face of it, such a scheme was fantastic. But British military
authorities in Cairo and London liked the idea. The victim decided
upon was a distinguished member of Hitler's *Wehrmacht*—Maj. Gen.
Karl Kreipe, one of the heroes of Leningrad, now in command of the
22,000 German troops on the Greek island of Crete. Capturing him
would upset German planning in the Mediterranean, and it would be
a poke in the ribs that would bring a chuckle to the rebellious millions
living under Nazi occupation. And people who laugh are not afraid.

One February night, therefore, a British plane roared over a guerrilla hideout in the mountains of Crete. Out of it parachuted one of
the two schemers—Maj. Patrick "Paddy" Leigh-Fermor, a handsome Irishman who was also a noted Greek scholar. But before his
companion, Maj. W. Stanley Moss, could jump, the plane got lost in
the clouds and was forced to turn back.

Moss came back 10 times in the next six weeks, through fog and
flak, but each time failed to make contact with Leigh-Fermor and the
Cretans. Finally, arranging for an approach by sea, he slipped past
the German coastal-patrol boats in a launch one night and waded
onto a mined beach. Leigh-Fermor and a band of murderous-looking
Cretan mountain men were waiting there to help Moss pull through
the surf the boatload of guns and ammunition he had brought. Then
they set out in pitch-darkness to climb the roller-coaster goat trails to
their first hideout. It would have been difficult going in daylight. At

383

night it was torture. When, at 4 A.M., they arrived at the cave, their feet were blistered, their bodies black-and-blue from falls.

For two more nights the band marched north, over trails used by German patrols. They hid out during the day with villagers. Moss and Leigh-Fermor passed the time reading *Alice in Wonderland* and *The Oxford Book of Verse* and listening to the clump of hobnailed boots as German soldiers tramped down the cobbled streets.

Now Paddy Leigh-Fermor rubbed his mustache with burnt cork, stuck his legs through ragged trousers, bound a kerchief over his head, and started down into Herakleion, the capital of Crete. He was to meet a guerrilla called "Micky" Akoumianakis. Micky knew more about the activities of General Kreipe than anyone else—he lived next door to him.

Quickly, Leigh-Fermor saw that a kidnaping raid on the general's residence was out of the question. The villa was surrounded by three rows of barbed wire charged with electricity and guarded by dogs and a platoon of troops. So, for the next four days, the young Irishman watched from Micky's window until he had a timetable of the general's movements.

Each morning the general drove from his villa to military headquarters, five miles away. Every evening he returned after dark. This suggested that some night the kidnapers could trap him in his car. Studying the road, Paddy and Micky found the perfect spot for a holdup—an L turn so sharp that all cars were obliged to brake there and shift gears.

Paddy then returned to the hideout to confer with Moss. Their evolving plan called for 12 men: 8 hidden in the ditches alongside the road and 4 stationed ahead to warn of the general's approach. The two British officers were to masquerade as German military police. For this purpose the guerrillas got hold of two German uniforms. Into the lapels of each, Micky's wife sewed suicide tablets to be used in case of capture.

By now the Germans had got wind of a British party of some sort on the island, and the little band was kept stumbling up and down the mountains each night to a new hideout. They slept in caves or lofts. Once they sat in a loft, their automatics trained on the door, while four Germans banged around downstairs demanding food.

By April 23 preparations were complete. The operation was scheduled for the following night. And then General Kreipe upset the timetable. For three nights in a row he came home while it was still light, as if he suspected something was afoot.

On the fourth day the British officers watched the daylight fade and darkness come—and no sign as yet of the general. This was it.

The 12 men took their places at the ambush. They waited an hour. Finally, the spotters' flashlights blinked. A car flying two metallic pennants came down the road.

As the car slowed for the L turn, Leigh-Fermor and Moss, wearing correct German MP uniforms, waved it to a halt. Paddy opened the right-hand door and pulled Kreipe out onto the road. The two rolled over and over, Kreipe cursing, kicking, and lashing out with his fists until three guerrillas handcuffed him and tossed him into the back of the car. When the chauffeur reached for a pistol, Moss blackjacked him and dumped him into a ditch.

Now Paddy put on the general's hat and took the general's place beside the driver's seat. Moss slid behind the wheel. Manoli Peterakis and George Tyrakis, two of the guerrillas, sat in the back, Kreipe between them.

Soon after they started down the road, they saw the swinging red lamp of a German control post. Tyrakis unsheathed his knife and made clear to Kreipe what would happen if he dared call for help. The sentry stepped to one side as the car approached; Moss slowed to let him see the flags on the fenders, then roared on.

When the kidnapping expedition came abreast of General Kreipe's home, the gates swung open, two guards stiffened to attention. Moss honked the horn, Leigh-Fermor motioned that he would not be entering, and the car whirled on.

Altogether, they went through 22 German control posts. Their worst moments were in Herakleion, where the movies had just let out. The streets swarmed with German soldiers. Moss tooted; the troops saluted. Paddy Leigh-Fermor, imposing in the general's hat, nodded back, stone-faced.

Once through the city, "we felt a terrific elation," wrote Moss in his book telling of the exploit. "We started discussing what sort of celebration we would have when we got back to Cairo."

But Cairo was still a long way off. They abandoned the car now and took to the mountains, knowing full well that every single one of the 22,000 Germans on Crete would soon be hunting the general throughout the island's 35-mile width and 165-mile length.

By midafternoon of the next day the sky was full of planes with observers scanning the countryside through binoculars. Every now and then they would let fall a snow of leaflets: "If General Kreipe is not returned within three days, all rebel villages in the Herakleion district will be razed." The Germans did dynamite Anoyia—a 900-year-old town—and then dive-bombed what masonry was left standing.

Each night the kidnapers fled east and south. The general turned out to be a rather pleasant fellow; he kept pace with the others on their nightly marches and accepted his embarrassing plight without complaint. Sometimes, however, he worried about his numerous sisters. He, a bachelor, had long provided for them; but in the German Army, allotments ceased the moment a soldier was taken prisoner.

Meanwhile, Leigh-Fermor and Moss were becoming haggard over their failure to contact a radio operator who could confirm arrangements with Cairo about their escape ship. Then one night, stumbling into a guerrilla hideout, they heard an English voice, and there was the man they were looking for. But when he tried to send their message, nothing happened. His transmitter was out of order!

It looked as if their early good fortune was finished. They dispatched runners to the only other two radiomen on the island, asking them to transmit a message to Cairo, but these operators were a long way off. And now the Germans were organizing for a massive drive up and through the mountains.

One afternoon an urgent message reached the weary band. One of the guerrillas, translating rapidly, reported that truckloads of soldiers were preparing to encircle the mountain on which they were hiding; they must make a break for the coast at once.

This meant climbing at night, at a fast clip, over Mount Ida, 8,000 feet high. They left at dusk and climbed for 12 hours. Soft snow concealed treacherously deep crevasses. At the summit it started drizzling. The men had no food, and for shelter they found only a shepherd's crumbled, roofless hut. There they waited until night, freezing, then started the descent.

"It took us two hours—stumbling and falling—to reach the bottom of the snow belt," wrote Moss in his diary, "and then we found ourselves groping through stunted trees. Twigs would snap back in your face, and brambles would tear at your clothes and hands."

The mood of the guerrillas became so ugly that Moss and Leigh-Fermor felt concerned for the safety of the general.

Sitting in a ditch 24 hours later, in a downpour, shivering and miserable after accomplishing what must have been a record-breaking ascent and descent, Leigh-Fermor reread the message that had sent them scrambling over Mount Ida. The guerrilla had made a mistake in translating it; far from urging them to go over the mountain, it had implored them not to move!

Then another piece of bad luck. When they got to the beach where they planned to wait for their getaway, they found 200 Germans encamped there. Now a whole new set of arrangements had to be made. When at last a radio operator was located, a new rendezvous was suggested.

"We are feeling the anticlimax of this business acutely," Moss wrote a week later. "It seems that we now have everything to lose and nothing whatever to gain."

But at this point, with the Germans sniffing in narrowing circles all around them, their luck turned. A murderer and two sheep thieves joined the group.

"They are the shiftiest-looking men I have ever set eyes upon," wrote Moss. "However, they have a matchless knowledge of every path and track, which makes them peerless as guides."

So, assisted by their new guides, the kidnapers continued to elude the German troops.

The night of May 14, after almost three weeks of flight, they were awakened by a messenger: "A boat is coming for you at Rodakino Beach tomorrow night. You'll have to hurry to get there on time."

Led by their sheep thieves, they raced up and down mountainsides hour after hour, arriving at noon on a hill overlooking the beach.

Downshore, in full view of their binoculars, was a German camp; less than a mile upshore was another. At 9 P.M. they slid down to the beach between the two. And then the most welcome sound in the world—a low throb of motors!

Safely in Cairo three days later, Paddy and Moss bade the general good-bye. "He smiled at us with a rueful though kindly expression," said Moss, "and then he was gone." Major General Kreipe was taken to a prison camp in England.

Leigh-Fermor and Moss were both awarded Britain's Distinguished Service Order. Kreipe became a bond salesman in Germany after the war. He held no grudge against Moss and Leigh-Fermor, for the adventure had saved his life. The other two German generals in command of the Cretan garrisons were executed as war criminals by sentence of a Greek tribunal.

*It seemed to be a devil's game that the major of
the Soviet security police was playing with
the helpless West German prisoner—until the interrogation
came to a sudden strange conclusion.*

Second Crossing

By Hans Hardt

IT WAS A CHILL SEPTEMBER evening in 1951. As I stepped off the westbound train at the last village in the Soviet Zone of East Germany, I cast a grateful glance at the dark clouds overhead. It was just the right weather to slip back across the border into Free Germany unnoticed.

I sought out a dimly lit café. There, nursing a glass of lemonade while I waited for night to close in, I relived the few days I had just spent with my parents and brother—our first family reunion in over seven years. It had been saddened by my parents' destitution. They had lost all their belongings when they fled from the Soviet armies in 1945, only to be overrun by the Red tide in the town where they were now living. Return to our native village of Fichtenhorst was unthinkable and forbidden: it now belonged to Communist Poland.

I had been living in West Germany since my release from a prisoner-of-war camp in Britain in 1948. Finally able to trace my parents' whereabouts, I learned that my father was now crippled with multiple sclerosis, and I determined to get him to West Germany for proper medical treatment. But, after months of waiting, my application for a Soviet visa had been turned down "on political grounds"— presumably because as a POW I had spent four years in England.

In May 1951 I had tried to slip into East Germany to see my parents, only to be stopped at the frontier and turned back with my passport stamped, "Illegal Crossing of the Border." Now, some four months later, I had tried again and had gotten through. I knew that to be caught a second time, trying to get out after several days' unreported sojourn in the Soviet Zone, would mean something worse than a stamp on my passport.

I was fairly hopeful of getting back into West Germany, however, because of the detailed map my brother had drawn for me. It plotted precisely the camouflaged positions of border guards, noted the hours when some posts were unmanned, and indicated various landmarks, such as the high chimneys of several factories near the border.

My watch showed 11. It was time to go.

For two hours I walked a deserted country road. When a hamlet came into view, I turned sharp right and minutes later entered the forest that stretched across the frontier. I crouched down and struck a

match for a last look at my map, stuffed the paper into my pocket, and resumed walking. Every few minutes I stood still and listened, to be sure that the rustling sounds were merely wind and leaves. Soon I was close to the path dividing East from West. And then:

"Stoi!" a voice shouted in Russian ("Stop!").

I threw myself on the ground, rolled a few yards, staggered to my feet, and ran. A tommy gun chattered, and two white flares plopped overhead. When the shooting stopped, I heard the terrifying noise of dogs in full cry. Something hit my back and knocked me headlong into a clump of bushes. When I lifted my head, I was looking into the panting jaws of a German shepherd.

Two Russian soldiers yanked me to my feet. While one of them held the warm barrel of his tommy gun under my chin, the other emptied my pockets. They bound my hands and marched me through the forest. Suddenly my blood froze—I remembered the map!

That night I paced a cold cellar room with barred windows, berating myself for not having destroyed that piece of paper. To the Russians, I felt sure, it would be conclusive proof that I was a spy.

Early next morning two guards hustled me to a little office upstairs. Behind a big black desk sat an officer in a major's uniform; the hated red tabs on the collar of his jacket betokened a member of the Soviet security police.

"Good morning, *kleiner Spion*," he said, with cold sarcasm. "Did you sleep well?"

I was startled to be addressed in good German, although I knew that the Soviet forces had been combed for men fluent in the language for service in East Germany. But the major's tactics were Russian enough: the contempt in the phrase *kleiner Spion* ("little spy"); the assumption of guilt; the apparent expectation that I would make a clean breast of things quickly.

"I am not a spy," I protested.

"I didn't ask your profession, *kleiner Spion*, but how you slept. So you crossed the border illegally four months ago! Please tell me, what did you try to find out this time?"

"Nothing. I went only to see my parents."

"And where do they live?"

"I won't tell."

"We have ways of finding out," the major said.

He was looking through my passport. "So you were born in Fichtenhorst?" He looked at me sharply for a moment, closed my passport, then picked up the hand-drawn map.

"Fine drawing, that. Roads, villages, our guard positions, even the location of some large factories. How much do the Americans give you for such a nice drawing?"

I was silent. I realized how feeble my explanation would sound.

"All right, little spy," he snapped. "Maybe you will talk in Siberia! Guards, take him away."

Cold fear gripped me at the dread word "Siberia." But dead tired, hungry, I was no sooner in my cell than I dozed off despite my fears. I could not tell how long I had slept when the guards woke me and led me before the major again. He lit a cigarette and studied me.

"We have checked the information on your passport. All lies. Now we know you are a spy. You had better talk."

391

I stood dumbfounded. "I have no reason to lie to you," I protested.
"We'll see about that. How long did you live in Fichtenhorst?"
"For the first 13 years of my life."
"All right, tell us about Fichtenhorst. We happen to know that village." He closed his eyes and leaned back in his chair.

I spoke of our village east of the river Oder, of the old church amid the lime trees. I told how we farm boys washed the horses at the riverbank in the evening. I mentioned the village priest, the local schoolteacher's foibles, my own grandmother, who owned a big farm and was loved for her good deeds.

Through it all the major's face remained a wooden mask. When I stopped, he opened his eyes and asked, "Then you knew Wolfgang Leuters, Magda Furst, and Walter Korb, for example?"

I wondered what devil's game he was playing. I remembered no such people in the village in my time.

"Or the farmer Stolpel—Ignaz Stolpel?" he continued.

"Yes, yes, that one I knew. Did you know him, Major?"

"Shut up!" His voice rasped. "I ask the questions here. Tell me what you know about this Stolpel."

"Well, he was the poorest farmer in Fichtenhorst. His land was so bad that even the weeds were scrawny. Everybody felt sorry for him because he worked hard. He never complained, though, and he was too proud to accept help. Frau Stolpel worked on the land every day, also, and Josef—that was his son. His father drove the boy as hard as he drove himself. Nobody thought that unjust. It was the lot of most boys in the village. When he was 16, Josef left home. It was said he had gone south to Czechoslovakia, but nobody knew for sure."

I paused, remembering the pity we had all felt for the Stolpels. "Go on!" the major ordered.

I told how the poor farmer had changed after losing his son. He turned against the village, refusing even to come to Mass and forbidding his wife to go. People said that on Sundays, when the bells rang out, she would cry her heart out, for she was very devout.

"Why wouldn't he let her go?" the major asked.

"They said she sided with the boy, and Stolpel was bitter about it. He didn't want her to talk with people. Two years after her son ran away, Frau Stolpel died. Her husband went to the funeral in his working clothes. Then he returned to his fields and worked long into the night. He became more silent and hostile than ever."

I paused. "Do you want me to go on, Major?"

"Yes."

My grandmother, I told him, wanted to help the lonely man. She offered him good land in exchange for his barren fields, but he shook his head and went on working. Then one day he was found face down on the ground. He was rushed to the hospital in a nearby town. He had had a stroke. His farm was auctioned off, but that didn't bring enough money even to pay the hospital.

"In the spring he came back," I went on. "My grandmother found him wandering on his old farm and led him to our house. She gave the old man a room, and he sat at our table. He rarely spoke, even in thanks, but he did everything he could to earn his food.

"To my boyish eyes he seemed very old, with his white hair and tottering step. At first I was a little afraid of him. Then one day, when I was trying to make my first fishing rod and bungling the job, he took it from me, finished it skillfully, and gave it back. He did all this without speaking, but with a gentleness that took away my fear. After that there was an unspoken friendship between us.

"When he died, Grandmother found his wife's prayer book sewn inside his mattress. In it was a scribbled note: 'Father, I go away now and will never come back. I go away because you do not love me. Please be good to Mother.' It was signed 'Josef.'

"Now do you believe I am from Fichtenhorst?" I finished, a bit embarrassed because I had let myself ramble on about an old man.

The major did not answer. "Go back to your cell!" he ordered harshly. As I turned to leave, he picked up the map. With dismay I realized that he had given me no chance to explain away that incriminating paper—and people had drawn sentences of from 5 to 10 years at hard labor on flimsier evidence of spying. I had fallen into his trap. The fact that he had not once mentioned the map proved to me that his mind was made up.

I slept through the night, stupefied by fatigue and hopelessness. Early in the morning a guard woke me. "Get ready!"

This was it. I was numb with despair.

"We will take you to the Western Zone," the guard said.

Throughout the hour's walk to the border between two soldiers I kept expecting to be turned back. This was some cruel trick, I was sure. And I still only half believed it when they handed me my papers and motioned for me to cross the line into West Germany.

"You are lucky," one of them said, not unkindly.

How right he was I understood only when I looked into my passport and saw there a new stamp: "Second Illegal Crossing of the Border." It was signed: "Major Josef Stolpel."

*A flamboyant German fighter pilot, captured
by the British in World War II, won his freedom
in a daring and ingenious escape feat.*

The One
That Got Away

*By Kendal Burt
and James Leasor*

OBERLEUTNANT FRANZ VON WERRA, marching between impassive
guards, traversed the long corridors of the British Air Interrogation Center at Cockfosters and was ushered into a pleasant, richly
paneled room. It was completely dark save for a powerful reading
lamp that cast a circle of light on a massive mahogany desk. Behind
this sat an RAF officer with a thin, lined face, bushy eyebrows, and
an upcurling mustache.

He spoke in fluent but slightly accented German. "I am Squadron
Leader Hawkes. Sit down, Oberleutnant."

As the prisoner clicked his heels and bowed stiffly, he noted a
silver-knobbed walking stick propped against the desk. It reminded
him of the foppish British officers of German newspaper cartoons.

"Oberleutnant, 13 English aircraft shot down and half a dozen
destroyed on the ground is quite a respectable score." There was cold
mockery in the interrogator's voice. "As a minor ace of the first war, I
am especially thrilled to meet one of the major aces of the second."

Von Werra mimicked the other's casual drawl. "I have not read of
your exploits in studying the Royal Flying Corps' fascinating history," he said, "and, intrigued as I am to meet you, I am not going to
reveal any military information."

Von Werra paused for a long moment, then added with sneering
insolence: "But how stupid of me, Herr Major! No doubt it was you
who shot me down!"

The squadron leader said nothing.

The long silence that ensued was finally broken by the wail of an
air-raid siren. Another siren began, and then another one, until the
screaming cacophony covered the whole London area. Von Werra

smirked: more German bombers overhead. It was September 7, 1940, and the all-out Battle of Britain was well under way.

Suddenly the squadron leader turned off the reading lamp, plunging the room into darkness. He pushed himself up from his chair, seized his walking stick, and walked over to the window. Despite the wailing sirens, Von Werra could hear that he limped heavily and that one of his boots squeaked. His interrogator was wearing an artificial leg. There was no doubt about it.

"Forgive me, Herr Major," Von Werra said impulsively. "I'm terribly sorry. I had no idea—"

There was no reply. The squadron leader had drawn back the blackout curtains and was staring into the London night.

Presently the wailing died down, siren by siren. Hawkes redrew the curtains and returned to his desk. As he snapped on the lamp, he tipped the shade so that Von Werra sat facing its harsh light.

"Tell me, Oberleutnant," he said casually, "which of your friends in the Headquarters Staffel of the Second Gruppe of No. 3 Fighter Geschwader will look after Simba, your pet lion cub? Will it be 'Sanni,' perhaps?"

Von Werra gasped. Since his capture two days before he had divulged only his name, rank, and serial number. Yet a British interrogator knew not only his unit but the name of his pet lion and the nickname of his best friend.

Nor was he bluffing; he seemed to know everything. He even commented on how slender was Von Werra's claim to being a baron, a title that the young flier often used.

For the next two hours Squadron Leader Hawkes continued his devastating attack, his sarcastic voice cutting deeply into the German's arrogance.

"I must congratulate you, Oberleutnant," he said, "on your flair for publicity."

He brought out a transcript of a German radio program on which Von Werra had told of shooting down five Hurricanes and destroying four more on the ground, all in one solo raid. Although there had been no witnesses, the feat had been lauded in Germany as "the greatest fighter exploit of the war."

Hawkes, half sitting on the edge of the desk, leaned over the prisoner. His voice was icy. "You know as well as I do, Oberleutnant 'Baron' von Werra, 'The Red Devil,' 'The Terror of the RAF,' that there was no incident even remotely resembling your alleged exploit."

The RAF could hardly have suffered the loss of nine Hurricanes without being aware of it, Hawkes said. And item by item he pointed out the absurdities and holes in the fabrication, including the discrepancies between what Von Werra had said over the radio and what he had told the press. In the end the spuriousness of the story was manifest, and Von Werra sat silent and abashed.

And now the squadron leader struck. "Suppose your fellow prisoners get to know what you and I know about your famous exploit—what sort of life would you lead in prison camp? You'd be the laughingstock of the place."

Von Werra smiled weakly, but smiled nevertheless. "Herr Major, I know what price you are likely to ask for keeping quiet—military information." His voice gathered firmness. "I assure you I will tell you nothing, Herr Major! You may make it impossible for me to live with my comrades, but the alternative would be worse. You see, I couldn't live with myself."

The interview was over. Von Werra had not broken under the grilling. And as Hawkes rang for the guard, the prisoner showed a flash of his irrepressible spirit.

"Herr Major, I'll wager a magnum of champagne against 10 cigarettes that I escape in six months."

It was as well that Squadron Leader Hawkes did not accept the wager. He would have lost.

Then 26 years old, willful, exuberant, intensely ambitious, Franz von Werra had been in the Luftwaffe since its inception more than five years earlier. He had quickly got the measure of that service: The only way to get ahead was to get oneself talked about. What impressed was dash, aggressiveness, a touch of daredeviltry. Von Werra tried to outfly all the others in mock combats and indulged in such prohibited stunting as diving under bridges and low aerobatics over his girl's house. Whereas other pilots had pet dogs, falcons, even pigs, Von Werra must keep a lion cub. To add to his glamour he adopted the title of Baron, which, despite its dubious legitimacy, had a certain snob value even in Hitler's forces.

When war came, the important thing, of course, was to become an ace, and Von Werra actually downed eight verified planes, which was not a bad record. But the Polish, Norwegian, Dutch, and Belgian air forces had been demolished in a matter of days, and the French Air Force was hard hit. In a few weeks the RAF too would be knocked out, and all the Nazi fliers were scrambling for honors before it was too late. Von Werra's boast of destroying nine Hurricanes in his famous unwitnessed raid put his score near the top. The authorities, after reducing his claim from nine planes to five, awarded him the Knight's Cross. But before he could receive it, on his 10th mission over England he was shot down.

However vainglorious his boasting, Von Werra had an acute sense of security. At a time when the supremely confident Nazis expected few losses and scarcely bothered to give their airmen security briefings, the carelessness of captured fliers was a boon to British Intelligence. They often carried secret documents, maps, strength reports, technical data, diaries, or tattered bus tickets, cinema ticket stubs, and crumpled sales slips from which it was possible to deduce the location of various units. But Von Werra burned all the papers on his person immediately after his plane crashed.

His first interrogation convinced him that the German leaders had been right: The British *were* stupid. A courteous, informal army captain with iron-gray hair offered him a cigarette and, ignoring their roles as captor and captive, seemed bent only on talking about German politics, Nazi ideals, Germany's claim to colonies, and the like. Vastly relieved not to be questioned on military matters, Von Werra had relaxed, become expansive, and had talked freely. Only later did he realize how astutely the interview had been managed and that the interrogator had simply been sizing him up to decide which techniques would yield the best results in future interrogations.

Although Von Werra had now successfully withstood the grueling frontal attack of Squadron Leader Hawkes, who was his second interrogator, RAF Intelligence was by no means finished with him. In the ensuing days he was questioned repeatedly at all hours of the day and night by half a dozen different German-speaking officers working separately and in collaboration. Between them they tried almost every trick in the business to get him to talk.

He was cajoled, flattered, tempted, and provoked. It was suggested that it might be possible to arrange for him to visit the West End—discreetly escorted, naturally, and wearing civilian clothes; everything would be laid on for him—dinner, a show, a visit to a nightclub. Another interrogation turned out to be a "friendly chat between flying types," with a bottle of whisky ("Help yourself, old man") and a box of cigars on the table. Von Werra would play none of these dangerous games.

Using yet another stratagem, his captors kept him in solitary confinement for several days, then placed him in a room with another member of his unit, Oberleutnant Carl Westerhoff. The two happened to be close comrades and, when they were alone, greeted each other warmly. Westerhoff immediately plied his friend with many questions, but Von Werra answered guardedly, glancing continually around the room. Suddenly, he pulled Westerhoff into a dark corner, climbed on his shoulders, and peered into a ventilator grill. When he got down, he whispered, "That's where it is. There's definitely a black thing in there and some wires. Let's lean out the window and talk. We'll be safe there."

The microphone in the ventilator was confirmed that very evening when the lights went on. From then on they did their talking leaning out the window.

Three mornings later Von Werra sat up in bed as though stuck with a pin. "God, what a fool I've been!"

The ventilator was the most obvious place in the room to put a microphone. The British had put it there *intending it to be found!* Moreover, the windows in other rooms he had been in at Cockfosters had all been fixed so they would not open. This one had been deliberately left in working order, doubtless with a microphone concealed under the ledge.

Von Werra leaned out the window and said in a loud clear voice: "Hallo, RAF Intelligence. Oberleutnant von Werra calling. I'm trying to find a microphone concealed near the window of my room. I am now tapping the hollow sash board on the left-hand side. Are you receiving me? Oberleutnant von Werra calling and testing. . . ."

It may have been pure coincidence, but that same morning Westerhoff and Von Werra were moved out of the room.

Before they had finally finished with him, the British interrogators had worked on Von Werra for a total of three weeks. During that period he had not knowingly given away any military information whatsoever. But in the process of questioning him, the British had unavoidably provided him with an almost complete picture of their methods and techniques. As it turned out, this information was of far greater importance than anything he could have told them. For Oberleutnant von Werra was profoundly impressed by the subtlety and the insidiousness of British interrogation methods, and he now knew more about them than did any other German—a fact that later had far-reaching consequences both for the Royal Air Force and for the Nazi Luftwaffe.

Von Werra was sent to Grizedale Hall, a prisoner-of-war camp situated in the wild moorland country, 20 miles from the Irish Sea. The building was a gaunt stone mansion of 40 rooms and was very closely guarded. A captured submarine commander, Kapitänleutnant

Werner Lott, had recently attempted to escape and had not succeeded in getting beyond even the inner ring of barbed wire.

There had been few determined escape efforts, however. As in other British POW camps at this time, most of the captured Nazis were content to sit tight and confidently await the arrival of German troops. But Von Werra no longer shared the belief that Britain would be defeated by Christmas. The surprising and unpleasant competence of the RAF, which had already cost his unit nearly 15 pilots, and the British defense measures he had observed—camouflaged pillboxes, blockhouses, antitank ditches, tall poles in fields as antiglider obstructions—had convinced him that the war would last a long time.

WITHIN 10 DAYS of his arrival at Grizedale Hall, Von Werra had devised a scheme for escaping. The senior German officer, Major Willibald Fanelsa, who with the aid of a three-man council passed on all escape plans, listened to it dubiously.

Every other day 24 prisoners were taken out on the road for exercise. They turned either north or south—apparently at the whim of the mounted sergeant who accompanied them—and were marched at a smart pace for about two miles, then rested at a bend in the road for 10 minutes, and were marched back.

Discipline was strict and surveillance heavy. In addition to the mounted sergeant there were an officer on foot in charge and four guards in front and four in the rear.

The rest area on the northern route, where a wire fence gave onto an open meadow, offered no possible cover. On the southern route, however, the rest area was beside a stone fence. If some of his fellow prisoners distracted the guards and others massed to shield his movements—and Von Werra had worked out the details of how this could be done—he might vault the fence and run crouched behind it until he reached a blind spot in the road, then escape into thick woods. Once free, he would make his way to the coast and try to stow away on a neutral vessel.

Major Fanelsa approved the plan as "by far the best that had been submitted" up to that time. The escape council provided a crude map and the heavy clothing needed for the rough moor country. Von Werra had already managed to acquire three shillings in English money and had saved his chocolate ration for food. Two days later the plan was put into action.

Major Fanelsa asked the camp commandant to change the exercise period from 10:30 A.M. to 2 P.M. on the ground that it interfered with camp educational classes in the morning; actually, to allow Von Werra to escape nearer to nightfall. At the camp gates, since there was danger that the northern route might be taken, one of the English-speaking prisoners gave the order to turn south. This was not challenged. The officer in charge thought the mounted sergeant had given the order; the sergeant assumed it had been given by the officer.

When the usual rest was called, the guards took their positions on one side of the road while the prisoners went to the opposite side and stood or milled about in front of the stone wall. The appearance of a greengrocer's cart on the usually deserted road was at first dismaying. But it proved the perfect distraction, for the guards bought apples from it, and the sergeant fed one to his horse. When the cart had gone, Von Werra moved in behind the tallest of his comrades, who by prearranged plan were carefully grouped together. He quickly hoisted himself up onto the wall. An elbow nudged him as a signal that no guards had been alerted, and he rolled over, dropping noiselessly into the field behind.

As the prisoners re-formed in column, the sergeant gave the order to march. When they had gone 300 yards, the Germans broke into a marching song—one of two alternative songs they had agreed to sing at this point. It was the favorable one, and it let Von Werra know that he had not yet been missed.

Now safely out of sight of his captors, who had disappeared around the bend, he stood up without further concealment and vaulted the stone fence. He then dashed across the road and disappeared into a thick pine wood on the other side.

Singing on the walks was strictly forbidden, and when the prisoners had suddenly burst into full-voiced song, the guards had been taken by surprise. Suspecting something amiss, the sergeant rode up and down the column trying to count the prisoners. But they kept moving from one rank to another and back again—a ruse suggested by Von Werra—so that it was difficult to tell how many there were. After a word with the officer, the sergeant finally rode ahead of the column, drew his revolver, and ordered a halt.

When the POW's shuffled to a stop, the officer went down the length of the column, counting. The count was 23 instead of 24. There could be no doubt about it: One prisoner was missing.

Local residents still recall the furor that ensued. By 5:30 the whole antiescape machinery of the area had been set in motion. The Home Guards and local police were brought into the hunt, and three bloodhounds were rushed by car from headquarters at Preston. Before the dogs arrived, a heavy rain fell and made them useless. Regular troops, at first held back lest they destroy the scent, were then lined up to beat through the woods.

Von Werra disappeared completely for three days and nights. The police suspected that someone was harboring him or that he had died from exposure or injury. Neither of these things had happened.

Even in the wildest parts of the Lake District there are many small stone huts, known as hoggasts, used for storing sheep fodder. Home

Guards visited in turn each hoggast in their area, however remote, and at about 11 P.M. of the fourth day two Home Guards patrolling the Broughton Mills area, only four or five miles from the coast, found a hut on which the padlocked door had been forced open. Shining a carbide bicycle lamp within, they discovered the fugitive.

While one of the Home Guards held a gun on him, the other tied a cord tightly around Von Werra's wrist, then tied it to his own wrist. But before they could lead him away, Von Werra in a perfectly timed maneuver sent the man he was tied to sprawling and at the same time knocked out the light. Then, leaping out of reach of the second man and jerking his bound wrist with all his might, he snatched the cord free and disappeared into the night.

He was not found again until after two more days of intensive search. At 2:30 P.M. on the sixth day of Von Werra's freedom, a shepherd spotted him sneaking through the bracken on a 1,200-foot hill overlooking the Duddon Valley. The shepherd notified a nearby contingent of the Cumberland and Westmorland Constabulary. They immediately threw a cordon around the base of the hill. When they had closed in on him, they took no chances; they at once put handcuffs on the captive.

This time he did not get away.

After serving 21 days of solitary confinement as punishment for his escape, Von Werra was removed from Grizedale Hall and sent to Swanwick, a POW camp in the Midlands. But having got away once, he was confident that he could do it again and was determined to give it a good try. So he at once carefully inspected the security setup of the new camp minutely.

Swanwick was surrounded by two heavy barbed-wire fences, and the narrow land between them was patrolled constantly. Watchtowers, set at intervals of 50 yards along the outside fence, were equipped with machine guns and searchlights, and the fences were floodlit at night except during air-raid alerts, at which time the guard was reinforced. The only possible means of escape, he decided, was by tunneling.

The building he was assigned to was only a yard or so from the inner boundary fence, and Von Werra figured that a tunnel measuring about 14 yards long, starting from a small unused room on the ground floor, would emerge beyond the outer fence. The exit would be uncomfortably close to one of the watchtowers, but a few shrubs and trees offered a little cover.

The project seemed possible, and within a few days five other officers enthusiastically joined with him to organize the Swanwick Tiefbau A.G. ("Swanwick Mining Co.")

From the first the undertaking went well, despite many obstacles. Von Werra found that by skipping lunch, at which he would hardly be missed since only one British officer was then in charge of 150 prisoners, he could devote six hours a day to digging. The short-handled scoops and fire buckets, thoughtfully provided by the War Office to cope with incendiary bombs, were perfect for excavating and carrying away dirt, and one of the tunnel team discovered a huge and partially empty catch basin for rainwater into which it could be dumped. After a time the air in the burrow became so nauseous that even a few minutes' work incurred retching and violent headaches, and a large cave-in invited complete disaster, since it left only a thin crust of earth above the tunnel. But no guard fell through this—fortunately, it was directly under the first security fence, and fresh air filtering down through the remaining thin, porous dome solved the problem of ventilation.

All the prisoners cooperated, standing lookout at strategic spots and shouting coded warnings when the noise of digging or prying out large stones threatened to reach the sentries' ears. When noise was unavoidable, it was drowned out by group singing, harmonica playing, loudly boisterous card games, even a staged free-for-all fight. The work went steadily forward, and just one month after it was started, the tunnel, a "rabbit hole" just big enough to crawl through, was completed.

Meanwhile, the five tunnelers (one of the original six pessimistically gave up midway) had made their plans for getting out of England. The sale of a diamond ring to a guard for a pound had given them each four shillings. With this scant fund for bus fare, two of the men hoped to reach Liverpool and stow away on a neutral ship for Ireland. Two others would make for Glasgow where they would also try to board a neutral ship. Only Von Werra decided to go it alone.

His experience while on the run in the Lake District had convinced him that a German escapee in Britain stood very little chance unless he could somehow get out of the country before the search for him got under way. The only means of doing this was by air. Von Werra therefore decided on the boldest possible course: He would make his way to the nearest RAF field and, relying on his wits when he got there, try to get his hands on a plane.

CASTING ABOUT FOR a simple but convincing masquerade, he decided to pass himself off as a Dutch pilot who had crashed in returning from a bombing mission. This was plausible, for there were now a great many Czech, Dutch, Norwegian, and Polish refugees serving in the RAF, speaking broken English (his own English was fair), and wearing relatively unfamiliar uniforms. Since few airmen in the Midlands were likely to know much about the workings of the Coastal Command, he would be from the "Mixed Special Bomber Squadron, Coastal Command," based at Aberdeen. Aberdeen would be a long way off, and the ambiguous designation "Mixed Special Bomber Squadron" would allow him a certain latitude for explanations.

For a uniform, one prisoner donated a flying suit that he had somehow managed to retain, a second supplied fur-lined flying boots, and a third leather gloves. To complete his wardrobe, Von Werra bought a woolen tartan scarf from the camp shop. He could forgo identification papers but would certainly need a British service identity disk, which was made of vulcanized fiber. This was impossible to obtain, but the camp's forgery department provided him with an exact replica made of cardboard.

At 9 P.M. on December 20, wearing black pajamas over his flying suit to protect it, Von Werra cautiously broke through the last layer of earth above the tunnel exit. Conditions were ideal. The night was dark, and an air-raid alert had caused the floodlights to be turned off. As he emerged to freedom, the camp chorus, greatly augmented for the occasion and singing with tremendous volume to obscure any sounds of the escape, burst forth with *Muss-i denn, Muss-i denn zum Städtele hinaus* ("I must away into the great wide world").

Silently Von Werra made his way through the darkness, and a few minutes later his four companions emerged one by one from the tunnel. At a barn some 200 yards distant, where they had agreed to rendezvous, they whispered their good-byes to Von Werra, shook his hand, and then went their separate ways.

Since the raid was still on, Von Werra decided to wait for the all-clear before venturing farther, lest he be picked up as a survivor of a crashed German aircraft. There was no hurry. With any luck, the escape would not be discovered until roll call next morning, which gave him at least 10 hours' start. He crouched down near the barn and anxiously waited.

At 3 o'clock the all-clear had still not sounded. Von Werra dared not wait any longer. He emerged from his hiding place, tucked the camp's copy of *The Times* under his arm as a prop, and set off across the fields.

He might have walked less jauntily had he known that the police were already scouring the district for him. Swanwick had been alerted to the escape shortly after midnight, when one of the escapees, Major Heinz Cramer, had been captured. Major Cramer had tried to steal a bicycle he found leaning against the wall of a shop. Unluckily, it belonged to the village policeman, who had left it there momentarily while he made a routine check of the shop's rear premises.

Von Werra walked for miles along country roads without encountering a soul. He now had only a few hours left and was beginning to worry. At 4:30 he heard a locomotive hissing on a nearby siding. He stepped over to it and climbed into the cab.

The engineer was startled. His jaw dropped. "What d'you think you're up to?" he demanded.

"I am Captain van Lott, formerly of the Royal Dutch Air Force, now with the RAF," Von Werra explained matter-of-factly. "I've just made a forced landing in a Wellington after being hit by flak in a raid over Denmark. I must get to the nearest RAF field quickly. Where is the nearest telephone, please?"

The engineer was helpful. "My mate Harold here's just going off duty. He'll walk you along to the station."

Walking along the track beside the engineer's mate, Von Werra reached the Codnor Park station at 5:30. But the telephone was in the booking office, which was locked, and the booking clerk, Sam Eaton, did not arrive till shortly before 6. Nervously, Von Werra waited.

When Eaton appeared, he was out of sorts, and he listened impatiently to Von Werra's story of crashing a bomber nearby and of leaving the uninjured crew at a farmhouse that had no telephone.

"Will you please ring up the nearest RAF field and ask them to send a car to fetch me?" Von Werra asked. "My base at Aberdeen will send a plane for me and my crew there."

Manifestly skeptical, the dapper little booking clerk asked several questions about the crash, then picked up the telephone. "Put me through to the police, please!"

Von Werra sat rigid while the other spoke at length into the telephone. But apparently Sam Eaton merely wanted to rid himself of the problem. For when he hung up the receiver, he said, "Don't worry. Somebody will be right along. They're in a much better position to help you than I am."

A porter now brewed tea. Eaton offered Von Werra a cup, took one himself, and as the three sat waiting for the police, Von Werra's magnetism and genial plausibility began to have their effect. For half an hour he answered questions about the crash and the bombing raid and talked expansively about the RAF. Finally he confided—"I really should not tell you this"—that he belonged to a special squadron and that the night's raid had been a test for a new bombsight. "Now you see why it is urgent that I get back quickly?"

Eaton was visibly impressed. "Really! I'm very sorry. If you'd said so before . . . Should I ring up the base?"

"Please do."

The clerk lifted the receiver and asked for Hucknall airdrome. When he finally got through to the duty officer, he explained briefly about Von Werra, then motioned Von Werra himself to the phone.

"He wants to speak to you, sir."

The Hucknall duty officer was hard to convince. He asked a great many questions about the crash and remarked that it was curious that he had not heard about it. But at last he said, "I suppose I'll have to do something about you. I'll send a vehicle to pick you up."

At one minute past 7 the police arrived. There were two plainclothesmen and a uniformed sergeant. For a time they eyed Von Werra in silence, their looks neither friendly nor hostile. Then one of the detectives suddenly rapped out:

"Sprechen Sie Deutsch?"

Von Werra answered in English, "Yes, I speak a little German. Most Dutch people do."

The detective grunted, and instantly the tension relaxed.

"Sprechen Sie Deutsch?" was evidently the only German they knew among them, for the second plainclothesman now said, "So you're one of the Coastal Command boys, eh?"

Von Werra now knew that they had not come to arrest him. They were simply checking on his story. He had read enough accounts of RAF bombing raids in the British papers to be convincing.

"Yes," he said, giving his most disarming smile. "Last night it was a wizard show, but we nearly bought it."

At this knowing RAF slang, the three policemen looked significantly from one to the other and grinned.

"Where are your papers?" the sergeant asked.

Von Werra was commendably patient. "Do you not know that it is forbidden to take personal papers into the air? With us, the special squadron, that rule is strictest."

After that they did not even ask to see his identity disk. And although they asked a great many more questions, Von Werra's answers, together with the fact that Hucknall was sending a car for him, seemed to satisfy them.

At length, one of the detectives clapped him on the back. "Grand types, you Coastal Command chaps."

"Yes. Jolly good luck to you," said the second detective. "Some Germans broke out of a prison camp near here last night. We thought at first you might be one of them."

Von Werra gulped, then covered his dismay by joining uneasily in their laughter. So their escape had already been discovered!

Five minutes after the police had left, an aircraftman came in and saluted smartly. "Transport for Hucknall, sir," he announced.

Von Werra's spirits soared again. As he settled himself comfortably for the 10-mile ride to the RAF base, he felt that he might yet steal that airplane.

Contrary to Von Werra's supposition, the Hucknall duty officer had not sent the car because he was convinced Captain van Lott was genuine but because he strongly suspected he was bogus. He had not heard of the escape from Swanwick, but Van Lott had talked too much and too garrulously. And it seemed incredible that a bomber could crash in the dark without injuring any of the crew. Still, aircrews sometimes had amazing luck when they crashed. The officer decided he'd better check Captain van Lott's story on the spot. If he was an imposter, his dress, his papers, and the way he told his story face to face would give him away.

As a precaution the duty officer gave the driver of the car a gun and warned him that Van Lott might be a saboteur or escaped prisoner. The windows of the station headquarters were barred, and he locked all the doors except the main entrance. In the adjutant's office, where the interview would be held, he built up a roaring fire so that Van Lott would be forced to take off his flying suit and thereby disclose his uniform.

It had just turned daylight when the driver drew up at headquarters and ushered Von Werra into the adjutant's office. The duty officer, who wanted to be occupied so that he could study his visitor covertly, was taking down the blackout shutters.

He saw a man of five feet seven inches with curly hair, a frank boyish face, and a pleasant smile. He looked neither villainous nor Teutonic. However, his flying suit was nonregulation and of a strange type—pale gray-green with a long diagonal zipper.

Still fumbling with the blackout shutters, the officer casually inquired: "Van Lott?—I won't keep you a moment. You may find it a bit stuffy in here. Take off your flying suit. Please sit down and make yourself at home!"

The room was in fact as stifling as the stokehold of a ship. But Von Werra replied: "It is not worth the trouble. My plane shall arrive any minute from Aberdeen." And, unobtrusively, he moved as far as possible from the fire.

The duty officer finished with the shutters, dusted his hands, and returned to his desk. Von Werra shook hands with him.

"I am sorry to bother you," he said. "I wish not to make you trouble. I shall go and wait by the control tower for my plane, yes?"

"That's not necessary. Stay in here where it's warm! Control will ring me as soon as contact is made with your aircraft."

Since his visitor betrayed no signs of discomfort at the heat and seemed to find it perfectly normal, the duty officer, who was also being grilled by his own coals, tried a new tack.

"You certainly had the most amazing luck with that crash," he said. "The details sounded very confusing over the phone. You'd better tell me the whole story again—you understand I will have to make a full report."

While Von Werra hurriedly described the raid and the crash, the officer made notes and asked probing questions. When Von Werra told of being interviewed by the police, it gave him pause. If true, this put a rather different complexion on the problem. If the CID had been satisfied with his story and had more or less vouched for him . . .

Nevertheless, the officer now picked up the phone and asked to have a call put through to the base at Aberdeen. A talk with the commanding officer there would settle the matter.

"Is that really necessary?" Von Werra asked. "My aircraft must arrive soon."

"Sorry. You know how it is—red tape and all that. And you realize," the duty officer added, "that you must identify yourself properly. Suppose you show me your identity disk."

Von Werra laughed tolerantly at this insistence on formality. He had worn his carefully forged cardboard disk suspended around his neck. Confidently, he unzipped the top of his flying suit and reached for it. As his fingers touched it, he gasped. Perspiration and the heat from his body had reduced the cardboad to a clammy pulp. He dare not produce it.

As he continued to fumble uncertainly, and the other waited patiently, the telephone rang. He was saved. The duty officer picked up the receiver.

"Right!" he said to the operator. "About time! Put me through. . . . Hallo, Aberdeen?" The connection was evidently a bad one, for he soon began shouting in exasperation.

But Von Werra had no desire to hear the conversation. Backing to the door, he caught the officer's eye, raised his eyebrows interrogatively, and went through the motions of washing his hands.

"Won't be long!" he said, and stomped down the corridor to the door marked "Gentlemen." This he opened and slammed—from the outside. Then he tiptoed on to the main door. When he opened it, he could hear the duty officer shouting:

"Captain van Lott . . . two words. . . . Hallo? . . . A Dutchman. . . ."

Once outside, Von Werra crouched low until he had passed under the adjutant's windows, then sprinted toward the hangars. Time was now the supremely vital factor. Near the first hangar he slowed to a brisk, purposeful walk.

Construction was under way here, and carpenters looked down curiously at him from scaffolding. Dodging around a cement mixer and almost bumping into a laborer who was cutting open a cement bag, he came upon a row of twin-engine bombers. These were no good to him, so he strode on.

Ahead, at the second hangar, was a group of Hurricanes. One part of Hucknall was an RAF training base for pilots; another part a highly secret Rolls-Royce experimental station. It was into this secret, heavily guarded section that Von Werra had now penetrated. The confusion of the construction area had provided a loophole in its normally faultless security.

He approached the only mechanic in sight. "Good morning," he said authoritatively. "I am Captain van Lott, a Dutch pilot. I have just been posted here. But Hurricanes I have not yet flown. The adjutant sent me here so you could show me the controls and make a practice flight. Which one is ready to take off?"

The mechanic, a civilian employee of Rolls-Royce, looked puzzled. "Haven't you come to the wrong place?" he asked. "This is a private firm, you know, sir."

"I know. But the adjutant said it was to you I should come. I haven't much time."

The mechanic pondered. Then the probable explanation dawned on him. The airman must be a civilian ferry pilot from the Air Transport Command, come to take delivery of a Hurricane. Such civilian pilots were known by the courtesy title of "Captain," and many of them were foreigners who spoke little English.

"I can't do anything for you until you've signed the visitors' book. It's regulations." he said. "Hang on a minute, Captain. I'll go fetch the manager."

When the mechanic hurried away into the hangar, Von Werra leaned against the fuselage of a Hurricane. A brand-new beautiful Hurricane with not a scratch on it! He was tempted to climb in and try to start the engine on his own. But this might wreck his chances altogether. There were certain controls he must be sure about before he attempted to take off.

The mechanic reappeared with a man in a khaki smock, presumably the manager. The official smiled and greeted him pleasantly.

"I hear you've come to collect a Hurricane. If you'll come with me, we'll get your paperwork fixed up."

"It shall take long? I have little time," Von Werra replied. "I just want to learn controls of the Hurricane."

"I'm afraid nothing can be done until you sign the visitors' book. We'll soon fix you up, though."

Reluctantly, Von Werra followed him into the hangar. The manager walked with infuriating slowness, and a clock in the hangar reminded Von Werra how much time had elapsed since the duty officer had put through that telephone call to Aberdeen. He almost lost his nerve.

The manager led Von Werra to an office where a man in a blue uniform, evidently a works policeman, presided over a large ledger.

The policeman now proceeded to take over. "If you'll sign along the next line, sir . . ."

The entry had to be made across two pages, which were divided into columns. Using printed characters, lest his German-style script betray him, Von Werra had no trouble with the first four headings, which were Date, Name, Nationality, and Station. The others were meaningless to him, but the policeman helped him fill them in, and presently the form was completed.

The manager now pronounced everything in order save for the receipt of the written orders covering the collection of the Hurricane. Von Werra said these were with his kit, which should arrive any moment by plane. Meanwhile, to save time, could he have instruction on the Hurricane controls?

"Righto," said the manager. "We can do that all right now you've signed the book."

As he emerged from the hangar with the mechanic, Von Werra glanced apprehensively about. No RAF uniforms were yet in sight. If the duty officer would only give him five more minutes!

The mechanic walked over to one of the new Hurricanes, slid back its hood, and Von Werra climbed in. The mechanic began to explain the unfamiliar instrument panel and controls.

Von Werra hung on every word. Much of it was confusing, but he tried to concentrate on essentials so that he would not stand the Hurricane on its nose in the takeoff.

Before the mechanic could anticipate his move, he reached forward and jabbed the starter button.

"Don't do that!" cried the mechanic in alarm. "Can't start without the trolley accumulator."

"Fetch it, then!" Von Werra ordered.

"Somebody else is using it."

Von Werra smiled warmly. "Please get it, yes? I really am in very much of a hurry."

Obligingly, the mechanic went to get it and presently returned driving the electric starter across the tarmac. He halted it under the engine of the Hurricane, jumped off, and raised the cable over his shoulder to plug it in.

As Von Werra began to operate the fuel-injection pump, the aircraft swayed slightly, and a voice above him ordered quietly: "Get out!"

Von Werra looked up and found himself facing the muzzle of an automatic pistol and the cold blue eyes of the duty officer, who was leaning over the rim of the cockpit.

"I spoke to Aberdeen," the officer said flatly.

The connection to Aberdeen had been very bad, and only by constant shouting and repetition had the duty officer been able to make himself understood, or to understand the man at the other end. Several times communication was cut altogether. But at long last he had learned that Van Lott was bogus.

In retrospect, the gaping holes in Von Werra's story were evident; one glaring implausibility, for example, being that there is no such rank as captain in the RAF. But the fact remains that it *did* succeed in getting him onto a British airfield, where he all but took off in a Hurricane. The British, always taken by audacity, enterprise, and an engaging personality, were inclined to admire the exploit. As one of the Rolls-Royce officials remarked, "A lot of us sporting types were rather sorry he didn't make it!"

The five escapees, all of whom were caught within 24 hours, were each given 14 days of solitary confinement at Swanwick. Perhaps the mildness of the punishment was due to the fact that the commandant knew he would soon be rid of the lot. In any case, on the last morning of their sentence he announced that they would be sent to Canada the next day with a batch of other prisoners.

To Von Werra this simply meant another opportunity to escape, and Canada had the great advantage of being adjacent to the then *neutral* United States. From one of the other prisoners who knew something of the country, he began at once to learn all he could about Canadian geography and customs.

"I've got a feeling," he said, "—it's more than a feeling—in Canada I shall be lucky!"

When the *Duchess of York* sailed from Greenock, Scotland, on

January 10, 1941, with 1,050 prisoners aboard, Von Werra was kept under special guard until the moment of departure, an attention he found rather flattering. During the voyage he spent long periods immersed in a bathtub filled from a tap that ran ice-cold seawater. He wanted to harden himself, in case he got a chance to leap overboard when the ship landed.

No such opportunity occurred at Halifax, where the vessel put in on January 21, and he now looked hopefully at the train into which the prisoners were shepherded. In Von Werra's coach there were 35 prisoners and 12 guards. Three guards were on duty at a time, and they stood in the center aisle: one at each end of the car and one in the middle. The prisoners were escorted to the toilet one at a time, and the lavatory door was always kept wide open. There was ice between the coach's double windows, and they were presumably frozen shut. But the prisoners were forbidden to tamper with them in any case.

Meals were served at the seats. When the first steaming containers of food were brought around, the meal was unexpectedly luxurious after the sparse British fare—thick slices of salt pork, crisp fried potatoes, baked beans, bread, butter, canned fruit, and piping-hot *real* coffee. After they had eaten, many of the prisoners became benign and expansive and forgot their ambitious escape plans.

But Von Werra did not forget. When he learned that the train was bound for a camp in Ontario, on the shore of Lake Superior, he guessed that it would pass near the border. If he could escape in a reasonably settled section, he might be able to hitchhike to the United States in a day or so.

The only feasible way to get away was to dive out the window into the snow. This would be suicidal while the train was at full speed; yet it couldn't be done during a halt, for the guards were then particularly alert, and additional guards were posted outside the train. The best moment would be just following a halt, before the train had gathered speed; the best time, shortly before dawn.

While his seatmates watched the guards, Von Werra knelt down and managed to raise the inside window a quarter of an inch. The opening was hardly noticeable, but it allowed the car heat to reach the ice on the outer window. Eventually a thin trickle of water resulted. The melting was a slow business, however, and after 24 hours Von Werra managed to send word to the other prisoners to turn up all their heat regulators full blast.

But once the window was melted free, how was he to evade the scrutiny of the three guards to open it? And how was he to put on his overcoat? Von Werra knew he would need it in the freezing Canadian winter, but if he donned it in the superheated car he would certainly arouse instant suspicion.

An escapee must have luck, and luck now solved these problems for Von Werra.

At the evening meal that day the prisoners were given a whole case of apples. They were starved for fruit and ate the lot. But apples, following the unaccustomedly rich and plentiful food, proved too much for their systems. From midnight onward long lines waited to go to the toilet, and such was the emergency that some prisoners had to be escorted to the guards' toilet. The three guards on duty were highly amused. Their attention was diverted, and frequently there was only one guard left in the coach.

Despite the heat in the car, some of the sicker prisoners, white-faced and shivering, wrapped their coats or blankets about them and sat hugging their stomachs. Thus it seemed natural for Von Werra to put on his overcoat. Afterward he sat with his head in his hands in an attitude of misery.

As the train slowed for the next station, he waited for a signal that the guards were occupied, then stood up, unfolded his blanket, and shook it out. Concealed behind this, one of his companions knelt down and slid the inner window open wide.

During the station stop, the remaining ice on the outside window melted quickly. The conspicuously clear glass now constituted a danger, but fortunately none of the guards noticed the window. When the train started up, several prisoners raised their hands to go to the toilet. While one of his companions repeated the blanket maneuver, Von Werra stood up, gripped the outside window, and jerked upward. It did not move. He tried again. The window finally opened smoothly.

The next moment Von Werra dove through the window head first and landed dazed but exhilarated in the snow. The others were able to close both windows unobserved, and his escape was not discovered until the train was several hundred miles away.

According to the Canadian authorities, Von Werra escaped from the train south of Smiths Falls, Ontario, when he was only 30 miles from the border. Characteristically, Von Werra later told the New York reporters that he left the train 100 miles north of Ottawa—a location that gave him a lot more elbow room for recounting extravagant Canadian adventures. In view of his talent for lying, how he actually got to the border is hard to say.

Indisputably, however, at 7 P.M. on January 24 he did arrive at

Johnstown, on the north bank of the St. Lawrence, and saw the twin-kling lights of Ogdensburg, New York, beckoning from the other side. The river was frozen, and he hoped at first to cross it on the ice. But a quarter of a mile from the American shore he came on a chan-nel of black, open water.

He returned to the Canadian bank and walked along it until he came to a deserted summer camp. Here he eventually found what he was looking for, a long cigar-shaped mound in the snow. It was an overturned rowboat.

Using heavy wooden fence palings as levers, he laboriously prized it free from the ice and righted it. Then, exerting all his strength to push it, he inched the heavy boat across the ice to the open channel. He had no oars, but again luck was with him; the rowboat drifted smoothly to the American shore.

The instant it scraped the shore ice, Von Werra leaped out and ran up the riverbank. At the first road he saw a parked car bearing New York license plates. The driver, a nurse from a nearby hospital, was just preparing to start it.

"Excuse me," he asked anxiously. "Is this America?"

He wanted to make sure, for he knew that in some places the Canadian border extended well below the St. Lawrence.

"Yes. You are in Ogdensburg," the nurse replied.

He smiled wearily. "I am an officer of the German Air Force. I am—" he corrected himself—"I *was* a prisoner of war."

He was by no means safe yet. A German prisoner who had recently escaped into Minnesota had been jailed there for three months, then returned to Canada. Von Werra was saved from a similar fate by his flair for publicity.

When U.S. Immigration authorities took him into custody, charging him with illegal entry, the reporters and feature writers quickly besieged Von Werra. His boasting, exaggerations, and colorful inventions gave them plenty to write about. Much of the newspaper comment was caustic. As the Ogdensburg *Journal* wrote: "At his mass press conference he spun stories that would have amazed Horatio Alger, Joseph Conrad, or the author of the *Arabian Nights*." But the publicity given to him by the press, newsreels, and radio made his case an international issue.

The German consul, anxious to muzzle his embarrassing indiscretions, posted a $5,000 bond, spirited him away to New York City, and for a time saw that he was entertained royally at theaters, nightclubs, and social functions. In Germany the publicity given to his escape quickly elevated him to a national figure. Meanwhile, Canada had tried to have him arrested for the theft of the $35 rowboat. And Britain, well aware of the threat he offered to British security (since he had coped with the entire interrogation gamut), was also making every effort to extradite Von Werra. On March 24 German consular officials told him certain new moves in Washington made it likely that he would soon be handed back to Canada. He was to forfeit his bond, which had now been raised to $15,000, and leave the country illegally at once.

FBI men had been detailed to follow Von Werra's movements, but he eluded them by a series of taxicab changes, took a train for El Paso, and crossed the international bridge disguised as a Mexican laborer. The German Embassy in Mexico arranged a passport for him under an assumed name and secured air passage to Germany via Rio de Janeiro and Rome. He reached Berlin on April 18, 1941.

For security reasons, Von Werra's return was for a time kept secret, and there was no public adulation. But Reichsmarshal Goering promoted him to Hauptmann (captain), and Adolf Hitler personally congratulated him on his escape and awarded him the long-delayed Knight's Cross for his supposed earlier exploit. And there were many private parties and receptions.

Von Werra's escape had consequences out of all proportion to its significance as an individual feat of daring. He was attached to the intelligence branch of the German Air Force, and his report on British interrogation procedures, subsequently expanded into a 12-page booklet that became standard issue for all German aircrews, had an immediate effect. Thereafter the British found the German airmen they captured extremely security-conscious.

AT GRIZEDALE HALL and other camps Von Werra had zealously collected the interrogation experiences of other prisoners to add to his own and had discussed the matter with captured staff officers. They too had been impressed by British interrogation methods and agreed that they greatly menaced German security. To most German pilots, who were inclined to dismiss the British interrogators as "old women" and "desk warriors," betraying secrets meant giving away names, strengths, and locations of units, drawing maps of airfields, and revealing technical data. But they gave away information without ever realizing that they had done so, such was the skill of these "desk warriors." Von Werra had learned at first hand that there was no scrap of apparently trivial and irrelevant information that the RAF did not record and eventually fit into the picture and that the only defense against such skillful interrogation was "complete and persistent silence."

He reported, for example, that British interrogators showed an extraordinary interest in prisoners' Field Post numbers, often taking great pains to get this apparently harmless and useless information. When the Germans looked into the matter, they realized that the

British could deduce a prisoner's unit and its location from his Field Post number. The system of numbering was changed forthwith.

Von Werra also visited Dulag Luft, the German air interrogation center, with far-reaching consequences. The Germans had not yet appreciated the immense importance of interrogation as a source of military information, and when Von Werra sat in on some of their interrogations, he found them so superficial as to be almost farcical. "I would rather be interrogated by half a dozen German inquisitors than by one British expert," he reported. As a result of his visit, Dulag Luft adopted many of the British interrogation techniques.

When he made a tour of German prisoner-of-war camps to suggest antiescape measures and found conditions worse than he had enjoyed in England, Von Werra made a number of recommendations for improving the lot of British prisoners. A book that he wrote about his escape experiences was surprisingly friendly in tone and appreciative of the British. He could not resist improving on reality in the title, however. He called it *Meine Flucht aus England* ("My Escape From England"), though he had escaped from Canada; as it happened, no German prisoner ever succeeded in escaping from England during the war. The Propaganda Ministry banned the book's publication. It was considered pro-British.

Two weeks after Germany attacked Russia, Von Werra maneuvered to be sent to the front there. As commanding officer of the First Gruppe of No. 53 Fighter Geschwader—famous as the "Ace of Spades" Geschwader—he was credited with eight more air victories within a few weeks, bringing his supposed total to 21.

In September his Gruppe was moved to Holland and assigned to coastal defense patrol. On October 25, during a routine patrol, Von Werra's plane developed an engine fault and dropped into the sea. German newspapers announced that he had been killed in action. But the court of inquiry that investigated the loss of the aircraft attributed the accident to "engine failure and the pilot's carelessness."

The young Chinese couple had long planned to make their escape
across the bay from mainland China to the British
colony of Hong Kong. And once the swim had begun, there could
be no turning back—not even in the presence of death.

The Deadly Struggle

By Pan Wan-chuang

T HE NIGHT OF November 9, 1970, was made for escape. As Lau
Ping-sang and I slipped into the water at Sheh Hau on the coast
of Kwangtung province at midnight, Deep Bay was black, silent, and
still. We had succeeded in eluding the guards and police dogs. No
patrol boat was in sight.

Laufaushan, a town in the British colony of Hong Kong, was three
miles away on the opposite side of the bay. By swimming with the
tide, we expected to reach it in six hours. As we waded out from the
shore, the water was piercingly cold, but I did not mind. I was intent
upon finding freedom. Ping-sang and I, both 22, planned to be married and to live in Hong Kong.

Ping-sang shivered uncontrollably and complained of feeling faint.
He had rheumatism, and his back was extremely painful. Since slipping away from Changmutou and walking some 40 miles to the seacoast, we had scarcely slept in nine days and had eaten nothing for the
past 24 hours. Now he seemed near exhaustion.

"Just think of the hot noodles we'll eat when we get there!" I said,
urging him on.

After an hour of wading, the water became deep enough to swim.
We inflated our three rubber basketball bladders and tied them to our
backs. I had learned to swim after we decided to escape, so I had two.
Ping-sang, who was a good swimmer, had the other. I was counting
on him to pull me through.

We had been swimming for about an hour when Ping-sang called.
His voice sounded hollow.

"Let's turn back," he gasped. "I can't make it. I just can't make it."
In the darkness I heard the inchoate sounds that came from his lungs

as he gasped for breath. I unfastened the strings of my two basketball bladders and exchanged them for his.

He lunged at me with an arm and hung onto me so heavily that I was almost bearing his full weight. Thinking I could swim for two, I began to paddle. I knew we must make it. We had waited too long, planned too hard, for this escape to fail, and we would be caught and killed if we went back.

I WAS BORN in Canton, the third of four daughters. When the Communists came to power in 1949, they called my father, who had been a prosperous Canton businessman, a capitalist. They confiscated all his property and left us only a dilapidated three-story wooden house. When I was three, Father died. Mother rented two stories of the house, cut stencils, and did handiwork to support us.

The state had complete control of our lives. Every move we made was right or wrong according to government rules. We were entitled to no opinions. From schoolmates who had been permitted to visit their families in Hong Kong, we heard of how people lived there. How wonderful it would be, I thought, to be able to think, talk, read, and work as one pleased! One day, I promised myself, I would escape.

In 1964, when I was 16, I graduated from junior middle school, but failed to enter senior middle. I was permitted to stay home for a full year before being assigned to work at the Huang-kang Commune in Tung Kuan county.

The commune had some 10,000 people divided into production brigades, subdivided into village squads, teams, and again into mountain squads. Each squad had about 200 people.

As a member of a commune I had to obtain permission even to go home. There were some 800 youths, ranging in age from 16 to 22, "educated youth" who had failed to enter senior middle school or college, and "social youth," drifters who had earlier refused to accept posts assigned to them.

I worked from 6 A.M. to 6 P.M., with one hour's break, planting and harvesting rice, litchis, peanuts, and sugarcane. I also carried mud. I worked about 20 days a month to earn about $7. After buying my rice ration of 43½ catties (a catty equals about 1½ pounds), I had about $4 left to buy oil, salt, sugar, and sundries. Three girls and I lived in a house with the barest minimum of furniture and grew our own vegetables.

Six nights a week there were meetings at which the thoughts of Mao Tse-tung were discussed. I did not contribute much to the discussions and was harshly criticized for not being active enough.

I had been at the commune for three years when Lau Ping-sang arrived, after graduating from middle school. I first met him in the fields when I asked him for a drink of water. After that we began to see a lot of each other.

We were opposites—I was the outgoing one, talkative and impulsive. He was a good athlete, well built, and of medium height. He was always self-disciplined.

Once I "borrowed" a farmer's bicycle to go for a ride, intending to return it later. When Ping-sang heard of it, he was angry with me. Sometimes, if the mood overtook me, I skipped meals. He knew that I had a history of tuberculosis. "You must learn to be stern with yourself to achieve anything in life," he would say.

I don't remember when we realized we were in love. But like most of the young people at the commune, Ping-sang and I could see no future for ourselves.

In the spring of 1970, when we visited our families in Canton, we discussed the idea of escaping to Hong Kong in whispers with our relatives and won their approval. Back at the commune, on long bicycle rides, we made careful plans.

In September I told my squad leader that I was ill and asked for permission to go home. I was granted a leave of 10 days. When it was up, I wrote the squad leader that I had not recovered. Ping-sang also asked for sick leave. He was suffering from rheumatism and was granted 20 days.

Once in Canton, friends helped. One gave us a compass. Another produced the basketball bladders. Another found us a map. Food was hidden in the house of a schoolmate who came from a "correct" proletarian family and therefore was not likely to be searched. During these days of hushed preparation Ping-sang, who had won several swimming prizes, taught me to swim. If I got into trouble, he assured my mother, he would be there to help.

So as not to be seen leaving Canton together, we arranged to meet in Changmutou. On November 1, I bade my mother and my sisters good-bye and boarded the train.

Ping-sang was at the Changmutou station when the train arrived, and we quickly disappeared into the mountains. It was 25-odd miles to the coast by highway, but to avoid detection we zigzagged across the mountains, almost doubling the distance. We traveled mostly by night, hiding in the woods by day.

We avoided a number of the villages, but we also boldly walked through some of them. Ping-sang's back was giving him a lot of pain, but he seldom complained. On the fourth day we reached Poon, and on the evening of the eighth day we came to Highway No. 125 on the seacoast. The area was heavily guarded. Rather than risk it, we decided to travel six miles more to Sheh Hau, even though we had no food.

I had been towing Ping-sang for what must have been two hours. At first he paddled, too. Then he stopped. Several times he fainted. Suddenly he put up a fierce resistance.

"You can't make it this way!" he gasped. "Leave me. Go on alone."

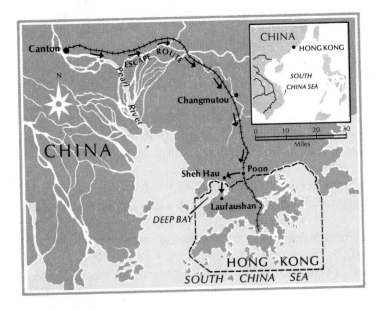

He wrenched himself from my grasp, gulping seawater as he went under. He was drowning himself!

I fought with him; I pleaded and pulled and kicked and clawed, but in the darkness it was like trying to fight a sea monster. I searched wildly for lights, hoping that even a Communist boat would detect us, but there was nothing. Again and again he slipped away and went under. How long this went on I do not know. Just as abruptly as it began, it stopped.

Ping-sang was prefectly still. He was dead.

I began to swim again, holding onto him by the strings that secured the bladders, paddling now with this arm, now with that. Now that I did not have to keep his head above water, the going got easier.

I lost track of time. It seemed like the longest night anyone ever lived and that I was the only person left in the world. I kept wondering if I was swimming in the right direction.

When I felt I was ready to collapse with exhaustion, I thought of all the hard times we had endured at the commune. Ping-sang had said that I must be stern with myself. His words exploded in my mind. I could yield to fatigue and fear, or I could try to make it to Hong Kong. *The choice was mine.*

Later, I do not know how much later, I saw three lights glimmering in the distance! Strength flooded back into me. I headed toward them, knowing no fatigue, feeling no weight, unthinking now. At last I saw that longed-for shore, limned as if by a ghost's brush against the paling sky. It was no longer the dream so often dreamed. I was seeing it with my own eyes.

Somewhere in the water was the dividing line between freedom and oppression, but Communist boats plied both sides of it. The bay was coming to life. I must be careful. I kept my head as low as possible, trying to appear like a piece of flotsam. Now I saw the little brown village nestled between the hills. The water was murky where Pearl River emptied into the sea.

I was only a few hundred yards away when a cramp developed in my leg. I could not move. Looking about desperately, I saw a pair of launches standing still. I dared not cry for help, but it was not long before one of them—belonging to the Hong Kong Marine Police—steamed toward me, and then I saw another launch manned by Communist militiamen.

Before the Communists saw me, the Hong Kong police fished me out of the sea and were helping me aboard.

"Wait!" I cried. "There is somebody else."

I raised my hand to show them the strings I was holding. They pulled Ping-sang's body aboard. We had made it together.

When we buried Ping-sang a few days later, someone asked me, "Why did you tow his body in the water for six hours? Wouldn't it have been easier for you to have continued alone?"

"Why, I couldn't leave him behind," I said. "I didn't want his body to be washed back to the China coast. If he couldn't make it alive, at least he could be buried in free soil!"

One of the greatest mass escapes in history took place in 1940. A third of a million Allied soldiers evaded a German trap on the coast of France and crossed the English Channel to safety.

The Sands of Dunkirk

By Richard Collier

IT WAS strangely silent as night came to northern France. Across the checkerboard of flat green fields and dark canals only a few sounds came faintly: the barking of hungry dogs and the lowing of unmilked cows, whose owners had already fled south. For a vast military disaster was in the making. The British, French, and Belgian Armies, deployed along a 150-mile front curving inward from the English Channel, had been surrounded and trapped by the Germans. And the exhausted troops, driven steadily back by enemy Panzers, now gripped their rifles and waited in silent fear.

Retreat was inevitable. Indeed, that very morning—it was Sunday, May 26, 1940—Anthony Eden, the Secretary for War, had authorized a complete British withdrawal to the coast. But was a successful retreat possible? General the Viscount Gort, the burly, plain-spoken commander in chief of the British Expeditionary Force, had doubts. "I must not conceal from you that a great part of the BEF and its

equipment will inevitably be lost in the best of circumstances," he cabled Eden. Then, because his whole life was the army, he turned to an aide and in a rare moment of self-revelation confided: "You know, the day I joined up I never thought I'd lead the British Army to its biggest defeat in history!"

The prospect of defeat had come with puzzling and terrifying suddenness. For eight months many of the 390,000 men of Lord Gort's army had had the time of their lives. Secure in the illusion that the 250-mile-long Maginot Line to the south was impregnable, they had built 400-odd concrete pillboxes, dug World War I-type slit trenches and antitank ditches, and waited for the Germans to attack. At night, during the long months of this "phony war," they drank and sang in 10,000 village cafés and made friends with the local girls. And the Germans encouraged this lightheartedness. When Lille housewives complained in a French newspaper that they could no longer obtain cosmetics, the Germans answered with a two-bomber raid—bombarding the town with face powder and vials of perfume.

Then suddenly, on May 10, World War II had erupted in deadly earnest. Ten German armored divisions and 117 infantry divisions smashed into neutral Holland, then made a wide sweep into neutral Belgium and Luxembourg. Soon after, seven tank divisions speared through the French Army at Sedan, moving easily through the hilly Ardennes Forest, a gap in the Allied defenses that the experts had believed impassable.

British troops rushed to the rescue, crossing Belgium with lilac blooms in their helmets and marching triumphantly to Brussels. Gort had been confident that his men would accomplish great things. But the campaign soon turned into a nightmare, and the Allied position was now desperate.

Both the English and the French had been equipped to refight World War I. Against the Germans' 2,700 modern tanks Gort could marshal only such lumbering, heavily armored tanks as the "Matilda," which carried a frail two-pounder gun. The French tanks also moved clumsily, were geared to infantry support, and often ran short of fuel during battle. British artillery was so outclassed that General Gort's best guns had little more than half the range of the latest German models.

In 10 days the Germans overran three-fourths of Belgium, and the Belgian Army, equipped with rusty rifles and horse-drawn cannon, began to crack. German tanks raced across France to the Channel and were now attacking the port of Calais.

Gort's only hope of escape lay in the port of Dunkirk. To reach it, he would have to fight down a corridor 50 miles long and 15 miles wide. And the odds were grim that more than 300,000 soldiers, the flower of the British Army, would be prisoners by the week's end.

But few knew this yet, and British units posting their sentries in a hundred vehicle parks and market towns and châteaus could only hope the top brass knew what they were about. "This is Mons all over again," a veteran assured Lance Cpl. Thomas Nicholls, a young anti-tank gunner defending Wormhout. "We're forming a thin red line to throw them out."

But at Ypres, when Maj. Cyril Huddlestone of the 4th East Yorks opened a War Office telegram routed to all units and read, "We are holding a National Day of Prayer for you," he snorted and crumpled it into his pocket. "Why don't they send us some 25-pounders instead?" he asked angrily.

South of Houthem, where the 43rd Light Infantry was bivouacked, Lance Cpl. John Linton, a regular of 11 years' standing, ignored personal fatigue and officers' orders in his efforts to protect his men. His unit, alternately digging in to fight desperately, then pulling out in haste, had retreated all the way from Brussels. And at each stop the officers issued the same grim warning: "All stragglers and wounded must be left behind. The Germans are on our heels."

When Private Curtis doubled up with appendicitis on the march, and the men grumbled that the dead weight of carrying him was too much, Linton said in his soft West Country accent, "All right, we'll leave him here." Then his voice hardened, and he looked every man straight in the eyes. "But *who's* going to do it? *Who'll* be the one to leave him behind, eh?"

And they shouldered Curtis anew, bound for the baggage truck that eventually carried him to England and safety.

Late Sunday night Capt. Harry Smith, stationed on the outskirts of Roncq, abruptly roused his East Surreys from sleep—for word of the disaster was spreading rapidly now. "We are making a general retreat to the coast," he announced when they had shuffled into an uneasy company parade. "The idea is to get back to England so we can return to France later."

To Pvt. Bill Hersey the news was spine-chilling. The instant the company was dismissed, he approached Captain Smith. "Sir," he asked, "is there anything you can do for my wife?"

The answer was succinct. "Go and get her."

Grabbing a bicycle, Bill Hersey pedaled for Tourcoing, two miles away, for his young French bride of 39 days. Their wildly improbable romance had started when Bill entered the Café l'Epi d'Or one quiet day during the "phony war." He had burned his hand on a camp stove, and when the proprietor saw the wound, he insisted that his daughter attend to it. Was not Augusta learning first aid and in need of practice?

Augusta's methods had seemed a shade primitive, for the alcohol she splashed on the burn sent Hersey leaping for the ceiling. Yet somehow, after that first meeting, Bill found that his wound needed dressing at least once a day.

Augusta spoke not a word of English, but Bill launched into a whirlwind courtship with the aid of a pocket dictionary. A handsome, devil-may-care regular who had soldiered all over India and spent many nights in the guardhouse, he secretly yearned for a wife and home. Soon he and Augusta fell deeply in love.

One night Bill went to Augusta's father, pointed to the word *marriage* in the dictionary, and said simply, "Your daughter."

Papa exploded. "He is no good, that fellow," he roared at Augusta. "He spends too much on cognac!"

"He'll change," Augusta said confidently.

The local clergy, too, had disapproved, but the priest from Bill's brigade interceded for the two young lovers, and Augusta and Bill were married on April 17.

And, strangely, the marriage seemed right from the start. The newlyweds shared warm moments at the café with Bill's friends: songs, quiet games of cards, and evenings on the café rifle range, locals versus troops, with Augusta handling her .22 as gamely as any man.

But now, pedaling furiously toward the café, Bill knew that those carefree evenings were ended. For the past two weeks they had been separated by the sudden, stunning war, and in the last 10 days he had fought through the exhausting retreat from Brussels. Tonight his one thought was to get Augusta safely away to England. At 11:30 P.M. he reached the café and knocked thunderously.

When Augusta opened the door and saw her husband's face, she knew immediately why he had come. "Get your things," he greeted her. "You're leaving."

Augusta swiftly dressed and packed a suitcase. Her father had already gone south to find safer quarters for his family, and her mother was too distressed to speak when Augusta wakened her to say goodbye. But when Bill Hersey urged, "Augusta is British now; only this way can she be safe," she seemed to understand.

"Dépêchez, dépêchez" ("Hurry, hurry"), Bill kept imploring as Augusta wheeled out her bicycle. It was a night for speed. Machine guns hammered faintly in the east, and sappers were laying mines by the roadside as they pedaled to Roncq. Transport was already moving off there, and Captain Smith made a quick decision. "Your wife can go with the driver in my truck," he told Hersey. "But first you had better get her fitted out."

Bill, a company storeman, outfitted Augusta as a British Tommy— rifle, steel helmet, khaki greatcoat. Then she climbed into the truck, and the captain signaled them off. For Hersey, who would be marching, the strangeness of it all almost numbed the pang of parting.

ACROSS THE CHANNEL, in an office carved into the damp chalk cliffs 500 feet above the sea, Adm. Sir Bertram Home Ramsay, flag officer commanding Dover, studied a nightmare assignment. Operation Dynamo, the evacuation of British troops from France, seemed to the aloof, silver-haired admiral to offer little chance of success.

Dunkirk, the one remaining bolt-hole in British hands, had already been bombed for a week by the Luftwaffe, and the fine harbor that had made it France's third port was now useless. The 25 miles of tortuous, shoal-ridden coast, known as "the graveyard of ships," was unapproachable with heavy craft, which meant that the evacuation would have to be a small-ship affair.

Quietly, clinically, Ramsay chewed it over with Capt. William Tennant, newly appointed senior naval officer at Dunkirk. Only 40 destroyers were now left from the 202 the navy had begun the war with; moreover, these slim, whippet-like vessels, crammed with guns and depth-charge racks, were not built to carry men. Thus the bulk of the lifting would have to fall on lightly armed merchant ships— coasters, cross-Channel ferries, flat-bottom Dutch barges. But only 129 such vessels were available on this warm May morning, though more were on the way from a score of ports.

To conduct the evacuation—which would continue for as long as Gort's men could hold off the Germans—the taciturn Tennant would be assisted by 12 naval officers and 150 ratings. Few on the ships knew about the project, but all through the navy there was a tingle of expectancy. If something strange was afoot, the navy was ready and waiting for it to happen.

Some learned the news in devious ways. CPO Wilfred Walters, summoned from a pub in North Shields on the Tyne and now en route for Harwich in the old coal-burning minesweeper *Ross*, had the romantic notion that they were speeding to the rescue of the Dutch royal family. Lt. Victor de Mauny, skipper of the contraband-control vessel *Ocean Breeze,* thought his mission was concerned with Belgian refugees—until, as he was having breakfast in the shore naval base at Ramsgate, a Scots Guard officer put him right with a withering: "Refugees? Good God, it isn't refugees—it's the BEF!"

Nobody hoped for too much from the operation. As Tennant left Ramsay's office, the admiral almost casually added one last word: At the most, Tennant and his staff could expect to bring off 45,000 men.

That any BEF troops whatever could be evacuated was amazing, for Dunkirk was held only because of an almost inexplicable turn in German strategy. On May 23, when the German tanks had come within 12 miles of Dunkirk, Gen. Gerd von Rundstedt issued a routine command: "Halt at the line of the Aa Canal and close up."

Unlike such dashing Panzer leaders as Rommel, Rundstedt, a cautious 65-year-old patrician, distrusted the new concept of independent tank warfare. Time and again in the Ardennes campaign he had clamped down brief "halt" orders, lest the tanks too far outrun the infantry, leaving a long, exposed flank. But on this occasion Hitler visited Rundstedt's headquarters, discussed the situation, then made the halt permanent. The tanks were to go no farther toward Dunkirk. The marshy Flanders plain was not tank country, Hitler said. The Panzers might bog down and endanger his plan for a Panzer strike into the heart of France.

"I believe we will soon come to an agreement with Great Britain," he had told Rundstedt a week earlier. And after an impassioned eulogy on the British Empire he had added, *"She* should rule the globe and the seas. I should rule Europe."

This story, quickly circulated among the generals, led Gen. Hans Jeschonnek, chief of staff to the Luftwaffe, to remark cynically: "Hitler has withheld the tanks from Dunkirk to save the British from a shameful defeat."

Perhaps Hitler's decision had been influenced by Hermann Goering, the vainglorious commander in chief of the Luftwaffe. When he heard the tanks were almost at Dunkirk, Goering pounded the table and cried: "I must talk to the Fuehrer immediately. This is a special job for the Luftwaffe."

He put through a telephone call, and within minutes Hitler agreed. Dunkirk should be left to the Luftwaffe.

The top German brass protested vigorously from every side. "But it's essential the tanks attack at once!" Gen. Fedor von Bock said angrily. "If Dunkirk isn't taken, the British can transport their army wherever they like."

"What is the meaning of this insane order?" General Greiffenberg, of Hitler's operations staff, said angrily. "Are we building golden bridges for the British?"

Field Marshal Albert Kesselring, chief of Air Fleet Two, telephoned Goering from Brussels to protest. Surely Goering realized that three weeks of air war had reduced some Luftwaffe units by 50 percent? That most available bombers were still based at airfields 300

miles from Dunkirk? When Hermann Goering remained adamant, Kesselring slammed down the telephone with a curt *"Nicht lösbar"* ("It won't work").

For three days the argument raged, while the British reorganized and regrouped their forces to defend the port. By Monday, May 27, Hitler had agreed to a limited use of tanks in the area, but they were still to bypass the port. Dunkirk remained the Luftwaffe's job.

Whatever their plight—and alarming rumors now sped along 100 miles of front—the British stubbornly refused to panic.

The units holding the perimeter fought with indifference to the odds. On the high ground above La Bassée Canal the Queen's Own Cameron Highlanders were almost surrounded and during two days faced the impossible task of stopping the 400 tanks of Rommel's 7th and 8th Panzer Divisons. But a battalion that had defied Gort himself would never yield to Germans. (Months ago General Gort had ordered the Highlanders not to wear kilts on active service; they were still wearing them.)

From his headquarters in a farmhouse cellar, Lt. Col. Peter Rose-Miller had telephoned in vain for artillery support and antitank guns. None was to be had. Then suddenly, watching the 400 tanks massed on the plain below him, Rose-Miller had a brainstorm. Summoning a score of sharpshooters, he ordered, "If you see a black hole, fire at it." To another group he passed out grenades with the advice: "Go out and see how many tanks you can bag!"

The results were better than he could have dreamed. When the tanks moved up, the Highlanders aimed for the black slits. As bullets whanged home, tank commander after tank commander shut down his periscope and visor. Shorn of vision, the tanks lurched drunkenly, and even a gunner seeking a breath of air risked a hastily lobbed grenade through the gun turret. "Prospects did not look good for an attack across the canal," Rommel later wrote. "The situation was extremely critical."

For 36 hours Rose-Miller fought a delaying action before the Panzers finally broke through and began to burn the roof of the farmhouse over his head. Rose-Miller, who had already seen his wounded out, then scrambled from his smoke-filled cellar, dived headfirst into the canal just as a tank closed in on him, and emerged triumphantly on the other side to fight again. His kilted Cameron Highlanders had cost Rommel 21 tanks.

Captain Tennant eventually set out for Dunkirk late Monday afternoon, May 27, on the destroyer *Wolfhound.* The ship had barely cleared Dover when she was attacked from the air, and for two hours, while her ack-ack guns pounded, she swerved almost continuously to dodge the rain of bombs.

As Dunkirk came in view, Tennant's heart sank. Never in his wildest dreams had he imagined such havoc. Black smoke from burning oil refineries enveloped the harbor, and the miles of warehouses and quays seemed on fire from end to end. In the sky above, dive bombers wheeled and turned, and bombs screamed down incessantly. Even as they watched, a stick of bombs fell beside the nearest quay with hammer blows, sending concrete and white water high in the air.

It was just 6 P.M. when Tennant landed and took swift stock of the situation. It was appalling. For four days there had been no water supply in Dunkirk. Only one telephone link remained open to London. Through an error in interpreting orders, 100-odd heavy antiair-craft guns had been destroyed, leaving almost no defense against planes. And on that Monday alone 30,000 incendiaries and 15,000 high-explosive bombs had been dropped. The 115 acres of docks and 5 miles of quays were reduced to rubble, and in the ruins of the town 1,000 men, women, and children lay dead.

Tennant gave crisp orders to his staff. The troops were to line up on the dunes and advance to the water's edge in groups of 50. No man was to embark without arms. The Admiralty's last order had been: "Mind you bring back the guns." If Britain itself was to be the last line of defense, even rifles might soon be at a premium.

Aside from the beaches, which lay open to the roaring northern winds, the sole remaining embarkation facilities were the east and west moles—long wooden gangways merging into solid concrete sub-structures that thrust 1,400 yards into the roadstead. These had been erected to protect the harbor and were not designed for berthing ships. At this season a surging three-knot tide raced between the concrete piles and made it extremely difficult for even the most ex-perienced seamen to bring craft alongside.

Later that evening Tennant saw that at low tide the Channel waters had receded a full half mile. Medical corpsmen, stretchers lifted head high, were struggling toward two solitary lifeboats that had been rowed within 100 yards of the shore. The parent ships were merely dark specks a mile offshore, and every lifeboat that rowed in would face a backbreaking 20-minute pull and could load, at most, 25 men.

With two of his staff Tennant thoughtfully tramped to the east mole. "It would certainly be quicker," he said, "if only we could get a ship alongside."

For a grim moment he considered the alternatives. "We'll try it," he announced. "Signal the nearest ship to come in."

As the *Queen of the Channel* responded, cutting a path toward them, the minutes seemed to crawl. First the bow had to be nosed in gingerly. Next a head rope was made fast. Then, as Tennant watched tensely, the ship's stern swung around against the pier. Minutes later she was secure fore and aft, and men were filing aboard.

Tennant breathed a sigh of relief. At least it *could* be done—with some sort of luck.

During that first experimental day, it was later established, 7,669 men were safely transported to England.

At 11 P.M. that Monday night General Gort, conferring in Bastion 32, received the disturbing news that Belgium had capitulated. King

Leopold had asked for an armistice, to begin at midnight. Now for 20 miles the whole left flank of the British Army lay open to the sea. Gort sat quite still, palms outspread on the table, staring into space.

The gap in the Allied lines was disastrous. But as Gort hastily set about closing it, his bright blue eyes were shining. He reacted to danger and the prospect of battle like a cavalry charger responding to the call of the bugle.

No news of the Belgian surrender reached Pvt. Bill Hersey's wife, Augusta, that night, yet somehow she had known. A French liaison

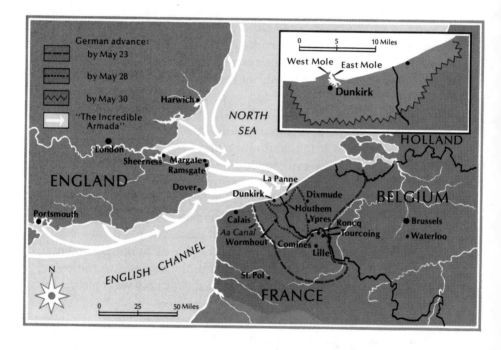

officer had sought shelter for her in a farmhouse east of Dixmude. But all his pleadings had not softened the Belgian farmer's heart; he had no beds for the British and their kind. Augusta had settled for a heap of dry straw in the farmyard. Next morning when she and driver Johnson sought to quench their thirst, they found that the farmer had locked the well.

Augusta understood his hostility. Being a Frenchwoman, she knew better than most the anguish that had befallen the land. Two weeks earlier the Belgians had pressed wine and flowers on the British, and priests had blessed the army as it streamed past. But now the liberators were pulling out, Belgium had surrendered, and for the second time in their lives these people were to be overrun by the Germans.

Sudden despairing signs of defeat were everywhere: white flags flapping from soldiers' bayonets; white sheets hanging from the windows of houses until it resembled washday; a Belgian general in a car, hastily changing to civilian clothes. And every village gave the British the same bitter, hostile glances.

Many Belgians took flight before the Germans. From Lille onward that Tuesday, May 28, some 800,000 refugees choked the roads in a chaotic cavalcade. Amid the confusion, rumors swept the countryside: English-speaking Germans dressed as officers were infiltrating the lines to misdirect convoys and spread panic. Near Dixmude an order from Divisional Headquarters warned that German parachutists were plummeting from the sky dressed as nuns.

Gunner William Brewer had dismissed all this as the tallest of tales. But when he and four mates were drinking tea near a farmhouse, Bombardier "Geordie" Allen ran up to them. "Did you ever see a nun shaving?" Geordie gasped. Stealing across the pasture, the party saw two German paratroopers, white coifs discarded, crucifixes dangling, shaving behind a haystack. Seconds later the "nuns" fell, riddled with rifle fire.

It was a day when it seemed the world had gone mad, and yet thousands of soldiers, torn by pity for the refugees, set aside their own troubles to help out. One staff sergeant stood by a roadside for hours, offering freshly brewed buckets of tea to the fleeing throngs. A nurse orderly emptied his field ambulance of almost all the bandages, ointment, and tinned milk it possessed. A chaplain, carrying bread supplies to the 6th Lincolns, found he couldn't resist the hunger in the people's eyes or the children's haunting cries. Although the unit hadn't seen bread in days, he doled out all 50 loaves.

For every man, pity took on a different guise. For some it was the dogs—homeless, shivering with fear, tagging onto any Tommy too merciful to shoo them away. To Lt. Gen. Alan Brooke, driving in his staff car along the Ypres-Comines line, it was the vacant smiles of lunatics freed from asylums, thronging the roadside.

IN LONDON there was no escaping the facts. On Tuesday at 2:45 P.M., packed tensely on the benches of the House of Commons, 600 Members of Parliament heard out Prime Minister Winston Churchill in shocked silence: Following a brave, unequal struggle, the Belgians had thrown in their hand. "Meanwhile," Churchill warned, "the

House should prepare itself for hard and heavy tidings. . . ." In just four minutes he had given them the worst.

Later, in the long Cabinet Room at 10 Downing Street, he called in 25 Ministers and told them plainly how bitter the future might be. Almost casually, he concluded with: "Of course, whatever happens at Dunkirk, we shall fight on."

There was a split second's silence. Then, to the old bulldog's astonishment, there were cheers. The 25 sober politicians were cheering as one, some pounding the table with their fists, others leaping up to slap Churchill on the back. The long room rang with their loyalty.

Although dozens of ships had now brought off grimy survivors from Dunkirk, the process was far too slow. The east mole could berth only 16 vessels at top high water, and Captain Tennant sent word to Admiral Ramsay that the crying need was for small ships—motorboats, whalers, lifeboats, any craft capable of inshore ferrying.

Ramsay called Rear Adm. Tom Phillips, vice chief of naval staff, then handed the telephone to Tennant's emissary, Capt. Eric Bush. "Here," he said, "you tell him."

Phillips listened to Bush for a time and then asked, "Well, how many small boats *do* you want? A hundred?"

To Bush it didn't seem that anyone as yet appreciated the full gravity of the situation. His voice tight with emotion, he answered, "Look, sir, not a hundred boats—*every* boat that can be found in the country should be sent if we're even to stand a chance!"

The Admiralty, which had already begun a register of privately owned craft two weeks earlier, agreed to call on every available small boat in England.

Meanwhile, Britain's finest troops were battling to hold the perimeter of the escape route open. The 3rd Grenadiers, after repulsing one German attack after another, were almost out of ammunition. When Capt. Stanton Starkey, head of one of the forward companies, opened the last ammo boxes available, an eerie chill settled over his men. The boxes contained Very signal lights.

But Starkey had noted one salient fact: The Germans were attacking by a rigid pattern. To keep the Grenadiers pinned down, they first called for a withering mortar barrage, signaled by a red-white-red Very light. Then another Very cartridge signaled the barrage to stop so the infantry could advance.

Starkey resolved on a last fling of the dice. When the German infantry again surged forward, he raised his pistol and sent a red-white-red pattern into the night sky. German mortar shells showered down on the German assault troops, throwing them into confusion.

From the German forward positions an imploring "stop" signal went soaring, and within seconds the barrage died. Recovering, the infantry once more moved forward. Again Starkey fired his Very pistol, signaling a mortar barrage.

Now, as the Germans strove to countermand the order, red and white signals spangled the sky. But as Starkey kept firing, the Ger-

mans gave up. Abruptly the mortaring ceased. For the moment the Ypres-Comines line was secure.

And on that Tuesday, the second day of the evacuation, 17,804 troops were lifted from Dunkirk.

Casualties in ships and men were already mounting. Consider the case of the destroyer H.M.S. *Wakeful.*

A cramped, fusty, 23-year-old war-horse built for a bygone age, the *Wakeful* had jettisoned all her torpedoes and depth charges in order to pack in more troops. On her first trip she delivered 600 men to Dover. Then, without waiting to refuel, she set off again within the hour, dodging some 70 bombs on the trip back to Dunkirk.

At 12:30 A.M. Wednesday the *Wakeful* was returning to England with 640 more soldiers aboard, churning on through the darkness as Capt. Ralph Fisher watched anxiously from the bridge. Admiral Ramsay had warned that the waters were now menaced by both U-boats and German destroyers, and for greater maneuverability Fisher had ordered all troops below decks.

Suddenly there were two light streaks in the water, coming straight toward the ship. "Hard-a-port!" Fisher yelled.

But it was too late. A torpedo struck *Wakeful* square amidships. With a rending of tortured ironwork, the old destroyer broke clean in two—bow and stern canting upward in the water like the twin peaks of a skyscraper.

The troops on board never stood a chance. More than 600 of them were trapped below decks, though it was to be hours before their agony was over. But Captain Fisher and other survivors were picked up by the Scottish drifter *Comfort*, and still others by the minesweeper *Gossamer*.

These two ships were joined by the destroyer *Grafton* and the minesweeper *Lydd*. At 2:50 A.M., however, two torpedoes struck the *Grafton*. The ship failed to sink, although one of the torpedoes, slicing through the wardroom, killed 35 officers.

Confusion was now complete, and in the chill darkness the *Lydd* opened fire on what appeared to be a German motor torpedo boat. The *Grafton*'s guns joined in, too, her crewmen cheering, convinced they were firing at *Wakeful*'s killer. But it was a tragic error—both were firing on the *Comfort*.

For the *Wakeful* survivors still below decks on *Comfort*, it was a moment of pure horror. Naked, their clothes still drying in the galley, they fled to the upper deck only to meet a fusillade of bullets. Frantically, Fisher yelled, "For God's sake, stop—we're all British!"

But no one heard. With a spine-jarring crash, *Lydd* rammed into the *Comfort*. It was only when her crew swarmed aboard to take prisoners—and found only two survivors—that they realized fully the enormity of their mistake.

A few hours later the tragedy was completed. En route for Dunkirk, the chief petty officer aboard H.M.S. *Ross* felt his spine prickle with horror. Out of the early-morning mist, like some grotesque leviathan, loomed the bow and stern of the *Wakeful*. From somewhere inside the hull came the unearthly cries of hopelessly trapped men.

A shocked moment passed. Then, quietly, Comdr. James Follington Apps addressed the *Ross*'s gun crew. His import was crystal clear. "I'm not giving any orders," he said, "but if a gun goes off by accident I shan't say anything about it."

Briefly, as the merciful guns blazed out, the echoes beat like thunder from the sky. Then, with a last flurry of bubbles, the destroyer *Wakeful* slid from sight.

In the last predawn darkness on Wednesday morning Capt. Eric Bush, having made his plea for small ships, returned to the evacuation area on the minesweeper *Hebe*. In the waters off La Panne—where Gort had established his headquarters, nine miles up the coast from Dunkirk—he sensed something strange about the beaches.

"What do you make of those dark shadows over there?" he asked Lt. Comdr. John Temple. For the dawn mists made it hard to see.

"I can't think what it might be, sir," Temple said, "unless it's shadows thrown by clouds."

But the sky was perfectly clear. Then the mists parted, the appalling truth became apparent, and the two men caught their breaths in awe. "By God," Captain Bush exclaimed, "it's soldiers!"

In huge dense squads they blocked the beaches, long queues of them winding like black serpents from the sandhills. Every few yards of the nine-mile stretch from La Panne to Dunkirk, piers seemed to jut a long way out into the sea—human piers, the front ranks up to their necks in the chill, gray water, patiently waiting for boats.

And more were coming, as Bush presently discovered—thousands more, streaming across the countryside toward Dunkirk, in the strangest retreat a modern army ever made. Some came on scooters and children's bicycles; some pushed their wounded in wheelbarrows. A sergeant rode on an enormous white hunter. A bombardier drove a tractor, towing a gun. One group journeyed in a Brussels garbage truck. "Make for the black smoke," they were instructed if they should lose the way; for the fiery destruction that was Dunkirk was visible almost 30 miles away.

One thought sustained them all: If they made it to Dunkirk, the navy would see them through.

To Captain Tennant's staff the tempo of the evacuation seemed maddeningly slow. At the east mole a 15-foot tide made it difficult to board ships at top speed, and a heavy surf thwarted loadings on the beach. By Wednesday afternoon 11 ships lay at the east mole's seaward end, and the inshore waters swarmed with destroyers, ferry-boats, and other craft. The weather was crystal clear, and the whole situation an invitation to General the Baron von Richthofen, who commanded a force of 180 Stuka dive bombers from his farmhouse headquarters near St. Pol, 50 miles away.

It was close to 4 P.M. when the attack came. The skies to the west seemed to darken, and within minutes the first wave of Stukas swelled into an inky cloud. Richthofen had rigged both the airplanes and their bombs with toy whistles, and as the bombers came hurtling lower and lower, their shrill screaming chilled the blood of the men on the beaches. In a long plummeting dive they fanned out over the harbor, over the nine miles of water between Dunkirk and La Panne.

The outnumbered Royal Air Force, though valiant in its attempts to provide air cover for the beleaguered British Army, had not yet learned to cope with Luftwaffe tactics, and the tightly packed ships at the east mole didn't stand a chance. As long as a boat remained afloat, however, the tired troops continued to file aboard in bold defiance of the bombs. From the personnel ship *Canterbury* Capt. Bernard Lockey watched them closing up their ranks, while man after man was blown to bits.

Close by, some Stukas dove for the destroyer *Grenade*. Three screeching bombs plunged home, one plummeting down her funnel, to leave the sailors floundering in a slippery film of blood and oil on her decks. Then, blazing like a pine brand from stem to stern, the *Grenade* swung slowly into the fairway out of control. For seconds it seemed certain the destroyer would sink, blocking the entrance to the harbor and bringing the entire evacuation to a standstill.

Comdr. Jack Clouston shouted for a trawler to take the destroyer in tow, and slowly the stricken ship was pulled clear of the fairway. The next instant her magazine ignited, and with a violence few men have ever witnessed, 1,000 rounds of ammunition went sky-high.

On the beaches vast columns of water geysered 100 feet skyward, as the Stukas pressed home their screaming attack. Tons of sand quaked, smothering those whose foxholes were too deep. An inferno of flame presently enveloped the harbor; molten metal dripped from buckled cranes. And as German fighters zoomed low, their machine guns firing, the bodies of dead men floated everywhere in the waters.

But for many the most harrowing sight was the bombed, blazing paddle steamer *Crested Eagle,* her plates glaring red-hot, her deck beams rising like a turtle's back in the heat. Thousands on shore stood aghast as her crewmen—on fire from head to toe—danced like dervishes, screaming and leaping into the sea.

Aboard the *Oriole* in the harbor Lt. Edwin Lacey Davies made a swift decision. The troops he saw massed along the beach needed a pier. But the only pier at Davies' disposal was his 432-ton *Oriole,* an old paddle steamer that had been converted to a minesweeper.

"There's only one thing to do," Davies told his sublieutenant. "I'm going to ground her until the next high water. Then others can send their boats to *me.* " Slowly, Davies brought *Oriole*'s head around until she faced the beach. Then, her paddles churning the water to froth, she roared toward the shore and jarred to a stop.

It was a gallant gesture. All that afternoon more than 2,500 troops scrambled over *Oriole*'s decking into the safety of other ships' whalers and lifeboats. And although the Luftwaffe kept pounding, not one bomb struck her.

At the next floodtide, with 600 troops aboard, the *Oriole* was again steaming for England, where Davies wrote a terse report to Admiral Ramsay: "Deliberately grounded H.M.S. *Oriole.* Objective: speedy evacuation of troops. Refloated; no apparent damage. Will again run aground if such course seems desirable."

Ramsay's reply summed up the whole spirit of Dunkirk: "Action fully approved!" And despite the Stuka attack, 47,310 troops were carried to England that Wednesday. This was more than the navy had expected to rescue altogether, and the cumulative total now amounted to 72,783 men.

Adm. Jean Abrial, the French commander at Dunkirk, had thought all along the British were pulling out only their nonessential troops. But on Thursday, the fourth day of the evacuation, the truth struck him with stunning impact: Gort's army was quitting en masse. Outraged, Abrial demanded an explanation. (Under the Allied setup Lord Gort was technically subordinate to the French high command.)

Gort replied bluntly that this was a matter for the French and British governments to unravel between them. This attitude so enraged Abrial that he later threatened to close the entire port and if necessary to place Gort under arrest. "Who does this Lord Gort think he is?" the admiral burst out to Capt. Harold Henderson, the British naval liaison officer.

Beseeching the admiral not to do anything hasty, Henderson immediately called Admiral Ramsay in Dover. "Look," he pleaded, "the evacuation has been going on for days, and nobody has told the French admiral a thing." Then he added a vital point: Not only should Abrial's government bring him up to date, but the French soldiers must have an equal chance to get away. Instantly, Admiral Ramsay agreed, promising to take up the matter personally with Winston Churchill.

Henderson felt better when he hung up. The evacuation was to proceed—British side by side with the French—though he would never forget Admiral Abrial's pained rebuke: "You owe loyalty to your country; yet you are a member of my staff. Couldn't you have summoned enough loyalty to let *me* know what was going on?"

But for Gort, immersed in the hour-by-hour crisis of commanding a beaten army, there was no question about where his first loyalty lay. So far, the fierce fighting of his front-line troops had kept the Germans from cutting off the retreat. Today almost 200,000 men were within the Dunkirk bridgehead—50,000 of them ready to embark—and, whatever their fate, Gort meant to share it.

"You can tell them back in England that nothing on God's earth will make me come home," he had warned his young aide, Captain the Viscount, Lord Munster, who had sailed for Dover the night before. "I'm going to stay and fight it out to the last round!"

But Lord Munster knew that if Britain was to survive, men of Gort's stature would be desperately needed in the struggle ahead. When he reached London on Thursday morning, the young lord went immediately to see Winston Churchill, the one man in England who could force Gort to change his mind.

The Prime Minister was dressed in pajamas and an ornate black-and-gold robe when Munster arrived, and he had just finished breakfast. Instantly, he rang for his valet and sent for dry underwear for his guest, who had waded out to a ship's whaler the night before and was still sopping wet.

The young lord lost no time in making his report, however: The commander in chief was bent on sacrificing his own life, he said, and he had to be brought home.

No man to deviate from his routine, Churchill was just about to take his bath. "I trust you are not overburdened with modesty, my young friend?" he asked. Munster said he wasn't.

A few moments later, clad in long woolen underwear that enveloped him like a sack, Munster perched on the edge of the bathtub while Churchill, wallowing happily in the water, heard him out in silence. "He needed only a pink celluloid duck to make the picture complete," Munster recalls affectionately.

But the old warrior at once saw Munster's point: For Gort to die at the head of his men would be a wanton waste. "We must put a stop to this," he growled, and the moment his bath was over, he penned a strongly worded order: Gort must nominate a successor and return home. "No personal discretion is left to you in this matter," the directive from Winston Churchill read. "It would be a needless triumph to the enemy to capture you."

For two days now small craft had been assembling along the coast. They came from Margate and Dover, from Portsmouth and Sheerness, from every possible port and down the tidal rivers, a fleet almost a thousand strong—salt-stained trawlers, motor launches, sleek cabin cruisers, barges, tugs, and lifeboats. And on Thursday afternoon officers attached to the Small Vessels Pool were given their final briefing at Ramsgate, a little fishing port near Dover.

"Now off you go," they were all told. "Good luck—steer for the sound of the guns!" And to the unmistakable concert of the Dunkirk guns, reverberating like thunder over the Channel water, the fleet of tiny boats moved out.

There had never been an armada like it before. Manned by the rich and famous, the poor and unknown, the old and young, it was an international mercy fleet—a true United Nations of boats and men. A Dominican monk skippered the yacht *Gulzar*. A Bank of England clerk reported for duty on a lifeboat with an umbrella, bowler hat, and pinstripe pants. Chinese steward Ah Fong brewed tea aboard the *Bideford*, and the Earl of Craven served as third engineer on the rescue tug *St. Olave*. California-born John Fernald commanded one of the 12 lifeboats towed by the tug *Racia*, and an Irish crew worked with its own Gaelic interpreter aboard the minesweeper *Fitzroy*.

Some had talked their way into it despite official qualms. Stewardess Amy Goodrich, the only woman to rate a Dunkirk decoration, had sworn that as long as nurses were sailing on the hospital ship *Dinard,* she'd sail, too. And she did.

Hundreds of boats, built for short-run river work, had never before put out to sea. Few had protection against mines, and almost all lacked adequate weapons or provisions. One crew set out with no more food than a bottle of malted-milk tablets. Aboard a tug an ambulance team discovered a shortage of surgical dressings; without further ado they stripped off their underclothes and began slicing them into bandages. Not to be outdone, the skipper soon had all the men shearing through towels, pillowcases, even the skipper's shirts.

And still the cockleshell fleet steamed across the waters: the *Count Dracula,* former launch of a German admiral, scuttled at Scapa Flow in 1919 but salvaged years later; the fishing trawler *Jacinta,* reeking of cod; the famous racing yacht *Endeavour;* the Yangtze gunboat *Mosquito,* bristling with armament to ward off Chinese river pirates; and the beach boat *Dumpling,* built in Napoleon's time, carrying a 70-year-old skipper.

As the fleet approached Dunkirk, even seasoned naval officers felt a lump rise in their throats; absurd yet magnificent, it was without precedent in the world's naval history. On the bridge of the destroyer *Malcolm* Lt. Ian Cox was almost moved to tears to see the boats led by the *Woolton,* an old, wallowing Isle of Wight car ferry. His voice trembling with emotion, Cox burst out with the classic lines from Shakespeare's *Henry V,* which spoke of another battle in France:

And gentlemen in England, now a-bed,
Shall think themselves accurs'd, they were not here;
And hold their manhoods cheap, whiles any speaks,
That fought with us upon Saint Crispin's day.

The rescue flotilla sailed into an inferno that was now almost beyond description. Two million tons of oil from the port's bomb-shattered tanks roared in a vast conflagration, 11,000 feet high and a mile wide. The air reeked with an unholy compound of smoke, putrid horseflesh, rank tobacco, cordite, garlic, and rancid oil. Unearthly sounds smote the ears: the whistling of bombs; the frenzied braying of a jammed klaxon in an abandoned ambulance; the screams of French cavalry horses, wheeling and plunging in panic; and, incongruously, the far keening of bagpipes from the dunes.

Along 20 miles of fog-shrouded beaches endless lines of men still stretched across the sands. Sometimes the seeming nearness of the waiting ships caused scores to throw aside all caution and rush into the waters—often to their deaths. From the deck of the destroyer *Impulsive* stoker Walter Perrier watched a slow-motion horror: Men in full kit, rifles raised above their heads, were wading out toward his ship. On and on they struggled, apparently completely bemused, until at last the sea engulfed them, and they drowned.

Sometimes, after flailing through the water, the troops scrambled into boats so fast that the crews couldn't handle the oars. Breasting a heavy surf, one whaler reached the shore only to be overturned by the thrashing fury of 20 Tommies. Before the crew could secure the boat, the soldiers had sunk like bullets in the churning water.

And by now thousands of troops were near starvation. With its railhead bombed out, Dunkirk had been cut off from almost all supplies for days, and the desperate men were scavenging anything their jaws could chew. Thirst, too, was a burning torment.

Yet humor was never lacking. From a vantage point on the dunes a sergeant couldn't stop laughing as he watched six landlubbers in a lifeboat, cursing and sweating, unable to row an inch. It took a naval launch's party, coming alongside, to explain that the boat was anchored fore and aft.

With a cheery flow of magician's patter, another sergeant stood waist-deep in the water, palming cards and coins. Close by, other men were listening to a harmonica concert. Four Royal Engineers did stunts on motorcycles, and a soldier on a chestnut horse went through the motions of a Cossack circus act. Farther on 22 men found stumps, bat, and ball and started a game of cricket. Every time a lone fighter swooped down to strafe, they scattered—briskly taking up positions again once the danger was past.

Gort had ordered all but essential transport destroyed so that nothing left behind would be useful to the Germans. "Burn, smash everything that belongs to Britain!" one officer had interpreted the order, and on all sides men had been savagely wielding sledgehammers and blowtorches with the fierce energy of vandals. Truck after truck was shunted into appointed fields and burned in great funeral pyres. Then Gen. Harold Alexander came up with a plan. If the navy had such a dire need for piers, he reasoned, why not drive a pier of trucks as far as possible into the sea?

And so it was done—one man grimly steering his vehicle far out into the shallow waters while a jolting, groaning line of trucks followed behind. Other men then took up the task, sawing planks and lashing them to the truck roofs until jetties 20 trucks in length had taken shape. Troops were soon marching three abreast on these gangways, out to lifeboats and whalers that they might never have reached.

Every hour now the traffic snarl along the retreat lines was getting worse. The rattletrap laundry vans and milk carts that had served the men as emergency transport were breaking down. Everywhere vital roads were blocked. At Watten and Moere the French had opened the lock gates, flooding the flat land for 15 miles. This proved a key factor in holding back the Germans, but it also meant one mighty and half-submerged traffic jam for the fleeing British.

THAT THURSDAY WAS the best day yet of the evacuation. The aid of the innumerable small craft, which were now busily ferrying troops out to the larger ships, made it possible to rescue 53,823 men.

But the cost was horrifying. By Friday the Dover waterfront had become a vast shipyard in which carpenters, engineers, and divers worked frantically to repair crippled vessels; and every approach to Dunkirk was a navigator's nightmare, a forest of sunken masts and superstructures. A high wind blew up that morning, and as the surf rose in the shallow waters, dozens of small craft veered and grounded. Moreover, the defense lines had contracted to the point where German guns were finding the range of the harbor, and all morning the docking berths rocked under artillery fire.

Rarely had ships or troops taken such a beating; to Ramsay and Tennant it seemed that only a miracle could save the men—more than 100,000 of them—who were still waiting for boats.

But England was in the mood for miracles. The crews of the little ships worked dazedly on, and more and more small craft joined them. All through the day they kept coming—river barges with massive oars and russet-colored sails; an RAF seaplane tender; the naval pinnace *Minotaur,* manned by teenage Sea Scouts; and even a fireboat from the London Fire Brigade.

Few of the crews had steel helmets to protect them against the hail of shells. The men on the oyster dredger *Vanguard* shielded their heads with enamel bowls and zinc buckets as they ferried troops to a yacht. Many boats returned to the shore again and again under shell-fire. One lifeboat alone—the *Prudential,* manned by a civilian crew—worked 30 nonstop hours between beach and destroyers, packing in 160 men at a time, towing other boats that had broken down, bringing off a peak total of 2,800 men.

And the troops, their hopes heightened by the ever swelling fleet, streamed forth to meet the boats. Many by now had found their own ways of leaving the shore. One man set sail on a door, another on a wooden locker, still others on rafts made from barrels. And from the minesweeper *Ross* a yeoman watched in admiration as a soldier sat on an inflated inner tube and rowed frantically with his rifle.

Thus, through sheer courage and resolve, the miracle of Dunkirk continued. Against almost impossible odds, 68,014 troops were ferried to England on that Friday, May 31—the highest 24-hour total achieved during the entire evacuation.

At 5 A.M. Saturday, June 1, Viscount Gort reluctantly stepped ashore at Dover from a motor antisubmarine boat. A Whitehall official met him with a government limousine and bustled forward to express relief that the commander in chief was safely back.

"That I've come back safe?" Gort flashed angrily. "That isn't what matters—it's that my army gets back!"

Much of it *was* back. Most of the BEF, as well as thousands of French troops (who Churchill had agreed were to be evacuated too) were now in England. But more than 65,000 British soldiers, including the best rearguard defense troops, were still at Dunkirk, as were 50,000 French soldiers. Gort feared that the Germans would soon be at the beaches and thus would end the evacuation.

The Luftwaffe certainly tried its best. At 7:20 A.M. Richthofen launched an all-out attack that was to continue most of the day. But this time his planes met stiffer opposition from the RAF, and when they zoomed low, they also encountered the massed rifle fire from thousands of angry soldiers. And hour after hour, as the Stukas kept diving, the troops moved patiently onto the ships.

An impressive number—64,429—were lifted to England that day. But by 6 P.M. it seemed to Captain Tennant that the navy was paying too dear a price for daylight evacuation. Only nine destroyers were left now, and other shipping losses were mounting out of all proportion to the number of men still to be saved.

Even as Tennant watched, six Stukas attacked the old destroyer *Worcester,* pounding her every five minutes without mercy, sending her staggering from the harbor with a casualty list of 350 dead, 400 wounded. Leaping to his feet, Tennant told Gort's successor, General Alexander, flatly: "I'm sorry, but that finishes it. I'm signaling Ramsay to stop any more stuff coming in by day."

Ironically, the Luftwaffe men ended the day with a sense of great disappointment and frustration. For when the last of his Stukas limped home in the dusk, Baron von Richthofen knew that the bombing of Dunkirk was all but over. Hitler had ordered a change of targets. From Monday on, all planes must be in readiness to bomb the airfields around Paris.

As the minesweeper *Speedwell* inched into Dover late Saturday afternoon, an embarkation officer hailed her captain from the quayside: "How many aboard?" By megaphone the reply boomed back: "Five hundred ninety-nine men—and one woman!" As a roar of laughter traveled through the ship, Augusta and Bill Hersey knew they were safely home at last.

It had been a harrowing trip. By pure luck Bill had caught up with his bride in time for them to embark together on the destroyer *Ivanhoe*. But hours later the *Ivanhoe* had been shattered by bombs. Bill and Augusta had made a split-second escape from the ship by jumping onto the rescuing *Speedwell*.

Now, at the end of the hellish journey, they reached an England that was bursting with welcome. As tens of thousands of troops continued to stream ashore, it was obvious that most of the British Army had been saved, and a joyous carnival atmosphere filled the port.

All day Sunday huge crowds lined every street and embankment along the 40 miles from Dover to London, cheering the troop trams. Everywhere there were signs of tribute: the gay bunting and flags of Coronation time, the slogan "Well Done, BEF" daubed on garden walls, bands playing "See the Conquering Heroes Come." The *Daily Mirror* summed up popular feeling with the big jubilant headline: BLOODY MARVELOUS!

That Sunday night 26,256 more men were returned to enjoy this adulation. But for 68,000 men—the troops killed or captured in the retreat—there would be no welcoming ovation. At the Dover railway station hundreds saw the same scene repeated time and again: the pale, strained faces of wives and sweethearts ducking through a forest of waving hands to ask their anxious questions.

"Have you seen my Johnny?"

"Don't know, love—what unit?"

"Dorsets—2nd Dorsets."

"Some Dorsets in the next coach—perhaps he's there."

And with luck, perhaps he was.

Amazingly, the evacuation, now conducted largely by night, continued until the early hours of Tuesday, June 4. During those last days the Germans had the range of the harbor down to perfection. At precise 10-minute intervals they sent shells screaming down on the closely packed craft. Scores of troops, cut off from their officers, hid out in the ruins of the town, unwilling to run this gauntlet of fire without a firm directive. But if troops were not in sight, the navy sent out search parties to find them. Stragglers were rounded up without incident, for discipline was rigid and impeccable to the end.

During those last days another 52,921 men were rescued, most of them French, bringing the final total to an almost incredible 338,226 men—of whom 139,911 were not British but other Allied troops.

But as Prime Minister Winston Churchill hastened to point out, "Wars are not won by evacuations." And Britain had paid a staggering price for the escape of her army. She had lost well over 200 ships and 177 planes, including 40 percent of her first-line bombers. The equipment of 10 divisions lay gutted or strewn across the fields of Flanders—a wreckage of more than 2,000 guns, 60,000 vehicles, 76,000 tons of ammunition, and almost 600,000 tons of stores and gasoline. Against Germany's 200 divisions there now remained equipment for only 2 British divisions. And in all of England, Churchill was later to reveal, there were only 500 18-pound guns and howitzers—many of these being stripped from museums.

England's life obviously hung in the balance, and to many Germans her finish seemed but a question of time. At dawn's first light on Tuesday Maj. Hans Sandar and his gunners, coming down to the shores of Dunkirk, stopped short in amazement as they beheld the thousands of vehicles littering the beaches. To his driver Hans Sandar cried out: "Exactly what we are looking for—scrap my car, fish that Buick out of the water, and get it working."

When his regimental commander Oberst Priesz noted, "So the British are out," Major Sandar jerked a thumb at the devastation. "The British are finished," he said.

The top brass felt the same, as did the Fuehrer himself. "We will not hear much more of the British in this war!" Hitler later told Gen. Ewald von Kleist.

Only the British themselves failed to realize that they were hopelessly beaten. Winston Churchill spoke for England when he announced to Parliament that afternoon: "We shall not flag or fail. We shall go on to the end. We shall fight in France, we shall fight in the seas and oceans. . . . We shall defend our Island whatever the cost may be. We shall fight on the beaches, we shall fight on the landing grounds, we shall fight in the fields and in the streets, we shall fight in the hills. . . . We shall never surrender."

And history has recorded that they never did.

*Hans Meyer was a man known for his great understanding
and forbearance—until the Communist authorities of
East Berlin committed the unforgivable sin of confiscating
his beautiful air-conditioned dream bus.*

Meyer's Caravan

By Norbert Muhlen

I HAD HEARD about Hans Meyer and his buses before I met him in a
little West German hotel. Friends in the Soviet Sector of Berlin
had told me his story, which had taken place in the days before the
Berlin Wall was built.

Meyer's story seemed to be widely known behind the Iron Curtain,
although people were not supposed to know it at all. The People's
Police file on the case is marked "Top Secret." A police informer
recently overheard a Soviet Berlin housewife saying to her butcher
that she found the story "awfully amusing"; she was arrested on the
spot and sent to prison for endangering the security of the state.

Meyer, a tall, 36-year-old man born in what is now Soviet Berlin,
likes to talk about the case that made him famous. "It all happened
because my best bus is the most beautiful bus in Germany," he told
me. "The seats are upholstered in blue leather, with blue silk cushions. There is a built-in coffee counter. It was the first bus in Germany with air conditioning and fluorescent lighting. As soon as I can
afford it, I'll fix my two other buses up the same way."

It was evident that buses were not only his business but his great
love. It was for this love that he set out to defeat the Communist
rulers who tried to take them away from him.

I asked him how he had gotten the buses in the first place.

"After the war," he said, "I salvaged an old bus that Soviet soldiers
had abandoned on the roadside. I had a job as a garage mechanic, and
I worked nights rebuilding the bus. When I'd turned it into a respectable vehicle, I operated it on a regular run in the Soviet Zone. Seems
that people had more confidence in my bus than in the state-run
buses, which never kept their schedules and often broke down. After

a while I was able to buy another bus and finally the third one—you know, the dream bus."

I asked him why the Communists had permitted this successful example of private enterprise in their Socialist state.

"They made a profit from my work," he said. "They granted me the right to run my buses from East to West Germany and back. The passengers were mainly Western businessmen with whom the Soviets wanted to deal. The catch was that they had to pay their bus fares in East marks; although these are worth only a quarter as much as West marks, they had to buy the East marks at an exchange rate of one to one. Thus they paid 40 marks for a trip priced at 10 marks, and the Soviets got the difference.

"But last year Communist newspapers began denouncing my outfit as antilabor and antipeace. Fact was, my drivers didn't want to join the state-run union because I paid them high salaries and their union fees would only have gone into the Communist treasure chest. It was also true that I never shouted 'Hurrah for Stalin,' just as years before I had never shouted 'Heil Hitler.' But I guess what they really wanted was my buses.

"In October 1950, when my three buses were about to cross the border into the West Zone, 15 People's Police boarded them with drawn pistols. My buses were then 'taken into the hands of the people.' And the Communist police issued a warrant against me as an 'economic criminal.'

"That's their term for a successful businessman," he explained. "At first they encouraged private business; but after we got it going, they accused the owners of 'economic crime' as a cover-up for the expropriation of their holdings."

How did he evade arrest?

"I was in West Germany at the time, waiting for my buses, and when they didn't arrive, I got suspicious. Then a former employee sent me a warning. Of course I didn't go back.

"Later I learned that, while the two older buses were now being run by the state, the third bus, the dream bus, had been taken out of circulation. The Communists considered it too fine to be used by the common people and decided to use it only when high party officials or foreign delegations were visiting the Soviet Zone. I think it was the worst moment of my life to have to stand by while they were doing things like that to my bus! I solemnly swore to return someday and get my buses.

"One of my former employees, now managing the bus line for the state, told me that the buses were still parked in my old garage in Soviet Berlin. But a guard of Soviet soldiers was stationed close by. Last February something like a miracle happened. My friend the manager phoned to let me know that the guard had been moved to a new post. I knew that the great moment had come—I had to steal my own buses from the thieves."

That night Herr Meyer had a meeting with his ex-employee. They studied maps, blueprinted their movements, and decided on the necessary preparations.

A few nights later the manager visited the garage to check on the buses, as was his custom. He carried several bottles of beer, one of them marked with a small red dot. This bottle he offered the night watchman, who fell asleep almost before he had finished drinking it.

While the watchman snored, the manager went to a nearby inn, where Hans Meyer and three friends, each a forbidding-looking six-footer, were waiting. Outside, a truck was parked, loaded with cans of gasoline. The manager reported that only the two regular buses were in the garage. The dream bus was being used by a delegation of Polish trade-union officials.

An hour later, when they drove over to the garage, the dream bus had still not come home. It seemed dangerous to wait longer. A few moments later a little caravan—the truck and two buses—left the garage, moving westward through the darkened city. Frequently, on frontier-crossing streets, the Communists throw up impromptu barricades and special control points. Meyer and his friends were taking a long chance.

Suddenly, less than two miles from the border, Meyer's heart leaped to his throat. Out of the darkness ahead came glaring headlights. If it was the police, they were sure to stop and examine a convoy so unusual.

But the oncoming vehicle did not slow down, and as it swept past, Meyer recognized the silhouette.

"It's my dream bus!" he shouted. He turned the truck around in pursuit. The buses followed.

Back at the garage, three determined-looking men surrounded the driver of the dream bus. One thrust the stem of a pipe into the side of the driver and mumbled: "If you come quietly, nothing'll happen to you." The driver gave himself up, and Meyer climbed proudly behind the wheel of his bus.

Once again the caravan swung westward. Many anxious minutes later they saw with relief the Soviet poster with its perverse proclamation: "You are now leaving the democratic sector." They had arrived in West Berlin, the free island surrounded by the "Red Sea."

But the most dangerous part of the escape still lay ahead—over 100 miles through Russian-held territory to the safety of West Germany. In a dark street Meyer and his friends exchanged the Eastern license plates of their vehicles for West Berlin licenses which they had prepared in advance. They had also forged documents certifying that these were West Berlin buses on a regular trip to West Germany. The captured driver was handed over to a friend, to be held in "protective custody" for another day. Then they moved out to the stretch of the famous Autobahn that links Berlin and West Germany.

At four in the morning Meyer's caravan arrived at the Dreilinden checkpoint, where Soviet soldiers carefully examined their papers, searched for contraband, and finally, not finding any irregularity, waved them on. At the border luck was still favoring Meyer. Everything went smoothly, and soon the buses sped swiftly over the invisible line to freedom.

Meyer drove straight to a telephone booth and put in a call to Soviet Berlin's People's Police Headquarters. To an amazed commissar he announced: "I've just liberated the buses that your state stole from me." Then he hung up.

Later Meyer penned a letter to the People's Police officer in charge of his prosecution for "economic crimes." "Dear Herr Kommissar Stanke," the letter went, "since I cannot recognize your illegal confiscation of my buses, I took the liberty today of recovering ownership."

Meyer chuckled as he finished his tale. "I still get many letters and phone calls from people living in the Soviet Zone congratulating me on my 'theft.' "

"Did the Communists take it lying down?" I asked.

"Well," he said, "they wanted the West German government to extradite me because I had committed, as they put it, the crimes of robbery, kidnapping, and attempted murder. But the West Germans ruled that my crime had been of a political nature and that I therefore deserved asylum, as did my buses, which, in a way, are the first buses to be political refugees.

"Since they could not take revenge on me, they punished a few People's Police whom they held responsible—Herr Kommissar Stanke has been demoted to sergeant. They also punished the night watchman—sent him to prison for six months because of his 'lack of proletarian vigilance.' I feel sorry for him. But anybody with a bus as beautiful as mine would have done what I did."

*Maybe he would never be able to evade
the North Vietnamese, the air force
captain told himself, but he'd sure make the
enemy work hard to catch him.*

Shot Down

By Joseph P. Blank

AS HE DANGLED in his parachute 40 miles northwest of Hanoi, Capt. Roger Locher's first stunned reaction was, *This can't be!* Getting shot down was something that happened to others. Like all fliers, he had never believed it could happen to him.

But it had. The gag of helpless fear he felt was real. So were the two sleek, silvery enemy MiG's whipping past him 1,000 feet away. Then jungle trees loomed below, and he crashed through branches to a halt—his boots barely touching the earth.

The tall, slim 25-year-old had taken off on the morning of May 10, 1972, from a Thailand air base and sped toward the Hanoi area. He was flying his 407th mission as a navigator-weapon-systems operator. The purpose of the mission was to prevent enemy fighters from attacking U.S. bombers. Backseater in the lead two-man F–4 Phantom jet, Locher had already been credited with shooting down two Vietnamese MiG-21's.

Now, as MiG's slashed down at the Phantom jets west of Hanoi, Locher destroyed the lead ship with two air-to-air missiles. Two other aircraft shot down two more MiG's before Roger Locher's pilot yelled, "We're hit!"

As flames swept the aircraft and it uncontrollably flipped over, Locher shouted, "I'm going to have to eject." He pulled hard on the ejection lever, heard a blast as he was shot earthward, and blacked out for a few seconds.

As he hit the trees, Locher was fully conscious. He knew that the MiG's had radioed his position, and the parachute, which he couldn't extricate from the tree, pinpointed his touchdown. Hastily, he unharnessed himself and began trudging up the side of a mountain, careful

455

not to leave any trail. In 10 minutes he was gasping for breath. He felt dizzy, his legs were turning rubbery, and his feet were very cold.

I'm in shock, he thought. *Stop. Calm down. Get your brains connected.* He crawled into dense jungle vegetation and lay down with his feet higher than his head.

Considering his predicament, he knew that things were bad. He was terribly far north; the closest pickup area where he could use his little battery-powered survival radio to contact over-flying comrades

was 90 miles to the south. *Ninety miles!* he thought. *Dodging and hiding. Have to stick to the mountains. Make two miles a day at the most. Forty-five days. No food. Strange terrain. But I'll give it a try. If they're going to capture me, I'll make them work.*

He slowly drank a half-pint of water from a bottle in his survival vest and adjusted the mosquito netting over his head. With a compass and map to guide him, he carefully set out southwest. Each step had to be reviewed for bootprints, broken twigs, or other signs that could easily betray him.

At noon he suddenly froze. He heard guttural and excited yelling coming straight at him. He crawled into some thick brush and lay still as the search parties came closer.

He remembered his youth around the Sabetha, Kansas, countryside and how game birds, frightened by approaching humans, would attempt to flee and thus reveal themselves. He told himself: *Breathe shallow. Don't give yourself away. Make them find you.* He sweated, prayed. He could smell the searchers' cigarettes. Then they passed.

Next day it happened again. He heard screams, shouts, rifle fire. *They are trying to flush me out like a pheasant,* he thought. *Stay put. They have practically got to step on you to find you.*

They almost did. He heard the crushing of leaves as two men sat down to rest just a few yards away. After a time they left. Silence. He strained his ears. Were they waiting for him to move? Was that a bird rustling leaves—or one of them? He stayed hidden for the remainder of the day, moving only to relieve cramped muscles.

On the third day he switched his radio to the survival frequency and picked up search pilots discussing the plight of a downed airman, who had apparently reported his pursuers closing in and requested that his location be strafed. He preferred death to imprisonment.

Then the transmission faded, and Locher switched off the radio. He heard search parties about 200 yards away and remained hidden. *What's the use?* he thought, as he pulled listlessly at leeches attacking his neck and wrists. *I haven't moved more than a mile in three days. Maybe I can't get out—but let's see how long I can delay the inevitable.*

Next day he plodded doggedly on, up and down mountain slope after mountain slope. Water was no problem. It rained every other night and, in the mornings, he had to dry out, being careful to avoid letting his boots and socks rot.

But he had no food. He tried three kinds of sparse, unripe jungle fruit. He took a nibble, then waited a half hour to see if it produced cramps. The fruit had no adverse effect. But he could never find more than a handful a day.

He could feel his strength seeping away. It would be so easy to surrender. *No,* he kept telling himself day after day. *Make them earn you.*

Shortly after dawn on the 12th day, Locher found a well-worn path leading south. It was a delicious relief from pushing through the jungle. Suddenly he heard voices coming toward him. Several youngsters were herding water buffalo to pasture. He dived into the bushes, crawled a few yards, and lay still.

The buffalo began grazing, some hardly 50 feet away. Time passed with excruciating slowness as he lay there hour after hour. Shortly before twilight, he heard the children's voices again. They had returned to herd the buffalo into the village corral. Then he heard one of the animals panting a few yards away and a boy beating him with a branch. The buffalo refused to budge. Then it snorted and stepped on a sapling, whacking it down on Locher's ankles. He opened his mouth in pain but stifled any sound. As the animal lumbered on, the boy stepped on the same sapling, slapping it against Locher's thighs. Finally, silence.

After dark, Locher wormed his way around the village and up the side of the mountain overlooking it. He fixed a bed of leaves. He awoke several times to pull away leeches. Each leech left a bloody sore. A drenching rain fell.

As he dried out in the morning, Locher carefully studied his map. He reached the dismaying conclusion that in 12 days he had progressed no more than seven straight-line miles.

He had no hope of being rescued this far north in enemy territory; he *had* to keep going south. But that way was the Red River plain, nearly 20 miles wide and filled with small communities. He could see no places for concealment.

Not knowing exactly what to do, he remained in his hiding place. The village sprawled 1,500 feet below him, and he could plainly hear the sound of the gong that ordained its daily routine—wake up, go to work, break for lunch.

One day fused with another. On the 20th day he knew he was

wasting away. He rubbed his buttocks and felt only skin and bones; he couldn't get food off his mind.

Either I starve to death here, he concluded, *or I get down to that plain and try to steal food there.*

He realized that once he started across the exposed valley he would almost certainly be captured. He speculated about horrors of imprisonment and determined that he would conduct himself with honor. He gave thanks for the 25 years of freedom he had enjoyed.

On the evening of his 21st day Locher decided that he would make for the plain at the first break of light. Thus committed, he felt at peace and contentedly watched a full, yellow moon float across the sky. He savored the freshness of the air and his isolation: It meant that he was still free.

A long, hard rain kept him awake most of the night, and he overslept his departure time. He was furious with himself, but he couldn't risk going past the village in daylight. *Another day of swatting damn mosquitoes with a damn banana leaf!*

LOCHER DOZED FITFULLY before he saw the flashes of surface-to-air missiles being fired from a village about eight miles away. The gunners had to be shooting at U.S. aircraft. Even if it also meant revealing his position to the North Vietnamese, he nevertheless had to inform his comrades that he was alive. He pressed the radio transmitter button and said: "Any U.S. aircraft that reads Oyster One Bravo, please come up voice." ("Oyster" was his flight call sign; "One" indicated lead aircraft and "Bravo" backseater.)

He switched to receive and heard, "Go ahead, Oyster One Bravo."

"Hey, man, I'm still down here after 22 days. Relay that I'm OK."

"Will pass on the contact."

Ten minutes later Locher was startled to hear a voice on his radio: "Rescue forces on the way."

But MiG's and heavy antiaircraft fire drove the first rescue effort off. Locher figured that his comrades might make one more attempt, probably on the following morning.

There'll be a hot reception committee waiting for them, he thought. Throughout the day he strained to hear the sound of enemy trucks bringing in search parties. At 9 that night he did hear two MiG's land at a nearby air base.

They know something is going to happen tomorrow, too, he worried.

On the morning of Locher's 23rd day in North Vietnam, 38 U.S. jet and piston fighters, helicopters, and tankers for aerial refueling took off from Thailand to pluck the waiting flier out. Two planes made radio contact with Locher and electronically zeroed in on his location. One pilot said, "We know where you are—now just stay put. We're going to get you out of there, buddy."

Chills rippled through Locher. *God, protect them. Don't let any get shot down because of me.*

Thirty minutes later two helicopters appeared. As Locher flashed his signal mirror, one slid toward him, while the other hung back, ready to act in an emergency. The lead ship hovered 50 feet above Locher and lowered a penetrator, a torpedo-shaped device with enough weight to break through jungle canopy. Automatic rifle fire broke out from the village, but it was quickly silenced by the chopper's miniguns.

Locher stumbled toward the penetrator. He yanked out the straps, secured himself, pulled down a paddle seat to sit on, and gave a joyous thumbs-up gesture. Quickly he was reeled into the ship, and they took off for home. Several MiG's buzzed far overhead, but they lacked the numbers to challenge the rescue mission, which returned to base safely.

It was a happy journey for Capt. Roger Locher, who had lost 30 pounds during his ordeal. He didn't know that he was the longest-surviving rescued airman in the war's history, and the chopper crew didn't know that they had probably made the deepest successful rescue penetration into enemy territory.

As they flew at top speed near ground level, roller-coastering into valleys and over ridges, using the terrain to block enemy gunners, they were proud of saving Locher, but they hid their pride behind a lot of banter and refused to give the rescued airman an opportunity to express his gratitude. All Locher could do was to look at them with a big, fat, loving grin and let the tears course down through his beard.

The saga of a young English parlormaid whose zeal for missionary work took her on a journey halfway around the world. Her life in war-ravaged China was one of extraordinary adventure and hair-raising escapes.

The Small Woman

By Alan Burgess

THE AFFAIR OF THE SMALL WOMAN both intrigued and concerned the senior physician of the Sian hospital in central China. That she was dying he did not doubt. Who she was, no one knew. Two unknown peasants had delivered her to the front gate of the Scandinavian-Alliance Mission that autumn day of 1941, heaving her out from the back of an oxcart.

When the senior physician examined her, he found on her undernourished body the scar of a recent bullet wound; she was suffering from severe internal injuries; there was a patch of pneumonia on one lung; and she had that dreadfully perilous disease, typhus. Her temperature was 105 degrees. She was in a raving delirium.

Then the Japanese began to bomb the city of Sian. The senior physician watched his patient's wasted form jerk in agony as each bomb whistled down. The small woman's body ran with a cold sweat; a spasm of pain crossed her face and a whisper came from her lips, "Where are my children? The Japanese will kill us!"

The whisper mounted to a scream, and then abruptly she was raving in an uncouth Chinese dialect that someone recognized as coming from a wild mountain region far to the north. The spasm of delirium passed, and a faint smile formed on her face at this clinical-smelling doctor who bent over her with such gentle insistence, saying, "Don't be frightened."

Frightened! She could tell him that being frightened hardly concerned her anymore after what she'd been through.

"Your name," said the insistent voice in her ear. But everyone knew her name. Ai-weh-deh, The Virtuous One! Only they did not want her Chinese name, but her English name.

It seemed such a silly question to ask. Surely they knew her name was Gladys Aylward and that she had been born in London. Her memory filtered back. She remembered the time of her great determination, when she was 26. A parlormaid, she had lacked the education to pass the examinations to become a missionary—but just the same, she was determined to go to China. She would have to do it entirely on her own, including saving enough money from her small wages to pay the fare for that frighteningly long journey.

She was at that time employed in the household of Sir Francis Younghusband, the eminent explorer. Dispirited, she sat on the bed in her servant's room and took out the black, well-thumbed Bible and put it on the dressing table. She turned out her purse, which contained all the money she possessed. There were two pennies and one halfpenny. She placed the coins on top of the Bible. She felt like weeping—China seemed so far away. But, suddenly conscious of her deep need, she cried out: "Oh, God, here's my Bible! Here's my money! Here's me! *Use me, God!*"

Gladys remembered her first encounter with the elderly clerk at the travel agency some months later. In all his years of advising on foreign travel, he had never heard such an outrageous demand. Had he not just finished patiently explaining that the cheapest route to China was overland through Russia to Tientsin via the Trans-Siberian Railway—the fare being 47 pounds, 10 shillings—*but* that it was now quite impossible to travel by that route because of the undeclared war between Russia and China?

"I couldn't really care about a silly old war," she said. "It's the cheapest way, isn't it? That's what I want."

Gladys reached into her purse and brought out three pound notes, the result of many weeks of saving. "Now if you'll book me a passage, I'll pay you three pounds on account and more every week."

"We do not," the clerk replied, carefully choosing his words, "like to deliver our customers *dead!*"

"Oh, they won't hurt me," she said. "I'm a woman. And anyway, the war will be over by the time I get the rest of the money, I'm sure."

The elderly clerk looked at her carefully. Then, in defeat, he picked up the three pounds.

Exactly what she thought she would be able to do when she arrived in China with little or no money, understanding not one word of the language, she hardly knew herself; but she could at least equip herself as an evangelist. "I must learn to preach," she said to herself. "I must learn to talk to the people."

With the essential simplicity that characterized her, in every moment of spare time she went to Hyde Park, where she mounted a soapbox and preached, often to a jeering audience. Tired Londoners moving homeward in the evenings were startled to find themselves exhorted by a small—five feet, 112 pounds—girl in a black dress to turn not homeward but to God.

Then she had her first piece of luck. From a friend she heard of Mrs. Jeannie Lawson. "Seventy-three years old, my dear, and still working away as a missionary in China. She wrote only a few days ago saying she wished she could find some younger woman who could carry on with her work."

Gladys Aylward remembered how all she could do was whisper weakly, "That's me! That's me!"

She wrote at once, eagerly, excitedly. Could she join Mrs. Lawson? Could she come to China?

Now it became imperative that she save the money for the train ticket. In the household she was willing to do anything; no chore was too arduous. She besieged employment agencies, offering her services to work on her day off, to serve at banquets, to work nights if necessary. By now the travel agency clerk was an old friend, accustomed to the enthusiastic young woman who appeared at his desk every Friday without fail, leaving sums that would be counted out in pennies and entered against that magical total—47 pounds, 10 shillings.

Then came that wonderful morning when the letter bearing the brightly colored Chinese stamps arrived. It told her that if she could manage to get to Tientsin by herself, a messenger would guide her to wherever Mrs. Lawson was working.

The excitement! She would get her passport at once! She would soon finish paying for the ticket! "I'm going to China," she said to all her friends. *"I'm going to China!"*

On Saturday, October 18, 1930, "Expedition Gladys Aylward" assembled on the platform at Liverpool Street Station. It must be numbered among the most ill-equipped expeditions ever to leave the shores of England, possessing in currency exactly ninepence in coin and a two-pound traveler's check, carefully sewn into her corset in the belief that even foreigners would not dare pry too closely into such an intimate feminine accessory; an old fur coat made into a rug; and two suitcases. One suitcase contained clothes, the other an odd assortment of cans of corned beef, fish, baked beans, crackers, meat cubes, coffee essence, tea, and hard-boiled eggs and a spirit stove. A kettle and a saucepan were tied to the handle of the suitcase.

Gladys sat cocooned in her fur rug as different trains rattled her across the Continent, through Germany, Poland, the great steppes of Russia, and into Siberia 10 days later. There she had her first scare, when soldiers began crowding onto the train, until at the city of Chita the cars were emptied of all civilians. That is, almost all, for Gladys refused to budge, and the packed train rumbled onward. A few hours later it halted again at a tiny station, and the soldiers got out and marched off into the darkness. The train lights went out. Gladys was the only person left aboard.

Then, borne on the thin, freezing wind, came a noise that, even though she had never heard it before, she recognized. The sound of gunfire! Ominous and terrifying, distant flashes lit the sky.

Realizing a little shamefacedly that the elderly clerk at the travel agency had been right after all, she gathered her belongings together. The conductor was now able to convince her, with gesticulations, that her only hope was to walk the tracks back to Chita.

So she set off into the night, the Siberian wind gusting the powdered snow around her heels, the fur rug over her shoulders, a suitcase in either hand—a slight, Chaplinesque figure, dwarfed by the tall, somber pines, the towering mountains, and the black sky diamond-bright with stars. When the cold and exhaustion became too much for her, she sat down on the icy rail, lit her spirit stove and, after melting some snow, boiled the water for her coffee essence. She ate two crackers and felt miserable. Then she arranged her suitcases into a windbreak, scooped up snow to fill the cracks, cramped herself firmly into her old fur rug, and lay down.

A pale dawn was lighting the mountains when she woke up, stiff but refreshed. She made herself more coffee, ate another cracker, gathered up her luggage, and set off again. Late that night, almost unconscious with cold and weariness, she lifted herself to the station platform at Chita. Next morning she got on another train that, after jolting interminably through the Siberian landscape, at last brought her to Vladivostok, on the shores of the Pacific.

She saw a poster advertising an Intourist hotel and went there. As the hotel clerk signed her in, a thickset man with a Mongolian face examined her passport and pocketed it. As far as Gladys could understand he had something to do with the police.

Next morning as she walked down the corridor she was suddenly conscious that someone was close behind her. It was an attractive girl, plainly dressed. She whispered in strongly accented English, "You are in danger. If you don't get out *now*, you never will. They need skilled factory workers desperately. They can send you off to the middle of Russia, and you'll never be heard of again."

"But what am I to do?" Gladys asked.

"Tonight at midnight be dressed and have your baggage ready. A knock will come on your door. Open it and follow the man outside. You understand?" Gladys nodded her head weakly and walked back to the foyer, where the OGPU man was sitting on a tilted chair smoking a cigarette. He looked contemptuously up at her.

"I would like my passport back," said Gladys.

He took the cigarette from his mouth and blew out smoke. "It is still being examined. I will bring it back to you—this evening."

THAT NIGHT GLADYS sat in the cold bedroom after eating her supper of crackers and canned fish. A knock came at the door. It was the OGPU man, grinning, waving her passport tantalizingly in one hand. Gladys snatched the passport from his hand with a quick movement and threw it back over her head. The grin on the man's face frightened her. He forced the door open and stepped inside.

"Don't you dare come in here," said Gladys simply. *"Get out!"*

"I am coming in," he snapped. His eyes flicked across to the bed and back to her.

Here was the absolute, the fundamental horror about which she had read in women's magazines all her life. She leapt backward like a small scalded cat. With inspired rhetoric she declaimed wildly: "God will protect me! God will protect me!"

The man stopped, puzzled. He stared at the small embodiment of virtue, rooted dramatically in front of him. Then, abruptly, his mood changed. He swore at her savagely. He waved his hand threateningly, then thought better of it and took a few steps backward out the door. Gladys slammed it shut.

She raced across the room, picked up her passport, and flipped through the pages. Her finger trembled with fright as she saw what they had done. The word "Missionary," in the line marked "Profession," had been altered to "Machinist."

She hauled her suitcases from under the bed and began to pile in her belongings. She must escape. She finished her packing, then sat down on the bed trembling, waiting for midnight and praying. The knock on the door was so gentle that she hardly heard it. A strange man in a drab mackintosh motioned to her to come and held the door open while she bundled through with her suitcases. She followed after him along a corridor and out into the cold night air.

465

They slipped through the dark side streets toward the sea. Near the docks, from the shadow of a pile of packing cases, the mysterious girl appeared. With a sigh of thankfulness Gladys hurried toward her.

"You see that ship?" The girl pointed. "It sails for Japan at dawn. You must be on it."

"But, Japan! I've got no money. . . ."

"You'll find the captain in that lighted hut over there. Plead with him, tell him you are in great trouble. You *must* leave on that ship."

"All right, I'll try." Gladys's voice was doubtful. "But what about you? Why have you helped me like this?"

"You needed help." The girl's voice was low and sad.

"But you. . . ?"

"I live here. I shall be all right."

"How can I thank you? What can I give you? I have no money."

"It does not matter."

Their hands touched for a moment in the darkness. "Good luck," the girl said.

Gladys pushed open the door of the hut and confronted a young Japanese in merchant-marine uniform.

"Please," she said, "are you the captain of that boat? I'm English and I *must* get on it!"

He looked at her impassively, then said in excellent English, "Have you money to pay your fare?"

"No." Gladys handed him her passport.

He leafed through it, taking his time.

"A British subject in trouble. We really cannot have that, can we?" he said at last. "I will take you on my ship."

Six hours later, as dawn lit the bare coastline, the ship slid out toward the open ocean. Gladys looked back at Vladivostok with tired eyes and wondered who the people were who had helped her. They would remain eternal enigmas in her past.

A week later Gladys stood on the deck of another Japanese ship, steaming west. Her luck had held good in Japan, where kind missionaries housed her and persuaded the tourist agency to exchange her tickets. Now she stared across the mud-yellow sea at a dark smudge on the horizon. Behind it the sun was setting with gaudy flamboyance. Gladys Aylward stared into the west until all the color had shredded out of the sky and the dark smudge was swallowed by the night. *It was China!*

Next day she went ashore, at last on the land of which she had dreamed for so many years. But her journey had only begun. At the mission in Tientsin they told her that Mrs. Lawson was at Yangcheng in the North China province of Shansi—wild and mountainous territory. The trip would involve weeks of travel; so the mission supplied a young Chinese Christian as a guide. They went by train to Peiping, by another train to the end of the line at Yütze, and from there on in ramshackle old buses. A full month later she arrived at Tsincheng, where she changed into rugged Chinese peasant clothing for the last leg of her journey by muleback. Two afternoons later, on rounding a

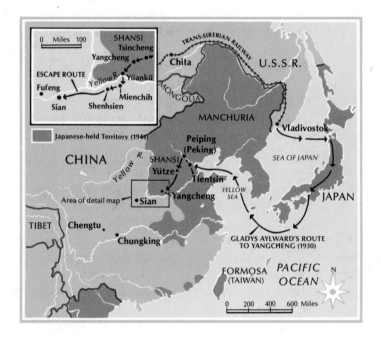

bend in the trail, the muleteer pointed ahead. "Yangcheng!" he said.

Yangcheng stood far off on its mountain peak like a castle in a fairy story. Its high walls grew from the natural rock and above them rose delicate pagodas and temples.

When they reached the Yangcheng mission, out of the door to meet them came a small lady with pure white hair.

"Well, and who are you?" she asked.

"I'm Gladys Aylward. You're Mrs. Lawson?"

"Yes, I am. Come in."

Gladys followed Mrs. Lawson into the house. Practically every door was off its hinges. There were piles of rubble on the flagstones, gaping holes in the tiled roof, dirt everywhere.

"I've only just managed to rent it," said Mrs. Lawson. "Got it cheap. Bit rough, but it'll be all right when it's cleaned up."

Gladys followed her into what appeared to be the only habitable place. In this room stood a table and two chairs. There was no other furniture. Mrs. Lawson called out in Chinese, and Yang, the old Chinese cook, came in bearing a large bowl of boiled dough strings and chopped vegetables. Gladys ate ravenously.

After her meal Gladys went out to get her baggage off the mule. A group of Chinese infants saw her and fled, howling. Two women picked up pieces of dried mud and flung them at her. In consternation, Gladys went back to Mrs. Lawson and told her what had occurred.

"It happens to me every time I go out," said Mrs. Lawson calmly. "I usually come back covered from head to foot with the filth they've thrown at me. They hate us here. They call us *Lao-yang-kwei*, foreign devils. It's something you'll have to get used to."

Jeannie Lawson explained their financial situation. She had a small income; the rent for the house had been paid for a year. Millet and wheat and vegetables cost only a few *cash*, copper coins with holes in the center that were strung in bunches on pieces of string. Two hundred of them were worth one Chinese dollar, or about one shilling and twopence. Thus, financially they were reasonably secure; but how were they to do the job for which both had come to China?

They arrived at the solution one day as they were watching a mule train pass by. "If we could only talk to the muleteers," Gladys said, "they'd carry our messages through the province."

"You've put your finger right on it," said Jeannie Lawson. "We'll open an inn! Why didn't I think of it before? Our house was built as an inn in the first place, hundreds of years ago. We've plenty of rooms and can sleep at least 50 men. We've already got a cook." Her voice was full of enthusiasm. "Once we've got the muleteers inside, we can tell them the Gospel stories. The Chinese all love stories."

Gladys was carried along on the flood tide of this enthusiasm. The roof was mended, the courtyard cleaned out. New doors were fixed. Large quantities of millet and maize and vegetables were stored.

"We must have a name," said Jeannie. "I've got it . . . The Inn of Eight Happinesses. Love, Virtue, Gentleness, Tolerance, Loyalty, Truth, Beauty, and Devotion."

The inn was now officially open. The smell of good food eddied out from Yang's kitchen, but the muleteers crowded into the other inns. No one came into the hostelry of the "foreign devils." Jeannie, Gladys, and Yang held a council of war.

"You," said Jeannie, leveling a stubby finger at Gladys, "have got to *drag* the customers into the courtyard."

"Drag them in?" Gladys's voice rose at least one octave.

Jeannie Lawson chattered questioningly to Yang in her fluent Chinese. He nodded in agreement. In the Yangcheng hostelry business, when a muleteer came down the street the innkeeper made a grab at the lead mule's head and tried to drag it in the direction of his own courtyard. The other mules were tethered behind with no choice but to follow along.

That, said Jeannie Lawson, was going to be Gladys's job. And she could expect to be aided by the mules. After a hard day on the mountain trails the poor beasts were only too anxious to be unloaded and given food and water.

Bolstered by this knowledge, Gladys stood gloomily at the doorway of the inn and waited for business. A mule train clip-clopped slowly down the street. Gladys waited tensed and poised in the doorway. The mule came level and Gladys grabbed its bridle. In a few seconds the startled muleteer and his train were in the courtyard.

Yang quickly explained to the muleteer and his companions that the "foreign devil" ladies offered good food and, as an extra attraction, stories which were to be told free of charge. As Yang knew well, and the muleteers also, that no human agency could lure the mules out of the courtyard until the sun rose next morning, there was nothing else for them to do but stay.

Yang brought in the steaming caldron of food and slopped it into their basins. They agreed that it was good food. But when Jeannie and Gladys entered, there was a perceptible movement toward the farthest corner of the room.

Jeannie was unabashed. "Don't be afraid," she said cheerfully. "I want to tell you a story which you will enjoy. All the stories we tell at the Inn of Eight Happinesses are free." The men looked a little more interested, and Jeannie perched herself on a stool. "The story I am going to tell you concerns a man named Jesus Christ who lived long ago in a faraway country called Palestine. . . ."

Their success as innkeepers was hard-earned. Evening after evening Gladys dragged in mules. But later, when the reputation of the inn was established, the courtyard was filled with teams, and the upper and lower floors were packed with muleteers.

Learning the Chinese language was also a slow business, but Yang was a willing teacher. Day after day, Gladys practiced. She learned some of the Bible stories in Chinese and relieved Mrs. Lawson from

time to time at the evening storytelling. In the years that followed she
was able to speak five different Shansi dialects fluently.

Gladys was now fully and completely absorbed with her way of
living. Her faith was like a warm blanket in which she could lie
enfolded and secure. This faith was to lead and sustain her through
many trying experiences during those early years.

The first of these was Jeannie Lawson's sudden death, following a
severe fall. The next few weeks were among the most precarious that
Gladys ever experienced in China. She was saved from possible disaster by one of the unlikeliest of people: the magistrate, who, called
the Mandarin of Yangcheng by the people, was an awesome figure
who commanded the powers of life and death.

One day soon after Jeannie's death, Gladys was in an upstairs room when she heard Yang shouting, "The mandarin's coming!"

Gladys straightened her hair, quickly smoothed her rather grubby native costume into place, and reached the courtyard just as the retinue trooped in. Coolies bore the luxurious sedan chair, painted gold and scarlet and curtained against prying eyes. Around it were grouped the mandarin's clerks in robes of dark blue silk, while gathered at a respectful distance were other retainers in magnificent costumes of yellow, orange, and scarlet. A clerk stepped forward and carefully opened the door of the chair. The mandarin descended.

He was quite magnificent: tall, with black hair, a pale ivory face, and a mustache that drooped at the corners. His gown, the wide sleeves encircled with band after band of beautifully embroidered silks of yellow, blue, green, and purple, fell smoothly to pointed black shoes. His three-cornered hat was black with a red pompon on the top. He carried a lacquered fan.

The mandarin's eyes caught Gladys's just as she came up from performing a deep bow.

"You are aware," he said, "that for many generations the custom of foot binding has been practiced in this province."

"Has it?" she murmured uncertainly.

"Now we have received a decree from the Central Government that all foot binding must cease immediately," he went on. "Every woman in this province has bound feet. Therefore, someone with big feet, unbound feet, must undertake the work of inspection."

With a sudden twinge of alarm Gladys looked down at her own size threes. In England they were reckoned quite small; here they were gargantuan.

"Obviously, no man can undertake this work. It must be a woman." The mandarin flicked his fan. "You," he said, "are the only woman in the province with big feet. *You* must take the job! You will be armed with my authority and report to me personally. Your wages will be one measure of millet a day and a farthing to buy vegetables. A mule will be supplied, and a guard of two soldiers will accompany you on your inspections."

It was an opportunity without parallel for her to visit every part of Shansi province, preaching wherever she went! If he would allow that. She did not know whether she could suggest "conditions" to the mandarin, but decided to risk his displeasure.

"You must realize," she said, "that if I accept this position I shall try to convert the people to Christianity wherever I go."

There was a short silence. She wondered if she had committed an unpardonable error. Then the mandarin said quietly, "I care nothing for your religion or to whom you preach. That is a matter for the conscience of each individual. But it is important that you should do this work. The Central Government is impatient!"

Gladys bowed low. "I am anxious to be of assistance, Excellency. I gladly accept the position." Everyone bowed and smiled. The deputation took its leave.

"You are now important," Yang told Gladys. "You are the mandarin's personal foot inspector." He bowed low and humbly.

Gladys never forgot the first village at which she arrived as official foot inspector. The village elder assembled the villagers in the square and informed them that foot binding must cease. The soldiers, who thoroughly enjoyed their small authority, made it quite clear that anyone who disobeyed would be thrown into prison. Gladys did not know quite what to do, but to make some sort of move she walked across the square and entered the first door she saw.

A dark-eyed, three-year-old girl, her feet bound, clung to her mother's trousers and looked up nervously.

"Unbind her feet!" said Gladys, trying to insert a note of authority into her voice.

The mother took the child on her lap and began to undo the bandages. They fell away, revealing tiny feet with the toes bent downward and up into the soles.

Kneeling down, Gladys gently pried the toes away from the sole and massaged the foot tenderly. Suddenly there was a giggle from the child, who wriggled with delight. "Oh, it tickles," she said.

The spell was broken. The village women gathered around, chattering happily. Everyone now wanted to tell of the pain and trouble her own feet had given for years. One of the neighbors rushed off to the next house to explain what had to be done, and soon all the housewives were exhibiting their little girls with unbound feet.

Gladys's visits to the villages became events of excitement. The children clamored around her. In the evenings the villagers crowded into the house where she would be staying to listen to the stories she told of a man called Jesus Christ, whose honorable ancestor was the great God who lived in the clouds. It appeared to these kindly people that this man Jesus had lived in a simple society closely akin to their own. He was an enthralling person, and the official foot inspector's supply of stories seemed inexhaustible.

The weeks passed into months and the months into years, and there was a harvest of happiness to be gathered from each day. In this wide terrain of high mountains and deep valleys, where the material way of living was meager and hard, Gladys grew to maturity. All that had gone before was a preparation for this, and this only a preparation for what was to come.

One day during Gladys's second year at Yangcheng a messenger from the *yamen*, the town hall, rushed into the courtyard waving a piece of scarlet paper. "An official summons from the *yamen*," he screamed. "A riot has broken out in the men's prison. You must come at once! It is an official order."

"All right," she said mildly. "I'll come. But I certainly don't see what a riot has to do with me."

They hurried to the prison. From the other side of the wall came screams, shouts, and yells. The governor of the prison, pale of face, met her at the entrance.

"The convicts are killing each other," he shouted. "You must go in and stop the fighting!"

"But I'm only the missionary woman," she said. "Why don't you send the soldiers in to stop it?"

"The soldiers are frightened. You must go in."

Gladys's mouth dropped open; her eyes rounded in amazement. "I go in there? Are you mad? If I went in, they'd kill me!"

"How can they kill you? You tell everybody you have the living God inside you—you preach it everywhere. If you preach the truth, if your God protects you from harm, then you can stop this riot."

Gladys stared at this simple man. "It's true!" she thought. "I have been preaching that my Christian God protects me from harm. Fail now, and I am finished in Yangcheng. Abandon my faith now, and I abandon it forever!"

But how could she go into the prison? Those men—murderers, thieves, bandits, rioting and killing each other inside those walls!

"Oh, God," said Gladys to herself, "give me strength!"

She looked at the governor. "All right," she said. "Open the door. I'll go in to them."

The immense iron-barred door swung open. Gladys was pushed into the courtyard. Then the door clanged shut behind her.

A WILD BATTLE was going on. Bodies were stretched out on the flagstones. One man, obviously dead, lay only a few feet away from her, blood still pouring from a great wound in his scalp. There was blood splattered everywhere.

The main group of men were watching one convict who brandished a large, bloodstained chopper. He suddenly rushed at them, and they scattered wildly to every part of the square. The man rushed again; the group parted; he singled out one man and chased him. The intended victim ran toward Gladys, then ducked away. The madman with the ax was now only a few feet from her.

Numbed with fear and hardly realizing what she was doing, she went toward him.

"Give me that chopper!" she said severely.

The man took two paces forward. For three long seconds his wild dark pupils staring from bloodshot eyes glared at her. Then suddenly, meekly, he held out the ax.

Gladys snatched the bloody weapon from his hand and held it rigidly by her side. The other convicts—there must have been 50 men cowering there—stared from every corner of the courtyard. All action was frozen in that one moment of intense drama.

"All of you!" she shouted, pressing her psychological advantage. "Come over here. Form into a line!"

Obediently the convicts shambled into a ragged group before her. For a moment she regarded them in stormy silence. Then suddenly her fear had gone. In its place was an immense, soul-searing pity that pricked the tears into her eyes. They were so wretched and hopeless! A mass of thin faces contorted with misery, pain, and hunger; remnants of humanity, half-men dressed in rags that were caked with dust, alive with lice. She could have wept openly. With an effort she pulled herself together.

"You should be ashamed of yourselves," she said, berating them like an irate mother scolding naughty children. "All this noise and all this mess! Now, if you clean up this courtyard and promise to behave in the future, I will ask the governor to deal leniently with all of you."

At that moment Gladys became conscious that the governor and his retinue were behind her. Through a small opening in the wall they had heard everything and now thought it safe to enter. The governor bowed to Gladys. "You have done well," he said.

"I have promised there will be no reprisals," she told him.

The governor nodded. "As long as there is no recurrence," he said, "we shall forget all about it."

"I'm glad," said Gladys. She turned to the prisoners. "I'm going now, but I shall be back and do all I can to help you."

"Thank you," one of them said. "Thank you, Ai-weh-deh."

She did not know at the time what the word "Ai-weh-deh" meant. That evening she asked Yang.

"Ai-weh-deh?" he said curiously. "It means The Virtuous One."

She was known as Ai-weh-deh for all her remaining years in China.

Becoming official foot inspector had given Gladys some importance in Yangcheng, but stopping a prison riot had raised her prestige enormously. Gone forever were the days when she was reviled in the streets. Even the merchants standing in their shop doorways now bowed politely as she passed.

She did not forget her promise to the prisoners. She visited them almost every day, taught them some facts about hygiene, brought them food, and read them stories. Whimsically she said to herself that they were the only parishioners she was certain of finding "at home."

It was also in her second year at Yangcheng that she began to gather together a family. She had just returned from a foot-inspection tour in the mountains and was walking down the main street when she saw a coarse, dirty woman sitting on the pavement. A child leaned against her knee, an appalling, sickly scrap of a child, clad in a dirty bit of loincloth. It had legs like stalks and a swollen belly, which told of malnutrition; the head and body were covered with running sores. Gladys was horrified.

"Woman, you have no right to sit in the baking sun with a child in that condition. It will die," she said sternly.

"If it dies, I'll soon get another one," said the woman.

Gladys glared at her. She had heard about such people—child dealers, people who bought and sold children.

The woman's next remark confirmed her thoughts. She said sneeringly, "You can have it for two dollars."

"I haven't got two dollars," Gladys answered.

"Lady with the heart of pity!" the woman said, "I will sell you the child for a shilling."

Gladys stopped and stared at her. "I haven't any money, and what would I do with the child?"

"But you want it, don't you?"

Gladys started to dispute the remark, then suddenly stopped. She did want the child.

"How much would you give?" said the woman.

Gladys had a few copper *cash* in her pocket, equal to about ninepence. "I'll give you this ninepence but not a penny more."

"She is yours," said the woman and hurried off down the street.

Gladys looked down at the child. Its age was indeterminate; roughly five years old, she reckoned. "Come with me," she said.

The child made no move. It seemed to comprehend little. Gladys had to more or less drag it to the inn. Inside the main room it ran to the darkest corner and crouched there, terrified.

At first the foundling reacted exactly like a wild animal, allowing no one to touch it. It was a girl child, a wild, dark-eyed outcast, hating everyone. But after three weeks of love and care Gladys produced another of her miracles. Ninepence—for that is what Gladys had nicknamed the child—was transformed. She now had a clean face, wore clean clothes, and announced she had come to stay. She was the first of five youngsters Gladys adopted.

If Gladys had ever had longing thoughts of home, they were dispelled forever by this growing family of chattering children around her. By 1936 her life was so tied up with China that she became a Chinese citizen. It made no difference to her work, but it made her feel as if she belonged.

No one in Yangcheng knew that the Japanese were now in power in Manchuria and were even then driving south along the age-old routes of the Mongol conquerors. So it was that one spring morning of 1938, when the little silver planes came buzzing in over the mountains, everyone ran out to watch them. Many had never seen an airplane before, and these looked pretty, swooping down out of the sun.

Gladys did not run out of the inn because, at the time, she was kneeling in prayer in an upstairs room with the cook and four converts. She did not hear the airplanes until the last minute, and then the whole world turned into a roaring, jumbled, falling, confused chaos that ended in blackness.

The people in the streets were still waving and shouting happily as the pointed metal cylinders from the bellies of the aircraft plummeted down into the town. Then the shouts turned to screams of pain and horror as chunks of flying masonry and hissing shrapnel ricocheted among them. The aircraft circled very low. It was almost impossible to miss.

One bomb struck a corner of the Inn of Eight Happinesses, killing nine people in the roadway outside. In the upstairs room where Gladys and the others were praying, the floor canted suddenly sideways, and they slid and fell downward in a welter of timber, tiles, dust, and plaster, to be buried among this debris in the room below.

Gladys lay face downward with a great beam pressing on her back. She felt no pain, but her breathing was difficult.

It seemed hours before the debris was hauled away and she was freed. She was battered and bruised, but she was able to help pull out the cook and the others.

Now there was panic and confusion everywhere.

"In the town it is dreadful," a man shouted. "All are killed!"

"We must go and see what we can do," said Gladys. Her medicine chest contained one large bottle of disinfectant (broken), one bottle of permanganate-of-potash crystals, a tin of boric powder, and some cotton. She rapidly tore her two sheets into bandage-sized strips and set off for the east gate.

Nothing in her life before had prepared her for the sight that confronted her. The center of the town appeared pulverized. Dead and dying, wounded and bomb-shocked lay everywhere, for the streets had been crowded. People still trapped were screaming for help.

"I need all of you," Gladys called to a group of onlookers. "Now get to work. Clear that rubble over there; someone is buried. Get buckets of hot water. Clear the main street so that there's a passage. Start at once."

In a distance of 10 yards she dressed the wounds of 12 people. A pail of hot water had appeared, and she emptied a few crystals from her precious bottle of permanganate into it. This she dabbed on as a rough antiseptic.

Her mouth was set in a firm line, her tunic stained with blood as she worked steadily on, bandaging and splinting and sponging with her bucket of permanganate. She kept working until late afternoon, when with a sinking heart she realized that she was still only three-quarters of the way up the main street.

Gladys went to the mandarin.

"There are still people alive under the ruins," she said. "We must get them out. We must pool the food supplies. Women must be enlisted to nurse the wounded. The town crier must make these announcements."

The mandarin nodded agreement. "I have other disturbing news," he said. "Reports have reached me that the Japanese are advancing toward Yangcheng. I understand that they are not merciful people."

"Then," said Gladys, "we ought not to waste any more time."

Clearance squads were organized. Muleteers, prisoners, and townspeople cleared the streets of rubble. The wounded were carried to the Buddhist temple, and there Gladys bathed them in her purple wash of permanganate, roughly splinted broken limbs, and comforted as best she could those who were about to die. That night a hundred flickering lamps burned within the thick walls of Yangcheng as the work progressed.

Victorious Japanese soldiers, in their khaki uniforms, swept over the mountain path five days later and entered a deserted city.

Out to the lonely villages and the mountain caves the people of Yangcheng had streamed, carrying what possessions they could. The governor of the prison and his guards had marched off with the convicts; the mandarin, with his wives, had moved to an isolated place nearby; Gladys, with her small Christian community of about 40 people, had left for a tiny walled village that lay on the side of a high peak like a swallow's nest on a sloping roof.

There she stayed for a week. Then, when news reached her that the Japanese Army had passed on through Yangcheng and that many of the people had come back, she and her charges returned.

She found the inn just as she had left it, the corner of the bombed building open toward the sky. She realized that she couldn't expect much business from then on. The mule traffic along the ancient route had fallen off. The time of peace was over. Now it would be war.

She was looking ruefully at the inn's gaping roof one day when a message arrived from the mandarin. "I am giving a feast that I would like you to attend. It will probably be the last ever held in Yangcheng. I have something I wish you to hear."

At the mandarin's feast Gladys, to her surprise, found that she was sitting in the seat of honor at her host's right. This had never happened before. All the important personages of Yangcheng were present, about a dozen in all. The meal was simple, unlike the sumptuous feasts she had enjoyed in early years.

At the end of it the mandarin stood up and made his speech. He told how Ai-weh-deh had first come to Yangcheng; what she had done for the poor and the sick and the imprisoned; of the new faith called Christianity which she had brought with her and which he had discussed with her on many occasions. Gladys was puzzled by his remarks. But at the end of his talk he turned toward her and said, "I would like, Ai-weh-deh, to embrace your faith. I would like to become a Christian."

Around the table everyone nodded and smiled as Gladys got up and stuttered her surprise, her appreciation, and her thanks. She had made the most important convert of all her years in China.

IN FEBRUARY 1940 Gladys decided to join David and Jean Davis, young Welsh missionaries, in Tsincheng, even though that city had been occupied by the Japanese. She arrived to find that David Davis was planning a trip to the coast, a month's journey away, and needed someone to help his wife run the mission while he was gone. The Japanese, he told her, had thus far respected the neutrality of the mission, which was now crowded with refugees, including some 200 children. But before Davis left, Gladys had a horrible experience from which came the injuries that were to trouble her for years.

She first heard the screams about midnight, when a party of Japanese soldiers who had crept in through the front gate began to smash down the doors of the rooms occupied by at least a hundred women—refugees, converts, visitors from villages. Gladys hurried into the women's courtyard. A Japanese officer snapped a command. Without warning, a soldier swung his rifle and crashed the butt against her head. She fell, barely conscious, realizing only that the rifle butt was still clumping into her body and that other Japanese soldiers were kicking her ruthlessly into unconsciousness. By the time David Davis, hearing the commotion, had raced to the courtyard, Gladys was a limp bundle of rags.

Davis stared aghast at the scene. There were at least 30 armed Japanese, intent on rape, struggling with screaming women in various stages of undress. The Japanese officer tugged his revolver from its holster. With the butt end he hit Davis across the mouth as hard as he could. The impact knocked Davis down, his cheek and mouth badly cut. But groggily, like a boxer, he pushed himself up to his knees, blood dripping down his tunic, and shouted: "Pray! Pray, all of you!"

And now the women were on their knees, their hands clasped together, praying loudly. It was a sight to baffle even the most lascivious. The Japanese soldiers stared stupidly, not knowing what to do. The officer shouted at them; they shambled out of the courtyard, the officer stalking after them.

The women carried Gladys to her room and revived her with cold water. She got up next morning feeling bruised and sore, and not certain what had happened. She suffered internal pains for many months afterward. But she did not let them interfere with her work.

In the spring the Japanese retreated from Tsincheng, and Nationalist troops entered the city. One day a Chinese officer came to the mission and asked for an audience with Gladys. He was young and in some indefinable way different from all the other men she had met during her stay in China. As he bowed and greeted her ceremoniously, she noticed the dark, shining hair brushed up from the high pale forehead, the dark almond-shaped eyes under black eyebrows, the clear golden skin.

With a dignity rather like that of the mandarin, he told her that his name was Linnan and that he was a colonel in Generalissimo Chiang Kai-shek's intelligence service. The situation in Shansi was confused, and he had been sent to find out what was going on. It was an area vital to the defense of China.

At last he asked simply, "Will you help China?"

Gladys frowned. "How can I help? You're fighting a war. This mission belongs to God."

"Does God insist on neutrality in all things?" he asked gently. "Is He not against evil?"

"Yes . . . but . . ." Gladys had never thought very precisely about the ethics of the conflict that had margined the past two years of her life. It was odd that this gentle-voiced young man should force her to confront these issues. At length she said, "I will help you as far as my conscience will allow."

He stood up and bowed. "That is most kind of you," he said softly. "I will come and talk with you further, if I may."

It was a week before he called again. This time he asked her many questions and told her how he yearned for a China strong and free and incorruptible. When he left, he asked if he might see her again. It was then that Gladys became aware, through some subtle nuance of his speech, that he had actually called to see *her!*

She shook her head in disbelief—then went to the cracked mirror in the corner of her room and stared at herself. Her eyes were large and dark and, although her skin was tanned by the sun, the years had chiseled only a few faint lines from their corners. But how somber was her dark blue high-necked tunic! Unthinkingly, she plucked a white flower from the vase in the corner and stuck it in her hair.

Linnan and Gladys became good friends. They were the same age; both had eager, inquisitive minds. In the evenings they would often walk through the narrow streets of Tsincheng, or in the fields around the old walled city, and watch the moon setting behind the tiled pagodas. Each time they met, the immense gulfs between their separate worlds grew narrower. She was a missionary dedicated to God. But God had also made her a woman full of the natural tides and forces that stir womankind. If she was falling in love, she reasoned, then it was God who had allowed it to happen.

Once when Gladys returned from a long trip into the mountains she told Linnan about two villages where Japanese troops had been billeted. Linnan questioned her closely about the number of troops, what weapons they had, where they were situated. The next time she went into territory occupied by the Japanese she made more careful note of their numbers and their armament. He had stirred in her a latent patriotism for her adopted country; if she could bring information through the Japanese lines unhindered and so help to defeat the common enemy, then she would be useful.

Few love affairs can have flourished in stranger circumstances. They met at odd moments in the mountains, in shattered villages, in the bombed towns. They talked when they could between battles and births and baptisms. His concern, his gentleness, his tenderness toward her never wavered. He was eager that they should marry at once, live together as man and wife as best they could, war or no war.

It was Gladys who said no. The war had to be won first. Marriage, their personal happiness, must wait.

With the coming of a new spring, word arrived that the Japanese were once again approaching and Tsincheng had to be evacuated. Gladys's first concern was for the 200 children she was caring for in the mission. She had written to the capital at Chungking and was assured that they would be fed, clothed, housed, and educated out of Madame Chiang Kai-shek's funds for refugee children—if they could get to Sian, across the Yellow River. So Gladys sent half the children to Sian under the guidance of a young Chinese convert.

Three weeks later Gladys heard that the children had been delivered safely and the guide was on his way back to get the other 100. Gladys waited impatiently; conditions at the mission were becoming more and more chaotic. But he never arrived. He was captured by the Japanese and presumably shot. Meanwhile, as the Japanese troops fought their way to within a few miles of the city, Gladys put the remaining children in the charge of two women mission workers and sent them off to the old inn at Yangcheng.

Gladys planned to stay in Tsincheng temporarily to help protect the mission. But the very night the children left, a Nationalist general sent his orderly to the mission to urge her to leave at once. When she refused, the orderly handed her a piece of paper. "These leaflets are being pasted up in the villages outside Tsincheng. They will appear on the gates of this city tomorrow, Ai-weh-deh," he said.

She read the handbill:

ONE HUNDRED DOLLAR'S REWARD WILL BE PAID BY THE JAPANESE ARMY FOR INFORMATION LEADING TO THE CAPTURE, ALIVE, OF ANY OF THE THREE PEOPLE LISTED BELOW.

First was the mandarin of Tsincheng. Second was the name of a well-known businessman, notorious for his Nationalist sympathies. The third line read simply:

THE SMALL WOMAN, KNOWN AS AI-WEH-DEH.

Gladys did not know what to do, but on impulse reached out for her Bible, flipped it open, then bent forward to read at random the line of Chinese characters. She did not remember ever having seen this passage before. Now she read it aloud in growing awe:

"Flee ye into the mountains! Dwell deeply in the hidden places because the King of Babylon has conceived a purpose against you!"

If she wanted a sign, was this not it?

She went into the compound, carrying her Bible, and peered out through the small spyhole in the gate. A party of Japanese soldiers was already marching into the city.

Gladys turned and began to walk across the compound. As she walked, panic began to build inside her. She broke into a run.

The back gate was her objective, the back gate through which by immemorial custom they carried out the dead. Outside lay the open stretch of the Strangers' Burying Ground. Beyond that was the shallow grass-grown moat that encircled the city, and away to the right stretched a large field of wheat.

But she had made one bad error of judgment. The route of escape from the back gate was in plain view of the advancing detachment of Japanese soldiers. She raced right into their vision.

She knew she was inviting a fusillade but she could not stop now; she was committed to flight.

As she raced through the graveyard she was conscious of the crack of rifles and the bee-whine of ricochets as bullets glanced off the tombstones around her. The edge of the moat was only a few yards away. She tried to spurt toward it, but something suddenly punched her in the back, knocking her flat on her face. She knew a bullet had hit her. "I'm dying," she thought.

Then she became aware of a burning sensation across her shoulder blades and realized that she was not dying at all, but soon might be, for bullets were still ricocheting all around her.

Her Bible had fallen with her; she could feel it pressing into her stomach. Using the Bible as a sled she wormed her way forward, pushing with her toes and tearing at the earth with her hands. Panting, she reached the moat and tumbled into it.

Doubled up, she scuttled along the moat until she could see the wheat growing above her head. She burrowed into it, edging backward so that she could replace the slender stalks and leave no telltale sign behind her. In the middle of the field she felt fairly safe.

Now she could feel the sting in her back. The bullet had skidded across the right shoulder blade. The wound had bled little, but she felt weak, as if all will had ebbed from her body. She closed her eyes.

When Gladys awoke, she felt much better. As night fell, she tunneled through the wheat to the farther edge of the field, then hurried toward the mountains. As she picked her way up the rocky slopes, she realized that she must leave this part of Shansi. If the Japanese knew she had remained, they might torture her friends or the children in her care. She herself would take the children to Sian.

Two days later Gladys was walking down the Yangcheng road to the Inn of Eight Happinesses. The children were overjoyed to see her. They crowded around in the courtyard, laughing and chattering.

"Tonight," she told them, "I want you all to go to bed early. Tomorrow we're going for a long walk across the mountains."

There was a burst of spontaneous cheering. A long walk was a wonderful adventure.

Later that night Gladys went to see the mandarin. She felt a sense of overwhelming sadness for the dying city. There was only one guard at the door of the mandarin's small chamber.

The mandarin was plainly dressed in a blue robe and a black skull-cap, and Gladys regretfully recalled those wonderful gowns of scarlet and gold of the past.

"Ai-weh-deh," he said gently, "it is good to see you!"

The mandarin was older. Like her, like all the Chinese people in Shansi, he had been living in an agony of doubt and fear. He had fled the city and carried on his civic business from a mountain village. When the enemy left his city, he had returned to its ruins.

He listened gravely as she told him what had happened and of her decision to try to reach Sian.

"I have heard that the Japanese armies have reached the Yellow River," the mandarin said. "You will have to cross their territory. It will be very dangerous."

"We shall stay away from all the known trails."

"With 100 children?"

"With 100 children," she said. "I dare not leave one behind."

"That is true," he agreed sadly. He paused for a second. "You have money, food for the journey?"

"Neither."

He smiled, then chuckled aloud. "You have a faculty for facing the formidable, Ai-weh-deh, with a calm which I have envied all these years."

"I've said it to you many times: 'God will provide.' "

"Yes," he answered, "but on this occasion, at least, let the mandarin of Yangcheng act as His agent. I can provide you with two baskets of millet and two men to carry them for the first part of your journey. It will take you weeks to reach Sian—you understand that?"

"I know."

"May God help you," the mandarin said. "May the good fortune you deserve be yours."

They bowed low to each other.

At dawn the young children were up and running around the

courtyard, behaving in the normal way of young children the world over. In vain Gladys tried to tell them they must save their energy for the long day ahead. Then the mandarin's two coolies, carrying the baskets of millet on their shoulder poles, arrived. Now they were on their way, the children scampering ahead, shouting that they could walk forever and ever.

At noon they stopped to eat their boiled millet. After filling the children's basins there wasn't much left for Gladys, and from then on that is the way it usually turned out. The children, revived after the meal, began again to make excited forays ahead, but as the afternoon progressed, these minor expeditions became fewer and fewer, and very soon she had four small ones hanging onto her coat. Gladys took turns with Ninepence and the older children carrying them.

It was getting dark when they came to a mountain village where she thought they might find shelter for the night. Help came from an unexpected quarter. A Buddhist priest, in his bright saffron robes, let them eat and sleep in his temple.

The next day was a replica of the first. That night, far from any village, Gladys and the children huddled together in the shelter of a semicircle of rocks to get out of the wind. In the morning the two coolies had to return to Yangcheng.

The next two nights were also spent in the open. This was new country to Gladys, but she knew by the direction of the sun that they were heading south. Much of the millet was used up now, and the food had to be carefully rationed for the wild and barren stretch of mountains that lay ahead.

Their thin cloth shoes were wearing through, and they were covered with dust and dirt. Nevertheless, they moved onward through the mountains until, on the 12th day, they emerged from the foothills and saw the Yellow River in the distance. At last, they thought, they were in sight of relief.

The road they followed led to the river town of Yüankü. But there was no one there. Rubble littered the streets, most of the houses were roofless. This meant the Japanese would soon arrive.

They trudged down a dusty path to the river only to discover that there the waters were almost a mile across, running swift and deep. There was no sign of boats. They huddled together in a hollow on the bank, and Gladys fell eventually into a deep but uneasy slumber.

When she woke next morning, the children were calling, "Ai-weh-deh, we are hungry. When shall we have something to eat?"

"Soon," she told them. "Soon."

She sent the older boys back to Yüankü to search the empty houses for food. Three hours later they came back triumphant with a few pounds of moldy millet and some dusty-looking cakes of dough, which she boiled and ladled carefully into the forest of waving basins. As usual, there was not enough for Gladys.

That night as the children huddled together on the bank of the river she comforted them as best she could.

At the end of four days there was still no sign of a boat. Even the youngest children had caught the mood of despair. Then one of them asked, "Ai-weh-deh, why does not God open the waters of the Yellow River for us to cross as He did for the Israelites?"

For a moment she paused. How to tell a hungry child that miracles

were not just for the asking? How to say, although I can face a mortal enemy wherever he may beset me, I cannot open these vast waters? I have no power other than the power of my own faith. What she said was: "Let us all sing a hymn to God. And perhaps soon our prayers will be answered."

A Chinese Nationalist officer commanding a platoon scouting the riverbank was suddenly jarred to a standstill by a far-off high-pitched sound, wavering and uncertain. A plane? His men thought so and thumbed back their helmets to cast their eyes over the cloudless sky. And yet this noise sounded almost like singing.

The young officer shook his head as though to clear it. Then he crawled up a slight rise in the bank and peered over the edge.

It was an astonishing sight. A great crowd of children were assembled on the bank, all seated in a circle and singing loudly. The officer motioned his men back with a hand signal. "Wait here," he said. "It may be a trick. Be alert." Then he walked farther along the bank, and the children saw him.

"Ai-weh-deh," they shouted with delight, "here's a soldier!"

The young officer noticed then for the first time the small woman sitting on the ground. She was thin and hungry-looking. She got to her feet as he approached, and with a shock of surprise he realized that she was a foreigner.

"Are you mad?" he said. "Who are you?"

"We are refugees trying to reach Sian," she said simply.

"This will soon be a battlefield. Don't you realize that?" he asked.

"All China is a battlefield," she replied wearily.

She looked steadily at him, until he said, "I will get a boat and try to ferry you across in three loads. But it is dangerous. If a Japanese plane comes over when we are halfway, there will be little hope."

He inserted his fingers in his mouth and whistled loudly. Soon two figures far away on the other bank pushed a boat into the water and began to scull it across.

Gladys swayed a little as one of the children pushed against her. The officer looked at her curiously. "You are ill," he said.

"I am fine," she said. "When we get to Sian I shall be all right."

When they were all safely across the river, the officer walked back to his platoon. It was curious about that foreigner. If this had been close to a large city he could have understood it, but wandering across a battlefield escorting an army of ragged Chinese children—that was, indeed, very curious.

At Mienchih next morning, Gladys loaded the children on railway cars—simple wooden boxes with roofs—and for four days they rattled slowly forward. At intervals along the line there were refugee feeding-camps. Gladys dozed a great deal of the time. It wasn't that she felt ill; it was as if a general weariness had settled in her bones.

They got off the train at Shenhsien, where the mountains rose steeply ahead of them. The peaks frightened Gladys. She didn't want to go on; she wanted to stop where she was and rest. But she knew it was impossible. Their only hope of permanent refuge was Sian.

They were all practically barefoot now and the sharp stones on the trail cut their feet, but they toiled upward. Next day found them among high peaks, intimidating and desolate. That afternoon, when Gladys was seated on a rock for one of their frequent rests, she looked around at the children. The eight- and nine-year-olds were still ahead, but two dozen of the little ones with mournful faces were gathered around her, almost too exhausted to plead to be carried. The older girls were slumped in attitudes of utter dejection, their chins in their cupped hands.

Gladys felt something wet flowing down her cheek. She tried to flick the tears away but they only came faster and faster. Soon she was sobbing aloud, abandoning herself to her grief, sobbing because she had no strength to stay her tears, sobbing from sheer weakness and exhaustion, sobbing for all the children, for all China, and for all the world. The children sobbed with her, and the little boys coming back down the trail stood openmouthed and they too began to wail. For many minutes the sound of their distress echoed in the valley.

When it was over, Gladys wiped her face with her coat sleeve and sniffed. The tears had cleansed her soul, washed away the bleak desperation. She smiled wanly.

"A good cry is always good for one," she said stoutly. "Now, that's enough, all of you. We'll sing a hymn, and while we're singing it we shall march along the trail."

Those old mountains in their long years of sun and wind and rain must have seen many strange sights, but it is doubtful if they had ever seen anything more unusual, or more gallant, than this column of singing children led by a small woman with a tearstained face.

Another two days, one without food, brought them through the mountains and onto the plain, where they again clambered aboard a freight train. Gladys did not really remember how many days the trip lasted. She only knew that it had been March when they set out and now it was late in April. But she did remember forming the children into a ragged line outside the Sian station and saying to them, "As we march at last through the gates of Sian, we shall sing a hymn."

An old Chinese lifted his head as she spoke. "Woman," he said, "you will never get into Sian. The gates are closed. No more refugees are allowed into the city!"

She did not believe him. She could not believe him. The mute faces of the children were turned up toward her. All these long weeks she had sustained them with the mirage of Sian.

"Where shall we go then?" she said desperately.

The old man pointed. "There is a refugee camp outside the walls yonder. They will feed you."

Gladys then led the children to the camp, and while they were being fed she herself went back along the road to the city. As she got closer she could see that the massive wooden gates were barred and shut. A watcher from the walls above shouted: "Woman, go away! The city is packed with refugees. No one comes in!"

She leaned her face against the hard surface of the gate and wept. So long a journey—and for this! For this!

Gladys walked slowly back to rejoin the children, not knowing what to tell them. But they had news for her instead. Representatives of Madame Chiang Kai-shek's New Life movement had discovered them and arranged to care for the children at nearby Fufeng.

Of the train journey to Fufeng she remembered only that there were pleasant young women wearing armbands of the New Life movement at the station to meet them. At the orphanage there the children were equipped with new clothes and shoes and alloted places to sleep. Gladys was given a little room in the temple, and the children came in all the time to show off their new clothes, or receive comfort for a new bruise, or just to tell "Mother" the latest news.

She dimly recalled that two Chinese women who ran a small Christian mission had invited her to preach at a nearby village. Of course, said Gladys. But as she walked along the sun-baked road she started having trouble with her feet. They did not want to go down in the right places. When she reached the village she was given a basin of food. But the food wouldn't go into her mouth: she could not control her hands. The others looked at her rather strangely. Would she like to lie down for a little while before she gave her sermon? Yes. It must be the heat that made her feel a little odd.

She stretched out wearily on the hard bed, her Bible by her side. The retinas of her eyeballs were shot with a great whirring blaze of colors—scarlets and purples and yellows. She felt hot. Then the great lights faded from the back of her eyes and she fell into darkness.

By the time they came to fetch her an hour or so later, Gladys was raving in delirium.

When at last the small woman stirred back into consciousness in her bed at the Baptist hospital in Sian, she and the kindly doctor to whom she owed her life were able to piece together the last link in the chain. Undoubtedly the distraught Christian women had prevailed upon the peasants to put Gladys into their oxcart and take her to the Scandinavian-Alliance Mission, where they had dumped her unceremoniously at the gate.

Gladys recovered sufficiently from her multiple wounds and diseases to leave the hospital. But she was still not really well; she had blackouts and spells of mental derangement. During this period Linnan came to Sian. He implored her to marry him and go with him to Chungking, where he was posted, but somehow their relationship had altered. Somewhere in the mountains between Yangcheng and the Yellow River and Sian, somewhere in the deep drifts of delirium and the fevers of her illness, certitude had been replaced by anxiety in Gladys's heart. All this, in tears, she tried to explain to Linnan; all this, in the despair of his love, he tried to brush aside. But it was no use. There was still so much work to be done for the Lord, and she, the small woman, the small disciple, had her part to play in that work. So she said good-bye to him with an overwhelming ache of loneliness in her heart, aware only that she would never know completely if she had acted wisely or not—only that through all the rest of her waking days she would remember Linnan as the one man she had loved.

When Linnan left to be caught up in the stream of war once more, Gladys set to work to provide for the five children she had adopted, earning a little money from the New Life movement and as a teacher of English. She also started a Christian church for refugees, in an unused factory. She kept at this until Ninepence got married and her four other children went away to school. Then Gladys went off to Chengtu, almost on the borders of Tibet, to work in a leper colony.

There she met an American missionary who, touched by her poverty and long years of service in China, managed to get funds to send Gladys Aylward home to England.

It did not, of course, work out quite as quickly as that. It took another three years of worry, indecision, and heartache before Gladys Aylward agreed to sail for England. Only after long consideration and prayer did she decide that God would wish her to return and therefore she should go.

Back in England Gladys Aylward continued her busy life—lecturing and preaching in churches, schools, and mission halls. She became a second mother to scores of Chinese students arriving in England for the first time. She also played a major role in setting up a hospital in Liverpool for Chinese seamen.

But for Gladys Aylward her dedication to China could not be denied. She went back again to where she believed she belonged. Because mainland China was now controlled by the Communists, she went to Taiwan (Formosa), where she founded an orphanage. She remained director of the Gladys Aylward Children's Home until her death of pneumonia at 68 in January 1970.

She was truly one of the most remarkable women of her generation.

*The revolutionaries who boarded the train
that night had come to rob and murder.
Only one faint hope of escape remained for the
occupants of the rear compartment.*

Night Train

By D. W. David

IT WAS BENGAL, 1942, a dark time for India. At our regimental
forward base depot in Dacca, the adjutant handed Captain N. and
me sets of identical papers, sealed and top secret. We were on our
way to join the regiment at Chittagong, and we had a very dangerous
railway journey ahead of us.

"I can't offer you any escort," the adjutant said. "I haven't a man
to spare. But these dispatches must reach our commanding officer
just as soon as possible. We aren't in wireless contact, so I must
depend on you two."

By this time Singapore had fallen, Malaya was overrun, and Japanese columns, driving through Burma, were poised to attack Assam,
the gateway to India. Added to this threat from the east, the country
harbored another menace within itself—militant activists who demanded immediate independence for India. The vast majority of
Indians were loyal to the British government, but a small, articulate
group of political extremists detested the British even more than the
Japanese aggressors. Long years of patronizing rebuffs had bred hatred of British rule, and pro-Axis riots were beginning to hamstring
the desperate efforts of the military.

Our journey to Chittagong involved a night on the train and a
crossing of the great Brahmaputra River—in ordinary circumstances
just a tiring ride of some 200 miles. But now there was the hazard of
encountering *goondas*—bands of hooligans, revolutionaries, and
thieves—carrying long cane-cutting machetes. They often waylaid
trains to rob and murder white occupants.

The adjutant was nervous. "These dispatches contain the names of
known Japanese sympathizers in Chittagong, who, in the event of a

Jap breakthrough, would be a ready-made fifth column," he said. "I've made two identical copies so that . . ."

His meaning was plain. If one of us fell afoul of the goondas, the other might with luck get through.

Captain N., a former tea planter, had little use for Indian aspirations and regarded all extreme nationalists as traitors. He was scornful of the adjutant's excessive caution.

"I'd like to see any goonda interfere with me," he growled.

I shared the captain's scorn, but for different reasons. A young subaltern, I was full of pride in British arms. If the "thin red line" had controlled the Indian masses for centuries, there was no reason now for an armed British officer to fear a few underfed zealots with knives. As to Indian politics, I knew little and certainly cared less; I was here to fight a war.

At the station Captain N. and I threaded our way through the swarming crowd and entered our respective compartments—his near the engine and mine at the rear. (More caution on the adjutant's part!) The porters stowed my luggage. I opened the screened windows of my carriage and, as the train lurched out of the station, poured myself a drink—whisky and cold water out of a Thermos. Then I lay down on my bunk. Soon the whisky and the low, pounding rhythm of the wheels were having their effect.

What woke me I do not know. The train was motionless, and the dim light in the compartment had gone out. The fan had stopped, too, and my bush jacket clung to me damply. A mosquito seemed to be droning near my ear—louder, louder, louder. Suddenly I sat bolt upright. I had heard that noise once before. It was the voice of a mob—an eerie, mindless sound like the roaring of the sea, but with a shrill counterpoint of hatred to fret the nerves.

We had stopped at a large station. The platform was a swaying mass of figures. *"Jai Hind!"* the mob was yelling ("Free India!"—the slogan of all Indian nationalists). I closed the windows and quick-ran to the door on the other side. No one was visible. The ground beyond the track fell away into open country.

A revolver cracked, once, twice, then twice more in rapid succession. I jumped down onto the track and looked up the long curved line of the train. Suddenly the door to Captain N.'s compartment burst open, and a mass of struggling figures spilled out. The figures dispersed and, in the gray light of early dawn, I could make out a body on the ground. I was alone.

At that instant I felt my arm gripped. I whipped around, prepared

494

to sell my life dearly, and confronted a terrified middle-aged Eurasian, a half-caste of mixed English and Indian blood. His topee was askew. His equally terrified wife cringed at his side.

"For God's sake, Mr. Officer, help us!" the man gasped.

"What's going on?"

"The goondas are attacking the Europeans on the train. They are working their way down from the engine. We shall all be murdered. Help us, sahib! In God's name, what to do?"

At 22 years of age, without experience in mob control, I didn't know. The cockiness I had shared with Captain N. died with him. But I couldn't admit my ignorance and fear, even to myself. I was British, a decision-maker (the Eurasian's use of "sahib" implied this).

"Quick, into my carriage!" I said.

The Eurasian and his wife scrambled in. I followed, locked the doors and windows, and sat down. I had no idea what to do. I lighted a cigarette. Trying to look impassive, I offered the Eurasian one, but he stared at me without comprehension. Fear had totally engulfed him. I felt my resentment rising as I looked at his ashen countenance. No man likes to see his own weakness reflected in another's face.

Crash!

An ax was being used on the door—blow after blow rained against it. I knew it could not last long, but with the crisis upon me I felt calmer. I reviewed the courses open to me. I could wait for them to burst in and slaughter us, as they surely would. I could open the window and fire at them, as Captain N. had done. Or perhaps I could persuade them that the police or military were on their way. A faint hope, but better than certain death.

I rose and approached the door. The Eurasian, realizing my intention, sprang at me and clawed my arm, gibbering in his terror and despair. I shook him off, and he sprawled against the bunk.

I opened the window. Immediately outside, the ax wielder paused, his ax raised in mid-stroke.

Just behind him, directing operations, stood three men, dressed in the invariable uniform of white trousers, white open-necked shirt, and white forage cap. Behind them stretched a sea of yelling, expectant faces: the eternal mob.

I addressed the nearest of the three leaders, a dark, intense youth; a student, perhaps, from some university.

"You can't come in," I said. "This is a first-class compartment."

The young man stared. "How dare you, a foreigner, tell us what we cannot do in our own country?"

We gazed at each other, a young Indian and a young Englishman of approximately the same age. Had I been older, more set in my beliefs, I might have reacted differently. As it was, I had an uneasy feeling his question made sense.

"What is it you want?"

"We want to travel to the river—in *this* compartment."

This was my last chance. A wrong decision could mean a horrible death for the two Eurasians who had trusted me, death as well for many who would face treachery if the papers I carried failed to reach their destination. I looked at the speaker for a long moment, and something I seemed to see in his eyes gave me hope. I stepped back and opened the door.

With deliberate dignity the three mounted the steps and entered the carriage. The last one turned and spoke swiftly to the waiting crowd, four of whom detached themselves and followed him. Dark, unsmiling men, gaunt with hunger and bitterness, they crowded into the compartment, waiting for orders. They kept their hands behind their backs, but I knew what they held.

As the train jolted into motion and pulled out of the station, I realized that all that stood between us and death was my own persuasiveness. No other help was possible now.

The dark youth opened the interrogation: "Where are you going?"

I explained.

"Why should you expect us Indians to fight your battles for you?"

The Japanese, I tried to tell him, were no respecters of persons. If they conquered India, they would enslave the whole population, native and European, whatever their political opinions.

"Even if that were true, why should we care? We are slaves now, to you British. Millions of us are starving. What could the Japanese do to us worse than you and your countrymen have already done?"

I had never looked at it that way, but I could see his point. Still, I didn't yield. I told him what the Japanese had done in their conquered territories.

"I do not believe you. The Japanese are Orientals like ourselves. They will welcome us as allies—we are fighting the same enemy."

How many hours we argued, I do not know. But I knew I had to keep talking whether I was making any impression or not. And, as we talked, I began to realize that the young man was uncertain of his theories—he seemed to need to talk to convince himself.

His companions required no such stimulus. Older, more sullen, they wanted to get the business over with. Their instinct was to kill, to wipe out the hated enemy. But the young man was their leader. He had been to college. He was India's future. They would not dare act without him.

The hatchet men remained standing, swaying to the rhythm of the train. The Eurasians huddled together in the corner. We talked on.

Looking back now, many years later, I can see the young Indian and myself in clearer perspective. We were playing cards with death as the stakes; but the bloom of youth and idealism had not quite left us, and we still believed in reason. I wanted desperately to change the young man's poor opinion of my people; he burned to show me the error of my countrymen's ways.

Then, as always, the hope of the world lay in the meeting of young people of different races—before their attitudes harden, before they identify themselves completely with their nation and background. Our conversation was just such a meeting.

We talked on.

Then, suddenly, the balance of power was reversed—the train came to an abrupt halt, and from outside came the sound of running feet and British voices shouting commands. The door was flung open. An enormous sergeant shouldered in, followed by an Indian noncommissioned officer who glared at my goonda companions like a wolf. Behind these two I could see a platoon of troops ranged along the side of the train.

The sergeant stared at me. "You all right, sir? We heard about the ambush, never expected to find anyone alive. I'll take these scoundrels to the civil police. You'll be making a charge, of course?"

I looked around the compartment. The Eurasian was transformed. Fear had left him; hatred now suffused his face. Without a word to me, he dragged his wife from the compartment. Pausing before the raiders, he spat out one word: "Bastards!"

I looked at the others. The hatchet men stood dully. They would accept whatever fate had in store for them. The two older goondas likewise seemed fatalistic; whether I charged them or not would not alter their attitudes in any way. The battle I had to win was for the mind of the young man.

Again, I read my answer in his eyes, eyes that appealed to me not for mercy but for understanding. I knew then that my next few words would be decisive. Would he become a rabid hater of "foreigners" like his companions, or an influence for the moderation and sanity the world so desperately needed?

I turned to the sergeant. "No," I said, "there will be no charge."

*Separated from his fiancée by the Iron
Curtain, a young Swede took matters
into his own hands and embarked on a gamble that
few would have dared to undertake.*

Fly by Night

By Hans Cars

THE PREDICAMENT IN WHICH ISOLDE and I found ourselves seemed fictional, fantastic, right from the start.

We met while I was on holiday behind the Iron Curtain. I was a Swedish student working for my doctorate in political science. She was a medical student from East Berlin: beautiful, slender, with dark hair and smiling eyes. In a few days we were in love, and three months later, while visiting her at her apartment in East Berlin, I asked her to marry me.

"But that's impossible," Isolde said, her eyes brimming with tears. "The authorities would never let me leave the country."

I refused to take no for an answer and finally convinced her that she must try to escape. On a map we examined the Communist borders stretching from the Baltic to the Black Sea and considered how we would slip out. By that time (July 1965) all the "standard" means of escape, such as a break through the Berlin Wall, were too risky.

Suddenly, to my own astonishment, I heard myself say, "I'll *fly* you out, Isolde."

Her eyebrows shot up. "But I didn't know you were a pilot."

"I'm not," I admitted. I had never been in a cockpit in my life. "But I'll go back to Sweden and learn to fly, and then I'll fetch you."

Isolde looked at me as if I were crazy. But before the evening was over, she agreed that a small plane was our best chance.

The trouble was that, within an hour of my first lesson in Stockholm, I learned that flying was not my strong point. My coordination was poor, my depth perception and sense of balance wretched.

But I kept at it, and eventually I was learning how to execute ludicrously inept landings. My instructor, however, was not encouraging. My persistence in flying too low over the treetops (one day I would have to fly that low to get in under the Communist radar beams) especially upset him. "Higher, higher!" he'd shout. "We don't want to lose our plane!"

It took me nearly a year, 40 training hours in the air, to get my pilot's certificate. One August day in 1966 I got the precious document. I was also successful in obtaining a tourist visa valid for entry into Czechoslovakia, which we had decided was the country best suited for the rescue flight.

Next morning, Sunday, August 14, I took the train to Vienna and on Monday drove from there to the nearby Czech border in a hired car. The frontier police examined my visa and painstakingly checked my car and luggage. I made myself relax. How were they to know that my real mission here was to find a suitable out-of-the-way field in which to land and pick up Isolde?

I selected an abandoned pasture north of Bratislava and about 25 miles east of Vienna, near a point where the somber wooden guard towers were a little farther apart than usual.

Although there were no Cessnas—the only plane with which I was familiar—available in Vienna, I learned that I could hire a similar type in Salzburg, 155 miles away. I took the train there and proved to an inspector at the airport that I could handle the plane. Then I managed to navigate the little aircraft back to Vienna.

Everything was now ready. From Salzburg I had sent Isolde the coded telegram she had awaited so long: "MAGNUS ARRIVES AT 1640. BRUNO." In the Swedish calendar, of which Isolde had a copy, each day has a special Christian name. Magnus was the following day, Friday, August 19, and I was asking Isolde to meet me at the railway station in Brno, Czechoslovakia.

On Friday afternoon I sped by car to Brno, 68 miles away. Isolde was there at the station. In our joy at being together again, we forgot for an hour or so that the night held any problems for us.

By dinner time our laughter was hollow, our smiles frozen. We were aware that we might be celebrating our last meal.

After dark we drove to the "escape field." I switched off the lights before leaving the road and crossed the pasture in the dark. There was no time to waste. At any moment the tower's searchlight, slashing about in circles just 330 yards away, might spot the car.

"Hide here in the trees until morning," I told Isolde. "I'll come just after dawn. When you see my plane, wave your red scarf to show me where you are. And remember, whatever happens, I love you."

Back in Vienna two hours later, I was far too excited to sleep. Instead, I wrote a letter to my parents in Sweden, telling them for the first time about Isolde and asking for their understanding in case anything went wrong. At about 3 A.M. I checked out of the hotel and went to the airport, where I explained that "urgent business in Salzburg" required me to take off just as soon as it was light. But I had hardly settled in the cockpit when the sky was split by jagged forks of lightning, followed by tremendous thunderclaps. Then the rain began to fall, and I was unable to take off.

For two more hours I fumed and fretted, waiting for the storm to abate. Finally, at 8 o'clock sharp, I was cleared for takeoff.

Once outside the traffic pattern, I dived to treetop level to slip under the radar surveillance at the border. Hedgehopping, I followed the main railway into Czechoslovakia, swept in between the two guard towers I'd chosen, and skimmed over the empty pasture at an altitude of only 65 feet.

No familiar waving red scarf. Isolde was not there! I banked and roared back toward the two guard towers. Terrified, I fully expected the soldiers, plainly visible on the towers, to open fire. But I caught them off guard.

Safely back in Vienna, I was utterly exhausted and worried sick about what might have happened to Isolde. There was only one thing to do. I hired a car and rushed back to Czechoslovakia, to the Bratislava hotel where we had planned to meet if anything went wrong. She was there, safe though badly shaken.

In her hiding place she had been drenched with rain, frightened by unfamiliar night sounds, and terrified when, at dawn, she had heard a burst of shots from the nearby border. Remembering our agreement that I would arrive shortly after dawn, she was afraid that something had happened to me. Yet she had waited for me until full daylight. Only then had she left her hiding place and found a road where, eventually, a motorist picked her up.

Despite her ordeal and knowing that a second attempt might be twice as dangerous, Isolde was eager to try again.

"What other chance will we ever have, Hans?" she asked.

The following morning we set out north along the border searching for a new "escape field." We found it near the little town of Mikulov. It was well marked by a small lake and a tall pine grove that I believed I could easily see from the air.

I left Isolde there about 3:30 P.M., again promising to pick her up at dawn the next day, Monday, August 22.

On the way back to Vienna I stopped briefly in several towns to make small sketches of the distinctive church steeples in each. These, I hoped, would help lead me back to the meadow. It was late afternoon when I stopped at the airport. Because the airport people were still friendly, I knew the Czech authorities had not lodged a complaint about my illegal morning flight.

Trying to sound casual, I asked the meteorologist, "What about the flying weather tomorrow, good?"

"No," he said. "Low-hanging clouds are moving in early tonight."

This meant that, with my limited experience, takeoff and landing might be impossible by morning. The news hit me like a blow in the stomach. If all our efforts were not to be in vain, I'd have to act quickly. It was now 5:30 P.M., and soon it would be getting dark.

I rushed over to the flight operations desk and tried to keep my voice level as I said, "I'd like to take a little exercise flight, just to see the sunset."

"All right," said the flight dispatcher, "but since you are not cleared for night flying, you must be back by dusk—no later!"

Even though I knew I couldn't get back before dark, and I'd never flown at night, I dashed for my plane and took off.

Following the church steeples I'd sketched, I found my stretch of frontier, dived to an altitude of only 30 feet, and leapfrogged a hill between two guard towers. Suddenly, right in front of me and less than 100 yards away was a third tower I hadn't seen before. I missed the tower top by what seemed inches. A soldier opened his eyes wide with terror as I practically flew into his open mouth.

But the near miss disorientated me. Where was the little lake, the tall pine grove where I had left Isolde? Circling, I found one lake, then another, but neither was *ours*. I broke into a cold sweat.

With shaking hands I took out my map and saw that there were only three lakes in the whole area. Climbing to get a broader view, I suddenly saw it and, to my enormous relief, saw *our* field beside it, *our* pine grove—and a tiny figure frantically waving a red scarf.

It was certainly one of the worst landings I ever made. I came in too high, overshot the field, and had to brake heavily to stop.

Without a word Isolde jumped into the seat beside me. Almost instantly we were roaring up into the dusk in a takeoff as bad as the landing. I could almost hear the sound of machine-gun fire as I spi-raled up as fast as I could. It was now quite dark, and all the familiar landmarks had vanished. I did the only thing I could: took a compass heading of the opposite direction from which I had come.

Luck was with us. After some 20 acutely anxious minutes we spotted in the distance a cluster of jeweled lights—Vienna!—then the straight, beaded strings of lights that marked the airport runway. I made my approach just as if it were daytime. When I thought the runway lights whizzing by looked big enough, I pulled up the plane's nose and made an amazingly smooth landing.

One last hurdle remained. The airport authorities must not see Isolde. We had planned for her to slip away into the darkness of the field. But, as she was getting out of the plane, a car from the control tower bore down on us with blazing headlights piercing the night.

"Hide!" I whispered. Isolde disappeared into the baggage compartment just before a furious air control officer pulled up.

"You've put us to a lot of bother," he snapped. "We contacted Czech Air Control to see if they'd seen or heard you. They said they had, but only over Austria, and that's a good thing for you, mister. You can get into serious trouble blundering across the border!"

He drove away, and I taxied the plane to a hangar. As an attendant, blinded by my lights, opened the hangar door, I told Isolde, "Quick, run for it!" She did, without being seen. I met her outside the field, and we drove jubilantly into town.

Next morning I sneaked Isolde back aboard and flew her to West Germany, where I landed in a field and let her out. After returning my plane to Salzburg, I rejoined her. It took her a month to get her papers, and on her 25th birthday, she arrived in Stockholm.

We were married in the white stone church where I had been christened and left on our honeymoon by car. I no longer fly.

An exchange of radio messages between the Arctic and the Antarctic had a strange aftermath many years later on the battlefields of Europe.

From the Ends of the Earth

By Vladimir Petrov

BORIS BEGICHEV, a good-natured, bold, and intelligent young Russian who knew English, spent the year 1929 as assistant operator at the radio station set up by the Soviet government on Franz Josef Land, about 700 miles from the North Pole.

Life became deadly monotonous there—until one day in October when this amazing message came over the airwaves:

"This is from the American expedition in the Antarctic.... Repeat your signals.... Where are you? ... That means you are near the North Pole. We are not far from the South Pole. This is perhaps the longest shortwave radio communication in history. I will try to reach you again. My name is John Tenner. What is yours?"

Boris Begichev could hardly believe that he had received a message from such a distance, but twice, later in the autumn, he again exchanged brief greetings with Tenner. Then on December 31 Begichev caught the friendly signal from the American in the Antarctic.

Tenner told Begichev that he lived in San Francisco. The Russian asked him about Jack London, whose stories he knew almost by heart. Tenner said that he, like Jack, had grown up on the Oakland waterfront, and he too loved London's tales. Begichev said he'd like to visit the United States, and Tenner invited him to San Francisco.

"To identify yourself," John Tenner said, "start your conversation when you call me by saying: 'Is it true that you have read Jack London's *The Scarlet Plague* 11 times?' "

"OK, that will be the password," Begichev replied.

In World War II Boris Begichev became an officer in the Russian Army. However, he hated Stalin's tyranny, deserted with General Vlassov, and joined the Russian Army of Liberation, which fought against the Communists. In the spring of 1945, after Germany's collapse, his unit retreated westward, hoping to find refuge with the American forces. Boris soon learned, however, that the Americans, fulfilling one of the agreements made with Stalin at Yalta, were handing over Army of Liberation escapees to the Red Army. He well knew that being caught meant either death or a concentration camp.

News soon came that General Vlassov had been captured and that part of the division was surrounded by Soviet tanks. From then on it was every man for himself. Begichev fled westward alone, walking by night and hiding during the day. At dusk one evening he came upon an American tank stopped on an old lumber road in a forest. A sergeant standing beside the tank said, "You're a Russian?"

"Yes," Begichev answered and explained that he was fleeing from the Communist troops. Just then two Soviet military police drove up in a car. The American tank captain asked them in sign language whether they would take the escapee with them. The Soviet policemen made it plain that they would be glad to. One of them drew his pistol and said to Begichev in Russian, "Get in our car."

As Begichev was about to obey, he heard the American sergeant say: "Captain Tenner, what's wrong with the Russians? A lot of them don't seem to like each other."

The captain shrugged, "Who can understand the Russians?"

The Soviet military policeman aimed his pistol at Begichev and shouted, "Get into this car!"

Without taking his eyes from the weapon, Begichev said in English: "Is it true, Captain Tenner, that you have read Jack London's *The Scarlet Plague* 11 times?"

Tenner stared at him for a second, then said brusquely to the military policeman, "*Nyet*—I'll take charge of this man." He motioned to Begichev and said. "In—quick!" Tenner and the sergeant followed Boris into the tank and slammed the turret shut.

While the tank rolled off, Begichev explained to Captain Tenner why he was fleeing from the "Scarlet Plague" of communism.

Finally Tenner said, "Let's stop here." He smiled, handed Begichev a carton of cigarettes, and said, "Mr. Begichev, we must turn back now. I think you can make it safely from here. If you ever come to the United States, don't forget to look me up." The two men shook hands, and Begichev struck off through the woods.

Begichev succeeded in escaping, for I saw him in Rome a year later, and he told me this story. Whether he ever got to the United States, I don't know.

The Germans considered Colditz Castle escapeproof. There they incarcerated Allied POW's who had escaped from other camps and been recaptured. This is the story of some of these men and their attempts to win their freedom.

The Colditz Story

By P. R. Reid

WHEN WORLD WAR II broke out in 1939, Patrick R. Reid, a captain in the Royal Army Service Corps, went to France with the British Expeditionary Force. In May 1940 Captain Reid was captured by advancing German troops and sent to Oflag VII C, a prison camp at Laufen, Germany. A bold and imaginative man, 30-year-old Reid managed to escape in September 1940, disguised as a woman, only to be recaptured before reaching his objective in Yugoslavia. As punishment, Reid was sent to the prison camp the Germans believed to be completely escapeproof—Colditz.

Patrick Reid wrote of his experiences as a prisoner of war in a book entitled *The Colditz Story*. Parts of his suspenseful account are printed here, beginning with Reid's arrival with other British officers at the grim medieval fortress known as Colditz.

THE FORTRESS PRISON

WE LEFT LAUFEN on November 7, 1940, and arrived three days later in Colditz, Oflag IV C.

There was little or no chance of escape on the journey. The guards were watchful, and we were always accompanied to the lavatory. We traveled sometimes in second class, sometimes in third, at all hours of the day and night. There were many changes and long waits, usually in the military waiting rooms of stations. Passersby eyed us curiously but without, I thought, great animosity.

We arrived at the small town of Colditz early one afternoon. Almost upon leaving the station, we saw looming above us our future prison: beautiful, serene, majestic, and yet forbidding enough to make our hearts sink into our boots. It towered above us, dominating the whole village—a magnificent castle built on the edge of a cliff. It was the real fairy castle of childhood's storybooks.

I thought of the dark, gloomy dungeons and of all the stories I had ever heard of prisoners in chains, pining away their lives, of rats and tortures, and of unspeakable cruelties and abominations.

In such a castle, through the centuries, everything had happened and anything might happen again. To friendly peasants and tradespeople in the houses nestling beneath its shadow, it may have signified protection and home, but to enemies from a distant country such a castle struck the note of doom and was a sight to make the bravest quail. Indeed, it was built with this end in view. About 1,000 years old, the castle had been preserved from destruction through the stormy centuries by its inherent strength.

It was built on the top of a high cliff promontory that jutted out over the River Mulde. The outside walls were on an average 7 feet thick, and the inner courtyard of the castle was about 250 feet above the river level. The rooms in which we were to live were about another 60 feet above the courtyard.

The town of Colditz was situated in the middle of a triangle formed by the three cities of Leipzig, Dresden, and Chemnitz, in the heart of the German Reich and 400 miles from any frontier not under the Nazi heel. There was little hope for would-be escapees.

We marched slowly up the steep and narrow cobbled streets from the station toward the castle. Entering the main arched gateway, we crossed a causeway astride what had once been a deep, wide moat— now devoid of water—and passed under a second cavernous archway whose oaken doors swung open and closed ominously behind us with the clanging of heavy iron bars in true medieval fashion. We were then in a courtyard about 45 yards square, with some grass lawn and flower beds, and surrounded on all four sides with buildings six stories high. This was the *Kommandantur,* or garrison area.

We were escorted farther, through a third cavernous archway with formidable doors, up an inclined cobbled coachway for about 50 yards, then through a fourth and last archway into the inner courtyard.

This was a cobbled space about 30 yards by 40 yards, surrounded on its four sides by buildings whose roof ridges must have been 90 feet above the cobbles. Little sun could ever penetrate here. It was an unspeakably grisly place, made none the less so by the pallid faces that we noticed peering at us through bars. There was not a sound in the courtyard. It was as if we were entering some ghostly ruin. Footsteps echoed, and the German words of command seemed distorted beyond reality.

I had reached the stage of commending my soul to the Almighty when the faces behind the bars suddenly took on life; eyes shone, teeth flashed from behind unkempt beards, and words passed backward into the inner depths:

"Anglicy! Anglicy!" ("English! English!")

Heads crowded each other out behind tiny, barred windows, and in less time than it took us to walk 30 yards, there was a cheering mob at every window. Not only at the small ones that we had first seen and would come to know so well, but at every other window that we could see there were jostling heads, laughing and cheering. Welcome was written on every face. We breathed again as we realized that we were among friends. They were Polish officers.

Relief was quickly followed by amazement as we heard the men behind the bars shout insults at the Germans in their own language, at the same time making violent gestures indicating throat-cutting of the unmistakable ear-to-ear variety. The Jerries were angry. They threatened reprisals and quickly hustled us away to a building and up many flights of stairs into a couple of attic rooms, where they left us under lock and key behind a wooden grill.

WE WERE NOT the first arrivals. Three Royal Air Force officers were there to greet us. They were Flying Officers Howard D. Wardle, Keith Milne, and Donald Middleton.

Wardle, or Hank, as he was called, was a Canadian who had joined the RAF shortly before the war. He was dropping propaganda leaflets over Germany in April 1940 when his bomber was shot down. He parachuted and landed in trees. Hank was one of the earliest British POW's of the war. He had managed to escape from the camp at Spangenberg, about 20 miles from Kassel, by climbing a high barricade while on the way to a gymnasium located just outside the camp precincts.

The other two, also Canadians, had escaped dressed as painters, complete with buckets of whitewash and a long ladder, which they carried between them. They had waited for a suitable moment when there appeared to be a particularly dumb Jerry on guard at the gate, marched up briskly, shouted the only words they knew in German, and filed out.

Having passed the gate, they continued jauntily until they were halfway down the hill on which the camp reposed. They then jettisoned ladder and buckets and bolted at top speed for the cover of the nearby woods.

These escapes were made in August 1940 and were probably the first escapes of the war from regular camps. None of the three traveled very far before recapture, and it was, alas, only a matter of hours before they were back behind bars.

They suffered badly at the hands of their captors, being severely kicked and battered with rifle butts. The local people were very bitter and revengeful.

The three RAF officers had arrived a couple of days before us at night and had seen no one. They were told that sentences awaited them and that they would probably be shot. On the first morning at dawn they had been marched out to some woods in a valley flanking one side of the castle, where they halted beside a high granite wall.

They had then been told to exercise themselves for half an hour. The Germans took a sadistic pleasure in terrifying the three of them. By the time they reached the high wall in the early half-light, they had given up hope of ever seeing another sunrise. The joke over, the Jerries took them back to the rooms in which we found them.

Later that evening we made our first acquaintance with the Poles. There were hushed voices on the staircase; then four of them appeared beyond the grill. They unlocked the door with ease and advanced to greet us.

We were the first English they had seen in the war, and the warmth of their welcome, coupled with their natural dignity of bearing, was touching. Each one of us might have been a hero, for to them we represented the friend who had come to their aid when in dire need, who had been prepared to fight in their cause. The Polish people are above all loyal, and they have long memories, too.

They brought food and some beer. Two of the four could speak English and the others French. They all spoke German. The meeting soon became noisy, and there was much laughter, which the Poles love. Suddenly there was a warning signal from a Pole on the lookout by the stairs, and in less than no time they were all hidden under beds in the corners of our two rooms, where suppressed laughter continued up to the instant of the entry of a German officer with his *Feldwebel* ("sergeant").

The attic door, and other doors below, had of course been locked by the Poles, so that there was nothing to cause suspicion other than our laughter, which the Germans had overheard and had come to investigate. The officer was shocked that we, reviled prisoners whose right to live depended on a word from him, should find occasion to laugh. It was like laughing in church, and he implied as much to us.

He noticed that we had shifted all the bunks to make more floor space and promptly commanded the *Feldwebel* to move them back again into orderly rows. The Poles moved with the beds. No sooner had the Germans departed than the Poles, like truant schoolboys, reappeared, laughing louder than ever at the joke.

The merriment continued for a while; then the Poles departed as they had come, leaving us to marvel at the facility with which they manipulated locks. In order to visit us, they had unlocked no fewer than five doors with a couple of instruments that looked like a pair of buttonhooks. Such was our introduction to Colditz, which was to be our prison house for several years.

There were about 80 Polish Army officers in the camp when we arrived. They were among the cream of the Polish Army, and some had undoubtedly charged German tanks at the head of their troop of horse during the Nazi attack on their country in 1939. Although stripped of much of their military attire, they were always smartly turned out on parade. They wore black riding boots, which they kept in beautiful condition.

The Polish officers had all committed offenses against the German Reich, and the majority had escaped unsuccessfully at least once. They had been prisoners since the end of September 1939. So many of them had prison sentences outstanding against them that the half-dozen cells normally set apart for solitary confinement housed about six officers each. The cells were about three yards square, and each cell had one heavily barred window. These were the windows we had seen, crammed with grimy faces, immediately upon entering the prison when we had arrived. Nearly half of their contingent was officially in solitary confinement.

Time passed quickly in our new surroundings and in making new friends. The Germans, after a week or so, gave us permanent quarters: a dormitory with two-tier bunks, a washroom, a kitchen, and a dayroom in a wing of the castle separated from the Poles. The courtyard was the exercise area. At first we were given different hours to exercise, but the Jerries eventually gave up trying to keep us apart. To do so would have meant a sentry at every courtyard door, and there were half a dozen of them. Moreover, the castle was a maze of staircases and intercommunicating doors, and the latter merely provided lock-picking practice for the Poles. We were so often found in each other's quarters that the Germans would have had to put the whole camp into solitary to carry out their intentions, so they gave it up as a bad job.

A trickle of new arrivals increased the British contingent, until by Christmas we numbered 16 officers. A few French and Belgian officers also appeared. All the newcomers were offenders, mostly escapees, and it was impressed upon us that our castle was "the bad boys' camp," the *Straflager* or *Sonderlager,* as the Germans called it.

At the same time we also began to appreciate its impregnability from the escape point of view. This was supposed to be the German fortress from which there was no escape, and for a long time it certainly looked as if it would live up to that reputation. The garrison manning the camp outnumbered the prisoners at all times; the castle was floodlit at night from every angle, despite the blackout. Notwithstanding the sheer drop of 100 feet or so on the outside from barred windows, sentries surrounded the camp within a palisade of barbed wire. The enemy seemed to have everything in his favor. Escape would be a formidable proposition indeed.

THE POLES ENTERTAINED us magnificently over the Christmas period. They had food parcels from their homes in Poland. We had nothing until, lo and behold, on Christmas Eve Red Cross parcels arrived from England. The excitement had to be seen to be believed. They were bulk parcels; that is to say, they were not addressed individually, nor did each parcel contain an assortment of food. There were parcels of tinned meat, of tea, of cocoa, and so on. We were also able to return, at least to a limited extent, the hospitality of the Poles, whose generosity was unbounded. We had to ration severely, for we could not count on a regular supply, and we made this first consignment, which we could have eaten in a few days, last for about two months. Our estimate was not far wrong.

Throughout the whole war, in fact, supplies of Red Cross parcels to Colditz were never regular, and a reserve always had to be stocked. Parcels were dispatched from England at the rate of one per person per week. In Colditz we normally received one a week, on rare occasions two parcels per person in three weeks.

The parcels both from the United Kingdom and from Canada were excellent in quality and variety. The individual, as opposed to the bulk, parcels weighed 10½ pounds each and contained a selection of tinned meat, vegetables, cheese, jam and butter, powdered egg, powdered milk, tea or cocoa, chocolate, sugar, and cooking fat. These parcels were paid for to a large extent by a prisoner's relatives, but it became almost a universal rule at all camps that individual parcels were put into a pool and everybody shared equally.

The Poles prepared a marionette show for Christmas. It was *Snow-White and the Seven Dwarfs*. They had the full text of the story, and the parts were spoken by people behind the screen. It was a picturesque show, professionally produced both as to the acting and the sets. The marionettes were beautifully dressed, and the frequently changing scenery was well painted. It lasted about two hours and was a great success. During the intermission sandwiches and beer were served, and afterward a feast was offered. The Poles had saved everything for months for this occasion. The beer was a ration, also saved. It was bottled lager that was handed out by the Jerries in exchange for prison money. To begin with, in Colditz it was not too scarce, but by the middle of 1941 it had disappeared completely.

513

Prisoners were not allowed so much as a look at a real reichsmark; instead, the special paper money known as *Lagergeld* was issued. *Lagergeld* did not go far. The canteen offered for sale the usual razor blades, toothpaste, shaving soap, and occasionally some turnip jam or beets in vinegar, and saccharine tablets. We could also buy musical instruments by order. They were very expensive—in fact, the prices were downright robbery—but they gave satisfaction to many amateur musicians.

During my sojourn in prison I bought two guitars, one for about £10 and the other for about £25, and a brass cornet for about £30. I must admit that the cornet was of good quality, and the more expensive guitar was a beauty. The instruments came from a well-known firm in Leipzig. I studied the guitar for a year and a half, becoming fairly proficient. I could read music slowly and could play some classical pieces by heart.

The cornet provided me with a means of letting off steam when I had nothing better to do. My colleagues limited the use of it to the washroom, with the door closed, in fine weather, at hours when they were normally out in the courtyard.

THE GERMAN FOOD was cooked in a large, well-equipped, and clean kitchen off the prison courtyard. Private cooking by the prisoners could also be done in our small kitchen, which was provided with a cooking stove and a hopelessly inadequate supply of coal. All loose and unessential items made of wood, together with large numbers of fixtures, partitions, floorboards, beds, and the like, quickly disappeared into the greedy mouth of our grubby little stove. However, the mouth-watering smells that exuded from that murky room invariably outweighed any pangs of conscience, not to mention fears of reprisals due to the dubious origin of most of our fuel. My favorite meal was corned beef fried with dried currants or sultanas. Even today my mouth waters in grateful memory of the delectable dish that warded off many an incipient depression. Capt. Rupert Barry was the *chef par excellence* for this *spécialité de la maison*. It was not an everyday meal—indeed, it was a rarity—which perhaps accounts for the poignant memories I still have of it.

The daily course of life, as may be expected, did not vary much. We awoke in the morning at 7:30 A.M. to shouts of *"Aufstehen"* ("Get up") from a couple of German noncommissioned officers who passed through the dormitories. At 8 A.M. breakfast orderlies (our own troops), helped by officers, carried up from the German kitchen a large cauldron of ersatz coffee (made from acorns), a number of loaves of bread, a small quantity of margarine, and on certain days a little sugar.

At 8:30 A.M. there was *Appell* ("roll call"). All ranks formed up in the courtyard, the Poles in one contingent, the British in another, with their respective senior officers in front. A German officer would appear. Everybody would salute everybody else, and the German NCO's would go through a painstaking count of the bodies. When all was found correct, there would be more saluting, and the parade would break up. As time went on, the first of four daily *Appells* was sounded at 7 A.M. by means of a factory siren. By 9 A.M. we were free to carry on any lawful pursuit such as reading, studying, language lessons, music lessons, or exercise.

The Poles knew almost every language imaginable, and most Englishmen took up a foreign language with a Polish teacher in exchange for English lessons.

When books started to arrive from the United Kingdom, study courses began. Later, a prison theater was opened, and plays, variety shows, and concerts occupied much of the time of officers with any talent for amateur theatricals or musicals.

One variety concert, arranged by Lt. Teddy Barton, played to packed houses for several nights. It was called *Ballet Nonsense*. Costumes were made mostly out of crepe paper, which seemed to serve the purpose well. The orchestra was of high quality, and the tunes and lyrics, composed by Jimmy Yule (Lt. J. Yule) and Teddy Barton, gave the show a professional touch that savored poignantly of Drury Lane and the Hippodrome.

The orchestral talent was provided by a mixture of all the nationalities under the able band leadership of John Wilkins, a submariner who had a fantastic aptitude for playing, in a matter of days, any wind instrument he chose to pick up. The underlying theme of *Ballet Nonsense* was provided by a corps de ballet consisting of the toughest-looking, heaviest-mustached officers available, who performed miracles of energetic grace and unsophisticated elegance upon the resounding boards of the Colditz theater stage attired in frilly crepe-paper ballet skirts and brassieres.

Ballet Nonsense very nearly never came off. A grand piano was to be installed for the occasion. When it arrived in the courtyard, the workmen engaged for the job of hauling it up the narrow stairs took off their jackets and vests. These, of course, were regarded as future escape gear and quickly disappeared. The contents of pockets were left intact, but the civilian clothing was considered fair game by the vast majority of the camp.

The commandant closed the theater and demanded the instant return of the clothing. Monetary compensation was offered by the POW's, but the return of the clothes—no!

After a month of futile searching for the clothes by the Jerries, our money was accepted and the theater finally reopened. *Ballet Nonsense* was a far greater success than anyone had dreamed, due to a month of extra rehearsals.

THE MIDDAY MEAL at Colditz was sounded at 12:30 P.M. and consisted of thick barley gruel. Occasionally, pieces of hog's hide were cut up and put into the soup, which gave it a delicious odor of pork, but that was about all. On such days the German menu on the blackboard outside the kitchen triumphantly announced *"Speck"*—in other words, bacon.

In the afternoon sports came to the fore. Foils made their appearance at one time, and many took up fencing. The little courtyard lent itself to games such as volleyball. Boxing was another favorite pastime among the POW's.

As time went on, the Jerries allowed us a couple of hours' exercise three times a week in a barbed-wire pen in the wooded grounds below the castle, but within the external castle walls. Here we played something resembling soccer—the hazards were the trees amongst which the game surged backward and forward. Our ball games amused the Jerries. Officers and NCO's were occasionally caught watching them surreptitiously—not because they were afraid of being seen as spectators, but because their vantage points were supposed to be secret and were used for spying upon us.

Toward afternoon musical instruments could be heard tuning up on all sides. As soon as instruments could be purchased, many officers started practicing one type or another. In the late afternoon, too, we could usually rely upon a *Sondermeldung* ("special announcement")—which was always a good diversion.

What happened was that the Germans, who had placed loudspeakers at strategic points throughout the castle, would switch on the power when a Special War Progress Bulletin was announced. These were calculated to raise German morale throughout the Reich to incredible heights and correspondingly to demoralize Germany's enemies to the point of throwing in the sponge.

The switching on of the power brought unmistakable crackling noises as the loudspeakers heated up. First a fanfare of trumpets sounded. Then the strains of Liszt's preludes would come over the air, followed by the announcer's proclamation in solemn tones:

THE WEHRMACHT HIGH COMMAND MAKES THE FOLLOWING AN-NOUNCEMENT. IN A FIERCE DAY-LONG BATTLE AGAINST A HEAVILY GUARDED CONVOY IN THE ATLANTIC, OUR SUBMARINES SANK 16 SHIPS TOTALING 150,000 GROSS REGISTERED TONS. IN ADDITION, 2 DESTROYERS WERE HEAVILY DAMAGED.

As soon as the announcer had ceased talking, German brass bands would strike up "Wir fahren gegen England" ("We're Marching Against England"), and to the accompaniment of the whine of descending bombs and the bursting of shells, the act would attain a crescendo of power and then end with trumpets heralding victory.

The show was intended to make the bravest quail. It regularly produced pandemonium in the camp. No sooner had the ominous crackle of the loudspeakers started than windows all over the castle would open and every musical instrument that could be mustered was requisitioned. As Liszt's preludes softened to give way to the announcer, this was the signal. Drums, cymbals, clarinets, cornets, trombones, and accordions all gave voice at once in a cacophony that could be heard reechoing from distant hills. The *Kommandantur* shook with reverberations. But the Germans persevered and the war went on in earnest for several months, until eventually they gave in, and the loudspeakers were forever silenced.

Of course they tried all means at first to stop our counterattack—but that was not easy. In the end, what broke the German morale over the battle was not so much the opposition we put up as the insidious counterpropaganda we produced. For we recorded the numbers of ships involved, until we could show the Germans that there could not be a British vessel left afloat, according to their figures.

In our less energetic moments, especially in the evenings, we played bridge and chess. Chess games, in a community where the passage of time was of no importance, went on for days. Players were known to sit up all night with a homemade, foul-smelling oil lamp (for the electricity was turned off). The light had to be shaded so as not to show through the windows and bring in the Jerries.

The last roll call of the day occurred usually at 9 P.M., after which soon came lights-out. At this "witching hour" many of the nefarious escape activities of the camp started up. They were lumped together under the general heading of "night shift."

WITH CHRISTMAS FARE inside us, optimism returned, and we began to wonder how the walls of our unbreachable fortress could be pierced. Tunneling seemed to be the only solution, and we (the British) were such a small number, and so united in our resolution to escape, that we worked as one team.

Our senior officer, who had the rather odd name under the circumstances of Lt. Col. Guy German, placed me in charge of operations. This enabled him to keep aloof from them himself so as to be in a strong position vis-à-vis the Jerries. Nevertheless, he was keen to take part in any escape into which he could be fitted.

We concentrated on parts of the castle not used by ourselves. Our debut was made early in January 1941 in a room on the ground floor under German lock and key. We were learning from the Poles their art of picking locks, and in this empty room, with our usual guards on the lookout for alarms, we started work. Pulling up floorboards, we came upon loose rubble and in a short time had a hole big enough for a man to work in, with the floorboards replaced over him.

I was dissatisfied with this tunnel entrance before long, because the boards were very old, and one of them could be lifted easily; moreover, they sounded ominously hollow underfoot. I made a sliding trapdoor out of bed boards, which fitted between the floor's supporting beams. The trapdoor itself was a long, open-topped box that slid horizontally on wooden runners. The box was filled with the under-floor rubble. When the trapdoor was in a closed position, a German could lift the floorboards and see nothing suspicious; he could even stand on the trapdoor. At the same time the rubble filling damped out the hollow sound. The trapdoor became known as Shovewood II, after a similar one I had built at Laufen, my first prison camp.

The trapdoor was soon tested in action. Hank Wardle and I were surprised one day when the Germans came to the room before we could disappear, but luckily not before we had closed the trapdoor and replaced the floorboards.

I do not know why they came directly to our room. It was most unlikely that they had then—as they had later—sound detectors around the castle walls, which picked up noises of tunneling. Their spies, set at various windows, may have remarked an unusual movement of British officers through certain doors in the buildings not previously employed.

In any event, it was an awkward moment when the Germans unlocked the empty room and gazed upon two British officers doing physical jerks and push-ups, counting audibly, "One—two—one—two—three and four—one—two—" with seraphic innocence written all over their faces. Luckily we spoke no German and had only to gesticulate in reply to their shouts. We were allowed to leave. The Germans searched the room after our departure, pried up floorboards, and then left without discovering the tunnel entrance. We heard no more of the incident. Even so, we felt that the tunnel would never succeed now, and we promptly gave it up.

We continued our search for the weak spots in the castle's armor. I was next attracted by the drains, and a trusted Polish orderly told me that once, when a certain manhole cover in the yard had been raised, he had seen small brick tunnels running in various directions. This sounded promising. There were two round manhole covers in the courtyard, but they were both in full view of spy windows and also of the spy hole in the main courtyard gate.

I decided to make a reconnaissance by night. In the darkness we could unlock our staircase door into the courtyard—we were always locked into our quarters at night—and, provided the guard outside the gate was not disturbed or tempted to switch on the courtyard lights, we could proceed with our examination.

The moon was not up. It was February and bitterly cold. We knew that the manhole covers were frozen solid to their bases, but we had prepared boiling water in our blacked-out kitchen. With Capt. Kenneth Lockwood acting as doorkeeper with the key, Rupert Barry made sorties at 10-minute intervals and poured the boiling contents of a kettle around the nearest cover. Then we both sortied, I with a stout piece of iron unscrewed from a door support, and together we managed to loosen and lift up the cover.

The hole was not deep, and there were tunnels as the orderly had said. I jumped in and Rupert replaced the lid and disappeared. He was to return in half an hour.

My reconnaissance along the slimy tunnels, which were about three feet by two feet in section, arched and flat-bottomed, revealed one leading up to the camp building in which the canteen was housed. This was bricked up at the canteen entrance, but obviously continued inside. Another led to the kitchen, which accounted for the slime. A third was the outfall sewer that ran under the courtyard to another manhole. It looked promising, and I followed it, but a couple of yards beyond the second manhole it, also, was bricked up with only a small pipe at the bottom serving to drain the system. The pipe headed out under the courtyard gateway. I had my iron tool, a cigarette lighter, and one of our homemade lamps. I tackled the brick; the joints were very tough indeed, and I made little impression. The wall had been recently built, obviously with special attention to strength.

Rupert returned on time and the two of us—myself pushing upward from within—managed to remove the heavy cover. I was filthy and I smelled bad, but there was hope in two directions.

During several nights following I took turns with Rupert and Capt. Dick Howe in attacking the brick wall in the tunnel with an assortment of steel bits and nails that we "won" by various means.

The task proved hopeless, especially as we dared make very little noise. In the silence of the night the sound of hammering could be plainly heard in the courtyard even from below ground. The tunnels and pipes echoed the sound and carried it a long way.

We thought of doing the job in daylight, and I actually descended two days running in full view of those officers who happened to be exercising in the yard, but protected from the direction of the main gate by a small knot of Britishers while the manhole cover was being removed. Although I hammered loudly enough to wake the dead, I made little impression. The joints in the brickwork were made with especially tough cement.

We tried the second direction. Inside the canteen, where we bought our razor blades and suchlike, was a manhole cover in front of the counter on the buyers' side. I had not far to seek for assistance in opening up this manhole, for Kenneth Lockwood had already provided the solution. Some weeks before he had had himself appointed assistant manager and accountant of the canteen.

Kenneth was a London Stock Exchange man, and the idea of keeping even the meager canteen accounts evidently made him feel a little nearer home. He was by nature a tidy person, meticulous in his ways and in his speech. He made a point of buckling the nib of the pen used by the German *Feldwebel* in charge of the canteen so that the unfortunate man invariably started his day's accounts with a large blot of ink at the top of his page. Kenneth explained to the *Feldwebel* on the first occasion that nibs made with poor wartime steel always buckled if used with bad wartime ink, owing to the "springiness" of the nib being affected by a film of corrosion.

The table that Kenneth and the *Feldwebel* used for writing was situated under the only window in the room, at some distance from the counter. While a few people stood at the counter and Kenneth distracted the German's attention with some accounting matter at the table, it was comparatively simple to tackle the manhole cover.

The cover came away after some persuasion. Sure enough, there were tunnels leading in two directions, one connecting with the tunnel already noticed from the yard and the other leading out under the window beside which Kenneth and the German worked. A second reconnaissance in more detail showed this latter to be about 18 yards long and built on a curve. Under the window it was blocked up with large hewn stones and mortar.

Outside the shop window and at the level of the canteen floor was a grass lawn, which also abutted the German section of the castle. At the outer edge of this lawn was a stone balustrade, and then a 40-foot drop over a retaining wall to the level of the roadway that led down to the valley in which our football ground was situated. Maybe the tunnel led out to this wall. We had to find out.

A few days later we managed to fashion from an iron bed piece a key that opened the canteen door. We could now leave our quarters at night and cross 10 yards or so of the courtyard to the canteen. It was simple then to open the door, slip inside, and lock the door behind us.

Entering our tunnel, we tackled the wall at the end. This time we were lucky. The mortar gave way easily, and we were soon loosening huge stones, which we removed to the other tunnel (the one leading back to the courtyard). Although the wall was four feet thick, we were able to get through it in a week of night shifts. Alas! the tunnel did not continue on the other side. Beyond the wall, under the grass, was sticky yellow clay.

My next idea was to make a vertical shaft that would bring the tunnel up to the grass. I decided to construct a trapdoor that would be covered with grass and yet would open when required, thus having the escape tunnel intact for further use. Escapes involving an immense amount of labor frequently serve in the freeing of only one or two men. I thought it worthwhile in this case to attempt to leave the escape exit ready for future use.

Once out on the grass patch we could creep along under the castle walls in the dark, descend the retaining wall with sheets, then continue past the guards' sleeping quarters to the last defense—the 12-foot wall of the castle park surmounted for much of its length with barbed wire. This obstacle would not be difficult provided there was complete concealment, which was possible at night, and provided there was plenty of time to deal with the barbed wire. We had to pass in full view of a sentry at one point. He was only 40 yards away, but as there were Germans who frequently passed the same point, this was not a serious difficulty.

I constructed out of bed boards and stolen screws a trap that looked like a small table with collapsible legs—collapsible so as to enter the tunnel. The legs were also telescopic; that is to say, they could be extended by degrees to five feet in length. The tabletop was a tray with vertical sides four inches deep. It sat in a frame and had shutters so that I could excavate upward from below, removing half the table area at a time. As soon as the edge of the tray came to within an inch of the surface of lawn, I merely had to close both shutters and cut the last inch of earth around the tray with a sharp knife. Then, pushing the tray up, I could lift it clear, still full of undisturbed grass. The last man out would replace the tray in the frame and patch up carefully any telltale marks around the edges. The frame, supported on its extended legs, set on stones at the bottom of the tunnel, would take the weight of a man standing on the tray. The tunnel floor (in the clay) was just five feet below the lawn surface. The contraption was christened Shovewood III.

Before all this happened, our plans were temporarily upset. Two Polish officers got into the canteen one night when we were not working and tried to cut the bars outside the window that I have mentioned before. Cutting bars cannot be done silently. They did not take the precaution of having their own stooges either distract the attention of the nearby sentry or give warning of his approach.

Throughout our work on the tunnel we had managed to establish a signaling system from our rooms above that gave warning of this sentry's approach. He was normally out of sight from where our tunnel exit was to be, but he only had to extend his beat a few yards in order to come into view.

The Poles were caught red-handed, and within a few days a huge floodlight was installed in such a position as to light up the whole lawn and all the prison windows opening onto it.

This was a good example of what was bound to happen in a camp holding none but officers bent on getting free. We had already asked the Poles for liaison on escape projects so that we would not step on each other's toes all the time, and now Colonel German called a meeting with their senior officers, at which an agreement was reached. The senior Polish officer was in a difficult position because he frankly could not fully control his officers; he knew that they might attempt to escape without telling him or anybody else. However, after this meeting the liaison improved, and when we offered some Poles places in our tunnel escape, mutual confidence was established.

Shortly after this incident about 250 French officers arrived at Colditz. They were not all escapees by any means, but about 100 of them were. Among the remainder were many French Jews who were segregated from the rest by the Germans and given their own quarters on the top floor of the castle.

We had to come to an arrangement with the French senior officer over escape projects similar to that agreed upon with the Poles, but unfortunately the French liaison system was also found wanting—at the expense of our tunnel—before a workable understanding was finally reached.

To RETURN TO THE THREAD of my story, we were not allowed by the Germans to store any canned food, expressly because it was potential escape rations. However, over a period of time we had all stinted ourselves to collect a reserve for distribution when our tunnel would be ready. It amounted to three heavy sack loads.

One night we were busy transporting the sacks into the tunnel from our quarters, where they were badly hidden. Rupert carried them one by one out of our courtyard door into the canteen. On the last trip all the courtyard lights were suddenly switched on from outside, and Rupert found himself caught between the doors. He made for the door of our quarters, which had to be unlocked again for him to reenter. To our astonishment, nothing further happened, so we completed our work for the night and returned to bed. Whether the Germans saw Rupert or not we shall never know, but since the Polish attempt they seemed to be more on the *qui vive*.

This incident was followed by one still more unfortunate. Although the Germans often paid nocturnal visits to our quarters without warning, this did not seriously bother us. If we were in the tunnel, the doors were locked as usual, and pillows were placed in our beds to pass the casual inspection of a flashlight's beam flicking along the rows of sleeping bodies.

One night, however, the Germans had been carousing—we could hear them. In fact, they kept our orderlies awake, and that was the start of the trouble. We had five staunch "game" orderlies, who had places reserved on our tunnel escape.

On this particular night, being unable to sleep because of the Germans, one of the orderlies named Goldman, who a had sense of humor, started to shout derisive remarks at the German sentry outside the nearest window. The jeering by Goldman must have been reported to the carousing goons, for after some time they arrived in the courtyard in force and headed for our quarters. Hauptmann Priem and another officer, the regimental sergeant major (Oberstabsfeldwebel Gephard), a corporal, and half a dozen goons entered and began shouting *"Aufstehen!"* They woke everyone up, poked the beds, and discovered that four officers were missing.

The Germans lost their heads. They had come upstairs drunk and disorderly, intent on having some fun at our expense, and they had not expected this new turn of affairs.

The confusion in the officers' dormitory became indescribable. Goons turned every bed inside out and emptied the contents of cupboards. Priem sent out orders for the whole camp to be paraded. It was about 2 A.M. by then.

Our "stooge," or lookout, at the canteen that night was a submarine officer named Wardle (not to be confused with Hank Wardle). He suddenly shouted, "They're heading for the canteen." He scarcely had time to jump down into the tunnel, and I had barely pulled the manhole cover over us, before the Jerries were in. They searched the canteen and tried hard to lift the manhole cover, but they were unable to do so as I was hanging onto it from underneath, my fingers wedged in a protruding lip of the cover.

As soon as we noticed that a general *Appell* had been called, I told Rupert and Dick (the others in the tunnel with me) to start at once building a false wall halfway up the tunnel, behind which they put our food store and other escape paraphernalia such as rucksacks, maps, compasses, and our civilian clothing, which we normally kept hidden there.

The hubbub continued in the courtyard for about an hour. The count was taken about half a dozen times amidst as much confusion as the prisoners could create without having themselves shot. They were aided in this by the chaos caused by the Germans themselves, who were rushing all over the camp searching every room and turning all movable objects upside down.

Rupert and Dick quietly continued their work and in a few hours had constructed a magnificent false wall with stones from the original wall that we had demolished, jointed with clay from under the lawn and coated with dust wherever the joints showed.

By 5 A.M. all was quiet again. We departed as we had come and went to bed wondering how the Germans would react to our appearance at morning *Appell*. We had apparently put them to a great deal of trouble, for we heard that, while the Jerries had had the whole camp on parade, they had carried out an individual identity check. Every officer paraded in front of a table where he was identified against his photograph and duly registered as present. We four were recorded as having escaped, and messages flashed to the OKW (Wehrmacht High Command) brought into action a network of precautions taken all over the country as a matter of routine for the recapture of prisoners.

At the morning *Appell*, when we were all found present again, confusion reigned once more. The goons decided to hold a second identification parade, which they completed in about two and a half hours. Then they called out our four names, which they had managed to segregate at last, and we were paraded in front of everybody. They dismissed the parade and led us to the little interview room, in which most of our fights with the *Kommandantur* took place.

We refused to explain our disappearance and were remanded for sentence for causing a disturbance and being absent from *Appell*. The OKW orders all had to be countermanded, and the commandant, we heard, received a "rap over the knuckles" for the incident.

The goons were upset and watchful during the next few days. They again visited the canteen, and this time the manhole cover came away—too easily for our liking, of course. But they had done some scraping around the edges before trying it and were apparently satisfied it was the result of their own efforts. The dust and grit, inserted around the manhole cover, were placed there by us, as a matter of routine after every working shift, so that the cover always looked as if it had not been touched for years. A goon descended and, after an examination, declared "nothing unusual" below. Kenneth, who was in the back of the shop, trying to appear occupied with his accounts, breathed an audible sigh of relief, which he quickly turned into a yawn for the benefit of his German colleague, busy at the same table.

The Germans were suspicious of this tunnel, either because they had seen Rupert in the courtyard or because they were warned by a spy in the camp. A third possibility would have been microphones, set to detect noises. Microphones were installed, to our knowledge, in many places later on, but it is doubtful whether the Jerries had them in Colditz at this period of the war. Microphones were installed in newly built hutted camps for the RAF, but their installation in an old castle would have left telltale marks that we could have traced.

The spy—that is to say, a stooge prisoner in the camp—set by the

Germans to report on us was a definite possibility, and our suspicions were later proved correct. Suffice it to say that we repeatedly found the goons very quick on the trail of our activities. We tried hard to make our actions look normal when among other prisoners, but it was not easy, especially on escapes such as tunnels, which involved preparation over a long period of time.

Incidentally, we employed the term stooge very loosely. Our stooge Wardle was certainly no spy.

The goons concreted four heavy clasps into the floor around the canteen manhole cover. However, we dealt with these forthwith by loosening them before the concrete was set, in such a way that they could be turned aside. This was done in daylight while Kenneth, as usual, occupied the goons and a few officers acted as cover at the counter. In their normal positions the clasps still held the cover quite firmly in place.

This done, we decided to give the tunnel a rest, as things were becoming too hot for our liking.

THE COMMUNITY OF NATIONS

IT WAS MARCH 1941. The camp was slowly filling up. The British contingent had increased by a steady trickle of new arrivals, escapees all, except for a sprinkling of "Saboteurs of the Reich"—we had three padres who were classed in the second category. One day about 60 Dutch officers arrived. Curiously enough, their senior officer was Major English (ours being Colonel German). The Dutchmen were a fine company of men and a credit to their country. They were all Netherlands East Indies officers. At the outbreak of the war they had sailed home with their troops to Holland in order to help the mother country. When Holland was occupied, the German High Command offered an amnesty to all those Dutch officers who would sign a certain document. This, if treated honorably, precluded an officer from acting in any way contrary to the wishes of the German Reich. It also laid down conditions relative to the maintenance of law, order, and subservience within the country. It was apparently a cleverly written document, and a number of Dutch officers of the home forces signed it.

The colonials, on the other hand, refused to sign it almost to a man and were promptly marched off to prison in Germany. After many vicissitudes, including unending wordy battles with the Germans as well as escape attempts, they finally ended up lock, stock, and barrel in Colditz. Since they all spoke German fluently, were as obstinate as mules and as brave as lions, heartily despised the Germans and showed it, they presented special difficulties as prisoners.

They were always impeccably turned out on parade and maintained a high standard of discipline among themselves. I regret to say that the French and we ourselves were the black sheep in matters of parade turnout. The average French officer is rarely, if ever, tidy. His uniform does not lend itself to smartness, and the French do not care about turnout anyway.

The British were more unfortunate and had an excuse for appearing a straggly-looking crowd. The British battle dress is not particularly smart, and most of us had lost a part of it at our time of capture—a cap, or jacket, or gaiters—and many of us had to wear wooden-soled clogs, given to us by the Germans. Occasionally a much-needed parcel came from home containing replacements for our worn-out kits, and the Red Cross once sent a bulk consignment of uniforms that were of great help. Still, we were a picturesque if not an unsightly company. The other nationalities had somehow succeeded in bringing much of their wardrobe with them, and, at any rate until time wore these out, they had a definite advantage over us. It was common for a Britisher to appear on parade, for instance, wearing a woolen balaclava or no cap at all, a khaki battle-dress blouse, blue RAF or red Czech Army trousers, home-knitted socks of almost any color, and trailing a pair of clogs on his feet.

Speaking of the picturesque, color was lent to our *Appell* parades by two Yugoslav officers who had joined our happy throng. Their uniform, consisting of voluminous red trousers and sky-blue embroidered vests, brought home to us what a community of nations we at Colditz had become.

First there was the Polish contingent. Then there were Englishmen, Irishmen, and Scotsmen. The Empire was represented by RAF officers from Canada, Australia, and New Zealand, and by an army doctor, Captain Mazumdar, from India. The French included some officers from Algeria and the Jewish contingent. There were the two Yugoslavs and some Belgian officers. The Netherlands were represented by an aide-de-camp of Queen Wilhelmina, and last, but decidedly not least, the Dutch East Indies officers completed this procession of nations.

Colditz was the only camp of this kind in Germany. The solidarity that existed among the various nationalities was always a matter of surprise to the Germans. The alliance amongst us was not fostered by any artificial means. It was natural, springing from something deep within us, and it withstood many tests. It was a sufficiently strong link to withstand any attempt by the Germans to alienate one nationality from another.

A favorite communal punishment meted out to any particular contingent was the curtailment of the hours of recreation allowed in the wooded park of the castle. When this happened, the recreation parade was ostracized by all until the Germans withdrew the ban. If an officer of any one nationality was unfairly treated, the whole camp would go on strike without hesitation.

On one occasion the German camp doctor worked himself into a Polish hate neurosis. He insisted that Poland no longer existed and that in consequence every Polish officer, of whatever rank, should salute him smartly. The staff physician was a captain. When he tried to make the Polish general salute and went into a tantrum about it, this was too much for the Poles. The whole contingent went on a hunger strike. The rest of the camp supported them in spirit. The senior officers of all the other nationalities sent parallel complaints to the German commandant concerning the doctor's attitude. After three days the commandant hauled his junior officer over the coals, and the famished Polish officers, having registered a grudgingly given salute from the camp doctor, took to their food again.

THE GERMAN SENTENCE upon the four of us who had disappeared for a night was two weeks' solitary confinement. During this confinement a third unlucky incident occurred that piled up further difficulties in the way of our canteen tunnel escape. A Frenchman and a Pole managed to disappear one day and were not missed until the evening *Appell.* The goons suspected a getaway during the return of the prisoners from their period of recreation in the park and searched all possible places of concealment in the proximity of the roadway leading down to it.

The two officers were found, hiding out until nightfall, in the seldom-used basement of a house near the path (it was used as an air-raid shelter), into which they had slipped undetected. This operation was by no means easy. It had been done by split-second timing, with the assistance of officers who had successfully distracted the attention of the guards accompanying the parade on the march. The assisting officers placed themselves in the ranks so as to be near the guards who walked at intervals on either side. When the officers who were to escape reached a predetermined spot on the march, the others made gestures or remarks calculated to draw the attention of their nearby guards away from the scene of action. Three seconds after the predetermined spot was reached, the escaping officers bolted. In five more seconds they were behind a wall. During these five seconds some eight guards had to be made to "look the other way."

The chances of success were very slight, but the trick worked. When the count was taken after the recreation period outside the courtyard gate, the assisting officers created confusion, and a German-speaking officer succeeded in browbeating the sergeant in charge into thinking that he had made a wrong count when he had come up with a discrepancy in numbers.

It was a pity that in this case a brilliant beginning was not carried through to a successful end and that the concealment of the count was not maintained at the later general *Appell*. The *Appell* normally called after dark in the lighted courtyard was, on this day, called in daylight, possibly due to the German sergeant's suspicions getting the better of him. *Appell* times were often changed without warning, especially to catch prisoners out, and this most assuredly should not have been overlooked.

Be that as it may, the officers, when caught, made up a story concealing their real method of escape and leading the Germans to suspect a rope descent from an attic skylight onto the grass lawn under which our tunnel exit lay hidden. A sentry was now placed on a beat that brought him in full view of our projected tunnel exit at intervals of one minute both day and night.

This incident led me to make a complaint through our senior officer, Colonel German, and to request closer liaison and more cooperation among the various nationalities so that we would not continually trip over each other in our hurry to leave the camp. Common sense prevailed, and from that date there were no further serious instances of overlapping escape plans.

As to our tunnel, I disliked the idea of lengthening it and making a long-term job of it, as any prolonged lapse of time worked against the success of the venture. The Germans also started gradually to install new locks on certain doors at key points throughout the camp. They began with the lock of the canteen, thereby foiling us temporarily in any attempt to spend long hours at work in the tunnel underneath it.

We called the new locks cruciform locks. The simplest description I can give of them is to compare them to four different Yale locks rolled into one. Kenneth Lockwood obtained an impression in candle wax of the four arms of the cruciform key to the canteen.

I worked for a long time on the manufacture of a false key. There was a dentist's room in the camp, which was normally locked, as was the dentist's cupboard of instruments, but these had presented little difficulty to budding burglars like ourselves. I wore out many of the bits of the dentist's electric drill in the process of making my key, but all my efforts were in vain.

I am afraid the drills were very blunt after I had finished with them. Ever afterwards when I heard the agonizing shrieks of sufferers in the dentist's chair, I felt a twinge of remorse that I should have been the cause of so much pain. I still often wonder what would have been my fate if all the dentist's visitors had known my secret sin. Luckily for me, only one or two of my trusted confederates knew, and they kept the secret.

The dentist, who was a French officer and fellow prisoner, must have thought little of German tool steel. He had filled one of my teeth excellently before I had ruined his drills.

At this unhappy stage, when we were debating what to do with our tunnel, Peter Allan and Howard Gee (a newcomer), both of whom spoke excellent German, reported the existence of a helpful goon sentry. He was a sympathetic type, and he started smuggling for us on a small scale: a fresh egg here and there in return for English chocolate, or a pound of real coffee in exchange for a tin of cocoa, and so on. He ran a terrific risk, but he seemed to do it with equanimity—perhaps too much equanimity—and we decided to take a chance.

At several clandestine meetings, in doorways and behind angles in the courtyard walls, Peter and Howard primed the sentry and eventually suggested that he might earn some big money if he once "looked the other way" for 10 minutes while on sentry duty.

The sentry apparently fell for the idea. He was told that we would have to arrange matters so that he did a tour of sentry duty for a given 2-hour period, on a given day, on a certain beat, and that in the 10-minute interval between two predetermined signals he was to stand (which was permitted) at one particular end of his beat. He was to receive an advance of 100 reichsmarks on his reward, which was settled at 500 reichsmarks (about £34), and the remainder would be dropped out of a convenient window an hour after the 10-minute interval. The sentry was also told that no traces would be left that could lead to suspicion or involve him in accusations of neglect of duty. To all this he listened and finally agreed. The escape was on.

The first escape party consisted of 12 officers, including 4 Poles. The French and Dutch officers were as yet newcomers, whereas the Poles were by now old and trusted comrades, which accounted for their inclusion. Further, the participation of officers of another nationality was decided upon for reasons of language facilities offered and for camp morale. The Poles had been most helpful since our arrival. The majority of them spoke German fluently, some of them knew Germany well, and those of us who thought of aiming for the North Sea or Poland took Poles as traveling companions. A few decided to travel alone.

My mind was occupied with another problem—how to arrange for the entry of 13 officers, 12 escaping and 1 sealing up the entrance, into the canteen? During open hours I examined the cruciform lock closely and came to the conclusion that, from the inside, I could dismount the lock almost completely, allowing the door to open.

The escape would have to be done after the evening roll call and under cover of darkness.

THE FATEFUL DAY was decided upon—May 29. I arranged to knock down the false wall the day before and to extricate all our provisions and escape material. This was to be accomplished during the two-hour lunch interval when the canteen was locked.

Just before lunch I hid in a triangular recess that was used as a store cupboard and to which I had the key. When the canteen was locked up, I had two clear hours to prepare everything. I removed the false wall, took out all of our escape paraphernalia, hiding it in the cupboard, and prepared the tunnel exit so as to give the minimum amount of work for the final opening. After 2 o'clock, with a suitable screen of officers, I came out of the cupboard, and all the stores were carried to our quarters.

The arrangements for the escape were as follows: Howard Gee, who was not in the first party, was to deal with the sentry. He would pass him the first signal upon receipt of a sign from us in the tunnel. This was to be given by me in the first instance at the opening end of the tunnel, passed to our 13th man on watch at the canteen window in the courtyard, who would then transmit it to our quarters by means of a shaded light. Gee could then signal to the sentry from an outside window. The "all clear" was to be given in the same way, except that our 13th man had to come to the tunnel exit and receive the word from me when I had properly sealed up the exit after all were out. I was to convey this information to him by pulling a piece of string up through the earth. Hopefully I would be over the wall at the far end of the lawn before the signal would be transferred to the sentry.

May 29 loomed overcast, and it soon began to rain. It rained all day in torrents, the heaviest rainfall we had ever had, but this would mean a dark night, and it did not upset our plans. The sentry was told during the course of the afternoon what post he was to occupy. He was given his advance in cash and instructed to avoid the end of his beat nearest to the canteen upon receipt of an agreed signal from a certain window and to remain away from that end until another signal was given.

As the evening approached, the excitement grew. The lucky 12 dressed themselves in kits prepared during many months of patient work. From out of astonishing hiding places came trousers and slouch caps made from gray German blankets, multicolored knitted sweaters, transformed and dyed army overcoats, windbreakers and mackintoshes, dyed khaki shirts, and home-knitted ties. These were donned and covered with army apparel. Maps and homemade compasses appeared, and subdued discussions took place concerning routes and escape instructions.

As the time passed, impatience to be off increased. I became alternately hot and cold, my hands were clammy, and my mouth was dry. We all felt the same, as I could tell by the forced laughs and the nervous jokes and banter that passed around.

I remained hidden in the canteen when it was locked up for the night and dismounted the lock. When the evening *Appell* sounded, I slipped out of the door behind a well-placed crowd of officers. If a goon pushed the door for any reason whatever, we were finished. A wedge of paper alone held it. Sentries were posted for the *Appell* at all vantage points, and one stood very close to the canteen. Immediately after the *Appell* we had to work fast, for all the prisoners then had to disperse to their rooms, the courtyard doors were locked, and every door was tried by the German duty officer. All 13 of us had to slip into the canteen behind the screen of assisting officers while German officers and NCO's were in the courtyard, and the lock had then to be remounted on the canteen door in double-quick time. The 12 escapees had to appear on parade dressed in their escape attire suitably covered with army overcoats and trousers. Assembled rucksacks had been placed in order in the tunnel during the lunchtime closing hours in the same way as before.

The *Appell* went off without a hitch. Colonel German, who had to stand alone in front, was looking remarkably fat, for he was escaping with us. He aroused no comment. Immediately after the "dismiss" order was given, and almost in front of the eyes of the sentry nearby, the 13 chosen ones slipped silently through the canteen door until all were inside. Luckily, the din in the courtyard covered any noise we made at this juncture.

While the lock was remounted on the door, I removed my army uniform and handed it to our 13th man. He was to collect all discarded clothes, conceal them in the cupboard, and remove them with assistance the next day. I went directly to the end of the tunnel, closely followed by Rupert Barry, for we were going together, and started work on the last few inches of earth beneath the surface of the opening. It was dark by now outside, and the rain was still pelting down. It began pouring through the earth covering of the exit, and within five minutes I was drenched to the skin with muddy water. The lock-testing German patrol tried the canteen door and passed on. Soon all was quiet in the camp. Within an hour the sentry was reported by light flashes to be at his post. I gave the signal for him to keep away from the canteen window.

I worked frenziedly at the surface of grass, cutting out my square, and then slowly heaved the tray of the exit upward. It came away, and as it did so a shaft of brilliant light shot down the tunnel. For a second I was bewildered and blinded. It was the light of the projector situated 10 yards away from the opening, which lit up the whole of the wall face on that particular side of the castle. I lifted the tray clear. Muddy water trickled into the tunnel around me. I pushed myself upward and, with Rupert's assistance from behind, scrambled out.

Once out, I looked around. I was like an actor standing on a stage. The floodlight made a huge grotesque image of my figure against the white wall. Row upon row of unfriendly windows, those of the German garrison area, frowned down upon me. The windows had no blackout curtains, and a wandering inquisitive eye from within might easily turn my way. It was an unavoidable risk.

Rupert began to climb out as I put the finishing touch to the tray for closing the hole. He was having some difficulty. He had handed up my rucksack and was levering himself upward when I happened to look at the wall in front of me. With a start I saw a second giant shadow outlined beside my own crouching figure. The second shadow held a revolver in his hand.

"Get back!" I yelled to Rupert, as a guttural voice behind me shouted: *"Hände hoch! Hände hoch!"* ("Hands up! Hands up!")

I turned to face a German officer leveling his pistol at my body, while another German officer leaped for the escape hole. He was about to shoot down the opening.

"Schiessen Sie nicht!" ("Don't shoot!") I screamed several times.

A bullet or two into the stone- and brick-walled tunnel might have wrought considerable damage, filled as it was with human bodies. The officer at the hole did not shoot.

German troops suddenly appeared from everywhere, and all the officers were giving orders at once. I was led off to the *Kommandantur* and conducted to a bathroom where I was stripped completely and allowed to wash. Then I was taken to an office where I was confronted by Hauptmann Priem.

He was evidently pleased with his night's work and in high spirits. *"Ah hah! Es ist Herr Hauptmann Reid. Das ist schön!"* ("Ah hah! It's Captain Reid. Splendid!") he said as I walked in, and continued: "Nobody could recognize who the villain was until he was washed! And now what has he got to say for himself?"

"I think the villain was a certain German sentry, was he not?" I questioned in reply.

"Yes, indeed, Herr Hauptmann. German sentries know their duty. The whole matter has been reported to me from the start."

"From before the start, maybe?"

"Herr Hauptmann Reid, that is not the point. Where does your tunnel come from?"

"That is obvious," I replied.

"From the canteen, then?"

"Yes."

"But you have been locked into your quarters. You have a tunnel from your rooms to the canteen?"

"No!"

"But yes! You have been counted on *Appell*. The canteen has been locked many hours ago. You have a tunnel?"

"No!"

"We shall see. How many of you are there?"

"So many I have never been able to count them properly!"

"Come now, Herr Hauptmann, the whole camp or just a few?"

"Just a few!"

"Good. Then I hope our solitary confinement accommodations will not be too overcrowded!" said Priem, grinning broadly. He added: "I was perturbed when first I saw you. I gave orders at once not to shoot. You see, I had my men posted at all windows and on the road. They were to shoot if any prisoners ran or struggled. I saw this figure that was you, writhing upon the ground. I thought that you had fallen from the roof and were in great pain."

While this was going on, hell had broken loose inside the prison. The courtyard was filled with troops, while posses dashed around wildly trying to locate the inside end of our rathole. In our quarters there was the usual parade in the dayroom while goons prodded beds and unearthed the customary 13 inert corpses made of coats and blankets. At first they were convinced the tunnel started in our quarters on the first floor, and they uprooted floorboards. Slowly it dawned upon them that it might be worthwhile to try the canteen.

Once there, as body after body issued from the manhole amidst shouts along the tunnel of "Goonery ahoy!" mingled with shouts from above of *"Hände hoch! Hände hoch!"* the goons began hopping with excitement, and revolvers were waving in all directions. The Jerry officer in charge was an elderly second lieutenant. His lips were white, and he was shaking all over. It was a miracle the weapons did not go off, for the Jerries were out of control. They stripped all the escapees naked in their anxiety not to miss any escape booty.

Eventually some semblance of order was restored, and each officer in turn, after a thorough inspection, was escorted back to our quarters garbed in his underclothes.

The next day the usual inquiry took place. The Germans had overhauled the tunnel, but what puzzled them was how 13 men could be inside the canteen, which was locked with their unbreakable cruciform lock, so soon after an *Appell* and after having been apparently closed up in their quarters for the night.

For a long time they searched for a tunnel connecting with our quarters, but eventually gave it up. I imagine that, finally, they worked out the method used—this was not difficult.

In due course we were all sentenced to two weeks' solitary, but as usual, the solitary cells were all occupied, and instead, we carried out the sentence in two small communal rooms. Funnily enough, one of these rooms was the one in which we had started our first tunnel and in which Hank and I had been caught.

Shovewood II was still in good working order, and as we had previously concealed some food reserves there, it at last came into its own—we were not short of extra rations during our term of solitary. The solitary, in this case, with 13 officers jammed into two small rooms, was of the Black Hole of Calcutta variety.

Needless to say, we never saw "our" sentry again. He did not receive his 400 reichsmarks, which was a good thing.

N o sooner were we all free again after our solitary confinement than a rare opportunity presented itself. One day, without warning, a large German truck was driven into the courtyard under guard and stopped outside the doorway to our quarters. Some French troop prisoners descended. We knew a couple of them. They were not lodged in the camp but lived somewhere in the town where they worked, and they occasionally came into the camp to do odd jobs. We had naturally made contact to nose out particulars concerning the orientation of the village and the life of its inhabitants. Unfortunately, these Frenchmen appeared so rarely that they were useless as trafficking agents.

This time they had come to collect a large number of straw palliasses—the standard prison mattresses consisting of large canvas sacks filled with straw—that were stored on the floor above the Dutch quarters. These mattresses were needed for troops' quarters being prepared in the village to house, as it turned out afterward, incoming Russian POW's.

The French prisoners each collected a mattress and, descending the winding staircase past our quarters, continued to the ground floor, then out through the main door where they swung the palliasses onto the truck.

There was no time to waste. After hasty consultation, Peter Allan was selected for the attempt. He was small and light and could speak German fluently, so he was an ideal candidate for a one-man effort. We were prepared to try more, but Peter was to be the guinea pig.

We rigged him out in what was left of our depleted stock of escape clothing, gave him money, packed him in one of our own mattresses, and then tackled the French.

On the stairway outside I stopped our most likely Frenchman as he descended and pulled him into our quarters with his mattress, saying: "I want you to carry an officer downstairs inside a mattress and load him onto the truck."

"Mais c'est impossible," said the Frenchman.

"It is simple," I assured him. "It will be over in two minutes; nobody will notice it."

"And if I am caught?"

"You will not be caught," I argued and pressed a tin of cigarettes into his hand.

"But the others?"

"They will not give you away. Offer them some of the cigarettes."

"I am not so sure," was his reply. "No! It is too dangerous. I shall be caught and flogged, or they may even shoot me."

"You know you will not be shot. Courage! Would you not risk a flogging for the Allies, for France?"

"I would not risk much for many Frenchmen," he said, cryptically, "and France is no more!"

"Come now!" I cajoled, "that is not a Frenchman speaking. That sounds like a collaborator. You are no collaborator. I know your reputation from Frenchmen in the camp who speak well of you. You have helped them. Can you not help us now?"

"*Eh bien!* I'll do it!" he consented, softening at last.

I breathed a sigh of relief and patted him on the shoulder. If he was caught, he was liable to suffer rough treatment.

Peter was already packed and waiting in a mattress, which was propped over the Frenchman's shoulder. I never saw a bundle of canvas and straw looking less like a mattress in my life, but the Frenchman made his exit to the courtyard.

Alas! he could not load the mattress onto the truck alone, so he did the sensible thing. Our Frenchman asked for help from a compatriot just relieved of his mattress. The two of them swung Peter, as if he were a feather, on top of the rapidly growing pile.

That was enough for the morning. We had no intention of risking another body on that truck. In due course it departed and was ineffectually prodded by guards at the various gates before trundling off down to the town below. Peter was duly unloaded by his guardian Frenchman in the town of Colditz. The mattresses and Peter were carried into a deserted house and left in a ground-floor room. The truck team then disappeared for lunch.

Peter wasted no time in extricating himself. He opened a window, climbed out into a small garden, and from there headed for a road.

Peter reached Stuttgart and then Vienna. His greatest thrill was when he was picked up by a senior German SS officer traveling in style in a large car and accompanied him for about 100 miles on his way. Only a man like Peter Allan, who had attended school in Germany, could have gotten away with the conversation involved in such a cheek-by-jowl car journey.

Meanwhile, in the afternoon work was resumed by the French on a second load of mattresses, and we resumed work on the preparation of a second "heavy" mattress. Peter had been instructed to make his getaway quickly for the reason that if we failed in the second attempt, we did not want the Germans to find Peter quietly lying in his mattress awaiting nightfall.

By now, however, the Frenchmen were frightened, and even our staunch French orderly wilted under the weight of the second mattress, duly prepared by us with Lt. J. Hyde-Thompson resting inside. Unfortunately Hyde-Thompson weighed nearly 175 pounds and was sufficiently tall to give the lie to the desired impression of a well-stuffed mattress. In the courtyard he was dumped on the ground next to the truck, and the Frenchmen refused to load him. Our distraction stooges worked overtime, but the French strike continued, and eventually the Jerries became suspicious. The NCO in charge called for an officer, and by the time the latter arrived, the truck was loaded and our "heavy" mattress still lay leadenly on the ground.

The officer prodded the mattress and then ordered the NCO to investigate, while he held his revolver cocked, expecting the worst. Hyde-Thompson duly appeared, covered with straw, and was ignominiously led away for examination and ultimately sentenced to a month's cooling off in the cells.

Fourteen days later we heard the sad and discouraging news that Peter Allan had been caught. His story was depressing.

He had reached Vienna and, having spent the last of his money, was looking around for ways and means to carry on to Poland. He thought of the American Consulate—for the United States was still not at war. He went there and disclosed his identity. The Americans politely but firmly refused him any kind of help. After this he became despondent. He was worn out from long trekking, and the insidious loneliness of the solitary fleeing refugee in an enemy land descended on him. This curious sensation has to be lived through to be appreciated. It can lead a man to give himself up voluntarily, despite the consequences; to talk and mix with other human beings—even his jailers—means something to a hunted man, particularly in a city. He who can withstand the temptation for long must have a strong inner fiber. It was for this reason, among others, that escapees found it advisable to travel in pairs whenever possible.

Peter Allan went into a park in Vienna and fell asleep on a bench. In the morning he awoke and found his legs paralyzed with cramps. He crawled to the nearest house and was taken to the hospital, where his resistance broke down. He was quite well looked after and was soon fit enough to be escorted back to Colditz, where the greater despondency of failure was to hold sway over him during a month's lonely imprisonment.

Two questions, at least, arise concerning this escape. First, why was a tall and heavy person selected for the second attempt? The answer is the same as that which accounts for pure strategy so frequently becoming modified by paramount policy, which often, as in this case, results in the failure of the project. Hyde-Thompson had arrived in Colditz with a considerable amount of German money in his possession, following an abortive escape attempt. Although the money was not officially his own, he had had the wit to save it through many searches, and he had a justifiable lien on it. Officers were searched upon departure from one camp and again upon arrival at a new one. This consisted of being stripped naked and having each piece of clothing carefully examined, while luggage was gone through with a fine-tooth comb. Hyde-Thompson had given a large proportion of the money to me with alacrity for the canteen tunnel attempt, and some more had gone with Peter Allan. It was time he should be rewarded, and the mattress escape was offered.

Second, one may wonder at the attitude of the Americans in Vienna. The explanation is probably twofold. The official one is that the Americans, though neutral, were having a hard time holding on to their Vienna consulate and were continually in danger of being ordered out of the country. They were doing important work and could not risk their position officially. The other explanation, which is quite plausible, is that Peter did not succeed in convincing the consulate that he was not a German agent provocateur. He had nothing to prove his case, and he spoke German perfectly.

Lt. MAIRESSE LEBRUN was a French cavalry officer, tall, handsome, and debonair. He had slipped the German leash from Colditz once already by what seems, in the telling, a simple ruse. In fact, it required quite expert handling. A very small Belgian officer was his confederate. On one of the park outings the Belgian officer concealed himself under the voluminous folds of a tall comrade's cloak at the outgoing "numbering off" parade and was not counted. Later, during the recreation period in the park, Lebrun, with the aid of diversions, climbed up among the rafters of an open-sided pavilion in the middle of the recreation pen. He was not missed because the Belgian provided the missing number, and the dogs did not get wind of him.

Later Lebrun descended and, smartly dressed in a gray flannel suit sent by a friend from France, walked to a local railway station and proffered a 100-mark note at the booking office in exchange for a ticket. Unfortunately, the note was an old one, no longer in circulation. The stationmaster became suspicious and finally locked Lebrun up in a cloakroom and telephoned the camp. The Colditz camp commandant replied that nothing was amiss and that his prisoner complement was complete.

While the stationmaster was telephoning, Lebrun wrenched open a window and leaped out on top of an old woman, who naturally became upset and gave tongue. A chase ensued. He was finally cornered by the station personnel and recaptured. In due course he was returned to the castle and handed over to the protesting commandant.

This adventure lost Lebrun his fine suit and found him doing a month's solitary confinement at the same time as Peter Allan.

One fine afternoon we heard many shots fired in the playground and rushed to the windows, but we could see nothing because of the foliage. Terrific excitement followed in the German quarters, and we saw posses of goons with dogs descending on the double from the castle and disappearing among the trees. Shouts and orders together with the barking of dogs continued for some time and eventually faded away in the distance.

We heard by message from Peter Allan what had happened. The solitaries—at the time a mere half dozen—were having their daily exercise in the park, during which period they could mix freely. Being only a few, they were sparsely guarded, though confined to one end of the compound, where the prisoners played football among the trees. Lebrun was in the habit of doing exercises with two other Frenchmen, which included much leapfrogging.

Now Lebrun was athletic. It was high summer, and he was dressed in what remained to him of his former finery—shorts, a yellow cardigan, an open-necked shirt, and gym shoes—not good escaping clothes, but that was also what he reckoned the Germans would think. While a couple of the latter were lolling rather sleepily outside the wire and looking at anything but the prisoners, Lebrun innocently leapfrogged with the other Frenchmen.

It all happened in a flash. A French colleague stood near the wire and, forming with his two hands a stirrup into which Lebrun placed his foot, catapulted Lebrun upward. Acrobats can heave each other tremendous distances by this method. Precision of timing of muscular effort is its secret. Lebrun and his friend managed it, and the former sailed in a headlong dive over the nine-foot wire.

This was only half the battle. Lebrun ran 20 yards along the fence to the main wall of the park. He had to reclimb the wire, using it as a ladder, in order to hoist himself onto the top of the wall, which was, at this point, about 13 feet high. Rather than present a slowly moving target during this climb, Lebrun deliberately attracted the fire of two of the nearest sentries by running backward and forward alongside the wall. Their carbines once fired (and having missed), the reloading gave him the extra seconds he needed. He was on top of the wall by the time they fired again and dropped to the ground on the other side in a hail of bullets as the more distant sentries joined in the fusillade.

He disappeared and was never recaught. He certainly deserves the greatest credit for this escape.

I met Mairesse Lebrun when the war was over, and here is the end of his story.

Lebrun escaped on July 1, 1941. Although he had the sleuth hounds and a posse of goons on his tail within 10 minutes, he managed to hide in a field of wheat. (You must walk in backward, rearranging the stalks as you go.) There he hid the whole afternoon while a search plane circled continuously above him. At 10 P.M. he set off. He had 20 German marks that had been smuggled into his prison cell from the camp. He walked about 50 miles, then stole a bicycle, and cycled between 60 and 100 miles a day. He posed as an Italian officer and begged or bought food at lonely farmhouses, making sure, by a stealthy watch beforehand, that there were only women in the house. When his bicycle had a flat tire, he abandoned it and stole a second. On the journey to the Swiss frontier he was stopped twice by guards and ran for it each time. On the second occasion, about 25 miles from the frontier, he tripped up the guard with the aid of his bicycle, then knocked him out with his bicycle pump. He took to the woods and crossed the frontier safely on July 8. He eventually reached Algeria to carry on the war.

If any German had examined Lebrun's cell at Colditz when he left for his daily exercise on July 1, he might have nipped Lebrun's escape in the bud. Lebrun had packed up his belongings and addressed them to himself in France. Months later they arrived—forwarded by Oberst Lieutenant Prawitt, the Colditz camp commandant.

THE GREATEST DAREDEVIL POLISH officer at Colditz among a bunch of daredevils was Niki, 2nd Lt. (Ensign) N. Surmanowicz. He was a small young man, a great friend of mine. We went on many marauding expeditions together through the forbidden parts of the camp. He taught me all I ever knew about lock-picking, at which he was an expert. It was Niki who had been one of our first visitors up in the loft upon our arrival at Colditz.

The manufacture of magnetic compasses was also a pastime of his. This he carried out with the aid of a homemade solenoid, employing the electric current of the main camp supply, which happened to be direct current. The number of compasses fabricated by him alone, together with their pivots, compass cards, and glass-covered boxes, numbered in the 50's.

His schemes for escaping were, to my mind, mostly too wild to bear serious examination. He, on the other hand, thought my ideas were prosaic, and I know he inwardly deprecated my painstaking way of setting about escape problems. Like Lebrun, he relied on dash, to which he added a depth of cunning hardly to be equaled.

Niki spent as much time in solitary confinement as he did with "the common herd." On one occasion, in the summer of 1941, he occupied a cell that had a small window, high up in the wall, opening onto our courtyard. Another Polish officer, Lt. Mietek Schmiel, a friend of Niki's, occupied the cell next door. I received a message from Niki one day, saying that he and Schmiel were going to escape that night and would I join them.

I declined the invitation for two reasons; first, I thought Niki was crazy, and second, I had given up the idea of escaping myself so long as I remained Escape Officer. With the British POW contingent rapidly on the increase, this latter course was the only one open to me if I wished to retain the confidence of our group as an impartial arbiter and helper.

I passed on Niki's invitation to join in the escape to a few of the most harebrained among our company, but his invitation was politely refused by all.

Nobody believed he was serious. Nobody believed he could ghost his way out of his heavily barred and padlocked cell, open his friend's cell, and then unlock the main door of the solitary cell corridor that opened onto the courtyard. Having accomplished this feat, he would still be inside the prison camp, the same as everyone else. Niki loved a challenge, and he would chuckle with laughter for the rest of his life if he could show the Jerries once and for all that it took more than they could contrive to keep a Pole down.

He left the invitation open, setting a rendezvous in the courtyard outside the solitary confinement cells for 11 P.M. that night.

I was at my window watching as 11 o'clock struck, and on the minute I saw the door of the cells open slowly. All was dark, and I could only faintly distinguish the two figures as they crept out. Then something dropped from a window high up in the Polish quarters. It was a rope made of sheets with a load strapped to the bottom—their escape kit, clothes, and rucksacks. Next I saw the figures climb the rope one after the other to a ledge 40 feet above the ground. What they were about to do was impossible, but they had achieved the impossible once already.

I could no longer believe my eyes. The ledge they were on jutted out four inches from the sheer face of the wall of the building. They both held the rope, which was still suspended from the window above them. My heart pounded against my ribs as I saw them with their backs against the wall, moving along the ledge inch by inch a distance of at least 10 yards before reaching the safety of a gutter on the eaves of the German guardhouse.

Once there they were comparatively safe and out of sight if the courtyard lights were turned on. I then saw them climb up the roof to a skylight, through which they disappeared. As they did so, they pulled the long rope of sheets, which was let loose by Polish confederates, after them.

Their next move, I knew, was to descend from a small window at the outer end of the attic of the German guardhouse. The drop was about 120 feet, continuing down the face of the cliff upon which the castle was built.

I retired to my bunk, weak in the knees and shaking, as if I had done the climb myself.

The next morning the two of them were back in their cells. I find it hard to tell the end of the story. Niki wore plimsolls (rubber-soled canvas shoes) for the climb, but his colleague, with Niki's agreement, preferred to wear boots of the mountaineering type. As they both descended the long drop from the guardhouse, the mountaineering boots made too much noise against the wall and awoke the German duty officer sleeping in the guardhouse. He opened his window to see the rope dangling beside him and a body a few yards below him. He drew his revolver and, true to type, shouted *"Hände hoch!"* several times and called out the guard.

I spent a month in Niki's cell later on without being able to discover how he had opened the door.

After this episode the Germans placed a sentry in the courtyard. He remained there all night with the lights full on, which was to prove a nuisance for later escape attempts.

THE SUMMER MONTHS WERE PASSING—slowly enough for us, yet too fast for all our plans. Winter, relatively speaking, is the escapees' "closed season," though World War II was to see many time-hallowed rules of this nature broken.

At this period of our captivity, escape equipment was becoming organized. Although not every officer had been equipped with identity papers yet, each had a homemade compass of one kind or another, a set of maps painfully traced over and over again from originals, and some German money.

Every officer possessed his private escape kit, which he had ample time to devise during the long hours of enforced idleness. And it was surprising what could be produced in the way of civilian clothing by dyeing and altering, by cutting up blankets, and by clever sewing and knitting. Many of our officers had their specialties and turned out articles in quantity.

I concentrated on the manufacture of caps and rucksacks. My particular brand of cap was cut out of any suitably colored blanket, had a peak stiffened with a piece of leather or other water-resistant material, and was lined with a portion of colored handkerchief and a soft-leather headband. They looked quite professional. My rucksacks were not always waterproof. They were made from dark-colored army material, with broad trouser suspenders adapted as straps, and the flaps and corners were neatly edged with leather strips cut from shoe tongues. They would pass in Germany as workmen's rucksacks.

Dyeing with ersatz coffee or purple pencil lead became a fine art. The blue Royal Air Force uniform was readily adaptable and with skillful tailoring could become a passable civilian suit. Of course, real civilian clothing was what every officer ultimately aimed at possessing. This urgent desire accounts for the high premium set on the workmen's clothing, which had given rise to the earlier "grand piano" incident.

A similar occasion arose once during one of the very rare visits of a German civilian dentist to supplement the work of our French Army dentist. He was accompanied by two leechlike sentries, who kept so close to him that he hardly had room to wield his forceps.

The dentist's torture chamber was approached through a maze of small rooms and had two doors, one of which was supposed to be permanently locked but which we opened on our nefarious occasions with the aid of our universal keys. On the back of this door was a coat hook, and on the hook our German dentist hung his Homburg hat and a fine fur-collared tweed overcoat.

This was indeed "big game," and Dick Howe, with another British officer, "Scorgie" Price, and a French officer named Jacques Prot were soon hot on the trail.

Dick arranged to pay an officer's dentist bill. The dentist was paid in *Lagergeld*, and Dick sought out an officer with a heavy bill—it came to 100 marks. He collected the whole sum in 1-mark notes. This would give him plenty of time. He arranged a signal with the other two. The operative word was "right." When Dick said "right" loudly, Price was to open the locked door and remove the hat and coat.

Dick went to the dentist's room and insisted on interrupting the dentist's work to pay his brother officer's bill. He drew him over to a table; the two sentries dutifully followed; and Dick started to count out his *Lagergeld* laboriously.

"*Eins, zwei, drei . . .*" he started and carried on to *zehn*, at which point he looked up to see if he had the full attention of the dentist and his guards. "Not quite," he thought, and he carried on painfully, "*elf, zwölf . . .*" By the time he reached *zwanzig*, he had all their eyes riveted on the slowly rising pile of notes, so he said, "right."

As he continued, he sensed that nothing had happened. At *dreiszig* he repeated "right" a little louder. Again nothing happened. At *vierzig* he filled his lungs and shouted "right" again. Still nothing happened. Doggedly he continued, holding the attention of all three, as the reserves of *Lagergeld* dwindled. As *fünfzig, sechzig, siebzig* passed, his "rights" crescendoed, to the amusement of his three spectators. Nothing happened. An operatic bass would have been proud of Dick's final rendering at *achtzig, neunzig,* and *hundert.* The scheme had failed, and the only people laughing at Dick's, by this time, comic act were the Germans.

The dentist, still guffawing, collected all the notes together and before Dick's crestfallen gaze started recounting them. As he reached *zehn*, he shouted, "r-r-right," and Dick, to his own utter astonishment, felt rather than heard the door open behind them and sensed an arm appearing around it. Before the dentist had reached *zwanzig*, the door had closed again. Dick continued the pantomime and eventually, after assuring himself that the hat and coat had really disappeared, retired from the scene with apologies—a shaken man.

The concealment of contraband material presented great difficulties, and many were the hours given to devising ingenious ways of hiding our precious work. The common hiding places and those at various times found out by the Germans were: behind false-backed cupboards and in trapdoor hides, under floorboards, and sewn into mattresses and overcoat linings. Small items were often sealed in cigarette tins, weighted, and dropped into lavatory cisterns or concealed in stores of food.

There were myriad possibilities, and it is appropriate that the better ways remain undisclosed for the present. Men who may have nothing to think about for many a long, weary day in the years to come will rediscover them and sharpen their wits in the exercise.

FROM THE BEGINNING close relations were maintained between the Dutch and the British. Although at the start this did not involve revealing the full details of our respective plans, it soon developed into a very close cooperation, which was headed on the Dutch side by a Captain Van den Heuvel.

The Dutch were not very long at Colditz before Van den Heuvel warned me of an impending attempt. "Vandy," as he was inevitably called, was a fairly tall, big-chested man with a round face, florid complexion, and an almost permanent broad grin. He spoke English well, but with a droll Dutch accent.

"Pat," he said to me one day, "we are about to try our first flight from Colditz. I can only say it is from the direction of the park, and it will take place on Sunday."

Sunday passed calmly, and in the evening I went to see Vandy.

"Well, Vandy, there's been no excitement. What have you got up your sleeve?" I asked.

"Ah! Pat," he replied, with a mischievous twinkle in his eye, "Two have already gone today!"

Sure enough, at the morning *Appell* on Monday two Dutchmen were missing. Some time later two more disappeared.

The Germans were worried enough over the first two. They were hopping mad when the number rose to four, then to six. There was a series of searches of the camp premises, and the park was given a very careful scrutiny. I noticed the Jerries placed bars across a small wooden manhole cover on the football ground that had, in any case, one large nut and bolt securing it.

Eventually I managed to worm out of Vandy how he, a comparative newcomer to the camp, had managed with such ease to arrange the escape of his six fellow Dutchmen from the fortress of Colditz.

His trick was so simple that it shook me to think that the rest of us—Poles, French, and British, numbering now some 250—had not thought of it. The various escapes were indeed made from the manhole on the football ground.

"All very well," I said to Vandy. "We've all looked at that manhole cover till we were blue in the face without arriving at any kind of a satisfactory scheme."

"Ah, Pat!" he replied, grinning broadly. "I looked at the manhole cover from another angle!"

On the first two occasions in question, a few Dutchmen, led by a venerable-looking bearded one by the name of Van Doorninck, had held Bible-reading meetings, curiously enough, around the manhole. Previously they had measured the size of the nut and bolt. During the Bible reading, the bolt was undone with a pair of large homemade wrenches filed out of iron bed parts. The bolt had about a ¾-inch diameter thread. When the sentries' notice was attracted to a football game in progress, two Dutchmen disappeared into the manhole. Now this was the crux. Immediately after the recreation, and before the prisoners returned to the castle, the football ground was carefully examined, invariably including the manhole, by two or three Jerries appointed for the purpose. They also let loose dogs to trace possible hideouts or graves among the trees.

"How," I asked, "did you conceal the opened manhole? That is what beats me."

"We made another bolt, a very special kind of bolt," Vandy replied. "It was made of glass tubing with a wooden head and painted just like the real one."

That in effect was the secret of this simple yet brilliantly conceived escape. The two escapees in the manhole had the real bolt with them. At nightfall they pushed up the lid, breaking the glass bolt. They cleaned away the bits as best they could before leaving and replaced the original bolt exactly as it was before, applying mud and dirt to cover any marks left on the iron.

Their exit thereafter, only impeded by a high wall and some barbed wire, presented no difficulty in the dark with the nearest guard over 400 yards away. By this time the Germans had enforced no fewer than four roll calls on the daily recreation parade—two in the park and two at the courtyard gate. How Vandy managed to cover these he kept a secret for a little while longer.

Two of the four who escaped reached Switzerland. The other two were caught at the frontier and eventually returned to Colditz. The third couple made their disappearance about a month after the others, during a Polish-Dutch international soccer match. They reached Switzerland safely.

The Germans still believed they could make Oflag IV C impregnable (from within), so escapees, when recaught, were not sent elsewhere according to normal custom but invariably returned to Colditz. For this reason it was always growing in population, a center of gravity toward which escapees moved from all over Germany, when not moving in the opposite direction under their own steam.

It was likewise a fortress, which required an ever-increasing garrison. The Germans continued to greatly outnumber the prisoners. Admittedly our jailers were not class A1 soldiers. The swollen number of the garrison was probably a source of irritation to the German High Command, because they held a series of inspections at one period, including a visit by two German officers who had escaped from Allied hands. One was Hauptmann Von Werra, the German airman who gave our POW authorities much trouble and eventually escaped from Canada to the United States. The story has it that he jumped from a train, crossed the St. Lawrence River in a stolen boat, and eventually contacted the German consulate in New York. He visited our camp during his leave to give the commandant advice. Shortly afterward he was reported to have been shot down and killed. (See "The One That Got Away," page 394.)

The return of escaped officers to their original camp provided certain advantages for the inmates, by which we were not slow to profit. It was inevitable, however, that, if the war lasted long enough, in the end the Germans would win the battle of Colditz and the camp would become practically unbreakable, but none of us thought that stage had arrived in the autumn of 1941. In fact, although every escape discovered meant that one more foxhole had been plugged, the prisoners really never gave up trying to find a way out until the Allied advance into Germany.

The *prominente*, as they were called by the Germans, also drifted gradually toward Colditz. Winston Churchill's nephew, Giles Romilly, arrived. He was given the honor and the inconvenience of a small cell to himself, which had a sentry outside it all night. He was free to mix with the other prisoners during the day, but he had to suffer the annoyance of being called for by his guardian angel—a heavy-booted Hun—every night at 9 P.M., escorted to his bedroom, and locked in until the next morning.

Like everybody else, he wanted to escape, but it was naturally more difficult to arrange. I once succeeded in substituting him for one of several French orderlies who were unloading coal from a truck in the courtyard. The coal dust was a helpful disguise—smeared over his face—but he did not even pass the first gateway. It was obvious that either he was watched from within the camp by other than his ostensible jailers, or, which is equally likely in this case, a French orderly—perhaps the one substituted—reported to the Germans what was happening, to save his own skin. We never found out, but it was Hauptmann Priem himself who entered the courtyard when the truck was ready to leave and calmly asked Romilly to step down from it. I think he was awarded only a week's solitary confinement and then returned to his normal routine.

IT WAS ALSO IN the late summer of 1941, when I was doing one of my customary periods of solitary—three weeks in this case—that the cells became overcrowded and Flight Lt. Norman Forbes joined me for a spell. The cells were tiny, about four yards by three yards. We were given a two-tier bed, however, which helped, but to compensate for this, our cell was built immediately over a semibasement cellar in which the camp garbage cans were housed.

Norman and I managed very well and did not get on each other's nerves. After Norman left, however, boredom settled in on me. I was studying economics, but found it heavy reading when continued for weeks on end. One day I thought of my cornet. As a concession I had been allowed to take into solitary, along with books and other paraphernalia, my guitar and my brass cornet.

Norman had only just managed to withstand my guitar crooning and categorically refused to let me practice my cornet. Now I was alone, I thought, and I could practice in peace. But so many objections were raised from nearby cells and also from the courtyard—which my cell faced—in the form of showers of pebbles, shouts, and insults, that I was driven to practicing my cornet at the only time (apart from the dead of night) when nobody could stop me, which was during the half hour of evening *Appell*.

This seemed to satisfy the POW's, since the German officers and NCO's taking the parade could hardly hear themselves speak, and the numbers invariably tallied up wrong, necessitating several recounts. By the third evening the hilarity grew to such an extent that the parade became almost a shambles. Apparently many of the German troops thought the cornet practice funny, too—which made it all the worse for the German officer in charge, who was beside himself. By the fourth day I was feeling so sorry for the Jerries having to put up with the ear-splitting noises that coincided with their commands that I decided to show a gentlemanly spirit and refrain from practicing on that evening.

Evidently I was not the only one who had been reflecting, for when the evening *Appell* was assembled and the German officer in charge entered the yard (Hauptmann Püpcke was his name), he made straight for my cell with two soldiers and swung open my door with considerable violence.

"Geben Sie mir sofort ihre Trompete" ("Give me your trumpet immediately"), he shouted.

I was so taken aback by his abruptness after my good intentions and sympathy for the German position that I thought it was my turn to feel insulted.

"Nein," I said. *"Ich will nicht; es ist meine Trompete. Sie haben kein Recht"* ("I don't want to; it's my trumpet. You have no right"). With that I hid the trumpet (cornet) behind my back. He seized it, and we began a violent tug-of-war. He ordered his two cohorts to intervene, which they did by clubbing my wrists and arms with their rifle butts, and I gave up the unlucky instrument.

"You will have a court-martial for this," the officer screamed as he slammed the door behind him.

The court-martial never came off, which was a pity, for it meant a journey, probably to Leipzig, and a chance of escape. Instead, I was awarded another month's solitary, which I began shortly afterward in a different cell.

IT WAS LATE SEPTEMBER, and the leaves were falling in the park, but all I could see from my tiny window by climbing onto my washstand was the wall of a section of our prison known as the theater block. It was during one of my long periods of blank staring at this wall that a light suddenly dawned upon me. If I had not been an engineer, familiar with plans and elevations and in the habit of mentally reconstructing the skeletons of buildings, the idea would probably never have occurred to me. I suddenly realized that the wooden stage of the theater was situated so that it protruded over a part of the castle, sealed off from the prisoners, which led by a corridor to the top of the German guardhouse immediately outside our courtyard.

This discovery was a little gold mine. I tucked it away and resolved to explore further as soon as I was free.

BEER HAD LONG SINCE disappeared from the camp, and with the thought of a dreary winter ahead, a few of us put our heads together. With the help of Niki, who had already managed to procure some yeast from a German, we started a brewing society. Someone unearthed a curious medal struck to commemorate a brewing exhibition. I, who was elected Chief Brewer and dispensed the yeast, wore the medal attached to the end of a large red ribbon. When asked by curious goons what the medal represented, I proudly told them it was a war decoration for distinguished service in the boosting of morale.

Brewing soon became a popular pastime and, with a little instruction by the Chief Brewer and his stewards, was highly successful. Soon, at nearly every bedside there were large jars or bottles, filled with water and containing at the bottom a mash of sultanas, currants, or dried figs—produced from our Red Cross parcels—together with the magic thimbleful of yeast. Curiously enough, it was eventually found that the yeast was unnecessary, for there was enough natural yeast already on the skins of the fruit to start the fermentation process without assistance. The one difficulty we experienced was the provision of gentle heat, because fermentation requires a fairly consistent temperature of about 27° C.

This problem was overcome by the simple use of body heat, or "hatching," as it was called. It was a normal sight to see rows of officers propped up in their beds for hours on end in the hatching position, with their jars and bottles nestling snugly under the blankets beside them. Fermentation was complete after two weeks. Some of our amateur brewers were luckier than the ordinary run of broody officers, as their bunks were situated near electric lights. Large incubating boxes were manufactured out of cardboard and lined with German blankets. Jars were arranged in tiers in the boxes, and the heat was turned on by placing the light bulbs in the boxes attached to lengths of "won" electric cable.

Soon we were having cheery evening parties and had started entertaining our fellow prisoners of other nationalities.

One day our brewing association invited a "brilliant lecturer" to expound the secrets of distillation. Human nature being what it is, we were soon distilling briskly. I tore down a long section of lead piping from one of our nonworking lavatories and made a coil, which was sealed into a large German jam can about 20 inches high. This still became the property of the Brewing and (now) Distilling Society. Almost every night distilling began after lights out and continued into the early hours. We worked shifts and charged a small percentage (of the resultant liquor) for the distilling of officers' brews.

I should explain that distillation is merely a method of concentrating any brew or wine. Brandy is distilled grape wine. We named our liquor simply firewater, for that undoubtedly is what it was.

Over a period of time we used up nearly all the bed boards in the British quarters as fuel for our witches' cauldron. Our rows of broody officers looked more odd than ever reposing on mattresses supported only by a minimum of bed boards with pendulous bulges in between the upper bunks and the lower ones. In vain did the Germans make periodical surveys of the bed boards, even to the extent of numbering them with chalk and indelible pencil. Alas! the numbers were consumed in the flames and did not survive the boards.

The distilling process was an eerie ceremony carried out in semidarkness around the kitchen stove, with the distillers listening over the cauldron for the telltale hiss of gentle distillation—their flickering giantlike shadows dancing on the walls—as the flames were carefully fed with fuel. Distilling required most concentrated attention because the work of a few weeks could be ruined in a minute if a brew, passing through the lead coils, became overheated and the alcohol boiled away. Distillation takes place between 80° and 90° C.

Having no thermometers, we learned to judge the temperature by sound alone—hence our expertise and our right to charge a premium for the process.

The liquor, as it appeared, drop by drop, from the bottom of the still, was pure white in color. It was bottled, and within a very short time the liquor became crystal clear, leaving a white sediment at the bottom. The clear liquid was run off and rebottled. This was firewater. The white sediment was probably lead oxide—pure poison—but I was not able to check this, and nobody every died to prove it.

With experience and Polish assistance we produced various flavored varieties, which the Poles insisted on calling vodka. We did not argue over the name, but I feel sure that our liquor would never have been a suitable accompaniment to caviar. It took the roof off one's mouth, anyway.

It was not long before the British had a good cellar and "vintages" accumulating. Christmas 1941 loomed rosily ahead of us.

SOON AFTER I WAS RELEASED from solitary, I made a reconnaissance of the stage in the theater, which was on the third floor of the theater block. By removing some of the wooden steps leading up to the stage from one of the dressing rooms, I was able to crawl underneath and examine that part of the floor over the sealed room leading to the German guardhouse. It was as I had hoped. There were no floorboards, only straw and rubble about four inches deep reposing on the lath-and-plaster ceiling of the room in question.

I next looked around for prospective candidates for the escape I was planning. I selected about half a dozen possibilities. I casually mentioned to them that I would get them out of Colditz if they, on the other hand, would produce first-class imitations of German officers' uniforms. It was a challenge and by no means an easy one.

We had made a start, however, on certain parts of German Army accoutrements, and this was reason for encouragement. What was left over from the lead piping that I had removed to make the still had already been melted down and recast into perfect imitations of German uniform buttons and one or two of their insignia. The lead, unfortunately, did not go very far when melted down.

My offer was a test of ingenuity and enterprise, and it produced Lt. Airey Neave, a comparative newcomer to the castle, and Hyde-Thompson of the mattress episode. They had teamed up, and Airey promised to make the uniforms. He said he could not make them, however, without Dutch assistance, so with Van den Heuvel's agreement, two Dutch officers were selected to make the team a foursome. The Dutch spoke German fluently, which was a great asset.

AIREY AND LT. W. L. B. "SCARLET" O'HARA came to me in distress one day soon afterward, while I was preparing our next evening's distilling operations. Airey said: " We're running short of lead."

Scarlet was our foundry foreman. He added: "The lead piping you gave me is finished. It didn't go very far. It's too darn thin—cheap German stuff—no weight in it." He looked toward the still.

"What are you looking at?" I asked. "I hope you're not hinting."

"Wouldn't dream of it," said Scarlet. "I just don't know where I'm going to get any lead from. We've only got three lavatories working as it is. That's not many for 40 officers. If I break one up, there will be a revolution."

"H'm! This is serious." I went into a huddle with Dick Howe, who was a keen distiller and was at that moment repairing a water leak at the bottom of our still.

"Dick, things look bad for the still. They've run out of lead. How much liquor have we? Is our cellar reasonably well stocked?"

"Our cellar is not at all well stocked," Dick replied, "for the simple reason that it's a bottomless pit. But if there's a greater need, I don't see how we can avoid the issue. We'll probably be able to recuperate our loss in due course—from, say, a Dutch or a French lavatory."

"Very good," I said to Airey, "your need is greater than ours. You'd better take the coil."

Then I told Dick: "It's probably just as well to lay up for the time being, as there's a search due one of these days, and we've got some stock to carry on with. The still would cause a lot of trouble if found, and it's useless trying to hide it."

Dick stopped tinkering and handed over the lead coil. It was melted down and poured into little white clay molds that were prepared from beautifully carved patterns, sculpted by a Dutchman. Replicas, conforming perfectly as to color (silver-gray) and size, were made of the various metal parts of German uniforms—swastikas and German eagles, tunic buttons by the score, and troops' belt clasps with the *Gott mit uns* monogram.

The most important item of the German uniform was the long greatcoat of field gray, and it was here that the Dutch came in; their greatcoats, with minor alterations, could pass in electric light as German greatcoats. The officers' service caps were cleverly manufactured by our specialists. Leather parts, such as belts and revolver holsters, were made from linoleum, and leggings were made from cardboard.

We had to compliment Airey and the various Dutch and Britishers who had done the work. The uniforms would pass—though not in broad daylight at close range, yet under almost any other conditions.

In the meantime I had not been idle, having my share of the bargain to accomplish. From thin plywood I cut out an irregular oblong shape, large enough to fill a hole through which a man could pass. The edge was beveled to assist in making a snug fit, and I gave one side a preliminary coat of white paint. To the reverse side I fixed a frame with swiveling wooden clamps, and I prepared wooden wedges. The result was christened Shovewood IV.

I asked Hank Wardle to help me in the preparation of the escape. This tall, robust Canadian, with his imperturbable manner and laconic remarks, could be relied upon to do the right thing in an awkward moment. His brain was not slow, though his casual and somewhat lazy manner belied it.

Under the stage in the theater we quietly sawed through the laths of the ceiling and then through the plaster. Small pieces of it fell to the floor with ominous crashes. Then I had to descend by a sheet rope to the room below, which was empty. The door connecting it to a corridor that passed over the main courtyard gate and thence to the attic of the guardroom was locked. I tested it with my "universal key." It opened easily, so I relocked it and began work.

I had prepared two collapsible stools that fitted one on top of the other. Standing on these, I could reach the ceiling. Hank held Shovewood IV in position while I carved out the plaster of the ceiling to fit it. Eventually, when pressed home and wedged from above, it fitted well enough to give the impression of an irregular oblong crack in the real ceiling. With a pencil I drew lines that looked like more cracks in various directions, to camouflage the shape of the oblong and to remove any impression that a casual observer might have of a concealed hole.

The color of the ceiling was exasperatingly difficult to match, and it took a long time to achieve a similarity of tint between it and Shovewood IV. This latter work necessitated many visits, as each coat of paint had to dry first and then be examined in place.

AIREY NEAVE WAS READY TO GO and was becoming impatient. "Look here, Pat," he protested, "I've got pieces of German clothing and gear lying about all over our quarters. It's tricky stuff to hide, and if the search comes, I'm finished. When will your hole be ready?"

"Keep your shirt on, Airey!" I retorted. "You'll go in due course, but not before it's a finished job. I want others to use this exit, too."

"I wish you'd get a move on, all the same," Airey Neave said. "The weather is fairly mild now, but remember, we've had snow already, and we're going to have a lot more soon. I don't want to freeze to death on a German hillside."

"Don't worry," I said. "I need two more days. You can reckon on leaving on Monday evening. The takeoff will be immediately after evening *Appell.*"

Even so I was not completely satisfied with my Shovewood IV. It was so nearly perfect that I wanted to make it absolutely foolproof. Its position in the sealed-off room was unique, and I felt we could unleash officers at intervals "until the cows came home."

I made a reconnaissance along the German corridor and, unlocking a further door, found myself in the attic over the German guardhouse. Probably nobody had been near the attic since Niki climbed in through the skylight and left by the window at the end. The window had not been touched, but that route was no longer possible since a sentry had been positioned to cover the whole of that wall face beneath the window. A staircase in the attic led down to the guards' quarters below. Layers of dust on everything, including the floor, were my greatest bugbear, and as I returned, I had to waft dust painstakingly over fingerprints and footprints by waving a handkerchief carefully in the air over the marks.

The plan was simple enough. I would send the escapees out in two pairs on successive evenings immediately after a change of the guard stationed at the front entrance to the guardhouse. Thus the new sentry would not know what German officers, if any, might have entered the guardhouse in the previous two hours. The two officers escaping would descend the guardhouse staircase and walk out through the hall. This was the most risky part of the attempt. The stairs and hall would be well lit, and a stray guardhouse goon might wonder where two strange German officers had suddenly descended from.

Therefore, the moment of descent from the attic had to be chosen when a period of comparative calm in guardhouse activity was anticipated. I insisted that the two officers, on reaching the guardhouse entrance, were to stop in full view of the sentry, put on their gloves, and exchange casual remarks in well-prepared German before marching boldly down the ramp to the first gateway. This act was calculated to absorb any shock of surprise that the sentry might have if, for instance, two strange officers were suddenly to issue from the entrance and quickly march away.

THE EVENING FOR THE ATTEMPT arrived. After the last *Appell* all of us concerned with the escape disappeared into the theater block instead of to our own quarters. Various senior officers and generals lived in the theater block, and movement in this direction did not arouse suspicion.

The two escapees who were to go that evening, Airey Neave and Lt. Tony Luteyn (Royal Netherlands Indies Army), were wearing no fewer than three sets of apparel—apart from some pieces of accoutrement, which were carried in a bag. Over everything they wore British Army greatcoats and trousers; underneath were their German uniforms, and underneath again was their civilian attire.

Although we thought highly of the German uniforms, they were not good enough for a permanent disguise. The cardboard leggings, for instance, would not have looked very convincing after a heavy rain, so they would be discarded in the woods outside the castle.

Our stooges were posted, and we climbed—the two escapees with some difficulty owing to their bulk—under the stage. I opened up Shovewood IV, and one after the other we dropped quietly into the room below. I led the way along the corridor and into the attic. British Army attire had already been discarded. The German uniforms were brushed, and everything was checked. I said to Airey Neave: "It takes me 11 minutes to return, clean up, and close Shovewood. Don't move before 11 minutes are up."

"Right!" replied Airey, "but I'm not going to hang around long after that. We'll take the first opportunity of a quiet period on the staircase and landings underneath us."

"Don't forget to take it easy at the guardhouse doorway," I said. "Remember, you own the place. Good-bye and good luck and don't come back. We don't want to see you again!"

We shook hands, and I left them in the attic. I relocked doors, redusted traces, mounted the rope of sheets, and, with Hank's assistance, wedged Shovewood IV firmly in place. Before Hank and I had issued from under the stage, our watchers reported a perfect exit from the guardhouse. The act went off, the German sentry saluted smartly, and our two escapees passed on.

We did not expect much difficulty from the first gate. The guard on duty would see the officers coming, and the gate itself was under a covered archway that was very dimly lit. After this the two were to pass through the German courtyard under another archway, the gates of which were open at this hour. They would then reach the bridge over the moat, before having to pass the last sentry at the outermost gate. There was a possibility, however, of bypassing this last gate, which might require a password.

I knew of the existence of a small garden gate in the parapet at the beginning of the moat bridge. I had remarked on it upon my first entry into the castle just a year before. This gate gave onto a small path that led downward into the moat. From what I knew of the geography of the camp, I always suspected this path might lead around to the roadway, down which we passed when going for exercise in the park. If our two officers could regain this roadway, they had merely to pass some occupied German barracks and proceed 100 yards to a locked gate in the outer wall around the castle grounds. This gate was not guarded as far as we knew, and with the area in pitch-darkness, the wall with its barbed wire could be climbed.

Our first two men disappeared toward the moat bridge, and we heard no more of them.

The next day we covered their absence at the two *Appells.* Van den Heuvel arranged this with perfect equanimity. It was another professional secret of his that he promised to reveal if I told him how I launched the escapees.

In the evening I repeated the performance of the night before, and Hyde-Thompson and his Dutch colleague departed from the camp.

We could not conceal four absences, so, at the next morning *Appell,* four officers were found missing. The Jerries became excited, and everyone was promptly confined to barracks.

As the day wore on and the German searches proved fruitless, their impatience grew. So did that of the prisoners. Every German who entered the courtyard was jeered at until, finally, the riot squad put in an appearance.

With rifles pointed at the windows, the Germans issued orders that nobody was to look out. Needless to say, this made matters worse. The French from their windows took up their favorite refrain: *"Où sont les Allemands?"* ("Where are the Germans?")

"Les Allemands sont dans le merde" ("The Germans are in the dung"), came the reply from about 40 windows. This was followed by, *"Qu'on les y enfonce"* ("Push 'em in deeper"). The shouted reply to that being, *"Jusqu'aux oreilles!"* ("Up to the ears!")

This chanted litany always provoked the Germans, who understood what it meant. The British began singing, *"Deutschland, Deutschland UNTER alles!"* ("Germany, Germany UNDER all!")— our revised version of the German national anthem—to the accompaniment of musical instruments imitating a German brass band. Fake heads began bobbing up and down at windows, and the inevitable shooting started, followed by the sounds of splintering glass.

From a protected vantage point I suddenly saw Van den Heuvel sally forth into the courtyard, having presumably opened the courtyard door with his own universal key. His face dark with anger, he headed for the German officer in charge. He told the Jerry in his own language what he thought of him and his race and their manner of treating defenseless prisoners. His anger was justified, for hardly had he finished speaking when the French announced from their windows that an officer had been hit.

This calmed the Jerries at once. The German officer removed his riot squad and went to investigate. Lt. Maurice Fahy had received a ricochet bullet under one of his shoulder blades. He was removed to the hospital, and peace settled on the camp once more. Fahy lost the use of one arm as a result of this episode.

IN THE MEANTIME our four escapees were continuing on their journey to the Swiss frontier. They traveled most of the way by train. Neave and Luteyn crossed the frontier safely. Airey Neave was the first Britisher to make a home run from Colditz.

Hyde-Thompson and his companion were caught by station controls at Ulm. They brought back the news that Neave and Luteyn had also been caught at the same station. There had been some RAF bombing, which was followed by heavy controls for the purpose of rounding up plane crews that had parachuted. Neave and Luteyn had, however, managed to escape again from the police station during a moment's laxness on the part of their guards. By the time Hyde-Thompson and his Dutch colleague reached Ulm, the Jerries were on their toes. Maybe they had received warning; in any case, once the two escapees were suspected, they had no real hope of success.

Hyde-Thompson's bad luck taught us a lesson. From now on no more than two escapees at a time would travel the same route.

THE INFORMER

B Y THE WINTER OF 1941–42, when Neave and Luteyn's escape took place, the forging of escapees' credentials had improved considerably. A number of expert forgers were at work, with the result that every British officer was eventually equipped with a set of papers, as well as maps, a small amount of German money, and an all-important compass.

Identity papers were reproduced by various means. The imitation by hand of a typewritten document is very difficult. There were only two officers in Colditz capable of doing it, and they worked overtime. The German Gothic script, commonly used on identity cards, while appearing to be even more difficult, is, in fact, easier to copy, and our staff employed on this form of printing was correspondingly larger.

The day arrived when a Polish officer, Lieutenant Niedenthal (nicknamed Sheriff), made a typewriter. This proved a great boon and speeded up the work of our printing department. The typewriter was of the one-finger variety, and its speed of reproduction could not be compared with any normal machine, but it had the great advantage of being dismountable into half a dozen innocent-looking pieces of wood that did not require concealment from the Germans. Only the letters attached to their delicate arms had to be hidden.

Each officer was responsible for the concealment of his own papers and aids, the idea being that, under such conditions, it was easier to make use of escape opportunities if they arose without warning. One or two such occasions did arise and were made good use of, thanks to this system. As for concealment of the contraband, many carried their papers about with them, relying on native wit to hide them in the event of a blitz search by the Jerries.

Searches occurred from time to time at unpredictable intervals. Sometimes we had warning; at other times none.

On one of the latter occasions I was busily doing some work with a large hammer when the goons entered our quarters.

I seized a towel lying on a nearby table and put the hammer in its folds. The method of search was systematic. All officers were herded into a room at one end of our quarters and locked in. The Germans then turned all the other rooms inside out. They tore up floorboards, knocked away chunks of plaster from the walls, jabbed the ceilings, examined electric lights and every piece of furniture, turned bed-clothes and mattresses inside out, removed all the contents of every cupboard, turned over the cupboards, emptied the solid contents of all cans onto the floor, poured our precious homemade brews down the sinks, broke up games, cut open pieces of soap, emptied water closets, opened chimney flues, and spread the kitchen fire and any other stove ashes all over the floor.

Then, coming to the last room, each prisoner was stripped in turn, and even the seams of his clothing were searched before he was re-leased into the main section of the quarters, there to be faced with the indescribable chaos of the Germans' handiwork. The Jerries usually found some contraband, though rarely anything of major importance.

On the particular occasion when I had the hammer wrapped up in the towel, as soon as my turn came to be searched, I put the towel casually on the table beside which the Jerry officer stood and began stripping. After my clothing had been thoroughly scrutinized, I dressed, picked up my "loaded" towel, and walked out of the room.

Then there was the time when the Gestapo decided to search the camp and show the German Wehrmacht how a search should be conducted. They employed flashlights to search remote crevices and borrowed the keys of the camp to make the rounds. Before they had finished, both the keys and the flashlights had disappeared, and they left with their tails between their legs. The German garrison was as pleased as Punch. We returned the keys, after making suitable im-pressions, of course, to their rightful guardians.

As I HAVE MENTIONED, I was not completely satisfied with Shovewood IV. When, after a week, the Germans had calmed down, Hank and I paid a surreptitious visit to the theater, and I applied a new coat of paint to the Shovewood, for I knew that when more officers escaped, the German efforts to discover the exit would be redoubled.

When the paint was dry, we paid still another visit to check the color, and during this visit I had a suspicion that we had been followed—a vague impression and nothing more. I was more careful than ever about our movements and disappearance under the stage. It was curious, though, that one particularly nosey German ferret paid a visit to the theater, and I even heard him speaking (presumably to a prisoner) close to the stage.

The next two officers were preparing for their exit, due for the following Sunday, when, on Saturday, we learned that the Jerries had been under the stage and had discovered my Shovewood. This was more suspicious than ever, since no traces were left to indicate the position of the Shovewood, buried as it was under a four-inch layer of dirt and rubble, which extended uniformly beneath the whole of the stage, an area of 100 square yards.

My suspicions were further increased when the German regimental sergeant major, Gephard, who on rare occasions became human, remarked in a conversation with Peter Allan: "The camouflage was *wunderbar!* I examined the ceiling myself and would not have suspected a hole."

"Well, how did you discover it then?" asked Peter.

"*Ach!* That cannot be revealed, but we would never have found it without help."

"Whose help? A spy?"

"I cannot say," replied Gephard with a meaningful look. Then, changing the subject: "The photographer has been called to take photographs of the camouflage for the escape museum."

"So you make records of our escapes?"

"*Jawohl!* We have a room kept as a museum. It is very interesting! After the war perhaps you shall see it."

The remark concerning "help" was reported to the various senior officers and escape officers. It meant that in the future we had to act under the assumption that there was a stooge or a man planted in the camp, and, sure enough, it transpired that there was.

Gephard was a strange character. He gave the impression of being sour and ruthless with his harsh, deep voice and unsmiling face. But he was probably the most intelligent of the Jerries at Colditz. I am sure he was one of the first to realize who would win the war. Apart from this, under his gruffness there was honesty, and it is possible he disliked the idea of sending blackmailed spies into a camp, enough to warrant his dropping hints about it.

The stooge was not unearthed for some time. There was no evidence from the theater escape to commit anyone. However, certain Poles had been keeping their eye on one of their own officers over an extended period and had slowly accumulated evidence.

Not very long after the theater escape, we heard a rumor that the Poles were about to hang one of their own officers. Later on the same day a Pole was hurriedly removed from the camp.

What I gleaned from Niki and others—the Poles were reticent about the whole incident—was that they had held a court-martial and had found the man guilty of aiding the enemy, though under duress. The officer had been blackmailed by the Germans, having been tempted in a weak moment while he was ill in a hospital somewhere in Germany. He was allowed to return home to see his family and thereafter was threatened with their disappearance if he did not act as an informer for the Germans.

I would go so far as to say that the German Army officers in the camp did not use him willingly. They were probably presented with an informer by the Gestapo and given orders to employ him. This would also account for Gephard's reaction in giving us the hint.

In any case, the upshot was that the Polish senior officer, rather than have a dead body on his hands, called on the German commandant, told him the facts—which the commandant did not deny—and gave him 24 hours to remove the man.

Toward the end of 1941 the goons also tried to persuade the French and Belgian officer prisoners to collaborate and work with them. Their efforts in Colditz had little success; only two or three Frenchmen disappeared. The Germans were very keen to employ engineers and chemical experts.

On a couple of days a goon officer addressed the French and Belgian officers at the midday *Appell* (by this time we were having only three *Appells* daily). The Jerry asked if there were any more volunteers for work, saying that officers should submit their names and state their professions in order to see if they could be fitted into the economy of the Reich. There was no response on the first day, except much laughter and derisive cheers. On the second day a French aspirant, Paul Durand, stepped smartly forward and said: "I would like to work for the Germans."

There was a gasp of surprise from the assembled parade and a beam from the goon officer.

"You really want to work for the Reich?"

"I would prefer to work for 20 Germans than for one Frenchman."

More gasps and looks of astonishment from the prisoners.

"All right! What is your name?"

"My name is Durand, and I wish to make it clearly understood that I would prefer to work for 20 Germans than for one Frenchman."

"Good! What is your profession?"

"Undertaker!"

Jacques Prot was another Frenchman whose puckishness was irrepressible and whose quick-wittedness won him freedom. Prot contrived to escape during a visit to the German dentist. The visit was made to the dentist's house in the village of Colditz rather than to the castle's torture chamber. Prot set off under heavy guard with another Frenchman, Guy de Frondeville, also suffering from some disease of the teeth. They managed to escape from the guards when leaving the dentist's house.

The two friends made it to Leipzig, then separated for safety. Prot, tall, dark, and well-built, aged about 26, went through Cologne to Aix-la-Chapelle. As he neared the frontier, he saw to his horror that his false papers were not at all like those in current use. The frontier station was heavily patrolled and guarded. He closely followed the crowd, mostly Belgian passengers, toward the barrier. He was at his wits' end. Then the light dawned. He grabbed a suitcase out of the hand of an astonished fellow passenger and took to his heels, through the barrier and away.

The psychology behind this move was inspired. For the passenger created a tremendous uproar, attracting everybody's attention for a few minutes—then, as soon as the Germans were fully aware of what had happened, they couldn't care less. An escaping French officer might have been something, but a thief running away with a Belgian's suitcase did not raise the slightest interest.

Nine days out from Colditz, Prot arrived in Paris, to the surprise and joy of his family, on Christmas Eve 1941.

He reached Tunis via the French Free Zone in 1942 and joined the 67th Artillery Regiment (Algerian). From Paris he returned the suitcase to its owner, whose address he found inside, and from Tunis he sent the German dentist a large consignment of real coffee with apologies for his abrupt departure. He fought through the Tunisian campaign to Cassino, where during the first offensive (Mount Belvedere) on January 29, 1944, he gave his life for France. May his honored memory remain long with his countrymen as it is cherished by every escapee of Colditz.

Christmas 1941 and New Year's Eve were happy affairs. There was deep snow everywhere and a spirit of hope, for the Germans were halted in Russia and were having a bad time.

Our cellar of wines and firewater added to the fun. Teddy Barton produced another good variety show that played to an overflowing house for three nights. On New Year's Eve, toward midnight, the British started a snake chain: men in single file, each with an arm on the shoulder of the man in front. Laughing and singing, the snake passed through the various quarters of the castle, growing in length all the time, until there must have been nearly 200 officers of all nationalities on it. At the stroke of midnight, the snake uncoiled itself into a great circle in the courtyard and struck up "Auld Lang Syne." The whole camp joined in, as the courtyard refrain was taken up from the windows in the castle. The snow was still falling. It had a peaceful and calming influence on everyone. If we prisoners could ever have felt happy and unrepressed, we were happy that evening.

THE DUTCH LIVED ON THE FLOOR just above us. They had discovered the existence of a hollow vertical shaft in the outer wall of the castle. It was a medieval lavatory. The castle had many curious buttresses and towers, and once before, during explorations, the Dutch had come across a secret staircase, bricked up in the thickness of one of the walls. As it only led to another floor level, it was of little use for escape purposes.

The vertical shaft, on the contrary, held definite promise. Vandy constructed a superbly camouflaged entrance to it in the urinal wall of the Dutch lavatory. As the urinal was kept wholesome by applications of a creosote-and-tar mixture, Vandy had little difficulty in obtaining a supply of it from the Jerries, which served to hide the shaft entrance from even the most experienced ferret. The entrance was about three feet from the ground and was closed with a thick concrete slab. Beyond the urinal was a small turret room. Through the outer wall of this turret Vandy pierced a second hole, which he camouflaged equally well by means of a door, made of the original stones of the wall cemented together. The door swung open on pivots and gave directly onto the vertical shaft, which was about one yard by four yards in size. The drop to the bottom was 70 feet. Vandy had a neat rope ladder made for the descent.

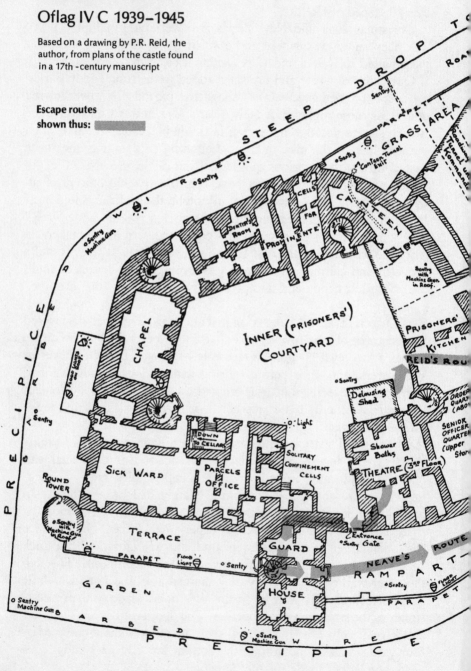

COLDITZ CASTLE

Oflag IV C 1939–1945

Based on a drawing by P.R. Reid, the
author, from plans of the castle found
in a 17th-century manuscript

**Escape routes
shown thus:**

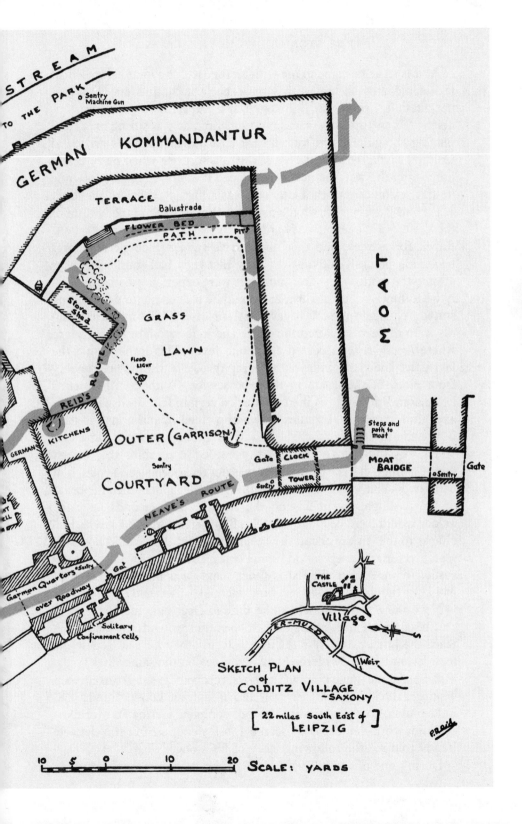

STREAM

TO THE PARK → ○ Sentry Machine Gun

GERMAN KOMMANDANTUR

TERRACE

Balustrade

FLOWER BED

PATH PITS

GRASS

LAWN

Store Shed

REID'S ROUTE

Flood Light

M O A T

KITCHENS

OUTER (GARRISON)

Steps and path to moat

GERMAN

Sentry ○

COURTYARD

Gate CLOCK

MOAT BRIDGE

Gate

Sentry ○

TOWER

○ Sentry

NEAVE'S ROUTE

German Quarters ○ Sentry

Gate

over Roadway

○ Solitary Confinement Cells

THE CASTLE

Village

RIVER MULDE

Weir

SKETCH PLAN
of
COLDITZ VILLAGE
~SAXONY

[22 miles South East of]
LEIPZIG

P.R.Reid

10 5 0   10   20   SCALE: YARDS

At this stage he came to me with a proposal for a joint escape effort if I would provide him with some experienced tunnelers. This was not difficult. I proposed Jim Rogers and Rupert Barry, our best tunnelers. When Jim Rogers was not tunneling, he was sitting on a stool playing the guitar. Jim took up the instrument upon his arrival at Colditz, saying he would give his wife a surprise when he returned home after the war. He never mentioned it in his letters. By the time he left prison camp years later, he was a highly proficient player.

He and Rupert, with Dutch assistants, set to work at the bottom of the shaft, but the going was hard and rocky in parts. Tunneling continued for a week, and then the Jerries suddenly pounced. It was becoming painfully obvious by now that they had sound detectors around the castle walls. Our tunnelers were experienced, knew exactly what they were up against, and could be trusted not to do anything stupid. Yet again they were taken by surprise. This time Priem and his team of ferrets entered the castle and made straight for the place where the shaft was located at ground level. This implied that the Germans knew the invisible geography of the camp, presumably from plans of the castle in their possession. Without a moment's hesitation, Priem set his men to attack a certain false wall with pickaxes. In less than 10 minutes they had pierced it, and a man put his head and arm through and shone a flashlight up and down the shaft.

The two tunnelers on shift had succeeded in climbing the 70 feet, one at a time—for the rope ladder was not reckoned strong enough to carry two—and Vandy was busy pulling up the ladder when the beam of the flashlight swept around the shaft. A few seconds later the ladder would have been out of sight. The Jerries would have had no clue as to the entrance, and the betting was that they would not have searched for an underground tunnel entrance on the third floor of the castle. It was such a close shave that Vandy was not even sure they had seen the dangling ladder, but, unluckily, they had.

Nevertheless, the tunnelers had time to clear out, and Vandy was able to complete the sealing of the two entrances, with the result that when the Jerries arrived in the upper stories, they were at a complete loss. Eventually they pierced new openings on the same lines as the blitz hole made down below. They first reached the small turret room where, unluckily for all, they found important booty. Vandy had hidden in this room no fewer than four complete German uniforms— our joint work—and also his secret *Appell* stooges. After this debacle Vandy told me the following story of his stooges.

During one of the periodic visits of the castle masons, doing repairs, he had managed to bribe one of them into giving him a large quantity of ceiling plaster. The Dutch amateur sculptor had carved a couple of life-size, officer-type busts that were cleverly painted (I saw one later) and as realistic as any of Madame Tussaud's wax-works. They were christened Max and Moritz by Vandy. Each bust had two iron hoops fixed underneath the pedestal, which was shaped to rest on a man's arm, either upright or upside-down hanging from the hoops. A shirt collar and tie were fitted to the bust, and, finally, a long Dutch overcoat was draped over the bust's shoulders.

When not in action the dummy hung suspended under the forearm of the bearer, concealed by the folds of the overcoat. In fact, to outward appearances the bearer was carrying an overcoat over his arm. When the *Appell* was called, officers would muster and fall into three lines. With a screen of two assistants and standing in the middle line of the three, the bearer unfurled the overcoat, an army cap was put on the dummy's head by one assistant, and a pair of top boots were placed neatly under the coat in the position of attention by the other assistant. The dummy was held shoulder-high, and the helpers formed up close to one another to camouflage the proximity of the "carrier" officer to his Siamese twin.

The ruse had worked perfectly for the *Appells* in connection with the Dutch park escape and the theater escape. Although Max and Moritz were discovered by the Jerries in Vandy's hideout, they were found as unclothed plaster busts, and Vandy hoped that he might be able to play the trick again.

THE RHINE MAIDEN

AFTER NIKI'S LAST ESCAPE attempt over the guardhouse roof and two successive attempts from hospitals by a Lt. Joseph Just, which took him to the Swiss border but not over it, the Poles seemed to retire from the escape front. Of course, they were pestered for a long time by the informer, whom they must have suspected and who must have hampered their efforts greatly. They were also liable to be blackmailed for the slightest offense, as their families were at the mercy of the Germans. In January 1942, without any warning, they were told to pack. With many regrets we said good-bye, and as we shook hands, we expressed the mutual wish: *"Auf wiedersehen—nach dem Krieg!"* ("Until we meet again—after the war!")

We saw very few of them again. They went to semiunderground fortress camps in the Posnan area. A very few managed to trek westward toward the end of the war. Niki died of tuberculosis.

For a long time the Polish rooms were vacant. Then French Jewish officers sifted out from many camps were gathered together and sent to Colditz. Why were they being incarcerated here? The question made one reflect a little as to what was to be the ultimate fate of all the Colditz inmates. We were "bad boys" and a public danger and nuisance. I, personally, did not think that we had much hope of surviving the war. If the Allies won, which we considered almost a certainty, Hitler and his maniacs would see that all possible revenge was wreaked before they descended the abyss and their fuehrer fulfilled the prophecy of his favorite opera, *Götterdämmerung.* The gathering of the French Jews was a bad omen. If the Germans won the war, they, at least, would not survive. Would we?

The French contingent had also been quiet for some time. They seemed to be resting on the laurels of Lebrun's escape. Then one spring afternoon a mixed batch of French, Dutch, and British were marching through the third gateway leading down to the exercise ground, or park, as it was called. The majority had just "wheeled right," down the ramp roadway, when a gorgeous-looking German fräulein passed by. She haughtily disdained to look at the prisoners and walked primly past, going up the ramp toward the German courtyard of the castle. There were low whistles of admiration from the prisoners—for she was a veritable Rhine maiden with golden-blonde hair. She wore a broad-brimmed hat, smart blouse and skirt, and high-heeled shoes; she was large as well as handsome—a fitting consort for a German demigod.

As she swept past us, her fashionable-looking wristwatch fell from her arm at the feet of Squadron Leader Paddon, who was marching in front of me. The Rhine maiden had not noticed her loss, but Paddon, being a gentleman, picked up the watch and shouted: "Hey, Miss! You've dropped your watch."

The Rhine maiden, like a ship under full sail, had already tacked to port and was out of sight. Paddon thereupon made frantic signs to the nearest guard, explaining: *"Das Fräulein hat ihre Uhr verloren. Ja!— Uhr—verloren"* ("The young lady has lost her watch. Yes!—lost— watch"), and he held up the dainty article.

"Ach so! Danke," replied the guard, grasping what had happened. He seized the watch from Paddon's hand and shouted to a sentry in the courtyard to stop the fräulein.

The fräulein was, by now, primly stepping toward the other (main) gateway that led out of the camp. The sentry stopped and immediately became affable, looking, no doubt, deeply into her eyes from which, unfortunately, no tender light responded.

He looked at her again and noticed something—maybe the blonde hair had gone awry. The second scrutiny, at a yard's distance, was enough for him. By the time our guard arrived panting with the watch, the Rhine maiden was a sorrowful sight, minus her wig and spring bonnet, revealing the head of Lieutenant Bouley, who unhappily did not speak or understand a word of German.

This escape attempt had been the result of months of patient effort and was prepared with the assistance of the officer's wife in France. The French were allowed to receive parcels directly from their next of kin, which made this possible. Bouley had a complete lady's outfit, including silk stockings. The golden hair was a triumph of the wigmaker's art: real hair that had been collected, bleached, curled, and sewn together. The wig was put together in Colditz. The straw hat was the product of French patterns and Colditz straw weaving.

The transformation had been practiced for weeks and was a conjuring trick that, I regret, I never saw enacted. The conjurer had three accomplices and the usual stooges to distract momentarily the attention of the guards as he turned the corner out of the gateway leading to the park. At this point the conjurer could count on a few seconds of blind spot, which might be drawn out to, say, 10 or 12 seconds by a good stooge attending to the guard behind him. The guards were ranged along the ranks on both sides at intervals of 10 yards.

Part of the transformation was done on the march, prior to arrival at the corner—for instance, strapping on the watch, pulling up the silk stockings, rouging the lips, and powdering the face. Once in the gateway, the high-heeled shoes were put on. The blouse and bosoms were in place, under a loose cloak around the escapee's shoulders. The skirt was tucked up around his waist. His accomplices held the wig, the hat, and the lady's bag.

There is a moral to this story that is worth recording. I had not been informed of the forthcoming attempt, and certainly I sympathized with the French in their desire for complete surprise. It was much better, for instance, that the parade going to the park should not be conscious of what was taking place. The participants behaved naturally in consequence, whereas the least whispering or craning of necks or rising on tiptoe—any conscious movement—might have upset the effort. Yet the fact of having informed me would not have made much difference to all this. Neither would I have been able to warn all the British on the parade; it would have been dangerous. Nevertheless, the moral emerges: the fateful coincidence that I happened to be behind Paddon on the walk; that, had I been warned, I might have nipped the watch incident in the bud, and the escape would probably have succeeded.

THIS ESCAPE, AS USUAL, closed the park to the prisoners for a period. Hardly had walks recommenced, however, when Vandy announced another attempt to be made by his contingent. I asked from what direction, and he answered, "From the park, of course!"

The "privilege" of going to the park for a two-hour walk around a barbed-wire enclosure at the bottom of the valley was continually being withdrawn by the goons, because of insubordination of the prisoners, in consequence of escapes, or just to annoy us. During those periods in the late spring of 1942 when the privilege was not withheld, the Dutch used to sit together on the grass in the middle of the wire enclosure while one of them would read to the others. Personally, I did not go very often to the park—it used to depress me. The goon sentries stood close to the wire, so that when officers walked around the path of the perimeter, they came within a few yards of them. I am sure the Germans put English-speaking sentries on this job who listened to one's every word. They could not have been edified, because many prisoners, for the benefit of the sentries, made a point of saying exactly what they thought of the goons, the German race, and the Third Reich in general.

On the day appointed by Vandy, I went to the park for a change and noticed the Dutch in their usual group, with a huge, black-bearded man in his army cloak sitting in the center, reading to them. I happened to notice also that he was fidgeting all the time, as if he had the itch. He held a book and continued reading for an hour and a half. The walk lasted officially two hours, but a quarter of an hour was allowed at the beginning and at the end to line us up and count the numbers present.

The whistle blew, and the prisoners slowly collected near the gate where they lined up to be counted before marching back to the castle. All went off as usual, and we started to march back. It was the custom that, as soon as the prisoners left the park, the goons unleashed their dogs. Suddenly hoarse shouts were heard behind us. We were halted and again counted. This time the goons found one prisoner missing.

What had happened was that the huge Dutchman with the black

beard had been sitting on a small Dutchman who had been entirely hidden by his black cloak (an alternative to the Dutch colonial army overcoat) and who had dug a "grave" for himself. The others had all helped to hide the earth and stones and to cover the small Dutchman with grass. When the whistle blew, they moved toward the gate, leaving the little man in his grave, ready to escape when the coast was clear. They managed to cover up the first count so that the goons did not notice that a man was missing. By bad luck, one of the Alsatian police dogs took it into his head to chase another. The leading animal ran straight over the grave and the other followed. When he reached the grave, the second dog, attracted possibly by the newly dug earth, started digging; in a few seconds he unearthed the Dutchman.

Vandy had once more employed a dummy Dutchman—the third he had made. When the alarm was raised, however, he had not used it again. He knew the parade would be carefully scrutinized, and he hoped to save the dummy. He was out of luck. The Germans searched all the officers carefully before they reentered the castle, and the dummy was found in its full regalia.

It was always questionable whether a dog was much use immediately after a parade, unless he found himself almost on top of a body, because the ground must have reeked with the scent of the many human beings who had just vacated the area. It cannot be denied, however, that in this case the dogs found the man; whether it was by coincidence or by astuteness, I do not know. The Germans were again having the better of the battle of Colditz. We would have to improve our technique.

ESCAPE STRATEGY

IN APRIL 1942 I ASKED to be released from the post of Escape Officer. It was high time someone else took on the job. I had visions of a month or two of rest, followed by an attempt in which I could take part myself. As Escape Officer it had become morally impossible for me to take part in any escape.

Colonel Stainer replaced Colonel German in the New Year as senior British officer, after the latter's departure to another camp. I think Colonel German was the only British officer who was removed from Colditz, once having been incarcerated there. Needless to say, he returned about a year later because of further "offenses" against the German Reich. I suggested Dick Howe as successor to the post of Escape Officer. I took over for him in July, while he did a month's solitary for some indiscretion. After that he carried on as Escape Officer for a long time.

Throughout 1941 the British contingent had slowly risen from a mere handful of 17 officers to about 45. During 1942 the number rose further, until by the summer there were about 60. Late arrivals included Maj. Ronnie Littledale, Lt. Michael Sinclair, and 10 naval officers and 2 petty officers from Marlag Nord. Group Capt. Douglas Bader of the RAF also arrived. Despite the loss of both legs in a prewar air accident, Bader had continued flying and had become one of Britain's famous aces. In August 1941 he was captured after parachuting from his disabled plane over France and was imprisoned by the Germans. Bader managed to escape twice, only to be recaptured and sent finally to Colditz. He had been in Colditz just a few weeks when he—a man with two artificial legs—volunteered for partnership in an escape attempt over the roofs of the castle.

Ronnie Littledale and Michael Sinclair had escaped together from a camp in the north of Poland and had traveled south. They were given assistance by Poles and lived in a large town somewhere in Poland for a while. When properly organized, they headed for Switzerland, but were trapped in Prague during a mass checkup of all its inhabitants because of the assassination of Heydrich. They were caught and put through the mill, including torture. They were then dispatched to Colditz.

Before long Michael Sinclair had a court-martial charge read against him for an offense he had committed in his earlier camp. We waved him good-bye as he left for his trial under guard. He was completely equipped for a getaway with transformable clothing, chiefly of RAF origin. His court-martial was to be held at Leipzig, but he managed to elude his guards in a lavatory at a Leipzig barracks before it took place, and a few days later he turned up in Cologne. There had been heavy Allied bombing, and the color of most of his clothing was unfortunate because a witch hunt for RAF parachute survivors was in progress. He was caught in the meshes and duly returned to Colditz under a three-man guard.

Returning escapees were bad for the morale of the prisoners. Michael Sinclair felt this very much, though he had no reason to. His record clearly showed that he was the type of man who would not miss a 100-to-1 chance of escape.

It was, nevertheless, becoming obvious to everybody that, once out of the castle, it was an escapee's duty to take very heavy risks rather than return to the fold within the oppressive walls of Colditz. I resolved I would not come back if I ever escaped again, and I know it was the decision that many others made as the months of 1942 dragged on. We already had one temporarily insane officer on our hands (he recovered after the war). He remained with us for months before the Germans were convinced he was not shamming, and we had to maintain a permanent guard from among our own number to see that he did not attempt suicide. The guard, which was worked on a roster, soon had to do double duty to cope with a second officer who tried to slash his wrist with a razor, but luckily he made a poor job of it and was discovered in a washroom before he had completed his work.

THE ARRIVAL OF the irrepressible Douglas Bader heralded an increase in practical joking of the type that was known as goon-baiting. Goon-baiting was a pastime indulged in when one had nothing better to do—a frequent occurrence in a POW camp. It varied from the most innocuous forms, such as dropping small pebbles from 100 feet or so onto the head of a sentry, through less innocent types such as the release of propaganda written on lavatory paper and dropped out of windows when the wind was favorable, up to the more staged variety such as the case of the "corpse."

A life-size "lay figure" was made out of mattresses and straw by Peter Storie Pugh and clothed in a worn-out battle dress. We were having frequent air-raid alarms by the summer of 1942, during which time the normally floodlit castle was blacked out. On one of these raids the "lay figure" was eased through the bars of a window and left suspended with a long length of twine attached, some of which was held in reserve.

As soon as the floodlights went on again, the figure was jerked into movement, and in less than no time the Jerries began firing.

After a good volley, the figure was allowed to drop to the ground. Goon sentries immediately rushed to recover the corpse, which thereupon came to life and rose high into the air again. A goon approached nearer, and the lay figure was promptly dropped squarely on his head.

It was difficult for the Jerries to find the culprits. It was even difficult for them to locate the window from which the figure had sallied, as thin twine was used. The result was the withdrawal of the park privilege for the whole camp for a month.

At first sight it might appear to be unfair that other nationalities should suffer for our sins, but we were not the only sinners, and we suffered reciprocally. It was the expression of our unity against the common enemy.

Mike Sinclair's fear that he had closed another avenue of escape for his fellow prisoners proved groundless. Soon after Sinclair's attempt, Squadron Leader Paddon was called to face a court-martial charge at a former prison camp in northeast Germany. He was duly equipped for an escape and left for his destination under heavy guard. It was a long journey, and he would be away several days. As the days turned into weeks, Colonel Stainer naturally became concerned and demanded an explanation from the camp commandant. The latter replied with a resigned shrug of the shoulders: *"Es war unmöglich, jedenfalls ist er geflüchtet!"* ("It was impossible; nonetheless he escaped!") Paddon eventually reached Sweden safely and then England. He was the second Englishman to do the home run from Colditz.

IT WAS HIGH TIME BRUCE, our "medium-sized" officer, who stood five feet one inch, was given a chance to escape. He had done much good work in helping others to get away. The opportunity arrived when the Germans decided we had too much personal property in our rooms. It was September, and they issued orders that all private kit not immediately required, as, for instance, summer clothing, was to be packed. The Jerries provided large boxes for the purpose. We were informed on the word of honor of the camp commandant that the cases would be stored in the German *Kommandantur* (the outer part of the castle) and would be made available again in the spring.

The cases were duly packed, closed, and removed on a truck. Several of them were Tate and Lyle sugar boxes, about three feet square by three feet high, which had contained bulk consignments of Red Cross food, and in one of these traveled our medium-sized officer.

He had his civilian clothes and escape equipment with him, as well as a knife to cut the cords holding down the lid of his case and about a 40-foot length of rope in the form of bed sheets. We knew the cases were to be stored in an attic at the top of a building that we could see from our windows.

Bruce escaped and reached Lübeck, bicycling much of the way. Unfortunately, he was recaught on the docks, trying to stow away on a neutral ship, and returned in due course to Colditz where he was placed in solitary confinement.

I would like to have heard his full story very much, but I never saw him again. I was doing two successive bouts of solitary in the "cooler" when he returned, and I did not even get the chance to meet him during the daily exercise hour.

My solitary was the result of two abortive escape attempts. The first was a short tunnel, mostly vertical, built to connect up with drains in the courtyard, which I have mentioned before. Rupert Barry and Colin McKenzie were my confederates. I had long ago noticed, on a photograph of the prisoners' courtyard taken before the war, a manhole cover near the entrance gateway. This manhole cover no longer existed, and I was sure it had been covered over for a good reason. We were trying to find out why, by means of the tunnel, when the unannounced arrival of a batch of Russian prisoners proved our undoing. Our vertical shaft began in what was known as the delousing shed, a temporary structure in the courtyard built to house the portable ovens, which looked like boilers and in which clothing was baked in order to kill lice and other pests.

The sudden arrival of the Russians necessitated the use of these portable ovens, and Rupert and I were caught red-handed. McKenzie was lucky. He was doing earth-disposal duty and was not in the shed. The boilers were hardly used once in six months, and it was unfortunate that the Russians arrived just during our working hours.

The incident, however, enabled us to meet the Russian soldiers, who were to be housed in the town, where normally we should never see them. They were a sight of which the Germans might well have been ashamed. Living skeletons, they dragged their fleshless feet along the ground in a decrepit slouch. These scarecrows were survivors of a batch 10 times their number that had started from the front. They were treated like animals, given no food, and put out into the fields to find fodder amidst the grass and roots. Their ghastly trek into Germany took weeks.

"Luckily," said one of them, "it was summertime. In the winter," he added, "nobody even bothered to move us to the hinterland from the front. Many died where they were captured."

How many times, in my life as a prisoner, did I murmur a prayer of thanksgiving for that blessed document, the Geneva Convention, and for its authors. But for its humane principles, I saw myself standing in the place of these wretched creatures. Needless to say, between Germany and Russia there were no recognized principles for the treatment of prisoners of war. Neither of these countries had signed the Geneva Convention.

My second bout of solitary was due to the fact that I tried to escape from my prison cell. It happened to be in the town jail because, as usual, all the solitary cells in Colditz were full, and the overflow nowadays went to the jail.

By placing a table on the bed, I could reach the ceiling of my cell. I had a small saw, which was normally hidden in my guitar. Breaking through the plaster one evening, I started to work on the wood. I had to work noiselessly, for the guards lived next door. In spite of every effort, I was not finished by morning, and, of course, the jailer saw my handiwork when he came with my bread and ersatz coffee.

I was evidently doomed to spend another winter in Colditz.

SEPTEMBER WAS NEARLY OVER. Dick Howe, our escape officer, came to me one day. "I have another job for you, Pat," he said. "Ronnie Littledale and Billie Stephens have teamed up and are clamoring to leave. Their idea isn't in the least bit original, but that doesn't stop their clamoring at all," he added.

He then described to me roughly what they intended to do.

"That old chestnut," I commented, "has grown a long beard by now. It doesn't stand a chance."

I knew the scheme well. A child could have thought of it. It involved making a sortie from one of the windows of the kitchen over the low roofs of various store buildings in the adjoining German *Kommandantur* courtyard. Then, descending to the ground, one had to cross over the path of a sentry's beat when his back was turned and crawl across the dimly lit area in front of the *Kommandantur* to a small open pit, in the far corner of the courtyard, which was visible from our windows. That was as far as the plan went. We would still be in the midst of the enemy, and how we were supposed to extricate ourselves was a mystery to me.

Dick, Ronnie, Billie Stephens, and I discussed the plan.

I suggested an addition to the team. "Why not add a fourth to our group of three? Then, when we get out, *if* we get out, we can travel in independent groups of two each."

"All right," said Dick, "do you have anyone particular in mind?"

"Well, if Ronnie and Billie are going to travel together, it's rather up to me, I suppose, to choose someone. I think Hank Wardle is the man. It's time he had a turn."

"Good. I don't think there will be any objections, but I'll just confirm this," rejoined Dick. "He's the right man as far as I'm concerned. He has all the qualifications; he's high on the roster and has helped in other escapes. But our two groups will have to travel by different routes, of course. What do you suggest?"

"Well, if it's all the same to Ronnie and Billie," I answered, "I've studied the route from Penig via Zwickau to Plauen, Regensburg, and Munich, and thence to Ulm and Tuttlingen. I'd like to stick to it. How about it, Ronnie? You could go from Leisnig to Döbeln, then via Chemnitz to Nuremberg and Stuttgart."

"That suits us," said Ronnie. "We prefer Leisnig, as it's only a few miles away, and we reckon to catch a train and be well on our way before the morning *Appell.*"

"All right," said Dick, "you're agreed then. We'll go into questions of detail, dress, food, and so on, nearer to the date for the 'off.' Let me know if you are stuck for anything."

Lt. Comdr. William (Billie) Stephens had been captured during the St. Nazaire raid, when the dock gates were blown up in an effort to imprison a large number of German U-boats. He had tried to escape twice and was a new arrival at Colditz. In fact, when he arrived, he was promptly put into solitary for several weeks to complete his sentences before he was let loose in the camp. He came from Northern Ireland. He was handsome, fair-haired, with piercing blue eyes and a Nelsonian nose. He walked as if he were permanently on the deck of a ship. He was a daredevil, and his main idea appeared to be to force his way into the German area of the camp and then hack his way out with a metaphorical cutlass.

The one hope I could see was of forcing an entry into the tall block of buildings, at the top of which Bruce, our "medium-sized" officer, had been deposited in his sugar box. As he had been able to make an exit from there, maybe we could also. It was important to have Bruce's comments, and I managed to pass a message to him in some food and, eventually, received an answer.

Once inside his building, he reported, it was possible to descend from unbarred windows on the far side into the moat of the castle. The top floors were unoccupied, but care was necessary to avoid noise as Germans occupied floors below. There was a large heavy door into the building that was visible from our quarters and that gave onto an unused staircase leading to the top.

There were two principal snags. First, the door mentioned above was visible from almost everywhere and in full view of the sentry in the German courtyard. Second, the door was locked. We could assume the lock was not cruciform in type, but beyond this we knew nothing. At night, when the floodlights were blazing, this door was in shadow. I might be able to work at the lock, but the risk was tremendous because the door was beside the main path, leading from the outer castle gateway to the entrance of the *Kommandantur*—all pedestrians passed within a yard of it. Besides, would the shadow be sufficient to hide a man from the eyes of the sentry? Lastly, the door was 20 yards from the pit of which I have spoken—and the nearest place of concealment—so that a person going to and from the door had to flit 20 yards each way through an area of half shadow where movement would be visible.

WHEN HANK WARDLE'S NOMINATION had been agreed upon, I broached the subject to him: "Ronnie and Billie want you and me to join them on one of the most absurd escape attempts I have ever heard," I opened by way of invitation.

"One thing seems to be as good or as bad as another in this camp nowadays," was Hank's reply.

"That means you're not fussy, I take it?"

Hank's answer was a typical shrug of the shoulders and "I couldn't care less. I've got nothing to do till the end of this man's war, so it's all the same to me!"

I described the plan to him in fair detail, and when I had finished he said: "I'll try it with you. I agree there's no hope of success, but we've got to keep on trying just the same."

The whole scheme assumed that we could reach the pit safely and hide inside it. For all we knew, it might have been deep. Our hope that it was shallow was based on the fact that the pit had no balustrade as a protection against anyone falling in. To reach the pit would be a prolonged nightmare.

The camp kitchen was in use all day. However, toward evening it was locked up. It was in full view of the sentry in the prisoners' courtyard. A pane of glass in one of the metal-framed windows was half broken. I had preparatory work to do in the kitchen, and this window was my only means of entry. I employed a stooge to help me. After the evening *Appell* on the first day of operations, he sat on a doorstep near the kitchen, watching the sentry, while I remained out of sight behind the protruding wall of the delousing shed, about five yards from the window. The sentry's beat varied between 8 and 12 seconds. I had to be inside before he turned around.

My stooge gave me the OK signal. I ran and hopped onto the sill. Reaching through the broken pane of glass on tiptoe, I could just grasp the lever that opened the window. I pulled it upward gently, withdrew my arm carefully so as not to break what was left of the glass pane, opened the window, and crept through. If the sentry stopped short or turned around in the middle of his beat, I was caught. I jumped down onto the kitchen floor and silently closed the window. I was safely inside, with a second to spare.

Leaving the kitchen was a little easier, as one faced the sentry and could see him through cracks in the white paint of the lower glass panes of the window.

I repeated this performance five evenings running, along with one assistant. We usually entered after the evening *Appell,* at about 6 P.M., and returned again before lockup time, at 9 P.M.

During these periods of three hours we worked hard. The windows on the opposite side of the kitchen opened onto the flat roofs of a jumble of outhouses in the German courtyard; all the roofs were about 12 feet above the ground. The kitchen windows on this side, as well as the whole wall of the building, were in bright floodlight from the time of dusk onward.

I opened one of the windows by removing a number of wire clips that were supposed to seal it and examined the bars beyond. I saw at once that, by removing one rivet, I could bend a bar inward, providing enough room for a body to pass through. The hole through the bars opened onto the flat roof.

The rivet was the next problem. I could saw off the head, but it was old and rusty and would obviously require great force to withdraw it. Yet the method would involve much less sawing. "Silence was golden." A sentry plied his beat just beyond the outbuildings, about 15 yards away. Luckily the window was not in his line of vision, unless he extended his beat to nearly double its normal length. This he did from time to time. Of course, the window and the flat roof were in full view of all the windows of the *Kommandantur* above the ground floor.

My assistant was Wally Hammond. He and his friend "Tubby" Lister arrived by mistake at Colditz, since it was an officers' camp and they were naval chief petty officers. They made good use of their sojourn with us.

Soon afterward, when they were removed to their rightful prison, they escaped and, with the advantage of their Colditz "education" behind them, reached Switzerland with comparative ease.

These two submarine men had a sense of humor that was unbeatable. During their escape, for lack of a better language they spoke Pidgin English with the Germans throughout, successfully posing as Latvian collaborators. They stayed at middle-class German hotels and, before leaving in the mornings, usually filled any army top boots that happened to be outside the doors of neighboring rooms with water, as a mark of their respect for the German High Command.

To return to the story of the rivet that required attention, the head was sawed through during the fourth evening shift. Next, we desperately needed a high-powered silent-working punch that would force the rivet out of its socket.

Wally Hammond made one in the space of a few hours out of a bar used for closing the grate door of a German heating stove. On the fifth evening of work I applied Hammond's punch and the rivet, which had been corroded in its position for probably 20 years, slid smoothly and silently out of its hole. The job was done, and I breathed a deep sigh of relief.

I camouflaged the joint with a clay rivet, sealed the window as usual, and, redusting everything carefully, we departed from the kitchen as we had come.

THE ESCAPE WAS ON, and we wasted no time. Our two groups would travel by different routes to the frontier crossing point on the Swiss border—a Colditz secret. Although I had never been there, I knew the area in my mind's eye like the back of my hand. Every Colditz escapee's first and last duty was to learn this crossing by heart. I had insisted months ago that no escapee should carry frontier-crossing maps on his person. We had the master map in the camp, and it was studied by all.

We each had our identity papers, our general maps, money, and compass. We usually kept them in small tubes. I had once received a present from friends in England that actually arrived—two boxes of 25 Upman Havana cigars. The cigars were in light metal containers about five inches long. These cases were much in demand. All the above documents, money, and a compass fitted into the metal tube, which was easily carried and could be easily concealed, even by sleight of hand if necessary.

I had printed my own identity papers. German Gothic script is not easy to copy, but it was possible with practice. We had a primitive, yet highly successful, system of duplicating, and we reproduced type-written orders and letters as desired. A multitude of lino-cut stamps provided all the officialdom necessary, and photographs were managed in various ways. The brown-colored *Ausweis* ("passport") was of thick white paper, dyed the correct tint with a patent mixture of our own manufacture.

Our clothes had long since been prepared. I would wear one of my mass-production cloth caps, converted RAF trousers, a fawn-colored windbreaker I had concealed for a year, and finally an overcoat (necessary at this time of year, early October) that I succeeded in buying from a French officer who had obtained it from a French orderly who, in turn, had access to the village.

It was a dark-blue civilian overcoat with black velvet lapels, and it buttoned, double-breasted, high up on the chest. I imagine it was a German fashion of about 1912. I wore black shoes.

It was essential to remove every single trace of the origin of anything we wore or carried, such as lettering inside shoes, name tags, and "Made in England" labels. We were to live our false identities and were prepared to challenge the Germans to prove the contrary, if we were held for questioning. Thus Hank and I became Flemish workmen collaborating with the Germans. As *Flamands* we could pass off our bad German and our bad French—a useful nationality. Since the nationality is not a common one, it would take the Germans a long time to find someone who spoke Flemish and could prove we were not *Flamands*.

We were concrete or engineering contractors' workmen. My German wallet contained my whole story. I was permitted to travel to Rottweil (some 30 miles from the Swiss border), in reply to newspaper advertisements—I had clippings—requiring contractors' men for construction work. I also had a special and very necessary permit to travel close to the frontier. Part of my story was that my fiancée worked at Besançon as a telephone operator for the Germans. She was a Walloon—or French-speaking Belgian girl. I kept a fictitious letter from her (prepared for me by a Frenchman) in my wallet, asking me to spend my few days' leave with her in Besançon before reporting for work in Rottweil. By a curious coincidence the railway line to Besançon from my direction passed within 15 miles of the Swiss frontier.

My trump card was a real photo, which I had, of a girl I had met in France. One day, while looking through a German weekly newspaper, I had come across a German propaganda photograph showing German and foreign girls working together for the Germans in a post office and telephone exchange. One of the girls in the picture was amazingly the double of the girl whose photo I carried. I immediately cut out the press photo and kept it as a treasured possession. It would prove to any German where my imaginary fiancée's loyalties lay. My private snapshot was conclusive evidence, and I was prepared to battle with any German who dared to doubt my identity.

The other three members of our team had different case histories, more or less as conclusive as mine.

Toward the end of our final preparations I held a last consultation, and, among many items, we discussed food.

"You all realize that we can't take anything with us by way of food except normal German rations," I pointed out.

"Yes, I agree," said Billie, "but all the same I'm taking enough corned beef and tinned cheese to make sure of one good meal before we board the train."

"Our sugar is all right, too," added Ronnie. "We can carry that with us indefinitely. It looks exactly the same as the German and would certainly pass."

"Now I've got a sticky proposition to make," I began, changing the subject. "There are a few of those small ersatz leather suitcases lying about—you know, the ones that came with that last batch of parcels. They had army clothing in them. I propose we each carry one."

"H'm! That's a tall order!" retorted Billie. "It's going to be hard enough to get out of the camp, climbing over roofs and walls and down ropes, without being pestered by suitcases in the bargain."

"I agree," I said. "But remember that when we do get outside the camp, a suitcase becomes the hallmark of respectability and honesty. How many people travel long journeys on main-line expresses in wartime with nothing at all in their hands? Only fugitives and railway officials. And the Germans know this well. They know that to look out for an escaped prisoner means to look out for a man traveling light, with no luggage—without a suitcase."

"I see your point, Pat," agreed Billie.

"At railway-station controls or in a roundup, a suitcase will be invaluable," I continued. "You can wave it about and make it prominent, and the betting is it'll help a lot. Moreover, it will be useful for carrying articles of respectabilty: pajamas—without tags and labels—razors, boot brushes, German boot polish, German soap, and, of course, your German food. Otherwise your pockets are going to be bulgy, untidy, and suspicious-looking. I know it's going to be hell lugging them with us out of the camp, but I think it will be worth the effort in the end."

They all agreed, and so it was fixed. We managed to procure four of the small fiberboard suitcases without any trouble and packed away our escape traveling kit.

I could hardly believe we were going to do the whole 400-mile journey by train.

It was October 14, 1942. As evening approached, Ronnie, Billie, Hank, and I made final preparations. Rupert was to be our kitchen-window stooge. We donned our civilian clothing and covered it with army trousers and greatcoats. Civilian overcoats were made into neat compact bundles.

I should explain why we had to wear the military clothes over everything. At any time a wandering goon might appear as we waited our moment to enter the kitchen, and there might even be delays. Further, we had to think of informers—among the foreign orderlies, for example, who were always wandering about.

Our suitcases were surrounded with blankets to muffle sound, and we carried enough sheets and blankets to make a 50-foot descent, if necessary. Later we would wear balaclava helmets and gloves; no white skin was to be visible. Darkness and the shadows were to be our friends. Only our eyes and noses would be exposed. All light-colored garments were excluded. We carried thick socks to put on over our shoes. This is the most silent method of movement I know, barring removal of one's shoes—which we were to do for the crossing of the sentry's path.

Squadron Leader MacColm was to accompany us into the kitchen in order to bend the window bar back into place and seal up the window after we had gone. He would have to conceal the military clothing we left behind in the kitchen and make his exit the next morning after the kitchen was unlocked. He could hide in one of the enormous cauldrons so long as he did not oversleep and have himself served up with the soup the next day.

Immediately after the evening *Appell* we were ready and started on the first leg of our journey. It was 6:30 P.M.

I was used to the drill of the entry window by now. At the nodded signal from Rupert, I acted automatically; a run, a leap to the sill, one arm through the cracked pane of glass, up with the window lever, then withdraw my arm again carefully, open window—without noise—jump through, and close window softly. I made it easily. Only two had done it before at any one session. The question now was whether five could succeed. One after another they came. At least they didn't have the window-lever latch to bother about.

The sentry was behaving himself. At regular intervals, as he turned his back, the signal was given. I could not see Rupert—but his timing was perfect. I was able to watch the sentry from behind the window throughout his beat.

Each time, as the sentry turned away, I heard a gentle scurry. I automatically opened the window, in jumped a body, and I closed the window again, breathing a heavy sigh. The drill was becoming automatic. It was taking as little as five seconds.

At last all five of us were safe.

We removed our military clothing and handed it to MacColm.

I set about the window overlooking the German courtyard, and as darkness fell and the floodlights went on, I heaved on the bar until it was bent horizontally and immediately attached to the unbent portion a long strip of black-painted cardboard resembling the bar. This hung downward in the correct position and camouflaged the opening.

"All set!" I whispered to the others. "I'm going out now. Hank, wait until I'm hidden by the shadow of the large ventilator. Then join me as quickly as you can. Billie and Ronnie, remember not to follow until we have crossed the sentry's path safely."

I squirmed through the hole in the bars onto the flat roof beyond. The roof joined the kitchen wall just below our windowsill. I crept quietly forward in a blaze of light. The eyes of 100 windows glared down upon me.

The impression was appalling. "Does nobody ever look out of a window at night?" I kept asking myself.

Happily there was shelter from the glare about halfway across the roof. The high square ventilator provided a deep shadow behind which I crawled. Hank soon followed. The sentry plied his beat not 15 yards away.

For several days we had arranged music practices in the evenings in the senior officers' quarters (the theater block). The music was used for signaling, and we had to accustom the sentry in front of us to a certain amount of noise. While Maj. Andy Anderson played the oboe, Col. George Young played the concertina, and Douglas Bader, keeping watch from a window, acted as conductor.

Their room was on the third floor, overlooking the German courtyard. Bader could see our sentry for the whole length of his beat. He was to start the practice at 7:30 P.M., when the traffic in the courtyard had died down. From 8 P.M. onward he was to keep a rigid control on the players so that they only stopped their music when the sentry was in a suitable position for us to cross his path. It was not imperative that they stop playing every time the sentry turned his back, but when they did stop playing, it meant that we could move. We arranged this signaling system because, once on the ground, we would have little concealment, and what little there was, provided by an angle in the wall of the outbuildings, prevented us from seeing the sentry on duty.

At 8 P.M. Hank and I crawled once more into the limelight and over the remainder of the roof, dropping to the ground over a loose, noisy gutter that gave me the jitters. In the dark angle of the wall, with our shoes around our necks and our suitcases under our arms, we waited for the music to stop. The musicians had been playing light jaunty airs at first and then had run the gamut of our popular songbooks. At 8 P.M. they changed to classical music; it gave them more excuse for stopping. Bader had seen us drop from the roof and would see us cross the sentry's path. The players were in the middle of Haydn's oboe concerto when they stopped.

"I shall make this a trial run," I thought.

I advanced quickly five yards to the end of the wall concealing us and regarded the sentry. He was fidgety and looked up at Bader's window twice during the five-second view I had of his back. Before me was the roadway, a cobbled surface seven yards wide. Beyond was the end of a shed and some friendly concealing shrubbery. As the sentry turned, the music started again. Our players had chosen a piece the Germans love. I only hoped the sentry would not become exasperated by their repeated interruptions. The next time they stopped, we would go.

The music ceased abruptly, and I ran—but it started again just as I reached the corner. I stopped dead and retired hurriedly. This happened twice. Then I heard German voices through the music. It was the duty officer on his rounds. He was questioning the sentry. He seemed suspicious. I heard gruff orders given.

Five minutes later I was caught napping—the music had stopped while I was ruminating on the cause of the duty officer's interrogation, and I was not on my toes. A late dash was worse than none. I stood still and waited. I waited a long time, but the music did not begin again. A quarter of an hour passed, and there was still no music. Obviously something had gone wrong upstairs. I decided therefore to wait an hour in order to let suspicions die down.

All this time Hank was beside me—not a word passed his lips, not a murmur or comment to distract us from the job at hand.

In the angle of the wall where we hid, there was a door. We tried the handle and found it was open, so we entered in pitch-darkness and, passing through a second door, took temporary refuge in a room that had a small window and contained, as far as we could see, only rubbish—wastepaper, empty bottles, and empty food cans. Outside, in the angle of the wall, any goon with extra-sharp eyesight, passing along the roadway, would spot us. The sentry himself was also liable to extend his beat without warning and take a look around the corner of the wall where we had been hiding. In the rubbish room we were certain to be much safer.

We had been in there five minutes when, suddenly, there was a rustling of paper, a crash of falling cans, and a jangling of overturned bottles—a noise fit to waken the dead. We froze with horror. A cat leaped out from among the refuse and tore out of the room as if the devil were after it.

"That's finished everything," I exclaimed. "The Jerries will be here in a moment to investigate."

"They may only flash a light around casually," Hank whispered, "and we may get away with it if we try to look like a couple of sacks in the corner."

"Quick, then," I said. "Grab those piles of newspapers and spread them over our heads. It's our only hope."

We did so and waited, our hearts thumping. Five minutes passed, then 10, and still nobody came. We began to breathe again.

Soon our hour's vigil was over. It was 9:45 P.M., and I resolved to carry on. All was silent in the courtyard. I could now hear the sentry's footsteps clearly—approaching and then receding. Choosing our moment, we advanced to the end of the wall as he turned on his beat.

I peeped around the corner. He was 10 yards off and marching away from us. The courtyard was empty. I tiptoed across the roadway with Hank at my heels. Reaching the wall of the shed on the other side, we just had time to crouch behind the shrubbery before he turned. He had heard nothing. On his next receding beat we crept behind the shed and hid in some small shrubbery, which bordered the main steps and veranda in front of the entrance to the *Kommandantur.*

The first leg of our escape was behind us. I dropped my suitcase and reconnoitered the next stage of our journey, which was to the pit. Watching the sentry, I crept quickly along the narrow grass strip at the edge of the path leading away from the main steps. On one side lay the path, and on the other side was a long flower bed. Beyond was the balustrade of the *Kommandantur* veranda. I was in light shadow and had to crouch as I moved. Reaching the pit, about 25 yards away, before the sentry turned, I looked over the edge. There was a wooden trestle with steps.

As we had figured, the pit was not deep. I dropped into it. A brick tunnel from the pit ran underneath the veranda and gave perfect concealment. That was enough. When I emerged again, I distinctly heard noises from the direction of the roofs over which we had climbed. Ronnie and Billie, who had witnessed our crossing of the roadway, were following. The sentry apparently had heard nothing.

I BEGAN TO CREEP BACK to the shrubbery where Hank was waiting. I was nearly halfway there when, without warning, heavy footsteps sounded. A goon was approaching quickly from the direction of the main castle gateway and around the corner of the castle building. In a flash I was flat on my face on the grass and lay rigid, just as he turned the corner and headed up the path straight toward me. He could not fail to see me. I waited for the end. He approached nearer and nearer with noisy footsteps crunching on the gravel. He was level with me. It was all over. I waited for his startled exclamation at my discovery—for his warning shout to the sentry—for the familiar *"Hände hoch!"*—and for the feel of his pistol jabbing into my back between the shoulder blades.

The crunching footsteps continued past me and retreated. He mounted the steps and entered the *Kommandantur*.

After a moment's pause to recover, I crept the remainder of the distance to the shrubbery and, as I did so, Ronnie and Billie appeared from the other direction.

Before long we were all safe in the pit without further alarms—the second lap completed. We had time to relax for a moment.

I asked Billie: "How did you manage crossing the sentry's beat?"

"We saw you two cross over, and it looked as easy as pie. That gave us confidence. We made one trial and then crossed the second time. Something went wrong with the music, didn't it?"

"Yes, that's why we held up proceedings so long," I answered. "We had a lucky break when they stopped for the last time. I thought it was the signal to move, but I was too late off the mark, thank God! I'd probably have run into the sentry's arms!"

"What do you think happened?" asked Ronnie.

"I heard the duty officer asking questions," I explained. "I think they suspected the music practice was phony. They probably went upstairs and stopped it."

My next job was to try to open the door of the building that I have described as the one from which our medium-sized officer escaped. The door was 15 yards away. It was in deep shadow, though the area between the door and the pit was only in semidarkness. Again watching the sentry, I crept carefully to the door and then started work with a set of master keys I had brought with me.

I worked for an hour on the door without success and finally gave up. We were checked and would have to find another exit.

We felt our way along the tunnel leading from the pit under the veranda and after eight yards came to a large cellar with a low arched ceiling supported on pillars. It had something to do with sewage, for Hank, at one point, stepped off solid ground and nearly fell into what might have been deep water. He must have disturbed a scum on top of the liquid because a dreadful stench arose. When I was well away from the entrance, I struck a match. There was a solitary wheelbarrow for furniture and, at the far end of the cavernlike cellar, a chimney flue. I had previously noticed a faint glimmer of light from this direction. Examining the flue, I found it was an air vent that led vertically upward from the ceiling of the cavern for about four feet and then curved outward toward the fresh air.

Hank pushed me up the flue. In plan it was about nine inches by three feet. I managed to wriggle myself high enough to see around the curve. The flue ended at the vertical face of a wall two feet away from me as a barred opening shaped like a letter-box slot. The opening was at the level of the ground outside and was situated on the far side of the building—the moat side for which we were heading. But it was practically impossible to negotiate this flue. There were bars, and in any case only a pygmy could have wriggled around the curve.

We held a conference.

"We seem to have struck a dead end," I started. "This place is a cul-de-sac, and I can't manage to open the door either. I'm terribly sorry, but there we are!"

"Can anyone think of another way out?" asked Ronnie.

"The main gateway is out of the question," I went on. "Since Neave escaped, they've locked the inner gate this side of the bridge over the moat. That means we can't reach the side gate leading down into the moat."

"Our only hope is through the *Kommandantur*," suggested Billie. "We can either try it now and hope to get through unseen—or else try it early in the morning when there's a little traffic about and some doors may be unlocked."

"Do you really think we'll ever pass scrutiny at that hour?" questioned Ronnie. "If we must take that route, I think it's better to try it at about 3 A.M. when the whole camp is sleeping soundly."

I was thinking how impossibly foolhardy was the idea of going through the *Kommandantur*. In desperation, I said: "I'm going to have another look at the flue."

This time I removed some of my top clothing and found I could slide more easily up the shaft. I examined the bars closely and found one was loose in its mortar socket. As I was doing this, I heard footsteps outside the opening, and a goon patrol approached. The goon had an Alsatian with him. A heavy pair of boots tramped past me. I could have touched them with my hand. The dog pattered behind and did not see me. I imagine the smell issuing from the flue obliterated my scent.

I succeeded in loosening one end of the bar and bent it nearly double. Slipping down into the cellar again, I whispered to the others: "There's a vague chance that we may be able to squeeze through the flue. Anyway, it's certainly worth trying. We shall have to strip ourselves completely naked."

"Hank and Billie will never make it," said Ronnie. "It's impossible; they're too big. You and I might possibly manage it with help at both ends—with someone pushing below and someone else pulling from above."

"I think I can get through," I said, "if someone stands on the wheelbarrow and helps push me. Once I'm out, I can do the pulling. Hank had better come next. If he can make it, we all can."

Hank was over six feet tall and Billie nearly six feet. Ronnie and I were smaller, and Ronnie was very thin.

"Neither Hank nor I," intervened Billie, "will ever squeeze around the curve on our stomachs. Our knees are not double-jointed, and our legs will stick. We'll have to come out on our backs."

"Agreed," I said. "Then I go first, Hank next, then Billie, and Ronnie last. Ronnie, you'll have no one to push you, but if two of us grab your arms and pull, we should manage it. Be careful undressing. Don't leave anything behind—we don't want to leave any traces. Hand me your clothes in neat bundles and your suitcases. I'll dispose of them temporarily outside."

After a tremendous struggle, I succeeded in squeezing through the chimney and sallied forth naked onto the path outside. Bending down into the flue again, I could just reach Hank's hand as he passed up my clothes and my suitcase, and then his own. I hid the kit in some bushes near the path and put on enough dark clothing to make me inconspicuous. Hank was stripped and struggling in the hole with his back toward me. I managed to grab one arm and heaved, while he was pushed from below. Inch by inch he advanced, and at the end of 20 minutes, with a last wrench, I pulled him clear. He was bruised all over and streaming with perspiration. During all that time we were at the mercy of any passerby. What a spectacle it must have been—a naked man being squeezed through a hole in the wall like toothpaste out of a tube.

Hank retired to the bushes to recover and to dress himself.

Next came Billie's clothes and suitcase, and then Billie himself. I got him out in about 15 minutes. Then Ronnie's kit arrived. I gave him a sheet on which to pull in order to begin his climb. After that, with two of us pulling, he was out in about 10 minutes. We all collapsed in the bushes for a breather. It was about 3:30 A.M., and we had completed the third leg of our marathon.

"What do you think of our chances now?" I asked Billie.

"I'm beyond thinking about chances," was his reply, "but I know I shall never forget this night as long as I live."

"I hope you've got all your kit," I said, smiling at him in the darkness. "I should certainly hate to have to push you back down the shaft to fetch it!"

"I'd give anything for a smoke," sighed Billie.

"I see no reason why you shouldn't smoke as we walk past the barracks if you feel like it. What cigarettes have you got?"

"Gold Flake, I think."

"Exactly! You'd better start chain-smoking, because you'll have to throw the rest away before you reach Leisnig."

"But I've got 50!"

"Too bad," I replied. "With luck you've got about three hours; that's 17 cigarettes an hour. Can you do it?"

"I'll try," said Billie ruefully.

A few yards away a German was snoring loudly in a room with the window open. The flue through which we had just climbed gave onto a narrow path running along the top of the moat immediately under the main castle walls. The bushes we hid in were on the edge of the moat. The moat wall was luckily stepped into three successive descents. The drops were each about 18 feet, and the steps were about two yards wide, with odd shrubs and grass growing on them. A couple of sheets were made ready. After half an hour's rest, and fully clothed once more, we dropped down one by one. I went last and fell into the arms of those below me.

On the way down Billie suddenly developed a tickle in his throat and started to cough, which disturbed the dogs. They began barking in their kennels, which we saw for the first time, uncomfortably near the route we were to take. Billie in desperation ate a quantity of grass and earth, which seemed to stop the irritation in his throat. By the time we reached the bottom of the moat, it was 4:30 A.M. The fourth leg was completed.

WE TIDIED OUR clothes and adjusted the socks over our shoes. In a few moments we would have to pass underneath a lamp at the corner of the road leading to the German barracks. This was the road leading to the double gates in the outer wall around the castle grounds. It was the road taken by Neave and by Van Doorninck.

The lamp was situated in full view of a sentry—luckily, some 45 yards away—who would be able to contemplate our back silhouettes as we turned the corner and faded into the darkness beyond.

The dogs had ceased barking. Hank and I moved off first—over a small railing, onto a path, past the kennels, down some steps, around the corner under the light, and away into the darkness. We walked leisurely, side by side, as if we were inmates of the barracks returning after a night's carousal in the town.

Before passing the barracks, I had one last duty to perform—to give those in the camp an idea as to what we had done, to indicate whether other escapees would be able to follow our route or not. I had half a dozen pieces of white cardboard cut into various shapes—a square, an oblong, a triangle, a circle, and so on. Dick Howe and I had arranged a code whereby each shape gave him some information.

I threw certain of the cards down onto a small grass patch below the road, past which our exercise parade marched on its way to the park. With luck, if the parade was not canceled for a week, Dick would see the cards. My message ran: "Exit from pit. Moat easy; no traces left."

Although I had pulled the bar of the flue exit back into place, we had, in truth, probably left minor traces. But as the alternative message was: "Exit obvious to goons"—which would have been the case, for instance, if we left 50 feet or so of sheet rope dangling from a window—I preferred to encourage other escapees to have a shot at following the route we'd taken.

We continued another 100 yards past the barracks, where the garrison was peacefully sleeping, and arrived at our last obstacle—the outer wall. It was only 10 feet high here, with coils of barbed wire stretched along the top. I was on the wall heaving Hank up, when, with a sudden pounding of my heart, I noticed the glow of a cigarette in the distance. It was approaching. Then I realized it was Billie. He and Ronnie had caught up to us. We had arranged a discreet gap between us so that we did not look like a regiment passing under the light of the corner lamp.

The barbed wire did not present a serious obstacle when tackled without hurry and with minute care. We were all eventually over the wall, but none too soon, because we had a long way to go in order to be safe before dawn. It was 5:15 in the morning, and the fifth leg of the marathon was over. The sixth and last stage—the long journey to Switzerland—lay ahead of us.

We shook hands all around, and with *"Au revoir*—see you in Switzerland in a few days," Hank and I set off along the road. Two hundred yards behind us, the other two followed. Soon they branched off on their route, and we took to the fields.

As we trudged along, Hank fumbled for a long time in his pockets and then uttered practically the first words he had spoken during the whole night. He said: "I reckon, Pat, I must have left my pipe at the top of the moat."

LIBERTY EXPRESS

HANK AND I WALKED FAST. We intended to lie low for a day. Therefore, in order to be at all safe we had to put the longest distance possible between ourselves and the camp. We judged the German search would be concentrated in the direction of a village about five miles away. Ronnie and Billie were headed for the railway station there. The first train was due shortly before morning *Appell.* Provided that there was no alarm in the camp before then and the two of them could reach the station in time for the train (which now seemed probable), Ronnie and Billie would be in Leipzig before the real search started.

Hank and I chose a difficult route, calculated to put the hunters off the scent. We headed south and then westward in a big sweep in the direction of the River Mulde, which ran due northward toward the Elbe. In order to reach a railway station, we had to trek about 20 miles or so and cross the river in the bargain. It was not an easy escape route, and we relied on the Germans thinking likewise.

We walked for about an hour and a half, and when it was almost daylight we entered a wood and hid in a thicket for the day. We must have been five miles away from the camp. Although we tried to sleep, our nerves were as taut as piano wires.

"A wild animal must have magnificent nerves," I said to Hank.

"Wild animals have nerves just like you and me. That's why they are not captured easily," was his comment.

Hank was not going to be easy to catch. His fiancée had been waiting for him since the night when he took off in his bomber in April 1940. It would plainly require more than a few tough Germans to recapture him. It gave me confidence to know he was beside me.

I mused for a long time over the queer twists that fate gives to our lives. I had always assumed that Rupert and I would finally escape together. Yet it happened to be Hank's turn, and here we were. I had left old and true friends behind me. Two years of constant companionship had cemented some of us together very closely—Rupert, Harry, Dick, Kenneth, and Peter. Would I ever see them again? Inside the camp the probability of early failure in the escape was so great that we brushed aside all serious thought of a long parting.

Here in the woods it was different. If I did my job properly from now on, it was probable that I would never see them again. We were not going back to Colditz; Hank was sure of that, too. I was rather shaken by the thought, realizing fully for the first time what these men meant to me. We had been through much together. I prayed that we might all survive the war and meet again.

As dusk fell, Hank and I set off across the fields. Sometimes when roads led in our direction we used them, but we had to be very careful. On one occasion we just barely left the road in time when we saw a light ahead (unusual in the blackout) and heard voices. A car approaching was stopped. As we bypassed the light by way of the fields, we saw an army motorcyclist talking to a sentry. It was a control, and they were after us. We passed within 50 yards of them.

It seemed a long way to the river. As the night wore on, I could hardly keep my eyes open. I stumbled and dozed as I walked, and finally I gave up.

"Hank, I'll have to lie down for an hour and sleep. I've been sleep-walking as it is. I don't know where we're going."

"OK. I'll stay on guard while you rest under the tree," said Hank, indicating a mound of grass looming ahead of us.

He woke me in an hour, and we continued, eventually reaching the river. It was in a deep cutting, down which we climbed, and there was a road that ran along its bank. To our left, spanning the river and the cutting, was a high-level railway bridge. I decided we would cross it. We had to reclimb the cutting. Sleep was overcoming me once more. The climb was steep and over huge rocks cut into steps like those of the pyramids. It was a nightmare climb in the pitch-darkness, as I repeatedly stumbled, fell down, and slept where I lay. Hank would tug at me, pull me over the next huge stone, and set me on my feet without a word, only to have to repeat the performance again in a few moments. Halfway up the embankment we stopped again to rest. I slept, but Hank was on the *qui vive* and, peering through the darkness, noticed a movement on the railway bridge. It needed a cat's eye to notice anything at all. He shook me and said: "Pat, we're not going over that bridge. It's guarded."

"How do you know for certain?" I asked. "And how are we going to cross the river, then?"

"I don't mind if we have to swim it," he said. "But I'm not going over that bridge."

I gave way, though it meant making a big half-circle, crossing the railway line, and descending to the river again somewhere near a road bridge that we knew existed farther upstream.

Reaching the top of the railway-bridge embankment, we crossed the lines, and as we did so, we saw in the distance from the direction of the bridge the flash of a lighted match.

"Did you see that?" I whispered.

"Yes."

"There's a sentry on the bridge, sure enough. You were right, Hank. Thank God you insisted."

Gradually we edged down the hill again where the river cutting was less steep and found that our bearings had not been too bad, for we saw the road bridge in the foreground. We inspected it carefully before crossing, listening for a long time for any sound of movement. It was unguarded. We crossed rapidly and took to the bushes on the far side, not a moment too soon; a motorcycle came roaring around a bend, its headlight blazing, and sped over the bridge in the direction from which we had come.

We tramped wearily across country on a compass bearing until dawn. Near the village of Penig, where our railway station was situated, we spruced ourselves up, attempted a shave, and polished our shoes. We entered the village—it was almost a small industrial town—and wended our way in the direction of the station. I was loath to ask our way at this time of the morning when few people were about. Instead, we wandered onward past some coal yards where a tramline started. The tracks ran alongside a large factory and then switched over to the other side of the road, passing under trees and beside a small river. We followed the lines, which eventually crossed a bridge and entered the town proper. I was sure the tramlines would lead us to the station.

The town was dingy, not at all like Colditz, which was of pleasing appearance. Upkeep had evidently gone to the dogs. Broken window-panes were filled with newspaper, ironwork was rusty, and the front doors of the houses, which opened directly on the street, badly needed a coat of paint.

We arrived at the railway station. It was on the far edge of the town and looked older than and out of keeping with the buildings around it. It had a staid respectable atmosphere and belonged to a period before industry had come to Penig. We entered and looked up the trains. Our route was Munich via Zwickau. I saw we had a three-hour wait, then another wait at Zwickau before the night express for Munich.

Leaving the station, we walked out into the country again and settled down for a meal and a rest behind a barn near the road. It is dangerous to wait in railway stations or public parks and advisable to keep moving under any circumstances when in a town.

We returned to the station toward midday. I bought two third-class tickets to Munich, and we caught the train comfortably. Our suitcases were a definite asset. My German accent was anything but perfect, but the brandishing of my suitcase on all occasions to emphasize whatever I was saying worked like a soporific on the Germans.

In Zwickau, having another long wait, we boarded a tram. I tripped on the mounting step and nearly knocked the conductress over. I apologized loudly. *"Entschuldigen Sie mir! Bitte! entschuldigen, entschuldigen. Ich bin ein Ausländer."* ("Excuse me! Please! excuse, excuse. I'm a foreigner.")

We sat down, and when the conductress came around, I beamed at her and asked in broken German: "Fräulein! If you please, where is the nearest cinema? We have a long time to wait for our train and would like to see a film and the newsreels. We are foreigners and do not know this town."

"The best cinema in Zwickau is five minutes from here. I shall tell you where to alight."

"How much is the fare, please, fräulein?"

"Twenty pfennigs each, if you please."

"Danke schön," I said, proffering the money.

After five minutes the tram stopped at a main thoroughfare junction, and the conductress beckoned to us. As we alighted, one of the passengers pointed out to us with a voluble and, to me, incoherent stream of German exactly where the cinema was. I could gather that he was proud to meet foreigners who were working for the victory of "Our Reich." He took off his moth-eaten hat as we parted and waved a courteous farewell.

ZWICKAU WAS JUST a greatly enlarged Penig as far as I could see. Dilapidation was visible everywhere. The inhabitants gave me an impression of impoverishment, and only the uniforms of officials, including the tram conductress, and those of the armed forces bore a semblance of smartness.

Hank and I spent a comfortable two hours in the cinema, which was no different from any other I have seen. German officers and troops were dotted about in seats all around us and made up 90 percent of the audience.

I dozed for a long time, and I noticed Hank's head drooping too. After two hours I whispered to him: "It's time to go. What did you think of the film?

"What I saw of it was a washout," Hank replied. "I must have slept through it, because I missed parts of it. It was incoherent."

"This cinema seems to be nothing more than impromptu sleeping quarters. Look around you," and I nudged Hank. Representatives of the German Wehrmacht and Luftwaffe were dozing around us in all sorts of postures.

"Let's go," I said.

Yawning repeatedly, we rose and left the auditorium.

Returning to the station in good time, we boarded the express to Munich. It was crowded, for which I was glad, and Hank and I spent the whole night standing in the corridor. Nobody paid us any attention. We might as well have been in an express bound from London to the north. The lighting, however, was so bad that few passengers attempted to read. It was intensely stuffy owing to the overcrowding, the cold outside, and the blackout curtains on all windows. The hypnotic drumming and swaying of the train pervaded all.

Our fellow travelers were a mixed bag: a few army and air force men, some workmen, and a majority of down-at-the-heel-looking businessmen or government officials. There was not a personality among them; all were sheep ready to be slaughtered at the altar of Hitler. There was a police control in the early hours. I produced my much-soiled German leather wallet, which exposed my identity card or *Ausweis* behind a grimy scratched piece of celluloid.

The police officer was curt in his questioning. *"Sie sind Ausländer?"* ("You're foreigners?")

"Jawohl." ("We are.")

"Wo fahren Sie hin?" ("Where are you traveling to?")

"Nach München und Rottweil." ("To Munich and Rottweil.")

"Warum?" ("Why?")

"Beton Arbeit" ("Concrete work").

Hank was slow in producing his papers.

I said: *"Wir sind zusammen. Er ist mein Kamerad."* ("We're together. He's my friend.")

Hank proffered his papers as I added, taking the officer into my confidence, *"Er ist etwas dumm, aber ein guter Kerl."* ("He's kind of dumb, but still a good fellow.")

The control passed on, and we relaxed, half dozing, as we roared through the night toward Munich—and Switzerland.

We arrived in Munich in the cold gray of the morning—several hours late. There had been bombing and train diversions.

I queued up at the booking office, telling Hank to stand by. When my turn came, I asked for *"Zweimal dritte Klasse, nach Rottweil."* ("Two third-class tickets to Rottweil.")

The woman behind the grill said: *"Fünfundsechzig Mark, bitte."* ("Sixty-five marks, please.")

I produced the 56 marks, which almost drained my fund.

The woman repeated, *"Fünfundsechzig Mark, bitte, noch neun Mark."* ("Sixty-five marks, please, you still owe me nine marks.")

I was confusing the German for 56 with 65.

"Karl," I shouted in Hank's direction, *"geben Sie mir noch Zehn Mark"* ("give me 10 more marks").

Hank produced a 10-mark note, which I handed to the woman.

"Ausweis bitte" ("Your papers, please"), she said.

I produced them.

"Gut," and she handed my wallet back to me.

I was so relieved that as I left the queue, forgetting my part completely, I said in a loud voice: "All right, Hank, I've got the tickets!"

I nearly froze in my tracks. As we hurried away, I felt the baleful glare of 100 eyes burning through my back. Hank and I were soon lost in the crowd, and what a crowd. Everybody seemed to be traveling. The station appeared to be untouched by bombing, and traffic was obviously running at high pressure. We had another long wait for the train that would take us to Rottweil via Ulm and Tuttlingen. I noted with relief that the wait in Ulm was only 10 minutes. Hyde-Thompson and his Dutch colleague, the second two officers of my theater escape, had been trapped in Ulm station. The name carried foreboding, and I prayed we would negotiate this junction safely. I also noticed with appreciation that there was a substantial wait at Tuttlingen for the train to Rottweil. It would give us a good excuse for leaving the station.

In Munich I felt safe. The waiting rooms were full to overflowing, and along with other passengers we were even shepherded by station police to an underground bombproof waiting room. It was prominently signposted for the use of all persons having longer than half an hour to wait for a train.

Before descending to this waiting room, however, I asked for the station restaurant, and roving along the counter I saw a large sign indicating coupon-free meals. I promptly asked for two and also two liters of beer. They were duly served, and Hank and I sat down at a table by ourselves to the best meal provided us by the Germans in two and a half years. It consisted of a very generous helping of thick stew—mostly vegetables and potatoes, but some good-tasting sausage meat was floating around as well. The beer seemed excellent to our parched gullets. We had not drunk anything since our repast on the outskirts of Penig when we had finished the water we carried with us.

We went to the underground waiting room. I was blasé by now and smiled benignly at the burly representative of the *Abwehr Polizei* ("security police") as he passed by, hardly glancing at the wallets we pushed under his nose.

In good time we boarded the train for Ulm. Arriving there at midday, we changed platforms without incident and quickly boarded our next train. This did not go directly to Rottweil, but necessitated changing at Tuttlingen. Rottweil was 30 miles from the frontier, but Tuttlingen only 15 miles away. My intention was to stroll out of the station at Tuttlingen with the excuse of waiting for the Rottweil train and never return.

This Hank and I duly did. As we walked off the station platform at Tuttlingen, through the barrier, we handed in our tickets. We had walked 10 yards when I heard shouts behind us: *"Kommen Sie her! Hier, kommen Sie zurück!"* ("Come here! Come back here!")

I turned around fearing the worst and saw the ticket collector frantically waving at us.

I returned to him, and he said: *"Sie haben Ihre Fahrkarten abgege-*

ben, aber Sie fahren nach Rottweil. Die müssen Sie noch behalten."
("You surrendered your tickets, but you're traveling on to Rottweil.
You have to keep them still.")

With almost visible relief I accepted the tickets once more. In my
anxiety I had forgotten that we were ostensibly due to return to catch
the Rottweil train and, of course, still needed our tickets.

FROM THE STATION we promptly took the wrong road; there were no
signposts. It was late afternoon and a Saturday (October 17). The
weather was fine. We walked for a long time along a road that refused
to turn in the direction in which we thought it ought to turn. It was
maddening. We passed a superbly camouflaged factory and sidings.
There must have been an area of 10 acres completely covered with a
false flat roof of what appeared to be rush matting. Even at the low
elevation at which we found ourselves looking down upon it, the
whole site looked like farmland. If the camouflage was actually rush
matting, I do not know how they provided against fire risks.

We were gradually being steered into a valley heading due south,
whereas we wished to travel westward. Leaving the road as soon as
possible without creating suspicion, we tried to take a shortcut across
country to another highway that we knew headed west. As a shortcut
it misfired, taking us over hilly country that prolonged our journey
considerably. Evening was drawing on by the time we reached the
correct road. We walked along this for several miles, and when it was
dark, we took to the woods to lie up for the night.

We passed a freezing, uncomfortable night on beds of leaves in the
forest and were glad to warm ourselves with a sharp walk the next
morning, which was Sunday. I was thankful it was a Sunday because
it gave us a good excuse to be out walking in the country.

We now headed along roads leading southwest, until at 8 A.M. we
retired again to the friendly shelter of the woods to eat our breakfast.
We consumed most of what was left of our supply of German bread,
sugar, and margarine.

We had almost finished our repast when we were disturbed by a
farmer who approached and eyed us curiously for a long time. He
wore close-fitting breeches and gaiters like a typical English gamekeeper. I did not like his attitude at all. He came close to us and
demanded to know what we were doing.

I said: *"Wir essen. Können Sie das nicht sehen?"* ("We're eating.
Can't you see that?")

"Warum sind Sie hier?" ("What are you doing here?") he asked, to

which I replied: *"Wir gehen spazieren; es ist Sonntag, nicht wahr?"* ("We're out on a walk; it's Sunday, isn't it?")

At this he retired. I watched him carefully. As soon as he was out of the woods and about 50 yards away, I saw him turn along a hedge and change his gait into a trot.

This was enough for me. In less than a minute we were packed and trotting fast in the opposite direction, which happened to be southward. We did not touch the road again for some time, but kept to the woods and lanes. Gradually, however, the countryside became open and cultivated, and we were forced once more to the road.

We passed a German soldier, who was smartly turned out in his Sunday best, and gave him a friendly "Heil Hitler!" Church bells were ringing out from steeples that rose head and shoulders above the roofs of several villages dotted here and there in the rolling countryside around us.

We walked through one of the villages as the people were coming out of church. I was terrified of the children, who ran out of the church shouting and laughing. They gamboled around us and eyed us curiously, although their elders took no notice of us at all. I was relieved when we left the village behind us. Soon afterward the country again became wooded and hilly, and we disappeared amongst the trees, heading now due south.

As THE AFTERNOON wore on, I picked up our bearings more accurately, and we aimed at the exact location of the frontier crossing. A little too soon—I thought—we reached the frontier road, running east and west. I could not be sure, so we continued eastward along it to where it entered some woods. We passed a fork where a forest track, which I recognized, joined it. I knew then that we were indeed on the frontier road and that we had gone too far eastward. At that moment there were people following us, and we could not break off into the woods without looking suspicious. We walked onward casually, and at the end of the wooded portion of the road we suddenly heard: *"Halt! Wer da!"* ("Halt! Who's there?") and then, more deliberately, *"Wo gehen Sie hin?"* ("Where are you going?")

A sentry box stood back from the road in a clump of trees, and a frontier guard stepped forth from it.

"Wir gehen nach Singen" ("We're going to Singen"), I said. *"Wir sind Ausländer."* ("We are foreigners.")

"Ihr Ausweis bitte." ("Your papers, please.")

We produced our papers, including the special permit allowing us to travel near the frontier. We were close to him. His rifle was slung over his shoulder. The people who had been following us had turned down a lane toward a cottage. We were alone with the sentry.

I chatted on, gesticulating, with my suitcase brazenly conspicuous.

"We are Flemish workmen. This evening we take the train to Rottweil, where there is much construction work. We must be there in the morning. Today we can rest, and we like your woods and your countryside very much."

He eyed us for a moment, handed back our papers, and let us go. As we walked on, I dreaded to hear another "Halt!" I imagined that if the sentry were not satisfied with us, he would, for his own safety, move us off a few yards so that he could unsling his rifle. But no command was given, and we continued our "Sunday afternoon stroll." As we moved out of earshot, Hank said to me: "If he'd reached for his gun when he was close to us just then, I would have knocked him to kingdom come."

I would not have relished being knocked to kingdom come by Hank, and I often wonder if the sentry did not notice a look in Hank's eye and think that discretion was perhaps the better part of valor. A lonely sentry is not all-powerful against two enemies, even with his gun leveled. Our story may have had a ring of truth, but, nonetheless, we were foreigners within half a mile of the Swiss frontier.

Soon we were able to leave the road and started to double back across country to our frontier crossing point. Just as we came to a railway line and climbed a small embankment, we nearly jumped out of our skins with fright as a figure darted from a bush in front of us, ran into a thicket, and disappeared. I could have assured him, if only he had stopped, that he gave us just as big a fright as we gave him.

By dusk we had found our exact location and waited in deep pine woods for darkness to descend. The frontier was scarcely a mile away. We ate a last meal nervously and without appetite. Our suitcases would not be required any more, so we buried them.

When it was pitch-dark, we pulled on socks over our shoes and set off. We had to negotiate the frontier crossing in inky blackness, entirely from memory of the maps studied in Colditz. We crossed over more railway lines and then continued, skirting the edge of a wood. We encountered a minor road, which foxed me for a while because it should not have been there according to my memory, but we moved on. Hearing a motorcycle pass along a road in front of us, a road running close to and parallel with the frontier, warned us of the proximity of our takeoff point.

We entered the woods to our left and proceeded parallel with the road eastward for about 100 yards and then approached it cautiously. Almost as we stumbled into it, I suddenly recognized the outline of a sentry box hidden among the trees straight in front of us.

We were within five yards of it when I recognized its angular roof. My hair stood on end. It was impossible to move without breaking twigs under our feet. They made noises like pistol shots, and we could be heard easily. We retreated with as much care as we could, but even the crackle of a dried leaf caused me to perspire freely.

To compensate for this unnerving encounter, however, I now knew exactly where we were, for the sentry box was marked on our Colditz map and provided me with a check bearing. We moved off 70 yards and approached the road again. Peering across it, we could discern fields and low hedges. In the distance was our goal: a wooded hill looming blacker than the darkness around it, with the woods ending abruptly halfway down its eastern slopes, to our left. There was no blackout in Switzerland, and beyond the hill was the faintest haze of light, indicating the existence of a Swiss village.

At 7:30 P.M. we moved off. Crouching low and on the double, we crossed the road and headed for our pointer. Without stopping for breath, we ran—through hedges—across ditches—wading through mud—and then on again. Dreading barbed wire that we could never have seen, we ran, panting with excitement as much as with breathlessness, across fields newly plowed, meadows, and marshland, until at last we rounded the corner of the woods. Here, for a moment, we halted for breath.

I felt that if I could not have a drink of water soon I would surely die. My throat was parched and swollen, and my tongue was choking me. My heart was pounding like a sledgehammer. I was gasping for breath. I had lived for two and a half years, both awake and in sleep, with the vision of this race before me, and now every nerve in my body was taut to the breaking point.

We were not yet "home." We had done about half a mile and could see the lights of the Swiss village ahead. Great care was now necessary, for we could easily recross the frontier into Germany without knowing it and stumble upon a guard post. From the corner of the wood we had to continue in a wide sweeping curve, first toward our right and then left again toward the village. Where we stood, we were actually in Switzerland, but in a direct line between us and the Swiss village lay German territory.

Why had we run instead of creeping forward warily? The answer is that instinct dictated it, and, I think in this case, instinct was right. Escapees' experience has borne out that the psychological reaction of a fleeing man to a shouted command, such as "Halt," varies. If a man is walking or creeping, the reaction is to stop. If he is running, the reaction is to run faster. It is in the split seconds of such instinctive decisions that success or failure may be determined.

We continued on our way at a rapid walk, over grass and boggy land, crouching low at every sound. It was important to avoid even Swiss frontier posts. We had heard curious rumors of escapees being returned to the Germans by unfriendly Swiss guards. However untrue, we were taking no risks.

We saw occasional shadowy forms, circled widely around them, and at last, at 8:30 P.M., approached the village along a sandy path.

We were about 1,000 yards inside the Swiss frontier. We had completed the 400-mile journey from Colditz in less than four days.

Under the first lamppost of the village street, Hank and I shook hands in silence.

We beat Ronnie and Billie by 26 hours. At 10:30 P.M. the following evening they also crossed the frontier safely!

Following his successful escape to Switzerland, Capt. Patrick Reid was granted a three-month recuperative leave. He was subsequently appointed British assistant military attaché in Berne, where he remained until 1946. During the postwar period Patrick Reid held diplomatic posts in Turkey and France before resuming residence in the United Kingdom. He is married and has three sons and two daughters. Reid has been awarded the MBE (Member of the British Empire) as well as the Military Cross.

His companion in escape, Howard "Hank" Wardle, eventually returned to his native Canada. He now lives in Ottawa.

Colditz Castle, Oflag IV C, continued as a German military prison until April 15, 1945, when it was liberated by advancing American troops and its POW's were finally freed.

CREDITS AND ACKNOWLEDGMENTS

Acknowledgments

THE JANUARY TUNNEL, by William A. H. Birnie, from "Eighty-Seven Feet to Freedom," *Reader's Digest*, Sept. 1962. BREAKOUT, by Christen Lyst Hansen, from "Ordeal in a Gestapo Attic," *Reader's Digest* (Great Britain), Mar. 1968. DESPERATE VOYAGE, by George Feifer, from "Fishing Boat to Freedom," *Reader's Digest* (Great Britain), July 1974. FIVE YEARS TO FREEDOM, by Maj. James N. Rowe, *Reader's Digest*, Jan. 1972, cond. from the book pub. by Little, Brown and Co. Copyright © 1971 by James N. Rowe. THE ELUSIVE FRENCH GENERAL, by Frederick C. Painton, from "Giraud's Brilliant Escape From a Nazi Prison," *Reader's Digest*, Sept. 1943. THE LONE SWIM, by Peter Döbler, from "Twenty-Eight Miles to Freedom," *Reader's Digest* (Great Britain), Oct. 1972. STOWAWAY, by Armando Socarras Ramírez as told to Denis Fodor and John Reddy, *Reader's Digest*, Jan. 1970. THE LIFELINE CALLED COMET, by W. E. Armstrong, from "Young Heroes of the Comet Life-Line," *Reader's Digest* (Great Britain), Oct. 1973. THE ONLY WAY, by Claus Gaedemann and Robert Littell, from "The Only Way Out," *Reader's Digest*, Sept. 1955. THE TRUCK THAT FLED, by William Schulz, from "The Truck That Fled Cuba," *Reader's Digest*, July 1969. OPERATION LIBERTY, by Frederic Sondern, Jr., and Norbert Muhlen, from "Comrade Lindemann's Conscience," *Reader's Digest*, Mar. 1953. RENDEZVOUS AT SEA, by Ken Agnew as told to Kenneth Schaefer, from "One of the Comrades Is Missing," *Reader's Digest*, Apr. 1971, cond. from *Argosy*. THE LONG WAY HOME, by John G. Hubbell, *Reader's Digest*, Apr. 1952. HOUSE OF ALPHONSE, by John G. Hubbell, from "Good Evening to the House of Alphonse . . . ," *Reader's Digest* (Canada), Sept. 1966. INCIDENT AT THE BORDER, by Lawrence Elliott, *Reader's Digest* (Canada), Mar. 1972. DRY GUILLOTINE, by René Belbenoit, *Reader's Digest*, June 1938, cond. from the book pub. by E. P. Dutton & Co., Inc., and Jonathan Cape, Ltd. Copyright 1938; renewal © 1966 by E. P. Dutton & Co., Inc., and reprinted with their permission. ESCAPE FROM CUBA, by Joseph P. Blank, *Reader's Digest*, May 1972. THE DOOMED PRISONERS, by Edwin Muller, from "The Doomed Prisoners of Differdange," *Reader's Digest*, Mar. 1956. TUNNEL TO FREEDOM, by Flight Lieutenant Paul Brickhill as told to Allan A. Michie, *Reader's Digest*, Dec. 1945. THE LION'S DEN, by C. Brian Kelly, from "Escape From the Lion's Den," *Reader's Digest*, Nov. 1976. SURVIVAL, by John Hersey, *Reader's Digest*, Aug. 1944, Feb. 1961. Originally pub. in *The New Yorker;* later in *Here to Stay*, Alfred A. Knopf, Inc. Copyright © 1944, 1962 by John Hersey. THE DOG FROM NO MAN'S LAND, by Anthony Richardson, *Reader's Digest*, Sept. 1960, cond. from *One Man and His Dog*, pub. by E. P. Dutton & Co., Inc., and

Art Credits